*Competing in a
global economy*

Competing in a global economy

AN EMPIRICAL STUDY ON SPECIALIZATION AND TRADE IN MANUFACTURES

Prepared for the United
Nations Industrial Development
Organization by

HELMUT FORSTNER

&

ROBERT BALLANCE

London
UNWIN HYMAN
Boston   Sydney   Wellington

Published by the Academic Division of
Unwin Hyman Ltd
15/17 Broadwick Street, London W1V 1FP, UK

Unwin Hyman Inc.,
8 Winchester Place, Winchester, Mass. 01890, USA

Allen & Unwin (Australia) Ltd,
8 Napier Street, North Sydney, NSW 2060, Australia

Allen & Unwin (New Zealand) Ltd in association with the
Port Nicholson Press Ltd,
Compusales Building, 75 Ghuznee Street, Wellington 1, New Zealand

First published in 1990

British Library Cataloguing in Publication Data

Forstner, Helmut
  Competing in a global economy : an empirical
  study on specialization and
  trade in manufactures.
  1. Foreign trade
  I. Title II. Ballance, Robert
  382

  ISBN 0-04-445619-0

Library of Congress Cataloging in Publication Data

APPLIED FOR

Typeset in 10/12 Bembo
Printed by Cambridge University Press

Contents

List of tables   ix

List of figures   xii

List of abbreviations   xiii

Preface   xv

1   The transformation of world industry: an introduction and summary   **1**

    The internationalization of industry   1
    Organization and summary of findings   8

2   Inter-industrial trends in manufacturing production   **20**

    Global pattern of manufacturing output   20
    Patterns of change and specialization   27
    Notes   35

3   Inter-industry trade in a global system   **36**

    Long-term trends in world trade   36
    The inter-industry structure of world trade in manufactures   43
    Stylized evidence of trading patterns   46
    Notes   58

4   Two-way trade in similar products   **59**

    An overview of two-way trade   60
    An industry-specific view of IIT   65
    Notes   68

5   International patterns of factor endowments   **70**

    The factor abundance theory in higher dimensions   71
    The measurement of factor abundance   72
    The changing basis for comparative advantage   75
    Factor abundance and the patterns of trade   82

Annex: The specific factors model 88
Notes 91

6 Factor requirements, output and trade **93**

Factor intensities and empirical evidence 93
Revealed comparative advantage and factor intensities 101
Annex: Technology and trade 109
Notes 112

7 Country differences, country similarities and the structure of trade **114**

Factor abundance and net trade 114
An empirical assessment of the factor abundance proposition 122
Country similarities and manufactured trade 125
Annex: Trade flows and factor movements 131
Notes 135

8 Economies of scale and market structure **137**

Hypotheses on increasing returns, market structure and trade 138
Concepts and measurement 140
International comparisons between industries 145
Export concentration and industrial concentration 154
Notes 158

9 Intra-industry trade revisited **160**

Intra-industry trade versus inter-industry trade 160
Determinants of IIT intensity in DMEs 164
The role of vertical product differentiation in IIT 166
Annex: Foreign direct investment versus trade 172
Notes 177

10 A retrospective view **178**

Sectoral comparative advantage 179
Inter-industry comparative advantage 179
Intra-industry specialization and trade 180

Appendix A (Technical) 182

Appendix B (Statistical) 187

Bibliography 214

Author index 221

List of tables *

2.1	Share of economic groups and developing regions in world MVA, 1970–86	*page* 21
2.2	Share of economic groups in world value added of selected manufacturing branches and years	23
2.3	Structure of MVA, by economic groups	24
2.4	Growth of output in selected industries and country groups, 1963–86	26
2.5	Test of comparative industry rankings	28
2.6	International patterns of specialization, by industry, 1986	29
2.7	An internationalized ranking of industries by growth of output, 1973–86	31
2.8	Indices of structural change, 1973–86	32
2.9	Change in output share in selected industry groups, 1973–86	34
3.1	Growth rates for GDP, MVA and exports of manufactures, 1960–86	37
3.2	Share of manufactures in total exports, by economic group, 1970–86	39
3.3	World exports of manufactures and the shares of the major economic groups	40
3.4	Share of manufactures in total exports of selected countries and areas	42
3.5	Net manufactured exports of developed countries, by trade category, 1970–85	50
3.6	Manufactured exports of developed market economies, by trade category, 1970–85	51
3.7	Net manufactured exports of developing countries and areas, by trade category, 1970–85	53
3.8	Manufactured exports of developing countries and areas, by trade category, 1970–85	54
3.9	Structural change in manufactured exports, 1970–2 to 1983–5	56

4.1 Average shares of IIT in manufactured goods, by country group, 1985   62

4.2 Change in the average share of IIT in manufactured goods between 1970 and 1985, by country group   64

4.3 Industries with high IIT shares in trade of DMEs and developing countries and areas, 1985   66

5.1 Distribution of factor endowments, 1970 and 1985   77

5.2 Dispersion of factor endowments within broad country groups, 1970 and 1985   81

5.3 Factor abundance and net trade by country or area, 1970 and 1985   83

5.4 Factor abundance and net trade, by country group, 1970 and 1985   87

6.1 Average factor intensities, by industry, 1970–7 and 1978–85   96

6.2 Correlations between factor intensity rankings of country groups, 1970–7 and 1978–85   99

6.3 Coefficients of variation of factor intensities, by industry, 1970–7 and 1978–85   100

6.4 Concordance of factory intensity rankings within country groups, 1970–7 and 1978–85   102

6.5 Output-based measures of RCA, by industry groups, 1970–2 and 1983–5   105

6.6 Export-based measures of RCA, by industry groups, 1970–2 and 1983–5   108

7.1 Factor orientation, in selected industries, 1970 and 1985   117

7.2 Correlations between factor orientation and factor intensity, 1985   124

7.3 Partial correlations between levels of bilateral intra-industry trade and country attributes, 1985   130

8.1 Size elasticities and industry rankings for years around 1985   146

8.2 Growth of the number of establishments and production, by industry, selected countries, 1977–82   149

8.3 International comparison of employment entropy indices in manufacturing industries, around 1985   152

8.4 Relationship between industrial concentration, the level of industrial development and country size, by industry, around 1985   153

8.5 Rank correlations between industry characteristics   155

8.6   Distribution of industries, by industrial concentration
and by export concentration   157

9.1   Impact of industry characteristics on the share of IIT,
by country group, 1985   163

9.2   Determinants of IIT intensity of selected DMEs, by
country, 1985   165

9.3   Impact of quality differences on two-way trade between
DMEs and developing countries and areas, 1985   170

B1   Availability of data on skilled labour, by country and year   189

B2   Composition of country groups   193

B3   Broad classification of industrial branches, by growth
performance and factor intensity   195

B4   Broad classes of manufactured goods   196

B5   DMEs' average factor intensities, 1970–7 and 1978–85   197

B6   NIEs' average factor intensities, 1970–7 and 1978–85   199

B7   Second-generation NIEs' average factor intensities,
1970–7 and 1978–85   201

B8   Selected developing countries' average factor intensities,
1970–7 and 1978–85   203

B9   Determinants of bilateral intra-industry trade, 1985   205

B10   Categorization of industries by economies of scale,
industrial concentration, product differentiation and
export concentration   210

List of figures

3.1 Net exports of developed market economies, by
     product category, 1970–85   *page* 47
3.2 Net exports of developing countries, by product
     category, 1970–85   48
4.1 Industries with significant increases of IIT, 1970–85   68

List of abbreviations

CA	current account
CPE	centrally planned economy
DME	developed market economy
FDI	foreign direct investment
GDP	gross domestic product
GNP	gross national product
H–O	Heckscher–Ohlin
H–O–V	Heckscher–Ohlin–Vanek
IIT	intra-industry trade
IITL	intra-industry trade level
IITS	intra–industry trade share
ISCO	International Standard Classification of Occupations
ISIC	International Standard Industrial Classification
MES	minimum efficient scale
MVA	manufacturing value added
NIE	newly industrializing economy
OLI	ownership location internalization
OLS	ordinary-least-squares
R and D	research and development
RCA	revealed comparative advantage
SITC	Standard International Trade Classification
TNC	transnational corporation
UDB	UNIDO data base
USSIC	US Standard Industrial Classification
UNIDO	United Nations Industrial Development Organization

Preface

Interest in the determinants of specialization and trade has a long tradition among economists. The past two decades, however, have brought substantial changes in the world trading system. Theoreticians and empiricists alike have been forced to modify their methods of analysis in an effort to stay abreast of all these changes. Theoreticians, for example, have constructed more elaborate models which better represent a trading system composed of multiple buyers and sellers who may or may not operate according to competitive dicta. Empiricists have resorted to more powerful econometric tools and have made use of data sets that are far larger than those available to their predecessors. An unintended result of all these advances is that the gap between theoreticians and empiricists has widened. This book is mainly empirical in approach. However, the compilation and analysis of quantitative material is closely linked to particular elements of economic theory. A major objective is to help bridge what we believe is a widening gap between the work of the theoretician and that of the empiricist.

This particular orientation lends itself to either of two methods of presentation. One would be to begin with a complete elaboration of the theoretical framework and then move on to empirical applications or tests. We have chosen not to do this in the present case. One reason has to do with the underlying theory. Several of the relevant models are set out in a formal manner and their distinguishing features can be easily presented. Others, however, are informal and do not lend themselves to a stylized presentation. This contrast makes it difficult to summarize concisely all the theoretical features that are relevant to an empirical study. A second reason is that even the most familiar trade models become complex once they are applied in a world of higher dimensions – one populated by a large number of buyers and sellers who trade a variety of products which, in turn, are produced with several factors of production. The complexity of the underlying theory makes it difficult for the reader to assess empirical evidence when this is separated from the conceptual framework.

The Heckscher–Ohlin approach provides much of the framework for analysis in this book. Its use leads naturally to an assessment of factor abundance as a determinant of specialization and trade. But the Heckscher–Ohlin model is not intended to suggest that factor abundance is the only relevant determinant. Once attention turns from inter-industry to intra-industry forms of specialization and trade, other less formal models may be relevant. One example is the 'economies-of-scale' model, which represents a world characterized by increasing returns to scale and imperfect competition.

Both types of models are used in the following account and their juxtaposition represents another distinguishing feature of the book. The two approaches differ in many ways. However, they can also be seen as offering complementary explanations for specialization and trade. The Heckscher–Ohlin model is interpreted as applying mainly to inter-industry patterns of change, while the economies-of-scale approach finds application in the analysis of intra-industry developments.

The book is intended to provide an empirical supplement to a more traditional analysis of specialization and trade. It is mainly, though not exclusively, concerned with subjects of interest to theoreticians, industrial economists and trade analysts. Finally, the book is designed as a global study rather than a treatise rooted in a single economy. This orientation is compatible with that of UNIDO, which is the international organization with responsibility for industry.

The contribution of various individuals is gratefully acknowledged. Charles Sawyer (University of Southern Mississippi) provided advice and comments on the entire manuscript and was the author of the annexes to the book. Tetsuo Yamada (UNIDO) was a major contributor to Chapter 8; in particular, he carried out most of the empirical analysis of that chapter. Extensive comments were also supplied by Tracy Murray (US International Trade Commission and University of Arkansas) and Mathew Tharakan (University of Antwerp). Finally, the book makes extensive use of the UNIDO Data Base, and the contributions of the statisticians and other staff of the Industrial Statistics and Sectoral Surveys Branch is gratefully acknowledged.

This publication has been prepared for the United Nations Industrial Development Organization by Helmut Forstner and Robert Ballance, who are responsible for the views and opinions expressed therein. These views and opinions do not necessarily represent those of other persons or institutions mentioned here.

CHAPTER 1

The transformation of world industry: an introduction and summary

The last thirty years have brought many fundamental changes in world industry. Two of the more important of these – the internationalization of markets, and the growing opportunities for firms to specialize – establish the themes around which this book is built. This chapter begins with a brief discussion of these two developments and some of their implications. The concluding section describes approaches and objectives of the book and summarizes the major findings.

The internationalization of industry

For nearly two centuries, manufacturers operated in a spatial context that was predominantly local. The search for inputs, materials and buyers seldom extended beyond regional markets, and it was rarer still that such activities were national in scope. This provincial character no longer applies. Whatever their country of origin, most large firms now tend to operate in an environment that is international, if not global, in scope. Crude evidence to support such a view of industry is found in the rapid growth of international trade, the development of international capital markets, the continued spread of foreign investment, and the accelerated transmission of technologies across national boundaries.

Greater internationalization has brought more opportunities for collaboration, but it has also created new types of rivalries. The traditional agent of competition in any market has always been the firm. Today, however, governments are intimately involved in the process. National policy-makers have always been concerned with their country's position in industrial hierarchies; but the potential rewards and losses of competition have risen as markets have become more integrated.

The degree of interdependence between countries has accentuated national rivalries. The expansion of an industry in one country (whether developed or developing) will often result in the contraction of the same industry elsewhere. Relative changes in any industrial hierarchy are therefore likely to induce policy responses in several countries. Such rivalries are found in both newly emerging industries and mature ones and have repercussions for producers throughout the world.

The integration of markets for manufactures has also changed the micro-economic environment. Foreign buyers of products or suppliers of raw materials and other inputs now constitute a significant part of any large firm's network for the exchange of factors and goods. The international dimension is equally evident in other types of inter-firm relationships. Manufacturers buy and sell process or product technologies from foreign counterparts. They embark on collaborative forms of R and D, share out production facilities and distribution systems, and engage in many other forms of cross-border co-operation.

Increased opportunities for inter-firm collaboration also have a competitive dimension. Foreign firms will unexpectedly challenge complacent suppliers in the latter's home or export markets. They sometimes go to great lengths to acquire vital technologies and secrets of their international competitors. Domestic firms, in turn, are often reluctant to provide the same proprietory knowledge to foreign firms that they share with their domestic collaborators. The steadily expanding network of inter-firm collaboration and competition has spilled across national boundaries. It has changed the ways firms operate, the types of strategies they adopt, and the very nature of business–government relations.

Greater market integration has brought more opportunities for specialization in particular products or product lines. The potential buyers in today's market represent a wider range of incomes, tastes and preferences. This diversity affords more opportunities to compete on the basis of non-price attributes. Buyers also become more demanding and discriminating as their incomes grow and as they become more experienced. These are but a few of the observable changes in demand patterns which have occurred as the incomes of households and firms have grown.

At the microeconomic level, the motives for specialization are known. Most firms choose to specialize because they accept the premise that low prices and high volumes are essential to the achievement of competitive superiority. According to conventional wisdom, firms that enlarge their market share will realize the benefits of economies of scale. Attempts to compete on the basis of other attributes such as timeliness, quality or variety have, in the past, been regarded with some scepticism. The reason for scepticism was the suspicion that in many industries the costs of achieving these goals will grow faster than the benefits they provide.

The alternative routes to specialization are contradictory in the sense that individual firms are forced to choose between them. They may compete on the basis of price (and therefore seek greater economies of scale), or they may choose non-price forms of product differentiation. That decision is a firm-specific one which lies outside the scope of this book. In another sense, however, the two views are not contradictory since both stress the importance of specialization, albeit of different types. The internationalization of markets is increasing the scope for specialization by offering firms in developing and developed countries more choice in the ways they compete.

Orientation and approach

Interest in the determinants of specialization and trade has a long tradition, but the changes that have taken place in the last thirty years have led to new theories and to revisions of existing ones. In an effort to explain the forces behind today's trading system, some trade specialists have gone outside their field by drawing on the work of analysts in the field of industrial organization. This approach is welcome: a compartmental relationship between the two broad lines of research serves no purpose in today's world.

But while some barriers have been torn down, others still exist. One division is between trade theoreticians and empiricists. Theoreticians have struggled to keep abreast of changes in the real world by constructing more realistic models of the trading system. Empiricists have launched increasingly sophisticated studies in order to identify and measure the determinants of trade. All this work has led to numerous refinements, both theoretical and empirical. However, the theoretician's task of modelling a world populated by a multiplicity of buyers and suppliers of commodities and factors of production is daunting. Progress has been achieved at the cost of much greater complexity. Empiricists, on the other hand, now have access to more powerful econometric methods and a growing volume of data. Yet their task is made no easier when they must utilize these tools within the confines of today's multi-dimensional models.

This book is mainly, though not exclusively, concerned with subjects of interest to theoreticians, industrial economists and trade analysts. It is empirical in approach, but is not intended to be merely a documentary account of long-term trends or recent developments. The compilation and analysis of quantitative material is closely linked to particular aspects of economic theory. In this sense, the book attempts to bridge the gap between the work of the theoretician and that of the empiricist.

The selection of themes had several implications. First, the emphasis placed on the internationalization of markets meant that the book should be designed as a global study and not as a treatise rooted in a single economy, however important. Issues relating to patterns of specialization and trade are just as vital for small, open economies as for large ones, and appear to have applicability whether the countries are rich or poor. Second, many of the questions arising in the book cannot be properly examined when the subject of analysis is the manufacturing sector in its entirety. Thus an industry-specific framework is adopted, and much of the subsequent discussion proceeds along that line. The following section considers some of the approaches and methods employed in the study in more detail.

The framework for analysis

The literature on international specialization can be interpreted in different ways. This book follows the practice of trade theorists who use the term to refer to production-related developments. That usage is in contrast to the work of empiricists, who often refer to specialization as a trade-related phenomenon, by which they usually mean changes in the composition of a country's exports and imports or other types of shifts in trading patterns.

Although theoretical discussions of specialization may be confined to shifts in production, supporting evidence can still be drawn from trade. In doing so, economists regard international trade as consisting of two distinct components. One of these components, inter-industry trade, figures prominently in studies of the international division of labour. The other is often referred to as two-way or intra-industry trade (IIT). It can be defined as the simultaneous import and export of products that are close substitutes, in terms of either their factor inputs or their final uses. That definition is operational in the sense that the intra-industry component of trade can be measured and distinguished from the inter-industry component.

Inter-industry trade is dependent on comparative advantage, and the structure of production is determined by a country's factor endowments. IIT, however, depends on economies of scale and perhaps other determinants not recognized by models based on comparative advantage (Krugman, 1983, p. 344). The same applies to the domestic equivalent of IIT in production, which is referred to here as intra-industrial specialization. Each industry will have a wide range of potential products, some of which will be produced under conditions of increasing returns. But the existence of scale economies implies that each country produces only a subset of the potential products available to it. Little can be said about expected patterns of intra-industrial specialization on the basis of such theories.

The distinction between inter-industry and intra-industry patterns of trade is clearly related to the issue of specialization but cannot be carried over easily to studies of the latter. Both types of trade are considered in this book, but no attempt is made to investigate intra-industrial specialization. There are several reasons for this. First, it is virtually impossible to assess the patterns of such specialization in production. The data requirements would be massive, including information on production technologies, product characteristics and inter-firm exchanges. Second, it is not possible to formulate a workable definition of an industry which would be equally applicable to a large number of countries. An unambiguous definition – even for a single country – is rarely possible, since industries consist of shifting groups of competitors which are clustered around specific products or processes. Nor are there objective criteria for such a definition. The assignment of products and/or activities to a particular industry depends instead on the researcher's subjective judgement of the extent of substitutability. Third, the usefulness of attempting any distinction between inter-industrial and intra-industrial specialization is questionable once it is recognized that the choice of products to be produced by each country is essentially arbitrary.

Trade analysts have addressed this problem in a pragmatic manner, often defining each 'industry' as the equivalent of a three-digit category in the Standard International Trade Classification (SITC). The method has not escaped criticism, but it is now a generally accepted part of the literature. This book follows the same practice, and the discussion of inter-industry and intra-industry trade patterns proceeds accordingly. The definitional problems are more serious when the subject of discussion is domestic production. The International Standard Industrial Classification (ISIC) offers the most comprehensive source of international data on production. However, each ISIC category is a heterogeneous mixture of products and activities which does not really approximate even the loosest definition of an industry. The ISIC serves as a basis for defining industries in the early parts of the book but in later stages more detailed industry descriptions are employed.

The conceptual basis for the distinction between international trade and inter-industrial specialization can be made clearer by drawing upon the tools used in the exposition of trade theory. Theoreticians, for example, usually begin their study of trade by assuming a state of autarky (that is, a hypothetical situation where the country engages in no trade whatsoever). They demonstrate the effects of trade by comparing a country's post-trade patterns of production and consumption with those that prevailed in autarky. The transition from autarky to trade is depicted as a two-step process. With no trade, patterns of production and consumption depend solely on domestic forces. Once the possibility of external demand and supply is acknowledged, patterns of consumption will change, giving rise to what is described as 'gains from international exchange'. The second step in the adjustment process involves a shift in patterns of production. After trade occurs, there is an incentive to specialize, which gives rise to 'gains from specialization'. Together, the two effects represent the 'gains from trade' and are part of the theoretician's toolkit to demonstrate the superiority of free trade rather than no trade. This book makes no attempt to measure the welfare effects of trade. Nor is it concerned with the identification of gains from specialization or international exchange. However, the theoretician's use of an imaginary two-step process is retained, since it provides a useful device to distinguish between the production and trade-related effects of specialization.

Mention should also be made of certain statistical and classificational issues. Because the volume of data included in the study is substantial, various summary measures must be used. These types of data aggregation are derived from the underlying theoretical and empirical literature. The arrangement of industry data according to factor intensity, or the categorization of trade in manufactures as resource-based, Heckscher–Ohlin and product-cycle goods, is common practice. The same applies to the distinction between intra-industry trade and inter-industry trade as well as other commonly used statistical and economic conventions.

Of more significance perhaps is the arrangement of country data used here. Information on a large number of countries is included in the book, and space constraints dictated that various country groupings be used. The most familiar of these groupings is the developed market economies (DMEs). These economies are a fairly homogeneous group, being similar in terms of

5

relative factor endowments, structure of manufacturing production, composition of trade and other attributes. The same degree of homogeneity does not apply to the developing countries. A certain amount of country-specific data is presented in the following chapters, but, more often, the developing countries are arranged in different sub-groups: newly industrializing economies (NIEs), second-generation NIEs, and other developing countries. These types of country groupings are familiar to most readers, although economic theory provides no clear criteria to determine group membership (see e.g. Bradford and Branson, 1987; Cline, 1982; Michaely, 1985).

No generally accepted definition of group membership is available. Instead, the selection of first- and second-generation NIEs has merely drawn upon the work of others. In the case of the first-generation NIEs, the group is pictured as consisting of countries that are 'super competitors' in many international markets for manufactures and are likely to embody production and trading attributes that distinguish them from most other developing countries. The same claims do not necessarily apply to second-generation NIEs, though their involvement in world exports would still seem to distinguish them from other developing countries.

Other elements of the book's framework are conceptual in nature and are drawn from the theoretical literature. The choice of theoretical tools is determined partly by the types of broad issues mentioned above. For example, the book's emphasis on empirical issues requires that theoretical tools be operational in the sense that data requirements are realistic and attainable. Propositions that can be closely linked with underlying theory are also favoured over those that can be stated only intuitively. Finally, because the study is international in scope, there is also a preference for theoretical material that is of general applicability rather than valid only for specific cases.

Based on these considerations, the H–O model (also described as the factor proportions, factor endowments or factor abundance approach) provides much of the theoretical framework for analysis. The factor abundance approach operates reasonably well when inter-industry aspects of trade and specialization are the subject of investigation and the scope of study is international or global. But the model is not intended to suggest that factor abundance is the only source of trade or specialization. Once attention turns to intra-industry aspects, it faces a strong challenge. A theoretical counter-culture has emerged which Krugman describes as being represented by 'a set of informal arguments stressing sources of trade other than those in formal models' (1987, p. 132).

The conceptual basis for analysis

The two approaches mentioned above are distinct in several ways, but they are also complementary in the sense that the H–O model is concerned with inter-industry characteristics while the alternative approaches referred to by Krugman are especially useful for an analysis of intra-industry forms of specialization and trade. Both lines of argument are utilized in the following account. Because several characteristic assumptions are the subject of empirical inquiry in later chapters, it is helpful to summarize them here.

The distinguishing assumptions of the H–O model as outlined in Chipman (1988) can be most easily described for the simple case involving only two countries which produce two goods and make use of two factors of production. The factors are assumed to be qualitatively identical between countries. They are completely mobile between industries but are immobile between countries. Goods, however, move freely between countries. The production functions for each good are the same in both countries and are subject to constant returns to scale. A further assumption is that factor requirements (intensities) will never be reversed between the two goods, no matter how factor prices change.

The H–O model goes on to assume perfect competition in markets for both goods and factors. This postulate, together with the insistence on constant returns to scale, enables the analyst to construct the general equilibrium framework for trade which the H–O model represents. In order to highlight the role of factor abundance, the possible impact of demand on trade patterns is excluded by the assumption that consumption patterns are identical between countries at any given set of goods' prices. Finally, it is assumed that trade in goods is balanced.

Differences in factor proportions – with respect to both country endowments and input requirements – are necessary for international trade to arise. Differences in factor endowments relate to factor abundance, while input requirements are represented by factor intensities. On the basis of these assumptions, factor abundance will determine the pattern of international trade. A country will export the good that uses its abundant factor most intensively and will import that which uses its scarce factor intensively.

The approaches that represent the alternative to the H–O model are referred to here as the 'economies-of-scale' models. Perhaps the best version is that presented by Krugman (1979a). He assumes that international trade takes place in the presence of increasing returns, product differentiation and monopolistic competition. In the simplest case, involving only two countries, each economy is capable of producing any of a large number of goods by using one factor of production. Production technology is the same for all (potential) goods in both countries, so that firms can differentiate their products costlessly. The decisive technological feature is that of increasing returns to scale: the cost functions in the two countries reflect decreasing average costs.

With regard to demand, all consumers of a country are assumed to have the same utility function, which treats goods (or rather, versions of one differentiated good) symmetrically. This concept represents the consumers' 'love of variety' – that is, the consumers have no overwhelming preferences for any particular version of the differentiated good. The market structure is assumed to be one of Chamberlinian monopolistic competition. Each producer faces a downward–sloping demand curve for his particular version of the differentiated good and can choose the output level that maximizes his profits. Since a great number of producers is assumed, no interaction between them takes place.

Even if the two countries are identical with regard to technologies and tastes, they will engage in international trade. This trade will take the form of intra-industrial exchange. The pattern of trade (which country exports or imports which version of the differentiated good) is indeterminate but the volume can be related to the size of the two trading partners. In general, the Krugman model depicts new forms of trade as 'a way of extending the market and allowing exploitation of scale economies' (Krugman, 1979a, p. 479).

Further contrasts between the H–O and economies–of–scale model are found in terms of their 'power' or explanatory capability. Krugman (1983) asserts that the factor endowments approach can not provide an adequate account of world trade. That criticism is perhaps fair when a 'strong version' of the H–O hypothesis is employed. But more general, and 'weaker', versions of the H–O proposition are also available. Models incorporating scale economies and product differentiation seem to perform no better than the weaker versions of the H–O model. The lack of more robust predictive abilities is due mainly to the fact that the scale economies model is concerned not so much with patterns of commodity production or trade but with the relative extent of inter-industry and intra-industry trade. The H–O approach is treated in a fairly rigorous manner, and weaker versions of the model are used extensively in the following account. Scale economies, product differentiation and other aspects of imperfect competition will necessarily receive less formal treatment.

Organization and summary of findings

The following chapters fall into three parts. Chapters 2, 3 and 4 are mainly documentary in nature. They represent an empirical survey of manufacturing production, inter-industry trade and intra-industry trade. Although the chapters are broad in scope, an industry-specific orientation is retained and various theoretical concepts find application.

Chapters 5, 6 and 7 constitute the second part of the study and make extensive use of the H–O model. Chapter 5 is concerned with country differences in factor endowments, while Chapter 6 focuses on the role of factor intensities. The results obtained in these two chapters are drawn together in Chapter 7 where a synopsis of the H–O model is presented. Most of this discussion is concerned with differences in the economic attributes of countries, but Chapter 7 also addresses the possibility that country similarities can influence specialization and trade.

This alternative line of reasoning is expanded in Chapters 8 and 9 as the discussion moves from an H–O framework to the 'economies-of-scale' model. Empirical evidence concerning economies of scale, market structure and product differentiation is examined for specific industries and groups of countries. Various attributes of intra-industry trade involving different sets of countries are studied, and some of its potential determinants are considered. Chapter 10 concludes the study by summarizing the major results and considering their implications for the future work of theorists and empiricists. Some of the main findings of later chapters are summarized below.

Inter-industrial trends in manufacturing production

The analysis begins with a survey of inter-industrial patterns in world industry in the DMEs and in several groups of developing countries. The main purpose is to provide an empirical backdrop for the more detailed analysis of specialization in production and trade in later chapters.

The DMEs' share of world manufacturing value added (MVA) is declining, though they continue to dominate almost all markets for manufactures. This decline, however, is not reflected by any change in the inter-industrial composition of output. Specific industries in specific countries have contracted substantially, but the inter-industrial structure of total manufacturing output in DMEs has proven to be relatively stable. The contradiction between these two trends is attributed to three factors. One is the decline in manufacturing relative to services, which seems to have affected several DMEs. A second is that a major source of contractive pressure is often competitors in other DMEs and the resultant shifts are not reflected in group averages. The third reason is that major firms in some industries have suffered not from inter-industry shifts in demand or supply, but from changes that are intra-industry in character.

Close agreement in national endowments and demand patterns should mean that the inter-industry structure of countries is similar. This prognosis, however, finds little support. The DMEs are the only group of countries that can claim more than a modest degree of similarity in inter-industry structure. Nor does the inter-temporal pattern of change show any evidence of a tendency for inter-industrial structures to converge, although differences in relative factor endowments and tastes have certainly narrowed.

The lack of any evidence of increasing similarity may imply that the inter-industry patterns are moving in the opposite direction, towards greater specialization in particular industries. Although the DMEs have the greatest degree of similarity, they also tend to specialize in much the same industries. Only the NIEs come close to matching the DMEs in terms of inter-industrial specialization. No similar evidence of specialization was found for second-generation NIEs.

These impressions are based on comparisons between individual countries or averages for country groups. However, the dynamics of inter-industry change can also be examined in relation to an international reference or norm. Here also, there is little agreement between patterns of change in DMEs and developing countries. Industries that tend to be expanding in DMEs (according to an internationalized measure) are often contracting in developing countries, and the reverse is also true. Nor do the internationalized patterns of change agree with measures expressed in purely 'domestic' terms. An industry that is faring poorly in relation to other parts of domestic manufacturing may still be performing better than competitors in other countries.

9

The pace of inter-industrial change is also considered. Indices of structural change show that inter-industry shifts are proceeding more rapidly among the NIEs and second-generation NIEs than in DMEs or in non-NIEs. This distinction must be discounted to some extent, however, since patterns of change in the two former country groups are comparatively erratic: periods of rapid growth in the NIEs and second-generation NIEs are often preceded or followed by equally abrupt periods of contraction.

Conventional analysis distinguishes between industries according to their factor intensities, growth elasticities or other characteristics. When industries are classified by such criteria, the results for various country groups are substantially different. Manufacturers in the DMEs have moved rather quickly out of industries that are relatively labour-intensive, but there has not been a concomitant rise in industries that are especially large users of capital. The developing countries have been comparatively slow to withdraw from labour-intensive operations, but the growth of capital-intensive industries has been rapid – proportionately much greater than the corresponding shift in DMEs. The move into capital-intensive industries has been fastest among the non-NIEs and was attributable mainly to trends in several of the larger countries (India, Pakistan and Turkey). Such a result is surprising, since the relative prices of investment goods are thought to be highest in developing countries other than the NIEs. Direct government action rather than differences in relative factor prices would seem to be the most likely explanation for this particular result.

Inter-industry trade in a global system

Chapter 3 begins with a survey of long-term trends in the world trade. The dynamic nature of trade in manufactures is impressive in comparison with growth in other parts of the world economy. Another prominent feature is the dominance of the DMEs: these countries have accounted for at least four-fifths of world exports of manufactures in every year between 1970 and 1982. The developing countries' share of world trade in manufactures remains small (13 per cent in 1985), although it has more than doubled since 1970.

The fact that the bulk of the DMEs' manufactured trade is with other members of the same group is somewhat of a theoretical curiosity. The factor proportions model predicts that countries with significant differences in factor endowments will have the greatest incentive to trade. The tendency towards factor convergence among the DMEs should have reduced the potential for trade between these countries, though, in fact, intra-DME trade has continued to grow rapidly.

A first attempt to link patterns of inter-industry trade with their underlying determinants makes use of three trade models. Statistics for 22 DMEs and more than 150 developing countries were compiled for all years during the period 1970–85 and were then arranged in product categories that approximate the Ricardian, H–O and product-cycle models. Net exports of Ricardian goods (i.e. resource-based products) have had little impact on world trade balances. The DMEs have usually had a slight deficit in their trade in Ricardian goods, while the developing countries have maintained a small, but favourable, trade balance.

Results for the two other trade categories are of more interest. The DMEs have long enjoyed a favourable – and relatively stable – balance of trade in H–O goods. That situation was reversed in the 1980s, and after 1984 the group became a net importer of H–O goods. The reversal did not apply to all DMEs, however. Among the six largest DMEs, the USA and the UK were the only ones to experience a significant deterioration in their trading position for H–O goods. By 1985, the US net imports of H–O goods exceeded the corresponding net exports of France, the Federal Republic of Germany, Italy and Japan combined.

The developing countries' trade in H–O goods is much different. They were traditionally net importers of such goods, and the size of their trade imbalance grew steadily during the 1970s. That relationship, too, had changed by 1985, when the developing countries became net exporters of H–O goods. The turnaround was due largely to trade successes of the NIEs. These countries had only modest net exports of H–O goods in 1975 ($0.5 billion), but ten years later their net exports exceeded $31 billion.

The pattern of world trade in product-cycle goods is the most volatile of the three categories. The DMEs excel in the production and export of these goods. Net exports of product-cycle goods from DMEs rose almost sixfold between 1970 and 1980. The value of the DMEs' net exports has fallen in the 1980s, but this was largely due to circumstances in the USA (which is now a net importer) and to a decline in the net exports of the UK.

As expected, the developing countries' net trade in product-cycle goods has been negative throughout the 1970s and 1980s. There was a steady increase in net imports of these countries in the 1970s, but, again, the beginning of the 1980s marked a watershed. The developing countries continue to be net importers of product-cycle goods, but the deficit is now lower than the level recorded in 1980. The pattern of trade in product-cycle goods differs among various groups of developing countries. The NIEs have the lowest level of net imports, and these have declined since 1980. In big countries such as India, Pakistan and Yugoslavia, net imports of product-cycle goods have increased modestly, while in many of the smaller and generally poorer developing countries, net imports of these goods have steadily grown.

Two-way trade in similar products

Chapter 4 completes the 'survey' portion of the book with an analysis of two-way trade. Such trade occurs in several forms. The chapter begins with a description of each of these and then goes on to discuss methods of measurement.

An examination of bilateral trade for developed countries and a sample of developing countries shows that IIT is most important among the DMEs, where it accounts for more than two-fifths of all trade in manufactures. This figure is substantially higher than the average for developing countries or any subset of these countries. The analysis of the pattern of IIT suggests that a positive relationship exists between a country's level of development and the share of IIT. Furthermore, similarity between trading partners fosters IIT. Support for these hypotheses is found in calculations of IIT shares in world trade, in the trade between different country groups, and in the figures for individual countries. In addition, an examination of trade growth shows that, almost without exception, IIT is growing more rapidly than its inter–industrial counterpart.

The second half of the chapter adopts an industry-specific view of IIT. Further support for the 'similarity hypothesis' mentioned above is obtained when the two-way trade of each industry is considered separately for the DMEs and developing countries. Although the extent of product differentiation is probably greatest in consumer goods industries, producers of capital goods are the most heavily involved in IIT. The prominence of capital goods producers results from their large share in the two-way trade of DMEs. Consumer goods figure most prominently in the IIT of developing countries.

Difficulties in the measurement of two-way trade arise from the fact that certain types of IIT are not statistically distinguishable. This has led to a tendency for analysts to focus on rates of change rather than levels of IIT. Of the 90 industries considered in this study, more than two-thirds experienced increases in the share of IIT in total trade between 1970 and 1985. More generally, two-way trade has become an important phenomenon and is not restricted to any particular group of countries or industries.

International patterns of factor endowments

Chapter 5 embarks on an analysis of inter-industry patterns by considering the role of factor endowments. The factors considered in this exercise are physical capital, skilled labour, semi-skilled labour, and unskilled labour. Prior to presenting the results, several conceptual and definitional issues are discussed.

The first step in the empirical analysis is to obtain a picture of the international distribution of factor endowments and to determine how the pattern has changed over time. The results for DMEs present no surprises. These countries are comparatively well endowed with physical capital. Their shares of skilled and semi-skilled labour are smaller but still high by international standards. The endowment pattern of developing countries is characterized by a relative scarcity of both skilled labour and physical capital.

More interesting is the distinction between various sets of developing countries. The NIEs have a fairly balanced resource structure with semi-skilled and

12

skilled labour being most important. The pattern is similar among second-generation NIEs. These countries, however, are relatively better endowed with unskilled and semi-skilled labour than are the NIEs. The remaining developing countries account for an overwhelming portion of unskilled labour while physical capital is relatively scarce.

Long-term shifts in the distribution of factor supplies reveal a significant trend which concerns the redistribution of factors between the two major country groups. Changes have not been great, but have clearly favoured the developing countries. The largest shifts were in the shares of physical capital, mainly owing to the rapid accumulation of this factor in several NIEs and second-generation NIEs. Changes in the endowment pattern for semi-skilled labour were also significant. In 1970 all the developing countries accounted for 46 per cent of the total supply in the country sample, but by 1985 they claimed 53 per cent.

In the closing section of Chapter 5, the discussion turns to the role of factor abundance (rather than factor endowments). Using dichotomous indicators of abundance/scarcity, trading patterns in broad product classes are examined. Three classes of traded products are identified: they include labour-intensive H–O goods, capital-intensive H–O goods, and product-cycle goods. Relationships in accordance with the factor abundance hypothesis are observed between skilled labour and net exports of product-cycle goods, as well as between semi-skilled or unskilled labour and net exports of labour-intensive H–O goods. Most of the countries that are net exporters of product-cycle goods are relatively well endowed with skilled labour, while most of the net exporters of labour-intensive H–O goods are characterized by an abundance of semi-skilled or unskilled labour.

Although the results linking endowments of physical capital with net exports offer less support for the factor abundance hypothesis, the 'weak' version of the hypothesis is not refuted. The reason is that this version depends not on a robust relationship between factor endowments and net trade but merely on a tendency, or an on-average association, between the two variables. A possible explanation for the results on physical capital is the H–O assumption that factors are not internationally mobile. Clearly, such an assumption does not apply to physical capital. It is more applicable to semi-skilled and unskilled labour, and the results for those two factors support the factor abundance hypothesis.

Factor requirements, output and trade

Chapter 6 provides a detailed account of factor intensities in specific industries. After discussing issues of measurement, the relationship between factor intensities and patterns of output and exports in specific industries are examined.

Ordinal comparisons of factor intensity are made for a large number of countries during the period 1970–85. Variations over time were not great: the industries that tended to be relatively heavy users of a particular factor during the 1970s remained so in the 1980s. Industry rankings by physical- and human-capital intensity were also similar, suggesting a close relationship between the two inputs. The cross-industry pattern confirms most casual impressions regarding factor requirements. Industries typically regarded as being heavy users of physical capital, human capital or labour generally matched expectations.

Contrasts are more apparent when variations in factor intensities across countries are examined on an industry-by-industry basis. Large differences in labour intensity are found – even among the most labour-intensive industries. Cross-country variations in physical- and human-capital intensity were similar in magnitude and considerably lower than those for labour. Statistical tests reveal a high level of agreement in the international rankings of industries, but in no instance is this agreement perfect.

The relationship between factor intensity on the one hand and specialization and trade on the other is tested with the help of an empirical hypothesis. This hypothesis is based on the premise that competitive advantage will be concentrated in a set or 'bloc' of industries which are intensive users of a country's abundant factor. Tests of the 'bloc hypothesis' are conducted for both output and trade. Predictions of the H–O model are confirmed for DMEs. The competitive strengths of these countries are determined by ample supplies of human and physical capital, while they are at a substantial disadvantage in the production of labour-intensive goods. The results for developing countries are somewhat different: the expectation that competitive advantages in production would be concentrated in labour-intensive manufactures is not borne out by the data. However, when tests of the bloc hypothesis are repeated with export data, some support for H–O propositions is obtained for the developing countries too. Thus, there is evidence for the NIEs' competitive advantage in activities using intensively labour or physical capital. Furthermore, shares in world exports of labour-intensive products were particularly high for one-half of the second-generation NIEs and some other developing countries in the 1980s.

The role of country differences and similarities

Chapter 7 begins with an examination of factor endowments as a determinant of net trade. The discussion is industry-specific, being based on data for 90 industries in each of 46 countries. Subsequent sections consider the interaction between factor endowments and factor intensities and how these variables influence patterns of trade and specialization.

The analysis makes use of the concept of 'factor orientation'. The term is employed in an industry-specific context and refers to those instances where the availability of a particular factor has a discernible impact on net trade. The 'direction' of the orientation may be either positive or negative depending on the availability of the particular factor and the industry's factor intensity. In other words, relative abundance of a factor may enhance an industry's competitive advantage, or, alternatively, its scarcity may result in a competitive disadvantage.

The overall impression obtained from these tests is that factor endowments do not exert an overwhelming impact on net trade. Less than half of the 90 industries considered are found to have any 'visible factor orientation'. That picture is altered somewhat when the volume of each industry's trade is taken into account. Industries with a visible factor orientation are found to account for over half of all manufactured trade in the country sample, and their share has been increasing over time.

Confirmation that factor abundance is an important determinant of trade patterns does not, by itself, provide much useful information to the analyst or policy-maker. It is more important to know which factors have the greatest influence on trade and whether their significance is changing over time. This issue is considered first in terms of the manufacturing sector as a whole. The same question is later addressed in an industry-specific context.

The sector-wide investigation of this issue demonstrates that in the 1970s physical capital had the greatest influence on sectoral comparative advantage in manufactures. The situation changed during the 1980s, however. Skilled labour replaced physical capital as the most important of the factors considered here. The two remaining factors – semi-skilled and unskilled labour – were of much less importance as determinants of comparative advantage in manufactured goods.

A related point concerns the way in which the two major factors affect trade in manufactures. Physical capital is generally found to make a positive contribution to trade performance. In countries with an abundance of physical capital, those industries with a matching orientation tended to excel. The same description does not apply to skilled labour: this factor usually had a negative impact on net exports.

The discussion goes on to analyse circumstances in specific industries. These results are too detailed to summarize here, though several generalizations can be made. First, the way in which each factor influences the trade of different industries varies over time. Second, the results show that only a portion of net trade is subject to factor-abundance effects. That is not surprising, since the factor abundance model considers only a single set of determinants (factor endowments).

Although factor endowments do not always yield a convincing or complete explanation of trading patterns, the results are sufficiently encouraging to attempt a more general application of the H–O model. A multi-dimensional version of the H–O model is used to assess the interaction between factor abundance, factor intensities and trade simultaneously. Results of the exercise support a weak (or on-average) interpretation of the H–O model. Even in a complex trading world of many factors, goods and countries, there is a tendency for net trade to be influenced by the interaction between factor endowments and factor intensities.

15

The results for semi–skilled labour match most closely with the predictions of the H–O model. Physical capital and skilled labour seem to be more important determinants of sector–wide trading patterns, although neither set of results fits comfortably with industry results. There may be several explanations for these ambiguities. Semi–skilled labour represents a category of workers whose skills are closely related to the production process. That factor is a vital input for many industries, and a large reservoir of semi–skilled labour would provide a solid basis for specialization and trade. Physical capital and highly skilled labour may be even more crucial to the operation of many industries, but it may also be very difficult for many countries (particularly developing countries) to develop adequate supplies of these factors. Here, it is relevant to note that neither of these two resources fulfils the H–O model's assumption of factor immobility.

In the concluding section of the chapter, interest turns from the issue of national differences in factor endowments to similarities. Studies based on models other than the H–O genre have concluded that country similarities actually contribute to the international exchange of goods. The two interpretations, however, are concerned with different types of specialization and trade. Inter–industry forms of specialization and trade are the primary concern of the factor abundance model, while explanations that stress the degree of similarity between countries focus on intra–industry forms of specialization and trade.

Bilateral patterns of trade in specific industries are used to examine the effects of country similarities. The hypothesis tested with this large body of data is that greater country similarities will give rise to larger amounts of bilateral IIT. The test confirms that similarities in income, market size or relative endowments are positively associated with the level of IIT. In fact, there is no industry where country similarities prove to have a negative impact on IIT.

Economies of scale, market structure and international trade

Chapter 8 moves from the H–O model to a set of issues more commonly associated with the new trade theories. These include scale economies, industrial concentration and product differentiation. A full–fledged empirical assessment of these topics is not attempted. Instead, the chapter represents an empirical excursion into a non–H–O world rather than an attempt to test existing theory.

The chapter begins with a series of inter–industry comparisons for each of the three variables mentioned above. The role of scale economies naturally varies across industries but generally tends to be of more significance in developing countries than in DMEs. The distinction appears to reflect the greater disparities between large and small establishments in the developing countries. Another reason is that large establishments in developing countries often operate in highly protected markets.

Scale economies may also represent a barrier to entry. The data presented in Chapter 8 indicate that manufacturers in developing countries face the highest entry barriers. This is especially true in industries requiring relatively large amounts of physical capital or depending on scale economies. The pattern in DMEs is much less clear. The existence of excess capacity in some industries along with capacity rationalization in others presents a very mixed picture.

Entropy indices are used to measure the degree of industrial concentration. The results reveal a much more consistent pattern than was found for scale economies. The same industries tend to be highly concentrated in both DMEs and developing countries. The degree of concentration in DMEs, however, is less than in developing countries. These impressions, however, are based on a set of industries that are defined in rather broad terms, which make it difficult to interpret the results. In order to remedy this weakness, similar tests are carried out with detailed data for over 400 US industries. The major finding of the exercise is that industrial concentration is positively correlated with both scale economies and capital intensity.

The concluding section of the chapter examines the relationship between industrial concentration and export concentration. It is shown that the two characteristics are positively correlated across industries. Furthermore, both domestic (industrial) and export concentration are high in Ricardian industries but low among H–O industries. Export concentration is also high in product-cycle industries, although the degree of domestic concentration seems to depend on the nature of research and development expenditures and the extent of scale economies.

Intra-industry trade revisited

Chapter 9 returns to the subject of IIT but examines it from a perspective that differs from the discussion in Chapter 4 and the approach used in other studies. Analysts have usually adopted a rather broad frame of reference by studying IIT in relation to total trade in manufactures. However, tthe present chapter is concerned with aspects of the new trade theories and an industry-by-industry approach is adopted. The main purpose is to gain some impression of how patterns of IIT are influenced by the types of industry-specific characteristics that were introduced in earlier parts of the book.

The analysis considers 90 industries located in 47 countries. Only a moderate portion of the variation in IIT shares across industries is explained by scale economies, product differentiation and industrial concentration. In the DMEs, the share of IIT appears to be positively related to scale economies. The relationship is a weak one, however, and does not apply to developing countries. Nor does product differentiation exert a particularly strong influence on IIT. That result is partially discounted, however, since methods of measurement can take account only of vertical (not horizontal) forms of differentiation. The relationship between industrial concentration and the share of IIT is much stronger. Higher levels of concentration reduce the share of IIT in total trade.

CHAPTER 2

Inter-industrial trends in manufacturing production

Patterns of change in manufactured output can be examined from either a domestic (i.e. national) or an international perspective, though the emphasis in this book is mainly on the latter. Moreover, attention is focused on long-term changes rather than on the sort of adjustments that occur over the course of the business cycle. Such an orientation leads to a discussion of industrial structure, structural change, and inter-industrial patterns of specialization.

The meaning of these structural terms can vary widely; and before embarking on this survey, some elaboration is helpful.[1] The notion of structural change may refer to either a relative or an absolute shift in output or employment. Absolute changes in output or employment are more relevant for studies of a single country. Though a decline in the share of output or employment could change the relative power of industrial workers or even the character of society, an absolute decrease in the level of output or employment involves greater, and more costly, adjustments.[2]

An emphasis on absolute shifts in output or employment is less appropriate when the subject of discussion is international in scope. Any deterioration in an industry's relative international standing is more likely to bring a response from policy-makers than if the industry were to decline in relation to other domestic industries. Public policies in support of a particular industry (e.g. import restrictions, favourable tax treatment, a relaxation of anti-trust laws or other methods) are more easily justified as a response to foreign competition than to competition between domestic firms.

This chapter begins by looking at inter-industrial patterns of specialization. The main purpose is to provide a comprehensive picture of world industry and patterns of change since the early 1970s. The subsequent discussion is concerned with the degree of industrial similarity between the developed and developing countries and some of the general factors that may influence patterns of specialization.

Global pattern of manufacturing output

The geographical distribution of world industry is well known. Table 2.1 shows the distribution of world MVA among major groups of countries

Table 2.1 Share of economic groups and developing regions in world MVA, 1970–86[a]/ (percentages)

Year	DMEs	CPEs	Developing countries/areas[b]/	Developing regions				
				Africa	West Asia	South and East Asia[b]/	Latin America	Europe
1970	74.3	15.2	10.5	0.8	0.7	2.4	6.1	0.5
1973	73.2	15.8	11.0	0.8	0.8	2.6	6.3	0.5
1975	69.0	18.9	12.2	0.9	0.9	2.9	6.8	0.6
1977	68.7	19.0	12.3	0.9	0.9	3.2	6.7	0.6
1979	68.2	19.1	12.7	0.9	0.9	3.4	6.8	0.7
1980	67.3	19.6	13.1	0.9	0.9	3.5	7.0	0.7
1981	67.0	19.9	13.0	1.0	1.0	3.7	6.6	0.7
1982	66.2	20.6	13.2	1.0	1.1	3.9	6.5	0.7
1983	66.3	20.7	13.1	1.0	1.1	4.1	6.2	0.7
1984	66.8	20.2	13.0	1.0	1.1	4.2	6.1	0.7
1985	66.7	20.4	12.9	1.0	1.1	4.1	6.0	0.7
1986	66.1	20.7	13.3	0.9	1.1	4.3	6.2	0.7

Source: UNIDO

a/ Percentages were calculated from data at 1980 prices. For a list of the countries and areas
included in each group, see the statistical appendix.

b/ Excluding Afghanistan, China and Taiwan Province.

and regions. The share of MVA in DMEs has fallen since 1970, while the shares of centrally planned economies (CPEs) and developing countries have risen. The most rapidly industrializing countries are in South and East Asia, but the industrial progress of other developing regions has been somewhat disappointing. For example, the share of Latin America – the most industrialized of the developing regions – has declined since 1980, and that of Africa has been virtually unchanged since 1970.

The relative importance of any group of countries will vary from industry to industry. Table 2.2 provides an overview of the global pattern of inter-industry specialization in a number of industries. The prominence of DMEs has waned but they continue to account for a disproportionate share of world output in many industries – notably paper, metal products, electrical machinery and transport equipment. The decline is explained primarily by the gains of CPEs. The latter countries have made considerable progress in industries such as textiles, industrial chemicals, non-ferrous metals and non-electrical machinery.

Figures for the developing countries present a somewhat different picture. Given the abundance of unskilled labour in these countries, it is logical to expect relative progress to be concentrated in labour-intensive industries. The most widely accepted example of such an industry is textiles. Though the developing countries have recorded modest gains in several labour-intensive industries (for example, wearing apparel and footwear), their share of world textile production has changed very little since 1965. In contrast to expectations, these countries' most impressive gains have been in resource-intensive industries such as petroleum refining, industrial chemicals and steel – none of which is labour-intensive.

Shifts in the inter-industry composition of world industry have their parallel at the domestic level. Table 2.3 summarizes the latter feature, showing the average structure of MVA in several country groups. The figures for DMEs are of some interest. The inter-industry structure of output in these countries has changed very little since 1970. Apart from a notable increase in the share of electrical machinery, the relative gains and losses of most industries were negligible. This fact runs counter to the claims of policy-makers and industrialists in some DMEs who describe the plight of various industries in alarming terms.

Foreign competitors are usually regarded as the major source of contractive pressures in specific industries. However, the fact that the DMEs' share of world MVA has fallen without accompanying changes in the structure of manufacturing suggests other reasons. One obvious explanation is that the service sector in DMEs has grown dramatically – and at the relative expense of manufacturing. Another possibility is that the major source of competitive pressure is the DMEs themselves. The list of senescent industries and industrial successes varies across DMEs, and their rise and fall may be concealed by group averages. A third reason could be that much of the structural change experienced by DMEs has been not inter-industry but rather intra-industry in

Table 2.2 Share of economic groups in world value added of selected manufacturing branches and years[a]/ (percentages)

Industry (ISIC)	DMEs			Developing countries/areas			CPEs		
	1965	1975	1986	1965	1975	1986	1965	1975	1986
Food products (311/2)	58.9	54.0	50.6	16.7	16.3	18.9	24.4	29.7	30.5
Beverages (313)	60.1	54.9	56.7	13.3	15.4	21.3	26.6	29.7	22.0
Tobacco (314)	49.4	50.4	42.9	35.8	33.0	37.6	14.8	16.6	19.5
Textiles (321)	54.8	47.6	43.8	21.5	21.3	22.7	23.7	31.1	33.5
Wearing apparel (322)	69.1	58.9	51.0	12.9	14.4	16.9	18.0	26.7	32.1
Footwear (324)	68.3	57.2	45.9	14.8	17.3	19.4	16.9	25.5	34.7
Paper products (341)	87.2	82.7	80.8	7.3	9.3	11.4	5.5	8.0	7.8
Industrial chemicals (351)	73.0	64.4	59.3	7.3	9.6	13.5	19.7	26.0	27.2
Other chemicals (352)	74.3	69.5	68.1	15.8	17.1	19.3	9.9	13.4	12.6
Petroleum refineries (353)	64.6	59.5	46.3	24.6	24.6	36.2	10.8	15.9	17.5
Rubber products (355)	70.8	62.9	57.1	11.9	13.9	16.6	17.3	23.2	26.3
Pottery,china,earthenware (361)	77.6	68.1	60.1	9.8	12.1	13.4	12.6	19.8	26.5
Glass products (362)	80.3	73.2	70.1	10.2	13.2	13.9	9.5	13.6	16.0
Other non-met.min.prod.(369)	71.5	61.6	54.3	10.9	14.7	20.5	17.6	23.7	25.2
Iron and steel (371)	81.3	74.7	67.7	5.8	8.9	13.3	12.9	16.4	19.0
Non-ferrous metals (372)	76.5	67.6	66.9	9.0	9.4	11.3	14.5	23.0	21.8
Metal products (381)	87.0	80.5	73.1	7.8	9.7	13.3	5.2	9.8	13.6
Non-electrical machinery (382)	79.3	67.6	59.5	3.2	4.9	4.5	17.5	27.5	36.0
Electrical machinery (383)	86.8	81.1	80.2	5.4	7.1	8.4	7.8	11.8	11.4
Transport equipment (384)	87.2	80.4	77.9	5.3	7.5	7.4	7.5	12.1	14.7

Source: UNIDO

a/ Percentages were calculated from data at 1980 prices. Owing to a lack of data, not all three-digit industries are shown here.

Table 2.3 Structure of MVA,a/ by economic groups (constant 1980 prices)

Industry (ISIC)	DMEs		CPEs		All developing countries b/		Advanced developing countries c/		Other developing countries d/	
	1970	1986	1970	1986	1970	1986	1970	1986	1970	1986
Food products (311/2)	8.8	8.8	18.3	15.0	18.6	15.9	16.6	14.7	24.8	20.3
Beverages (313)	1.9	1.9	3.6	2.0	3.0	3.4	2.8	2.8	3.6	5.5
Tobacco (314)	0.7	0.6	1.0	0.7	3.3	2.4	1.9	1.7	7.6	4.7
Textiles (321)	4.6	3.5	10.1	7.6	12.3	8.7	13.3	8.8	9.3	8.6
Wearing apparel (322)	2.9	2.2	4.8	4.0	4.0	3.4	4.3	3.7	3.1	2.4
Leather and fur products (323)	0.6	0.4	0.9	0.6	0.9	0.6	1.0	0.6	0.7	0.6
Footwear (324)	0.9	0.5	1.3	1.1	1.6	1.0	1.6	1.0	1.5	1.1
Wood and cork products (331)	2.9	2.4	1.9	1.5	2.9	2.4	2.8	2.5	3.1	1.9
Furniture, fixtures, excl. metal (332)	2.0	1.9	1.0	1.2	1.4	1.1	1.5	1.2	1.3	1.1
Paper products (341)	3.5	3.6	1.0	1.0	2.3	2.5	2.3	2.4	2.0	2.8
Printing and publishing (342)	4.6	4.9	0.9	0.7	3.7	2.5	4.3	2.6	2.0	1.9
Industrial chemicals (351)	3.9	4.3	5.0	5.7	2.6	4.7	2.8	5.3	1.9	2.3
Other chemicals (352)	3.1	3.9	2.1	2.0	3.9	5.0	4.0	5.3	3.7	4.3
Petroleum refineries (353)	2.4	1.7	2.2	1.8	6.3	6.1	3.7	3.4	14.4	15.9
Products of petroleum and coal (354)	0.4	0.3	2.5	1.9	0.7	0.7	0.7	0.7	0.7	0.5
Rubber products (355)	1.3	1.1	1.5	1.5	1.6	1.6	1.8	1.8	1.1	1.0
Plastic products (356)	1.4	2.3	0.6	0.8	1.5	1.6	1.4	1.7	1.6	1.4
Pottery, china, earthenware (361)	0.5	0.4	0.5	0.5	0.5	0.5	0.6	0.5	0.3	0.3
Glass products (362)	0.9	0.9	0.5	0.6	0.9	0.8	1.0	0.9	0.5	0.6
Other non-metallic min.products (369)	3.0	2.4	3.8	3.2	3.6	4.3	3.6	4.1	3.6	5.2
Iron and steel (371)	7.5	4.9	5.4	3.9	4.5	4.8	5.3	5.4	2.1	2.4
Non-ferrous metals (372)	2.2	2.1	2.5	1.9	1.9	1.7	1.6	1.5	2.8	2.4
Metal products (381)	7.0	6.1	2.4	3.2	4.5	5.4	4.9	5.8	3.2	3.8
Non-electrical machinery (382)	11.5	12.5	13.5	21.4	3.2	4.7	4.0	5.3	0.8	2.4
Electrical machinery (383)	8.1	12.1	3.5	4.9	3.5	6.1	4.2	7.1	1.2	2.4
Transport equipment (384)	10.0	10.6	5.1	5.7	4.7	5.0	5.6	5.7	1.9	2.5
Professional scientific equipment (385)	2.0	2.3	2.1	2.8	0.3	0.6	0.4	0.8	0.1	0.1
Other manufactures (390)	1.4	1.4	2.0	2.8	1.8	2.5	2.0	2.7	1.1	1.6
Total manufacturing (300)	100.0	100.0	100.0	100.0	100.0	100.0	100.0	100.0	100.0	100.0

Source: UNIDO

a/ In deriving these figures, all data were first expressed in 1980 United States dollars and shares weighted by the value of each industry's output were then calculated.
b/ Percentages were calculated from data for 69 developing countries and areas which, together, accounted for 95 per cent of that group's total MVA in 1980, the latest year for which base weights were available.
c/ Countries and areas include NIEs, second generation NIEs, India, Pakistan, Turkey and Yugoslavia.
d/ Includes 47 countries.

character. Ready examples would be the emergence of the mini–steel sector at the expense of integrated producers and the successes of specialized automobile producers at times when the major automobile firms were experiencing severe pressure.

Table 2.3 also shows the structure of output for all developing countries and for two subsets. The first of these subsets is made up of the 'more advanced' countries,[3] while the second is a heterogeneous group which includes many of the smaller and often poorer developing countries. The structure of the advanced developing countries is close to the average for all developing countries, a result that reflects the importance of the former group in the total.

The most significant inter-industry shift is the substantial drop in the share of textiles in total MVA. The industry's share declined by roughly one-third in both subsets of developing countries. This deterioration was balanced by modest gains spread across several industries including chemicals, electrical machinery, transport and steel. The composition of MVA in the advanced developing countries is also more diversified than in the poorer ones. A disproportionate amount of MVA in the poorer countries is accounted for by only five industries – food, beverages, tobacco, textiles and petroleum – which supplied 55 per cent of MVA in 1986. Only one of the remaining 23 industries produced more than 5 per cent of MVA.

These results show an inter-industry pattern that is most diversified in the DMEs, moderately so in the advanced developing countries, and highly concentrated in the poorer ones. Such a generalization is based on group averages and does not necessarily imply that inter-industry diversification is systematically related to a country's level of development. It may, however, suggest that economic growth is first reflected by greater inter-industry diversification, while intra-industry forms of diversification are more important among DMEs.

Structural trends and inter-industry specialization are, of course, partially determined by the overall performance of the world economy. The early 1970s were characterized by dramatic increases in the price of oil and other commodities followed by a period of rapid inflation. These developments subsequently led to a slow-down in growth of investment, productivity and income. An international comparison of growth rates vividly illustrates the marked difference between the present economic climate and that prevailing before 1973.

Table 2.4 documents some of these changes, showing growth of output in key industries for 1963–73 and 1973–86. No industry proved to be exempt from the slow-down. Food products are the only field that has not experienced a substantial absolute fall in rates of growth after 1973. Electrical machinery, on the other hand, continues to be one of the most dynamic industries (especially in the developing countries), although in some instances growth rates fell by almost one-half after 1973.

Japan's performance continues to surpass that of other DMEs though recent experience has brought that country's rates of growth more closely in line with

Table 2.4 Growth of output in selected industries and country groups, 1963–86 (average annual percentage rates of growth)

Economic group and countries/areas	Food products (311)[a]	Textiles and wearing apparel (321+322)[a]	Industrial chemicals and products (351+352)[a]	Fabricated metal products (381)[a]	Non-electrical machinery (382)[a]	Electrical machinery (383)[a]	Transport equipment (384)[a]
DMEs							
1963–1973	3.81	3.49	7.87	5.28	5.67	8.21	5.50
1973–1986	1.91	−0.39	2.54	0.53	2.30	4.75	1.60
United States							
1963–1973	3.01	3.80	7.51	3.79	5.53	6.99	2.89
1973–1986	2.61	0.27	3.72	0.98	2.72	4.08	2.07
Japan							
1963–1973	5.39	7.13	15.14	15.53	14.43	20.22	16.58
1973–1986	1.41	−0.33	3.66	0.85	6.01	11.90	2.77
Germany, Fed.Rep.of							
1963–1973	3.51	2.05	7.69	3.36	3.68	7.32	6.22
1973–1986	1.93	−1.81	1.58	0.76	1.43	2.71	3.70
Developing countries[b]							
1963–1973	5.29	3.96	10.91	7.66	10.49	11.72	7.80
1973–1986	4.52	2.39	6.32	4.72	3.00	7.29	2.30
NIEs[c]							
1963–1973	5.21	5.67	13.44	8.81	13.50	12.12	11.31
1973–1986	2.58	1.83	6.35	3.45	1.60	6.53	1.33
Second-generation NIEs[d]							
1963–1973	5.83	6.11	8.78	4.53	2.83	10.40	8.34
1973–1986	7.70	4.73	5.96	9.35	5.04	10.54	2.26

Source: UNIDO

[a] Numbers in parentheses refer to ISIC code.
[b] Figures are based on data for 31 countries which accounted for 79 per cent of MVA in all developing countries in 1980, the latest year for which base weights are available.
[c] Figures for China (Taiwan Province) were not available.
[d] Data were not available for Jordan, Sri Lanka and Thailand.

those of the USA and the Federal Republic of Germany. The deceleration of growth in the developing countries was milder than in the DMEs. The consequences, however, are no less severe, given the former countries' relatively small industrial base. Only the second-generation NIEs seem to have avoided the effects of the slow-down. In that group the growth of output in several industries – food products, fabricated metal products and electrical machinery – actually accelerated after 1973.

Patterns of change and specialization

A survey of trends in manufacturing output can begin by posing several questions. First, are patterns of specialization similar across countries or, if not, are they becoming more similar over time? Second, is the pace of industrial change accelerating or slowing in relation to past experience? Third, can these patterns of change be related to broad industry characteristics such as relative factor intensity?

The expectation that industrial structures are becoming more similar is based on two broad lines of reasoning. First, international differences in tastes, preferences and other demand characteristics have narrowed over the past two decades. The technological revolutions in communications and transport are important reasons for closer agreement between demand patterns. Other contributing factors include the increasing international mobility of firms and the growth of foreign direct investment. Second, studies of the relative endowments of capital and skilled and unskilled labour in Japan, the USA, Western Europe and even some developing countries have found a tendency towards convergence (Bowen, 1983a, pp. 403–5; Aho and Bayard, 1982, p. 383; Cline, 1982, p. 39). A country's factor endowments are an important determinant of the inter-industry structure, and these supply-side changes should give rise to a greater degree of output similarity.

In order to test for greater similarity, the 28 industries that make up the manufacturing sector were first ranked by level of value added in each country. These rankings were then compared for all members of each country group using Kendall's coefficient of concordance. Table 2.5 shows the results. Agreement between industry rankings is closest for the DMEs. Rankings for the advanced developing countries are less similar, and disparity is even greater when the remaining developing countries are considered as a group. Since convergence in demand patterns and relative factor endowments is likely to have gone furthest in DMEs, these results are not surprising. However, intertemporal changes in coefficients were also negligible, giving no support to the expectation that structures converged during the period 1970–86. Only the more advanced developing countries report any noticeable increase in the agreement between industry rankings.

If the similarity in industrial structures is neither great nor rising, what are the specific industries in which countries specialize? An answer to this question

Table 2.5 Test of comparative industry rankings[a]

Country group (number of countries/areas)	Kendall's coefficient of concordance[b]	
	1970	1986
DMEs (22)	0.774	0.758
Advanced developing countries (21)[c]	0.507	0.542
Other developing countries (40)	0.481	0.485
All countries (83)	0.460	0.466

Source: UNIDO

a/ Industry rankings are based on value added in constant United States dollars.

b/ Kendall's coefficient (W) is defined as:

$$W = \frac{12\ (S - 1)}{k^2\ (n^3 - n) + 24}$$

where S is the sum of the squares of the deviations of the total of the ranks obtained by each industry from the average of these totals, k is the number of countries and n is the number of industries.

c/ Includes six NIEs, eleven second generation NIEs, India, Pakistan, Turkey and Yugoslavia.

can be obtained by comparing each industry's unweighted share in the total MVA of a given country group with the corresponding world totals. An indicator having a value of unity would mean that the industry's importance in the country group exactly matches its global contribution to world MVA. Values substantially greater than unity indicate areas of specialization, while those substantially less than unity represent industries in which the country group has no specialization. For illustrative purposes, it is assumed that any indicator with a value below 0.50 (i.e. where the industry's contribution to the group's MVA is less than half of its global contribution to world MVA) represents an instance of underspecialization. The corresponding case of specialization is represented by values in excess of 1.50.

Calculations of the above type were carried out for DMEs, NIEs and second-generation NIEs and are shown in Table 2.6. Although the composition of output is most similar among the DMEs, that group's structure is also the most distinct in comparison with world averages. The DMEs specialize in eight of 28 industries, while in another three industries they are underspecialized. The pattern found for the NIEs is similar. These countries

Table 2.6 International patterns of specialization,[a] by industry, 1986 (industry and index of specialization)

Industry characterization[b]	DMEs	NIEs	NIEs, second generation
Under-specialization	beverages (0.453) tobacco (0.197) petroleum refineries (0.263)	beverages (0.394) tobacco (0.257) wood products (0.445)	non-electrical machinery (0.460)
Specialization	paper products (1.743) printing, publishing (1.628) plastic products (1.511) iron and steel (1.629) non-electrical machinery (2.454) electrical machinery (1.874) transport equipment (1.788) scientific equipment (2.258)	wearing apparel (1.644) plastic products (2.205) iron and steel (1.871) electrical machinery (2.483) transport equipment (1.605) scientific equipment (2.692)	tobacco (1.521) rubber products (2.011) other non-metallic mineral products (1.842)

Source: UNIDO

a/ The index of specialization (S) is the ratio between two shares defined as: $S = a_{ij}/a_{iw}$ where a_{ij} is the unweighted share of industry i in the MVA of country group j and a_{iw} is the corresponding share of industry i's worldwide output in world MVA.

b/ Underspecialization is defined by an index of 0.50 or less. Specialization refers to those industries having an index of 1.50 or more.

are specialized in six industries, only one of which (clothing) is not among the same list of DMEs. The second-generation NIEs are quite different. Figures for this group deviate very little from the corresponding world figures, meaning that there is no true pattern of specialization. Of the three industries that do qualify as areas of specialization, all rely heavily on inputs from mining or agriculture.

The results in Table 2.6 contrast with those of other studies of inter-industry specialization based on trade (not output) data. Trade-related studies have concluded that inter-industrial specialization among DMEs was never great and probably declined in the 1960s and early 1970s (see, e.g., Aquino, 1978, p. 294). The lack of any distinct pattern of specialization among second-generation NIEs offers another contrast. Some analysts have regarded the export gains of this group as evidence that they are gradually emerging as competitive suppliers of certain manufactures. For this interpretation to be true, numerous supply-side adjustments should have occurred. Without supporting evidence of specialization in output, a more likely explanation for the export achievements of second-generation NIEs may be the rapid growth of intra-industry trade. Such trade would require substantial imports of components and other inputs but may result in only modest additions to local value added.

The foregoing description relies upon the national economy as the reference for measuring inter-industry specialization. A more complete picture can be obtained if patterns of specialization are examined from an international perspective as well. Conventional bases for determining industrial change (for example, in relation to a country's GDP or total MVA) are not appropriate for such a purpose. Another reference, or norm, is needed for an international assessment. In the case of the DMEs, the norm chosen as a basis of comparison is the world. The norm adopted for developing countries, however, is different. Since the question is whether the industrial structure of the developing countries is becoming more similar to that of the DMEs, the latter group of countries is used as the norm.

An international measure of structural change can be based on differences between growth rates. First, the difference between an industry's growth of output in a country group and the same industry's growth in the appropriate reference group is taken. From this expression the difference between the growth of MVA in the country group and the reference group is subtracted. The resultant index would show the advance or decline of the industry, in relation to changes in the reference group.[4]

Table 2.7 identifies industries in DMEs and developing countries according to whether they are expanding or contracting in relation to the corresponding norm. There are few industries where the direction of change in the DMEs agrees with that of the developing countries. Of the 28 industries in the manufacturing sector, the DMEEs have ten that are expanding in relation to world trends. Eight of these were found to be contracting in the developing countries. Similarly, among the DMEs' 18 contracting

Table 2.7   An internationalized ranking[a/] of industries by growth of output,[b/] 1973–86

	DMEs	Developing countries[c/]	
Expanding industries	Printing and publishing Non-electrical machinery Transport equipment Plastics Electrical machinery Glass products* Paper products Furniture, fixtures* Scientific equipment Leather products*	Petroleum products Scientific equipment Petroleum refining* Non-metal products Iron and steel Miscellaneous industries Industrial chemicals Tobacco* Metal products Wood products*	Expanding industries
Contracting industries	Non-ferrous metals* Non-industrial chemicals Pottery, china* Metal products* Food products Wood products* Iron and steel* Industrial chemicals Rubber products* Wearing apparel* Beverages Textiles* Footwear* Miscellaneous industries Non-metal products* Tobacco* Petroleum refining* Petroleum products*	Rubber products* Beverages Wearing apparel* Non-ferrous metals* Footwear* Pottery, china* Furniture, fixtures* Paper products Textiles* Electrical machinery Food products* Non-industrial chemicals Glass products* Leather products* Plastic products* Non-electrical machinery Transport equipment* Printing and publishing*	Contracting industries

Source: UNIDO

a/ Industries are ranked in declining order by their relative rate of
   international expansion/contraction. An asterisk indicates that the
   industry's share of MVA in the country group declined between 1973 and 1986.

b/ The measure (I) is defined in terms of rates of growth (r) where i is the
   industry, j is the country group, n is the reference group (world or DMEs)
   and M refers to the entire manufacturing sector. Thus, $I = (r_{ij} - r_{Mj}) - (r_{in} - r_{Mn})$. In calculating I, all growth rates for country groups were
   weighted by output.

c/ Data was available for 32 developing countries which accounted for
   79 per cent of that group's MVA in the 1980 base weights.

industries, 15 appear in the list of expanding industries in the developing
countries.

Table 2.7 also identifies contracting and expanding industries in more
conventional terms (by each industry's weighted share in the MVA of the
country group). In the DMEs, 16 industries are identified as contracting by this
method, though three are found to be expanding relative to world norms. In
the developing countries, nine of the 16 industries that are contracting relative
to group averages are found to be expanding in comparison with international
standards.

More insights regarding industrial patterns can be obtained by considering the pace of change rather than the extent of agreement. In order to address this question, indices of structural change have been calculated and are reported in Table 2.8. The pace of change has been greatest in the two groups of NIEs. Moreover, the pattern appears to differ depending on the size of the countries concerned. This fact can be seen by a comparison between the two sets of indices, since the weighted measures are dominated by trends in the larger economies while unweighted measures give equal importance to large and small ones. The distinction on the basis of market size applies mainly to the DMEs and second-generation NIEs. In both groups, the extent of structural change in the larger countries has exceeded that in smaller countries. The opposite relationship is found for the NIEs, although this group is not a representative one in terms of market size as it consists mainly of economies that are either extremely small or relatively large.

The structural indices used here can be unduly sensitive to cyclical events. For example, an industry reporting an increasing share of MVA over several years may contract in later years. In order to account for cyclical differences, an index of consistency has been calculated and reported in Table 2.8. The

Table 2.8 Indices of structural change, 1973–86 (percentages)

Country grouping (number of countries)	Index of structural change[a]		Index of consistency[b]	
	weighted[c]	unweighted	weighted[c]	unweighted
DMEs (23)	6.83	5.34	0.51	0.49
NIEs (6)	8.30	8.56	0.38	0.40
Second generation NIEs (12)	9.29	6.55	0.33	0.32
Other developing countries (51)	7.28	5.65	0.43	0.47

Source: UNIDO

a/ The index of structural change (C) is defined as: $C = 0.5 \sum_{i=1}^{28} |a_{iT} - a_{i0}|$

where a_{it} is a three-year average of the share of industrial branch i (i = 1,2,...,28) in MVA for the periods t = T (1984–86) and t = 0 (1973–75).

b/ The index of consistency (K) is defined as: $K = \dfrac{\sum_{i=1}^{28} |a_{iT} - a_{i0}|}{\sum_{i=1}^{28} \sum_{t=0}^{T-1} |a_{i t+1} - a_{it}|}$

c/ Weighted shares were obtained by summing value added in constant United States dollars over each industry in the respective country group.

32

index takes a value of unity when there have been no reversals in movements of industry shares and a value of zero when year-to-year changes cancel out completely. The pattern of structural change is most consistent for the DMEs. Trends in NIEs and second-generation NIEs have been somewhat more erratic, as periods of rapid growth have often been preceded or followed by a relative contraction. The degree of consistency is little affected by the size of the economies concerned.

The last question raised at the beginning of this section concerned the extent to which patterns of change can be related to the input requirements of various industries. In order to study this aspect, several overlapping categories of industries were created. One consists of industries with a high growth potential. These are thought to require comparatively large outlays for R and D and to have rapid rates of technological innovation. A second category is composed of industries that are growing slowly and have relatively modest requirements for R and D. The two remaining categories are made up of industries generally regarded as being either labour-intensive or capital-intensive.

Table 2.9 reports the output shares of each category and the percentage change in these shares between 1973 and 1986. The increase of high-growth industries in the DMEs (20.74 per cent) was nearly equivalent to the relative decline in slower-growing industries (-25.47 per cent). The DMEs have also moved quickly out of the labour-intensive fields but have been far slower to boost the share of output in capital-intensive industries. The experience of individual countries varies, however. In Japan, the movement into high-growth industries and the exit from labour-intensive operations have proceeded at a torrid pace. The movement out of low-growth industries has also been rapid in the USA, but the relative contraction of labour-intensive activities was not large and was accompanied by a decline in the share of capital-intensive industries. Much of the change in the Federal Republic of Germany has been a withdrawal from low-growth industries and/or labour-intensive industries.

For completeness, Table 2.9 also gives estimates for the developing countries. These figures, however, should be viewed with caution, since the industry classification is intended for DMEs and may not be suitable for developing countries. One reason is that an industry's factor intensity and production technologies can vary, depending on domestic availability of factors and relative prices. Subject to this qualification, the calculations tell an interesting story.

The developing countries have been relatively slow to withdraw from low-growth industries, but the expansion of high-growth industries has matched that in DMEs. Also remarkable is the expansion of capital-intensive industries (8.51 per cent), which has been proportionately greater than for the DMEs. Trends in several of the larger non-NIEs (India, Pakistan and Turkey) were the main reason for this shift.

The overall results of this survey have already been summarized in Chapter 1 and need not be repeated here. It is sufficient to note that the inter-industrial pattern of world production has changed substantially since the early 1970s but that the experiences of different country groups bear little resemblance.

Table 2.9 Change in output share in selected industry groups, 1973–86 (percentages and percentage changes[a/])

	Industry categories[b/]			
	High-growth industries	Low-growth industries	Labour-intensive industries	Capital-intensive industries
DMEs				
1973	30.96	18.14	13.53	49.50
1986	37.38	13.52	10.91	50.01
Percentage change	+20.74	−25.47	−19.36	+1.03
United States				
1973	32.00	17.55	12.21	53.30
1986	37.38	10.87	10.98	49.87
Percentage change	+16.81	−38.06	−10.07	−6.44
Japan				
1973	29.04	22.11	12.27	53.53
1986	45.65	15.38	6.91	60.99
Percentage change	+57.20	−30.44	−43.68	+13.94
Germany, Fed.Rep.of				
1973	38.26	17.32	10.87	55.13
1986	42.86	12.28	7.61	57.84
Percentage change	+12.02	−29.10	−29.99	+4.92
Developing countries[c/]				
1973	17.94	24.11	21.92	31.01
1986	22.71	20.29	17.35	33.65
Percentage change	+26.59	−15.84	−20.85	+8.51
NIEs[d/]				
1973	22.09	22.54	19.14	33.56
1986	29.19	20.25	16.04	35.49
Percentage change	+32.14	−10.16	−16.20	+5.75
Second-generation NIEs				
1973	13.17	18.14	19.94	27.31
1986	15.21	16.07	17.11	28.64
Percentage change	+15.49	−11.41	−14.19	+4.87
Other developing countries[e/]				
1973	15.01	27.59	25.44	29.47
1986	19.07	21.88	18.73	33.67
Percentage change	+27.05	−20.70	−26.38	+14.25

Source: UNIDO.

a/ Percentage change was calculated as $[(S_2 - S_1)/S_1]100$ where $S_1(S_2)$ is the output share in 1973 (1986).
b/ Industry categories were adapted from Lawrence (1984, pp.33–35). The categories overlap and do not include all output of the manufacturing sector. For a listing of the industries included in each category, see table B.3 of the statistical appendix.
c/ Totals refer to 69 countries which, together, accounted for 95 per cent of the base weights for MVA in all developing countries in 1980.
d/ Figures exclude Taiwan Province.
e/ Figures refer to 51 developing countries.

The following chapter considers inter-industry patterns of specialization in world trade.

Notes: Chapter 2

1 For an early but incisive critique of the uses and abuses of structuralist termi-nology, see Machlup, 1958.
2 Lawrence, 1984, adopts this interpretation in his study of the US economy.
3 Included in this group are NIEs and second-generation NIEs.
4 Assume, for example, that the food products industry in the DMEs grew at a rate of 2.2 per cent in 1973–86 while the industry's worldwide growth rate was 2.7 per cent. The difference in growth rates (−0.5 per cent) must then be corrected for growth of total MVA in the DMEs and the world. If these two rates are 1.6 and 1.9 per cent respectively, the industry is identified as a contracting one:

$$(2.2 - 2.7) - (1.6 - 1.9) = -0.2$$

Note that the industry would be identified as an expanding one if the conventional practice of comparing industry growth (2.2 per cent) with growth of MVA (1.6 per cent) were used.

CHAPTER 3

Inter-industry trade
in a global system

Trade in manufactures has always been subject to substantial fluctuations during the business cycle. More stable trends can be observed, however, when trading patterns are examined over longer periods of time. The chapter begins with an overview of long-term trends in inter-industry trade. The remainder of the chapter is devoted to a discussion of some of the main features of inter-industry trade among developed and developing countries.

Long-term trends in world trade

Table 3.1 shows growth in GDP, total exports, MVA and exports of manufactures in each of the three major economic groupings. The high rates of growth in total income during the 1960s and early 1970s reflect the exceptional nature of that period. The subsequent slow-down in world growth is also evident: the growth of income in developing and developed countries has fallen significantly since 1975. The pattern is similar in the case of exports (SITC 0–9), though rates of growth have generally been more volatile.

Neither MVA nor exports of manufactures were immune to the slow-down in the world economy. However, these activities were not so hard hit by the slow-down as other economic sectors. MVA has tended to grow at a more rapid pace than income. The difference between the two rates of growth was greatest in the 1960s, but even during the 1980s the gap remained. Manufactured exports, in turn, have expanded at a pace exceeding the growth of MVA. Other studies spanning even longer periods of time have also found a stable relationship between growth of manufacturing production and exports, the latter expanding more rapidly than production (e.g. Batchelor, Major and Morgan, 1980, pp. 16-17). The impression that emerges from these comparisons is that manufacturing has provided much of the impetus for overall growth and that exporting has been a major reason for this sector's prominence.

These features of the world economy are well-known, but they have received comparatively little attention in the work of most trade theories. The theoretical literature reveals only a passing interest in issues such as

Table 3.1 Growth rates for GDP, MVA and exports of manufactures,[a] 1960–86 (percentages)

Indicator[b]	1960–70	1970–75	1975–80	1980–86
Developing countries/areas				
GDP	5.6	6.1	5.1	3.0
Total exports	7.3	4.1	4.0	1.5
MVA	7.1	7.2	6.1	3.5
Manufactured exports[c]	...	11.6	14.0	10.4
DMEs				
GDP	5.1	3.2	3.4	2.5
Total exports	8.0	6.8	6.0	3.8
MVA	6.3	3.3	3.8	3.0
Manufactured exports[c]	10.0	6.6	6.5	3.4
CPEs				
NMP[d]	6.7	6.2	4.3	3.6
Total exports[e]	9.8	22.4	16.2	3.8
Index of industrial production	9.0	9.0	5.6	4.0
Manufactured exports[e]	10.0	20.6	14.2	3.8

Sources: GDP and data for total exports: UNIDO and United Nations, Yearbook of National Accounts Statistics, Vol. II, international tables, various issues. Index of industrial production, manufactured exports and exports in current dollars: United Nations, Monthly Bulletin of Statistics, various issues.

a/ SITC 5–8 less 68.
b/ Growth rates are derived from data expressed in constant dollars.
c/ Quantum index.
d/ Net material product.
e/ Growth rates are derived from data expressed in current dollars.

the level of trade between countries or changes in those levels over time. Empiricists and policy analysts have had more to say about these particular features. They suggest that the rate of growth in manufactured exports is tied to the rate of expansion in foreign markets, which in turn is tied to consumption patterns. In particular, since income elasticities of demand are higher for manufactured products than for non-manufactures, manufactured exports would grow more rapidly during periods when income is growing at normal or high rates. Conversely, when the rate of growth in income slows, manufactured exports will be adversely effected.

Those focusing on policy matters have stressed that the international arrangements in force during much of this period contributed to the rapid growth of trade. The removal of trade barriers on manufactures was one of the relevant policy features. However, the period was also marked by a relatively free movement of international capital and floating exchange rates.

Governments often preferred to manipulate capital flows and exchange rates to resolve balance of payments problems rather than use import restraints.

Table 3.2 provides a different view of world trade. The figures show manufactured exports both as a share of total exports and as a percentage of non-oil exports (i.e. excluding SITC 3). The share of manufactures in total exports has tended to rise throughout the world. By 1986, three-quarters of all exports from DMEs were manufactures. The proportion of manufactures in the exports of developing countries, though much lower, has also risen since 1970. Figures for the CPEs reflect a somewhat different trend. These countries are somewhat less dependent than the DMEs on manufactured exports. The share of manufactures in their total exports fell during the last ten years.

Dramatic changes in the price of oil are the major reason for the sometimes erratic movement in the share of manufactures. The effects of oil price increases in 1973 and again in 1978–9 can be seen from the year-to-year changes in the figures in Table 3.2. The importance of this commodity in the exports of developing countries (and, to a lesser extent, in CPEs) explains the sharp drop in the share of manufactures during these two periods. Owing to the significance and volatility of oil prices, a clearer indication of the manufacturing sector's contribution to world exports is obtained when trade in crude oil and refined petroleum (SITC 3) is excluded. The long-term rise in the share of manufactures in non-oil exports is readily apparent. Manufactures accounted for two-thirds of the world's non-oil exports in 1970, but by the mid-1980s more than three-quarters of the total was in this form.

The exclusion of oil reveals a modest rise in the share of manufactured exports of CPEs since 1970. The increase is much sharper, however, in the case of developing countries. By 1985 the share of manufactures in the non-oil exports of these countries was approaching that of industrialized countries. This result should dispel the notion that developing countries are dependent on exports of agricultural products. Furthermore, the rise in the share of fuel exports in the 1970s was due largely to price effects and did not reflect any shift in the underlying composition of the commodities being exported by developing countries. The same observation would not apply to manufactures. The rising share of manufactures in the exports of developing countries cannot be attributed primarily to price effects, but was the result of more fundamental changes in the structure of production.

Other features of world trade in manufactures are given in Table 3.3. The value of manufactured exports rose impressively throughout the 1970s. This is a continuation of a trend dating back to the 1950s. Growth faltered in the early 1980s but then resumed its upward movement, recovering dramatically in 1986. The predominance of DMEs is also clear from the table. These countries have accounted for 80–85 per cent of world trade in manufactures in almost every year since 1970. In contrast, the CPEs' share of world trade in manufactures has steadily declined. By the early 1980s, the value of this group's manufactured exports had fallen below that of the developing countries.

Table 3.2 Share of manufactures[a] in total exports, by economic group, 1970–86 (percentages)

Economic group	Basis[b]	1970	1975	1976	1977	1978	1979	1980	1981	1982	1983	1984	1985	1986
World	A	60.9	57.4	57.0	57.5	60.4	57.5	54.2	55.1	56.3	57.8	59.3	61.4	66.6
	B	67.1	71.1	71.5	71.7	72.9	72.2	71.4	72.6	73.3	73.4	73.9	75.6	76.1
DMEs	A	71.9	73.1	73.5	74.1	74.8	72.8	70.9	71.1	71.5	71.5	71.9	73.5	75.6
	B	74.4	77.0	77.4	78.0	78.4	77.3	76.2	77.1	78.0	77.8	78.1	79.8	79.6
CPEs	A	58.2	55.2	54.5	53.9	54.9	52.5	49.8	49.1	47.5	47.1	47.0	47.2	51.2
	B	63.9	66.8	67.1	66.7	67.9	68.0	67.2	67.8	67.8	68.3	68.4	67.5	68.1
Developing countries	A	17.3	15.1	16.6	17.3	21.0	19.8	17.7	20.6	22.8	27.4	31.4	34.6	43.6
	B	25.9	37.0	40.3	40.3	44.5	46.1	47.1	51.9	53.0	55.4	58.4	61.2	63.7

Source: United Nations, Monthly Bulletin of Statistics, various issues.

a/ SITC 5 through 8 less 68.

b/ A = manufactures as percentage of total exports; B = manufactures as percentage of total exports excluding SITC 3, mineral fuels and related materials. All figures calculated from data expressed in current prices.

Table 3.3 World exports of manufacturesa/ and the shares of the major economic groups (US$ billion and percentages)

Year	World exports of manufactures		Developing countries/areas		CPEs		DMEs	
	Total US$ billions	Percentage increase over preceding year	Share in world exports	Exports to DMEs	Share in world exports	Exports to DMEs	Share in world exports	Exports to DMEs
1970	189.9	15.2	5.0	3.1	10.0	1.5	85.0	63.9
1971	216.0	13.7	5.2	2.7	9.6	1.5	85.2	64.2
1972	258.9	19.9	5.7	3.6	9.9	1.5	84.4	64.1
1973	346.9	34.0	6.7	4.5	9.4	1.6	83.9	63.2
1974	458.4	32.2	6.8	4.3	8.5	1.7	84.7	60.6
1975	500.1	9.1	6.3	3.7	9.3	1.6	84.4	56.4
1976	564.4	12.8	7.5	4.8	8.9	1.6	83.6	57.2
1977	647.3	14.7	7.8	4.8	8.9	1.6	83.3	56.9
1978	784.0	21.1	8.1	5.1	8.7	1.5	83.2	57.1
1979	941.0	20.0	8.7	5.4	8.4	1.7	82.9	58.5
1980	1 085.9	15.4	9.1	5.3	8.1	1.5	82.8	57.2
1981	1 083.2	-0.3	10.3	5.8	8.2	1.5	81.5	54.1
1982	1 040.4	-4.0	10.7	6.2	8.5	1.6	80.8	54.3
1983	1 048.6	0.8	11.8	7.4	9.0	1.6	79.2	55.3
1984	1 132.1	8.0	13.1	8.5	8.4	1.5	78.5	56.5
1985	1 186.2	4.8	13.5	8.3	8.0	1.3	78.5	57.3
1986	1 411.4	19.0	13.1	8.5	8.1	1.4	78.8	59.9

Source: United Nations, Monthly Bulletin of Statistics, various issues.

a/ SITC 5 through 8 less 68.

Curiously, the export shares in the two groups of developed countries have evolved along lines that are different from the corresponding trends in world production of manufactures. In the case of MVA, CPEs have claimed a steadily growing proportion of the world total while the dominance of DMEs has waned (see Table 2.1). The situation is different in the developing countries. Their share of manufactured exports has grown modestly but steadily and roughly parallels movements in world MVA.

A third view of trading patterns is given in Table 3.3, which shows the direction of trade. Because the DMEs are the largest importers of manufactures, their share in each group's exports is shown separately. In every year since 1970, more than one-half of the world's exports of manufactures have been intra-trade between DMEs. In contrast, the proportion of CPEs' exports to DMEs is negligible and has remained so since 1970. The developing countries, too, are only minor suppliers of manufactures to DMEs. Their share, however, rose rapidly after 1975.

The disproportionately large amount of manufactured trade among DMEs is inconsistent with the most popular model to explain the commodity pattern of world trade. According to the H–O model, factor requirements differ across products and factor endowments differ across countries. Therefore, a country will have a comparative advantage in (and will export) those products that require the country's abundant factors of production. The theory would predict, for example, that China, a labour-abundant country, would export textiles and apparel, labour-intensive products, whereas the USA, a capital-abundant country, would export aircraft and heavy machinery or other capital-intensive products. A second prediction is that the bulk of world trade would be bilateral trade between countries with different factor endowments. A corollary is that there would be little trade between countries with similar factor endowments. Although the factor endowments of DMEs are similar, the share of world exports of manufactures accounted for by trade among DMEs has been invariably high.

Because the trends described in the foregoing tables are merely averages for groups of countries, they may conceal large shifts in individual economies. This introductory section concludes with a brief look at movements in the share of manufactured exports in selected countries. Table 3.4 shows that among the DMEs the rise in the share of manufactured trade was greatest for Japan, although substantial increases were also recorded in other countries. The lowest shares in 1986 are shown for the UK, which is an oil exporter, and the USA – a major exporter of agricultural products. In several developing countries the rise in the share of manufactures has been even more dramatic. The exports of Brazil, Malaysia and Thailand included very few manufactures in 1965, but by the mid-1980s these goods were an important source of foreign exchange. Progress was no less impressive in other countries (for example, Pakistan, the Republic of Korea and Singapore) which already had a significant base of manufactured exports.

Table 3.4 Share of manufactures[a/] in total exports of selected countries and areas (percentages)

	1965	1970	1975	1980	1986
DMEs					
France	60.9	73.7	75.5	73.1	75.6
Germany, Federal Republic of	78.8	87.5	86.8	84.3	87.6
Italy	71.4	82.9	82.8	83.7	87.1
Japan	73.3	92.5	94.4	94.5	96.5
United Kingdom	76.0	80.1	80.6	71.5	72.8
United States	59.7	66.5	65.7	64.4	70.6
Developing countries and areas					
Brazil	5.0	13.4	25.3	37.2	35.1[b/]
Hong Kong	92.4	92.6	92.9	91.1	91.2
India	46.7	51.9	44.9	58.6	49.2[c/]
Malaysia	5.6[d/]	9.7	17.3	18.8	26.5[a/]
Pakistan	36.0	58.8	54.4	48.7	67.2[e/]
Republic of Korea	52.0	76.7	81.4	89.6	91.8
Singapore	28.9	27.5	41.5	43.1	58.8
Taiwan Province[f/]	...	84.8	83.6	90.8	93.3
Thailand	2.0	5.4	15.1	25.0	38.1[a/]

Sources: United Nations, <u>Yearbook of International Trade Statistics</u>, various issues.

a/   SITC 5 through 8 less 68
b/   1983
c/   1982
d/   1968
e/   1984
f/   Data are derived from the <u>Statistical Yearbook of the Republic of China,</u> various issues. Trade data follow the Chinese Commodity Classification which is not comparable to the SITC classification. Manufactured exports were regarded as being represented by section 3-4 after exclusion of processed food exports.
g/   1985

   In conclusion, the figures presented here represent only a brief survey of global trends in manufactured trade. It is clear, however, that the growth of world income and the internationalization of markets have contributed to a dramatic increase in manufactured exports. The growth of trade in manufactures was most rapid when the world economy itself was growing rapidly. Once that rate slowed, the pace of manufactured exports also subsided. But even during this later period, exports of manufactures continued to expand at rates exceeding those of non-manufactured exports or manufactured production.

   The growing share of manufactures in total exports represents only part of the overall adjustment process. Of equal importance are the underlying shifts that must have occurred in order to accommodate a reorientation of this magnitude. Trade theory offers a natural point of departure for an examination of these issues. The following section considers trading patterns in terms of alternative trade theories.

The inter–industry structure of world trade in manufactures

Long-term patterns of trade in manufactures can be more easily linked with underlying determinants if traded goods are grouped in a relatively few categories which, in turn, can be associated with existing trade models. The Ricardian, H–O and product-cycle models were chosen for this purpose. When industries are arranged in such a manner, they represent a continuum of trade which reflects the importance of various factors of production. Although these factors can be identified only in generic terms, the results provide a rough indication of the types of industries in which countries specialize. The statistical classification used to construct these three trade categories draws upon previous studies (Hufbauer and Chilas, 1974; Hirsch, 1974; UNIDO, 1981) and is presented in the statistical appendix (Appendix B).

A Ricardian interpretation

Manufactures containing a high proportion of domestic natural resources are described as Ricardian goods. A country's ability to produce these goods and to compete in international markets is determined largely by the quality and amounts of its resource endowments. The direction of world trade in Ricardian goods is generally expected to be from developing to developed countries, because much of the world's supply of natural resources is found in developing countries. The existing distribution of natural resources is due primarily to chance, as in the case of oil, where the bulk of world reserves are located in the Middle East. In the case of some resources, the domestic supplies of developed countries provided the original impetus for industrialization and were subsequently depleted – for example, the oil reserves of the USA or coal and other minerals in Europe.

Although the world's distribution of resource endowments is usually pictured as being static, international patterns of comparative advantage in Ricardian goods may change over time. For example, the discovery of new resource deposits – particularly those that are easily extracted or of a superior quality – can shift the pattern of international trade. The development of new technologies for extraction, steady reductions in the cost of transport, and the emergence of substitutes will also affect various suppliers.

Broad shifts in the priorities of the state have also altered the global distribution of natural resources. Beginning in the 1970s, governments in several developing countries made the exploitation of their natural resources a high priority. Chile, for instance, is presently the world's largest producer of copper. Roughly 80 per cent of this production is controlled by Codelco, the state-owned mining corporation. Similarly, Brazil's state-owned Carajás mine is the world's largest supplier of iron. The mine, which contains 20 billion tonnes of high-quality iron ore, has an annual output nearly matching production of the entire US industry in 1983. In fact, developing countries that are rich in natural resources often find that this richness represents a

43

disincentive in the choice of appropriate development policies and trade strategies. They will frequently encounter a natural resource bias (Ranis, 1981, pp. 215–20) and will fail to develop fully the exports of simple, labour-intensive manufactures (Bradford, 1987, pp. 302–5). Such a bias is not observed among the resource-poor countries of Asia, but it does seem to have occurred in Latin America.

An H–O interpretation

H–O goods lack the resource dependency associated with Ricardian goods. One distinguishing characteristic is that these goods are produced with production technologies that are everywhere the same. Economies of scale are assumed to be absent, while product specifications are simple or at least universally accepted. In other words, H–O goods represent a fairly orthodox set of manufactures where the ability to compete in international markets depends not on natural resource endowments but on the country's availability of labour and capital. The real marginal product of each factor depends on the ratio in which labour and capital are combined. Even though the relative prices of the two factors may differ between countries, a good whose production in one country is labour-intensive, for example, will be labour-intensive when produced elsewhere.

The likely direction of trade in H–O goods is not so clear-cut as in the case of Ricardian goods. Developing countries are expected to be relatively labour-abundant and therefore important exporters of labour-intensive goods. Developed countries, on the other hand, are usually well endowed with capital relative to labour and should excel in the export of capital-intensive goods.

A product-cycle interpretation

The characteristics of the third category, product-cycle goods, involve production technologies that are neither stable nor universally available. Instead, they are possessed by the firms that have designed and developed the product or the crucial production process. Access to this knowledge is limited through patent protection or because the research costs required for duplication are great. The prominent role accorded technology means that a third factor of production becomes an important determinant of competitive ability. In addition to unskilled labour and capital, a country's availability of skilled labour (managers, scientists and engineers) will determine export prospects.

Most versions of the product cycle assume that products systematically pass through several stages. Production in the first stage is characterized by the 'instability' of product design, a heavy dependence on skilled engineers and relatively large outlays for research and development. A second stage is entered once product characteristics are standardized. Input requirements then become more capital-intensive and long production runs are common.

Eventually, the product becomes a mature one with the labour-intensive parts of the production process (for example, the testing of parts and components and their assembly) being carried out in developing countries.

As products pass through these stages, a process of maturation occurs which alters the relative importance of the different factors of production. The technologies and know-how that generated economic rents for innovators and fast imitators become diffused as patents expire or as the knowledge is transferred to others in the form of licences, joint ventures or other types of inter-firm collaboration.

Once production is characterized by a series of standardized operations, the availability of skilled labour is less critical. As with H–O goods, the availability of unskilled labour and physical capital becomes the major determinant of comparative advantage. Not all phases of the production process – from conception to final assembly – are necessarily subject to this sort of evolution. Nevertheless, it is likely that specific production stages may be converted into mature, standardized operations.

The conception and development of new products and processes will continue to make considerable use of engineering skills and to require significant outlays for R and D. Later stages, such as the production of components and parts, often come to be characterized by much longer production runs. As the size of production facilities is expanded, the possibilities for automation grow and input requirements become more capital-intensive. Still other stages will consist in the testing of parts and components and their assembly into finished goods. After standardization, these operations will be relatively intensive in their use of unskilled labour. Developments such as these have had a profound effect on the selection of production sites. Various stages of production are located in countries that are endowed with specific factors.

The direction of trade will depend on the position of the product in the cycle. Mature goods, components and semi-finished products will conform to the trade predictions of the H–O model. Relative costs of labour and capital will determine comparative advantage. Developed countries should be the major suppliers of mature goods that have capital-intensive requirements, while developing countries are expected to export mature labour-intensive products. Expectations are different for product-cycle goods that are not mature. The ability to compete in international markets will depend not only on the availability of capital, skilled labour and unskilled labour, but also on access to the relevant technologies and related know-how. Some countries try to secure this information through foreign investment or by arranging joint ventures, licensing agreements and other forms of collaboration with technological leaders. However, because innovators are often reluctant to see their knowledge dispersed, they do not always supply the most vital technologies and related information.

The effects of these informal barriers are compounded by other difficulties inherent in the nature of the technology. Scientific knowledge, or know-how, may be transferred or taught. But mastery of the necessary scientific principles is not always sufficient for their application in manufacturing operations. There is also a 'know-why' component, which is required for adaptation and modification of products and processes in new locations and markets. This element is often locked in the experience of individuals and is less easily conveyed. The only alternative may then be to replicate the necessary know-how or to develop rival versions. This approach can be costly for countries having a shortage of scientists and engineers. The problems involved in the transfer of technology imply that products may not always move smoothly through the cycle described here. Countries that are the technological leaders in particular product lines may continue to be the major suppliers for long periods of time.

The foregoing description is merely a stylistic representation of the three trade models of interest here. The actual number of theoretical expositions and interpretations of each model are many. Each model is distinguishable in terms of those factors of production that will be the most important determinants of the composition of trade. Based on very general impressions of the international distribution of factors and factor requirements, the expected directions of trade have been hypothesized.[1]

Stylized evidence of trading patterns

A picture of international trading patterns in each of these product categories is assembled in this section. Conventional statistical definitions of trade in manufactures are not suitable for this purpose. Instead, an 'ISIC equivalent' of manufactured trade is used and can be found in the statistical appendix (Appendix B). Figures 3.1 and 3.2 refer to the trade of DMEs and developing countries, respectively. They show year-to-year changes in the composition of manufactured trade in each of the three product categories described above.

The two figures paint a very clear picture. In the case of Ricardian (resource-based) goods, comparative advantage did not change during the 1970–85 period. Developed countries are small net importers and developing countries are small net exporters. The experience for H–O goods is different. Net exports of developed countries increased steadily during the 1970s. However, there was a definite break in the trend in the early 1980s in favour of developing countries. By 1983 the developing countries were net exporters rather than net importers. A similar pattern exists for product-cycle goods, except that the developed countries remain significant net exporters.

These figures provide a basis for several general impressions. First, the data for Ricardian and product-cycle goods show that trade has been in the expected direction for both country groups. Although the H–O theory provides no explicit indication of the direction of trade, the results obtained are not surprising. Second, net trade in total manufactures in both groups of countries is determined primarily by performance in product-cycle goods

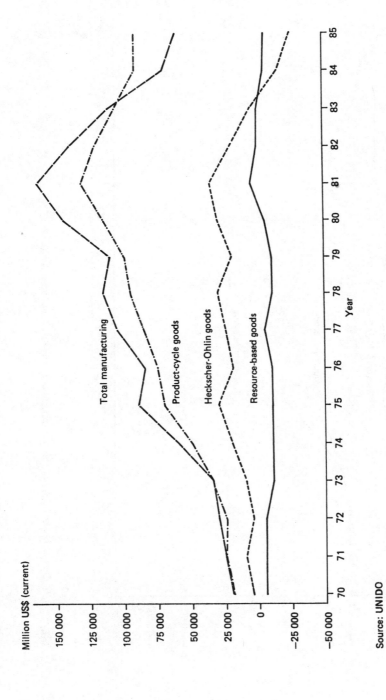

Million US$ (current)

150 000

125 000

100 000

75 000

50 000

25 000

0

−25 000

−50 000

Total manufacturing

Product-cycle goods

Heckscher-Ohlin goods

Resource-based goods

70 71 72 73 74 75 76 77 78 79 80 81 82 83 84 85

Year

Source: UNIDO

Figure 3.1 Net exports of developed market economies, by product category, 1970–85

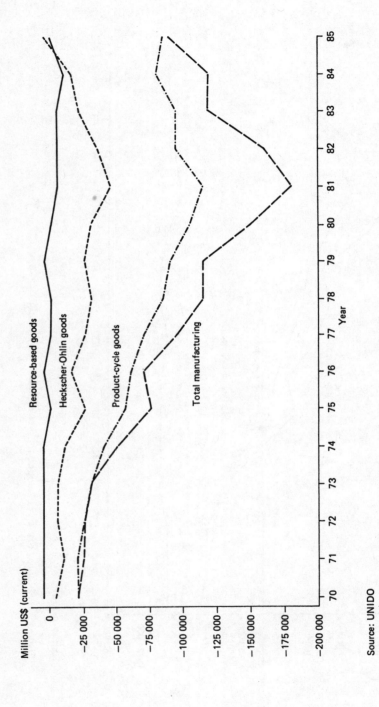

Source: UNIDO

Figure 3.2 Net exports of developing countries, by product category, 1970–85

and, to a lesser extent, by H–O goods. Ricardian goods play only a minor role. Third, a similar relationship applies when year-to-year changes in net exports of each trade category are considered. Ricardian goods exhibit a fairly stable trend. Curiously, perhaps, the wide swings in commodity prices that characterized much of the 1970s and 1980s are not reflected in the aggregate figure for trade in this category. Year-to-year movements in net exports of H–O goods have been more volatile, with even greater swings for product-cycle goods.

The evidence summarized in Figures 3.1 and 3.2 refers to a large number of diverse countries. More specific data are desirable in order to obtain a clear picture of trade performance in each of these categories. Table 3.5 provides figures on the net trade of individual countries. The comparative abundance of natural resources in several countries included among 'other DMEs' (e.g. Australia, Canada, New Zealand and Norway) is reflected by the favourable trade position of that sub-group with regard to Ricardian goods. The resource abundance of the USA, on the other hand, is negated by the large amounts of oil imports (SITC 331 and 332). CPEs are also net importers of Ricardian goods, although these results may be partly a statistical anomaly owing to the lack of data on trade between these countries.[2]

Trade patterns for H–O goods are of more interest. The increase in net exports during the 1970s can be attributed largely to Japan, with smaller increases being recorded by the Federal Republic of Germany and Italy. These developments were outweighed by a steady rise in net imports of the USA. The net trading position of the USA gradually deteriorated during the 1970s but net imports of H–O goods soared in the 1980s. By 1985 the country's imbalance in H–O trade exceeded the combined net exports of France, the Federal Republic of Germany, Italy and Japan.

Of the three categories, net trade in product-cycle goods has been the most volatile. Between 1970 and 1980, the DMEs' net exports rose almost sixfold. Later years brought further improvements in three of the six large countries. Surprisingly, the USA recorded a trade surplus of $44 billion in 1980 but had become a net importer of product-cycle goods by the middle of the decade. This turnaround, which occurred during a period of significant dollar appreciation, was very abrupt: by 1985 US net imports almost equalled the combined figure for all CPEs. Despite the US downturn, net exports of product-cycle goods by all DMEs were $91 billion, a total that was 47 per cent larger than net exports of all manufactures in 1985.

Swings of this magnitude would be due to multiple causes. The totals reported here for net exports in all product categories combined must reflect, and be influenced by, exchange rates, international capital flows and other determinants of the balance of trade. The relative importance of each respective trade category, however, depends on the underlying determinants of comparative advantage. These, in turn, are indicated by the data in Table 3.6. The percentages reveal little of the volatility typical of net exports. The decline in the share of Ricardian exports has been gradual

Table 3.5 New manufactured exports of developed countries, by trade category,[a] 1970–85 (US$ million)

Economic group/country	Ricardian goods				Heckscher–Ohlin goods			
	1970	1975	1980	1985	1970	1975	1980	1985
DMEs total	-6 075	-7 883	-3 821	-6 071	7 287	29 349	30 366	-23 099
France	-1 110	-1 280	-2 762	-2 213	2 560	8 042	9 363	5 017
Germany, Fed. Rep. of	-3 787	-4 572	-7 525	-4 183	4 957	11 189	17 867	23 955
Italy	-2 290	-4 397	-9 954	-7 522	3 570	11 699	17 534	18 593
Japan	-1 858	-4 884	-10 040	-9 041	7 419	21 904	45 138	56 280
United Kingdom	-4 641	-7 701	-11 069	-8 559	3 330	3 142	657	-8 763
United States	-1 348	-977	1 400	-10 240	-6 863	-10 637	-37 400	-108 872
Other	8 960	15 929	36 130	35 686	-7 685	-15 991	-22 794	-9 309
CPEs, total	442	-1 850	-5 031	62	-123	-2 091	2 962	4 548

Economic group/country	Product-cycle goods				Total manufactures			
	1970	1975	1980	1985	1970	1975	1980	1985
DMEs total	19 589	68 041	11 6871	90 856	20 801	89 507	143 416	61 687
France	-59	3 318	2 221	3 838	1 392	10 080	8 822	6 642
Germany, Fed. Rep. of	9 439	26 144	39 716	35 992	10 609	32 760	50 057	55 764
Italy	1 172	3 361	3 721	5 884	2 452	10 663	11 302	16 955
Japan	5 416	19 731	45 907	75 636	10 977	36 751	81 005	122 875
United Kingdom	3 486	7 693	13 504	3 557	2 174	3 135	3 092	-13 764
United States	10 495	26 858	44 597	-6 070	2 284	15 244	8 597	-125 182
Other	-10 361	-19 064	-32 794	-27 980	-9 086	-19 126	-19 459	-1 603
CPEs total	-1 587	-7 644	-8 315	-8 626	-1 244	-11 761	-10 384	-4 016

Source: UNIDO

a/ Trade categories and country groups are defined in the statistical appendix.

Table 3.6 Manufactured exports of developed market economies, by trade category, 1970–85 (percentages)

	Ricardian goods				Product-cycle goods				Heckscher–Ohlin goods			
	1970	1975	1980	1985	1970	1975	1980	1985	1970	1975	1980	1985
DMEs total	16.3	13.6	14.5	12.1	42.6	44.0	42.8	45.7	41.0	42.5	42.7	42.2
France	12.5	12.2	13.4	12.0	36.0	38.0	37.2	41.1	51.5	49.8	49.4	46.9
Germany, Federal Republic of	5.9	6.9	8.9	8.4	50.5	49.9	46.2	46.7	43.6	43.2	44.9	44.9
Italy	5.3	5.2	5.5	6.2	39.8	36.5	34.7	37.0	54.9	58.2	59.8	56.7
Japan	4.8	3.2	3.3	2.1	45.3	46.8	47.9	54.8	49.8	49.9	48.8	43.1
United Kingdom	9.6	8.8	10.5	8.5	47.6	51.3	51.6	55.3	42.8	39.9	37.9	36.2
United States	15.5	12.8	15.5	10.8	56.3	56.9	58.0	61.9	28.2	30.3	26.5	27.3
Other	30.9	24.9	25.1	22.0	31.2	34.5	32.3	33.4	37.9	40.7	42.7	44.6

Source: UNIDO.

and reflects the comparative scarcity of resources in West Europe and Japan. The share of product–cycle goods has tended to rise, while that of H–O exports has declined slightly in most developed countries. In 1985 product-cycle goods accounted for more than half of all manufactured exports by the USA, Japan and the UK. Changes in the composition of US exports are also noteworthy when considered in relation to the figures in Table 3.5. Despite a significant fall in net exports of product–cycle goods, the category's share in the country's total manufactured exports is large and growing. By 1985, nearly two-thirds of US manufactured exports were product–cycle goods. A similar pattern applied to trade in H–O goods. Although the US net exports of H–O goods declined by $102 billion between 1970 and 1985, their share in the country's total manufactured exports fell only marginally.

Table 3.7 provides evidence for the developing countries which is comparable to that in Table 3.5. Because trade performance in these countries varies so widely, selected sub-groups have been singled out for attention. Both first- and second-generation NIEs have consistently been modest net exporters of Ricardian goods. Few of these economies are particularly well endowed with natural resources, and some (e.g. Hong Kong and Singapore) have almost none. Instead, the favourable trade balances achieved by these countries result from the fact that they are efficient processors of imported materials from which higher-stage goods are then exported. The remainder of developing countries have an unfavourable balance of trade in Ricardian goods and this total has risen over time.

In the case of H–O goods, the model suggests that developing countries will be important exporters of labour-intensive goods. This expectation, which has been confirmed by other studies (e.g. Lary, 1968; Tuong and Yeats, 1980), should be consistent with the figures in Table 3.7. Although the classification used here does not distinguish between labour- and capital-intensive H–O products, a switch in the developing countries' trade position from a deficit of $32 billion in 1980 to a surplus of $4.5 billion in 1985 can be observed. The improvement was due predominantly to the gains of the NIEs. Other developing country groups were net importers, though the size of these deficits fell between 1980 and 1985.

Data for product–cycle goods show that net imports rose significantly in 1970–80 but declined slightly in later years. Imports are nevertheless substantial (more than $84 billion in 1985) and explain much of the overall trade deficit of developing countries. In 1970 net imports of product–cycle goods were equivalent to 86 per cent of the overall net trade deficit of developing countries, and by 1985 they amounted to 96 per cent of this total. Among the sub-groups of developing countries, only the NIEs appear to have managed a moderate improvement in their trade position, though they too are still net importers.

These trends may be re-examined in terms of the composition of manufactured exports from developing countries. Table 3.8 shows large changes in the export composition in comparison with those observed for DMEs

Table 3.7 Net manufactured exports of developing countries and areas, by trade category,[a] 1970–85 (US$ million)

Economic group/subgroup	Ricardian goods				Heckscher–Ohlin goods			
	1970	1975	1980	1985	1970	1975	1980	1985
Developing countries and areas Total	4 456	1 851	-1 474	-396	-7 354	-25 140	-32 130	4 510
NIEs	455	935	2 448	2 630	-424	543	12 456	31 552
Second-generation NIEs	1 225	1 904	4 487	5 412	-1 946	-5 781	-11 587	-3 742
Other developing countries	2 275	-989	-8 410	-8 439	-4 984	-19 902	-33 000	-23 300

Economic group/subgroup	Product–cycle goods				Total manufacturing			
	1970	1975	1980	1985	1970	1975	1980	1985
Developing countries and areas Total	-17 511	-53 223	-103 756	-84 333	-20 381	-75 755	-148 586	-87 721
NIEs	-5 367	-12 696	-23 438	-8 808	-4 989	-11 219	-8 534	25 374
Second generation NIEs	-2 523	-8 277	-16 893	-12 252	-3 110	-12 153	-23 992	-10 582
Other developing countries	-96 211	-32 250	-63 425	-63 273	-12 283	-52 383	-116 060	-102 512

Source: UNIDO

a/ Trade categories and economic groups of developing countries and areas are defined in the statistical appendix.

Table 3.8 Manufactured exports of developing countries and areas, by trade category, 1970–85 (percentages of total manufactured exports)

	Ricardian goods				Product-cycle goods				Heckscher-Ohlin goods			
	1970	1975	1980	1985	1970	1975	1980	1985	1970	1975	1980	1985
Developing countries/areas, total	46.8	36.7	25.6	13.3	11.6	13.3	16.6	20.2	43.3	48.4	57.7	66.5
NIEs	32.9	21.9	16.6	7.4	19.6	23.6	27.5	31.0	53.4	54.6	55.9	61.6
Second-generation NIEs	80.4	66.3	51.2	31.4	2.5	8.6	14.6	7.6	17.1	25.1	34.2	61.1
Other developing countries	47.1	38.8	28.7	20.0	9.6	9.9	10.9	16.4	43.4	51.3	60.4	63.6

Source: UNIDO

(see Table 3.6). The share of Ricardian goods in manufactured exports has declined significantly, and the average for all developing countries is now little more than the corresponding figure for DMEs. The decline was proportionately greatest among second–generation NIEs but also occurred in both other country groups. Among the NIEs, the decline in Ricardian exports was largely offset by a rise in the share of product–cycle goods. The same was not true of second–generation NIEs or other developing countries. In these countries, exports of H–O goods accounted for most of the shift away from Ricardian exports. The increase in the share of product–cycle goods was less impressive.

One feature that reappears throughout the evidence assembled in this chapter concerns the dynamic character of world trade. Before turning to more detailed aspects of trade and specialization, it would be helpful to obtain a comparative picture of the pace of change in the export composition of DMEs and developing countries. For this purpose, summary measures of structural change (expressed in percentage points) have been calculated and are shown in Table 3.9. Also given in the table are calculations showing the extent to which changes in export structure have been consistent over time. The latter index takes a value of unity when there have been no reversals in movements of industry shares (that is, when there has been total consistency over time) and of zero when year–to–year changes cancel out completely.

When group averages are compared, the results match casual expectations. The degree of change has been greatest for the second–generation NIEs, followed by first–generation NIEs and DMEs. Among individual countries, those experiencing a substantial degree of change also tend to have relatively high rates of export growth within the respective groups. Exceptions to this pattern can be noted, however. The composition of Argentina's exports, for example, has changed considerably, though the rate of export growth has been lowest of all NIEs. Similar comments apply to Australia, Colombia and Peru.

In conclusion, this survey has found a large measure of agreement between the interpretations offered by various trade models and the observed patterns of inter–industry trade. There was, however, a degree of unpredictability for both developing countries and DMEs. Changes in the composition of trade were sometimes substantial (whether measured in relative or absolute terms) and occurred over surprisingly brief time spans. The dynamic character of trade in manufactures may be more closely examined by restricting attention to the fastest–growing trade component.

Table 3.9 Structural change in manufactured exports 1970–2 to 1983–5 (DMEs and selected developing countries and areas)

Countries and areas[a]	Structural change indicator[b]	Indicator of consistency[c]
DMEs[d]	23.6	0.16
Ireland	44.6	0.25
Iceland	16.7	0.07
Israel	36.6	0.17
Spain	34.3	0.20
Greece	42.6	0.17
Japan	28.2	0.20
Finland	23.3	0.14
Portugal	30.9	0.17
Austria	16.2	0.14
Italy	13.0	0.10
Canada	16.6	0.12
Netherlands	20.4	0.16
United States	14.7	0.11
France	15.2	0.13
Germany, Federal Republic of	12.7	0.11
Switzerland	17.7	0.15
Denmark	20.0	0.16
Sweden	16.7	0.14
New Zealand	28.0	0.18
Belgium	22.6	0.18
United Kingdom	21.1	0.16
Australia	32.1	0.17
Norway	19.0	0.10
NIEs	36.2	0.17
Republic of Korea	48.1	0.23
Singapore	27.5	0.16
Mexico	42.2	0.14
Brazil	44.4	0.15
Taiwan Province	22.2	0.18
Hong Kong	25.3	0.18
Argentina	43.8	0.15
Second-generation NIEs[e]	51.3	0.16
Jordan	51.5	0.11
Indonesia	32.4	0.08
Cyprus	57.6	0.23
Thailand	48.6	0.22
Malaysia	49.9	0.21
Tunisia	62.7	0.12
Morocco	54.4	0.21
Philippines	47.1	0.19
Colombia	52.2	0.12
Sri Lanka	43.7	0.19
Peru	63.7	0.06

Table 3.9 continued

Countries and areas[a]	Structural change indicator[b]	Indicator of consistency[c]
Other significant exporters		
of manufactures	36.6	0.13
China	37.5	0.11
Yugoslavia	28.4	0.15
Turkey	62.6	0.21
Pakistan	25.7	0.11
India	28.9	0.08

Source: UNIDO.

a/ Countries are ranked within each group by the rate of growth of manufactured exports between 1970–1972 and 1983–1985.

b/ The indicator of structural change (C) is defined as

$$C = \frac{1}{2} \sum_{i=1}^{m} | a_{iT} - a_{io} |$$

where m is the number of industries and a_{it} is the share of industry i in total manufactured exports in period t. Industries were defined at the three-digit level of the SITC and shares were calculated as three-year averages for 1970–72 (t = 0) and 1983–85 (t = T).

c/ The index of consistency (K) is defined as

$$K = \frac{\sum_{i=1}^{m} | a_{iT} - a_{io} |}{\sum_{i=1}^{m} \sum_{t=0}^{T-1} | a_{it+1} - a_{it} |}$$

where t runs through all years between 1970 (t = 0) and 1984 (t = T–1).

d/ Group averages are unweighted means of the respective indicators.

e/ Uruguay was omitted owing to a lack of sufficiently detailed data.

Notes: Chapter 3

1 These insights, while useful, tell us nothing about the level of trade between countries. Such a lacuna is a serious one but is shared by all fundamental theories of international trade.
2 Because few CPEs provide detailed figures on their international trade, many of the data have been derived from partner-country statistics. Use of this method leads to an underestimation and does not take account of trade between CPEs.

CHAPTER 4

Two-way trade in similar products

The previous chapter portrayed world trade in terms of inter-industry exchanges. Although much world trade is of that form, a large and growing portion takes place within industries. Known as two-way or intra-industry trade (IIT), this is the fastest growing component of global trade in manufactures.

The portion of a country's trade that takes place within, rather than between, industries obviously depends on how industries are delineated. The statistical definition of an industry, however, seldom agrees with its theoretical counterpart. Putting aside this difficulty for the moment, IIT can be defined as the simultaneous import and export of products that are close substitutes, in terms of either factor inputs or consumption, or both. Because trade of this type can not be easily explained in terms of comparative advantages, IIT has played the role of an irritating but stimulating phenomenon for both theorists and empiricists.[1]

Formal models were initially developed in order to identify the circumstances under which IIT would occur. More recently, attention has turned to other aspects of IIT – the gains from trade, the consequences of trade intervention, and the implications for structural adjustment. The interest in IIT grew as its importance in world trade increased and as economists came to realize that certain theoretical and policy implications are different from those associated with inter-industry trade.

The empirical analysis of IIT is complicated by the fact that it occurs in many forms. A number of product categories are likely to exhibit IIT. They include the following:

(a) homogeneous products involved in border trade, entrepôt trade or seasonal trade;
(b) heterogeneous products made in the same industry at vertically adjacent or complementary stages of production;
(c) heterogeneous or differentiated products that are close substitutes in production, consumption or both.

The main determinants of IIT in category (a) are transport costs and seasonal differences in production. Labour cost differentials are the primary reason for the type of IIT described in category (b). This type of trade is sometimes referred to as 'vertical' or 'complementary' IIT, and tends to be of greatest significance in industries dominated by multinational corporations. Because intra-firm IIT depends partly on the complex objectives of multinationals, inferences with regard to its economic determinants are difficult.

The type of IIT described in category (c) can be further divided into the following sub-categories:

(i) products with different input requirements but high elasticities of substitution: examples are furniture made from different materials (steel, plastic, timber or cane), textile yarn from natural or man-made fibres, and footwear of leather or synthetic materials;

(ii) products being produced by industries that transform identical inputs into a range of outputs with different end-uses. For example, the basic iron and steel industry may supply both railway sleepers and heavy plates for shipbuilding; the petroleum industry may produce gasoline or tar but also supply a range of petrochemical products;

(iii) similar products made by similar processes from similar materials. Industries in which this type of IIT occurs are processed food, beverages, textiles, clothing, shoes, cars, furniture, tobacco products, appliances, hand tools, boats, electronic and mechanical data processing equipment and communications equipment.

It is mainly the types of IIT in sub-categories (ii) and (iii) that cannot be easily explained by conventional trade theory and most of its extensions. The basis for this trade seems to be the interaction between a variety of circumstances, many of which are insignificant when considered in isolation. Examples are small changes in production processes or special conditions surrounding the sale of the product. The resulting product differentiation often leads to a situation where plants in different countries produce product varieties that are close substitutes.

Such specialization is inevitable. The production of all varieties would be too costly because it would increase the down-time of machines, the size of inventories and the selling costs. If economies of scale are to be achieved, not all product varieties can be produced in every country. Simultaneous import and export of different product varieties is the result. The following section provides a survey of this type of trade.

An overview of two-way trade

An empirical indicator of IIT should measure 'trade overlap'. Although methods of measurement have been the subject of extensive debate in the literature, the only aspect of particular relevance to this discussion is the need to standardize the value of trade overlap in order to permit cross-country comparisons.

Trade overlap is best expressed as that portion of an industry's exports (imports) which is matched by imports (exports) of the same industry, depending on which of the two values is larger. In mathematical notation, the measure can be stated as

$$\min (X_{ij}, M_{ij})$$

where X_{ij} represents country j's exports of industry i and M_{ij} refers to the corresponding imports. The value chosen to represent two-way trade is then the lower of these two figures.

The popular share measure of IIT introduced by Grubel and Lloyd (1975) is easily derived from the above minimum expression. In the same way as the share of net exports in the sum of exports and imports is used to measure the relative size of 'one-way' trade, the share of IIT in the same total serves as an indicator of the relative size of two-way trade. After multiplying this ratio by 2, the upper bound becomes unity and the lower bound is zero. The expression, which is identical to the Grubel–Lloyd measure,[2] can be written as:

$$\frac{\min (X_{ij}, M_{ij})}{X_{ij} + M_{ij}} \times 2.$$

Much of the literature dealing with the measure concerns the advisability of adjustments to account for trade imbalances. In most applications, however, a correction for trade imbalance is not advisable. The present study will make use of an unadjusted measure of IIT shares, together with a corresponding unadjusted indicator of IIT levels.

Estimates of IIT shares in 1985 are given in Table 4.1. The table is organized as a matrix which shows the proportion of two-way trade between various country groups and among the members of each group. The share of IIT in world trade of the DMEs (42.8 per cent) is considerably higher than that among developing countries (16.3 per cent). Among the developing countries, the NIEs have the largest share of two-way trade. This type of trade is far less important for second-generation NIEs and other developing countries. However, these broad averages conceal substantial variations in the figures for individual countries and country groups. Particularly noteworthy is the case of Japan, which is the only one of the six largest DMEs that does not engage in a relatively large amount of IIT.

The aggregate figures suggest a positive relationship between the level of development and the share of IIT in manufactured trade. Whatever the actual determinants of IIT, the literature on the subject clearly demonstrates that some of them are country-specific or bilateral in nature. Accordingly, the most desirable means of assessing IIT is in terms of bilateral trade flows between countries or country groups. The types of predictions that would

Table 4.1   Average shares of IIT[a] in manufactured goods, by country group,[b] 1985 (percentages)

Economic group/country (number of countries)	Trade with:								
	World	DMEs	Six major exporters	Other DMEs	CPEs	Developing countries	NIEs	Second-generation NIEs	Other developing countries
DMEs (22)	42.8	47.1	45.3	48.3	16.1	15.1	21.6	11.6	12.3
Six major exporters	47.8	54.4	52.8	55.6	20.8	19.9	30.8	19.1	14.3
France	60.1	70.2	69.6	71.3	33.5	13.7	28.2	13.5	10.8
Germany, Fed. Rep. of	56.0	63.9	63.9	62.9	23.4	17.0	27.6	17.9	13.6
Italy	48.0	55.1	55.7	54.0	23.4	19.1	35.7	12.3	16.5
Japan	17.8	22.4	24.0	16.3	6.4	10.3	22.0	7.0	4.2
United Kingdom	60.2	67.7	66.5	69.3	22.5	22.7	26.9	25.3	20.5
United States	44.6	47.6	37.3	59.6	15.2	36.5	44.3	38.7	20.0
Other DMEs (16)	40.9	44.4	42.5	45.5	14.4	13.3	18.2	8.7	11.5
Developing countries and areas (25)	16.3	14.9	15.3	12.5	2.5	16.7	15.8	14.0	18.8
NIEs (6)	29.3	29.8	30.4	26.4	2.7	29.6	32.7	29.0	24.0
Second-generation NIEs (9)	13.3	11.3	11.9	7.9	0.6	17.5	18.2	11.5	13.5
Other developing countries (10)	11.4	9.6	9.7	8.8	4.3	12.8	3.8	7.5	15.5

Source: UNIDO

a/ In general, the averages of the Grubel-Lloyd measure used in this table are based on data at the four-digit level of the SITC. Determination of these averages consisted of three steps. First, for each of the 47 countries in the sample and for each of the six 'basic' subgroups of trading partners (identified in columns 3, 4, 5, 7, 8 and 9) the IIT share of all manufactures was calculated as a weighted average where the sum of exports and imports was used as the weight. Second, IIT-shares for the 'broad' partner country groups (DMEs, developing countries and world) were derived from the foregoing figures as the same type of weighted average. Third, figures for the groupings of the 47 countries were obtained as unweighted averages of the indices derived in steps one and/or two.

b/ The composition of country groups is given in table 5.1.

result from such an exercise are based on the premise that trading partners that are similar with regard to income levels and market size will tend to have larger shares of IIT in their bilateral trade than those that are not similar.

When trade between a heterogeneous sample of countries is analysed, the similarity hypothesis should lead to substantial variation in the IIT shares for many pairs of countries (or country groups). The results in Table 4.1 bear out this expectation. Looking first at the figures for DMEs, 47 per cent of their intra-trade was in the form of two-way trade. This compares with a share of 15 per cent in the same group's trade with developing countries. In contrast, the developing countries had a slightly higher IIT share in their intra-trade (16.7 per cent) than in their trade with DMEs (14.9 per cent).

Further support for the hypothesis is obtained from data for more narrowly defined groups of countries. Two-way trade between the six largest DMEs accounted for 53 per cent of the group's total intra-trade. With the exception of Japan, all these DMEs report large shares for IIT. The corresponding estimates for the major exporters among developing countries also conform to the hypothesis. The NIEs occupy a middle position between the DMEs and the second-generation NIEs. In terms of the country-similarity hypothesis, the group's shares with 'surrounding' partner groups should be of similar magnitudes, and this is exactly what the figures for the NIEs in Table 4.1 reflect.

Country data also provide evidence supporting the hypothesis. The two-way trade of France, the Federal Republic of Germany and the UK accounts for a substantial portion of all their trade with DMEs and with each other. Results for the USA are somewhat different. The proportion of IIT in that country's trade with developing countries (in particular, the NIEs and second-generation NIEs) is remarkably high. In this instance, country similarities may be of less importance than other economic and/or political factors. The same may apply to the IIT shares of Japan, which in general are far smaller than those of other DMEs.

Although there is wide variation in IIT shares, almost all countries have experienced a rapid increase in this type of trade. Table 4.2 documents the growth in IIT between 1970 and 1985. Increases in the IIT shares were of a similar magnitude for DMEs and developing countries. However, there are fairly wide differences between particular country groups and individual countries. Between 1970 and 1985 the share of IIT in Japan's trade with the world was unchanged, while its share of IIT in trade with other DMEs actually declined. At the other extreme is the UK, where the portion of IIT in world trade rose by nearly 15 percentage points.

Among the developing countries, the increase in the two-way trade of the NIEs was over 15 percentage points, another indication of this group's trade dynamism. The share for second-generation NIEs rose by slightly more than the average for all developing countries, while among the non-NIEs the increase was negligible. These figures suggest that many developing countries have yet to realize the potential for trade expansion that is inherent in two-way trade.

Table 4.2 Change in the average share of IIT in manufactured goods between 1970 and 1985, by country group^a/ (differences in percentage points^b/)

Economic group/country (number of countries)	Trade with:								
	World	DMEs	Six major exporters	Other DMEs	CPEs	Developing countries	NIEs	Second-generation NIEs	Other developing countries
DMEs (22)	7.7	8.1	7.8	7.3	3.3	7.4	13.5	6.6	4.4
Six major exporters	6.7	5.7	1.8	10.2	3.8	10.9	18.7	15.7	5.9
France	8.2	9.2	8.4	10.4	11.2	7.8	17.3	9.7	5.4
Germany, Fed. Rep. of	5.0	5.4	0.3	9.9	0.1	8.5	20.0	16.1	3.6
Italy	3.7	2.9	0.2	9.5	5.5	10.9	26.7	8.3	8.0
Japan	0.1	-2.9	-3.8	-2.2	-2.7	6.1	15.5	5.1	0.5
United Kingdom	14.9	13.4	2.5	21.8	2.2	11.5	12.5	19.9	9.4
United States	8.6	6.1	3.0	11.9	6.8	20.5	20.0	34.7	8.4
Other DMEs (16)	8.1	9.0	10.1	6.2	3.1	6.1	11.6	3.3	3.8
Developing countries and areas (25)	8.2	8.9	9.2	6.8	0.5	3.7	4.4	8.0	2.0
NIEs (6)	15.4	18.1	18.2	18.5	1.7	8.0	7.6	17.3	5.5
Second-generation NIEs (9)	9.9	8.6	9.2	4.1	0.1	7.6	7.7	7.1	4.6
Other developing countries (10)	2.5	4.0	4.2	2.7	0.0	-2.5	0.1	3.8	-2.5

Source: UNIDO

a/ The composition of country groups is given in table 5.1.

b/ Figures represent absolute change in percentage points between the beginning and ending year. A minus indicates a decline in the share.

With regard to two-way trade between different country groups, the fastest growing component was the DMEs' trade with NIEs. This applies even to Japan, where the strong emphasis on inter-industry specialization leaves comparatively little room for IIT. A similarly high increase in IIT was observed for the NIEs' trade with second-generation NIEs, while the figures for trade between other groups of developing countries present a mixed picture.

The impression that emerges from this exercise is that the level of IIT is especially sensitive to the economic characteristics of the trading partners. Various economic attributes may be determinants of two-way trade, but the most obvious is the level of income. The estimates of IIT shares and their changes over time suggest a systematic relationship between these two variables. The more developed a country, the greater the portion of IIT in its manufactured trade.[3] Furthermore, when trading partners are similar, the share of IIT in bilateral trade tends to be higher. A more extensive investigation of these generalizations will be carried out in a later chapter.

An industry-specific view of IIT

The discussion in the previous section was concerned mainly with the direction of trade. An alternative line of investigation would focus on the product composition of trade. Much of the theory is concerned with the product structure of inter-industry trade, although the product pattern of IIT is also of interest. The present section provides a documentary account of this aspect.

Table 4.3 shows those industries reporting relatively large shares of IIT in 1985 and accounting for at least 1 per cent of the total in the respective country group. One point that is immediately apparent from this table is the re-emergence of country similarities as a determinant of IIT shares. The share of two-way trade in particular industries tended to be higher for trade within each country group than for trade between DMEs and developing countries. This was particularly true for developing countries, although, on average, this group engages in less two-way trade for all manufactures than DMEs.

From the description of IIT at the beginning of this chapter, it is clear that certain industries are more likely to figure prominently in two-way trade than others. Such industries are identified here on the basis of average shares of IIT calculated over all 47 countries in the sample. According to these global figures (which are not shown), eight industries, which accounted for at least 1 per cent of world trade in manufactures, had IIT shares in excess of 50 per cent. The largest shares were recorded for miscellaneous electrical machinery (SITC 729), plastic materials (SITC 581) and office machines (SITC 714).

When industries were grouped by end-use into capital goods, consumer goods and intermediate goods, high global shares of IIT were found in all three classes. This result is somewhat surprising. Given the variety of differentiated products in consumer-goods industries, the proportion of two-way trade in

65

Table 4.3 Industries[a] with high IIT shares[b] in trade of DMEs and developing countries and areas, 1985 (percentages)

Country group	SITC	Trade with DMEs	SITC	Trade with developing countries and areas
	581	Plastic materials (74.3)	714	Office machines (53.7)
	729	Other electrical machinery (66.2)	729	Other electric machinery (51.8)
	722	Electric power machinery (66.2)	512	Organic chemicals (41.7)
	734	Aircraft (64.8)	723	Equipment for distributing electricity (32.5)
	512	Organic chemicals (64.3)	722	Electric power machinery (32.3)
DMEs	711	Non-electric power generating machinery (64.0)	711	Power generating machinery (25.5)
	651	Textile yarn and thread (64.0	653	Woven textile fabrics (25.3)
	719	Non-electric machinery and appliances (63.0)	894	Perambulators, toys, games (22.4)
	714	Office machines (62.3)	891	Musical instruments, etc. (22.0)
	541	Medicinal and pharmaceutical products (62.3)	861	Scientific, medical and optical instruments (20.6)
			735	Ships and boats (74.3)
			864	Watches and clocks (69.1)
			894	Perambulators, toys, games (60.2)
Developing countries and areas[c]			729	Other electrical machinery (59.6)
			722	Electric power machinery (50.4)
			714	Office machines (39.3)
			724	Telecommunications apparatus (35.7)
			652	Cotton, fabrics, woven (33.0)
			541	Medicinal and pharmaceutical products (31.8)
			891	Musical instruments (31.0)

Source: UNIDO

a/ Only industries which accounted for at least one per cent of total trade between or within the respective country groups in 1985 are included.

b/ IIT shares, given in parentheses, are weighted averages of four-digit SITC subgroups within each given three-digit group.

c/ The figures in the lower right hand block refer to trade between the 25 developing countries included in the sample and all developing countries for which partner country data were available.

that group was expected to be greatest. Consumer goods, however, do not figure as prominently in two-way trade as expected. Among the top ten industries in the ranking by global IIT shares, only two – pharmaceutical products (SITC 541) and furniture (SITC 821) – fall in this category. By contrast, five out of the top ten were producers of capital goods. They include: non-electric power generating machinery (SITC 711), office machines (SITC 714), electric power machinery (SITC 722), miscellaneous electric machinery (SITC 729) and aircraft (SITC 734). The remaining three industries in this list – organic chemicals (SITC 712), plastic materials (SITC 581) and miscellaneous chemical products (SITC 599) – produce intermediate goods.

The data in Table 4.3 show that the large shares recorded for capital goods result from their prominence in the two-way trade of DMEs – in particular, the trade within that country group. In contrast, the role of consumer goods in two-way trade is positively associated with the developing countries' involvement in world trade. Only one consumer-goods industry (pharmaceutical products) figured prominently in IIT among DMEs. Three others (toys and games, musical instruments, and photographic equipment) had relatively high IIT shares in trade between DMEs and developing countries. And the number increased to five (pharmaceutical products, consumer electronics, watches and clocks, musical instruments, and toys and games) in the trade of developing countries among themselves.

As an indicator of IIT, the empirical measure of 'trade overlap' suffers from certain statistical shortcomings. Depending on the data used to calculate IIT shares, different types of two-way trade flows may sometimes be lumped together. Some of the reasons for the resulting statistical untidiness of measures of IIT have already been mentioned in the introduction to this chapter. The measurement difficulties arising from the fact that different types of IIT are statistically indistinguishable have led some researchers to conclude that an empirical assessment of IIT may be futile. Instead, it has been suggested that empiricists should investigate patterns of change in two-way trade rather than focus on the level or share of such trade (Deardorff, 1984). While the present study does not quite share the pessimism regarding measurement issues, the last part of this chapter considers changes in IIT over time.

Figure 4.1 shows those industries that accounted for at least a moderate portion of world trade in 1970 and experienced substantial increases in IIT shares by 1985. In the case of the aircraft industry (SITC 734), the global share of IIT rose more than 26 percentage points. Gains in the other industries shown in the figure ranged from 10 to 20 percentage points. The industries shown include representatives from all three end-user groups – capital goods, consumer goods and intermediates.

Overall, the trade composition of 90 industries was considered in drawing up Figure 4.1. Of these, 67 recorded an increase in IIT shares between 1970 and 1985. On average, the increases were of a much greater magnitude than decreases. Not only does two-way trade account for a significant portion of

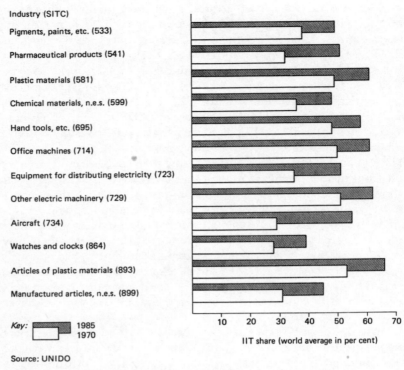

Figure 4.1 Industries with significant increases of IIT, 1970–85

world trade, but its effects are widespread and apply to most of the world's industries.

This chapter completes the 'survey' portion of the book. The evidence of IIT has been examined in a way that highlights particular features that are relevant to the discussion in later chapters. The relationships between country similarities and two-way trade are reconsidered in Chapters 7 and 9 where an empirical investigation of the economies-of-scale model is the focus of discussion. The intervening chapters return to the topics of inter-industrial specialization and inter-industry trade and rely primarily on an H–O framework.

Notes: Chapter 4

1 The subject owes its origins to the unexpected empirical finding that the formation of the Benelux Union and the consequent dismantling of trade obstacles led to greater amounts of intra-industry trade rather than to inter-industry specialization and trade among members; see Verdoorn, 1960. Previous work had acknowledged the role of preference similarities and the interaction between product differentiation and economies of scale as determinants of the composition

of trade in manufactures. However, the link between these hypotheses and IIT had yet to be made explicit.

2   In most studies the expression used is:

$$\frac{(X_{ij} + M_{ij}) - |X_{ij} - M_{ij}|}{X_{ij} + M_{ij}}.$$

This version obscures the character of the trade overlap. It is useful in another sense, however; it highlights the complementarity between IIT and net trade, an aspect that is stressed in later parts of the book.

3   Japan is an exception. Its IIT share is far below that of other DMEs. One explanation may be that trade impediments restrict IIT more severely than inter-industry trade. The result could also simply reflect the fact that the country's immense export capacity in most industries tends to dwarf competing imports.

CHAPTER 5

International patterns of factor endowments

This chapter, together with the following one, turns from a discussion of the more readily observable features of specialization and trade to their underlying determinants. The chapter begins with an empirical analysis of the distribution of factor endowments and then moves on to the subject of factor abundance. The theoretical models which serve as a framework for the organization and interpretation of the evidence receive particular attention in the following discussion.

In order to explain the pattern of international trade, theorists have considered three broad sets of determinants. One set is technological. These determinants can be represented by inter-country variations in (relative) efficiencies and give rise to comparative advantages through differences in production functions. The Ricardian model of trade provides an example of this line of reasoning. Factor endowments are a second set of determinants. Their effects are highlighted by the factor abundance model, which provides much of the framework for the present study. The third group of determinants is demand-related forces. Although these phenomena have now claimed a place in the literature on trade, there is no equivalent demand-oriented theory of international trade, since the results it could produce are trivial (Dixit and Norman, 1980, p. 3).

Theorists have acknowledged that one deficiency of their work is the lack of a universal model of comparative advantage. In the absence of such a model, the usual practice is to explain comparative advantage in terms of only one set of determinants. The most striking example of this practice is found in the factor abundance approach. In order to highlight the role of inter-country differences in factor abundance, other determinants of comparative advantage are neutralized with the help of specific assumptions. The effects of technology are excluded by the assumption that all countries have access to the same pool of technological knowledge, i.e. share the same production functions which in additon exhibit constant returns to scale. The role of demand is neutralized by the assumption that consumers' tastes are similar, both between countries and across income levels. In theoretical parlance, the latter assumption is known as the postulate of 'identical homothetic preferences'.

Stringent assumptions like these have led to misunderstandings of the role that theory may play in empirical work on trade. Rigorous empirical testing of any trade theory is questionable if the crucial assumptions are far removed from reality. Refutation of such theories would come as no surprise, whereas support would mean little in view of the extreme and often unrealistic assumptions they embody. All this seems to suggest that the prospects for carrying out a convincing empirical application of a particular theory are not bright.

Concerns such as these are valid, but they also ignore one of the main functions of trade theory. The true purpose of most models is to highlight a particular characteristic of trade and not to represent the complete workings of the world trading system. So long as an 'application' is not regarded as a rigorous test of a theory's validity, theoretical propositions can play a constructive role in empirical investigations. The propositions – even if they depend on questionable assumptions – can serve as a guide for the organization and systematic presentation of empirical information. Furthermore, data that are organized and presented along the lines suggested by a given theory either lend themselves to interpretation in the spirit of that theory or reveal facts of real life that are at variance with the theory's predictions. Both outcomes are of interest to the analyst.

The present chapter represents an example of an empirical application which makes use of a particular trade model in the sense described here. In view of the dominant role that the factor abundance theory plays in this chapter, the first section considers some of its empirical implications. This is followed by an examination of empirical methods to measure countries' factor endowments and to assess factor abundance. The third section applies these methods to data for a large sample of countries. The chapter concludes with some documentary evidence on the relationship between factor abundance and the commodity structure of net trade.

The factor abundance theory in higher dimensions

The theory's central proposition is an unambiguous prediction of the direction of trade. In a world of two countries, two goods and two factors, each country will export that good which makes intensive use of its abundant factor. In order for trade to occur, the two countries must differ in factor abundance.

The direction of trade in this $2\times2\times2$ model can be predicted unequivocally. What happens, however, if the trading world is more complex, involving a multitude of countries, goods and factors? This question had long puzzled both theorists and empirical researchers. Theorists must grapple with the fact that their basic model yields determinate solutions only for the 'laboratory case of twoness'. Empiricists are compelled to rely on a narrow, two-dimensional theoretical framework as a basis for analysis of a higher-dimensional world. It is only recently that refinements in the theory have promised a solution to some of these problems. The work of Dixit and Norman (1980) and Deardorff (1980, 1982) has produced a more general set of results on factor abundance trade, albeit at some cost in predictive power.[1] In a somewhat diluted form, the law of comparative advantage and the proposition of factor abundance are shown to be valid in a world populated by many countries, goods and factors.

The original, 'strong' version of the factor abundance proposition rests on the condition of twoness. The new, 'weak' version, however, is derived from a more general model. It asserts that comparative advantage (or, more specifically, factor abundance) determines trade patterns only in an 'on-average' sense. Countries have a tendency to export the goods they would produce relatively cheaply in autarky. And to the extent that comparative advantage is based on factor abundance, countries tend to export those goods that use abundant factors relatively intensively.

In more formal terms, these generalizations can be expressed as correlations between net exports and their determinants. A weak version of the law of comparative advantage implies a negative correlation between each country's autarky prices and net exports when trade is in equilibrium. Likewise, in an H–O setting with many countries, goods and factors, the factor abundance proposition implies a positive (correlation-like) association between net exports, factor intensities and factor abundance (Deardorff, 1982). It is important to note that these correlation results not only refer to the direction of trade (as the 'strong' version of the proposition) but also take into account the volume of trade in the various goods. This feature is especially useful in the interpretation of empirical results later in the book.[2]

A final point concerns the flexibility of the theoretical framework for any empirical study. Once a particular model has been selected as the conceptual basis of study, its theoretical content will usually require some modification in order to be accessible to empirical methods. In the present case the modification entails a compromise between the simplistic but 'strong' relationships that emerge from the 2×2×2 model and the complex but 'weak' relationships that characterize larger models. The reason for such a compromise is simple. Precise predictions regarding the structure of trade are not possible, owing to the indeterminacy of patterns of production and trade in models with more goods than factors. Moreover, the weak version of the factor abundance proposition yields hypotheses that are so complex that they prevent the direct application to real-world data. Because of these limitations the present study is modest in its methodological claims. The main objective is to portray patterns of international specialization and trade in such a way that some of the traits suggested by theory can be assessed approximately.

The measurement of factor abundance

A satisfactory method of determining factor endowments and factor abundance must deal with at least three issues. These relate to the selection and definition of the factors to be studied, the appropriate use of data to measure endowment levels, and the derivation of factor abundance indicators.

Capital and labour were the factors traditionally considered in applications of the classic two-dimensional model. However, the puzzling empirical results obtained with two-factor models eventually led economists to extend the framework.[3] One extension was to redefine capital to include both physical and human capital. The two types of capital endowments could then be compared with labour endowments in order to reassess the basis for comparative advantage.

The present exercise uses a similar approach, distinguishing between four broadly defined factors of production: physical capital, skilled labour, semi-skilled labour, and unskilled labour. In the case of physical capital, problems arise because capital stock is a heterogeneous collection of machinery and equipment, and not a primary input. The conceptual difficulties resulting from these circumstances have been extensively debated in the literature.[4] But a simplistic view of (physical) capital is still justified so long as it does not invalidate major propositions about the relationship between factor abundance and international specialization and trade (Ethier, 1979).

The second factor inherited from the original H–O model is unskilled or 'raw' labour. Unlike physical capital, this factor's services clearly meet the requirement of being a primary input. Unskilled labour also comes closest to fulfilling the theoretical postulate that factors are homogeneous and qualitatively alike across different countries. Hence many of the conceptual complications arising in connection with physical capital are absent. Unskilled labour, however, represents only a portion of the country's labour force. Human capital acquired through education and training is embodied in the labour force, and the unskilled or raw labour component is not directly observable.

The inclusion of human capital as a separate factor of production serves to distinguish between the original factor proportions model and its extensions. The basic notion is simple: human capital is formed through schooling, training and related forms of investment in workers. An early version of the extended model (Leontief, 1953) used the concept of 'labour efficiency' to distinguish between various types of labour. Later contributions, however, focused on skill differentials to represent different rates of human capital formation.

Prior to the development of a generalized factor abundance theory the inclusion of human and physical capital complicated the analysis by increasing the number of factors to three. In order to retain the 'twoness' of the original model, some analysts sought to merge human and physical capital into one broad aggregate of total capital. This method, however, had its own problems. It was necessary that the two types of capital be close substitutes. Moreover, the use of a composite measure of capital yielded results that were inferior to those obtained when human and physical capital were separately recognized as determinants of trade patterns (Branson and Monoyios, 1977). Finally, in order to determine the stock of the capital composite, estimates of aggregate investment in human as well as physical capital were needed. Such estimates are more difficult than a straightforward assessment of the size of various skill classes within the total labour force of a country.

In the present study the identification of skill classes forms the basis for treatment of human capital. The actual number of classes to be considered is primarily a matter of data availability.[5] The present exercise employs data for unskilled (or raw) labour, semi-skilled and skilled workers. These categories represent the entire labour force and together with physical capital serve as the conceptual framework for an extended factor proportions model.

Having determined the factors to be considered, attention turns to the method of assessing abundance (or scarcity). Factor abundance can be pictured in at least two ways. One is to define abundance (or scarcity) in terms of physical endowments of factors. Factor abundance could then be determined from cross-country comparisons of endowment levels. The alternative method employs an 'economic' definition of abundance based on factor prices. According to that approach, an abundant (scarce) factor will command a relatively low (high) price in an autarky state. The two views yield the same theoretical relationship between factor abundance and the composition of trade.

In empirical studies, the distinction between a physical and a price-based definition of abundance translates into the choice between a 'stock' measure of factor endowments and a measure based on the relative price of factor services. A preference for either has obvious data implications. The physical approach yields estimates that are appropriate for a country operating in an autarky state and for all conceivable trading equilibria. Most analysts shunned the use of price-based measures. They argued that such measures must reflect autarky relationships if they were to serve as predictors of patterns of specialization and trade. Recent theoretical work, however, has shown that factor prices observed in trading equilibria can perform the same function.[6] As a result, the empiricists have a real choice which is not constrained by the lack of data on autarky prices.[7]

For reasons of data availability, the present study relies on factor endowments and uses conventional methods of estimation. Following others (Balassa, 1979; Bowen, 1983a; Leamer, 1984; and Bowen, Leamer and Sveikauskas, 1987), the stock of physical capital is determined from accumulated gross domestic investment. An estimate of the net capital stock in current US dollars is derived by applying a depreciation factor to annual gross domestic investment (prior to accumulation) and assuming an asset life of 15 years. This method was employed to obtain estimates of physical capital stock in 47 countries for 1970 and 1985.[8]

An ideal complement to estimates for the stock of physical capital would be corresponding information on human capital. Such figures, however, would require economy-wide information on investment in human capital and are not available. Nor is it practical to estimate the returns on investment in human capital, as these cannot be defined in an empirically operational way. The only feasible alternative is to employ a stock-related measure which depends on the number of workers with certain labour skills. These figures serve as a proxy measure for human capital. They cannot be precise indicators, since they neglect differences between workers' 'personal' levels of human capital. And consequently, the count of skilled labourers leads to biases in inter-country comparisons of human capital endowments to the extent that the distribution of human capital among skilled workers differs between countries. Despite this potential measurement bias, it has become common practice to define skilled labour as the number of professional or technical workers. The same practice is followed in the present study. By contrast, the unskilled labour category is defined narrowly to consist of illiterate workers. The residual category of semi-skilled labour then becomes a fairly broad one comprising all literate, non-professional workers.

In the H–O framework, measurement of a country's total factor supplies is not suitable to indicate factor abundance. Due to the assumption of constant returns to scale, it is relative endowments which matter, so that absolute levels must be judged in relation to the country's overall size. In the simplest $(2 \times 2 \times 2)$ model several alternative expressions for factor abundance are available. These include the endowment ratio between the two factors in a single country, the endowment ratio between country A and country B for a single factor, and the share of country A's endowment of one factor in corresponding world endowments. Measures based on any of these ratios will provide an unequivocal indication of factor abundance or scarcity. But complications emerge once the model is extended to include more than two factors. In that case, not all three of the above ratios will yield useful measures of abundance.

A 'naive' approach to the measurement of factor abundance in the extended model is to follow the practices used in the two-factor case. Accordingly, empiricists will often replace the capital-labour ratio of the original 'small' model with ratios between different types of capital and labour. Such measures, even if they are appropriately scaled, result in asymmetric treatment of factors and cannot be justified by rigorous derivation from the underlying formal model. By contrast, the last one of the above indicators can serve to compare the relative endowments of more than two factors for a single country. This indicator, which is expressed in terms of the country's share in world endowments, yields a measure that treats all factors symmetrically. Yet another measure is the ratio between a country's share in world supply of a given factor and its share in world expenditure (Leamer and Bowen, 1981). This expression can be used in an ordinal manner to determine a factor's relative abundance across countries. It may also be treated as a dichotomous indicator of factor abundance or scarcity in a country.

The changing basis for comparative advantage

The following analysis of the international distribution of factor supplies makes use of each of the three measures described above. Information of this type is

75

required if variations in resource availability are to be related to levels of trade. Leamer (1984), for example, has shown that in an H–O setting an industry's net exports can be expressed as a linear function of factor supplies. Such a relationship incorporates two effects, one relating to factor abundance and the other to country size. The information on international differences in factor endowments presented here will be used in the analysis of net trade in manufactures reported in Chapter 7.

Table 5.1 summarizes the endowment pattern in 1970 and 1985. The figures show the expected high concentration of physical capital in the DMEs. These countries also accounted for a large share of all skilled labour and a significant portion of semi-skilled labour in the country sample. The shifts during this period were not great but have clearly favoured the developing countries. The DMEs' share of physical capital declined slightly although by 1985 they still claimed 85 per cent of the total. Unskilled labour is the only factor for which these countries had a marginal share of total supply (2.5 per cent in 1985).

When absolute changes in factor shares are considered, the trend towards lesser concentration among the DMEs is reconfirmed. The DMEs' decline is most pronounced for semi-skilled labour with lesser – and roughly equal – shifts for skilled labour and physical capital. However, the wide disparity in the distribution of resources between DMEs and developing countries means that differences in factor abundance will continue to be a paramount source of trade between the two country groups for some time.

Differences in the endowment patterns of the developing countries are as interesting as the distinctions between the two major country groups. The NIEs have a fairly balanced resource structure with semi-skilled and skilled labour being relatively important. The pattern of change in NIEs is characterized by relative increases in the shares of physical capital, skilled and semi-skilled labour and a decline in the share of unskilled labour. A similar pattern is found among second-generation NIEs. These countries are relatively better endowed with unskilled and semi-skilled labour than are the NIEs, although increases in the share of physical capital matched that reported for the richer group. The remaining developing countries account for an overwhelming portion of unskilled labour in the sample and the share has risen since 1970. Physical capital is by far the scarcest factor among the non-NIEs, although its rate of increase between 1970 and 1985 was high. In general, the distribution of productive factors reveals substantial differences between the country groups. These variations seem to agree with casual impressions regarding levels of economic development.

Figures for individual countries reveal very few instances of extremely high concentration of factor endowments. The most striking example is that of India, whose share of unskilled labour accounted for over 62 per cent of the entire country sample in 1970, rising to 65 per cent in 1985. Although lower, India's shares of skilled and semi-skilled labour were also remarkable. Figures for the USA represent another instance of factor concentration. The country began the 1970s with large shares of physical capital, skilled labour

Table 5.1 Distribution of factor endowments, 1970 and 1985

Country group, country or area	Percentage in total country sample (country ranking in parentheses)							
	Physical capital[a/] 1970	1985	Skilled labour[b/] 1970	1985	Semi-skilled labour[c/] 1970	1985	Unskilled labour[d/] 1970	1985
All DMEs of which:	90.53	85.27	66.03	62.87	54.18	46.71	3.37	2.47
Six largest DMEs	74.03	70.16	52.31	48.55	43.82	38.20	1.66	1.20
France	7.38 (4)	5.13 (4)	5.33 (6)	4.65 (7)	4.15 (7)	3.36 (9)	0.09(33)	0.09(32)
Germany, Fed. Rep. of	9.71 (3)	6.62 (3)	5.83 (5)	5.60 (6)	4.92 (6)	4.13 (6)	0.11(31)	0.11(30)
Italy	4.02 (6)	3.48 (6)	3.25 (8)	2.71 (9)	3.91 (9)	3.02(11)	0.54(13)	0.24(23)
Japan	11.17 (2)	17.62 (2)	6.59 (3)	7.08 (3)	10.74 (3)	8.48 (3)	0.23(27)	0.22(26)
United Kingdom	4.80 (5)	3.91 (5)	6.40 (4)	5.74 (5)	5.00 (5)	3.61 (7)	0.34(21)	0.10(31)
United States	36.95 (1)	33.40 (1)	24.91 (1)	22.77 (1)	15.10 (2)	15.60 (2)	0.35(20)	0.44(13)
Other DMEs	16.50	15.11	13.72	14.32	10.36	8.51	1.71	1.27
Australia[e/]	1.79 (8)	1.72(12)	1.26(18)	1.34(17)	0.64(27)	0.46(32)	.	0.01(43)
Austria	0.75(19)	0.78(19)	0.61(29)	0.58(31)	0.72(22)	0.53(29)	0.01(42)	0.02(38)
Belgium	1.19(13)	0.72(21)	0.90(21)	0.84(25)	1.57(17)	1.54(16)	0.27(26)	0.33(19)
Canada	3.75 (7)	3.29 (7)	2.38 (9)	2.61(10)	0.45(33)	0.34(34)	0.01(42)	0.01(43)
Denmark	0.65(21)	0.55(25)	0.63(26)	0.78(26)	0.42(34)	0.29(36)	0.01(42)	0.01(43)
Finland	0.60(23)	0.64(22)	0.56(30)	0.64(29)	0.65(26)	0.49(30)	0.01(42)	0.01(43)
Greece	0.48(24)	0.49(28)	0.47(32)	0.54(33)	0.22(39)	0.17(41)	0.30(24)	0.14(28)
Ireland	0.17(38)	0.21(40)	0.23(40)	0.23(40)	0.16(42)	0.16(42)	0.01(42)	0.01(43)
Israel	0.25(32)	0.24(38)	0.33(37)	0.43(35)	0.94(20)	0.75(22)	0.05(35)	0.04(34)
Netherlands	1.61 (9)	1.28(13)	1.44(17)	1.45(15)	0.22(39)	0.19(39)	0.02(38)	0.02(38)
New Zealand	0.32(26)	0.28(36)	0.29(38)	0.26(39)	0.29(36)	0.25(37)	0.00(46)	0.01(43)
Norway	0.66(20)	0.77(20)	0.40(34)	0.57(32)	0.52(30)	0.58(26)	0.01(42)	0.01(43)
Portugal	0.20(35)	0.29(35)	0.27(39)	0.38(37)	2.28(11)	1.81(15)	0.44(17)	0.28(22)
Spain	2.38(12)	1.82(11)	1.47(16)	1.26(18)	0.69(24)	0.49(30)	0.53(14)	0.35(17)
Sweden	1.55(11)	0.94(16)	1.67(11)	1.72(13)	0.59(28)	0.46(32)	0.02(38)	0.02(38)
Switzerland	1.15(16)	1.09(14)	0.81(23)	0.69(28)	0.59(28)	0.46(32)	0.01(42)	0.01(43)

Table 5.1 continued

Country group, country or area	Physical capital[a] 1970	1985	Skilled labour[b] 1970	1985	Semi-skilled labour[c] 1970	1985	Unskilled labour[d] 1970	1985
				Percentage in total country sample (country ranking in parentheses)				
Developing country or area	9.48	14.73	33.96	37.11	45.82	53.28	96.62	97.54
NIEs	3.68	6.46	8.54	10.87	9.95	12.12	7.01	5.71
Argentina	0.91(17)	0.52(26)	1.51(14)	1.06(22)	1.74(15)	1.50(17)	0.28(25)	0.24(23)
Brazil	1.16(14)	2.21 (9)	4.26 (7)	6.22 (4)	3.98 (8)	4.92 (5)	4.49 (4)	3.76 (4)
Hong Kong	0.10(40)	0.35(32)	0.18(42)	0.22(41)	0.27(37)	0.30(35)	0.16(28)	0.22(26)
Mexico	1.16(14)	2.02(10)	1.64(12)	2.07(11)	2.00(13)	3.16(10)	1.51 (8)	0.89 (9)
Republic of Korea	0.30(27)	1.02(15)	0.82(22)	1.14(20)	1.86(14)	2.10(14)	0.52(15)	0.52(12)
Singapore	0.05(43)	0.34(33)	0.13(43)	0.16(42)	0.10(44)	0.14(44)	0.10(32)	0.08(33)
Second-generation NIEs	1.49	3.00	6.42	7.91	13.28	16.22	13.50	12.53
Colombia	0.29(28)	0.32(34)	0.62(28)	0.92(24)	1.04(19)	1.32(19)	0.76(10)	0.59(11)
Indonesia	0.19(36)	0.92(17)	2.02(10)	2.83 (8)	5.14 (4)	6.2 (4)	8.30 (2)	7.83 (2)
Malaysia	0.12(39)	0.40(31)	0.34(36)	0.45(34)	0.42(34)	0.56(27)	0.65(12)	0.62(10)
Peru	0.19(36)	0.28(36)	0.64(25)	0.60(30)	0.56(29)	0.72(23)	0.48(16)	0.41(15)
Philippines	0.27(29)	0.45(29)	1.49(15)	1.54(14)	2.16(12)	2.69(12)	0.93 (9)	1.29 (7)
Sri Lanka	0.04(46)	0.08(44)	0.37(35)	0.36(38)	0.70(23)	0.78(21)	0.41(18)	0.29(21)
Thailand	0.26(30)	0.42(30)	0.63(26)	1.03(23)	2.95(10)	3.43 (8)	1.58 (7)	1.14 (8)
Tunisia	0.07(41)	0.11(42)	0.12(45)	0.05(47)	0.09(45)	0.14(44)	0.34(21)	0.33(19)
Uruguay	0.06(42)	0.03(47)	0.19(41)	0.13(44)	0.22(39)	0.16(42)	0.05(35)	0.03(35)
Other developing countries	4.31	5.27	19.00	18.33	22.59	24.94	76.06	79.30
Chile	0.26(30)	0.13(41)	0.41(33)	0.40(36)	0.48(31)	0.56(27)	0.13(30)	0.14(28)
Dominican Republic	0.04(46)	0.04(46)	0.08(46)	0.09(45)	0.16(42)	0.19(39)	0.16(28)	0.22(26)
Egypt	0.22(34)	0.63(23	1.26(18)	1.81(12)	0.67(25)	0.63(25)	2.58 (6)	2.99 (5)
Guatemala	0.05(43)	0.09(43)	0.13(43)	0.16(42)	0.16(42)	0.20(38)	0.38(19)	0.42(14)
India	1.61 (9)	2.23 (8)	13.06 (2)	11.30 (2)	16.44 (1)	17.84 (1)	62.38 (1)	65.00 (1)

Table 5.1 continued

	Percentage in total country sample (country ranking in parentheses)							
	Physical capital [a]		Skilled labour [b]		Semi-skilled labour [c]		Unskilled labour [d]	
Country group, country or area	1970	1985	1970	1985	1970	1985	1970	1985
Pakistan	0.24(33)	0.22(39)	0.78(24)	1.11(21)	0.86(21)	1.08(20)	5.90 (3)	7.74 (3)
Panama	0.04(46)	0.05(45)	0.07(47)	0.09(45)	0.08(46)	0.09(46)	0.05(35)	0.03(35)
Turkey	0.40(25)	0.51(27)	1.12(20)	1.21(19)	1.71(16)	2.31(13)	3.47 (5)	2.03 (6)
Venezuela	0.62(22)	0.57(24)	0.52(31)	0.77(27)	0.47(32)	0.69(24)	0.31(23)	0.33(19)
Yugoslavia	0.83(18)	0.80(18)	1.57(13)	1.39(16)	1.56(18)	1.35(18)	0.70(11)	0.40(16)

Source: UNIDO (based on supplementary data sources documented in the statistical appendix).

a/ Net capital stocks were computed by summing depreciated flows of annual real gross domestic investment. For technical details of the computation see the statistical appendix.

b/ Skilled labour is defined as the number of professional/technical workers (ISCO 0/1).

c/ Semi-skilled labour is the number of literate workers who do not belong to the professional/technical category.

d/ Unskilled labour is the number of illiterate workers.

e/ Endowments of semi-skilled labour and unskilled labour could not be estimated due to a lack of information on literacy rates.

and semi-skilled labour. However, its shares of physical capital and skilled labour had declined somewhat by 1985. A third remarkable case is Japan's share of physical capital, which rose from over 11 per cent in 1970 to over 17 per cent in 1985. These three countries were the only cases where factor shares of more than 10 per cent were recorded.

Changes in the international distribution of factors can be judged on the basis of absolute differences in country shares. The largest shifts were in national endowments of physical capital, a result reflecting wide differences in rates of capital accumulation. Singapore's gains, which even surpassed those of Japan, were the most impressive: the country increased its share of physical capital almost sevenfold between 1970 and 1985. The share of physical capital at least tripled in five other developing economies (Egypt, Hong Kong, Indonesia, Malaysia, and Republic of Korea). Of the ten developing countries experiencing the largest increases in this factor, five were NIEs and three were second-generation NIEs. Among the DMEs, Japan was the only country where the share of physical capital increased by more than a half. The factor's share actually declined in 14 DMEs, with the steepest fall recorded for Belgium.

Changes in country shares for the three labour categories were not great. All NIEs other than Argentina increased their shares of skilled labour though only about half of the second-generation NIEs reported relative increases in this factor. Japan was the only large DME to report a higher share of skilled labour in 1985 than in 1970, although about two-thirds of the smaller DMEs met this criterion.[9] Relative endowments of semi-skilled labour declined in all DMEs except Portugal and the USA. Shifts were in the opposite direction in NIEs and second-generation NIEs (other than Argentina and Uruguay), while the distribution of unskilled labour changed very little in comparison with other factors. In a third of the countries, the share of unskilled labour was virtually unchanged between 1970 and 1985.[10]

Summary measures of the dispersion of resource endowments between the members of each country group are a useful supplement to the data in Table 5.1. Although country groups were drawn up to ensure a degree of homogeneity, intra-group dispersion of endowments was sometimes large. The figures in the first part of Table 5.2 illustrate this feature. Among the DMEs, the dispersion of physical capital is largest and appears to be associated with that of country size. The six largest DMEs are similar in their endowments of physical capital as are the 16 smaller economies, but coefficients of variation for the group as a whole are much larger. The figures for developing countries tell a quite different story. Physical capital, skilled labour and semi-skilled labour are comparatively equitably dispersed among the NIEs and between the second-generation NIEs. The same was not true for other developing countries. Unskilled labour was the most unevenly distributed resource of all the four factors, and its dispersion widened over time.

The types of data shown in Table 5.1 and the first part of Table 5.2 offer some preliminary evidence regarding the distribution of factor endowments.

Table 5.2 Dispersion of factor endowments[a] within broad country groups, 1970 and 1985

Country group	Physical capital 1970	Physical capital 1985	Skilled labour 1970	Skilled labour 1985	Semi-skilled labour 1970	Semi-skilled labour 1985	Unskilled labour 1970	Unskilled labour 1985
A. Variation of endowment levels (coefficients of variation in per cent)[b]								
DMEs	193.7	196.4	177.7	170.9	149.3	165.2	116.9	116.0
Six largest DMEs	100.2	101.4	92.0	90.7	62.8	77.8	61.2	67.0
Other DMEs	87.2	84.1	72.3	70.9	81.4	85.0	156.7	149.9
Developing countries and areas	112.3	110.0	191.5	162.6	180.2	171.0	319.9	330.8
NIEs	85.2	78.4	107.4	125.3	84.9	89.9	144.8	147.7
Second-generation NIEs	58.3	80.7	88.9	98.9	113.2	114.7	172.4	175.8
Other developing countries	113.3	124.8	208.2	184.4	222.0	217.8	254.3	254.6
B. Variation of endowment levels relative to variation in GNP (ratio of the respective coefficients of variation)								
DMEs	0.88	0.89	0.81	0.78	0.68	0.75	0.53	0.53
Six largest DMEs	0.84	0.87	0.77	0.78	0.53	0.67	0.51	0.58
Other DMEs	0.98	0.91	0.81	0.77	0.91	0.92	1.76	1.63
Developing countries and areas	0.94	0.96	1.61	1.43	1.51	1.50	2.69	2.90
NIEs	0.96	0.96	1.20	1.32	0.96	1.11	1.63	1.83
Second-generation NIEs	1.05	0.93	1.62	1.14	2.05	1.32	3.12	2.02
Other developing countries	0.89	1.01	1.63	1.49	1.74	1.76	1.99	2.06

Source: UNIDO (based on supplementary data sources documented in the statistical appendix).

a/ Underlying factor endowment data are those of table 5.1.

b/ Ratio between standard deviation and mean expressed in per cent.

However, they do not provide the explicit information on factor abundance which is needed to answer fundamental questions regarding the H–O pattern of trade. A first impression regarding the dispersion of factor abundance (rather than factor endowments) is obtained from the second part of Table 5.2. The indicators, which correct resource variation for differences in country size, show a much more equitable pattern of factor abundance in DMEs than in the developing countries. This result conforms with the impression that DMEs are relatively homogeneous in terms of their basic economic characteristics while developing countries are not.

At least three general observations can be made on the basis of the data presented in this section. First, because the diversity of factor endowments is great, a strong H–O component should be present among the determinants of the commodity composition of trade. Second, the variation in factor abundance differs among factors and H–O influences should reflect this fact. Third, the distribution of resources across countries is changing over time but the pace of change is different for each resource. Patterns of specialization and trade should be altered as a result of these shifts.

Factor abundance and the patterns of trade

National differences in factor abundance offer plausible partial explanations for international variations in patterns of specialization and trade. The point of empirical interest is whether these differences are mirrored in the structure of production and trade and, if they are, whether their role coincides with the predictions of the H–O theory. These questions are addressed in a later chapter with the help of more detailed data. The present section has a related, but more limited, objective – to consider how factor abundance may influence trade in broad groups of manufactures.

From the previous discussion, it is clear that any 'application' of the factor abundance hypothesis requires three types of data. Information on factor endowments, factor intensities and the structure of trade is needed to forge a link between factor abundance and trade patterns. In the present exercise, a classification of goods according to relative factor requirements is established. The classification yields three broad product categories. H–O trade is represented by two categories which consist of labour-intensive and capital-intensive goods, while the third refers to product-cycle goods. Countries were arranged in three groups based on this product classification. They include net exporters of product-cycle goods, net exporters of capital-intensive H–O goods that were importers of product-cycle goods, and net exporters of labour-intensive H–O goods that were also importers of both product-cycle and capital-intensive H–O goods.[11] Economic theory suggests a loose connection between factor abundance and trade in these country groups.

Table 5.3 shows the relationship between net trade and factor abundance, where an ordinal measure is used for the latter. Based on this measure a

Table 5.3 Factor abundance and net trade by country or area, 1970 and 1985

Net exporters by product class	Ranking of factors by abundance ratio[a]							
	Physical capital		Skilled labour		Semi-skilled labour		Unskilled labour	
	1970	1985	1970	1985	1970	1985	1970	1985
A. Product-cycle goods[b]								
Denmark	1-	2+	2-	1+	3-	3-	4-	4-
France	1+	1+	2-	2-	3-	3-	4-	4-
Germany, Fed. Rep. of	1+	1+	2-	2-	3-	3-	4-	4-
Ireland	3+	2+	1+	1+	2+	3+	4-	4-
Italy	1-	1-	3-	3-	2+	2-	4-	4-
Japan	1+	1+	3-	3-	2+	2-	4-	4-
Netherlands	1+	2+	2+	1+	3-	3-	4-	4-
Sweden	2+	2-	1+	1+	3-	3-	4-	4-
Switzerland	1+	1+	2-	2-	3-	3-	4-	4-
United Kingdom	3-	2-	1+	1+	2-	3-	4-	4-
United States	1-	1-	2-	2-	3-	3-	4-	4-
Yugoslavia	3+	3+	1+	1+	2+	2+	4+	4-
B. Capital-intensive H-O goods								
Argentina	3+	3-	2+	2+	1+	1+	4-	4-
Belgium	1+	2-	2-	1+	3-	3-	4-	4-
Brazil	4-	4+	2+	1+	3+	2+	1+	3+
Canada	1+	1-	2-	2-	3-	3-	4-	4-
Indonesia	4-	4+	3+	3+	2+	2+	1+	1+
Peru	4-	4+	1+	2+	2+	1+	3+	3+
Republic of Korea	4-	3+	2+	2+	1+	1+	3+	4-
Singapore	4-	1+	1+	2-	2+	3-	3+	4-
Spain	3-	1+	2-	3-	1+	2+	4-	4-
Venezuela	1+	3+	2+	1+	3+	2+	4-	4-

Table 5.3 continued

| Net exporters by product class | Ranking of factors by abundance ratio [a] | | | | | | | |
| | Physical capital | | Skilled labour | | Semi-skilled labour | | Unskilled labour | |
	1970	1985	1970	1985	1970	1985	1970	1985
C. Labour-intensive H-O goods								
Austria	1+	1+	3+	2-	2+	3-	4-	4-
Colombia	4-	4-	3+	2+	1+	1+	2+	3+
Egypt	4-	3+	2+	2+	3+	4+	1+	1+
Finland	1+	1+	2+	1+	3-	3-	4-	4-
Greece	2+	2+	3+	1+	1+	3+	4-	4-
Hong Kong	4-	1+	2+	3-	1+	2-	3+	4-
India	4-	4+	3+	3+	2+	2+	1+	1+
Israel	2+	2+	1+	1+	3-	3-	4-	4-
Malaysia	4-	4+	3+	3+	2+	2+	1+	1+
Mexico	4-	3+	2+	2+	1+	1+	3+	4-
Pakistan	4-	4-	3+	2+	2+	3+	1+	1+
Philippines	4-	4+	2+	2+	1+	1+	3+	3+
Portugal	4-	3+	3+	2+	1+	1+	2+	4+
Sri Lanka	4-	4+	3+	2+	1+	1+	2+	3+
Thailand	4-	4+	3+	3+	1+	1+	2+	2+
Tunisia	4+	3+	2+	4-	3+	2+	1+	1+
Turkey	4-	4-	3+	3+	2+	1+	1+	2+
Uruguay	3-	3-	2+	2+	1+	1+	4-	4-

Sources: UNIDO and supplementary data sources documented in the statistical appendix.

a/ Ranks 1 or 2 indicate relative factor abundance. Ranks 3 or 4 denote relative scarcity. The sign accompanying each rank denotes absolute abundance (+) or scarcity (-). Both the ordinal and dichotomous measures used here are derived from normalized factor shares. These normalized shares are obtained as the ratio of a country's share in world supply of the given factor and its share in world GNP.

b/ Group A consists of all net exporters of product cycle goods, irrespective of trade in the other two types of goods. Group B is composed of net exporters of capital-intensive H-O goods that imported product cycle goods. Finally, group C is made up of net exporters of labour-intensive H-O goods that imported the other two types of goods. If a country's assignment to one of the three groups was different between 1970 and 1985, the more 'advanced' group was chosen for representation in the table. Countries that were net importers of all three types of goods are not shown.

ranking of 1 or 2 may be interpreted as an indication of relative abundance, while a ranking of 3 or 4 suggests relative scarcity. In addition, a plus or minus denotes factor abundance (+) or scarcity (−) measured in an absolute sense. When considered in relation to the type of trade, these factor abundance profiles provide the basis for a prima facie judgement of H–O forces.

The results provide some empirical support for the generalized version of the factor abundance proposition. That proposition suggests a tendency for countries to be net exporters of goods that use their abundant factors intensively. Similarly, countries will be net importers of goods that use their scarce factors intensively. The insistence that there is no more than 'a tendency' for this proposition to hold means that predictions of the trade pattern are not necessarily applicable to a specific country, good or factor. Bearing this qualification in mind, the theory's assertion concerning average factor characteristics of trade is confirmed by Table 5.3.

The generalized factor abundance hypothesis is broad enough to allow for differences in the 'contribution' of various factors to an overall H–O scheme. Such differences can be observed from comparisons between net exports and factor abundance. If the factor rankings in Table 5.3 are considered in conjunction with the indicators of absolute abundance, a broad pattern of differentiation emerges. The expectation that skilled labour conveys a competitive advantage in product–cycle goods is corroborated in ten out of the 12 countries. All such exporters of product–cycle goods (other than Yugoslavia) are DMEs and include the six largest countries in this group. Italy and Japan are the exceptions to this broad interpretation of the product–cycle hypothesis in the sense that skilled labour is relatively scarce in the two countries. The relative availability of semi–skilled labour,[12] however, is much greater than that of skilled labour. The results for these two countries may reflect the fact that the degree of international competitiveness in product–cycle goods depends on more than the availability of skilled labour. The innovative capacity of skilled labour is crucial for product development, but other labour skills which are even more closely tied to production processes can also convey a competitive advantage in product–cycle goods. Confirmation of the important role that is suggested for semi–skilled labour requires more evidence and is the subject of further analysis later in this book.

The results for net exporters of capital–intensive goods provide only modest support for a (partial) factor abundance hypothesis. There is limited evidence that capital exerts a substantial effect on net exports – mainly in the form of a positive sign of the dichotomous indicator. An unambiguous relationship between capital abundance and trade does not appear to be a general characteristic of the ten countries in this group. There can be at least two reasons for these poor results. First, an H–O outcome would be observed only in terms of an on–average relationship or tendency. A positive interaction between capital abundance and capital intensity will yield a comparative advantage, but there may still be numerous exceptions for countries, goods or factors. Second, the H–O model assumes that physical capital is not internationally mobile,

85

though in reality, to a considerable extent, it is. For both reasons, the H–O link between capital abundance and product structure of net trade may be a rather weak one.[13]

International flows of capital and skilled labour violate the assumption of factor immobility between countries, but the same may not apply to semi-skilled or unskilled labour.[14] Certainly, the empirical relationship between these two factors and the net trade of labour-intensive products conforms to H–O predictions. This fact can be seen from the results for country group C in Table 5.3. The group consists of 18 countries which are both net exporters of labour-intensive goods and net importers of capital-intensive goods. With very few exceptions, the dichotomous indicator for semi-skilled labour had the expected sign. Most countries in this group can be distinguished according to whether semi-skilled labour, unskilled labour or both are important determinants of international competitiveness. Semi-skilled labour seems to dominate in Austria, Greece, Hong Kong, Mexico, the Philippines and Uruguay, while unskilled labour is important for Egypt. Other countries (India, Malaysia, Thailand and Turkey) appear to rely on both types of labour.

In strict terms, the modern version of the H–O theory says that factor abundance will also be an on-average determinant of the volume of net trade in the various product groups. As a final step in this preliminary analysis, Table 5.4 summarizes the evidence on this aspect. Countries are again divided into groups, this time according to 'factor dominance'. Countries characterized by a dominance of physical capital are all those for which this factor is ranked highest in Table 5.3. The same criterion is applied analogously to other factors. Net exports were then aggregated across each of the three product categories to determine whether the direction and volume of trade agree, on average, with an H–O pattern.

Only some of the estimates compiled in Table 5.4 support a factor abundance explanation. When the volume and direction of trade are considered simultaneously, the abundance of semi-skilled or unskilled labour is still the major determinant of trade. The importance of skilled labour is weakened in this set of comparisons. One reason may be the nature of trade in product-cycle goods. A country with ample innovative capacity will have high rates of product development in at least some of these industries, but it may simultaneously import other product-cycle goods where its innovative base is weak. On balance, the country is likely to be a net exporter of product-cycle goods, though perhaps not in large volumes. Finally, the relatively weak performance of physical capital as a determinant of the direction and volume of net trade may again be explained by its greater mobility among countries.

Though not a rigorous test, factor abundance effects of varying strengths can be observed in these results. The strength of these effects varies between the four factors. Labour other than the most skilled appears to be the prominent source of comparative advantages. By contrast, the extent to which physical capital endowments determine comparative advantage is ambiguous. The following chapter considers the role of factor intensities while Chapter 7

Table 5.4 Factor abundance and net trade, by country group, 1970 and 1985 (percentages)

| Year | Countries/areas with dominant abundance of:[a/] | Net exports ratio[b/] | | |
		H-O goods, capital intensive[c/]	Product-cycle goods	H-O goods, labour intensive[c/]
1970	Physical capital	7.8	17.6	0.6
	Skilled labour	10.7	6.9	-3.2
	Semi-skilled labour	-30.5	-71.3	21.3
	Unskilled labour	-54.4	-84.5	47.9
1985	Physical capital	1.8	12.1	-11.1
	Skilled labour	3.8	0.4	-5.1
	Semi-skilled labour	-12.5	-25.4	62.6
	Unskilled labour	-65.4	-55.9	37.8

Sources: UNIDO and supplementary data sources documented in the statistical appendix.

a/ A country or area is defined to have dominant abundance of that factor for which the country's share in world supply is relatively highest.

b/ The net exports ratio is defined as the ratio of exports minus imports over exports plus imports.

c/ The classification of H-O goods into capital intensive and labour intensive is based on United States data for 1982. For details see the statistical appendix.

draws together all these results for a more comprehensive application of the factor abundance hypothesis.

Annex: The specific factors model

In the preceding chapter, the analysis of international specialization and trade utilized the factor abundance approach. In general, the focus until now has been on how the relative abundance of various factors of production creates comparative advantage. The existence of diverse patterns of comparative advantage among countries or groups of countries lies at the basis of an explanation of international specialization and trade, where the H–O model provides the theoretical framework. In this section we will relax one of the major assumptions that was implicitly made in our analysis, in order to reconcile some of the predictions of the H–O model with real-world situations.

A crucial assumption of the H–O model demands that factors of production can be shifted costlessly from one industry to another in response to changes in domestic supplies of various factors. As factor supplies change, factor prices may change, leading to changes in specialization and patterns of trade. In this process reallocation of resources at little or no cost appears to be possible in the long run. Accordingly, the above assumption should not substantially affect results that are representative of a relatively long time period like that covered by the analysis of this chapter.

Over shorter periods of time, however, the assumption of costless reallocation may be less plausible. A short-run change in the relative price of commodities produces changes in the relative price of factors of production which induce an intersectoral reallocation of resources. Over short periods of time such reallocations may be difficult, as some factors may be immobile within the economy and/or specific to a particular use. Immobility may be due to geographic considerations. The expanding and contracting sectors of the economy may be in separate locations, making it difficult to reallocate labour and/or capital. In the case of labour, contracting industries may also lobby for legislation concerning plant closings and layoffs, which may hinder the movement of factors of production from one industry to another.

Aside from geographic or legal restraints on resource reallocation, a more fundamental problem lies in the specificity of various resources to particular industries or uses. Certain types of semi-skilled or skilled labour provide examples of such specificity. Thus, workers in a particular industry may develop forms of human capital that are specific to that industry. In general, human capital may be thought of as being composed of two components. First, workers may develop generic human capital such as basic literacy, which is easily transferable across industries. Other types of education, skills and training may be more sector-specific and difficult to transfer across industries. As a result, as economic circumstances change, labour may become 'trapped' in a particular industry in the short run even if no legal or geographic barriers to labour mobility exist. Over time, however, worker retraining and geographic mobility should overcome much of this type of labour immobility. In summary, this implies that even in the long run only half of the H–O assumption of intersectoral mobility of resources would seem plausible for the majority of the labour force.

The issue of factor specificity may be more important with respect to capital. It has long been recognized that various forms of capital may not be intersectorally mobile in the short run, for example, for geographic reasons similar to those outlined above. More importantly, capital may be specific to a particular kind of use such as producing food, and may be partially or totally unsuited to the production of another commodity such as textiles. In such cases it would be difficult to reallocate capital in the short run from one sector to another in response to a change in relative commodity prices. And again, the brisk reallocation of resources envisioned in the H–O model may be realistic only over the long run. As a practical matter, the actual speed of reallocation in response to changes in commodity prices may be related to the speed with which sector-specific capital is depreciated in the contracting industry. If, for instance, the relative price of food rises and that of textiles falls, then the medium–term response may be a faster rate of new investment in the food industry. Put another way, net investment (new investment minus depreciation) may be positive in the food industry. In the contracting textile industry, net investment may become negative. This process would continue until a new long–run equilibrium is reached in both industries. Thus, capital would not be 'released' from one sector to another in a strict sense, but the reallocation would be a dynamic process occurring over time.

There are obvious effects on the economy as a whole of such impediments to reallocation. Since capital cannot be reallocated over the short run, the economy will not be able to produce an optimal quantity of food and the supply of tradable goods will be suboptimal. Further, since capital allocation is temporarily suboptimal, the economy will operate inside its production possibility frontier, or in other words at less than full employment. These conditions are clearly at variance with those postulated for the H–O model.

In order to assess the effects of the presence of specific factors on the patterns of trade and the prices and returns to factors of production, the previous example has to be analysed in a more formal framework. Following most previous work on the subject, three factors of production will be considered. Labour is assumed to be intersectorally mobile between both the food and textile industries, even in the short run. However, instead of capital being homogeneous, the capital stock is divided between the two sectors and is assumed to be immobile between them in the short run. The model thus contains two countries, two products and three factors of production.

One of the main results of the H–O model used for the major part of the study was that it can predict trade patterns from the knowledge of factor endowments alone. Would the same be true in a specific factors model?

In an H–O world, where countries have identical factor endowments and preferences, no trade would take place. In such a situation trade is still possible, however, if in the short run capital has been allocated differently between the two industries in the two countries. Comparative advantage would then depend upon which industry in which country is better endowed with specific capital. The result is that in a specific factors model trade patterns cannot be predicted from knowledge of total factor endowments alone; one must also know how capital is allocated among industries.

To gain more insight into the working of the model, an increase in the supply of labour in one country will be assumed. Under H–O conditions, the result would be that this country would now be relatively well endowed with labour so that it would export the labour-intensive product. In the specific factors model, however, this result does not necessarily hold. All that can be said is that the labour-abundant country would produce more of both goods. Trading patterns depend on how the specific capital is allocated between industries, and are much less sensitive to the overall endowments of labour and capital in the two countries. If specific factors are present, one should not be too surprised to observe instances where a country is exporting a commodity that seems to run against the grain of its total factor endowments. This does not imply that the H–O model is incorrect; rather, it simply means that its predictions may not hold in every short-run situation, especially in the presence of specific factors.

As an extension, it can be shown that trade does not equalize factor prices across countries within the context of the specific factors model. It may be assumed, for instance, that countries A and B have identical endowments of labour, but that country A is relatively well endowed with capital specific to the production of food. Country A will then export food and import textiles. If trade continues unimpeded, commodity prices will be equalized across countries. Does this also imply that factor prices will be equalized across countries? Labour is now relatively productive in country A, which has more capital to work with than in country B. Trade would not equalize wages across the two countries in this case. However, it may be that trade would reduce factor price differences between countries relative to the factor price differences that prevail in autarky. This would seem to be consistent with the fact that, while trade does not equalize factor prices, it seems to move factor prices in that direction.

The above results are useful in order to sort out some anomalies in the patterns of international trade and specialization. As mentioned before, the presence of specific factors would help to explain, in many cases, instances where a country can be observed exporting a product that would seem to run counter to its comparative advantage. Even in a labour-abundant country, the presence of sector-specific capital could lead to the export of capital-intensive products. This does not mean that the H–O model is incorrect; it simply implies that there may be exceptions attributable to the presence of specific factors.

The existence of specific factors might help to explain some of the anomalies present in this chapter. Although the analysis uses more than just two factors of production, the data do not permit inferences concerning the allocation of the various types of labour and capital to the various industries. They allow for measuring the abundance of three separate classes of labour, but capital must, of necessity, be considered homogeneous. Some types of physical capital may be mobile across all classes of goods, but a reasonable assumption is that some forms of capital are not. Since capital was defined to be homogeneous, it was expected that it would confer comparative advantage most heavily to the production of capital-intensive H–O goods. While the results in Table 5.3 do not refute this proposition, the results for capital are weaker than those for the various classes of labour. Some countries that are abundant in capital may have a substantial portion of this capital allocated to the production of product-cycle goods. In this case the presence of capital may be conferring some comparative advantage that cannot be readily discerned owing to data limitations. Given the existence of sector-specific capital, it is not surprising that the H–O results with respect to undifferentiated capital are weaker than for various types of labour, which can be reasonably posited to contribute to comparative advantages in broadly defined sectors.

In the preceding chapter, the weaker results for physical capital were explained in terms of the international mobility of this factor. It may well be that capital mobility and the existence of sector-specific capital may be related. Sector-specific capital may be difficult to reallocate between two disparate industries in the same country. However, it is quite plausible that mobility could occur between countries for the same sector. Thus, the existence of capital mobility and sector-specific capital may both contribute in a complementary way to the relatively weaker results obtained for the H–O predictions for physical capital.

The specific factors model can serve to explain some of the deviations from the predictions of the H–O model. Further, it can help to explain how economies adapt to changing patterns of comparative advantage. Over longer periods of time it becomes a less useful device, as capital and labour are reallocated and become less 'specific'. In the long run, relative supplies of factors determine – at least in part – how international trade and specialization evolve.

Notes: Chapter 5

1 Dixit and Norman, 1980, provide a wealth of generally valid relationships which describe general equilibrium in an open-economy world with many factors and many goods. Deardorff, 1980, restates the law of comparative advantage for a fairly general model of world trade. Deardorff's later work (1982) is a logical extension of his general model, which provides a detailed account of the role of factor proportions in a high-dimensional world.
2 The hypothesis discussed here is the 'commodity version' of the factor abundance proposition. The underlying model is used to predict the commodity

(or product) pattern of (net) trade on the basis of country attributes and characteristics of production processes. An alternative formulation, the 'factor content version', was suggested by Vanek, 1968. Vanek's interpretation also depends on a systematic relationship between factor abundance, factor intensities and trade; however, it lacks the intuitive appeal of the commodity version. The message of the factor content proposition is that a country's exports will embody the services of its abundant factors, while its imports will embody the services of scarce factors.

3 An often cited example of such surprising empirical results is the so-called Leontief paradox. Leontief, 1953, had carried out factor content calculations which apparently revealed the USA as labour- rather than capital-abundant.

4 Arguing from a neo-Ricardian point of view, Steedman, 1979, p. 64, has asserted 'that the existence of heterogeneous capital goods does lead to a breakdown of the logic of the Heckscher–Ohlin–Samuelson theory and hence to that of its major conclusions'. By contrast, Ethier, 1979 and 1981, demonstrated that, if the factor abundance model's basic assumptions are not violated by the introduction of capital, the core theorems remain valid.

5 An early example of the distinction between unskilled and skilled labour is found in Hufbauer, 1970. The maximum number of seven labour categories appears in Bowen, Leamer and Sveikauskas, 1987.

6 Helpman, 1984, demonstrated 'that in the absence of factor price equalization the factor content of bilateral trade patterns can be predicted from post-trade data' (p. 93) on factor prices. These predictions are again of the weak (correlation) type and can easily be extended to a country's aggregate trade with the rest of the world. Their attractiveness is twofold: they state factor abundance attributes of bilateral trade flows, and their empirical validation can be performed in a direct manner.

7 It would have been interesting to compare the empirical performance of the physical–abundance hypothesis with that of the price–abundance hypothesis, if data availability had allowed to do so. However, such a comparison must be left for the research agenda of future studies.

8 These countries accounted for over 88 per cent of world exports of manufactures in 1979. More technical and statistical details on the compilation of capital stock estimates are provided in the statistical appendix (Appendix B).

9 Among individual countries, the largest increases were recorded by Thailand, followed by Colombia, Venezuela, Brazil and Egypt. Among the DMEs, Norway had the largest relative increase in skilled labour.

10 A major exception was the Philippines, which experienced a particularly large increase in the share of unskilled labour. Modest increases were observed for Canada, Hong Kong, Pakistan and the USA.

11 The classification can be loosely associated with stages of development where exporters of product-cycle goods are regarded as the most advanced and exporters of labour-intensive H–O goods as the least advanced. If a country's trade type changed between 1970 and 1985, it was assigned to the more advanced of the two groups. In setting up this country classification, trade in Ricardian (resource-based) goods was disregarded, as no indicator of natural resource endowments was used in the analysis.

12 Semi-skilled labour as defined here is an amalgamation of labour categories of differing skill levels. A plausible hypothesis may be to assume that this factor has a higher skill content in DMEs than in developing countries.

13 Recent general results on these points are found in Ethier and Svensson 1986.

14 There are exceptions e.g. Latin American and Asian immigration to the USA, or the European guest labour programme.

CHAPTER 6

Factor requirements, output and trade

The previous chapter was concerned with the role of factor endowments, but obviously more information is required for an empirical assessment of patterns of specialization and trade. In particular, the factor abundance theory assigns a big role to factor intensities.

The present chapter provides a detailed account of factor intensities in specific industries. The first section deals with the measurement of factor intensities and considers the extent to which intensities vary across industries and between countries. The second section examines the relationships between factor intensities on the one hand and output and trade on the other hand.

Factor intensities and empirical evidence

Previous discussion has made implicit use of the fact that the relative factor requirements of industries differ. Terms like 'resource-based', 'capital-intensive' or 'labour-intensive' are used to suggest systematic differences in the relative input requirements of industries. Such terms can be associated with quantifiable characteristics.

From the economist's point of view, factor intensities characterize a production technique rather than the underlying 'technology'. It is quite possible, for example, that two factories sited in different countries would have identical production functions but operate with different factor intensities, for the simple reason that factor prices in the two countries differ. Profit-maximizing producers would choose different production techniques even though they share the same technology.

In reality, both technological possibilities and factor returns are likely to vary across countries. The factor abundance model nevertheless makes use of certain restrictions on inter-country differences in production techniques in order to obtain predictions on trade patterns. One such restriction is that of identical techniques for all countries as a result of identical technologies and equalized factor prices. Another (weaker) restriction appears in the H–O model with two countries, two factors and two goods: it rules out the possibility that factor intensities are reversed between industries when factor prices change.

The absence of 'factor intensity reversals' ensures that the rankings of industries by factor intensities are everywhere the same.

Theoretical assumptions about production techniques raise several empirical questions. First, what is the extent of inter-country variations in factor intensities of particular industries? Second, is it sensible to construct an industry typology based on factor requirements that is not country-specific? That is, can industries be classified universally by their factor intensities?[1]

Measuring factor intensities

Before answers to the above questions can be attempted, some measurement issues must be clarified. Like the measurement of factor abundance, that of factor intensity is not a trivial matter. In the simplest case – that of a single industry – a knowledge of factor requirements per (physical) unit of output is sufficient to permit comparisons of factor intensities between countries. But when two or more industries are compared, input–output ratios stated in physical quantities are inappropriate for obvious reasons.

The basic two–factors, two–goods model provides a point of departure for discussion of measurement questions. Based on a comparison of factor–input ratios, the two industries can be identified as relatively labour-intensive and relatively capital-intensive. These ratios provide a precise characterization of factor intensity so long as only two factors are considered. A ranking of industries by a single factor-input ratio contains all the information required by the analyst.

When more than two factors of production are admitted, several types of factor-input ratios can be calculated and the measurement of factor intensities on the basis of such ratios becomes problematic. In this case the factor shares approach offers a way out of the dilemma. The value of a factor's input in relation to the value of the industry's output provides a measure of intensity which is free from the ambiguities associated with other expressions (Jones and Scheinkman, 1977). In general, the factor shares yield a measure of intensities which permits generalization and empirical application of the model's basic propositions.

Estimates of factor intensities can be used, for instance, to judge the extent to which reversals in industry rankings occur in the real world. Because such reversals would have significant repercussions for the basic model with two factors and two goods, they have received considerable attention in the literature. The importance of this phenomenon is diminished, however, in models with more than two goods. The possibility that industry rankings by factor intensities will differ between countries is then of less consequence to predictions about trade (Deardoff, 1986). A cross-country comparison of factor intensities is nevertheless of interest, as it provides a basis for developing a typology of industries.

The cross-country pattern of factor intensities

Table 6.1 presents industry rankings by average factor intensities for 43 countries. The methods of compilation are imperfect, however, and before examining the results, three qualifications should be noted. First, factor-input ratios rather than factor shares were the basis of calculations. This departure from the ideal was dictated by data availability; use of factor shares would have meant that a smaller number of factors could be studied. Instead, a more conventional approach which uses labour-based factor ratios as proxy measures of intensities was employed.[2] Non-wage value added per employee and wages per employee are taken as indicators of the relative intensities of physical capital and human capital, respectively. In addition, a simple, globally applicable indicator of labour intensity was calculated in the form of the reciprocal of total value added per employee.[3] All three factor-input ratios are proxies rather than actual measures of physical-capital, human-capital and labour intensities. Their limitations have been discussed repeatedly in the literature (Balassa, 1979, pp. 260–1; UNIDO, 1986, pp. 164–5; Bowden, 1983, pp. 218–19).

A second qualification is that the data underlying the present exercise are highly aggregated. Therefore, they can hardly serve to assess factor intensities of industries defined in a manner that would accord with theoretical models. Nevertheless, the attention that trade theorists have paid recently to the issues of aggregation (Neary, 1985; Deardorff, 1986) and of average relationships (Dixit and Norman, 1980; Deardorff, 1982) seems to justify also a discussion of averages of factor intensities.

A third qualification is that in Table 6.1 cross-country variations in factor intensities are disregarded. Instead, the estimates are expressed as world averages (both unweighted and weighted). Subsequent analysis of the cross-country variations will provide some means of assessing the validity of this step. A concession that is intended to address these departures from preferred practice is to focus attention on ordinal rather than cardinal expressions of factor intensities.

The unweighted estimates of physical capital intensity proved to be quite stable over time. The same six industries were the most intensive users of physical capital in both time periods. These industries, in decreasing order of capital intensity, were petroleum refining, petroleum, coal and related products, industrial chemicals, beverages, tobacco and 'other chemical products' (including pharmaceuticals). Additional industries appearing in the highest quarter of the distribution were non-ferrous metals (1970–7) and paper products (1978–85).

Steel products and transport equipment are still other industries that are widely regarded as heavy users of capital. The results, however, are ambiguous. Unweighted estimates indicate that neither of the two industries is a particularly large user of capital. When weighted estimates are considered, the results fit more closely with conventional expectations. This discrepancy

Table 6.1 Average factor intensities, by industry,[a] 1970–7 and 1978–85 (unweighted and weighted industry rankings)

Industry (ISIC)	Intensity in the use of					
	Physical capital[b]		Human capital[c]		Labour[d]	
	1970–1977	1978–1985	1970–1977	1978–1985	1970–1977	1978–1985
Food products (311)	9 (11)	8 (12)	20 (26)	19 (24)	18 (9)	18 (10)
Beverages (313)	4 (4)	4 (4)	24 (24)	17 (21)	23 (23)	23 (24)
Tobacco etc. (314)	5 (12)	5 (20)	27 (28)	21 (28)	24 (4)	24 (4)
Textiles (321)	26 (28)	24 (28)	26 (27)	23 (27)	2 (1)	4 (1)
Wearing apparel (322)	28 (27)	28 (27)	28 (25)	28 (26)	1 (2)	1 (2)
Leather and fur products (323)	23 (23)	23 (25)	21 (18)	26 (23)	5 (7)	5 (5)
Footwear (324)	27 (26)	27 (26)	25 (23)	27 (25)	3 (3)	2 (3)
Wood and cork products (331)	17 (19)	22 (23)	18 (15)	22 (15)	10 (10)	7 (9)
Furniture fixtures excl. metal (332)	25 (17)	26 (18)	16 (8)	24 (8)	4 (16)	3 (15)
Paper (341)	11 (8)	7 (7)	9 (9)	7 (7)	19 (22)	22 (21)
Printing and publishing (342)	16 (14)	19 (13)	3 (6)	9 (11)	16 (18)	11 (16)
Industrial chemicals (351)	3 (3)	3 (3)	8 (11)	1 (5)	26 (25)	27 (27)
Other chemicals (352)	6 (6)	6 (5)	11 (20)	4 (16)	25 (21)	25 (22)
Petroleum refineries (353)	1 (1)	1 (1)	1 (1)	2 (2)	28 (28)	28 (28)
Products of petroleum and coal (354)	2 (2)	2 (2)	2 (7)	8 (17)	27 (27)	26 (26)
Rubber products (355)	14 (24)	14 (24)	22 (21)	12 (20)	12 (6)	16 (6)
Plastic products (356)	12 (20)	18 (19)	23 (22)	25 (19)	14 (8)	9 (8)
Pottery, china, earthenware (361)	24 (25)	25 (22)	14 (17)	20 (18)	8 (5)	6 (7)
Glass (362)	20 (18)	15 (15)	12 (16)	11 (12)	6 (12)	14 (14)
Other non-metallic min. products (369)	8 (9)	9 (16)	10 (19)	13 (22)	20 (15)	19 (11)
Iron and steel (371)	10 (7)	10 (8)	5 (3)	3 (3)	21 (24)	21 (23)
Non-ferrous metals (372)	7 (5)	11 (6)	7 (2)	6 (1)	22 (26)	20 (25)
Metal products (381)	22 (21)	21 (21)	13 (10)	18 (13)	7 (13)	8 (12)

Table 6.1 continued

Industry (ISIC)	Physical capital[b]		Human capital[c]		Labour[d]	
	1970–1977	1978–1985	1970–1977	1978–1985	1970–1977	1978–1985
Non-electrical machinery (382)	15 (13)	17 (10)	6 (5)	10 (4)	17 (20)	12 (19)
Electrical machinery (383)	21 (22)	13 (11)	15 (13)	14 (9)	9 (11)	15 (18)
Transport equipment (384)	19 (15)	20 (17)	4 (4)	5 (6)	15 (19)	13 (17)
Professional scientific equipment (385)	18 (10)	16 (9)	17 (12)	16 (10)	11 (17)	10 (20)
Other manufactures (390)	13 (16)	12 (14)	19 (14)	15 (14)	13 (14)	17 (13)

(Column group heading: Intensity in the use of)

Source: UNIDO

a/ Averages were taken over a sample of 43 developed and developing countries. To derive the unweighted measure, industries (i=1,2,...,m) were first ranked by factor intensity for each country (j=1,2,...n) separately to obtain ranks r_{ij}. The average ranking of each industry over all countries in the sample was then calculated simply as the arithmetic mean:

$$\bar{r}_i = \frac{1}{n} \sum_{j=1}^{n} r_{ij}$$

Finally, industry rankings were based on the world averages $\bar{r}_i$. The ranks in terms of weighted averages of factor intensities are given in parentheses. These averages were derived from aggregate data on value added, wages and employment.

b/ Physical-capital intensity is measured by non-wage value added per employee.

c/ Human-capital intensity is measured by wages per employee.

d/ Labour intensity is measured by the reciprocal of total value added per employee.

between weighted and unweighted estimates points to the possibility of variations between countries in factor intensities.

Unweighted estimates for human capital showed consistently high factor intensities for industrial chemicals, petroleum refining, petroleum and coal products, iron and steel, non-ferrous metals and transport equipment. A high ranking was also obtained for non-electrical machinery (including computers), when weighted averages were calculated. Many of these same industries were also in the highest quarter of the ranking for physical capital. Spearman correlations between industry rankings by human- and physical-capital intensity were 0.41 for 1970–7 and 0.67 in 1978–85. These results suggest a positive association between the two factor intensities – at least when global averages are considered.

The industries that were found to be heavy users of labour closely matched with a priori expectations. Wearing apparel, footwear, furniture, textiles, leather and leather products, pottery and metal products all have large requirements for labour relative to total (i.e. physical and human) capital. Rankings changed only slightly when weighted averages were used.

International differences in factor intensities

Table 6.2 provides an indication of differences in factor intensities among country groups. Spearman correlations measure the agreement between the industry rankings of a reference group (the DMEs) and three groups of developing countries. The figures show that rankings of the latter countries differed, sometimes substantially, from the DME average. This result can partly be explained by differences in the basic economic attributes of the various developing countries. The greater the disparity in the relative factor abundance of countries, the more likely it is that there will be substantial differences in factor prices. Significant cross-country differences in factor intensities will be the result.

Cross-country variation in factor intensities can also be represented on an industry-by-industry basis. Table 6.3 documents this feature, showing for each of the 28 industries coefficients of variation of factor intensities across the 43 studied countries. Labour has the largest coefficients, with the maximum being reported for industrial chemicals in 1970–7. Wide differences in labour intensity can be observed even among the most labour-intensive industries such as wearing apparel, leather and leather products, footwear and pottery. These particular results indicate the need for caution when categorizing industries as 'labour-intensive'.

Variations in physical and human capital intensity were similar in magnitude and considerably lower than those for labour. Most industries that are extensive users of either factor reported a relatively narrow range for the corresponding intensities. This result would seem to imply that a general classification of industries in terms of human or physical capital requirements is more appropriate than one based on labour intensity.

Table 6.2 Correlations between factor intensity rankings of country groups, 1970–7 and 1978–85

	Spearman correlations between country group[a] and DME average					
	Physical-capital intensity		Human-capital intensity		Labour intensity	
Country group (no. of countries/areas)	1970–1977	1978–1985	1970–1977	1978–1985	1970–1977	1970–1985
Developed market economies (20)	1.00	1.00	1.00	1.00	1.00	1.00
NIEs (6)	0.79	0.84	0.64	0.84	0.70	0.86
Second-generation NIEs (7)	0.76	0.76	0.61	0.46	0.81	0.81
Other developing countries/areas (10)	0.60	0.73	0.27	0.57	0.53	0.69

Source: UNIDO

a/ The group averages of factor intensities underlying the above correlations are of the unweighted ordinal type. They were derived by first ranking industries (i = 1,2, ... m) by factor intensity separately for each country (j = 1, 2, ..., n) to obtain ranks r_{ij}. The average ranking of each industry over all countries in the group was then calculated simply as the arithmetic mean:

$$\bar{r_i} = \frac{1}{n} \sum_{j=1}^{n} r_{ij}$$

Finally, industry rankings were based on the group averages $\bar{r_i}$.

Table 6.3 Coefficients of variation of factor intensities, by industry, 1970–7 and 1978–85

Industry (ISIC)	Physical capital		Human capital		Labour	
	1970–1977	1978–1985	1970–1977	1978–1985	1970–1977	1978–1985
Food products (311)	66.0	68.5	71.7	76.5	111.4	112.0
Beverages (313)	59.7	61.7	76.2	80.1	118.0	117.6
Tobacco etc. (314)	85.1	88.8	99.5	87.4	159.4	176.7
Textiles (321)	48.0	56.5	61.3	71.4	93.1	93.4
Wearing apparel (322)	100.2	73.3	103.7	82.7	131.7	227.2
Leather and fur products (323)	73.3	77.3	73.6	90.4	321.7	145.1
Footwear (324)	90.9	72.3	72.4	72.7	250.3	163.1
Wood and cork products (331)	87.8	105.3	88.7	100.5	80.0	128.0
Furniture fixtures excl. metal (332)	82.2	82.2	72.3	81.4	89.7	145.6
Paper (341)	70.6	72.4	74.1	76.7	82.0	108.8
Printing and publishing (342)	63.9	67.3	73.0	78.6	101.9	256.7
Industrial chemicals (351)	83.3	65.4	67.3	71.5	334.0	275.6
Other chemicals (352)	47.1	56.5	64.7	67.6	70.4	72.0
Petroleum refineries (353)	99.1	115.6	79.6	201.4	151.5	214.5
Products of petroleum and coal (354)	175.8	174.7	90.5	83.2	95.2	76.0
Rubber products (355)	62.1	59.5	69.8	73.9	90.8	78.0
Plastic products (356)	64.4	70.9	75.5	87.9	245.7	131.7
Pottery, china, earthenware (366)	68.9	81.9	73.5	80.4	126.2	315.6
Glass (362)	67.6	66.3	69.2	76.6	85.0	94.8
Other non-metallic min. products (369)	53.1	50.7	68.4	70.1	73.3	86.0
Iron and steel (371)	62.7	69.1	68.3	76.4	91.6	143.2
Non-ferrous metals (372)	114.7	145.9	69.9	82.2	185.5	163.1
Metal products (381)	56.9	59.7	71.0	77.6	91.1	102.3
Non-electrical machinery (382)	53.5	67.6	72.0	77.1	102.9	101.8
Electrical machinery (383)	58.4	51.3	76.3	79.1	90.6	126.1
Transport equipment (384)	78.3	57.0	72.5	72.0	81.5	74.4
Professional scientific equipment (385)	95.8	63.6	80.1	73.3	77.5	72.5
Other manufactures (390)	113.8	101.5	160.3	113.5	89.4	112.2

Source: UNIDO

a/ Coefficients of variation (ratios between standard deviations and means) were calculated using the entire country sample of 43 countries and areas.

This assessment of factor intensities concludes with an examination of the consistency in industry rankings across countries. Measures of concordance were calculated for members of each country group and are reported in Table 6.4. They reveal a high degree of agreement in the industry rankings. The null hypothesis of no relationship between countries' industry rankings is rejected, as all coefficients are positive and statistically significant. Furthermore, the coefficients are stable over time and differ very little, either between factors or between country groups.

Although the concordance is strong, the coefficients for each country group do not support an extreme assumption of perfect agreement in industry rankings. Such an outcome would be indicated by a coefficient of unity, but the estimates in Table 6.4 are much lower. Unequal factor prices and technological differences may provide sufficient reasons for a diverse range of production techniques. Such diversity is likely to account for patterns of specialization and trade which are more complex than suggested by theoretical models.

The imperfect concordances in Table 6.4 indicate the existence of reversals between countries in the rankings of industries by factor intensities.[4] The extent of such reversals was examined with the help of clustering techniques. The most surprising result of the cluster analysis was the 'omnipresence' of reversals. There was no pair of countries throughout the entire sample where reversals did not occur for each factor. In other words, no two countries had identical industry rankings for at least one factor of production in either of the two time periods.[5]

Revealed comparative advantage and factor intensities

Factor intensities provide the theoretical link between endowments and patterns of output and trade. But in empirical work they have often played a more prominent role. In fact, most empirical studies of trade have been country-specific and have left aside any explicit assessment of factor abundance – the major characteristic in the underlying theory.[6] They have focused instead on the relationship between factor intensities and levels of output or trade in specific industries. Although the concept of factor intensities is by no means assigned a secondary role in the H–O literature, there are two reasons to regard this approach as an improper test of the theory. First, any test of the H–O proposition must explicitly incorporate data on trade, factor intensities and factor abundance. Second, when analysts focus exclusively on the interaction between factor intensities and trade, they obtain only indirect evidence on the operation of H–O forces. More specifically, factor abundance cannot usually be inferred with precision from the relationship between factor intensities and trade patterns (Leamer and Bowen, 1981; Aw, 1983).

Analysts may wish to study the technical characteristics of specific industries for other reasons, however. One is that factor intensities are useful in

Table 6.4 Concordance of factor intensity rankings within country groups, 1970–7 and 1978–85

Country group (number of countries/areas)	Kendall's coefficient of concordance[a]					
	Physical capital		Human capital		Labour	
	1970–1977	1978–1985	1970–1977	1978–1985	1970–1977	1978–1985
Developed market economies (20)	0.65	0.65	0.73	0.74	0.69	0.68
NIEs (6)	0.74	0.74	0.68	0.66	0.67	0.68
Second-generation NIEs (7)	0.69	0.78	0.66	0.70	0.60	0.68
Other developing countries (10)	0.62	0.60	0.63	0.63	0.66	0.64

Source: UNIDO

a/ The (adjusted) coefficient of concordance (W) is defined as:

$$W = \frac{12 \, (S - 1)}{k^2 \, (n^3 - n) + 24}$$

where S is the sum of squares of the deviations of the total of the ranks obtained by each industry from the average of these totals. The number of countries is n and m is the number of industries. For more details, see Maxwell (1967), pp. 117–121. A coefficient of zero would indicate complete randomness while a coefficient of unity would signify complete agreement in the rankings.

describing a country's involvement in the international division of labour. Another is that the theory poses questions that are applicable mainly to single countries (for example, the types of commodities to be produced and exported), and factor intensities have an important role to play in this regard.[7]

Methodological considerations

The role of factor intensities is encapsulated in the expectation that the composition of national output will be weighted in favour of those industries that use the country's abundant factors most intensively. This relationship – which is usually associated with the work of Rybczynski (1955) – lies at the heart of the factor abundance theory. In the high–dimensional version of the theory it takes the form of a correlation or on–average result (Ethier, 1984). For such an on–average relationship to hold, it is sufficient that production be concentrated in a few industries which use an abundant factor intensively. Thus, the output structure in a relatively capital-abundant country is expected to be dominated by relatively capital-intensive industries and analogously for other countries and factors. Demand conditions permitting, the commodity patterns of exports are expected to reflect the interaction between factor intensity and factor abundance in a way similar to output.

The static framework which yields the sorts of relationships described here can be easily extended to a model expressed in comparative-static terms. An example is Krueger's (1977) model of complete global specialization with three factors and two sectors. By providing a theoretical framework to describe the changes in output and trade that occur as a consequence of factor growth, the model serves as a means for analysing shifts in factor intensities over time.[8] Krueger's model predicts that, as economic development continues, the absolute and relative amounts of accumuulated capital will increase. The share of capital-intensive industries will tend to rise (on average) as relative factor endowments change. Similar changes will occur in the structure of exports unless shifts in domestic demand offset this tendency.

Most of the arguments depend on the existence of an on–average rather than a determinate relationship between variables. A given set of factor intensities may impose only a weak restriction on the structure of output and trade, though the possibility of a much stronger association is not precluded. The strength of the hypotheses relating factor intensities to output and trade is then open to question. Three stylistic interpretations are possible. The strongest of these would be one postulating a monotonic relationship: the more intensively an industry uses an abundant factor, the higher are its values of output and exports. A second, and weaker, relationship can be stated as a 'bloc' hypothesis: depending on a country's factor abundance, comparative advantage is expected to be concentrated in the set (or bloc) of industries that use a given abundant factor most intensively. The third hypothesis is even weaker. It merely postulates the existence of an on–average association between factor intensity and the structure of output or trade. Empirically, this last hypothesis depends merely on a test of the sign of a correlation coefficient. The theory of high dimensional trade models implies that a monotonic hypothesis is inappropriate for an empirical study of this type. Tests of the third hypothesis are faced with serious problems of econometric specification (Anderson, 1981). Consequently, the second version is chosen as the basis for analysis in this section.

Testing the 'bloc' hypothesis

An analysis of the output structure is a natural starting point for an investigation of the bloc hypothesis.[9] A set of 'commodity composites' which can be associated with each factor was first identified. The composites were made up of those industries in the highest quarter of each factor intensity ranking. Each composite consists of seven of the 28 industries included in the manufacturing sector. The second step was to calculate output-based measures of revealed comparative advantage (RCA) for the three 'factor-intensive' composites and for all countries in the sample.[10] The RCA indicator is defined as the ratio between a country's share in world output of the composite and the country's share in world GDP.[11] In countries where manufacturing output is relatively concentrated in industries that are intensive users of abundant factors, the H–O relationship between factor intensities and output should be borne out by the above indicator.

Table 6.5 summarizes the results, showing RCA indicators for the entire country sample in 1970–2 and 1983–5. At first glance the figures present a diffuse picture. Much of this diffuseness may be due to the shortcomings of the RCA indicator as an 'absolute' measure of comparative advantage. Nevertheless, simple ordinal comparisons between RCA values of the three commodity composites reveal some systematic relationships. In particular, if for each country the highest (lowest) of the three RCA values is taken as indicating comparative advantage (disadvantage) in the corresponding type of goods, the expected association between factor intensities and output is confirmed for almost all DMEs. The comparative disadvantage of these countries in production of labour-intensive manufactures was pronounced and pervasive. Shares in world output for the labour-intensive composite reveal that only a few DMEs (Belgium, Greece, Israel and New Zealand) had a comparative advantage in this type of goods and that, except for Israel, this was the case only in one time period. The competitive strengths of most DMEs are in industries that use large amounts of physical or human capital.

Of the two capital-intensive composites, one usually dominates over the other. Human capital was the major contributor to comparative advantage in one-half of the DMEs, while physical capital played this role in about one-quarter of these countries. In particular, comparative advantage in production was closely associated with human-capital intensity in nine DMEs (including most of the largest exporters of manufactures) in both time periods.

Although the results for DMEs agree with theoretical expectations, the situation was different for the developing countries. The expectation that comparative advantage would be associated with labour-intensive manufactures was only partly supported by empirical evidence. The most labour-intensive industries are not necessarily those in which the developing countries have the highest shares in world output. Only the results for Hong Kong, the Republic of Korea and several of the larger developing countries (India, Pakistan and Yugoslavia) in part conform with expectations, showing a substantial bias in favour of labour-intensive industries in the second time period. Among second-generation NIEs, only Indonesia had a significant comparative

Table 6.5 Output-based measures of RCA,[a] by industry groups, 1970–2 and 1983–5 (percentages)

Country group/ Country and area	Aggregate RCA (per cent) for 'commodity composites'[b] which are intensive users of:					
	1970–1972			1983–1985		
	Physical capital	Human capital	Labour	Physical capital	Human capital	Labour
DMEs						
Australia	77.9	113.0	59.6	70.4	80.1	41.6
Austria	127.1	147.2	121.8	148.6	151.3	114.0
Belgium	145.9	124.0	141.0	122.7	119.3	127.8
Canada	133.9	110.1	60.8	96.9	113.8	68.1
Denmark	111.3	98.5	44.7	59.1	69.9	25.1
Finland	218.0	175.9	86.8	160.5	159.9	70.3
Germany, Fed.Rep.of	83.5	140.5	75.2	85.1	153.9	100.4
Greece	65.3	55.2	113.1	121.2	109.4	61.2
Ireland	114.3	75.3	42.3	121.1	54.3	49.9
Israel	93.6	147.4	171.2	141.2	115.5	224.4
Italy	103.7	115.7	89.7	156.1	156.7	92.3
Japan	154.9	165.1	124.9	117.6	168.0	76.0
Netherlands	103.2	109.0	72.1	163.8	168.1	72.2
New Zealand[c]	65.4	138.2	114.9	50.1	80.7	94.5
Norway	135.5	104.2	72.6	112.8	448.5	55.5
Portugal[c]	59.2	65.9	58.1	141.6	197.6	69.5
Spain	172.2	134.2	98.2	115.9	159.8	88.8
Sweden	114.2	164.3	56.5	105.2	164.0	37.6
United Kingdom	140.8	146.4	91.6	107.5	105.8	69.4
United States	86.5	94.7	54.1	91.8	95.1	60.1
NIEs						
Argentina	98.9	116.8	77.3	99.9	86.7	54.0
Brazil[c]	144.9	103.6	67.5	127.8	113.7	87.9
Hong Kong[d]	38.3	198.5	37.4	41.4	109.0	164.4
Mexico	110.6	98.3	64.3	64.4	89.7	48.8
Republic of Korea	92.2	57.8	33.4	133.0	134.8	143.0
Singapore	274.3	291.5	156.3	221.5	223.7	53.3
Second-generation NIEs						
Colombia	194.9	148.1	25.8	200.7	191.3	30.8
Indonesia[c]	26.2	21.7	20.4	27.6	25.6	31.2
Malaysia	266.8	255.0	115.2	213.2	122.8	86.1
Peru[c]	164.2	119.3	46.0	157.5	240.4	78.6
Philippines	154.6	89.5	63.7	459.2	365.3	96.9
Thailand[c]	219.0	191.7	35.8	124.9	120.0	16.4
Tunisia[c]	236.8	218.5	60.4	116.6	124.0	43.9

Table 6.5 continued

| Country group/ Country and area | Aggregate RCA (per cent) for 'commodity composites'[b] which are intensive users of: | | | | | |
| | 1970–1972 | | | 1983–1985 | | |
	Physical capital	Human capital	Labour	Physical capital	Human capital	Labour
Other developing countries						
Chile	119.1	98.0	32.2	114.7	98.7	49.6
Dominican Republic[c]	51.4	21.1	190.2	71.8	60.7	106.7
Egypt	123.9	218.5	27.7	108.0	56.9	50.9
Guatemala[c]	151.1	181.5	31.5	108.8	142.9	22.6
India	204.3	183.1	96.5	196.1	212.0	162.6
Pakistan[c]	139.5	68.4	14.7	91.7	66.6	126.9
Panama	204.8	153.9	42.3	70.0	63.6	10.6
Turkey[c]	85.7	85.7	16.5	84.0	90.8	49.2
Venezuela[c]	189.0	111.2	27.7	122.1	111.3	24.8
Yugoslavia	128.6	137.3	116.4	213.1	175.3	295.8

Source: UNIDO

a/ The output-based indicator of RCA can be written as:

$$RCA_{hj} = \frac{Q_{hj}}{Q_{hw}} \bigg/ \frac{Y_j}{Y_w} \times 100$$

where Q is output, Y is GDP, h refers to a given factor, j represents a country and w refers to world totals. In particular, Q_{hj} is output in country j of those (seven) industries in the upper quartile of the distribution of industries by h-intensity in country j. Aggregate Q_{hw} is defined analogously for the whole sample w. For more details on the underlying data see the statistical appendix.

b/ For a description of the construction of each commodity composite, see the text.

c/ Data for the second time period are for 1980.

d/ Data for the first time period are for 1973.

advantage in the production of labour-intensive goods (and only for 1983–5). Aside from these instances of corroboration, evidence of a consistently high concentration of output in labour-intensive areas of manufacturing was noted for one developing country (the Dominican Republic). In summary, the structure of manufacturing output in developing countries only partially matched H–O expectations regarding the relationship between factor abundance and factor intensity. The strength of the association between the two variables was weakest in 1970–2 and particularly so among second-generation NIEs.

The same tests were repeated after replacing the output-based measure of RCA by indicators derived from export data.[12] The results are reported in Table 6.6. As far as the DMEs are concerned, the figures agree largely with the pattern that emerged from output-based measures. In particular, the data for 1983–5 support H–O propositions about labour intensity as a source of comparative disadvantage[13] and capital intensity as a source of comparative advantage of these countries.

Among the NIEs, the export-based measure of RCA produces marginally better evidence of H–O relationships than the output-based version in as much as physical capital and labour are more frequently identified as sources of comparative advantage. Furthermore, the figures for second-generation NIEs show that the rapid growth of manufactured exports of these countries during the 1970s was based on a comparative advantage in relatively labour-intensive industries. Unlike the results for output, those for exports indicate that at the beginning of the 1980s a number of second-generation NIEs (Indonesia,

Table 6.6 Export-based measures of RCA,[a] by industry groups, 1970–2 and 1983–5 (percentages)

Country group/ Country and area	Aggregate RCA (per cent) for 'commodity composites'[b] which are intensive users of:					
	1970–1972			1983–1985		
	Physical capital	Human capital	Labour	Physical capital	Human capital	Labour
DMEs						
Australia	80.5	49.6	24.7	89.3	74.3	14.6
Austria	208.7	226.9	196.1	160.3	164.0	136.4
Belgium	269.3	250.4	523.7	317.9	333.1	402.6
Canada	346.6	244.8	43.4	214.1	251.7	39.4
Denmark	290.9	137.0	79.6	239.3	102.5	87.5
Finland	352.1	245.6	89.7	331.1	203.3	111.6
Germany, Fed.Rep.of	69.9	168.9	87.5	89.3	184.8	129.0
Greece	78.6	41.2	43.8	77.5	79.1	36.9
Ireland	156.1	73.6	97.6	535.5	134.1	235.4
Israel	81.0	93.1	220.9	286.8	189.0	133.8
Italy	86.0	146.2	100.4	106.9	142.0	86.6
Japan	83.5	96.9	125.6	62.9	121.0	46.5
Netherlands	330.0	179.5	214.0	554.2	303.6	144.3
New Zealand[c]	26.4	19.9	111.4	41.1	68.9	23.2
Norway	282.1	180.7	45.9	165.5	125.0	22.5
Portugal[c]	114.8	138.3	367.2	152.6	106.0	92.4
Spain	34.0	29.1	95.7	82.1	82.7	69.2
Sweden	208.6	210.6	164.3	195.9	215.9	162.1
United Kingdom	136.6	131.2	126.1	134.8	109.7	83.1
United States	35.1	51.2	14.7	39.7	47.6	17.0
NIEs						
Argentina	10.9	6.1	13.1	26.7	15.4	16.4
Brazil[c]	187.7	17.9	16.2	93.7	28.5	38.8
Hong Kong[d]	51.3	536.9	293.2	69.2	34.6	754.7
Mexico[e]	26.0	24.4	24.7	12.3	12.2	9.9
Republic of Korea	18.1	24.0	116.7	153.5	156.4	690.6
Singapore	1134.3	959.0	687.5	1037.3	992.4	598.2
Second generation NIEs						
Colombia	272.1	277.2	14.8	203.0	279.3	8.1
Indonesia[c]	1.7	0.2	44.8	10.6	10.2	10.8
Malaysia	275.2	220.3	224.1	295.1	54.9	298.3
Peru[c]	149.5	142.9	3.0	121.9	233.1	35.9
Philippines	130.0	149.8	12.4	100.9	14.7	99.4
Thailand[c]	27.1	25.3	18.0	8.5	10.3	22.8
Tunisia[c]	78.6	29.1	15.9	113.3	124.9	183.3

Table 6.6 continued

Country group/ Country and area	Aggregate RCA (per cent) for 'commodity composites'[b] which are intensive users of:					
	1970–1972			1983–1985		
	Physical capital	Human capital	Labour	Physical capital	Human capital	Labour
Other developing countries						
Chile	647.6	32.5	6.0	327.2	32.4	13.4
Dominican Republic[c]	3.0	18.9	442.9	5.3	13.9	207.6
Egypt	6.8	32.8	51.5	30.4	36.1	7.0
Guatemala[e]	273.9	372.5	63.8	35.9	56.4	51.2
India[e]	18.4	55.0	27.3	19.6	21.7	16.4
Pakistan[e]	55.3	7.2	10.4	59.4	14.3	128.4
Panama	157.7	64.2	3.3	38.9	37.6	11.0
Turkey[e]	6.3	2.0	5.1	6.3	4.8	17.2
Venezuela[e]	302.3	236.9	0.7	407.1	404.3	2.0
Yugoslavia	69.6	67.8	88.8	103.8	96.0	238.4

Source: UNIDO

a/ The export–RCA indicator can be written as:

$$RCA_{hj} = \frac{X_{hj}}{X_{hw}} \Big/ \frac{Y_j}{Y_w} \times 100$$

where X are exports, Y is GDP, h refers to a given factor, j to a country and w to the world. In particular X_{hj} are the exports by country j of those (seven) industries that appear in the upper quartile of the distribution of industries by h–intensity in country j. Variable X_{hw} is defined analogously for the whole sample w. For more details on the underlying data see the statistical appendix.

b/ For a description of the construction of each commodity composite, see the text.

c/ Data for the second time period are for 1980.

d/ Data for the first time period are for 1973.

e/ Data for the second time period are for 1979.

Malaysia, Philippines, Thailand and Tunisia) had attained an international comparative advantage in labour–intensive goods. Similarly, export data of non-NIEs reveal more cases of this type of comparative advantage than do output data.

From the previous results it can be concluded that the bloc hypothesis performs well for the DMEs, irrespective of whether output or export data are the basis for determining RCA. For the developing countries, export figures provide relatively stronger support for the hypothesis than do output figures. Thus, an overall comparison between Tables 6.5 and 6.6 suggests that the H–O traits that characterize patterns of exchange (exports) are somewhat stronger than those for output. This distinction is of interest since the factor abundance theory maintains that national differences in factor endowments generate differences in output structure. Differences in output structure should translate directly into trading patterns if patterns of consumption are uniform. But in a world of differing consumption patterns, it would be no surprise if the vagaries of demand blurred the expected H–O relationship between output and trade. Such a possibility, however, is not observed. Instead, the structure of demand for manufactures seems to accentuate the H–O traits of trade as compared with those of output.

In summary, a moderately strong hypothesis of an H–O-like relationship between factor input requirements and comparative advantage receives partial support from the foregoing analysis. This support comes mainly from the relationship between labour inputs and comparative advantage. Whether such a partial concordance between theoretical expectations and empirical evidence warrants an endorsement of the H–O model of the trading world at large is considered in the following chapter.

Annex: Technology and trade

The H–O model of trade posits that a country will tend to specialize in and export products that intensively use its relatively abundant and thus relatively cheap factors of production. The reverse would also hold, as a country would tend to import a product that intensively utilizes its relatively scarce (expensive) factors of production. Among the assumptions from which these propositions are derived is that production functions are the same everywhere. Alternatively, the technology of production for a particular commodity is assumed to be known and fixed both domestically and internationally. Under such restrictive conditions, which seem at variance with casual observation, the only basis for trade is differences in the prices of the factors of production.

In this section the effects of relaxing the above assumption concerning technology will be discussed. A framework for this discussion is provided by models that incorporate changes in technology as well as technological differences between countries. In response to the Leontief paradox, a fairly large amount of work has been done regarding the effects of technological change in a standard H–O model. The common feature of these theories is an emphasis on such change and the resulting pattern of trade in new products. While the details of the process differ among theories, all are designed to explain the pattern of trade of the USA.

The first major theoretical effort to explain the observed patterns of trade in terms of technical progress was the technology gap model sketched by Posner (1961). The basic idea is that, as new products and processes are being developed, the country in which these innovations occur will temporarily possess a technological advantage over its trading partners in these products. This advantage will last only until the new technology is initiated in other countries. But before that happens, the innovating country may export the good even though it has no obvious basis for comparative advantage in terms of factor endowments. As time passes, each individual innovation is eventually diffused around the world and the initial advantage is lost. However, as progress continues, new products and processes are being discovered. This implies that there exists a constantly changing list of new products in which the innovating country has a competitive advantage.

A difficulty with the technology gap model is that it fails to explain why a new innovation is not produced immediately in the least cost-location. Put another way, new products and production processes are transferred to the developing countries only after a substantial amount of time has lapsed. In a world where firms operate only domestically, this would be understandable, as firms would be reluctant to share their knowledge with others. However, in a world of transnational corporations (TNCs), it is difficult to see why a firm would not go abroad immediately to produce in the lowest-cost location. In this way it could potentially reap an even larger reward from the innovation and prevent the diffusion of the knowledge because production would be internalized within the firm.

The most commonly used approach to technology and trade is that developed by Vernon (1966). Vernon departs from the strict theory of comparative advantage to construct the product-cycle hypothesis which was outlined in Chapter 3. While comparative costs are important for standardized (H–O) goods, for new and maturing (product-cycle) goods the patterns of trade are to some extent outside the traditional H–O model. Vernon's product-cycle theory might also provide an explanation of the Leontief paradox. If DMEs are heavy exporters of product-cycle goods, then their exports would embody labour and human capital rather than physical capital, as the theory predicts.

While these theories are intuitively appealing, it is necessary to attempt to test their validity empirically. Several empirical studies have included R and D as a factor explaining trade within a multi-factor proportions model. Stern (1976) found that R and D expenditures had a positive and significant effect on West Germany's exports. Similar results for the USA were obtained by Baldwin (1971, 1979) and by Stern and Maskus (1981). Maskus (1983) found that for the USA the importance of R and D as a determinant of trade may be growing over time. Based on a different methodology, the results obtained by Sveikauskas (1983) indicate that science and technology are what differentiates the US economy from that of the rest of the world.

The conclusion of this empirical work is that the technology gap and product-cycle explanations of trade flows seem to have some validity for DMEs. This conclusion is rather tentative, as most of the empirical work has been done only for the USA. A loose implication of the results is that new technology, products and processes have become important determinants of the patterns of trade. The gross quantities of labour and capital are still important, but other factors matter as well. It would thus seem likely that the transfer of technology to the developing countries would tend to improve their competitive advantage relative to the DMEs. A number of recent theoretical models of North–South trade also support this (Krugman, 1979b; Dollar, 1986).

The H–O assumption that technology is virtually identical across countries for a given industry may be appropriate for the technology necessary to produce labour-intensive or capital-intensive H–O goods. By contrast, for countries to develop competitive advantage in product–cycle goods, the transfer of proprietary technology may be essential. A general definition of such transfer is: the development by people in one country of the capacity on the part of nationals of another country to use, adapt, replicate, modify or further expand the knowledge and skills associated with a different method of manufacture of a product. Technology transfer is inherently difficult to measure as it is more a relationship or process rather than a simple economic exchange of quantities. One cannot define a standard unit of technology in the same fashion that one can define goods.

In more concrete terms, it is frequently useful to think of technology transfer as a package. A technology transfer package may contain one or more of the following components: (1) technology transferred via technical documents, blueprints, etc.; (2) permission to use various rights, knowledge, or assets; (3) use of capital, intermediate or final goods; (4) transfer of training, etc. Such transfers may be either proprietary or non-proprietary. In the former case the technology may be associated with some form of monopoly rent, which means that cost and price may be distorted. The technology package, or its components, may be transferred either via a foreign direct investment (FDI) 'bundle' or by means of some sort of contractual arrangement, i.e. 'unbundled'. Some of the components of a technology transfer bundle could be: export of hardware, licence, technical assistance contract, contract manufacturing, management contract, marketing agreement, training contract, consulting contract, architectural and engineering contract, research and development contract, construction supervision contract, construction contract, turnkey contract, production-sharing, and co-operation. The above list is of course not all-inclusive, but it serves to illustrate the variety of forms that technology transfer may take and to explain why the concept is difficult to define in a precise way. Additionally, one has to consider indirect technology transfer, which occurs through publicly accessible channels or through training in DMEs.

If the transfer of technology is potentially beneficial to developing countries, then it is appropriate to consider its cost. Theoretically, the price of technology should be an approximation of the present discounted value of the anticipated royalties or fees and other benefits derived from the technology, net of all costs. To the seller, the cost of technology would include all direct costs, overhead costs and the cost of forgone profits on exports or direct investment. Both the price and the cost are subject to much judgement because they contain implicit forecasts and include costs that are difficult to allocate in an accounting sense. All one can conclude is that the value of technology transfer is very difficult to calculate with any degree of precision. This fact alone constitutes a major impediment to technology transfer.

Since much of the technology transfer to developing countries occurs through TNCs, it is useful to look at technology transfer as an interaction between the two. Ultimately, developing countries would like to be able to generate their own technology. In the interim, such countries must be concerned primarily with the availability of technology. Using FDI as a proxy for 'bundled' technology transfer, it may appear that the rate of growth of access is slowing down. During the 1970s international direct investment in developing countries was growing at 29 per cent per year. The share of developing countries as recipients of international direct investment increased from an average level of about 20 per cent in the first half of the 1970s to a level above 32 per cent in the late 1970s. Since that time there has clearly been a reduction of significant proportions, with the 1984 level of international direct investment being only $9.5 billion as compared with $16.7 billion in 1981 (OECD, 1987).

The transfer of technology will almost always involve a contest between the desire of the TNC to maximize rents from technology and the desire of developing countries to obtain technology cheaply and/or on very favourable terms. The major issue here seems to be the 'unbundling' of FDI. TNCs would frequently prefer to exploit their monopoly power through FDI; on the other side, developing countries feel that this may be an expensive way to obtain technology and that it carries non-economic costs. However, attempts to unbundle FDI through licensing or joint ventures will probably slow technology transfers or restrict the availability of the newest technology. Furthermore, within the current institutional framework of world trade, increasing the amount of technology transfers may not be a simple policy task. However, given the current slow growth of world trade, this transfer is essential.

Notes: Chapter 6

1 In relation to empirical tests of the H–O proposition, the question is sometimes raised whether a matrix of factor intensities can be found that would be 'representative' of the world. Indications are that matrices pertaining to individual countries (e.g. the USA) usually cannot play this role (Anderson, 1987).

2 Factor shares of unskilled labour require data on wages paid to unskilled workers. These data are not available for a broad range of countries. The alternative of factor-input ratios has the disadvantages of treating factors asymmetrically and depends on factor price ratios; see Bowden, 1983.

3 Total value added per employee was introduced as a measure of total (physical and human) capital intensity by Lary, 1968. Its reciprocal can loosely be interpreted as an indicator of labour intensity in the underlying factor proportions model. On the other hand, non-wage value added and wages are usually taken broadly to represent the returns to physical capital and human capital, respectively. On these grounds, they serve as proxy measures of the input values of the two types of capital.

4   Here the term 'reversal' is used in a descriptive way. It doses not reflect properly the generalized definition of a factor intensity reversal in high dimensions (Ethier, 1984).

5   The final results of the clustering procedure were rather inconclusive as regards the formation of broad groups of countries with similar factor intensity attributes. This was particularly evident when an ordinal measure of factor intensity was employed. That measure yielded an 'atomistic' portrait of the whole country sample. Most steps in the process of hierarchical clustering merely linked one additional individual country to the existing single cluster. Additional details on the techniques applied can be found in the technical appendix (Appendix A).

6   Deardorff, 1984 provides a comprehensive overview of empirical studies on trade patterns. His article lays out the relationship between theoretical models and empirical work and summarizes the main results obtained by the latter. The priority placed on factor intensities in the empirical analyses of specific countries is evident from this summary.

7   Although a contrary view has sometimes been expressed (Leamer, 1974), both the structure and the methodology of trade theory emphasize a country-specific orientation. This applies in particular to results that have been obtained on the basis of the duality approach to general equilibrium analysis; see Dixit and Norman, 1980.

8   The model has a primary sector and a manufacturing sector producing many commodities. Land is a specific input to the primary sector, capital is a specific input to manufacturing, and labour is mobile between the two sectors. The basic propositions derived from the model concern the successive stages of output specialization that accompany capital accumulation. For details on this comparative-static approach, see Jones, 1971, and Krueger, 1977.

9   Another rationale for emphasizing the relationship between output and factor intensities concerns the choice of the factor intensity measure. The present study makes use of a measure of factor intensities that is based only on direct factor inputs to the production of a given industry. Hamilton and Svensson, 1983, argue that direct factor intensities are best suited to explain the structure of production.

10   Bowen, 1983a, suggests use of a composite commodity to indicate international comparative advantage. A recent theoretical application of the composite commodity (together with the composite factor) approach is found in Neary, 1985.

11   This particular version of an RCA indicator has been suggested by Bowen, 1983b. It is a straightforward generalization of Balassa's 1965 original indicator, and can be interpreted in at least three different ways. First, the measure can be assumed to indicate comparative advantage in an 'absolute' sense, where the value of 100 per cent represents the dividing line between comparative advantage and comparative disadvantage of a given country in a given industry. Second, it can serve to rank, for a given industry, countries in terms of comparative advantage. Third, it can provide, for a given country, a ranking of industries in terms of comparative advantage. The present discussion adopts the last (and least controversial) of the three views, where commodity composites are considered instead of industries.

12   Exports rather than net exports were chosen for the exercise on trade, since it was easier to calculate RCA indicators from the former data (Balassa, 1965).

13   Only Belgium (in both time periods) and Japan (in 1970–2) showed surprisingly high values for exports of labour-intensive industries. In the case of Japan, this is due mainly to exports of electrical machinery – an industry where value added per employee was relatively low in 1970–2.

CHAPTER 7

Country differences, country similarities and the structure of trade

Trade analysts have usually chosen to explain inter-industry patterns of specialization and trade in terms of differences in the economic characteristics of trading partners. Such an approach is found in the first section of this chapter, where the relationship between factor endowments and net trade is examined for a large number of countries. The results of that investigation are used in the second section to assess the extent to which a generalized version of the H–O theory provides an explanation for patterns of world trade.

The discussion in the third section takes up a different issue, intra–industrial specialization and trade. The rapid growth of IIT is an empirical fact for which conventional factor abundance theory does not offer a satisfactory explanation. In searching for an adequate explanation for IIT, theorists have concluded that similarities rather than differences between countries are conducive to intra-industry forms of specialization. This possibility seems paradoxical in light of the conclusions of the factor abundance theory. Nevertheless, it is quite plausible from the viewpoint of the new theories which emphasize the role of scale economies and product differentiation. The concluding section of the chapter is devoted to an empirical analysis of some of these issues.

The theoretical basis for this chapter draws upon both the H–O and the economies-of-scale models. Such an approach is in line with the observation made by Helpman and Krugman (1985, p. 262) that 'the pattern of trade is shaped by the underlying exchange of factors but with an overlay of additional specialization to realize economies of scale'. The pattern of trade referred to here is explained by the conventional H–O model, which depends on country differences, while the overlay of additional specialization is intra-industry in scope and its extent is dependent upon country similarities.

Factor abundance and net trade

The present empirical application of the factor abundance model rests upon two points of logic. First, if country differences in factor endowments are a major determinant of comparative advantage, they should be systematically related to the pattern of trade of the various industries. Second, some knowledge of an industry's factor input characteristics would permit inferences about the relationship between factor supplies and trade. The first half of this argument serves as the basic premise for analysis in this section, while the second half will be treated in the following section.

Both propositions are integral parts of the argument and are needed to reflect the full content of the basic H–O hypothesis. Consequently, the analysis in this section is partial in the sense that it focuses on industry-specific linkages between factor supplies and trading patterns but only casually attempts to explain these linkages in terms of the underlying industry characteristics. The view that emerges from this exercise should, nevertheless, lead to some impression of the extent to which factor abundance influences specialization and trade.

Methodological background

Evidence of industry-specific relationships between net exports and factor endowments can be obtained from cross-country regressions in the tradition of Leamer (1984).[1] The researcher can choose from several regression models in order to demonstrate that differences in relative factor supplies are systematically related to variations in trading patterns. The model used here follows Leamer (1984) in that it makes no explicit use of factor abundance indicators. Instead, it attempts to assess the impact of levels of factor supplies on the size of net exports for each particular industry. Such an assessment is expected to answer two basic questions: (a) Is the cross–country variation in a given industry's net exports systematically related to variations in the endowments of certain factors? (b) How do industries differ with respect to the factor endowments effects on trade?

In order to describe these relationships, use is made of the notion of 'factor orientation'.[2] The term is an illustrative label referring to the association between factor endowments and trade. Its meaning can best be defined in geometric terms. In a space where the dimensionality equals the number of countries, two types of vectors can be visualized. One represents the cross-country distribution of a given resource. The components of this vector are the countries' levels of endowment for that resource. The second vector provides an analogous representation of the cross–country pattern of trade for a particular industry. The generalized factor abundance theory will then suggest a statement about the way in which the directions of the two vectors are related. The statement will be an on-average one, referring to all industries and all factors. Alternatively, if the resource distribution vectors are given, the underlying theory permits the user to draw inferences about the 'orientation' of industries' trade vectors.

A narrow definition of factor orientation can be stated in terms of the angle between the net exports vector and the resource distribution vector. There is, however, a close relationship between this geometric definition and the more familiar usage of correlation and regression coefficients.[3] The generalized H–O theory employs covariances or correlations to assess its basic relationships

115

(Deardorff, 1982). These tools, however, are limited, as they do not permit the user to isolate the impact of each individual factor on trade. Accordingly, the present analysis makes use of regression techniques and depicts factor orientation as equivalent to a regression coefficient which associates net trade with levels of factor supply.

The factor orientation of an industry's net exports is expressed in terms of beta coefficients. These show the change in standard deviations of the trade variable that is induced by a change of one standard deviation of the respective factor endowment variable. The meaning of the coefficients is straightforward: they indicate both the direction and the strength of the abundance effect which a given factor exerts on the net exports in a particular industry. The abundance effects may be positive, negative or non–existent. In geometric parlance, the corresponding 'orientation' of the net export vector with respect to the factor endowments vector would be termed near-parallel, near-anti-parallel or virtually orthogonal.

Estimates of factor orientation

Table 7.1 presents industry data which have been compiled in accordance with this interpretation. The estimates are based on a sample of 46 countries and 90 industries. The table shows only those industries with beta coefficients that were statistically significant in at least one of the two years considered. The rationale for such a selection is that a coefficient with a sufficiently large t-value can confidently be assumed to carry the correct sign. If a statistically significant coefficient also has a large absolute value, the factor abundance impact on net exports is appreciable. Coefficients that meet both criteria would indicate that the industry's net trade has a marked factor orientation.

A first glance at the figures of Table 7.1 suggests that the factor abundance impact on net trade is not overwhelming. Of the 90 industries considered, 41 had a marked factor orientation in 1970 and the number dropped to 35 in 1985. A total of 54 industries exhibited a significant factor orientation in at least one of the two years, but only 22 revealed such a relationship in both 1970 and 1985.

The impression conveyed by these statistics is not complete, however. The sheer number of categories (or industries) having a marked factor orientation is not a good indication of the role played by factor abundance. A more accurate picture is obtained by considering the share of world trade accounted for by products with a marked factor orientation. This share was found to be 54 per cent of total net trade in 1970 and 63 per cent in 1985. In other words, differences in factor abundance exerted some influence on more than one-half of the value of the net trade of the sample countries, and the significance rose over time.

A comparison between the four factors reveals pronounced differences in factor orientation. The contribution to comparative advantage/disadvantage can be determined by ranking each factor according to absolute values of beta

Table 7.1 Factor orientation[a] in selected industries, 1970 and 1985

Industry (SITC)	Physical capital[b]		Skilled labour[c]		Semi-skilled labour[d]		Unskilled labour[e]		Adjusted R² [f]	
	1970	1985	1970	1985	1970	1985	1970	1985	1970	1985
Organic chemicals (512)	1.976*	0.346	-1.146*	0.411	-0.291	-0.744***	0.581	0.193	0.478	0.013
Other inorganic chemicals (514)	1.797*	0.430	-0.934	0.510	-0.150	-0.403	0.432	0.022	0.196	0.109
Radioactive and associated materials (515)	-1.064	-0.387	2.215***	0.055	-0.685***	0.019	-2.143	-0.027	0.511	–
Mineral tar and crude chemical (521)	2.582*	-0.272	-2.099**	0.438	-0.556	-0.330	1.247*	0.045	0.345	–
Pigments, points, varnishes and related materials (533)	0.527	0.405	0.200	0.264	-0.350***	-0.286	0.128	0.024	0.008	–
Essential oils, perfume and flavour materials (551)	-0.513	-0.532	1.854***	1.406	-1.377**	-0.844	0.156	0.053	0.026	–
Fertilizers, manufactured (561)	1.998***	0.912	-1.673	-0.126	-0.292	-0.495	0.380	0.029	0.058	0.152
Plastic materials, regenerated (581)	1.404*	0.277	-0.878	0.126	0.258	-0.178	0.198	-0.008	0.375	–
Chemical materials and products (599)	0.905***	0.128	-0.127	0.982**	-0.354	-0.583***	0.201	-0.053	0.102	0.252
Leather (611)	-0.467	-0.134	0.385	0.140	-0.063	-0.224	0.628**	0.559	0.443	0.068
Manufactures of leather or reconstitutes (612)	-0.474	-0.535	-0.258	-0.237	0.938**	0.508***	-0.461	-0.021	0.059	0.149
Articles of rubber (629)	-0.320	0.546	-0.501	-0.674***	1.367*	0.443***	-0.653**	-0.055	0.224	0.046
Veneers, plywood boards, reconstituted wood (631)	0.424	-0.870	-1.534***	-0.590	0.480	1.044*	0.347	-0.403	0.220	0.173
Wood manufactures (632)	0.329	-0.758***	-2.069*	-0.130	1.524*	0.393	-0.106	-0.194	0.393	0.219
Cotton fabrics, woven (652)	1.134	0.150	-2.061**	-0.453	0.995***	0.192	0.630	0.311	0.227	0.013
Textile fabrics, woven other than cotton (653)	0.286	0.591	-2.052*	-0.716	2.232*	0.645	-0.368	-0.124	0.504	–
Made-up articles, chiefly of textiles (656)	1.177	-0.515***	-1.754***	-0.923**	0.601	0.828***	1.087*	-0.087	0.396	0.655
Lime, cement, building materials excluding glass and clay (661)	0.528	0.040	-0.852	-1.132***	0.511	1.067**	0.067	-0.313	–	0.065
Clay and refractory construction materials (662)	0.670	0.408	-1.253	-0.276	1.235*	0.270	-0.296	-0.110	0.214	–
Mineral manufactures (663)	0.679	1.051**	-0.342	-0.179	0.002	-0.135	0.129	0.110	–	0.099
Pottery (666)	0.113	-0.051	-1.058***	-0.381	1.107*	0.334	-0.261	-0.072	0.286	–
Pig iron, spiegeleisen, sponge (671)	0.143	-1.469**	0.703	0.947	-1.510*	-0.161	0.828***	-0.226	0.283	0.095

Table 7.1 continued

Industry (SITC)	Physical capital [h/] 1970	1985	Skilled labour [g/] 1970	1985	Semi-skilled labour [d/] 1970	1985	Unskilled labour [e/] 1970	1985	Adjusted [f/] R² 1970	1985
Ingots and forms of iron or steel (672)	1.340***	-0.193	-0.607	1.103	-0.718	-0.776	0.734**	0.055	0.095	0.003
Universals, plates and sheets (674)	0.959***	0.690	-1.059	-0.695	0.537	0.161	0.040	0.076	0.053	-
Tubes, pipes and fittings of iron or steel (678)	1.101**	0.919**	-0.704	-0.709***	0.317	0.325	0.078	-0.024	0.166	0.170
Iron and steel castings, forgings, unworked (679)	-0.125	0.223	1.047***	-0.322	-0.218	0.731	-0.390***	-0.450	0.452	0.023
Nails, screws, nuts, bolts, rivets, etc. (694)	0.556	0.309	-1.598	-0.852**	1.151*	0.438	-0.056	0.042	0.218	0.077
Cutlery (696)	0.312	0.278	-0.743	-0.745***	0.707**	0.484***	-0.137	-0.033	0.096	0.003
Household equipment of base metals (697)	0.205	-0.030	-0.060	-0.829***	0.180	0.600***	-0.049	-0.019	-	0.110
Office machines (714)	1.100*	1.677**	-0.396	-1.559*	-0.287	0.462	0.352***	0.255	0.322	0.459
Metalworking machinery (715)	0.604	0.982**	-0.535	-0.679	-0.053	0.089	0.215	0.131	-	0.067
Textile and leather machinery (717)	1.381***	0.854	-0.211	-0.341	-0.480	-0.040	0.293	0.078	0.063	0.023
Machines for special industry (718)	1.015**	0.761	-0.050	0.013	-0.233	-0.157	0.124	-0.028	0.314	0.051
Machines and appliances (excl. electric.) parts (719)	0.856***	0.859***	0.395	-0.138	-0.162	-0.107	0.206	0.034	0.052	0.050
Electric power machinery, switchgear (722)	1.597**	1.210**	-0.725	-0.708***	-0.212	0.120	0.376	0.094	0.191	0.163
Telecommunications apparatus (724)	1.089***	0.824**	-2.017*	-0.804**	1.381*	0.211	-0.052	0.129	0.369	0.091
Domestic electrical equipment (725)	0.193	0.871**	-0.259	-1.241*	0.500	0.500***	-0.202	0.122	-	0.109
Electric apparatus for medical purposes (726)	1.374**	0.799	-0.436	0.081	-0.464	-0.330	0.421	0.101	0.072	0.057
Other electrical machinery and apparatus (729)	1.113*	-1.010	-0.075	0.257	-0.264	0.006	0.175	-0.090	0.693	-
Railway vehicles (731)	2.044**	1.188**	-1.104***	0.324	-0.096	-0.012	0.442	0.056	0.316	0.145
Road motor vehicles (732)	0.801	0.656**	-0.284	-0.689***	0.043	0.253	0.078	0.078	0.030	0.030
Road vehicles other than motor vehicles (733)	-0.162	0.684***	0.464	-0.428	0.224	0.129	-0.285	0.027	0.027	0.014
Aircraft (734)	0.538***	0.196	0.934*	0.664***	-0.984*	-0.349***	0.229	-0.044	0.788	0.463
Ships and boats (735)	0.968	1.439*	-1.942**	-1.620*	1.641*	0.768***	-0.255	0.020	0.358	0.326
Travel goods, handbags and similar articles (831)	-0.201	-0.559***	-0.827	-0.680***	0.820**	0.713***	-0.167	-0.172	0.051	0.436
Clothing, except fur clothing (841)	-0.370	-0.410	-0.872	-0.900**	0.895	0.736**	-0.197	-0.095	0.007	0.420

Table 7.1 continued

Industry (SITC)	Physical capital[b]		Skilled labour[c]		Semi-skilled labour[d]		Unskilled labour[e]		Adjusted[f] R^2	
	1970	1985	1970	1985	1970	1985	1970	1985	1970	1985
Fur clothing and articles made of fur skins (842)	-0.874	-0.732*	0.418	0.065	0.367	-0.187	-0.264	0.082	–	0.937
Footwear (851)	-0.128	-0.667***	-0.098	-0.511	0.253	0.759***	-0.105	-0.299	–	0.307
Scientific, medical, optical measuring instruments (861)	1.250**	1.020*	-1.129***	-0.762**	0.639***	0.150	0.047	0.146	0.414	0.126
Watches and clocks (864)	0.585	0.931***	-1.140	-1.310**	0.414	0.344	0.196	0.245	–	0.018
Musical instruments, sound recorders and reproducers (891)	0.938***	0.942*	-2.273*	-1.086*	1.588*	0.358***	-0.055	0.163	0.419	0.179
Perambulators, toys, games, sporting goods (894)	0.217	-0.068	-0.730	-0.998*	0.392	0.531***	0.042	0.036	–	0.392
Office and stationery supplies (895)	0.958	0.848***	-0.750	-0.490	0.519	0.135	0.002	0.076	0.279	0.019
Manufactured articles (899)	-0.073	-0.559***	-1.626**	-0.394	1.452*	0.613*	-0.251	-0.246	0.473	0.224

Source: UNIDO

a/ Factor orientation coefficients are regression coefficients estimated from a sample of 46 countries. The regression equation used is

$$T_{ij} = a_i + b_i K_{ij} + c_i H_{ij} + d_i S_{ij} + e_i U_{ij} + u_{ij}$$

where T_{ij} are net exports of industry i by country j, K, H, S and U are stock measures of physical capital, skilled labour, semi-skilled labour and unskilled labour, respectively, and u is the disturbance term. Both the dependent and the independent variables are standardized to unit variance, so that the regression coefficents are beta coefficents. Asterisks indicate statistical significance at the 1(*), 5(**) or 10(***) per cent level. Only those industries are shown for which at least one statistically significant coefficient obtained in at least one year.

b/ Net capital stocks are aggregated depreciated flows of real gross domestic investment.
c/ Skilled labour is the number of professional/technical workers (ISCO 0/1).
d/ Semi-skilled labour is the number of literate workers who do not belong to the professional/technical category.
e/ Unskilled labour is the number of illiterate workers.
f/ In several cases the values of R^2 were low and, after adjustment, were negative. These observations are indicated by a dash (–).

coefficients. On this basis, physical capital was the most important in 1970. Coefficients for physical capital were dominant; that is, they had the highest absolute value in 47 of the 90 industries in 1970. In almost all these cases (43) the beta coefficients were positive, indicating that physical capital made a significant contribution to comparative advantage. The factor's significance had diminished somewhat by 1985. Physical capital had the highest ranking in only 35 industries, of which 28 coefficients were positive.

Skilled labour was second in importance to physical capital in 1970. But in 20 of the 32 industries where this factor was dominant, its influence was negative, meaning that abundance of skilled labour resulted in a comparative disadvantage.[4] By 1985 skilled labour had replaced physical capital as the most important determinant of net trade. In 26 out of the 40 industries where net exports were influenced by endowments of skilled labour, the factor was a source of comparative disadvantage. The impact of the two remaining factors on net trade was less important. The beta coefficients for semi-skilled labour revealed only ten industries (in both years) with a visible factor orientation. Unskilled labour played a minor role: the factor was dominant in only one industry in 1970 and five industries in 1985.

The pattern of industry rankings summarized here includes no test to determine whether the beta coefficients are significantly different from zero. Inclusion of this criterion leaves the picture virtually unchanged. The number of occurrences of both dominant and significantly positive (negative) beta coefficients for each of the factors were as follows: for physical capital, 17 (0) in 1970 and 11 (3) in 1985; for skilled labour, 3 (8) in 1970 and 2 (13) in 1985; for semi-skilled labour, 4 (2) in 1970 and 4 (1) in 1985; and for unskilled labour, 1 (0) in 1970 and none in 1985.

The relatively important role of physical capital is reconfirmed by the results for broad groups of industries. The factor is an important source of comparative advantage in industries producing chemicals (SITC 5) and machinery and transport equipment (SITC 7). It is of less significance for basic manufactures (SITC 6) and miscellaneous manufactured goods (SITC 8). This broad pattern fits with the casual impression that chemicals and machinery and transport equipment tend to be relatively large users of physical capital. In the case of machinery and transport equipment, the relationship between physical capital and net trade was unchanged between 1970 and 1985. The same was not true for chemicals, where the factor's significance has declined over time.

The contribution of each factor to comparative advantage can be assessed when the trade shares of various industries are considered. The largest shares of net trade are in motor vehicles and non-electrical machinery. The fact that the abundance of physical capital exerts a strong influence on the trade patterns of these two industries fits comfortably with a conventional H–O model. Similar observations apply to other widely traded manufactures such as universals, plates and sheets of iron or steel, and ships and boats. In contrast, the finding that physical-capital abundance is the prime source of comparative advantage in certain engineering industries is surprising. Many types of the engineering activities are thought to depend heavily on the availability of human capital and are regarded as product–cycle industries. Nevertheless, two engineering industries – machines for special industries and telecommunications apparatus – had large volumes of net trade and their trading patterns had a close positive association with the distribution of physical capital.

The results are even more ambiguous among industries with low to moderate levels of net trade. In some (for example, plastics, steel tubes and pipes, paints and fertilizers), the expected relationship between physical–capital intensity and factor supplies is obtained. In others, elements of the product–cycle model might be expected to operate although the availability of physical capital again exerted a strong positive influence on net exports. Examples are organic chemicals, office machinery, electric power machinery and scientific instruments.

In the case of skilled labour, the negative effects of resource abundance were observed most frequently among industries producing basic manufactures (SITC 6). In other words, the factor had an anti–parallel orientation which might have to do with specific use of skilled labour in other industries. A similar, though less pronounced, result was observed for industries producing miscellaneous manufactured goods (SITC 8). Among the industries with an anti–parallel orientation for skilled labour, those classified as basic manufactures generally reflect features of the H–O model. This is true for various textile industries like woven cotton fabrics, textile fabrics and made–up articles of textiles as well as for cement and pottery.

Gauged in terms of the volume of trade, the aircraft industry was the most significant instance where skilled labour made a positive contribution to net trade performance. Other industries where this factor was a source of comparative advantage included some of the smaller chemical industries: inorganic chemicals, radioactive materials, essential oils, and miscellaneous chemical materials and products. Results such as these support H–O premises, but evidence for other industries is counter to expectations. The most striking contradiction occurs in engineering industries. The competitive abilities of these industries are thought to depend mainly on the availability of skilled labour. Most coefficients, however, were negative (and often statistically significant). Examples include telecommunications apparatus, office machines, electric power machinery and domestic electrical equipment.

Judging from the size of orientation coefficients, semi–skilled labour appears to be a less important source of comparative advantage than either physical capital or skilled labour. Clothing was the most important industry for which semi–skilled labour was a prominent source of comparative advantage. Other industries with modest amounts of net trade and a parallel orientation for semi–skilled labour were musical instruments, footwear, ships and boats, and domestic electrical equipment. Also included in this category were several industries that are widely regarded as being labour–intensive – cotton fabrics, textile fabrics and made–up articles of textiles. One impression that emerges from this set of coefficients is that much of the comparative advantage usually attributed to an abundance of 'raw' labour actually depends on the availability of labour with some degree of skills.[5]

The fact that unskilled labour had little impact on comparative advantage is not explained by an examination of the detailed regression results. In some instances the relationship was expected; for example, unskilled labour was a source of comparative advantage for producers of leather or made-up articles of textiles. In other instances the factor's positive contribution to comparative advantage is puzzling in terms of the H–O model. Examples are organic chemicals, mineral tar, some iron and steel industries, and even office machines.

An even more detailed analysis of factor orientation could yield further insights with regard to industry-specific relationships. However, the overall impression of the role that factor abundance plays as a determinant of trade patterns would probably not change significantly. This role can be summed up in terms of a few statements. First, the factor abundance impact on net trade in manufactures is of moderate strength. This can be attributed to the fact that the relationships identified in the factor abundance theory are of an on-average nature. Consequently, no more than a portion of net trade in manufactures is likely to be subject to factor abundance effects. That portion, however, was relatively large in terms of the total value of trade considered.

Second, the strength of the abundance effect varies depending on the factor considered. From a sector-wide perspective, the results reported here suggest that physical-capital abundance is a source of comparative advantage in manufactures at large,[6] while the role played by skilled labour in this respect is ambiguous. Semi-skilled and unskilled labour are of less significance when the manufacturing sector as a whole is the focus of discussion.[7] These impressions are altered somewhat by the results reported in the following section, where the role of factor intensities is incorporated. They are not sufficient to judge which factors best accord with the H–O prediction of the product composition of manufactured trade. A more definitive statement requires information on factor intensities as well as factor orientation. The following section incorporates data on factor intensities, with the result that impressions regarding the relative importance of various factors are altered.

An empirical assessment of the factor abundance proposition

Empirical investigations of the factor abundance hypothesis require data on factor endowments, factor intensities and trade. Such a comprehensive application of the H–O model raises at least two problems. First, it has to be decided how the full, complex hypothesis should be evaluated on the basis of available data. Second, the correct interpretation of outcomes is not straightforward when the application of the model is less than complete.

In view of these points, the objective of the following exercise is a modest, descriptive one. It is to determine whether a particular kind of systematic overall relationship exists between empirical measures of factor abundance, factor intensity and net trade, and if so whether the sign of the relationship agrees with H–O predictions. A mosaic of data on factor abundance, factor intensity and net trade is first assembled. The evidence is then examined to determine the extent of agreement with one of the model's general predictions. Credible results will require the researcher to follow a precise set of rules when assembling the H–O 'mosaic'. Consequently, some thought must be given to the method of validation.

The general theory of comparative advantage can be stated in the form of correlations between the variables involved. All correlations that relate directly to the law of comparative advantage apply to pairs of variables (for example, autarky prices and net exports). In order to extend this method to a complete H–O framework, the analyst must be able to assess the relationship between the three variables, factor intensity, factor abundance and trade.

The association between factor abundance and trade was established in the previous section on the basis of the factor orientation concept. If factor orientation is also related systematically to factor intensity, the basic requirements of an application of the H–O proposition are met. As shown in the technical appendix (Appendix A), a correlation between factor orientation and factor intensity – extended over all factors and goods – serves to establish such a comprehensive relationship. The correlation is expected to be positive if the factor abundance proposition holds in its generalized form. In addition, the same type of correlation – if restricted to one particular factor – enables the analyst to assess the factor's contribution to an H–O version of the trading world.

The immediate requirement is to find appropriate data for factor intensities. Common practice was followed by employing US data. Direct factor shares were derived from US data for 1982 and used as a measure of relative factor intensities in each industry. The shares were calculated to reflect, as accurately as possible, the factor definitions used in the compilation of data on endowments.[8] Altogether, the data on factor intensities represent the technical characteristics for a large portion of the 90 industries treated in the present study.[9]

Table 7.2 summarizes the results of what can be termed a broad application of the factor abundance theory.[10] The first four rows and columns of the table show correlations between factor orientation and factor intensity for 1985. The entry in the last row and column of the table represents the weak global H–O proposition outlined in the technical appendix. The simple correlation coefficient carries a positive sign as predicted by the generalized factor abundance hypothesis and is significantly different from zero. This result is regarded as an indication that the pattern of net trade in manufactures carries features that conform with a weak prediction of the factor abundance model. Even in a complex trading world of many factors, goods and countries, net trade appears to be influenced (in an on-average sense) by the interaction between factor intensities and factor endowments. More generally, not only

Table 7.2 Correlations[a] between factor orientation and factor intensity, 1985[b] (Pearson correlation coefficients)

	Factor orientation				
	Physical capital	Skilled labour	Semi-skilled labour	Unskilled labour	All factors[c]
Factor intensity					
Physical capital	−0.009	0.250**	−0.340*	0.063	
Skilled labour	0.194***	0.020	−0.094	0.017	
Semi-skilled labour	−0.005	−0.215***	0.284**	−0.048	
Unskilled labour	−0.248**	−0.381*	0.618*	−0.127	
All factors[c]					0.246*

Sources: Table 7.1 and United States, Bureau of the Census (1984).

a/ Asterisks indicate statistical significance at the 1(*), 5(**) or 10(***) per cent level.

b/ Estimates of factor orientation are for 1985. All factor intensities were calculated from United States data for 1982. The measurement concept is that of shares of factor rewards in value added. The proxy measures of factor rewards used in this exercise are imputed factor incomes. The income imputed to capital is estimated by the non-wage portion of value added. The income of semi-skilled labour is proxied by wages of production workers, that of skilled labour by the difference between the total payroll and these wages. Both types of wages have been corrected for the income of unskilled labour embodied in the corresponding categories of employees. This correction is based on an estimate of the wage rate for unskilled labour which has also been used to calculate the income of that factor at large. More details on the underlying data and on estimation procedures can be found in note 6/ and in the statistical appendix.

c/ The correlation for all factors simultaneously was obtained by pooling the observations on all four types of factor intensity/factor orientation.

does factor abundance exert a visible effect on a substantial portion of net trade, but its overall impact is of a form predicted by the generalized H–O theory.

At least two remarks on the above results seem to be in place. First, its support for a general H–O proposition contrasts sharply with the rejections reported for recent tests of the factor abundance theory.[11] However, this is not surprising, if differences in concepts as well as in data are taken into account. While in other empirical contributions exact relationships (between supply of factors and indirect factor trade) were usually tested, the present exercise attempts to validate a prediction about the sign of a correlation–like expression. Furthermore, there are differences in the data underlying the various studies. Second, the present validation of a weak H–O proposition is partial in character in that it comprises only forty-six countries, only four broad factors of production, and only manufactured goods.

The other diagonal entries of the correlation matrix of Table 7.2 serve to assess the role of the studied four factors individually. The result for semi-skilled labour conformed most closely to the H–O model. The correlation tests for other factors were much less convincing. A tentative judgement of the relative significance of the four factors within an H–O world would be that basically all H–O regularity of the commodity composition of net trade relates to semi-skilled labour. Yet this regularity is strong enough to produce an overall relationship of the H–O type between factor endowments, factor intensities and trade flows.

A result that suggests that the H–O model can be closely associated with only one factor of production is surprising. However, the fact that this particular resource is semi-skilled labour does not appear to be counter-intuitive, for at least two reasons. First, of the factors considered here, semi-skilled labour comes closest to fulfilling the assumption of immobility between countries and is therefore most likely to impact trade patterns in an H–O manner.[12] The movement of highly skilled labour from developing to developed countries (i.e. the 'brain drain'), as well as the large amounts of unskilled labour moving (both legally and illegally) to North America, West Europe and now Japan, make the immobility assumption questionable for those two factors. Second, semi-skilled labour represents a broad category of workers whose abilities are closely related to production processes so that this type of labour is a vital input in many industries. A large reservoir of workers with production-oriented skills should provide a solid basis for comparative advantage. For these reasons, a strong relationship between net trade and abundance of this factor can be expected.

The results obtained for physical capital are nevertheless disappointing – despite the fact that the factor's high degree of international mobility violates a basic assumption of the model. The orientation coefficients of Table 7.1 showed that physical-capital abundance played a prominent role in sector-wide patterns of comparative advantage. This raised expectations about the factor's significance for the inter-industry composition of trade. The expectations, however, were not fulfilled by the correlation results in Table 7.2.

Country similarities and manufactured trade

The factor abundance model yields the proposition that differences in factor endowments are the basis for trade. However, similarities in factor endowments are also relevant. The role of endowment similarities is observed, for example, in the factor content version of the H–O model. One of the main features of this version is that under certain conditions international trade will lead to the international equalization not only of prices for goods but also of factor rewards. The necessary conditions for such an outcome include a minimum degree of similarity in relative factor endowments of countries.[13] In this sense, the factor content version embraces two paradoxical features. Countries must differ in terms of their factor abundance if the main motive for international trade is to be preserved. The differences, however, cannot be too large, or international equalization of factor rewards will not be guaranteed.

New theories of international trade

The above line of reasoning is quite different from the theoretical approaches lumped together under what is sometimes called the 'new theories of international trade'. An obvious contrast between these theories and the orthodox H–O approach lies in the fact that different types of specialization and trade are explained. While the factor abundance model is concerned with the inter-industry pattern of trade, the new models focus on intra-industrial forms of specialization and IIT.

The forerunner to much of the new theorizing is Linder's preference-similarity theory. A central tenet of this theory is that the type and quality of the manufactures consumed within a country reflect its level of development and structure of production. Per capita income is a useful proxy for both these characteristics, since a close correspondence is expected between this measure and the domestic pattern of consumption of manufactures. With regard to trade, the composition and quality of manufactured exports (which is a close correlate to domestic production) reflect the characteristic tastes of the majority of the country's consumers. Imports, on the other hand, are viewed as catering to slightly different sets of preferences for a consumer minority.

The link between Linder's ideas and the more formal theoretical work in recent years is the concept of 'international trade in manufactures . . . as an extension of the internal market' (Hufbauer, 1970, p. 197). Among other hypotheses relationships between country similarities and trade can be developed from this literature. One is that similarity in levels of per capita income should foster bilateral trade, given that other determinants (for example, geographical distance) remain constant. A second is that the composition of one country's exports will more closely resemble the composition of another's imports if the two countries have similar levels of per capita income and production structures. A logical consequence of the latter hypothesis is that the composition of a country's exports and imports are quite similar. On the whole, Linder's theory gives rise to the expectation that much of the trade between similar countries will be in similar goods.

Linder's arguments suggest that consumer preferences are an important determinant of the intensity and composition of international trade. It was not until more recent contributions to trade theory accorded a similar role to consumer tastes that the link between Linder's ideas and the new theories of trade became evident. Another element that figures prominently in the new theories is monopolistic competition, which to some extent was also reflected in the Linder model. What distinguishes the newer models from Linder's original work is their formal rigour, a feature that they have in common with the conventional factor abundance theory.

The literature on the new trade theories is broad in scope. For the present study one of its aspects – the relationship between country similarities and trading patterns – has been chosen as the subject of analysis. The underlying theoretical model assumes monopolistic competition and describes an interaction between economies of scale on the supply side and preference diversity on the demand side. Krugman's version of such a model (1979a) is one of the more concise and was outlined in Chapter 1. Its simplicity, and the fact that it focuses on trade between similar countries, illustrates clearly the main points of interest for the present study.

The main purpose of Krugman's model is to analyse the effects of scale economies, preference diversity and product differentiation on international trade. However, it also provides insights regarding the role of country similarities. The outcome is that the share of total trade (which is entirely IIT) in world income will be greatest when the two countries are of equal size and possess equal endowments of labour, the only factor of production that is recognized in the Krugman model.

Krugman's results have been criticized for their simplicity, particularly with regard to consumer preferences. But other models which take a more sophisticated view of demand yield similar results. Helpman (1981), for example, has shown that, when IIT occurs in differentiated products, the source of trade is economies of scale in production. This analysis also leads to the conclusion that in industries with increasing returns the share of IIT in bilateral trade will be higher when the factor endowments or per capita incomes of trading partners become more similar.

The growing importance of IIT is increasingly matched by a new appreciation of the country similarities that foster this form of trade. While large 'distances' between the H–O attributes of countries will create inter-industry trade, small distances are conducive to relatively high volumes of IIT. The first aspect was the subject of the previous section. The remainder of this section focuses on the second aspect.

Empirical evidence

The identification of empirically testable relationships in the generalized factor abundance theory is difficult owing to the complexity of the subject. That task becomes even more problematic in the case of the new trade theories. The major reason for added complications is that the new approaches concern very narrow aspects of international trade. And sometimes, the choice of a particular model to analyse trade is motivated by the desire for theoretical tractability rather than empirical relevance. The empiricist who chooses to work with the new theories must then consider the empirical 'applic-ability' of a given hypothesis rather than attempting a more wide-ranging analysis.

The recent empirical literature is full of attempts to explain IIT in terms of the concepts of the new trade theories. The most successful among these attempts had as their objective an explanation of the intra-industry compo-nent of bilateral trade, mainly in terms of country attributes.[14] This line of reasoning has a parallel in recent empirical work conducted in a fac-tor abundance framework. In that case, investigations of partial relation-ships between country attributes and trade patterns (similar to those pres-ented in the previous section) have produced interesting and stimulating results.

Building on such analogy, the present exercise introduces two novel features. One is the examination of relationships between country attributes and IIT in an industry-specific context. This approach contrasts with previous empirical studies which considered the whole of manufacturing, either by aggregating the measure of IIT across all industries or by pooling industry-specific observa-tions into one huge sample. Although no model provides a rigorous framework for an industry-specific investigation, theoretical work seems to suggest that such a distinction can be helpful in identifying the influence of country attrib-utes on IIT. Helpman (1981), for example, distinguishes between two sectors where only one produces differentiated manufactures with increasing returns to scale. The trade of this sector is likely to be influenced by the types of country attributes stressed by the new theories. Trade of the other (constant-returns) sector would follow H–O rules. More generally, the eclectic character of the new theoretical framework suggests that the distinctive features of any model will be more visible in some industries than in others. Visibility would also depend on the extent of agreement between theoretical assumptions and industrial realities.

A second distinctive feature of the following exercise is in the way trade flows are measured. Previous studies have dealt almost exclusively with the IIT component's share in total trade. The practice is due partly to the nature of theoretical results and partly to the fact that analysts were usually interested in the relative size of the inter-industry and intra-industry components in exports or imports. Nevertheless for descriptive purposes the absolute amount of intra-industry exchange for a given product category is of interest too. The present exercise adopts the second approach, examining levels of IIT under the hypothesis that, other things being equal, greater country similarities yield larger absolute levels of bilateral IIT. Such a premise seems plausible in light of the Linder theory and the central message contained in later attempts to explain IIT.[15]

Because country similarities are the primary concern of this section, bilateral comparisons between countries are employed. The level of the intra-industry component in bilateral trade (IITL) can be measured by the extent of trade overlap (see Chapter 4) as

$$IITL = \min (X, M)$$

where X (M) are exports (imports) by country 1 to (from) country 2 and trade flows pertain to a given product group or industry.

A comparison of trading partners in terms of the attributes that determine IIT is less straightforward. First, selection of relevant attributes suggested by theory would include relative factor endowments and country size. In order to streamline statistical procedures, the choice is usually narrowed to two country characteristics: per capita GDP, and market size measured by total GDP. Per capita GDP is employed because similarities in both factor endowments and demand patterns are normally mirrored by similarities in per capita income. Total GDP is used as a proxy for market size because it reflects economic size differences between countries while other alternatives such as population represent an indication of demographic size. Similarities are measured by the negative of the absolute difference between countries in each of the two variables.

Two other possible determinants of IIT are included in the regression analysis. These are average per capita GDP and average total GDP of the two countries involved in each bilateral comparison. The former variable reflects the expectation that demand for differentiated products is great in the trade between countries with high levels of income (Linder, 1961). The corresponding empirical hypothesis is that higher levels of income will result in larger amounts of IIT. The latter variable, average total GDP of trading partners, is expected to capture the size effect. In addition, it may be hypothesized that large countries tend to have a greater IIT component in their trade. This outcome can be attributed to the possibility that, with increasing returns to scale, large countries will be able to produce a wider variety of differentiated products than smaller countries (Lancaster, 1980).[16]

Construction of appropriate statistical tests is hindered because the new theories have little to say about the possible algebraic relationship between trade variables and country attributes. While the general impact of country similarities on new forms of trade is clear, an equation that would reflect this relationship in a cross-country framework can be formulated only in an ad hoc manner. The present exercise makes no attempt to fit complicated equational forms which may have little or no theoretical foundation. Instead, partial correlations of the data are examined to determine whether they show the expected signs.

Table 7.3 presents a summary of partial correlations between IITL and the four variables described above. The results are in almost perfect agreement with theoretical expectations. When country similarities are expressed in terms of income levels and market size, their impact is overwhelmingly positive. In fact, there is no industry where country similarities had a significantly negative influence on the level of bilateral IIT. Coefficients relating bilateral IIT to similarities in per capita GDP were significantly positive for 70 of the

Table 7.3 Partial correlations[a] between levels of bilateral intra-industry trade and country attributes, 1985 (number of significant coefficients)

Level of significance (percentage)	Partial correlation between IITL[b] and:							
	Income similarity[c]		Size similarity[d]		Average income[e]		Average size[f]	
	+	−	+	−	+	−	+	−
1	37	0	81	0	44	2	85	0
5	20	0	5	0	13	2	2	0
10	13	0	0	0	6	0	1	0
Total	70	0	86	0	63	4	88	0

Source: UNIDO

a/ Partial correlation coefficients were calculated for a total of 90 industries (SITC three-digit groups). For each industry bilateral IIT between all pairs formed out of the 47 countries in the sample was analyzed. The coefficients underlying the present summary table are shown in the statistical appendix (table B.9).
b/ IITL = min (X,M) where X(M) are bilateral exports (imports).
c/ Income similarity is measured by the negative of the absolute difference in per capita GDP between the two trading partners.
d/ Size similarity is measured by the negative of the absolute difference in GDP between trading partners.
e/ Average income is the arithmetic mean of per capita GDP of trading partners.
f/ Average size is the arithmetic mean of GDP of trading partners.

90 industries tested, while those referring to similarities in market size were significantly positive for all but four industries.

The strongly positive correlations between IIT and average market size may be due to nothing more than a scale effect, but the positive coefficients associated with average per capita GDP lend direct support to a general hypothesis on intra-industry specialization. Linder, for example, argues that demand for (horizontally) differentiated products rises as per capita income grows. Consequently, the intra-industry exchange of (differentiated) products should increase as the per capita incomes of trading partners rise. This expectation is corroborated by the results in Table 7.3, which shows that 63 of the partial correlations are significantly positive.

In summary, the effects of country similarities on levels of IIT are pervasive. Similarities in income levels or market size breed intra-industry specialization and trade, irrespective of trends in inter-industry trade. However, this is only one aspect of the IIT phenomenon. Theory proposes that in addition to country attributes there are also quantifiable industry characteristics that have a significant impact on two-way trade. The following chapter considers this latter point by examining some of the industry characteristics that may act as determinants of the (relative) extent of IIT.

Annex: Trade flows and factor movements

In this chapter the impact of country differences and similarities on patterns of trade was considered. As is usual, it was assumed that the factors of production were mobile between industries but immobile internationally. Thus, countries export goods that intensively utilize their relatively cheap factors of production. If factors are allowed to move internationally, then capital and labour would migrate from those areas where their returns are low to areas where their returns are higher. To the extent that this is not possible, trade in goods becomes a substitute for the migration of factors. In reality, factors of production are not perfectly immobile internationally. The increasing mobility of capital and to a lesser extent labour needs to be considered to gain a more realistic picture of the structure of world trade. As was pointed out in the preceding chapter, the weak results obtained for physical capital and skilled labour (Table 7.2) may reflect the relatively high mobility of these factors. Furthermore, the migration of factors would tend to reduce differences in the endowment of factors across countries over time. This lessening of differences in endowments may partially account for the increasing importance of intra-industry trade over time.

The study of international trade has been traditionally concerned with cross-border transactions of goods and to a much lesser extent of services. Further, the way in which these cross-border transactions affect an economy's production structure and factor markets is usually examined. The monetary side of international economics deals with the way cross-border financial transactions affect an economy's interest rate, exchange rate and financial markets. In practice, the real and the monetary sides of international economics have developed almost independently of one another.

On the real side, exchange rates, interest rates and capital movements are generally considered irrelevant. Exchange rates are ignored because they are assumed to be the relative price of two monies, both of which are 'veils' which have no real effects. Interest rates do not matter, as it is assumed that they represent the long-run price of money with only negligible effects on intersectoral prices and relative factor prices. Financial capital movements may matter over a period that is long enough for them to influence an economy's endowment of productive capital. However, if this endowment is assumed to be initially large, then changes arising from financial flows can likewise be ignored. More generally, international trade in productive capital may also be ignored if commodity trade eliminates the factor-price differentials which stimulate the migration of factors across borders. Thus, for a variety of reasons, the study of international trade has been able comfortably to ignore international movements of capital.

Over the last twenty years, this split between the real and monetary sides of international economics has become increasingly less realistic. Since the advent of generalized exchange rate floating in the early 1970s, it has become more difficult to ignore changes in exchange rates. Recognizing this difficulty,

131

theoretical and empirical research is now progressing on the issue of real and financial linkages among open economies. In this annex, the determinants of short-run flows of financial capital are considered. We shall also examine how these flows and other factors influence changes in exchange rates. Such changes in turn affect short- to medium-run trade flows in ways that may differ from predictions generated by a more long-run H–O model.

The current account balance can be defined as the difference between total imports and total exports. Using simple GNP accounting terms, the current account (CA) can be expressed as

$$CA = Y - (C + I + G),$$

where Y is national income, C is consumption by the public, I is investment spending and G is government spending. Another way of stating the same definitional identity is to set CA equal to the difference between national income (Y) and domestic residents' spending $(C + I + G)$. If income is larger (smaller) than spending, a CA surplus (deficit) is created. Saving (S) is equal to $Y - C - G$. In a closed economy, it would be true that saving (S) must equal investment (I). For an open economy, only the following identity must hold:

$$S = I + CA.$$

If S is smaller (larger) than I in an open economy, a capital account surplus (deficit) occurs. Since in an open economy total outflows must equal total inflows, a current account surplus (deficit) creates a capital account deficit (surplus). A capital account surplus indicates that inflows of capital are larger than outflows; the reverse is true for a capital account deficit. Thus, in an economy where domestic saving is larger than investment, a current account surplus occurs. To balance overall inflows and outflows, the country exports capital (a capital account deficit).

Since governments rarely run balanced budgets, the above identity can be modified to reflect the influence of the government budget on the current and capital accounts. If we assume that the difference between government spending (G) and tax revenue (T) is borrowed by the government, then the current account (CA) can be written as

$$CA = S - I - (G - T).$$

The current account, or alternatively the capital account, thus becomes directly related to saving, investment, government spending and taxation.

Obviously, a current account deficit (surplus) must be financed by a capital account surplus (deficit). These capital movements necessary to offset imbalances in the current account may take several forms. In the older, fixed exchange rate system capital movements were primarily official. CA surpluses meant an accumulation of official reserves, while a CA deficit meant a loss of reserves. Increasingly, capital movements are non-official in nature. Among these movements, short-term capital flows involve assets with maturities of less than a year while long-term capital flows involve assets with maturities greater than a year. If the purchaser of the asset has operating control over the issuer of the asset, then the capital movement is direct. If not, the investment is referred to as portfolio investment, which may be either short-term or long-term.

Inflows and outflows of short-term and long-term capital obviously create capital account surpluses and deficits. In the case of a capital inflow, foreign investors must purchase the domestic currency in order to transfer the capital. The short-run effect is to increase the supply of foreign exchange and to cause the domestic currency to appreciate. The resulting appreciation of the currency reduces exports and increases imports. As exports contract and imports expand, the widening current account deficit mirrors the capital account surplus. For a capital account deficit (outflows larger than inflows), the buying of foreign exchange causes the capital-exporting country's currency to depreciate. This depreciation increases exports and reduces imports, creating a current account surplus.

The above scenario concerning capital flows and the current account balance represents the 'conventional wisdom' about how capital flows impact imports, exports and the current account balance. In an economy with a flexible exchange rate and open capital markets, changes in the exchange rate and the current account balance reflect changes in capital flows. This chain of causation is admittedly complex. Empirical evidence on the subject is limited, but one recent test seems to support the view that in the short run changes in capital flows determine the exchange rate and the current account (Hutchinson and Piggott, 1985). In the short run, monetary and fiscal policies that influence interest rates will tend to impact capital flows, the exchange rate and the current account balance.

These policy-induced changes in trade flows can in turn have a major impact on industrial structure and the ability of domestic industries to compete in international markets. Large exchange rate depreciations (appreciations) can enlarge (reduce) the size of the tradable goods sector of the economy (Dornbusch, 1973). Essentially the older form of 'crowding out' has moved. In a closed economy, policies that influence interest rates impact primarily on the interest-rate-sensitive sectors of the economy. However, in an open economy interest rate changes influence the exchange rate, and the structure of the economy changes as the relative prices of tradable and nontradable goods change.

Recent changes in the world capital markets have led to a worldwide increase in the mobility of short-run portfolio capital (Obstfeld, 1986). While these changes improved the worldwide efficiency of capital markets, the cost has been an increase in exchange rate volatility. These effects can be offset only to the extent that flows of capital not involving traded goods are restricted (i.e. by exchange controls). This insulation may be more apparent than real if the exchange rate is pegged to another country's currency which is floating. Variations in this latter exchange rate lead to implicit changes in the exchange rate and the value of reserves of the country.

One of the most important questions in the present context is whether or not the increased mobility of capital and the associated exchange rate changes have had a measurable impact on international specialization. Increased exchange rate variability could adversely impact investment in the tradable goods sector and distort patterns of comparative advantage. Although the proposition is inherently difficult to test, the available evidence appears to be that it does not (IMF, 1984a). However, it would be desirable if capital could flow freely internationally *and* exchange rates would fluctuate less. Such a change would require a new type of exchange rate system (IMF, 1984b). This change from official to unofficial capital flows may also influence the H–O results presented in the previous chapter. With fixed exchange rates, changes in a country's current account would change the level of private investment *and* official reserves. In a floating-rate system, virtually all of the changes in the current account would lead to changes in private investment. This would affect H–O-type empirical results because the new exchange rate system would lead to relatively large movements of the world's productive capital.

Another example of international factor mobility – besides capital movements – is the migration of labour. Unlike international flows of capital, labour migration involves the movement of both the factor of production and the owner of the factor, so that the source country loses both. In the standard H–O model of international trade, it is normally assumed that labour can be costlessly reallocated among industries domestically but that it is immobile internationally. In a modern economy labour is not typically homogeneous, and occupational classifications frequently define separate labour markets. The extent of international labour mobility also varies from occupation to occupation. Some skills form an almost world market as opposed to a purely domestic labour market, while other skills (or lack thereof) are characterized by almost H–O-like labour immobility. In occupations containing a large investment in education or training, significant migration from countries where such skills are poorly rewarded to countries where the remuneration is higher may be significant. In many cases, well trained migrants easily assimilate into their chosen countries, and social and cultural problems may be minimal. Most countries have notably more lenient immigration laws for such individuals. This may not be accidental for developed countries. A developed country may have a comparative advantage in the production of goods that contain relatively large amounts of human capital and/or have a large research and development component. The immigration of labour containing a large amount of human capital might thus augment the country's comparative advantage. The issue is far from trivial, as the USA alone admits nearly 50,000 professional immigrants per year.

The movements of labour may account for some of the results shown in Table 7.2. As pointed out, skilled labour is now quite mobile in the world economy, and this mobility may be partially responsible for the relatively poor results obtained for that factor in the previous chapter. The same seems to be true for unskilled labour. Both legal and illegal migration of this factor may be distorting the H–O results.

The empirical research on this issue tends to confirm that relative wage differentials affect labour migration. The key variable is the wage differential rather than just the relative income differential between countries. Furthermore, the relative wage elasticity seems to be greater than one implying a high degree of responsiveness of professional immigration to changes in relative wages (Agarwal and Winkler, 1984). However, non-economic variables in the home country also seem to have a significant impact on the migration of professionals (Huang, 1987).

A final point shall be made about the general relationship between trade and factor movements. The H–O model is based on the view that factor movements and (inter-industry) trade in goods are substitutes. If over time labour and/or capital is allowed to migrate between countries, then the differences in relative factor prices will decrease and the amount of inter-industry trade will diminish. Trade between the two countries will increasingly become intra-industry trade as the basis for trade moves from factor-price differentials to economies of scale, product differentiation or differences in product technology. If labour can migrate to countries whose exporting industries derive their comparative advantage from something other than differences in factor endowments, such migration could increase output and exports. In such a circumstance, migration would be trade-expanding. This result seems to hold for a wide variety of models where the basis of trade is something other than differences in factor endowments (Markusen, 1983). Thus, if trade is intra-industry rather than inter-industry, trade and factor movements may be complements rather than substitutes.

Notes: Chapter 7

1   For the case of more goods than factors – which seems to be representative of the real world – the underlying regression equations cannot be derived rigorously from the formal H–O model (Anderson, 1987). Nevertheless, the regressions can be useful to describe certain features of the trading world in the spirit of the H–O theory.
2   This terminology is inspired by the recent general formulations of the factor abundance theory which can be stated as geometric relationships between vectors in a high dimensional Euclidean space.
3   In the case of correlation coefficients, the relationship is straightforward. The cosine of the angle between the net exports and the factor endowments vectors is formally equivalent to the Pearson correlation coefficient, once net exports and factor endowment measures have been standardized to zero means.
4   A negative impact of a factor on an industry's comparative advantage is most likely the consequence of the factor's specificity of use in other industries (see Leamer, 1984, pp. 32-3 and the Annex to Chapter 5).
5   Semi-skilled labour could unambiguously be identified as a source of comparative disadvantage in very few industries, among them certain chemical industries, pig iron and the aircraft industry. The results for this last industry illustrate how two

different categories of labour – skilled and semi-skilled labour – can significantly influence net trade patterns in opposite ways.

6   Tamor, 1987, in a critical appraisal of the regression approach used here, maintains that endowment levels merely explain the level of total manufacturing activity (and thus sectoral comparative advantage), but not the industry composition of such activity (or inter-industry comparative advantage).

7   The sector-wide interpretation of comparative advantage in manufacturing largely agrees with the findings reported in Leamer, 1984, pp. 170–4. There it is shown that physical capital was the major source of comparative advantage in manufacturing in the 1970s, while skilled labour was more often associated with a comparative disadvantage. The latter feature seems to have become even more striking in the 1980s.

8   The major difficulties arose in connection with input requirements of the various skill categories of labour. Factor income of unskilled labour was estimated as the product of employment and a proxy for the unskilled wage rate, of which several alternatives were tested. Income of semi-skilled labour was defined as the wage sum of production workers with a minimum degree of labour skills. Finally, income of skilled labour was crudely proxied by the difference between total payroll and wages of production workers, with a correction for income of unskilled workers covered by this residual income value. Accordingly, the correlations relating to skilled labour are the least reliable part of the exercise.

9   For statistical details on this factor intensity matrix see the statistical appendix (Appendix B).

10   Only one of several tested alternatives of a correlation matrix is shown in the Table. The alternatives differ in terms of the minimum wage rate used to estimate the income of unskilled labour. Sector-wide, the wage rate of unskilled labour was assumed to be a fraction of the minimum (across all four-digit SIC categories) of the wage rates of production workers. By choosing alternative values for this fraction ranging between 0 and 1, the sensitivity of correlation results was tested. The outcome of this testing was that the correlation results remained qualitatively unchanged for all versions of the definiton of the return to unskilled labour.

11   An overview of such tests and their major results is given in Bowen, Leamer and Sveikauskas, 1987.

12   The basic results on patterns of trade in the presence of factor mobility are found in Ethier and Svensson, 1986. There it is shown, for example, that a weak form of the H–O theorem continues to hold in that 'a country will on average export those goods that make relatively intensive use of the country's relatively abundant non-traded factors' (p. 38).

13   In technical-theoretical parlance, countries are required to have factor endowments in the same 'cone of diversification'.

14   A recent example of an empirical analysis of this type is found in Balassa and Bauwens, 1987, where a huge sample of observations on bilateral IIT flows was related to a fairly long list of explanatory variables. And among these variables, country attributes yielded plausible results in terms of the signs and significance levels of their coefficients.

15   The present approach can also be seen as being motivated by symmetry considerations, since it mirrors the 'Leamer regressions' of the first section of the present chapter.

16   The present formulations of 'explanatory' variables are basically those used by Loertscher and Wolter, 1980. Some later studies adopted more complicated approaches to the measurement issue, but with little improvement in empirical results.

CHAPTER 8

Economies of scale and market structure

A factor abundance interpretation of international specialization and trade has served as the primary source of theoretical guidance throughout previous chapters. This chapter and the following one explore a different set of issues which are drawn from the new theories of trade. Though the discussion moves outside an H–O world, reference to that model is not discarded.

It has been suggested that the H–O model is most accurately pictured as an attempt to isolate the effects of factor abundance on patterns of specialization. To do so, it employs several assumptions which neutralize the effects of other determinants. The approach and rationale behind the new theories of trade are quite different. To appreciate better the distinction between the two approaches, several of the more stringent assumptions of the H–O model can be briefly recalled. One is the requirement that industry production functions exhibit constant returns to scale. A second is the stipulation that each good is homogeneous and that the consumer encounters no product diversity. Finally, perfect competition is assumed to prevail in all markets. The distinction between the factor proportions model and the new models is highlighted by the latter's treatment of these assumptions. By allowing for increasing returns to scale, product differentiation and various forms of imperfect competition, the new models recognize types of trade that depend on determinants other than factor endowments.

In contrasting these two approaches, the present chapter serves a dual purpose. One is to consider the degree to which the H–O view must be tempered and its predictions qualified if it is to approximate better the microeconomic realities of world industry. The second is to assemble some fragmentary evidence regarding the extent to which conditions in various industries depart from the H–O postulates. Such evidence can be helpful in determining the relevance of alternative trade models. A thorough empirical assessment of non-H–O determinants of specialization and trade would be valuable. However, the difficulties of measurement, data availability and comparability are severe, and the evidence assembled here is mainly inferential. The approach of this chapter is best described as an empirical excursion into a non-H–O world rather than an attempt to explain new forms of international trade.

The first section of this chapter summarizes some of the main hypotheses about the relationships between increasing returns, market structure and trade. The second section reviews the subjects of scale economies, industrial concentration and product differentiation as they are set out in the literature on industrial organization. It also describes the methods of measurement and discusses their strengths and weaknesses. The third section presents industry-specific estimates for each of the three characteristics mentioned above. The concluding section looks at the relationship between industrial concentration and export concentration.

Hypotheses on increasing returns, market structure and trade

The theoretical alternatives to an H–O world are many. In principle, there can be as many models of specialization and trade as there are models of imperfect competition. Faced with this multitude of alternatives, Dixit and Norman concluded that 'to arrive at a general theory of trade with imperfect competition is . . . impossible; the most one can hope for is a catalogue of special models' (1980, p. 265). The common features of these special models include production with increasing returns, various types of market structure, and product differentiation.

Recognition of the importance of increasing returns to scale for international trade long precedes the new models of trade. Adam Smith's familiar dictum that the division of labour is limited by the extent of the market points to the potential gains from trade which can be associated with scale economies. Smith's observation was extended by Ohlin (1933) and Drèze (1960), who noted that economies of scale may influence the pattern of trade. Other things being equal, industries that can benefit from scale economies will tend to have lower autarky prices in countries with large markets than in countries with small ones.

These ideas have been carried still further by economists who constructed formal models which relate economies of scale to imperfect competition (e.g. Negishi, 1972, or Dixit and Norman, 1980). Their work has led to more explicit statements regarding trade under increasing returns. Krugman (1980), for example, has put forward a 'larger domestic market hypothesis'. He suggests that a country will tend to be a net exporter of products that have relatively large domestic markets. Large countries are expected to have a competitive advantage in industries where scale economies are prominent. Conversely, countries with small domestic markets are at a disadvantage unless they produce standardized goods and then realize scale economies by exporting.

The relationship between scale economies and trade assumes other characteristics when attention focuses on the individual firm. There is empirical evidence to indicate that, on average, large firms tend to export a greater portion of their output than small firms and that the percentage of exporters in the industry tends to rise as firm size increases (e.g. Gleijser, Jacquemin and Petit, 1980; Auquier, 1980). This finding is often regarded as a confirmation that the export efficiency of large firms derives from cost advantages obtained through their involvement in international markets. Such evidence is used to justify the government's support for large firms or to show the benefits of mergers among directly competing firms.

The degree of industrial concentration will also affect the export capabilities of firms. Large firms operating in a highly concentrated domestic market will have considerable market power. The degree of market power will depend not only on the number of firms in the domestic market but also on the industry's size distribution. Firms with domestic market power enjoy several advantages over their weaker domestic rivals. They may engage in price discrimination because they are better able to segment domestic and international markets than are small firms operating in a highly competitive domestic market. They will also have better access to the sources of credit which are needed to finance export operations. These are only some of the reasons to expect industrial concentration to influence an industry's export performance.

However, the line of causation does not run in only one direction – from industrial concentration to export performance. The extent to which firms depend on exports will also affect the pattern of industrial concentration. For example, as an industry becomes more dependent on exports, the number of firms competing – not only in the domestic market but also in export markets – will rise. Trade ultimately will lead to a larger equilibrium number of firms and to greater competition (Dixit and Norman, 1980, pp. 267–72), and both characteristics imply a reduction of industrial concentration.

Observations such as these apply to markets where entry is relatively easy. But an industry may consist of only a few firms characterized by entry regulations, large investment to achieve minimum efficient scale (MES), or other entry-limiting practices. If factor supplies and production functions are otherwise comparable, increasing returns to scale in such industries can mean that higher concentration is associated with a greater comparative advantage (Das, 1982).[1]

Aside from scale economies and market structure, the possibility of product differentiation is relevant. The new theories of trade usually deal with products that are horizontally differentiated in terms of actual or perceived characteristics and assume a market structure of monopolistic competition. Each firm will produce one version of a differentiated product (with increasing returns) and face a downward-sloping demand curve. The firm may have some degree of market power, although this is limited by the existence of imperfect substitutes – real or potential. Entry usually depends not on the imitation of an existing product but on the development of a new product variant. Firms compete, then, not just on the basis of price but also in terms of consumer preferences[2] – that is, with regard to design, quality, presentation, and other features that make their products distinguishable from those of rivals.

Concepts and measurement

The literature on industrial organization suggests a number of possible measures for economies of scale, market concentration and product differentiation. Most international data, however, are ill-suited for such purposes. The statistics are based on industry definitions which are stated in very broad terms (for example, the three-digit level of the ISIC). This characteristic is hardly compatible with the models which assume that products are either homogeneous or highly substitutable. A related problem is that the researcher is often forced to work with product classes that represent different types of production processes, multiple stages of production, and a variety of inputs. A third troublesome characteristic is that indicators based on a broad definition of an industry are sensitive to the composition of products and activities in a particular country. As a result, the empirical evidence considered here is subject to many qualifications. The results are still useful so long as systematic differences in the indicators for various industries can be identified with reasonable statistical certainty.

Economies of scale

Increased specialization is the source of economies of scale within a plant or firm. The larger the firm, the greater are the opportunities to achieve worker specialization or to utilize productive, special-purpose machinery to its maximum potential. Long production runs and mass production techniques are therefore common methods of reducing unit costs. In industries where fixed costs are a large portion of the total, the unit costs of batch production will be high. Long production runs will yield even greater reductions in unit costs if the variable cost component is not especially sensitive to an increase in the firm's output (that is, if there is a substantial degree of competition in markets for labour and other inputs).

The fact that a firm's production function does not exhibit constant returns to scale throughout is usually depicted by the familiar U-shaped average cost curve. The curve implies that economies of scale will eventually be contained by diminishing returns, since the opportunity to realize additional reductions in unit costs will eventually be exhausted. In a perfectly competitive market, firms operating on such cost curves will expand output until marginal costs rise to the point where they equal marginal revenue. The outcome is different, however, if marginal costs carry on falling as output is increased. It then makes sense for the firm to expand output indefinitely. The only check on the firm's growth would be the size of the market. In these circumstances, a rational firm would raise output until it was the only producer in the industry.

At least two features of the U-shaped average cost curve seem to conflict with reality. First, empirical estimates of long-run average cost curves generally suggest that many cost curves are L-shaped rather than U-shaped (Schmalensee, 1988, p. 653). Average costs will fall as small producers raise output but will remain approximately constant for levels of output above some MES. Second, the theoretical concept of single-product firms fits awkwardly with the reality of product differentiation and multiple-product plants. These circumstances give rise to another concept, that of economies of scope. If scale economies are realized in the provision of inputs used in more than one product, economies of scope are possible. More generally, the cost function of a multiple-product firm appears to be sensitive to the composition as well as the scale of output (Bailey and Friedlander, 1982, p. 1032).

Neither the shape of the cost curve nor the prevalence of multi-product firms can be separated from underlying patterns of technological development. Indeed, the types of technologies developed during the past two decades may have had the result (intended or otherwise) of enlarging the range of output for which increasing returns are applicable or at least postponing the onset of diminishing returns. Some support for this impression can be found in both industry-specific studies (e.g. McGee, 1973; Ayler, 1981) and more general investigations (Griliches and Ringstad, 1971). Certainly, improvements in information technology are intended to remove many of the managerial diseconomies of scale associated with communications and control in large organizations. It is these types of diseconomies that were traditionally thought to be the main cause of diminishing returns at higher levels of output.

A clear picture of the relationships between cost curves and concepts such as economies of scale, economies of scope and technological change cannot be assembled. However, there seem to be grounds to make the (comparatively weak) assertion that the incidence of decreasing returns within the manufacturing sector has been reduced. As a result, the economies-of-scale model poses a serious challenge to the assumption of non-increasing returns which is so firmly embedded in the H-0 theory. Such a possibility makes it important to obtain some impression about cross-country patterns of scale economies, however crudely derived.

The extent of scale economies can be measured by various methods. Estimates of the MES may be obtained by interviewing engineers or executives, by studying the variation of costs with scale, by relating profitability to the size of plants or firms, or by assuming that some fraction of an industry's output is produced in efficient plants in a given country. Answers given in interviews may be speculative when the information required goes beyond design decisions, while evidence gathered from real data is subject to competitive conditions and historical circumstances. All these problems are magnified in the case of a cross-country study.

Following Hufbauer (1970, pp. 178–9), the present study uses size elasticities of output per person engaged as a proxy for scale economies. Once firms are classified by size, variations in value added per person engaged are regarded as an inverse measure of variations in average unit costs (Caves, Khalizadeh-Shirazi and Porter, 1975, p. 133). Estimates of these elasticities are obtained from the following regression equation:

141

$$v_i = kn_i^a$$

where v_i is value added per person engaged in a given size class i, n_i is the average number of persons engaged per establishment in size class i, k is a constant, and a is the size elasticity parameter for the industry which is assumed to be constant.

Estimates of size elasticity are subject to certain biases. The products and production technologies associated with a given 'industry' category will inevitably vary. Large establishments will tend to have relatively capital-intensive and/or skill-intensive methods of production, while small establishments rely more heavily on inputs of unskilled labour. The distinction will distort industry-wide estimates of size elasticity, exaggerating the significance of scale economies among large firms but underestimating their role for small firms. A related difficulty is that establishments classified as members of a given industry will differ with regard to age, product mix, quality of labour and other factors, all of which may be associated with firm size. The assumption that size elasticity is constant for a given industry can also be violated. For example, because market power is often related to establishment size, estimates of the parameter may reflect an element of monopoly profit. Considerations such as these obviously call for cautious treatment of the results.

Industrial concentration

Industrial concentration refers to the number and size distribution of firms supplying a particular product or a group of highly substitutable products. Concentration may be related to both the market power and growth performance of firms in an industry and is often treated as an indicator of the former.

Most industries are neither perfectly competitive nor monopolies and the distribution of firm size is frequently skewed. Typically, the number of establishments falls off abruptly for the larger size categories (that is, the distribution is log-normal with respect to firm size). This result contradicts the natural expectation that firms would be clustered around an optimal size or that a majority would operate at or above the industry MES owing to competitive forces. Such expectations might be confirmed only if the investigation is narrow in scope (e.g. at the level of products rather than an industry). So long as the focus of discussion is industry-wide, factors other than scale are important and a log-normal distribution is not surprising. Numerous firms, for example, may have secured a market niche through the production of high quality products – a strategy that would allow them to operate with small plants although at relatively high costs (Müller and Owen, 1985, p. 45). Whatever the industry's actual distribution of firm size, this feature, along with the number of firms in the industry, provides a means of determining industrial concentration.

There are various country-specific factors (the size of domestic and foreign markets, the level of industrialization and government policies) which may influence concentration. In addition to these, the growth of an industry will itself alter concentration patterns over time. Over the medium term, rapid

142

growth may reduce concentration if large firms are unable to take advantage of all opportunities for expansion. Rapid growth will also induce new entry, particularly in industries producing differentiated products. Finally, in the long run, changes in production technologies emerge as a determinant of concentration (Curry and George, 1983, pp. 217–27).

A measure of industrial concentration is therefore a summary statistic which would take into account both the number of firms and the inequalities in the firm distribution of market shares. When the number of firms is small and inequality in market shares is large, the market power exerted by a group of firms is great and the concentration measure would be large. Several alternative measures of concentration can be constructed from these facts. Differences between the measures result mainly from the choice of relative weights assigned to the two variables.[3] All measures nevertheless display similar patterns, which means that a choice can usually be made dependent on data availability. The current study makes use of employment statistics for establishments rather than firms or enterprises. This decision, which was due to data limitations, has some potential drawbacks.[4] Establishment data, for example, may best capture the effects of scale economies at the plant level. Alternative measures based on data for firms or enterprises will include multiple plants producing different products with different technologies.

The actual expression used here is the employment entropy measure.[5] Computation requires information on the total number of establishments and the number of persons engaged by size class. The expression, which indicates the shape of the frequency distribution of establishments by size, is an inverse measure of relative concentration. Each establishment's share in the industry's total employment is weighted by the logarithm of its reciprocal. In its simplest form, the entropy measure (E) is defined as

$$E = \sum_{i=1}^{n} x_i \ln \frac{1}{x_i} = - \sum_{i=1}^{n} x_i \ln x_i$$

where x_i is the share of establishment i in the industry's total number of persons engaged and n is the number of establishments in the industry. The higher the value of E, the lower the degree of concentration. The measure takes its maximum value ($\ln n$) when the shares of all establishments are equal, and it is zero when there is only one establishment in the industry.

With the help of size distribution data, the measure for each industry can be decomposed into two additive components representing between–group and within–group entropy. In its decomposed form, the measure is defined as:

$$E = - \sum_{j=1}^{m} s_j \ln s_j + \sum_{j=1}^{m} s_j E_j$$

where s_j is the share of size class j in the industry's total number of persons engaged, m is the number of size classes, and E_j is the entropy of size class

143

j. The first term represents between-class entropy, while the second refers to within-class entropy.[6]

Several remarks should be made with respect to the measurement of concentration. First, industries and markets are often defined differently. Industries are described in terms of their production processes or raw material requirements. Markets, however, are usually identified from the standpoint of the consumer, meaning that they consist of goods that are close substitutes in consumption. For example, metal products and plastic items may compete in the same market although they are supplied by different industries. It follows that industry data are not the preferred source of information to assess or interpret market characteristics. They are used because no other form of information is readily available. Second, because entropy typically refers to domestic production and ignores imports, evidence of concentration can be misleading. Accordingly, the measure employed here is regarded as an indicator of industrial concentration rather than market concentration. Third, measures of concentration are sensitive to the level of industry aggregation. Estimates derived from highly aggregated data will have a downward bias as they incorporate not only the effects of economies of scale and entry barriers but also the degree of product diversification. Finally, establishments may be separated according to regional rather than national markets. The degree of competition between geographically scattered establishments is sometimes modest, and the market power of these establishments could be large.

Product differentiation

Many (but not all) manufactured products become differentiated over time. Because of its nature, product differentiation is generally greater among consumer goods than among either capital goods or intermediate goods. Ready-to-eat food products, consumer electrical equipment, cosmetics and passenger cars are just a few examples of highly differentiated products. Such products are no longer perfect substitutes in consumption, although producers compete among themselves in the same market.

In order to compete on characteristics other than price, firms will try to differentiate their products in terms of design, quality and presentation. These efforts serve to lower the price elasticity of demand, to shift demand curves to the right, and to increase the firm's market share. With a greater degree of differentiation, rival products become poorer substitutes and the price elasticity of demand for a given product is reduced. Thus, product differentiation represents a departure from perfect competition (see e.g. Sherman, 1974, pp. 227–9; Howe, 1978, pp. 57–9; and Caves and Williamson, 1985).

It is customary to distinguish between horizontal, vertical and technological forms of differentiation. Horizontal differentiation refers to a combination of 'core' attributes found in all products within a given group. A particular product variety is determined by the way in which these attributes are combined. Vertical differentiation reflects differences in quality and

144

can usually be attributed to absolute differences between the core attributes of product varieties. Finally, technological differentiation is the result of innovation. Products in a given group have distinct technical attributes or are produced by technologically different processes to combine attributes. Technological differentiation leads to product improvements across the entire quality range.

Product differentiation is easy to observe but difficult to measure. In theoretical terms, elasticities of substitution with respect to prices reveal the extent of product differentiation in a specific market. In practice, the multitude of markets and product varieties to be considered demands a much simpler approach. The current study makes use of data on the unit values of exports (stated at f.o.b. prices) as a proxy for the extent of product differentiation. With the assumption that unit values of non-differentiated exports are similar, coefficients of variation are calculated across export destinations.[7] The nature of this approach means that it focuses mainly on the extent of vertical product differentiation. The resultant measure depends largely on the number of export destinations and absolute differences in the unit values. Because market power and discriminatory export practices may influence the variation in unit values, the measure's use as an indicator of product differentiation may involve some distortion.

International comparisons between industries

The measures described above are employed to gain some impression of the extent to which industries deviate from the H–O assumptions of constant returns, perfect competition and product homogeneity. Attention focuses on inter-industry comparisons, as these can help to identify those industries for which a particular assumption may be especially inappropriate.

Industries' size elasticities

Evidence for scale economies is presented in the form of size elasticities of value added per person. These were calculated for 24 industries in selected DMEs and developing countries. The results, which relate to information for years around 1985, are shown in Table 8.1.

Industries with relatively large size elasticities in both country groups are non-industrial chemicals, petroleum and coal products, and glass. Those with consistently low elasticities include textiles, wearing apparel, and rubber products. In many cases, however, the relative values of the elasticity estimates differed between the two groups of countries. Electrical machinery proved to have a high elasticity in DMEs though not in developing countries, while the reverse was true for non-metallic minerals and basic metals. Footwear, plastics and non-metallic minerals reported relatively

145

Table 8.1 Size elasticities[a] and industry rankings for years around 1985

Industry (ISIC code)	Developed market economies			Developing countries and areas			All countries		
	Number of countries	Average size elasticity[b]	Industry ranking	Number of countries	Average size elasticity[b]	Industry ranking	Number of countries	Average size elasticity[b]	Industry ranking
Food products (311/2)	6	0.089	14	11	0.144	15	17	0.101	17
Beverages and tobacco (313/4)	4	0.137	6	11	0.391	3	15	0.322	1
Textiles (321)	6	0.031	24	12	0.097	22	18	0.059	24
Wearing apparel (322)	6	0.077	18	10	0.139	17	16	0.091	22
Leather and fur products (323)	5	0.085	15	11	0.157	13	16	0.126	8
Footwear (324)	5	0.056	23	9	0.212	8	14	0.111	13
Wood and cork products (331)	6	0.120	8	11	0.097	23	17	0.116	10
Furniture, excl. metal (332)	6	0.085	16	12	0.198	10	18	0.103	16
Pulp and paper (341)	7	0.157	3	12	0.279	5	19	0.172	4
Printing and publishing (342)	6	0.126	7	12	0.123	19	18	0.125	9
Industrial chemicals (351)	3	0.076	19	8	0.219	7	11	0.112	12
Other chemicals (352)	4	0.139	5	8	0.205	9	12	0.160	5
Petroleum and coal products (353/4)	6	0.234	1	6	0.409	1	12	0.255	2
Rubber products (355)	6	0.071	21	12	0.100	21	18	0.083	23
Plastic products (356)	5	0.070	22	11	0.176	12	16	0.098	19
Pottery, china, earthenware (361)	4	0.103	10	6	0.151	14	10	0.111	14
Glass (362)	5	0.191	2	5	0.392	2	10	0.226	3
Other non-metal. min. products (369)	5	0.072	20	9	0.391	4	14	0.133	7

Table 8.1 continued

Industry (ISIC code)	Developed market economies			Developing countries and areas			All countries		
	Number of countries	Average size elasticity[b]	Industry ranking	Number of countries	Average size elasticity[b]	Industry ranking	Number of countries	Average size elasticity[b]	Industry ranking
Basic metals (371/2)	7	0.084	17	11	0.233	6	18	0.110	15
Metal products (381)	6	0.095	12	11	0.141	16	17	0.100	18
Non-electrical machinery (382)	7	0.091	13	12	0.119	20	19	0.094	21
Electrical machinery (383)	7	0.155	4	12	0.180	11	19	0.158	6
Transport equipment (384)	7	0.111	9	11	0.129	18	18	0.112	11
Prof. and scient. equipment (385)	7	0.100	11	9	0.079	24	16	0.097	20

Source: UNIDO

a/ Estimates of size elasticities were obtained on the basis of the regression equation

$$v_i = k \, n_i^a$$

where v_i is value added per person engaged for establishment size class i, n_i is the corresponding average number of persons engaged, k is a constant and a is the size elasticity which is assumed to be constant.

b/ Individual countries' data were weighted by the number of persons engaged in the industry in question.

low elasticities in the DMEs but comparatively high values in developing countries.

In general, size elasticities tend to be significantly higher in developing countries than in DMEs. This contrast reflects the greater disparities between small and large establishments in the former countries. Scale economies could be one reason for the marked difference between large and small establishments in the two country groups. Another is that larger establishments in developing countries tend to have more highly protected markets. In comparison with their smaller competitors, they are able to generate relatively greater monopoly profits. Large firms operating in DMEs may not receive the same, relatively generous, levels of protection.

Indirect evidence on entry barriers

Scale economies are often regarded as a natural barrier to entry. But there are artificial entry barriers as well, some of which have already been mentioned. A rough impression of the effects of entry barriers can be obtained by considering the increase in the number of firms/establishments in an industry in relation to its growth of output. Increases in output can be attributed to the expansion of existing establishments and/or new entrants, while the relative contribution to growth from either source will be subject to the effectiveness of entry barriers. A low ratio would imply that entry barriers are restrictive. Slow growth in the number of establishments relative to growth of output can also reflect an increase in the average value added per establishment. In either case, industries experiencing this type of growth pattern are expected to be relatively concentrated.

In order to examine inter-industry differences, the relationship between growth of output and growth in the number of establishments was estimated for 24 industries during the period 1977–82. The results are reported in Table 8.2 for 15 DMEs and 18 developing countries. In the developing countries, the industries with the highest entry barriers are relatively intensive users of physical capital and/or they depend on scale economies. They include: food processing, beverages and tobacco, petroleum and coal products, and basic metals.

A somewhat different picture emerges in the DMEs. Stagnating growth is a major entry barrier, particularly for industries that are resource-based or labour-intensive. In many of these industries the number of establishments did not decrease in proportion to production cuts. And in some cases the number of establishments actually rose, implying a fall in output per establishment. Such trends suggest the emergence of excess capacity in some firms along with the rationalization of existing capacity in others. The DMEs reported a decline in the number of establishments in 11 of the 24 industries shown in Table 8.2. In four of these industries – furniture, pulp and paper, non-industrial chemicals, and glass – an increase in output was associated with the fall in number of establishments. Apart from the possible effects of the slow market

Table 8.2 Growth of the number of establishments and production, by industry, selected countries,[a] 1977–82

Industry (ISIC code)	Selected developed market economies			Selected developing countries and areas		
	Growth of the number of establishments[b]	Growth of production[c]	Growth of the number of establishments relative to production growth[d]	Growth of the number of establishments[b]	Growth of production[c]	Growth of the number of establishments relative to production growth[d]
Food products (311/2)	1.370	1.100	1.246	1.072	1.478	0.726
Beverages and tobacco (313/4)	1.169	1.097	1.066	1.055	1.406	0.750
Textiles (321)	0.925	0.940	0.984	1.119	1.066	1.049
Wearing apparel (322)	0.936	0.861	1.086	1.002	1.140	0.879
Leather and fur products (323)	0.776	0.895	0.867	1.209	1.191	1.016
Footwear (324)	0.825	0.948	0.870	1.212	1.075	1.127
Wood and cork products (331)	1.381	0.871	1.586	1.068	1.117	0.956
Furniture, excl. metal (332)	0.670	1.020	0.657	1.176	1.057	1.112
Pulp and paper (341)	0.936	1.089	0.859	1.276	1.288	0.991
Printing and publishing (342)	1.043	1.105	0.943	1.182	1.332	0.888
Industrial chemicals (351)	0.966	0.983	0.982	1.225	1.352	0.906
Other chemicals (352)	0.935	1.107	0.845	1.179	1.340	0.880
Petroleum and coal products (353/4)	1.062	0.865	1.227	1.024	1.395	0.735
Rubber products (355)	1.031	0.873	1.181	1.373	1.411	0.973
Plastic products (356)	1.110	1.130	0.983	1.391	1.281	1.085
Pottery, china and earthenware (361)	0.631	0.882	0.716	1.107	1.196	0.925
Glass (362)	0.932	1.002	0.930	1.258	1.377	0.914
Other non-metallic mineral products (369)	0.995	0.905	1.100	1.238	1.343	0.921
Basic metals (371/2)	1.113	0.799	1.393	1.177	1.355	0.869

Table 8.2 continued

Industry (ISIC code)	Selected developed market economies			Selected developing countries and areas		
	Growth of the number of establishments[b]	Growth of production[c]	Growth of the number of establishments relative to production growth[d]	Growth of the number of establishments[b]	Growth of production[c]	Growth of the number of establishments relative to production growth[d]
Metal products, excl. machinery (381)	1.148	0.928	1.238	1.214	1.431	0.848
Non-electrical machinery (382)	1.052	1.024	1.028	1.332	1.417	0.940
Electrical machinery (383)	1.125	1.107	1.017	1.500	1.328	1.130
Transport equipment (384)	1.011	0.957	1.056	1.248	1.235	1.011
Professional and scientific equipment (385)	1.033	1.016	1.017	1.820	1.911	0.952

Source: UNIDO

a/ The countries included are as follows: 14 DMEs - Australia, Austria, Belgium, Denmark, Finland, Federal Republic of Germany, Iceland, Ireland, Italy, Norway, Spain, Sweden, United Kingdom and the United States; and 18 developing countries - Chile, Colombia, Cyprus, Ethiopia, Ghana, Haiti, Hong Kong, India, Indonesia, Kenya, Malta, Peru, the Philippines, Republic of Korea, Singapore, Turkey, Venezuela and Yugoslavia. However, the number of countries included differs slightly from industry to industry.

b/ In symbols,

$$gE = \sum_{j=1}^{n} E82_j \bigg/ \sum_{j=1}^{n} E77_j$$

where $E82_j$ and $E77_j$ are, respectively, the number of establishments in 1982 and in 1977 in country j, and n is the number of countries included.

c/ In symbols,

$$gV = \sum_{j=1}^{n} V82_j \bigg/ \sum_{j=1}^{n} V77_j$$

where V82 and V77 are, respectively, value added in constant 1980 United States dollars in 1982 and in 1977.

d/ In symbols, gE/gV.

growth, these shifts can be attributed to entry barriers such as heavy initial capital requirements and economies of scale.

Industrial concentration

Barriers to entry affect the degree of industrial concentration. The latter can be measured by the employment entropy index. Indices of this type were calculated for the individual industries in all DMEs and developing countries for which data were available. The results, which are given in Table 8.3, reveal a more consistent pattern for concentration than was found for size elasticities. The weighted averages show that the most highly concentrated industries are beverages and tobacco, footwear, industrial chemicals, petroleum and coal, rubber, and glass. Those that are not highly concentrated include food products, wearing apparel, wood, printing and publishing, metal products, and non-electrical machinery.

When industries are ranked by industrial concentration, the coefficients of concordance between DMEs, between developing countries and for the total sample were 0.850, 0.722 and 0.753, respectively. In other words, industries that are highly concentrated in one country tend to be highly concentrated in others, although absolute degrees of concentration differ.[8] The relationship between industrial concentration and size elasticities is also of interest. Correlation coefficients between the two indicators were positive but weak. The rank correlation for DMEs was statistically insignificant, while that for developing countries was significant at the 5 per cent level. This result may indicate that economies of scale are a somewhat more significant entry barrier in developing countries than in the DMEs.

Another distinctive feature of Table 8.3 is that industries in DMEs are less concentrated than those in developing countries. This result may be due partly to systematic differences in the market size of the two country groups. Industrial concentration, for example, may be less pronounced in large countries than in small ones owing to the interaction between economies of scale and the size of the domestic market. A simple cross–country regression analysis was conducted to determine the effects on industrial concentration of the level of industrial development and country size. The following equation was used for the test:

$$- \ln E_{ij} = a_i + b_i \ln V_j + c_i \ln N_j + u_{ij}$$

where i stands for an industry, j for a country, E is the employment entropy index, V is per capita MVA (a proxy of the level of industrial development), N is population (country size), and u is the disturbance term.

Regression results are summarized in Table 8.4. The two explanatory variables have a strong negative effect on industrial concentration. They also explain more than half of the variation in the entropy index for all industries other than footwear and petroleum and coal products. High absolute values of elasticities of industrial concentration with respect to both independent

Table 8.3 International comparison of employment entropy indices[a] in manufacturing industries, around 1985

Industry (ISIC code)	Developed market economies			Developing countries/areas			All countries		
	Number of countries	Average entropy index	Industry ranking	Number of countries	Average entropy index	Industry ranking	Number of countries	Average entropy index	Industry ranking
Food products (311/2)	9	8.16	22	10	6.00	21	19	7.87	22
Beverages and tobacco (313/4)	7	5.44	7	10	4.38	9	17	4.90	4
Textiles (321)	8	7.58	18	10	6.19	23	18	7.14	17
Wearing apparel (322)	8	8.57	24	10	6.96	24	18	8.21	24
Leather and fur products (323)	8	5.59	10	10	4.74	10	18	5.33	9
Footwear (324)	8	5.38	6	10	3.97	4	18	4.96	5
Wood and cork products (331)	8	8.13	21	10	5.16	15	18	7.86	21
Furniture, excl. metal (332)	8	7.48	17	10	4.92	12	18	7.28	18
Pulp and paper (341)	9	6.84	13	10	4.96	13	19	6.72	13
Printing and publishing (342)	9	7.84	20	10	5.29	16	19	7.66	20
Industrial chemicals (351)	7	5.20	5	9	4.21	8	16	5.03	6
Other chemicals (352)	9	5.82	11	9	4.80	11	16	5.55	11
Petroleum and coal products (353/4)	9	4.55	2	8	3.22	2	17	4.41	2
Rubber products (355)	8	4.67	3	10	4.06	6	18	4.45	3
Plastic products (356)	8	7.24	15	10	6.02	22	18	6.97	15
Pottery, china, earthenware (361)	7	5.48	8	8	3.20	3	15	5.23	8
Glass (362)	7	4.41	1	8	3.53	1	15	4.25	1
Other non-metal. min. products (369)	7	7.32	16	9	5.60	17	16	6.98	16
Basic metals (371/2)	9	5.55	9	10	4.14	7	19	5.47	10
Metal products (381)	9	8.20	23	10	5.97	20	19	8.02	23
Non-electrical machinery (382)	9	7.61	19	10	5.65	19	19	7.54	19
Electrical machinery (383)	9	6.87	14	10	5.62	18	19	6.77	14
Transport equipment (384)	9	5.12	4	10	4.05	5	19	5.06	7
Prof. and scient. equipment (385)	9	6.30	12	10	5.07	14	19	6.22	12

Source: UNIDO

a/ Industry averages for country groups were obtained by weighting values by the number of persons engaged in each country in the particular industry. Details of the computational procedure are given in the text.

Table 8.4 Relationship between industrial concentration, the level of industrial development and country size,[a] by industry, around 1985

Industry (ISIC)	Estimated regression coefficient[b] of:		Number of countries in the sample	Adjusted R^2
	ln V	ln N		
Food products (311/2)	−0.1384	−0.1473	42	0.841
Beverages and tobacco (313/4)	−0.1565	−0.1733	43	0.605
Textiles (321)	−0.2016	−0.1943	42	0.706
Wearing apparel (322)	−0.2173	−0.0889	41	0.653
Leather and fur products (323)	−0.2453	−0.2223	40	0.715
Footwear (324)	−0.3159	−0.1647	38	0.481
Wood and cork products (331)	−0.2358	−0.2510	42	0.577
Furniture, excl. metal (332)	−0.1613	−0.1121	41	0.664
Pulp and paper (341)	−0.2833	−0.2233	45	0.765
Printing and publishing (342)	−0.1713	−0.1747	44	0.822
Industrial chemicals (351)	−0.2718	−0.3215	35	0.663
Other chemicals (352)	−0.1520	−0.1708	34	0.730
Petroleum and coal products (353/4)	−0.2058	−0.2363	25	0.222
Rubber products (355)	−0.1987	−0.1878	42	0.566
Plastic products (356)	−0.2550	−0.1661	42	0.774
Pottery, china, earthenware (361)	−0.1474	−0.3027	24	0.542
Glass (362)	−0.3110	−0.3122	29	0.665
Other non−metal. min. products (369)	−0.1813	−0.1493	36	0.758
Basic metals (371/2)	−0.2558	−0.2393	41	0.649
Metal products (381)	−0.1832	−0.1572	44	0.839
Non−electrical machinery (382)	−0.1968	−0.2091	43	0.703
Electrical machinery (383)	−0.2842	−0.1814	45	0.664
Transport equipment (384)	−0.1430	−0.1912	44	0.517
Prof. and scient. equipment (385)	−0.3246	−0.3294	33	0.645

Source: UNIDO

a/ The regression equation used here is

$$-\ln E_{ij} = a_i + b_i \ln V_j + c_i \ln N_j + u_{ij}$$

where i stands for an industry, j for a country, E is the employment entropy index, V is per capita MVA, N is population and u is the disturbance term.

b/ All coefficients were statistically significant at the ten per cent level. Out of the 48 estimates 44 were significantly different from zero even at the one per cent level.

variables are observed for industrial chemicals, glass, and professional and scientific equipment. Industries where concentration can be explained mainly on the basis of the level of industrial development include wearing apparel, footwear, pulp and paper, plastic and electrical machinery. Country size was the more important explanatory variable for industrial concentration of wood and pottery, china and earthenware.

The relationship between concentration and the level of industrial development may depend on the fact that skill and technology requirements sometimes act as a barrier to entry. In the case of country size, an analogous role would be played by economies of scale. The assumptions underlying these interpretations are that skill and technology requirements act as an important barrier in developing countries, whereas a domestic market of limited size has a similar effect in small countries.[9]

US industry characteristics

The empirical evidence assembled here is based on very broad definitions of industries. This fact obscures much of the effects of product differentiation. It also results in substantial variation in the cross-industry estimates for scale economies and industrial concentration. Ideally, the boundaries of each industry would be determined in such a way that all varieties would be produced with similar technologies and products were close substitutes. The first stipulation would permit a more accurate assessment of scale economies, while the second would yield greater precision in the determination of patterns of industrial concentration.

Although any single-country assessment has obvious drawbacks, this approach is necessary if precise industry definitions are to be obtained. The similarity in rankings for concentration and (to a lesser extent) scale economies which were obtained from the cross-country analysis described above provides a partial justification of this approach. The following paragraphs are based on an analysis of detailed industry data for the USA. This data source offers several technical advantages such as a good coverage of establishments, ample detail, and consistency between size categories as well as a minimum of data suppression.

Information on 439 US industries provided the basis for estimates of size elasticities (economies of scale), employment entropy indices (industrial concentration) and total capital intensity. A proxy for product differentiation was derived from coefficients of variation in unit values of US exports.[10]

The results are summarized in Table 8.5, which shows rank correlation coefficients between pairs of industry measures. The positive association of industrial concentration with both scale economies and capital intensity is the major finding of the exercise. This result provides additional empirical support for the view that increasing returns and high (initial) capital requirements can be effective entry barriers and important determinants of market structure. By contrast, the association between product differentiation and other industry characteristics is weak. This may be due partly to the fact that the measure used here is most appropriately interpreted as an indicator of vertical differentiation, although horizontal differentiation is thought to be more common. Vertical differentiation may nevertheless have a role to play, and this possibility is explored in the following chapter.

Export concentration and industrial concentration

The foregoing discussion was concerned with particular features of the scale economies model. The relevance of some of these features for patterns of

Table 8.5 Rank correlations between industry characteristics[a]

	Spearman correlation coefficients[b]		
	Total capital[c] intensity	Industrial[d] concentration	Product[e] differentiation
Economies of scale[f]	0.410*	0.219**	−0.182***
Total capital intensity		0.325*	0.012
Industrial concentration			0.052

Sources: UNIDO and United States, Bureau of the Census (1984)

a/ Correlations are based on United States data for 1982, aggregated into SITC three-digit groups.

b/ Asterisks denote statistical significance at the 1(*), 5(**), or 10(***) per cent level.

c/ Value added per employee.

d/ Employment entropy index.

e/ Coefficient of variation of unit values of exports to different destinations.

f/ Size elasticity.

IIT will be assessed in the following chapter. The present section considers a narrow issue – the possible relationship between export concentration and industrial concentration in domestic markets.

Since large firms in oligopolistic industries often rely on foreign sales to realize economies of scale, the degree of concentration may be high in domestic and export markets. It can also be the case that major exporting countries (particularly large ones) have a substantial degree of hegemonic power in certain international markets, or that international collaboration is great and borders on cartel-like behaviour. Typically, a few existing internationally oligopolistic producers (and exporters) compete under a regime established to maintain profits, stability or other goals.[11]

There will be other industries, of course, where domestic markets are not concentrated although exporters are limited to a very few suppliers. In these industries, the major exporting countries will often dominate international markets through economies of scale which are external to the firms but internal to domestic industries. Marketing and trade operations can be the responsibility of a few large companies even though the industry is not concentrated in its domestic market. In such cases, trade assumes oligopolistic characteristics which are not observed in production (Dixit, 1984).

155

Entropy indices are used to examine the relationship between domestic industrial concentration and export concentration. Employment entropy indices based on US data for 1982 (discussed in the previous section) represent the first element in this comparison. The second is an export entropy index of the form

$$- \sum_{j=1}^{n} x_{ij} \log x_{ij}$$

where x_{ij} is the share of country j in the value of world exports of industry i and n is the total number of exporting countries. United Nations trade statistics for 91 countries and 113 industries (SITC three-digit groups) in 1983 were the data source for this measure.

The two concentration measures revealed a significantly positive correlation (a Spearman correlation coefficient of 0.381) across industries. That result seems to support Dixit's observation (1984, p. 2) that entry barriers in international markets are closely associated with economies of scale – just as in domestic markets – and that a few large multinational firms dominate both markets. A more detailed picture of the association between industrial concentration and export concentration is obtained from Table 8.6, which is based on a two-way classification of the data taken from the source described above. The industry ranking by type of concentration was first condensed into five categories where each category represents one-fifth of the entire industry distribution. Industries were also arranged by product category – Ricardian, H–O and product-cycle – using a classification scheme described in earlier chapters.

Whatever the reasons for the similarities between export and industrial concentration, the data summarized in Table 8.6[12] reveal some interesting features. Both industrial and export concentration are high in resource-based industries but low among H–O industries.[13] Export concentration was generally high among product-cycle industries, whereas the degree of industrial concentration seems to depend on the importance of R and D and the extent of plant scale economies. Some product-cycle industries (for example, aircraft, photographic and cinematographic supplies, sound recorders and reproducers) are highly concentrated in both domestic and international markets; others, such as mineral manufactures, tools for use in the hand or in machines, and wire products, are not.[14]

The results outlined here yield some support for the assertion that external economies of scale, R and D capabilities relating to product development or differentiation, and natural resource endowments are more important for successful entry in international markets than for domestic market entry. In general, neither the extent of product differentiation nor plant economies of scale can fully explain the export concentration among countries. Their effects on trade patterns depend largely on technologies and skills used in the development of products and processes, all of which are subject to external economies of scale. These elements, then, should be considered

Table 8.6 Distribution of industries,[a] by industrial concentration and by export concentration (number of industries[b])

	Export concentration[b]					Type of industry[e]		
	High	Medium high	Medium	Medium low	Low	R	H-O	PC
Industrial concentration[c]								
high	10	6	3	3	1	11	6	6
medium high	6	3	7	2	4	5	12	5
medium	4	4	3	4	8	5	12	6
medium low	2	6	6	5	3	5	10	7
low	1	3	4	8	7	4	15	4
Type of industry R	12	4	3	3	8			
H-O	4	10	14	14	13			
PC	7	8	6	5	2			

Sources: UNIDO and United States, Bureau of the Census (1984).

a/ A total of 113 industries defined as SITC three-digit categories, is covered.

b/ Each cell of the two-way classification table gives the number of industries falling in the respective categories. Each of the categories 'high', 'medium high', etc. comprises 20 per cent of the total number of industries. The detailed categorical data are shown in the statistical appendix (table B.10).

c/ Industrial concentration is measured by the employment entropy index and refers to data for the United States, 1982.

d/ Export concentration is measured by the export entropy index, which has been derived from data of 91 countries for 1983.

e/ The types of industries are designated by R (Ricardian), H-O and PC (product-cycle), where the definitions are those given in the statistical appendix.

as determinants of location of export capacities in conjunction with factor proportions and R and D intensity.

Notes: Chapter 8

1   These points refer to economies of scale that are internal to a firm or plant. But economies of scale that are external to the firm (though internal to the domestic industry) are also important. A relatively large industry may have more opportunities for within-industry specialization and easy access to public inputs. The sources of such scale economies include various types of industry-specific infrastructure (physical and institutional), industry-wide R and D activities, and accumulation of industry-wide technological information. It follows that firms in relatively large industries have more potential for cost savings than those in a smaller industry. In general, the size of the domestic industry is expected to determine the extent of external economies of scale.

2   The treatment of consumer preferences varies. In neo–Chamberlinian models (e.g. Krugman, 1979a, 1980, 1981; Dixit and Norman, 1980, pp. 281–93) consumers are assumed to demand all available varieties. All product varieties then enter the utility function symmetrically. In neo–Hotelling models (e.g. Lancaster, 1980; Helpman, 1981) consumers are assumed to demand a single variety; that is, varieties enter the utility function asymmetrically.

3   For various concentration measures and their characteristics, see e.g. Davies, 1979, and Curry and George, 1983, pp. 204–17.

4   The use of employment data may underestimate the relative importance of large establishments since these firms tend to use less labour and more capital than small establishments. However, this bias can be assumed to be insignificant since employment data are also highly correlated with other statistics such as sales or output.

5   Entropy is a concept of information theory that can be used to measure the degree of uncertainty. For a thorough review of the entropy concept and its application in economics, see Theil, 1967, ch. 8; 1971, pp. 636–46.

6   For details on the mathematical procedure of decomposition, see Jacquemin and Kumps, 1971, p. 61. In order to obtain the industry-wide estimate (E), it was necessary to calculate entropy (E_j) for each size class. The computation of E_j was based on the extreme values for entropy within size class j as suggested by Meller, 1978, pp. 46–7.

7   This approach is taken from Hufbauer, 1970, pp. 190–3. An alternative measure of product differentiation makes use of the relative amount spent on advertising. The underlying assumption for the latter proxy is that inherent product complexities/characteristics and diverse tastes of consumers require producers to provide information on their varieties in order to promote sales.

8   At the four-digit level of ISIC, rankings of the 80 industries in different large countries are also similar. Spearman rank correlation coefficients between Japan and the USA, Japan and the Republic of Korea and the Republic of Korea and the USA are 0.751, 0.779 and 0.660 respectively. These calculations were based on data provided in Ministry of International Trade and Industry, Japan, 1986; Economic Planning Board, Republic of Korea, 1987; and a magnetic tape with data of the *US Census of Manufactures 1982* provided by the US Department of Commerce, 1984.

9   It should be noted that this argument refers to domestic markets only; i.e. it does not take into account the size of export markets.

10 All four measures of industry characteristics were aggregated to the SITC three-digit level. Partial evidence at this level of detail is found in the statistical appendix, which shows categorical measures of industry characteristics.

11 Such a regime usually concerns 'stability', 'basically co-operative arrangements', and 'specific roles and norms': Cowhey and Long, 1983, p. 158. Examples are the iron and steel industry or the automobile industry.

12 Details on industry coverage of each of the five categories of industrial concentration and export concentration can be obtained from Table B10 of the statistical appendix (Appendix B).

13 Food-processing industries were one exception. These are resource-based but are close to H–O operations. H–O industries that did not fit the general pattern were either partially dependent on natural resources (construction materials, pottery, ingots of iron or steel) or characterized by large economies of scale (perfumery and cosmetics, road vehicles, finished steel products).

14 These product-cycle industries also reflect various H–O characteristics, a fact that may be related to the result.

CHAPTER 9

Intra-industry trade revisited

The role played by industry-specific characteristics is quite different in the new theories of trade from their function in the factor abundance theory. In the H–O model, industries' factor intensities provide a precise link between endowments and trade patterns. By contrast, the new theories do not build on an interaction between industry characteristics and country attributes to explain trade. Instead, the presence of some combination of industry characteristics is shown to be sufficient to establish two-way trade. Such an outcome is possible even in the case where the economic attributes of trading partners are not distinguishable in any significant way (Krugman, 1979a). More generally, the new theories assign a more important role to industry characteristics as determinants of trading patterns.

The shift in emphasis complicates empirical analyses based on the new theories. One problem is to construct measures of the variables that are thought to determine patterns of trade. A second is that certain hypotheses regarding the relationship between industry characteristics and trade cannot be readily expressed in the form of algebraic relationships. Examples are the impact of product differentiation or of increasing returns on trade. The present chapter addresses these problems. The scope of discussion, however, is limited to a set of issues where the theory is fairly precise and the empirical difficulties are manageable. Such an approach is not comprehensive but is still helpful in obtaining an impression of the extent to which economies of scale and product differentiation may affect the relative extent of IIT. The first section of the chapter presents the test results for several broad hypotheses. The second section looks at the industry-specific determinants of IIT in DMEs, while the third section focuses on the role of vertical product differentiation in two-way trade between DMEs and developing countries.

Intra-industry trade versus inter-industry trade

The tendency for analysts to focus on the share of IIT in total trade (exports plus imports) was noted in Chapter 4. The most popular measure of IIT shares was proposed by Grubel and Lloyd (1975). Though not intended for such a purpose, the Grubel-Lloyd index shows the breakdown of total trade into its inter-industry (H–O) and intra-industry (non H–O) components. By

160

indicating which of the two components dominates, the measure can be useful in identifying the types of determinants that are likely to influence trade in a specific industry.

The underlying question concerns the type of trade (inter-industry or intra-industry) that can be associated with a particular industry. One limiting case is described by the factor abundance model, which depends on assumptions that exclude the possibility of IIT. The other, represented for instance by the Krugman model, describes a world where all trade is IIT. In reality, both types of trade will co-exist, and this outcome, too, has been anticipated by several theoretical models. Rather than attempting to distinguish between inter-industry and intra-industry trade in a dichotomous manner, the following discussion focuses on the degree to which either component is present in the trade of various countries.

The methodological problem that arises in this context concerns the appropriateness of trade-overlap measures. In describing IIT as 'an untidy phenomenon', Gray (1988) called attention to an issue that is often neglected. Overlapping exports and imports within narrowly defined product categories represent the 'classical' case of two-way trade in horizontally differentiated products. However, the high level of aggregation in trade statistics, along with other statistical anomalies, means that the available data do not match the concepts of industry or product used in new trade theories. These discrepancies give rise to 'impure forms' of IIT; for example, the exchange of products at different stages of processing.

Most empiricists play down the statistical difficulties associated with the measurement of IIT and regard their measures as compatible with the theoretical concept. This pragmatic approach concedes that little can be done to reconcile the information demands of theory with the available data. Nevertheless, it is difficult to ignore the occurrence of impure forms of IIT, particularly since some of the reasons for the overlap are integral parts of non-H–O models. An eclectic approach is adopted here – one that attempts to assess the ability of various theoretical hypotheses to explain an intrinsically 'untidy' statistical phenomenon.

One such hypothesis concerns the interaction between scale economies and product differentiation. The mere fact that firms produce differentiated versions of a product with increasing returns to scale can result in two-way trade. Ideally, the analyst would wish to relate the presence or absence of scale economies or product differentiation to evidence of the presence or absence of IIT. Such a test could best be expressed as a relationship between dichotomous variables. The available evidence, however, can be stated only in terms of continuous (not dichotomous) measures. An empirically operational version of such a hypothesis would postulate that the cross-industry pattern of IIT is positively related to the extent of scale economies and the degree of product differentiation. Such a proposition – though it cannot be rigorously concluded from the underlying model – would reflect the spirit of the foregoing discussion.

A second hypothesis concerns the role of industrial concentration. Theories of IIT do not usually posit a direct link between industrial concentration and two-way trade. Product differentiation may nevertheless be related to industrial concentration in a systematic manner. Product differentiation is likely to be high in industries whose market structure approximates monopolistic competition, leading to a low degree of industrial concentration. Ample opportunities for product differentiation, on the other hand, are likely to reduce the extent of concentration. Accordingly, a measure of industrial concentration is expected to be negatively related to IIT (Greenaway and Milner, 1984).

These hypotheses were tested using data for 80 SITC three-digit categories. Measures of industry characteristics were computed from US information for 1982, while IIT shares are weighted averages for country groups drawn from a sample of 47 countries. The coefficients of linear regressions presented in Table 9.1 show how each industry characteristic impacts on IIT shares. Only a small portion of the variation in IIT shares across industries is explained by the three industry characteristics. The poor results may reflect the untidiness of IIT as well as the limited applicability of any particular theoretical account.

Given the eclectic approach that is adopted here, the individual coefficients are of more interest than the overall fit of the regression equation. Theory suggests that economies of scale are the major source of non-comparative-advantage trade. However, there is only a weak positive relationship between size elasticities and the share of IIT, and even this result seems to apply only to the DMEs. Findings of this type are common in the empirical literature. In some cases they have led researchers to recast the measure of plant scale economies as another indicator of product standardization – an extreme form of redressing unexpected results. More plausible is the suggestion that the scale economies being measured by size elasticities are not those stressed by the relevant theory. IIT may depend on economies of scale obtained from long production runs rather than a large scale of operations (Toh, 1982).

In the case of product differentiation, the weak (and mainly positive) association with IIT is not surprising. The interpretation, however, is clouded by the same types of problems that arise with the economies-of-scale variable. The measure used here represents vertical rather than horizontal forms of differentiation. Thus, it is not ideally suited to explain the 'classic' type of IIT which occurs between similar countries in a Chamberlinian setting. The expression used here may be a more appropriate indicator of H–O forms of IIT which occur when products are differentiated in terms of quality. It is this type of IIT in which developing countries are expected to engage. The positive coefficients for second-generation NIEs and for other developing countries are compatible with this interpretation, and this point is considered further in the last section of the chapter.

While Table 9.1 shows only weak support for the role of scale economies and product differentiation, the expected negative relationship between the share of IIT and industrial concentration emerges clearly from the estimates.

Table 9.1 Impact of industry characteristics on the share of IIT,[a/] by country group, 1985 (beta coefficients)

Country sample (number of countries and areas)	Independent variables[b/]			Adjusted R²	F-value
	Scale economies	Product differentiation	Industrial concentration		
A. Underlined: All industries[c/]					
All countries (47)	0.158	0.022	−0.374*	0.08	3.46**
DMEs (22)	0.152	−0.088	−0.359*	0.14	5.24*
NIEs (6)	−0.024	0.006	−0.267**	0.04	2.24***
Second-generation NIEs (9)	−0.021	0.207***	−0.130	0.21	1.45
Other developing countries (10)	0.150	0.144	−0.271**	0.04	2.11
B. Low-concentration industries[d/]					
All countries (47)	0.278	−0.030	−	0.02	1.35
DMEs (22)	0.358**	−0.003	−	0.09	2.95***

Sources: UNIDO and United States, Bureau of the Census (1984).

a/ The dependent variable in the underlying linear regressions was the unweighted average of the IIT share for each country group in 1985. Scale economies are measured by size elasticities of per person value added, product differentiation by coefficients of variation of export unit values, industry concentration by employment entropy indices. All measures of industry characteristics are as defined in the text and based on 1982 United States data.

b/ Variables have been standardized to unit variance so that parameter estimates are beta coefficents. The sign of the coefficient of the entropy index was reversed, in order to reflect the impact of concentration. Asterisks denote statistical significance at the 1(*), 5(**) and 10(***) per cent levels.

c/ Estimates of part A were obtained on the basis of data for 80 industries defined in terms of SITC three-digit groups.

d/ Estimates of part B were derived from data on those 41 industries whose employment entropy indices exceeded the arithmetic mean of all 80 industries. Results for subsets of developing countries are not shown, as they were not statistically significant.

Such a relationship appears in all five regressions of Table 9.1, with four out of five coefficients being statistically significant. The negative impact of industrial concentration on IIT is strongest for the DMEs.

As mentioned before, industrial concentration has to do with a particular feature of the underlying model of monopolistic competition. This model specifies a market structure of numerous suppliers and a low degree of industrial concentration. Industries of this type are likely candidates for two-way trade in horizontally differentiated products. A modified hypothesis which would reflect this view focuses on industries where concentration is low. In these industries, scale economies and product differentiation may exert a positive influence on IIT which is not detected when the entire sample

163

of industries is considered. The second half of Table 9.1 presents empirical evidence which provides partial support for this modified proposition. In DMEs, the two-way trade of industries with low concentration is significantly and positively influenced by the extent of economies of scale. An analogous, though weaker, effect was observed for the NIEs, while the IIT of other developing countries reveals no similar evidence.[1]

Determinants of IIT intensity in DMEs

Since the DMEs account for the bulk of two-way trade, most analyses focus on these countries. The present section adds to these studies by considering patterns of IIT in individual DMEs. In doing so, a measurement novelty is introduced. Rather than dealing with the level or share of IIT in total trade, an attempt is made to measure and analyse the intensity of IIT in various industries.

Intensity measures have become familiar tools in the study of (gross) exports and net trade. There, the term 'revealed comparative advantage' (RCA) is often used to refer to measures that require a normalization of trade flows with respect to country size and industry size. An analogous (RCA-like) approach is adopted here to derive a measure of IIT intensity which is both country and industry-specific. The resulting indicator has the following form:

$$\text{ITTI} = \frac{\min\ (X_{ij},\ M_{ij})}{(X_{mj}\ +\ M_{mj})\ (X_{iw}\ +\ M_{iw})}$$

where X is exports, M represents imports, i is an industry, j is a country, m refers to total manufactures and w stands for world totals.[2]

The present analysis differs from that of the previous section by offering an analysis of individual countries. Hence, the relative weight of each potential determinant of IIT intensity is assessed for each DME. The resulting picture of two-way trade of the DMEs supplements the (more aggregated) country-specific analysis of specialization and trade in comparative-advantage goods in Chapter 6.

To the extent that measures of the intensity of net trade can be regarded as indicators of comparative advantage, they represent the potential of a country to succeed as a net exporter of particular product groups. This interpretation must be altered somewhat in order to examine trade in non–comparative-advantage goods. However, the intensity of IIT in a given product group can be loosely regarded as an indication of the country's potential to engage in non-comparative-advantage trade. Although the determinants of IIT carry no labels as concise and informative as the classic trade determinants, they play a role similar to that of factor intensities in the study of comparative advantage.

Table 9.2 presents the results of country-specific regressions of IIT intensity on the set of potential determinants analysed in the previous section. A

Table 9.2 Determinants of IIT intensity[a] of selected DMEs, by country, 1985 (beta coefficients)

Country[b]	All industries[c] Independent variables[e]				Low-concentration industries[d] Independent variables[e]		
	Scale economies	Product differentiation	Industrial concentration	Adjusted R²	Scale economies	Product differentiation	Adjusted R²
Australia	-	-	-	-	0.494**	0.031	0.11
Austria	-0.016	-0.057	-0.341*	0.09	-	-	-
Belgium	0.009	0.022	-0.172*	0.05	-	-	-
Denmark	0.185	-0.048	-0.504*	0.21	-	-	-
Finland	0.235**	-0.096	-0.379*	0.15	0.520**	-0.028	0.09
France	-	-	-	-	0.302***	0.011	0.03
Ireland	-0.112	-0.102	-0.188***	0.04	-	-	-
Italy	-0.130	-0.215***	0.028	0.02	-	-	-
Netherlands	0.124	0.055	-0.247*	0.09	0.280***	0.132	0.03
New Zealand	0.147***	-0.049	-0.211*	0.11	0.363**	-0.031	0.13
Norway	-	-	-	0.00	0.376**	0.152	0.10
Portugal	-0.123	-0.218***	0.071	0.00	-	-	-
Sweden	0.083	-0.005	-0.290**	0.05	-	-	-
Switzerland	0.034	-0.090	-0.212*	0.20	0.278***	-0.132	0.15
United Kingdom	-	-	-	-	-	-	-
United States	0.243***	-0.125	-0.055	0.04	0.391***	-0.134	0.10

Sources: UNIDO and United States, Bureau of the Census (1984).

a/ For a definition of IIT intensity, see the text. All other measures are as defined in the text and based on 1982 United States data.

b/ Only those regressions are shown which yielded at least one significant coefficient estimate. This rule led to the exclusion of Canada, the Federal Republic of Germany, Greece, Israel, Japan and Spain.

c/ Estimates for 'all industries' were obtained on the basis of data for 80 SITC three-digit groups.

d/ Estimates for 'low-concentration industries' were derived from data for those 41 industries whose entropy indices exceeded the arithmetic mean of all 80 industries.

e/ Variables have been standardized to unit variance so that parameter estimates are beta coefficients. The sign of the coefficient of the employment entropy index was reversed, in order to reflect the impact of concentration. Asterisks denote statistical significance at the 1(*), 5(**) and 10(***) per cent levels.

remarkable variation in the strength of the impact of the various industry characteristics on IIT intensity is observed. In particular, for six out of the 22 DME countries considered here (Canada, the Federal Republic of Germany, Greece, Israel, Japan and Spain) the independent variables had no significant impact on competitiveness in non-comparative-advantage forms of trade.

On the whole, the results in Table 9.2 corroborate and extend those of Table 9.1. Like the earlier regressions, the present ones clearly bear out the hypothesis of a negative impact of industrial concentration on IIT. This impact was most evident among the smaller DMEs. A possible explanation for the distinction between large and small DMEs can be based on the argument that a large home market offers more opportunities to increase product variety. A large country could be expected to have a greater demand for imports of differentiated products because of its extended preference diversity. And the high potential for IIT may be spread more evenly across the entire range of manufactures than is true for a small country, where competitiveness in IIT appears to depend more strongly on the type of industry.

A significantly positive coefficient for scale economies was frequently obtained and usually associated with low-concentration industries. Even in those countries (Finland, New Zealand and the USA) where statistical significance of the scale-economies coefficient applied to all industries, the strongest results applied to the restricted sample of low-concentration industries. Moreover, the prominence of scale economies in low-concentration industries was not confined to the smaller DMEs but can be observed for France, the UK and the USA.

In summary, there is empirical evidence that the intensity of two-way trade of DMEs is subject to the types of determinants employed in a model of IIT under monopolistic competition. The degree of international competitiveness in two-way trade – particularly in small DMEs – appears to be greatest in industries where concentration is low and the scope for product differentiation is high. The degree of competitiveness in the two-way trade of these industries is often positively influenced by economies of scale.

The role of vertical product differentiation in IIT

The foregoing analysis suggests that both product differentiation and scale economies influence IIT. The first part of this conclusion, however, must be qualified since a precise measure of the degree of horizontal differentiation in an industry is not available. In fact, the extent to which product differentiation influences IIT depends upon the variable's assumed relationship with industrial concentration. Further ambiguity arises from the fact that the measure of vertical (not horizontal) differentiation introduced in Chapter 8 was of little importance as a determinant of IIT shares in broad groups of countries.

This state of empirical affairs is unsatisfactory. Despite indirect evidence that product differentiation seems to influence IIT, there is a lacuna as far as measures of differentiation and their relation to trade are concerned. No quantitative indicator that would permit a comprehensive assessment of the impact of horizontal differentiation on patterns of trade is available. Nevertheless, there is scope for a more detailed analysis of the way in which vertical differentiation affects two-way trade, in particular the trade between DMEs and developing countries.

A 'factor abundance' model of IIT developed by Falvey (1981) can serve as the backdrop for this tentative analysis. The model focuses attention on a particular industry operating in a two-country world. The industry is assumed to use a given stock of (industry-specific) capital in combination with labour, and product differentiation over a whole range of qualities is possible. Different product specifications (quality levels) are distinguished by the capital–labour ratios used in production. As a general rule, it is assumed that higher quality requires a higher capital–labour ratio.

When the endowments of the two countries differ, the capital-abundant country will have a comparative advantage in high-quality products and the labour-abundant country in low-quality products. This creates a potential for intra-industry specialization based on factor abundance. If demand conditions permit, the two-way trade of the countries will reflect this pattern of specialization. Such a model is best suited to the analysis of IIT between DMEs and developing countries where differences in factor abundance are substantial. The concept of vertical differentiation then provides an explanatory device to bridge the gap between conventional and modern views of international specialization and trade.

Additional insight into the sources of IIT between DMEs and developing countries can be gained from a second model developed by Flam and Helpman (1987). Their simplified approach to trade in vertically differentiated products differs from Falvey's by assuming that labour is the only factor of production. The Flam–Helpman model recognizes two countries, both producing the same product but with different levels of efficiency. International specialization takes the form of product differentiation by quality types. Such specialization is assumed to be Ricardian, or technology-based. The comparative advantage of one country (the 'North') is in high-quality versions of the differentiated product, while that of the other country (the 'South') is in low-quality versions. Two-way trade will occur if the quality range being produced in each country does not match the product versions that are demanded.

Flam and Helpman go on to assume that higher quality versions of the product require larger labour inputs per unit of output than do lower-quality versions. In a competitive equilibrium, the higher-quality versions of the differentiated product command a higher price. Based on the assumed pattern of specialization and IIT, it follows that the South will export products of low quality and low price to the North and will import versions of high quality and high price.

Testable hypotheses about IIT between a DME and a developing country can be developed on the basis of the latter model. As in previous instances, such hypotheses are only formulated 'in the spirit' of the underlying theory and not rigorously derived from a formal model. The theory implies that the probability of bilateral IIT in a particular industry will be larger if there are substantial opportunities for vertical differentiation between North and South. More specifically, there will be a difference between the quality of the DME's exports to the developing country and the quality of its imports, and this difference can be related to the extent of bilateral IIT.

The role of quality differences as a determinant of bilateral IIT can be described in terms of two alternative propositions. One concerns the 'direction' of quality differences. If the quality of the DME's exports to the developing country is superior to that of its imports from the latter, a relatively high share of IIT in bilateral trade obtains. In this sense, the mere direction of a quality difference is expected to impact on the share of IIT between pairs of trading partners. Second, not only the direction but also the extent of differences in quality may have a predictable impact on bilateral IIT. The wider the gap in quality between the two trade flows, the higher will be the portion of IIT in bilateral trade (provided that qualities of the DME's exports and imports differ in the way described).

Empirical tests of these hypotheses are carried out by linear regression. The dependent variable is the share of IIT in bilateral trade of a given product group between a DME and a developing country. The independent variable, reflecting the impact of quality difference, is defined in accordance with the arguments of Flam and Helpman (1987). Price differences are used as a proxy for differences in quality where, for reasons of data availability, prices are expressed as trade unit values. For a given pair of countries (one DME and one developing country) and a given product group, quality differences are proxied by the ratio between the unit value of the DME's exports to the developing country and the unit value of its imports from the developing country.[3] Corresponding to the two versions of the quality difference hypothesis, the independent variable is expressed in two alternative forms. First, the direction of quality differences is represented by a dummy variable which takes the value of 1 if the ratio of unit values exceeds unity and assumes a value of 0 otherwise. Second, the extent of quality differences is measured by that ratio itself.

Other independent variables used in the present regressions are those introduced in the last section of Chapter 7. They include: the negative of the absolute difference between trading partners in per capita GDP (a measure of income similarity), the negative of the absolute difference in total GDP (a measure of similarity in size), the arithmetic mean of per capita GDP of the two trading partners (a measure of the average income level), and the arithmetic mean of total GDP (a measure of average size).

The data set underlying the estimation of regression coefficients is very large. Individual observations relate to the bilateral trade of a DME and a developing country where each trade flow is expressed at the four-digit sub-group of the SITC. All trade in manufactures is considered, and the country pairings are exhaustive (22 DMEs and 25 developing countries). Thus, the analysis provides a comprehensive documentation of IIT in manufactures between North and South in 1985.

The results obtained from this sample of over 20,000 observations are summarized in Table 9.3. They show very clearly that 'conventional' forces such as country similarity in terms of income and market size, average income and average market size influence two-way trade between North and South in much the same way as they affect IIT in general. All four coefficients are highly significant and carry the expected signs.

The role of quality difference is also apparent from the regression coefficients of Table 9.3. The direction of quality difference is seen to have a significant impact on the share of IIT between DMEs and developing countries. When the extent of quality differences is taken into account, the overall impact is weaker though the regression coefficient is still statistically significant.

The results of Table 9.3 provide a general impression of the way determinants (and, particularly, quality differences) influence the IIT between DMEs and developing countries. Because the extent of vertical differentiation varies widely among industries, a more detailed examination of the results is desirable. That step would help to identify the industries where vertical differentiation makes the most important positive contribution to two-way trade. Such industries might be promising fields for developing countries that hope to build new trade relationships with DMEs.

This question can be addressed by breaking up the present sample into industries defined at the three-digit level of the SITC and re-estimating the first of the two relationships shown in Table 9.3 for each industry. The regression coefficients of the direction of quality difference (shown in Table B9 of the statistical appendix) yield interesting evidence on IIT of individual industries. The quality difference variable performed contrary to expectations (that is, it carried a negative sign) for less than one-third of the 87 industries considered. However, the negative coefficients were statistically significant in only four of these cases. For another one-third of the industry observations, the quality difference coefficient was significantly positive. Not all the industries in this subset accounted for large portions of the total value of two-way trade between DMEs and developing countries. The following discussion focuses on those industries where two-way trade between DMEs and developing countries exceeded the mean value for the entire sample of industries.

Because the models dealing with quality differentiation as a source of IIT recognize only final goods, it is appropriate to begin this summary by considering the results for consumer-goods industries. Trade in telecommunications apparatus – which includes most consumer electronics products – accounts for the largest portion of IIT between DMEs and developing countries in final products. The significantly positive coefficient for the quality difference variable indicates a distinct division of labour between DMEs and developing countries. This result is especially important in view of the industry's prominence in the total IIT between the two country groups. The balance of trade in

Table 9.3 Impact of quality differences on two-way trade between DMEs and developing countries and areas,[a] 1985

Dependent variable[c]	Independent variables[b]						
	Income[d] similarity	Size[e] similarity	Average[f] income	Average[g] size	Direction of quality difference[h]	Extent of quality difference[i]	F- value
IIT-share	0.026*	0.096*	0.016*	0.109*	0.028*	–	44.73*
	0.026*	0.106*	0.016*	0.120*	–	0.003***	36.02*

Source: UNIDO

a/ The number of bilateral trade flows (21904) considered in the two linear regressions is much less than the theoretical maximum which would apply for trade in all four-digit SITC categories involving 22 DME countries and 25 developing countries. The reason is that only non-zero values of IIT could be considered due to the definition of the quality-difference variables.

b/ Independent variables (other than the dummy variable indicating the direction of quality difference) have been standardized to unit variance. Asterisks denote statistical significance at the 1(*), 5(**) and 10(***) per cent levels.

c/ IIT-share in bilateral trade of a four-digit SITC category between a DME and a developing country.

d/ Negative of the absolute difference in per capita GDP of trading partners.

e/ Negative of the absolute difference in total GDP.

f/ Arithmetic mean of per capita GDP of trading partner countries.

g/ Arithmetic mean of total GDP.

h/ The dummy variable used to indicate the direction of quality difference assumes a value of 1 if the unit value ratio (exports/imports) of the DME's trade with the developing country exceeds unity and the value of 0 otherwise.

i/ Ratio between the unit value of the DME's exports to the developing country and that of its imports from the latter.

telecommunications apparatus was slightly in favour of developing countries, and the industry appears as a quite promising area of trade expansion for this group.

Similar results were obtained for trade in domestic electrical equipment. Although the total value of IIT is substantially less than for telecommunications apparatus, the developing countries are net exporters and quality differences exert the expected influence. Other types of consumer goods where vertical differentiation is an important determinant of two-way trade are rubber articles and plastic articles.

The most striking exception among consumer goods was the clothing industry. The quality difference variable had a significantly negative impact on the share of North–South IIT. This means that, in cases where the quality of a DME's exports to a developing country is superior to that of the reverse trade flow, the share of IIT tends to be low. Viewed from a different angle, the net exports of developing countries are higher if the relative quality of their gross exports is low. An explanation for this negative (positive) impact of quality difference on IIT (net exports) can be stated in terms of price differentials. As the developing countries' gross exports become cheaper in relation to those of the DMEs, their net exports rise.

Other instances of a statistically significant impact of quality difference on the share of IIT were detected among capital goods or industrial intermediates. Although they are not truly represented in the formal model outlined previously, the intuitive reasoning is similar to that for consumer goods. It is best expressed in the words of Flam and Helpman (1987, p. 821), who state that IIT in vertically differentiated products (of all types) is bound to arise 'because in a given country the range of produced qualities does not correspond precisely to the demanded range of qualities'. If demand for intermediate and capital goods as well as demand for final goods is considered, the same basis for IIT in vertically differentiated products still applies. And quality difference plays the same role in the two-way trade of these goods as it does in consumer products.

The results of industry-specific regressions seem to support this view. The category with the largest value of IIT between North and South is electrical machinery and apparatus. These products consist mainly of capital equipment and related equipment components. Similarly, the sixth-largest trade category by value of IIT ('other non-electrical machinery') is also a capital-goods industry. The quality difference variable for both industries was positive and statistically significant. Three other capital-goods industries with significantly positive coefficients have lower trade levels, though these are by no means negligible; they include textile and leather machinery, machines for special industries, and ships and boats.

The occurrence of significantly positive coefficients was greatest among producers of intermediate goods, and many of these industries accounted for substantial amounts of IIT. Examples include organic chemicals, plastic materials, paper and paperboard, glass, and two steel categories (universals, plates and sheets and tubes, pipes and fittings). Other instances of quality differentiation in the IIT of industries producing intermediate goods were noted for metal manufactures and for equipment for distributing electricity. From such results, evidence of quality differentiation on the basis of technological differences may be inferred.

The role of quality difference in IIT could be discussed at greater length but would probably reinforce the general impression that the effects are not uniform across a broad spectrum of manufacturing industries. More detailed industry-specific studies would shed light on the particular characteristics of IIT. However, such an approach would go far beyond the scope of the present study, and the industry-specific regressions reported previously mark the end point of this exercise. Though not comprehensive and highly tentative, the foregoing results reveal several insights regarding the relationship between vertical differentiation and IIT. The most important is that, on average, quality difference has the expected impact on North–South IIT. Moreover, this impact is not restricted to consumer goods – as theoretical models might suggest – but holds also for industries producing intermediates and capital goods.

Annex: Foreign direct investment versus trade

In this chapter statistical tests were performed to ascertain whether or not the variables that have been theoretically linked to intra-industry trade influence this type of trade. As pointed out above, the empirical results obtained are not particularly strong. If the role of scale economies and product differentiation appears somewhat ambiguous, then are there other factors that might at least partially account for IIT?

In a standard H–O model, differences in factor endowments produce differences in factor prices and product prices. If resources are immobile, trade in goods takes place. If factors are allowed to move between countries, factors (in particular capital) will move in response to international differences in factor prices until all differences in factor rewards are arbitraged away. And inter-industry trade and FDI, for instance, act as substitutes for each other. As was mentioned earlier, the international movement of physical capital may have accounted for the weaker results obtained for this factor in attempting to explain inter-industry trade.

The situation is much more ambiguous with respect to intra-industry trade and specialization. Since this type of trade can occur where no significant differences in factor rewards exist, FDI can also occur in a similar environment. In this case, does FDI act as a substitute for trade or as a complement? At this point even the theoretical work on this question is not clear. On the one hand, Agmon (1979) argues that FDI and intra-industry trade are strong complements. The reasoning behind his conclusion is that the same factors that have led to the growth of TNCs are also the factors that stimulate intra-industry trade. This would seem intuitively plausible as the volume of world trade and the volume of FDI have both been expanding in the postwar era. On the other hand, Norman and Dunning (1984) in a recent survey reach no firm conclusion on the issue. In some cases FDI is a substitute for trade and in other cases it is complementary to it. The result depends on the type of product being traded, the size of transaction costs, and the extent of scale economies. A similar result can be obtained within the standard H–O framework. Markusen (1983) has recently found that a suitably modified H–O model can yield a variety of circumstances where FDI and trade are either substitutes or complements. He also shows that differences in production technology between countries and a variety of product and factor market distortions can lead to situations where FDI and intra-industry trade are complements rather than substitutes.

Empirical studies on this issue are at this point scarce. Norman and Dunning (1984) find that intra-industry FDI tends to be greatest in technology-intensive industries such as chemicals and allied products, engineering products, and electrical and electronic products. In a recent survey on intra-industry FDI, Rugman (1985) concludes that this type of FDI would be most common among high-income countries. The primary industry characteristics would be a high-income elasticity and a high level of technology. Intra-industry FDI would seem to be determined by the same factors that determine intra-industry trade.

Over the last thirty years, the H–O model has been refined to deal with the international mobility of capital. This development has been part of a more general line of research aimed at investigating the effects on predicted patterns of trade of relaxing some of the more restrictive assumptions of the H–O model. The advantage of starting with the H–O model is that it concentrates on the relationship between a country's pattern of international trade and specialization and its endowment of factors of production, such as capital. The international movement of capital, such as FDI, can be treated in a manner similar to changes in the factor endowments of the sending and receiving countries. Thus, the relationship between international trade and foreign investment can be analysed in an integrated fashion rather than treated as separate and relatively unrelated phenomena. From these propositions it can be established how FDI flows affect patterns of trade.

In an H–O framework, trade and FDI are potential substitutes. The greater the volume of trade, the lower the volume of FDI and vice versa. It can also be anticipated that FDI flows from relatively capital-abundant countries to relatively capital-scarce countries. FDI, like trade, also affects the relative prices of factors of production. As seen above, international capital movements tend to equalize factor prices across countries. Like trade, FDI would tend to raise the return to the relatively abundant factor in both countries.

The H–O framework also yields testable hypotheses concerning the flows of FDI. From the model one would assume that FDI would tend to originate in capital-abundant countries and flow to capital-scarce countries. The empirical evidence on FDI seems broadly consistent with this hypothesis. Gross inflows and outflows of FDI on a per capita basis seem to vary systematically with income per capita. Gross outflows are high for the highest-income countries, but then fall off sharply as a country's per capita income declines. Gross inflows also decline systematically with per capita income, but not as rapidly as outflows. As a result, only the richest countries have net outflows, and the middle-income countries tend to have the highest net inflows (Dunning, 1981). Further Baldwin (1979) has shown that FDI of the USA tends to be highest in labour-intensive industries, which generally conforms to the predictions of the H–O model. It was also hypothesized that tariffs (and other barriers to trade) would tend to stimulate FDI. Empirically this seems to be the case, as tariff and non-tariff barriers have been found to promote FDI, at least in developing countries.

The familiar model thus provides a simple explanation of FDI as a process of arbitrage where firms move capital from a location where its return is low to a location where its return is higher. As a consequence, the explanation for FDI can be tied to the existing and well developed theory of international trade. This explanation, however, may be somewhat too neat. Several obvious anomalies appear with respect to the international movement of capital.

It has been observed that the USA tends to have net outflows of FDI and net imports of portfolio capital. This poses the question of whether it is possible for equity capital to be cheap (abundant) and portfolio capital to be expensive (scarce) simultaneously. Furthermore, many developed countries simultaneously attract FDI and export capital abroad. Such behaviour does not seem to be consistent with the export of capital from capital-abundant countries to capital-scarce countries. The existence of such anomalies has led to a considerable amount of theoretical work concerning non-traditional explanations of FDI. As a starting point, most of this work assumes that the major vehicle for FDI is the TNC. Since it has been shown that the existence of TNCs is incompatible with the assumption of perfect competition, it is not surprising that at least some observed FDI flows are inconsistent with the results obtained from the H–O model. For example, if perfect competition prevails in capital markets, any differentials between the returns to capital engaged in various activities would be briskly competed away. If this is not the case, capital may not earn a homogeneous rate of return within a country, and thus capital flows may become difficult to predict.

Moving away from the assumption of perfect competition has yielded several other explanations of FDI which focus on the operation of the TNC. One of the earliest explanations of FDI is the product-cycle hypothesis. According to this hypothesis, new products are initially produced in the developed countries owing to the availability of research and development facilities and the locational advantages of being close to the expected market. As the production process becomes standardized and the domestic market becomes saturated, firms begin to export the product. If successful, firms may start to invest in plant and equipment abroad where costs may be lower. The final stage of the process may involve FDI flows into developing countries with

174

the production being exported to the market where the product was originally produced. According to the product–cycle hypothesis, FDI could occur either as a result of the interpenetration of developed countries' markets or the development of lower-cost production sites. The former would involve FDI among capital-abundant countries and thus would not be easily explainable in a more traditional capital-arbitrage framework.

The idea of a cycle can also be found in Kojima (1978). In Kojima's model FDI flows from developed countries into developing countries on the basis of comparative advantage. This type of FDI is 'trade-oriented', in the sense that it allows previously unexploited resources to be used. Therefore flows of FDI in this model result mainly from the evolution of the international division of labour. This is an 'industry-cycle' approach as opposed to Vernon's 'product-cycle' approach. The model, while appealing, is not particularly general as much FDI does not fit this pattern. However, it was developed to explain Japanese FDI and explicitly recognizes that other forms of FDI may call for other explanations.

The product–cycle and industry–cycle hypotheses, while seemingly capable of explaining some forms of FDI, are not particularly useful. Most recent work has built on the explanations provided by Hymer (1976) and Kindleberger (1969). The starting point of these explanations is that firms undertake FDI in order to capture larger profits from a monopoly over rent–yielding assets. Some of these advantages may include patents, access to technology, managerial skills, marketing skills, or a recognizable brand name. In this situation, rent is defined as a rate of return greater than that which would occur in a perfectly competitive market. If capturing the rents available from such rent-yielding assets outweighs the disadvantages of operating in a foreign market, FDI may occur. A weakness of this explanation lies in the question of why firms would bother with FDI when these rents could theoretically be captured via selling or leasing intangible assets. However, if markets for these assets are imperfect, rents can be received by the owners of the assets. Market imperfections generally occur because of the special characteristics of intangible assets which make arms-length transactions difficult. Many of these assets, especially technology, have public-goods characteristics in the sense that their use does not diminish their stock. Also, once developed, technology may be reproduced at little cost. If such assets were sold in the open market, their availability would quickly become such that the innovating firm could gain little by selling them. A second problem is that if prospective buyers are fully informed about the product, the firm's market power might vanish. Thus, exporting or FDI flows become more attractive alternatives.

Another quite popular explanation of FDI is the internalization theory formulated by Buckley and Casson (1976). This model emphasizes the aforementioned market failures for technology and intermediate inputs. The corresponding markets are considered imperfect in the sense that they are difficult to organize, pose serious problems of uncertainty, and often make it difficult to exploit fully the value of intangible assets. In order to bypass these imperfections, firms internalize their operations. This involves the familiar forward and/or backward integration of production activities. The internalization of markets, if it occurs across national boundaries, results in FDI flows. In the market for various types of knowledge, the incentive to internalize is particularly strong. The creation of innovative production processes or products involves lengthy time lags, considerable investment, and sometimes a high degree of uncertainty. Under these circumstances, the firm may well be able to reduce its outlays by internalizing its operations rather than using external markets. A further possible benefit of international internalization is that the firm may be able to set intra-firm prices in such a way as to avoid certain types of government intervention (i.e. transfer pricing).

The most recent approach to FDI involves pulling together various explanations of such investment in order to attempt to formulate a more unified explanation. This eclectic theory of FDI, which is also sometimes referred to as the OLI (ownership location internalization) paradigm, has been developed by Dunning (1977, 1981). In this model, three essential conditions must be met for FDI to occur. First, the firms should possess ownership advantages associated with intangible assets mentioned earlier. Second, locational considerations such as tariffs and transportation costs should dictate whether a firm pursues FDI rather than exports the product. In engaging in FDI, the firm must consider whether it can overcome the locational disadvantages of operating in a foreign location. Dunning also emphasizes the opportunities of combining ownership advantages with the favourable factor endowment advantages of foreign countries; while factor endowments are considered, they enter the model in a different way from in the H–O model. Finally, internalization must be considerably more beneficial to the firm than selling the advantages it possesses on the open market through licensing.

What seems clear is that many of the difficulties associated with explaining the patterns of FDI are associated with intra-industry trade. This type of trade is difficult to reconcile with the standard H–O model, as it clearly implies that a country has a simultaneous competitive advantage and disadvantage in the same product category. Intra-industry trade can occur in a world where there are no differences in factor endowments and thus no differences in factor prices between countries.

At this point it should be clear that the knowledge concerning the determinants of FDI is incomplete at best. In the most general terms, it seems that the H–O prediction that FDI will flow from capital-abundant countries to capital-scarce countries seems to be correct in the long run. Since in the book the focus has been on long-run changes in specialization and trade, the H–O model may not be totally inaccurate. However, a simple H–O story of FDI may be less well suited to explain the flow of FDI among capital-abundant countries, where there seems to be more going on than simple capital arbitrage. Many of these flows may be intra-industry FDI, which is more difficult to explain. Attempts at an explanation usually rely on some form of internalization of intangible assets. However, at this point the literature lacks an overall theory of FDI. Progress in this area is further hampered by data limitations which constrain the possibilities to test various theories empirically.

Notes: Chapter 9

1 The role of vertical differentiation for low-concentration industries cannot be accurately assessed on the basis of the results of Table 9.1.
2 This measure of IIT intensity is analogous to the RCA indicator introduced in UNIDO, 1986. The definition also reflects Deardorff's 1984 suggestions on the preferred way to design dependent variables in regression analyses of international trade.
3 In order to correct partially for differences between f.o.b. and c.i.f. reported data, the unit values of bilateral exports/imports are first divided by those of the corresponding trade flows between the DME country and all its trading partners. Thus, the ratio actually takes the form of a pair of 'normalized' unit values.

CHAPTER 10

A retrospective view

Previous chapters have reported on a wide range of findings. An empirical examination of mainstream models suggests the existence of a set of 'core' determinants which govern patterns of specialization and trade. The strength of these determinants varies depending on whether inter-industry or intra-industry aspects are being considered and on the degree of similarity between trading partners. National differences in relative factor abundance have a perceptible impact on net trade and inter-industry specialization which partly conforms with the spirit of the factor abundance theory. Similarities between countries impact specialization and trade when intra-industry trends are examined.

The description and analysis of these relationships leads to several generalizations which can be condensed into a three-part thesis. The thesis consists of the following statements on patterns of output and trade at three different levels of aggregation:

(a) At the level of the manufacturing sector, comparative advantage is positively influenced by abundance of physical capital; the role of highly skilled labour is ambiguous.

(b) At the level of particular industries, inter-industry patterns of comparative advantage on average follow H–O predictions where the 'human factor' of semi-skilled labour plays an important part.

(c) The degree of intra-industrial specialization tends to be greatest among countries that are similar in their economic characteristics. Intra-industrial specialization is also positively associated with higher levels of income, with greater economies of scale and with low levels of industrial concentration.

The structure of this empirical thesis is clear. It starts from the broadest level of aggregation – the pattern of specialization distinguishing between manufacturing and other sectors of the economy. Having identified the determinants at this level, attention turns to the inter-industry structure and isolates the major forces that determine the composition of the manufacturing sector. Finally, the thesis considers the intra-industrial pattern of specialization and the relevant determinants. Each of the three components of the thesis is briefly considered below.

Sectoral comparative advantage

The assertion that abundance of capital is a source of sectoral comparative advantage is supported by several pieces of evidence. The DMEs' overwhelming shares in global production and exports are matched by an equally large proportion of the world's supply of physical capital. The abundance of physical capital is a general characteristic of the pattern of factor endowments which applies to all DMEs.

The results of the cross–country analyses of net trade in various industries lend further support to this view. Physical capital and highly skilled labour are both important determinants of net exports: the former usually has a positive impact, while the latter generally has a negative impact. As there are a number of reasons to interpret these cross–country results as a reflection of sector-wide determinants, physical capital stands out as the major source of comparative advantage in manufactures. In fact, of the four factors considered in this study, physical capital was the one that was mainly responsible for significant differences in the cross–country pattern of factor abundance.

Inter-industry comparative advantage

The statement that the inter-industry pattern of comparative advantage on average follows factor abundance rules receives support from several parts of the study. A comprehensive test was conducted for 46 countries, 90 industries and four factors. On average, net trade and factor endowments were found to be related as predicted by the generalized H–O theory.

The factor abundance proposition appears to enjoy a considerable degree of empirical support despite the unrealistic nature of some of the assumptions required for its formal derivation. In fact, at least one of the assumptions usually made to derive H–O results is grossly violated in the real world. The postulate that factor intensities of industries are the same in all countries (even in the weak sense of an ordinal equivalence) is clearly refuted by the evidence compiled here.

Further support for this interpretation is derived from the country-specific results on inter-industry patterns of output and trade. Because the H–O theory in higher dimensions is country-oriented rather than industry-oriented (Deardorff, 1980, 1982), the results for individual countries are especially relevant. There is a distinction, however, between patterns of specialization in output and trade: the evidence pertaining to exports exhibits slightly stronger H–O traits than patterns of output.

The analysis of inter-industry patterns of comparative advantage reveals other, more detailed, features. Among the four factors of production studied, only semi-skilled labour behaves in a typical H–O fashion. The basis for this assertion is found in the general test of the factor abundance proposition in Chapter 7. Additional support is obtained from the country-specific results (mentioned above) which assign an important role to a broad class of labour as a source of inter-industry comparative advantage.

Two other remarks on the role of semi-skilled labour in an H–O context are useful to bear in mind. One is that the dominant role of this particular factor may partly depend on its low degree of international mobility – a characteristic that conforms to H–O standards. A second, and somewhat contradictory, characteristic is that the factor is probably not perfectly mobile between domestic industries, and that to the extent that it is not, another H–O assumption seems to be violated.

Intra-industry specialization and trade

The intra-industry picture is a detailed mosaic of specialization and trade in differentiated products. Except for special cases – for example, two-way trade between DMEs and developing countries – the precise pattern of intra-industrial specialization (which country produces and exports which product) is arbitrary. The extent of such specialization and trade is nevertheless influenced by several forces, some of which are country-specific while others are industry-specific.

Country-specific factors were shown to exert a strong influence on the level of IIT. Income levels are positively associated with IIT in almost all industries. Similarities between trading partners (with regard to both income and market size) also have a strong positive impact on levels of bilateral IIT. In addition, industry-specific factors influence the intra-industry share in the whole of an industry's exports and imports. The intensity of IIT is systematically higher in industries that are relatively less concentrated (particularly among the DMEs). And within this class of industries, IIT intensity is sensitive to economies of scale. This pattern of 'nested' effects on the share of IIT is largely in the spirit of the major models of intra-industrial specialization.

Finally, the analysis of two-way trade between the DMEs and developing countries provides results that represent a point of tangency between the theory of comparative advantage and its alternatives. Differences in specialization are influenced by quality difference between versions of an industry's products. This result may well have its roots in factor abundance which may affect patterns of specialization even at the most detailed level.

In conclusion, the focus of this book has been on the presentation of empirical data and on the interface between empirical and theoretical aspects of specialization and trade. The need to bring these two lines of research more closely together offers a rich agenda for further work. Because the scope of the study has been rather broad, no particular aspect could be treated in the depth that a more narrowly focused study would afford. Therefore one objective of further work along the lines of the present book would be to deepen the analysis of certain subjects.

Further progress on the methodological tools of trade analysis is also desirable – and most likely. There are opportunities to improve on the empirical measurement of a number of concepts, for example. Measures that would better reflect the underlying theoretical concepts are expected to provide a clearer understanding of the forces driving today's world economy and serve as a much stronger bridge between theory and empirical work. Examples relate to the assessment of countries' resource bases, the measurement of industries' factor requirements and, in particular, the measurement of industry characteristics from the realm of new trade theories. Progress in the area of country analyses is also important, as the underlying factor abundance theory is country-oriented. The types of results that can be expected might be more relevant to policy issues than the sweeping conclusions usually drawn from cross-country studies.

As far as the results on factor abundance and trade are concerned, the major point of interest concerns the role of semi-skilled labour. Much of the evidence analysed here was based on a very broad concept of this type of labour. Future research could be directed towards examining the relationship between trade and semi-skilled labour in a more detailed fashion. Refinements in the measurement of labour categories that embody skills closely related to the production process would be desirable. In this connection a more extensive analysis of the relationship between trade and semi-skilled labour from both an industry-specific and a country-specific view should be attempted.

Among the many possibilities to improve on the analysis of IIT, two can be mentioned. First, new insights could be expected from more extensive investigations of industry-specific IIT. Case studies might be particularly useful in order to get a grasp on the precise type of two-way trade under study. Second, the role of vertical differentiation in IIT deserves more attention than it has sometimes received. More evidence is needed on intra-industrial variations in factor intensities, on ranges of product quality, and on the ensuing potential for developing countries to participate in two-way trade in manufactures. With these new tools, the two bodies of theory considered here can be fitted more closely with empirical accounts of trade and specialization.

Appendix A (Technical)

A procedure for validating the H–O proposition

The propositions of the generalized version of the theory of comparative advantage can be expressed in terms of covariances or correlations. The simplest correlation result is that of a non-positive relationship between the autarky prices and net exports of each country. The corresponding inequality reads

$$\mathbf{p}_j^{a\prime} \mathbf{t}_j \leq 0 \qquad (j = 1, 2, \ldots, n) \tag{1}$$

where $\mathbf{p}_j^a$ and $\mathbf{t}_j$ are two column vectors and $\prime$ designates the transpose. The first of these vectors represents the autarky prices of m goods. The second refers to the net exports of country j, which has been chosen arbitrarily from among the n countries of the model. In order to obtain a relationship that simultaneously embraces all m goods and n countries, two matrices can be formed, namely

$$\mathbf{P}^a = [\mathbf{p}_1^a \ \mathbf{p}_2^a \ldots \ \mathbf{p}_n^a] \tag{2}$$

and

$$\mathbf{T} = [\mathbf{t}_1 \ \mathbf{t}_2 \ldots \ \mathbf{t}_n]. \tag{3}$$

The two matrices combine the autarky prices and the net exports of all countries.

A statement of comparative advantage which holds under fairly general assumptions can then be written as a matrix inequality of the following form:

$$\mathbf{u}_m^{\prime} \left(\mathbf{P}^a \ \# \ \mathbf{T} \right) \mathbf{u}_n \leq 0 \tag{4}$$

where $\mathbf{u}_m$ and $\mathbf{u}_n$ are vectors containing only 1s and of lengths m and n, respectively. Multiplication of the two matrices $\mathbf{P}^a$ and $\mathbf{T}$ is carried out in an element-by-element fashion, giving rise to the Schur product specified by $\#$. In the literature, (4) is usually presented in the form of an inner product between two expanded vectors so as to retain the correlation character of the hypothesis (Deardorff, 1980). The equivalence between such extended correlations and the present reformulation as a matrix inequality is easily established.

Starting from (4), the basic H–O relationship for higher dimensions can be easily stated. The generalized H–O proposition must be of the same form as the generalized law of comparative advantage. In other words, a linkage is required between a trade matrix ($\mathbf{T}$ in the above example) and another matrix representing the determinants of this trade ($\mathbf{P}^a$ in the case of the law of comparative advantage). The statement of H-0 relationships must incorporate variables representing factor abundance and factor intensities as well as trade. In order to simplify the exposition and to retain a close link with the empirical results of Chapter 7, factor intensities are assumed to be the same for all countries. In that case, such intensities can be represented by a matrix

$$\mathbf{A} = [a_{hi}] \tag{5}$$

where a_{hi} is the share of factor h in the value of output of good i, and h runs from 1 to k. The abundance of factor h in country j is measured by the variable v and is summarized in the matrix

$$\mathbf{V} = [v_{hj}]. \tag{6}$$

The factor abundance proposition can then be stated as

$$\mathbf{u}'_k (\mathbf{V} \# \mathbf{AT}) \mathbf{u}_n \geq 0, \tag{7}$$

in close analogy to (4). From (7) it can be seen that the generalized H–O proposition can be expressed in the same 'correlation-like' form as the law of comparative advantage (4).

The major differences between the hypotheses represented by equations (4) and (7) can be easily summarized. First, in the H–O framework the matrix of determinants is represented by the factor abundance matrix $\mathbf{V}$ rather than p^a, the autarky price matrix. Second, the impact of factor abundance on trade is 'filtered' by factor intensities. This yields the familiar relationship between factor abundance ($\mathbf{V}$) and net exports of factor services embodied in traded goods ($\mathbf{AT}$). Third, because conditions of factor abundance convey comparative advantage and trade is expressed as net exports, the sign of the inequality in (7) is reversed as compared with (4).

The relationship between the basic law of comparative advantage and the H–O hypothesis is apparent from a comparison between the inequalities in (4) and (7). The hypothesis employs the law of comparative advantage to explain trade in terms of a 'primitive' set of characteristics such as factor endowments. One of the essential methodological steps for the factor abundance theory to be operative is to move from the space of direct goods trade (represented by $\mathbf{T}$) to the space of indirect trade in factor services (represented by $\mathbf{AT}$). Following that step, it is a simple matter to show that relative factor endowments determine indirect trade in factor services and (somewhat less precisely) trade in goods. The change in space of the 'dependent variable' is suggested by the Heckscher–Ohlin–Vanek (H–O–V) or factor content version of the factor abundance hypothesis as the 'natural' formulation of a generalized proposition. The present discussion builds on a commodity version for the reason that a commodity version seems to have more intuitive appeal than a factor content version, even if the stated hypothesis is expressed in a weak (on average) form.

The generalized H–O proposition in (7) suggests an empirical procedure to assess the relationship between factor abundance and the factor content of traded goods. However, the empirical results in the first section of Chapter 7 concern the relationship between factor endowments and international trade in goods. In order to make use of the earlier results when equation (7) is the basis for a proximate validation of the H–O proposition, the inequality can be rewritten in the following way:

$$\mathbf{u}'_k \; (\mathbf{VT}' \; \# \; \mathbf{A}) \; \mathbf{u}_m \geq 0. \tag{8}$$

$\mathbf{T}$ is the transposed matrix of trade flows and $\mathbf{u}_m$ is a vector of length m consisting only of 1s. The elements of the $(k \times m)$ matrix $\mathbf{VT}'$ in this equation (where k represents the number of factors and m is the number of goods) are closely related to the concept of factor orientation on which Table 7.1 is based. Hence (8) can loosely be interpreted as an H–O restriction on the (generalized) correlation between factor orientation and factor intensity when all factors and all goods are considered simultaneously.

Finally, the form of (8) suggests a way to assess each factor's contribution to the overall H–O correlation. The k elements in the vector $(\mathbf{VT}' \; \# \; A)\mathbf{u}_m$, which shall be named $\mathbf{C}_h$, $(h = 1, 2, \ldots, k)$, reflect each individual factor's role in this regard.

Econometric methods

The following paragraphs present the technicalities behind some of the results reported in the book. Together with the details given in the text, they provide a complete description of the statistical/econometric procedures that were applied to the data.

An application of clustering techniques

Chapter 6 reports an attempt at grouping countries according to similarity of their factor intensity profiles. The method employed is that of clustering the 43 countries in the sample by ordinal factor intensity variables, where for each of the three factors 28 variables are used simultaneously. In the case of clustering by labour intensity, for instance, the ith variable is the rank of the ith industrial branch in terms of labour intensity, determined for a given country. Application of hierarchical clustering with the centroid method for measuring distance is expected to identify groups of countries that have similar rankings of industrial branches by labour intensity. In particular, the initial steps in the clustering procedure would by necessity identify countries that have identical rankings of industrial branches by factor intensity.

As was mentioned in Chapter 6, no pair of countries could be found for which the rankings of the 28 industrial branches were identical at least in terms of one type of factor intensity. In technical parlance, each hierarchical clustering exercise started with combining two countries that were somewhat apart in terms of factor intensity rankings.

Regression techniques

Tables 7.1, 7.3, 8.1, 8.4, 9.1, 9.2, 9.3 and B9 report results of regression analyses. The purpose of these analyses – which generally used linear regression equations – was to test hypotheses about determinants of specialization and trade but not to predict such patterns. As a consequence, economic theory served as the sole guide for specifying the underlying relationships, and no particular emphasis was laid on goodness of fit of the tested equations. Given the complexity and eclectic nature of the relevant theories, the analysis almost by necessity is plagued by the problem of omitted variables. In this respect, the usual assumption was made that the omitted variables are virtually uncorrelated with the included ones.

A special feature of the presentation of regression results in the book is that of writing coefficient estimates in the form of beta coefficients. Accordingly, the coefficients indicate the number of standard deviation changes in the dependent variable induced by a change of one standard deviation of the corresponding independent variable. Since the tests usually cover a large number of countries and industries as well as several factors, beta coefficients appear as the appropriate analytical tool that permits – owing to its inherent standardization – meaningful comparisons.

Most of the reported regression coefficients were obtained (sometimes after appropriate transformations of variables) on the basis of the ordinary-least-squares (OLS) estimation technique. However, in one case weighted-least-squares estimation was applied in order to correct for potential biases arising from systematic heteroscedasticity.

In the regression of an industry's net trade on factor endowments, the problem of heteroscedasticity is likely to arise. One reason is that large countries must be expected to have large amounts of unmeasured factor endowments and therefore high residual variances. Therefore, it may be assumed that a country's residual variance is systematically related to its size. More specifically, the assumption of 'multiplicative heteroscedasticity' can be made and the variance of residual j (var_j) modelled as

$$\mathrm{var}_j = a \cdot Y_j^b$$

with Y_j being GDP of country j and a and b unknown parameters.

In order to obtain weighted-least-squares estimates of the regression coefficients of Table 7.1, a three-step procedure (suggested by Leamer, 1984, p. 122) has been applied. As a first step in this procedure, the logarithms of the squared OLS residuals were regressed against the logarithms of GDP to obtain estimates for a and b in the above equation. In a second step, these estimates were used to derive predicted values of residual variances.

Finally, these predicted values were used as weights in the re-estimation of the regression of net trade on factor endowments.

Finally, it should be noted that all regression exercises reported in the book left one methodological problem – coefficient estimation in the presence of measurement errors – unresolved. The broad coverage of countries, factors and industries meant that elaborate treatment of errors in variables was precluded by the dimension of the exercise. It must be left for the agenda of future research to take up some of the approaches outlined in the study and to apply more sophisticated econometric techniques to possibly more reliable data.

Appendix B (Statistical)

Data sources

The data used in this study can be divided into primary and secondary sources. Primary sources are all data available in the UNIDO data base (UDB) and in related computer data sets maintained by the UNIDO Secretariat. Secondary data sources – for example, various national and international statistical publications – were used to supplement the main body of information. For information on how to acquire the general industry statistics used in the study, readers may write to: Head, Industrial Statistics and Sector Surveys Branch, UNIDO, Box 300, A-1400 Vienna, Austria.

Primary sources

The UDB contains statistics on national accounts, trade, employment and population as well as industrial statistics. In the case of industry data, the information is collected by the Statistical Office of the United Nations in collaboration with UNIDO and with estimates by the UNIDO Secretariat. In the course of the present study, the following variables have been used:

(a) GNP and GDP, exports and imports of goods and services in current US dollars (Chapters 5, 6 and 7);
(b) MVA in constant US dollars at 1980 prices (Chapters 2 and 8);
(c) population in thousands (Chapters 7 and 8);
(d) total labour force in thousands (Chapter 5);
(e) information at the level of industrial branches (three–digit ISIC) on gross output, value added and wages in constant US dollars (1980 prices), as well as on the number of employees (Chapters 2 and 6).

As regards gross output and value added, valuation for some countries is in producers' prices while others are at factor values. The main criterion for using either valuation concept has been to assure maximum consistency within a country both between variables and over time. In the case of employment data, the preferred indicator is the average number of employees, although the number of persons engaged is accepted if it is the only data available. More detail on concepts and data coverage is given in UNIDO (1989).

All information on international trade flows is taken from the UN trade data tapes. This vast data collection contains information on the current value of annual imports (c.i.f.) and exports (f.o.b.) in thousands of US dollars as well as on the physical quantities of such trade. The level of detail reaches the five-digit (item) level of SITC. In cases where reported country data were not available, gaps were filled by information from trading partner countries. The coverage of countries and years treated in the present study can be obtained from the tables in the text. Trade data for Belgium cover the Belgium–Luxembourg Economic Union, while those for the USA also cover Puerto Rico.

For part of the analysis in Chapter 6, trade flows had to be aggregated into ISIC three-digit categories. To achieve this goal, a concordance was established between the ISIC and the SITC, Revised. The concordance was based on a correspondence table provided by OECD. The table, which is a modified version of a concordance scheme developed by the World Bank, assigns to each four-digit ISIC category those categories of the SITC whose products fall, either entirely or partly, in the range of outputs of the ISIC category under consideration. In cases where only part of the SITC category is to be included in the ISIC category, an estimate of this part in percentage terms is provided. Aggregation of trade flows according to this scheme has been carried out by the UNIDO Secretariat on the basis of the UN trade data tapes.

A third primary source of information used in the present context is a UNIDO data set of industrial statistics containing additional details on the distribution of variables by size of establishments. This data set formed the basis of much of the analysis of Chapter 8.

Finally, compilation of factor endowments data (Chapter 5) was based on three primary data sources. The basic data for computing stocks of physical capital came from World Bank (1976, 1987). The underlying computer tapes contain information in national currency on countries' annual gross domestic investment both in current and in constant terms for the period 1955–85. They also provide a time series of exchange rates between national currencies and US dollars, so that capital stocks in current US dollars can be estimated by the method described below. The same tapes provide country data on the percentage of literate population which was used as supplementary information in the computation of unskilled-labour endowments.

Information on numbers of workers refers to the three skill categories (skilled, semi-skilled and unskilled) and was based on data taken from ILO, *Yearbook of Labour Statistics*, various issues. These data cover most of the countries studied in Chapter 5. Where data were not available for the two years under consideration, information on neighbouring years was substituted or figures were estimated. Table B1 reflects the availability of occupational data for the country sample of Chapter 5. Literacy rates were needed to compute the number of illiterate workers. These were taken from UNESCO, *Statistical Yearbook*, various issues, supplemented by information from World Bank (1976, 1987).

Table B1 Availability of data on skilled labour,[a] by country and year

Country or area	Years[b]
Argentina	1970
Australia	1970, 1985
Austria	1971, 1985
Belgium	1970, 1981
Brazil	1970
Canada	1971, 1985
Chile	1970, 1985
Colombia	1973, 1981
Denmark	1970, 1985
Dominican Republic	1970, 1981
Egypt	1975, 1983
Finland	1970, 1986
France	1968, 1982
Federal Republic of Germany	1970, 1984
Greece	1971, 1985
Guatemala	1973, 1981
Hong Kong	1971, 1985
India	1971, 1981
Indonesia	1971, 1985
Ireland	1971, 1985
Israel	1970, 1985
Italy	1971, 1981
Japan	1970, 1985
Malaysia	1970, 1980
Mexico	1970, 1980
Netherlands	1971, 1985
New Zealand	1971, 1981
Norway	1970, 1985
Pakistan	1972, 1985
Panama	1970, 1985
Peru	1972, 1981
Portugal	1970, 1985
Philippines	1970, 1985
Republic of Korea	1970, 1985
Singapore	1970, 1985
Spain	1970, 1985
Sri Lanka	1971, 1985
Sweden	1970, 1985
Switzerland	1970, 1980
Thailand	1970, 1984
Tunisia	1975, 1980
Turkey	1970, 1980
United Kingdom	1971, 1981
United States	1970, 1985
Uruguay	1975, 1985
Venezuela	1971, 1985
Yugoslavia	1971, 1981

a/ Data availability refers to ILO, Yearbook of Labour Statistics, various issues.

b/ The years indicated are those required in the study or neighbouring years which were used as a basis for estimation.

Secondary sources

To supplement the data sources listed above, a number of international and national sources have been used. International sources included United Nations, *Monthly Bulletin of Statistics*, various issues, United Nations, *Yearbook of National Accounts*, vol. II, various issues, and United Nations, *Yearbook of International Trade Statistics*, various issues, all of which have been used to provide data for Chapter 3. Among the supplementary national data sources, the computer tape containing the Geographic Area and Industry File of the US *Census of Manufactures, 1982* was the most extensively used. In particular, the following variables were of interest: number of employees (total and by size class of establishments), number of production workers, payroll, wages for production workers, and value added. The above variables served to calculate proxy measures of scale economies, industrial concentration and factor intensities for US industries.

The compilation of measures of industrial concentration also made use of census data: Ministry of International Trade and Industry, Japan, *Census of Manufactures 1984, Report by Industries*, (1986), and Economic Planning Board, Republic of Korea, *Report on Mining and Manufacturing Survey 1985* (1987). To supplement the data in Table 3.4 on trade in manufactures, information from the *Statistical Yearbook of the Republic of China, 1986* was employed.

Estimation methods

The following sections describe the methods used to derive estimates of countries' factor endowments and industries' factor input requirements.

Physical capital endowment

For each country in the sample, two estimates (1970 and 1985) of the net stock of capital were derived by summing depreciated annual gross domestic investment. The average asset life was assumed to be 15 years with a depreciation rate of 13.3 per cent. As the objective was to express capital stocks in current US dollars, the real value of the capital stock was first computed in national currency by accumulating depreciated real values of gross domestic investment in that currency. Second, the current value in national currency of the capital stock was obtained by applying the implicit deflator for gross domestic investment to the real figure described above. Third, the current US dollar value was derived by use of the exchange rate of that year for which the stock of capital was to be computed.

Time series on gross domestic investment for 13 countries were incomplete for the first time period. After inspection of data plots, missing values for seven of these countries (Egypt, Indonesia, Malaysia, Pakistan, Singapore, Thailand and Tunisia) were estimated on the basis of a semi-logarithmic regression of real domestic investment on time. For the remaining six countries (Chile, Hong Kong, Mexico, Peru, Sweden and Venezuela), data gaps were filled by use of annual average growth rates.

Skill categories of labour

As outlined in Chapter 5, the total labour force of each country was subdivided into three categories of skilled workers, semi-skilled workers and unskilled workers. The basis of this categorization was occupational and demographic data.

'Skilled labour' was defined in a narrow way as that portion of the labour force with the relatively highest skill content. As the statistical equivalent of this high-skill category, the number of economically active people in major labour force group 0/1 (professional, technical and related workers) in the International Standard Classification of Occupations (ISCO) was chosen, following the practice of similar empirical studies. Whenever data for the required year (1970 or 1985) were not available, the share of skilled labour in the total labour force was calculated for the year closest to the missing one. This share was then applied to total labour force data (taken from the UDB) for the year in question. Missing data for Argentina and Brazil for the year 1985 were estimated on the basis of cross-country regressions. These regressions were log-linear relationships between relative capital endowments (measured by capital stock per worker) and relative skill endowments (measured by the share of skilled workers in total labour force).

'Unskilled labour' was defined as the number of illiterate workers. It was obtained by subtracting from total labour force the portion of literate workers (derived on the basis of the country-wide literacy rate). Finally, the category of 'semi-skilled labour' was defined as that portion of workers who are literate, but do not belong to the professional/technical group. Accordingly, their number was obtained by subtracting the numbers of professional workers and illiterate workers from the total labour force.

Factor input requirements

In order to derive measures of factor input requirements and factor intensities at the three-digit level of the ISIC (Chapter 6), data on value added and wages were used. To facilitate comparison as well as render possible aggregation across countries and over time, constant dollar figures were needed both for value added and wages (used to compute factor inputs). Data on value added in 1980 dollars were taken directly from the UDB, while corresponding figures for wages had to be estimated. In this estimation the implicit deflator for value added (derived from current-price and constant-price data in national currency) was first applied to national currency data on wages; the resultant real values in national currency were then converted to US dollars by use of the exchange rate for 1980.

191

For the test of the H–O proposition in Chapter 7, US census information of 1982 was used to obtain estimates of factor input requirements at the SITC three-digit level in the form of imputed factor incomes. For physical capital, the flow measure of non-wage value added was used. To indicate factor input requirements of the three skill classes of labour for which factor endowments had been measured, proxy variables had to be employed, as there was no exact correspondence between those three classes and the census data used.

The first step in the estimation of income for the various labour categories was to choose a proxy for the wage of unskilled labour. This proxy was taken to be the minimum (across all US Standard Industrial Classification (USSIC) four-digit categories) of the wage rates of production workers. In tests of the sensitivity of results to the choice of this proxy, fractions of the above minimum were also used. Imputed income of unskilled labour was obtained by multiplying the unskilled wage rate by employment of each industry. The basic data for imputed income of semi-skilled labour were wages for production workers. These wages were adjusted for the income accruing to unskilled workers by subtracting the product of the unskilled wage rate (as defined previously) and the number of production workers.

With regard to skilled labour, the data situation was most difficult, as the US census data contain no information that would approximately reflect the narrow definition of this type of labour used in the compilation of endowment figures. For want of more appropriate information, the difference between total payroll and wages for production workers was taken as a starting point to estimate income of skilled labour for each industry. This broad income aggregate was corrected for income of unskilled labour by the same method that was applied to semi-skilled labour. Still, the income estimate for skilled labour must be expected to be strongly upward-biased. Thus, the data on skilled labour requirements appear to be the most fragile part of the information on factor input requirements underlying the results of Table 7.2.

In order to aggregate data on value added, wages and employment to the three-digit level of the SITC, the concordance between the USSIC and the SITC given in Hufbauer (1970) was used.

Classifications

Tables B2–B4 give classifications of countries on the one hand, and of industries on the other hand, which have been used recurrently throughout the book. Together with details specified in the tables included in the text, these appendix tables provide the full background of typologies used in the analyses.

Table B2 gives the universe of countries from which samples for the various parts of the analysis were selected mainly on the basis of data availability. For

Chapter 5, the selection criterion was availability of resource endowment and trade data for the years studied. To ensure maximum comparability of results, the same criterion was applied in Chapters 4, 7 and 9. A slightly narrower selection of countries for Chapter 6 resulted from the availability constraints regarding detailed industrial statistics. The country samples analysed in Chapter 8 were designed on the basis of availability of data on the size distribution of establishments.

Table B2 Composition of country groups

Developing Countries and Areas

Africa

Algeria	Gambia	Réunion
Angola	Ghana	Rwanda
Benin	Guinea	Sao Tome and Principe
Botswana	Guinea-Bissau	Senegal
Burkina Faso	Kenya	Seychelles
Burundi	Lesotho	Sierra Leone
Cameroon	Liberia	Somalia
Cape Verde	Libyan Arab Jamahiriya	Sudan
Central African Republic	Madagascar	Swaziland
Chad	Malawi	Togo
Comoros	Mali	Tunisia[b]
Congo	Mauritania	Uganda
Côte d'Ivoire	Mauritius	United Republic of
Djibouti	Morocco[b]	Tanzania
Egypt	Mozambique	Zaire
Equatorial Guinea	Namibia	Zambia
Ethiopia	Niger	Zimbabwe
Gabon	Nigeria	

West Asia

Bahrain	Kuwait	Syrian Arab Republic
Cyprus[b]	Lebanon	Turkey
Democratic Yemen	Oman	United Arab Emirates
Iraq[b]	Qatar	Yemen
Jordan[b]	Saudi Arabia	

South and East Asia

Afghanistan	Indonesia[b]	Philippines[b]
Bangladesh	Iran (Islamic Rep. of)	Republic of Korea[a]
Bhutan	Malaysia[b]	Singapore[a]
Brunei Darussalam	Maldives	Sri Lanka[b]
Burma	Mongolia	China (Taiwan Province)[a]
China	Nepal	Thailand[b]
Democratic Kampuchea	New Caledonia	Tonga
Fiji	Pakistan	Vanuatu
French Polynesia	Papua New Guinea	
Hong Kong[a]		
India		

193

Developing Countries and Areas

Latin America

Anguilla	Dominican Republic	Netherlands Antilles
Antigua and Barbuda	Ecuador	Nicaragua
Argentina[a]	El Salvador	Panama
Barbados	French Guyana	Paraguay
Belize	Grenada	Peru[b]
Bermuda	Guadeloupe	Puerto Rico
Bolivia	Guatemala	Saint Lucia
Brazil[a]	Guyana	St. Vincent-Grenadines
British Virgin Islands	Haiti	St. Kitts-Nevis
Chile	Honduras	Suriname
Colombia[b]	Jamaica	Trinidad and Tobago
Costa Rica	Martinique	Uruguay[b]
Cuba	Mexico[a]	United States Virgin Islands
Dominica	Montserrat	Venezuela

Europe

Malta
Yugoslavia

Developed countries

CPEs	DMEs	
Albania	Australia	Japan
Bulgaria	Austria	Luxembourg
Czechoslovakia	Belgium	Netherlands
German Democratic Republic	Canada	New Zealand
Hungary	Denmark	Norway
Poland	Finland	Portugal
Romania	France	South Africa
Union of Soviet Socialist	Germany, Federal Republic of	Spain
Republics	Greece	Sweden
	Iceland	Switzerland
	Ireland	United Kingdom
	Israel	United States
	Italy	

---

a/ Included among the NIEs. As there is no clear-cut quantitative criterion
   to define this country/area group, common practice was followed (see e.g.,
   UNIDO, 1985, p. 116).

b/ Included among second generation NIEs. The definition adopted for this
   group is that of the 'new exporting countries' of Havrylyshyn and Alikhani
   (1982).

Table B3 Broad classification of industrial branches, by growth performance and factor intensity

Industry class	ISIC
High-growth:	351, 352, 356, 382, 383, 385
Low-growth:	321, 322, 323, 324, 371, 372
Labour-intensive:	321, 322, 323, 324, 331, 332
Capital-intensive:	353, 371, 372, 381, 382, 383, 384

In addition to listing those countries whose data have been used at least for part of the study, groupings that provided the framework of large parts of the discussion are specified in Table B2. Table B3 presents a broad classification of industries by growth performance and factor intensity. This classification has been used to summarize some of the results of Chapter 2. Finally, Table B4 provides the details of a classification of SITC three-digit industries into Ricardian, H–O and product-cycle industries. In addition, the second of the above industry groups is subdivided into a capital-intensive and a labour-intensive group.

Supplemental tables

Tables B5–B10 present background information to some of the results discussed in the main text. Tables B5–B8 give actual measures of physical capital intensity and human capital intensity for the 28 industrial branches studied in Chapter 6. The figures are weighted averages representative of four country groups (DMEs, NIEs, second-generation NIEs, and a sample of ten non-NIEs). Table B9 presents in detail the partial correlations between bilateral IIT and country characteristics (summarized in Table 7.3) as well as industry-specific regression coefficients indicating the influence of vertical differentiation on bilateral IIT (discussed also in connection with the results of Table 9.3). Finally, Table B10 gives the details of a classification of industries in terms of scale economies, industrial concentration, product differentiation and export concentration discussed in Chapter 8.

Table B4 Broad classes of manufactured goods

Class of goods[a]	SITC codes[b]				
Ricardian goods	011,	012,	013,	022,	023,
	024,	025,	032,	0422,	046,
	047,	048,	052,	053,	055,
	061,	062,	0713,	0722,	0723,
	073,	074,	081,	091,	099,
	122,	2219,	2312,	2313,	2314,
	243,	251,	2626,	2627,	2628,
	2629,	263,	267,	411,	421,
	422,	431,	633,	641,	681,
	682,	683,	684,	685,	686,
	687,	688,	689,		
Heckscher-Ohlin goods	111,	112,	332,	533,	551,
	553,	554,	561,	581,	611*,
	612*,	613*,	621*,	629,	631*
	632*,	642,	651* (less 6516 and 6517),		
	652*,	653*,	654*,	655*,	656*,
	657*,	661,	662*,	664,	665,
	666*,	671,	672,	673,	674,
	675,	676,	677,	678,	679,
	691*,	692*,	694*,	696,	698,
	731*,	732,	733*,	812*,	821*,
	831*,	841*,	842*,	851*,	892,
	893*,	894*,	895*,	897*,	899*,
Product-cycle goods	266,	512,	513,	514,	515,
	521,	531,	532,	541,	571,
	599,	6516,	6517,	663,	693,
	695,	697,	711,	712,	714,
	715,	717,	718,	719,	722,
	723,	724,	725,	726,	729,
	734,	735,	861,	862,	864,
	891.				

a/ The major source for the classification in Ricardian (resource-based), H-O and product-cycle goods was UNIDO (1981, pp. 103–108). The partitioning of H-O goods into a capital intensive and a labour intensive class was mainly based on data on value added per employee from United States, Bureau of the Census (1984). The resultant sub-classes were finally reconciled with the classification given in UNIDO (1981).

b/ An asterisk indicates a product group pertaining to a labour-intensive H-O industry.

Table B5 DMEs' average factor intensities,[a] 1970–7 and 1978–85 (thousands of 1980 US dollars)

Industry (ISIC)	Non-wage value added per employee[b]		Wages per employee[c]	
	1970–1977	1978–1985	1970–1977	1978–1985
Food products (311)	15.3	19.0	8.8	10.4
Beverages (313)	21.7	29.0	9.2	12.0
Tobacco etc. (314)	24.8	32.0	9.6	11.1
Textiles (321)	7.1	9.6	7.1	9.1
Wearing apparel (322)	6.1	7.6	7.0	7.6
Leather and fur products (323)	11.5	13.8	10.2	11.8
Footwear (324)	7.5	9.2	8.9	9.4
Wood and cork products (331)	11.9	13.5	10.7	12.5
Furniture fixtures excl. metal (332)	11.7	14.1	11.7	13.6
Paper (341)	14.5	19.7	11.3	14.2
Printing and publishing (342)	12.0	15.0	11.8	12.4
Industrial chemicals (351)	20.9	28.4	10.8	15.4
Other chemicals (352)	18.1	26.5	9.4	12.6
Petroleum refineries (353)	93.6	94.0	20.6	18.0
Products of petroleum and coal (354)[d]	37.8	35.3	13.8	13.0
Rubber products (355)	9.5	12.8	9.5	12.1
Plastic products (356)	11.1	13.1	8.6	10.4
Pottery, china, earthenware (361)	8.5	13.9	9.5	11.8
Glass (362)	11.8	16.4	10.1	13.6
Other non-metallic min. products (369)	15.0	17.7	10.2	11.4
Iron and steel (371)	16.6	21.1	15.5	18.1
Non-ferrous metals (372)	18.9	22.6	15.5	19.7
Metal products (381)	10.4	12.8	10.9	12.5

Table B5 continued

Industry (ISIC)	Non-wage value added per employee [b]		Wages per employee [c]	
	1970-1977	1978-1985	1970-1977	1978-1985
Non-electrical machinery (382)	12.1	16.0	12.3	14.7
Electrical machinery (383)	9.9	15.7	10.4	13.3
Transport equipment (384)	11.9	14.7	12.9	14.6
Professional scientific equipment (385)	12.7	17.0	10.1	12.2
Other manufactures (390)	11.5	14.8	9.8	11.1

Source: UNIDO

a/ The figures in the present table are weighted averages over the 20 DMEs shown in tables 6.5 to 6.7 and over the years within each time period for which data were available, with the weights being numbers of employees. For more details on country coverage and methods of computation see the text of the present appendix.

b/ Non-wage value added per employee is taken to be a proxy for physical-capital intensity.

c/ Wages per employee are taken to be a proxy for human-capital intensity.

d/ Group averages exclude Ireland and Portugal.

Table B6 NIEs' average factor intensities,[a] 1970–7 and 1978–85 (thousands of 1980 US dollars)

Industry (ISIC)	Non-wage value added per employee[b]		Wages per employee[c]	
	1970–1977	1978–1985	1970–1977	1978–1985
Food products (311)	11.2	12.8	3.6	3.2
Beverages (313)	9.1	11.4	2.8	2.6
Tobacco etc. (314)	14.9	16.6	4.4	4.1
Textiles (321)	6.2	6.5	2.8	2.5
Wearing apparel (322)	3.7	3.5	2.4	2.3
Leather and fur products (323)	5.4	5.1	4.8	2.7
Footwear (324)	4.0	3.5	3.6	2.5
Wood and cork products (331)	5.6	5.5	2.4	2.4
Furniture fixtures excl. metal (332)	5.3	7.2	3.1	2.7
Paper (341)	9.8	11.2	4.0	3.7
Printing and publishing (342)	11.4	9.6	6.9	4.7
Industrial chemicals (351)	16.6	25.8	5.6	6.0
Other chemicals (352)	13.7	18.9	5.0	5.1
Petroleum refineries (353)[d]	42.1	51.4	6.0	5.5
Products of petroleum and coal (354)[e]	13.1	21.3	3.8	4.4
Rubber products (355)	10.2	9.2	2.9	2.9
Plastic products (356)	7.5	6.5	3.3	2.7
Pottery, china, earthenware (361)	7.0	7.3	3.6	2.9
Glass (362)	10.9	11.1	6.0	4.5
Other non-metallic min. products (369)	7.8	8.8	3.1	2.8
Iron and steel (371)	15.9	17.8	5.1	4.7
Non-ferrous metals (372)	12.5	12.4	7.1	4.0
Metal products (381)	6.5	6.9	3.5	3.0

Table B6 continued

Industry (ISIC)	Non-wage value added per employee [b/]		Wages per employee [e/]	
	1970–1977	1978–1985	1970–1977	1978–1985
Non-electrical machinery (382)	8.9	7.2	4.7	3.8
Electrical machinery (383)	5.9	7.4	3.5	3.1
Transport equipment (384)	7.6	8.5	5.0	4.2
Professional scientific equipment (385)	4.4	6.2	3.2	3.6
Other manufactures (390)	4.7	6.7	3.1	2.9

Source: UNIDO

a/ The figures in the present table are weighted averages over the six NIEs shown in tables 6.5 to 6.7 and over the years within each time period for which data were available, with the weights being numbers of employees. For more details on country coverage and methods of computation see the text of the present appendix.

b/ Non-wage value added per employee is taken to be a proxy for physical-capital intensity.

c/ Wages per employee are taken to be a proxy for human-capital intensity.

d/ Group averages exclude Hong Kong.

e/ Group averages exclude Hong Kong and Singapore.

Table B7 Second-generation NIEs' average factor intensities,[a] 1970–7 and 1978–85 (thousands of 1980 US dollars)

Industry (ISIC)	Non-wage value added per employee[b]		Wages per employee[c]	
	1970–1977	1978–1985	1970–1977	1978–1985
Food products (311)	5.1	7.2	1.4	2.0
Beverages (313)	12.4	18.4	1.9	2.8
Tobacco etc. (314)	4.5	7.4	0.8	1.0
Textiles (321)	2.4	3.2	1.1	1.4
Wearing apparel (322)	3.5	2.5	2.2	2.0
Leather and fur products (323)	3.2	4.4	1.5	2.1
Footwear (324)	1.8	2.6	1.4	1.7
Wood and cork products (331)	2.7	3.6	1.7	1.8
Furniture fixtures excl. metal (332)	2.4	2.0	1.9	1.6
Paper (341)	4.7	5.9	1.6	1.8
Printing and publishing (342)	4.2	4.7	2.4	2.7
Industrial chemicals (351)	7.2	10.4	1.7	2.3
Other chemicals (352)	6.5	7.9	2.3	2.6
Petroleum refineries (353)[d]	164.1	115.9	13.6	8.6
Products of petroleum and coal (354)[e]	145.9	101.8	13.8	9.6
Rubber products (355)	4.8	4.9	1.6	1.8
Plastic products (356)	2.3	3.9	1.1	1.5
Pottery, china, earthenware (361)	3.9	3.8	1.9	1.9
Glass (362)	4.0	5.2	1.8	2.2
Other non-metallic min. products (369)	6.7	9.1	2.4	3.2
Iron and steel (371)	6.0	8.6	2.3	2.6
Non-ferrous metals (372)[d]	6.3	17.0	1.5	1.5
Metal products (381)	3.3	4.7	1.6	2.1

Table B7 continued

Industry (ISIC)	Non-wage value added per employee [b/]		Wages per employee [c/]	
	1970–1977	1978–1985	1970–1977	1978–1985
Non-electrical machinery (382)	3.2	4.6	1.7	2.1
Electrical machinery (383)	4.9	5.2	1.9	2.2
Transport equipment (384)	5.1	5.5	2.2	2.2
Professional scientific equipment (385)	8.6	6.9	4.0	3.2
Other manufactures (390)	4.0	4.6	1.3	2.3

Source: UNIDO

a/ The figures in the present table are weighted averages over the seven second-generation NIEs shown in tables 6.5 to 6.7 and over the years within each time period for which data were available, with the weights being numbers of employees. For more details on country coverage and methods of computation see the text of the present appendix.

b/ Non-wage value added per employee is taken to be a proxy for physical-capital intensity.

c/ Wages per employee are taken to be a proxy for human-capital intensity.

d/ Group averages exclude Indonesia.

e/ Group averages exclude Indonesia and Tunisia.

Table B8 Selected developing countries' average factor intensities,[a] 1970–7 and 1978–85 (thousands of 1980 US dollars)

Industry (ISIC)	Non-wage value added per employee[b]		Wages per employee[c]	
	1970–1977	1978–1985	1970–1977	1978–1985
Food products (311)	3.4	4.0	1.7	2.0
Beverages (313)	9.0	12.0	2.5	3.4
Tobacco etc. (314)	3.4	2.3	0.9	1.1
Textiles (321)	2.4	2.2	2.3	2.2
Wearing apparel (322)	9.7	5.7	9.0	6.0
Leather and fur products (323)	4.6	4.1	2.3	2.1
Footwear (324)	6.3	4.2	5.9	4.1
Wood and cork products (331)	5.0	6.3	3.8	4.1
Furniture fixtures excl. metal (332)	3.7	4.2	2.9	3.3
Paper (341)	5.7	6.5	2.7	3.7
Printing and publishing (342)	3.1	4.0	2.8	3.1
Industrial chemicals (351)	7.1	9.1	2.8	3.7
Other chemicals (352)	5.4	6.2	2.4	2.8
Petroleum refineries (353)	52.8	67.2	7.2	5.5
Products of petroleum and coal (354)[d]	12.5	11.0	4.8	3.1
Rubber products (355)	4.3	5.3	2.7	2.9
Plastic products (356)[e]	3.7	5.3	2.0	2.6
Pottery, china, earthenware (361)[f]	3.7	3.4	3.3	2.6
Glass (362)	2.3	3.6	1.9	2.6
Other non-metallic min. products (369)	3.8	4.3	2.5	2.5
Iron and steel (371)	3.6	3.7	2.6	2.7
Non-ferrous metals (372)	9.9	11.8	3.1	4.0
Metal products (381)	3.9	5.0	2.7	3.1

Table **B8** continued

Industry (ISIC)	Non-wage value added per employee [b]		Wages per employee [c]	
	1970–1977	1978–1985	1970–1977	1978–1985
Non-electrical machinery (382)	2.8	3.6	2.5	2.7
Electrical machinery (383)	3.6	4.9	2.6	2.9
Transport equipment (384)[a]	2.9	3.5	2.7	3.0
Professional scientific equipment (385)	2.0	2.8	1.9	2.1
Other manufactures (390)	13.2	22.7	15.1	21.7

Source: UNIDO

a/ The figures in the present table are weighted averages over the ten non-NIEs shown in tables 6.5 to 6.7 and over the years within each time period for which data were available, with the weights being numbers of employees. For more details on country coverage and methods of computation see the present appendix.

b/ Non-wage value added per employee is taken to be a proxy for physical-capital intensity.

c/ Wages per employee are taken to be a proxy for human-capital intensity.

d/ Group averages exclude the Dominican Republic and Guatemala.

e/ Group averages exclude Pakistan.

f/ Group averages exclude the Dominican Republic and Panama.

g/ Group averages exclude the Dominican Republic.

Table B9 Determinants of bilateral intra-industry trade, [a] 1985

Industry (SITC)	Partial correlations [b] between the level of bilateral IIT and:				Impact of quality difference on the share of bilateral IIT between DMEs and developing countries/areas [a]
	Income [c] similarity	Size [e] similarity	Average income [d]	Average size [d]	
Organic chemicals (512)	0.100*	0.435*	0.115*	0.487*	0.068**
Inorganic chemicals: elements, oxides & halides (513)	0.120*	0.333*	0.101*	0.392*	-0.083
Other inorganic chemicals (514)	0.102*	0.232*	0.053***	0.316*	0.000
Radioactive and associated materials (515)	0.071***	0.289*	0.041	0.340*	.
Mineral tar and crude chemical (521)	0.102**	0.119**	0.040	0.163*	-0.089
Synthetic organic dyestuffs (531)	0.064***	0.260*	0.171*	0.287*	0.122**
Dyeing & tanning extracts and materials (532)	0.005	0.193*	-0.051	0.223*	0.010
Pigments, paints varnishes and related materials (533)	0.140*	0.354*	0.164*	0.390*	0.034
Medical and pharmaceutical products (541)	0.161*	0.393*	0.241*	0.451*	-0.031
Essential oils, perfume and flavour materials (551)	0.066***	0.424*	0.027	0.501*	-0.136*
Perfumery and cosmetics except soaps (553)	0.096**	0.416*	0.107*	0.443*	0.059
Soaps, cleansing and polishing preparations (554)	0.150*	0.279*	0.172*	0.307*	0.109**
Fertilizers, manufactured (561)	0.073***	-0.013	0.120*	0.025	0.055
Explosives and pyrotechnic products (571)	0.088**	0.114***	0.064***	0.187*	0.206**
Plastic materials, regenerated (581)	0.122*	0.359*	0.110*	0.404*	0.091*
Chemical materials and products (599)	0.116*	0.404*	0.087**	0.462*	0.076*
Leather (611)	0.095**	0.773*	0.025	0.420*	0.061
Manufactures of leather or reconstitutes (612)	-0.005	0.340*	0.010	0.181*	0.037

Table B9 continued

Industry (SITC)	Partial correlations[b] between the level of bilateral IIT and:				Impact of quality difference on the share of bilateral IIT between DMEs and developing countries/areas[a]
	Income[c] similarity	Size[c] similarity	Average income[d]	Average size[d]	
Fur skins, tanned or dressed (613)	-0.043	0.446*	0.016	0.235*	0.033
Materials of rubber (621)	0.099*	0.361*	0.102*	0.404*	0.141**
Articles of rubber (629)	0.101*	0.357*	0.089*	0.397*	0.058***
Veneers, plywood boards, reconstituted wood (631)	0.100***	0.140*	0.079**	0.187*	-0.036
Wood manufactures (632)	0.123*	0.114*	0.141*	0.153*	-0.039
Cork manufactures (633)	0.016	0.146*	-0.007	0.158*	-0.165***
Paper and paperboard (641)	0.084**	0.249*	0.100*	0.290*	0.132*
Articles of pulp, paper or paperboard (642)	0.168*	0.218*	0.193*	0.245*	-0.028
Textile, yarn & thread (651)	0.106*	0.340*	0.149*	0.360*	0.052
Cotton fabrics, woven (652)	0.072**	0.290*	0.111*	0.306*	-0.037
Textile fabrics, woven other than cotton (653)	0.109*	0.272*	0.133*	0.305*	0.037
Tulle, lace, embroidery, ribbons, etc. (654)	0.075***	0.258*	0.132*	0.293*	-0.030
Special textile fabrics and related products (655)	0.110*	0.388*	0.135*	0.436*	0.031
Made-up articles, chiefly of textiles (656)	0.157*	0.186*	0.171*	0.226*	-0.084*
Floor coverings, tapestries etc. (657)	0.079***	0.108*	0.116*	0.154*	-0.012
Lime, cement, building materials excluding glass and clay (661)	0.117*	0.082**	0.100**	0.111*	-0.033
Clay and refractory construction materials (662)	0.056***	0.303*	0.093**	0.321*	0.048
Mineral manufactures (663)	0.109*	0.427*	0.132*	0.471*	-0.014
Glass (664)	0.084***	0.225*	0.044	0.278*	0.110**
Glassware (665)	0.115*	0.285*	0.099*	0.329*	0.019
Pottery (666)	-0.051	0.510*	-0.143*	0.559*	0.059
Pig iron, spiegeleisen, sponge (671)	0.078***	0.289*	0.152*	0.308*	0.049

Table B9 continued

Industry (SITC)	Partial correlations[b/] between the level of bilateral IIT and:				Impact of quality difference on the share of bilateral IIT between DMEs and developing countries/areas[a/]
	Income[c/] similarity	Size[c/] similarity	Average income[d/]	Average size[d/]	
Office machines (714)	0.051***	0.433*	-0.017	0.507*	-0.021
Metalworking machinery (715)	0.060***	0.332*	0.094**	0.391*	0.071
Textile & leather machinery (717)	0.043	0.370*	0.093**	0.421*	0.075**
Machines for special industries (718)	0.092*	0.352*	0.068**	0.432*	0.069*
Machines, appliances (excl. electric.) parts (719)	0.106*	0.453*	0.083***	0.522*	0.035*
Electric power machinery, switchgear (722)	0.077**	0.443*	0.059***	0.522*	0.026
Equipment for distributing electricity (723)	0.079**	0.232*	0.069***	0.290*	0.136*
Telecommunications apparatus (724)	0.085**	0.277*	0.056***	0.356*	0.059**
Domestic electr. equipment (725)	0.112*	0.343*	0.164*	0.381*	0.063**
Electric apparatus for medical purposes (726)	0.019	0.570*	-0.032	0.633*	-0.004
Other electrical machinery and apparatus (729)	0.017	0.497*	-0.062**	0.578*	0.033***
Railway vehicles (731)	0.001	0.044	-0.001	0.106**	-0.090
Road motor vehicles (732)	0.054***	0.077***	0.024	0.118*	0.020
Road vehicles other than motor vehicles (733)	0.135*	0.221*	0.154*	0.247*	0.124**
Aircraft (734)	0.027	0.259*	0.001	0.307*	-0.125**
Ships and boats (735)	0.040	0.082***	-0.165*	0.098**	0.172**
Sanitary, plumbing, heating and lighting fixtures (812)	0.129*	0.219*	0.154*	0.254*	0.055
Furniture (821)	0.167*	0.185*	0.203*	0.221*	0.023
Railway vehicles (831)	0.145*	0.275*	0.152*	0.307*	-0.061
Clothing, excl. fur clothing (841)	0.145*	0.195*	0.166*	0.213*	-0.067*
Fur clothing and articles made of fur skins (842)	0.033	0.183*	0.088**	0.241*	0.051

Table B9 continued

Industry (SITC)	Partial correlations[b] between the level of bilateral IIT and:				Impact of quality difference on the share of bilateral IIT between DMEs and developing countries/areas[e]
	Income[c] similarity	Size[c] similarity	Average income[d]	Average size[d]	
Footwear (851)	0.117*	0.237*	0.137*	0.262*	0.047
Scientific, medical, optical measuring instruments (861)	0.042	0.662*	-0.031	0.707*	0.002
Photographic and cinematographic supplies (862)	0.046	0.637*	-0.039	0.685*	-0.066
Watches and clocks (864)	0.028	0.029	0.125*	0.055***	.
Musical instruments, sound recorders & reproducers (891)	0.076**	0.549*	0.028	0.600*	0.013
Printed matter (892)	0.125*	0.223*	0.088*	0.286*	-0.003
Articles of artificial plastic materials (893)	0.149*	0.338*	0.156*	0.388*	0.125*
Perambulators, toys, games, sporting goods (894)	0.107*	0.455*	0.060***	0.519*	-0.027
Office & stationery supplies (895)	0.077**	0.556*	0.072**	0.605*	0.080**
Jewellery, gold and silverwares (897)	0.063***	0.171*	0.165*	0.223*	.
Manufactured articles (899)	0.170*	0.476*	0.167*	0.549*	0.033

Source: UNIDO

<u>a</u>/ Results were derived from observations on trade between all pairs of members of a sample of 22 DMEs and 25 developing countries and areas.

<u>b</u>/ Asterisks indicate statistical significance at the 1(*), 5(**) or 10(***) per cent level.

<u>c</u>/ Similarity between countries in terms of income (size) was measured by the negative of the absolute difference in GDP per capita (total GDP).

<u>d</u>/ Average income (size) was indicated by the arithmetic mean of GDP per capita (total GDP).

<u>e</u>/ The figures shown in this column are coefficient estimates obtained from a linear regression of IIT shares on income similarity, size similarity, average income, average size and the direction of quality difference. Only the coefficients of the last independent variable are presented in this table. This variable took the form of a dummy variable which assumed the value of 1 if the unit value of the DME's exports to the developing country exceeded that of its imports from the latter and the value of 0 otherwise.

Table B9 continued

Industry (SITC)	Partial correlations[b] between the level of bilateral IIT and:				Impact of quality difference on the share of bilateral IIT between DMEs and developing countries/areas[e]
	Income[a] similarity	Size[c] similarity	Average income[d]	Average size[d]	
Ingots and forms of iron or steel (672)	0.052	0.130*	0.007	0.150*	0.040
Iron and steel bars, rods, angles, etc. (673)	0.092**	0.262*	0.159*	0.273*	0.064
Universals, plates & sheets (674)	-0.009	0.529*	-0.093*	0.594*	0.243*
Hoop & strip/iron or steel (675)	0.069***	0.259*	0.122*	0.273*	0.030
Rails and railway track construction materials (676)	0.057	-0.043	-0.064	-0.015	0.042
Iron and steel wire (677)	0.088**	0.239*	0.129*	0.256*	0.091
Tubes, pipes and fittings of iron or steel (678)	0.124*	0.248*	0.174*	0.289*	0.175*
Iron and steel castings, forgings, unworked (679)	0.089***	0.129*	0.065	0.186*	0.200
Finished structures and structural parts (691)	0.094**	0.120*	0.156*	0.148*	0.086
Metal containers for storage and transport (692)	0.125*	0.167*	0.125*	0.210*	0.070
Wire products (excluding electric), fencing grills (693)	0.109*	0.256*	0.098**	0.291*	0.100
Nails, screws, nuts, bolts, rivets, etc. (694)	-0.034	0.433*	-0.088**	0.488*	0.125**
Tools for use in the hand or in machines (695)	0.128*	0.387*	0.172*	0.454*	0.147*
Cutlery (696)	-0.004	0.580*	-0.013	0.618*	-0.032
Household equipment of base metals (697)	0.081**	0.416*	0.058***	0.457*	0.007
Manufacture of metals (698)	0.112*	0.271*	0.111*	0.328*	0.064*
Power generating machinery, excl. electric (711)	0.059***	0.227*	0.004	0.299*	-0.003
Agricultural machinery and implements (712)	0.070**	0.122*	0.038	0.170*	0.121**

Table B10 Categorization of industries by economies of scale, industrial concentration, product differentiation and export concentration

Industry (SITC)	Scale [a] economies	Industrial [b] concentration	Product [c] differentiation	Export [d] concentration
Meat, fresh, chilled or frozen (011)	5	4	4	4
Meat in airtight containers, n.e.s. (013)	1	5	5	2
Milk and cream (022)	3	5	1	1
Butter (023)	1	1	5	1
Cheese and curd (024)	2	4	5	1
Fish preparations (032)	5	4	1	5
Rice, glazed or polished (0422)	5	1	.	1
Meal and flour of wheat or of meslin (046)	4	2	1	1
Cereal preparations and starch (048)	1	5	4	5
Fruit, preserved and fruit preparations (053)	5	4	1	5
Vegetables, roots and tubers, preserved or prepared (055)	1	2	1	5
Sugar and honey (061)	1	1	1	5
Sugar preparations (062)	1	4	4	5
Chocolate (073)	1	5	5	4
Feeding-stuff for animals (081)	2	5	1	3
Margarine and shortening (091)	1	2	3	2
Food preparations, n.e.s. (099)	2	5	2	5
Non-alcoholic beverages, n.e.s. (111)	3	5	4	3
Alcoholic beverages (112)	1	1	5	1
Tobacco manufactures (122)	1	1	5	1
Synthetic and reclaimed rubber and substitutes (231)	1	5	5	2
Wood shaped or simply worked (243)	3	5	3	1
Pulp and waste paper (251)	2	1	2	1
Synthetic and regenerated fibres (266)	2	1	4	3
Petroleum products (332)	1	3	2	5
Animal oils and fats (411)	2	4	2	1
Fixed vegetable oils and fats (421)	5	2	2	3
Other fixed vegetable oils (422)	5	1	2	1
Inorganic chemicals: elements, oxides and halides (513)	5	2	.	5
Other inorganic chemicals (514)	5	3	1	3
Pigments, paints, varnishes and related materials (533)	2	5	4	3

Table B10 continued

Industry (SITC)	Scale[b] economies	Categorical measure of [a] Industrial[b] concentration	Product[c] differentiation	Export[d] concentration
Medicinal and pharmaceutical products (541)	2	3	3	4
Essential oil, perfume and flavour materials (551)	5	2	1	3
Perfumery and cosmetics, except soaps (553)	2	3	4	1
Soaps, cleansing and polishing preparations (554)	2	5	4	3
Fertilizers, manufactured (561)	1	2	1	5
Explosives and pyrotechnic products (571)	4	1	1	4
Plastic materials, regenerated cellulose, etc. (581)	4	3	3	3
Chemical materials and products, n.e.s. (599)	5	4	1	3
Leather (611)	2	3	5	5
Manufactures of leather or reconstituted (612)	1	2	4	5
Articles of rubber, n.e.s. (629)	4	3	5	3
Veneers, plywood boards, reconstituted wood (631)	4	5	2	5
Wood manufactures, n.e.s. (632)	4	5	2	5
Paper and paperboard (641)	2	3	2	3
Articles of pulp, paper or paperboard (642)	3	4	2	4
Textile yarn & thread (excl.synthetic or regenerated) (651)	5	3	4	5
Cotton fabrics, woven (652)	5	3	5	5
Textile fabrics, woven other than cotton (653)	5	3	5	4
Tulle, lace, embroidery, ribbons, etc. (654)	4	3	2	3
Special textile fabrics and related products (655)	1	2	4	4
Made-up articles, chiefly of textiles (656)	4	4	3	5
Floor coverings, tapestries, etc. (657)	3	3	4	4
Lime, cement, building materials, excl. glass & clay (661)	5	4	1	5
Clay and refractory construction materials (662)	3	2	3	2
Mineral manufactures, n.e.s. (663)	4	5	1	4
Glass (664)	1	2	1	3
Glassware (665)	5	3	1	4
Pottery (666)	1	1	2	2
Pig iron, spiegeleisen, sponge iron, etc. (671)	4	2	3	5
Ingots and forms of iron or steel (672)	4	2	5	2
Iron and steel bars, rods, angles, etc. (673)	1	2	1	4
Universals, plates and sheets of iron or steel (674)	1	1	4	2
Hoop and strip of iron or steel (675)	5	2	4	1
Rails and railway track construction materials (676)	.	1	4	2
Iron and steel wire (677)	3	3	4	3
Tubes, pipes and fittings of iron or steel (678)	2	3	1	2

Table B10 continued

Industry (SITC)	Scale[1/] economies	Categorical measure of[a/] Industrial[1/] concentration	Product[2/] differentiation	Export[1/] concentration
Iron and steel castings, forgings, unworked (679)	4	4	1	3
Copper (682)	5	2	4	4
Nickel (683)	2	1	3	1
Aluminium (684)	1	1	3	5
Zinc (686)	3	2	3	2
Tin (687)	2	1	5	1
Finished structures and structural parts, n.e.s. (691)	4	5	2	4
Metal containers for storage and transport (692)	4	5	3	4
Wire products (excl. electric). fencing grills (693)	2	4	2	5
Nails, screws, nuts, bolts, etc. (694)	5	5	3	3
Tools for use in the hand or in machines (695)	3	3	3	4
Cutlery (696)	2	2	4	3
Manufacture of metals, n.e.s. (698)	3	5	3	4
Power generating machinery, excl. electric (711)	2	1	3	2
Agricultural machinery and implements (712)	1	4	5	2
Office machines (714)	4	4	2	1
Metalworking machinery (715)	3	5	4	2
Textile and leather machinery (717)	5	4	4	1
Machines for special industries (718)	3	4	2	2
Machines, appliances (excl. electric.), parts (719)	3	5	4	3
Electric power machinery, switchgear (722)	3	3	4	3
Equipment for distributing electricity (723)	4	3	2	4
Telecommunications apparatus (724)	3	4	3	2
Domestic electrical equipment (725)	3	1	4	3
Electric apparatus for medical purposes (726)	2	2	5	1
Other electrical machinery and apparatus (729)	4	3	2	2
Railway vehicles (731)	4	1	1	3
Road motor vehicles (732)	2	3	5	1
Road vehicles other than motor vehicles (733)	2	4	4	2
Aircraft (734)	3	1	2	1
Ships and boats (735)	4	2	2	2
Sanitary, plumbing, heating and lighting fixtures (812)	3	4	3	4
Furniture (821)	5	5	3	4

Table B10 continued

Industry (SITC)	Scale economies [b]	Categorical measure of [a]		Export [d] concentration
		Industrial [b] concentration	Product [c] differentiation	
Travel goods, handbags and similar articles (831)	5	3	3	3
Clothing, except fur clothing (841)	5	5	5	5
Footwear (851)	5	3	5	2
Scientific, medical, optical, measuring instruments (861)	4	3	.	2
Photographic and cinematographic supplies (862)	3	1	.	1
Watches and clocks (864)	4	2	.	1
Musical instruments, sound recorders & reproducers (891)	4	3	3	4
Printed matter (892)	3	5	5	4
Articles of artificial plastic materials, n.e.s. (893)	3	5	3	4
Perambulators, toys, games, sporting goods (894)	2	4	3	4
Office and stationery supplies, n.e.s. (895)	3	2	.	2
Jewellery, gold and silver wares (897)	3	4	.	2
Manufactured articles, n.e.s. (899)	2	5	2	5

Sources: UNIDO and United States, Bureau of the Census (1984).

a/ Each variable takes values, 1, 2, 3, 4 or 5, indicating the magnitude for the respective industrial characteristic, where 1=high, 2=medium high, 3=medium, 4=medium low and 5=low. Each category is made up of 20 per cent of the distribution of industries in the respective variable.

b/ The measures of scale economies (size elasticity) and of industrial concentration (employment entropy index) were derived from United States census data for 1982. These measures were first calculated at the most detailed level of industry classification. Results were then aggregated to the three-digit level of the SITC using the concordance with the USSIC given in Hufbauer (1970). The proxies for scale economies and industrial concentration were expressed as weighted averages, where the weights were the total number of persons engaged in each four-digit category of the USSIC which fell within a three-digit SITC category.

c/ (Vertical) product differentiation was proxied by the coefficient of variation of unit values of United States exports to various destinations for 1982. Such coefficients were first calculated at the five-digit SITC level and then aggregated to the three-digit SITC level in the form of weighted averages, where export values were used as weights.

d/ The proxy variable for export concentration was the export entropy index, calculated on the basis of three-digit SITC data for 91 countries and areas in 1983.

Bibliography

Agarwal, V., and Winkler, D. (1984), 'Migration of professional manpower to the United States', *Southern Economic Journal*, vol. 50, no. 3, pp. 814–30.

Agmon, T. (1979), 'Direct investment and intra-industry trade: substitutes or complements?', in H. Giersch (ed.), *On the Economics of Intra-Industry Trade* (Tübingen: J.C.B. Mohr).

Aho, C., and Bayard, T. (1982), 'The 1980s: twilight of the open trading system?', *The World Economy*, vol. 5, no. 4, pp. 379–406.

Anderson, J. (1981), 'Cross section tests of the Heckscher–Ohlin theorem: comment', *American Economic Review*, vol. 71, no. 5, pp. 1037–9.

Anderson, J. (1987), 'Sources of international comparative advantage: theory and evidence' (book review), *Journal of Economic Literature*, vol. 25, no. 1, pp. 146–7.

Aquino, A. (1978), 'Intra-industry trade and inter-industry specialization as concurrent sources of international trade in manufacturers', *Weltwirtschaftliches Archiv*, vol. 114, no. 2, pp. 275–94.

Auquier, A. (1980), 'Sizes of firms, exporting behaviour, and the structure of French industry', *Journal of Industrial Economics*, vol. 29, no. 2, pp. 203–19.

Aw, B. (1983), 'The interpretation of cross-section regression tests of the Heckscher–Ohlin theorem with many goods and factors', *Journal of International Economics*, vol. 14, pp. 163–7.

Ayler, J. (1981), *Plant Size and Efficiency in the Steel Industry: An International Comparison* (Salford: University of Salford).

Bailey, E., and Friedlander, A. (1982), 'Market structure and multiproduct industries', *Journal of Economic Literature*, vol. 20, no. 3, pp. 1024–48.

Balassa, B. (1965), 'Trade liberalization and "revealed" comparative advantage', *Manchester School of Economic and Social Studies*, vol. 33, no. 2, pp. 99-123.

Balassa, B. (1979), 'The changing pattern of comparative advantage in manufactured goods', *Review of Economics and Statistics*, vol. 61, no. 2, pp. 259–66.

Balassa, B., and Bauwens, L. (1987), 'Intra-industry specialization in a multi-country and multi-industry framework', *Economic Journal*, vol. 97, no. 388, pp. 921–39.

Baldwin, R. (1971), 'Determinants of the commodity structure of US trade', *American Economic Review*, vol. 61, no. 1, pp. 126–46.

Baldwin, R. (1979), 'Determinants of trade and foreign investment: further evidence', *Review of Economics and Statistics*, vol. 61, no. 1, pp. 40–8.

Batchelor, R., Major, R., and Morgan, A. (1980), *Industrialization and the Basis for Trade* (London: Cambridge University Press), pp. 16-17.

Bowden, R. (1983), 'The conceptual basis of empirical studies of trade in manufactured commodities: a constructive critique', *Manchester School of Economic and Social Studies*, vol. 51, no. 3, pp. 209–34.

Bowen, H. (1983a), 'Changes in the international distribution of resources and the impact on US comparative advantage', *Review of Economics and Statistics*, vol. 65, no. 3, pp. 402–14.

Bowen, H. (1983b), 'On the theoretical interpretation of indices of trade intensity and revealed comparative advantage', *Weltwirtschaftliches Archiv*, vol. 119, no. 3, pp. 464–72.

Bowen, H., Leamer, E., and Sveikauskas, L. (1987), 'Multicountry, multifactor tests of the factor abundance theory', *American Economic Review*, vol. 77, no. 5, pp. 791–809.

Bradford, C. (1987), 'Trade and structural change: NICs and next tier NICs as transitional economies', *World Development*, vol. 15, no. 3, pp. 299–316.

Bradford, C., and Branson, W. (1987), *Trade and Structural Change in Pacific Asia* (Chicago: University of Chicago Press).

Branson, W., and Monoyios, N. (1977), 'Factor inputs in US trade', *Journal of International Economics*, vol. 7, pp. 111–31.

Buckley, P., and Casson, M. (1976), *The Future of Multinational Enterprise* (London: Macmillan).

Caves, R., Khalizadeh-Shirazi, J., and Porter, M. (1975), 'Scale economies in statistical analyses of market power', *Review of Economics and Statistics*, vol. 57, no. 2, pp. 133–40

Caves, R., and Williamson, P. (1985), 'What is product differentiation, really?', *Journal of Industrial Economics*, vol. 34, no. 2, pp. 113–33.

Chipman, J., 'International trade', in J. Eatwell, M. Milgate and P. Newman (eds), *The New Palgrave: A Dictionary of Economics*, vol. 2 (London: Macmillan), pp. 922–55.

Cline, W. (1982), '"Reciprocity": a new approach to world trade policy', in *Policy Analyses in International Economics* (Washington, DC: Institute for International Economics).

Cowhey, P., and Long, E. (1983), 'Testing theories of regime change: hegemonic decline or surplus capacity?' *International Organization*, vol. 37, no. 2, pp. 157–87.

Curry, B., and George, K. (1983), 'Industrial concentration: a survey', *Journal of Industrial Economics*, vol. 31, no. 3, pp. 203–55.

Das, S. (1982), 'Economies of scale, imperfect competition, and the pattern of trade', *Economic Journal*, vol. 92, no. 367, pp. 684–93.

Davies, S. (1979), 'Choosing between concentration indices: the iso-concentration curve', *Economica*, vol. 46, no. 2, pp. 67–75.

Deardorff, A. (1980), 'The general validity of the law of comparative advantage', *Journal of Political Economy*, vol. 88, no. 5, pp. 941–57.

Deardorff, A. (1982), 'The general validity of the Heckscher–Ohlin theorem', *American Economic Review*, vol. 72, no. 4, pp. 683–94.

Deardorff, A. (1984), 'Testing trade theories and predicting trade flows', in R. Jones and P. B. Kenen (eds), *Handbook of International Economics*, Vol. I (Amsterdam: North-Holland).

Deardorff, A. (1986), 'FIRless FIRwoes: how preferences can interfere with the theorems of international trade', *Journal of International Economics*, vol. 20, pp. 131–42.

Directorate-General of Budget, Accounting and Statistics, Executive Yuan (1986), *Statistical Yearbook of the Republic of China 1986* (Taipei: Republic of China).

Dixit, A. (1984), 'International trade policy for oligopolistic industries', *Conference Papers*, supplement to the *Economic Journal*, vol. 94, pp. 1–16.

Dixit, A., and Norman, V. (1980), *Theory of International Trade* (Cambridge: Cambridge University Press).

Dollar, D. (1986), 'Technological innovation, capital mobility, and the product cycle in North–South trade', *American Economic Review*, vol. 76, no. 1, pp. 177–90.

Dornbusch, R. (1973), 'Devaluation, money and non-trade goods', *American Economic Review*, vol. 63, no. 4, pp. 871–80.

215

Drèze, J. (1960), 'Quelques réflexions sereines sur l'adaptation de l'industrie belge au Marché Commun', *Comptes rendus des Travaux de la Société Royale d'Economie Politique de Belgique*, no. 275.

Dunning, J. (1977), 'Trade, location of economic activity and the MNE: a search for an eclectic approach', in B. Ohlin, P. O. Hesselborn, and P. J. Wikiman (eds), *The International Allocation of Economic Activity* (London: Macmillan).

Dunning, J. (1981), 'Explaining the international direct investment position of countries: towards a dynamic or developmental approach', *Weltwirtschaftliches Archiv*, vol. 117, no. 1, pp. 30–64.

Economic Planning Board, Republic of Korea (1987), *Report on Mining and Manufacturing Survey 1985* (Seoul: Republic of Korea).

Ethier, W. (1979), 'The theorems of international trade in time-phased economies', *Journal of International Economics*, vol. 9, pp. 225–38.

Ethier, W. (1981), 'A reply to Professors Metcalfe and Steedman', *Journal of International Economics*, vol. 11, pp. 273–7.

Ethier, W. (1984), 'Higher-dimensional issues in trade theory', in R. W. Jones and P. P. Kenen (eds), *Handbook of International Economics* (Amsterdam: North-Holland), pp. 131-84.

Ethier, W. and Svensson, L. (1986). 'The theorems of international trade with factor mobility', *Journal of International Economics*, vol. 20, pp. 21–42.

Falvey, R. (1981), 'Commercial policy and intra-industry trade', *Journal of International Economics*, vol. 11, pp. 495–511.

Flam, H., and Helpman, E. (1987), 'Vertical product differentiation and North–South trade', *American Economic Review*, vol. 77, no. 5, pp. 810–22.

Gleijser, H., Jacquemin, A., and Petit, J. (1980), 'Exports in an imperfect competition framework: an analysis of 1,446 exporters', *Quarterly Journal of Economics*, vol. 94, no. 3, pp. 507–24.

Gray, H. P. (1988), 'Intra-industry trade: an "untidy" phenomenon', *Weltwirtschaftliches Archiv*, vol. 124, no. 2, pp. 211–29.

Greenaway, D., and Milner, C. (1984), 'A cross section analysis of intra-industry trade in the UK', *European Economic Review*, vol. 25, no. 2, pp. 319–44.

Griliches, Z., and Ringstad, V. (1971), *Economies of Scale and the Form of the Production Function* (Amsterdam: North-Holland).

Grubel, H., and Lloyd, P. (1975), *Intra-Industry Trade* (London: Macmillan).

Hamilton, C., and Svensson, L. (1983), 'Should direct or total factor intensities be used in tests of the factor proportions hypothesis?', *Weltwirtschaftliches Archiv*, vol. 119, no. 3, pp. 453–63.

Havrylyshyn, O., and Alikhani, I. (1982), 'Is there cause for export optimism? An inquiry into the existence of a second generation of successful exporters', *Weltwirtschaftliches Archiv*, vol. 118, no. 4, pp. 651-63.

Helpman, E. (1981), 'International trade in the presence of product differentiation, economies of scale and monopolistic competition', *Journal of International Economics*, vol. 11, pp. 305–40.

Helpman, E. (1984), 'The factor content of foreign trade', *Economic Journal*, vol. 94, no. 373, pp. 84–94.

Helpman, E., and Krugman, P. (1985), *Market Structure and Foreign Trade* (Cambridge, Mass.: MIT Press).

Hirsch, S. (1974) 'Hypotheses regarding trade between developing and industrial countries', in H. Giersch (ed.), *The International Division of Labour: Problems and Prospects* (Tübingen: J.C.B. Mohr).

Howe, W. (1978), *Industrial Economics, an Applied Approach* (London: Macmillan).

Huang, W-C. (1987), 'A pooled cross-section and time-series study of professional indirect immigration to the United States', *Southern Economic Journal*, vol. 54, no. 1, pp. 95-109.

Hufbauer, G. (1970), 'The impact of national characteristics and technology on the commodity composition of trade in manufactured goods', in R. Vernon (ed.), *The Technology Factor in International Trade* (New York: National Bureau of Economic Research), pp. 145-231.

Hufbauer, G., and Chilas, J. (1974), 'Specialization by industrial countries: extent and consequences', in H. Giersch (ed.), *The International Division of Labour: Problems and Perspectives* (Tübingen: J.C.B. Mohr), pp. 3-38.

Hutchinson, M., and Piggott, C. (1985), 'Real and financial linkages in the macroeconomic response to budget deficits: an empirical investigation', in S. W. Arndt and J. D. Richardson (eds), *Exchange Rates, Trade and the US Economy* (Washington, DC: AEI).

Hymer, S. (1976), *The International Operations of National Firms: A Study of Foreign Direct Investment* (Cambridge, Mass.: MIT Press).

ILO, *Yearbook of Labour Statistics*, various issues (Geneva).

IMF (1984a), *Exchange Rate Volatility and World Trade*, Occasional Paper no. 28 (Washington, DC).

IMF (1984b), *The Exchange Rate System: Lessons of the Past and Options for the Future*, Occasional Paper no. 30 (Washington, DC).

Jacquemin, A., and Kumps, A-M. (1971), 'Changes in the size structure of the largest European firms: an entropy measure', *Journal of Industrial Economics*, vol. 20, no. 1, pp. 59-70.

Jones, R. (1971), 'A three-factor model in theory, trade and history', in J.A.N. Bhagwati, R. W. Jones, R. A. Mundell and J. Vanek (eds), *Trade, Balance of Payments and Growth* (Amsterdam: North-Holland), pp. 3-21.

Jones, R., and Scheinkman, J. (1977), 'The relevance of the two-sector production model in trade theory', *Journal of Political Economy*, vol. 85, no. 5, pp. 909-35.

Kindleberger, C. (1969), *American Business Abroad: Six Lectures on Direct Investment* (New Haven, Conn.: Yale University Press).

Kojima, K. (1978), *Direct Foreign Investment: A Japanese Model of Multinational Business* (New York: Praeger).

Krueger, A. (1977), *Growth Distortions and Patterns of Trade among Many Countries*, Princeton Studies in International Finance, no. 40 (Princeton, NJ: Princeton University Press).

Krugman, P. (1979a), 'Increasing returns, monopolistic competition and international trade', *Journal of International Economics*, vol. 9, pp. 469-79 .

Krugman, P. (1979b), 'A model of innovation, technology transfer and the world distribution of income', *Journal of Political Economy*, vol. 87, no. 2, pp. 253-66.

Krugman, P. (1980), 'Scale economies, product differentiation, and the pattern of trade', *American Economic Review*, vol. 70, no. 5, pp. 950-9.

Krugman, P. (1981), 'Intra-industry specialization and the gains from trade', *Journal of Political Economy*, vol. 89, no. 5, pp. 959-73.

Krugman, P. (1983), 'New theories of trade among industrial countries', *American Economic Review*, vol. 73, no. 2, pp. 343-7.

Krugman, P. (1987), 'Is free trade passé?' *Journal of Economic Perspectives*, vol. 1, no. 2, pp. 131-44.

Lancaster, K. (1980), 'Intra-industry trade under perfect monopolistic competition', *Journal of International Economics*, vol. 10, no. 2, pp. 151–75.

Lary, H. (1968), *Imports of Manufactures from the Less Developed Countries* (New York: NBER).

Lawrence, C. (1984), *Can America Compete?* (Washington, DC: Brookings Institution).

Leamer, E. (1974), 'The commodity composition of international trade in manufactures: an empirical analysis', *Oxford Economic Papers*, vol. 26, no. 3, pp. 350–74.

Leamer, E. (1980), 'The Leontief paradox reconsidered', *Journal of Political Economy*, vol. 88, no. 3, pp. 495–503.

Leamer, E. (1984), *Sources of International Comparative Advantage* (Cambridge, Mass: MIT Press).

Leamer, E., and Bowen, H. (1981), 'Cross-section tests of the Heckscher–Ohlin theorem: comment', *American Economic Review*, vol. 71, no. 5, pp. 1041-3.

Leontief, W. (1953), 'Domestic production and foreign trade: the American capital position re-examined', *Proceedings of the American Philosophical Society*, vol. 97, pp. 332–49.

Linder, S. (1961), *An Essay on Trade and Transportation* (New York: John Wiley).

Loertscher, R., and Wolter, F. (1980), 'Determinants of intra-industry trade: among countries and across industries', *Weltwirtschaftliches Archiv*, vol. 116, no. 2, pp. 280–92.

Machlup, F. (1958), 'Structure and structural change: weaselwords and jargon', *Zeitschrift für Nationalökonomie*, vol. 18, pp. 280–98.

Markusen, J. (1983), 'Factor movements and commodity trade as complements', *Journal of International Economics*, vol. 13, no. 3/4, pp. 341-56.

Maskus, K. (1983), 'Evidence on shifts in the determinants of the structure of US manufacturing foreign trade, 1958-1976', *Review of Economics and Statistics*, vol. 65, no. 3, pp. 415–22.

Maxwell, A. (1967), *Analysing Qualitative Data* (London: Methuen), pp. 117–21.

McGee, J. (1973), 'Economies of size in auto body manufactures', *Journal of Law and Economics*, vol. 16, no. 3, pp. 239–73.

Meller, P. (1978), 'The pattern of industrial concentration in Latin America', *Journal of Industrial Economics*, vol. 27, no. 1, pp. 41–7.

Michaely, M. (1985), 'The demand for protection against exports of newly industrializing countries', *Journal of Policy Modeling*, vol. 7, no. 1, pp. 123–32.

Ministry of International Trade and Industry, Japan (1986), *Census of Manufactures 1984, Report by Industries* (Tokyo).

Müller, J., and Owen, N. (1985), 'The effect of trade on plant size,' in Joachim Schwalbach (ed.), *Industry Structure and Performance* (West Berlin: International Institute of Management/Industrial Policy), p. 45.

Neary, J. (1985), 'Two-by-two international trade theory with many goods and factors', *Econometrica*, vol. 53, no. 5, pp. 1233–47.

Negishi, T. (1972), *General Equilibrium Theory and International Trade* (Amsterdam: North-Holland).

Norman, G., and Dunning, J. (1984), 'Intra-industry foreign direct investment: its rationale and trade effects', *Weltwirtschaftliches Archiv*, vol. 120, no. 3, pp. 522–40.

Obstfeld, M. (1986), 'Capital mobility in the world economy: theory and measurement', *Carnegie-Rochester Conference Series on Public Policy*, vol. 24, pp. 55–104.

OECD (1987), *Recent Trends in International Direct Investment* (Paris).

Ohlin, B. (1933), *Interregional and International Trade* (Cambridge, Mass.: Harvard University Press).

Posner, M. (1961), 'International trade and technical change', *Oxford Economic Papers*, vol. 13, pp. 323–41.

Ranis, G. (1981), 'Challenges and opportunities by Asia's superexporters: implications from Latin America', in W. Baer and M. Gillis (eds), *Export Diversification and the New Protectionism*, (Urbana, Ill.: University of Illinois), pp. 204–21.

Roskamp, K., and McMeekin, G. (1968), 'Factor proportions, human capital and foreign trade: the case of West Germany reconsidered', *Quarterly Journal of Economics*, vol. 82, no. 1, pp. 152-60.

Rugman, A. (1985), 'The determinants of intra-industry direct foreign investment', in A. Erdilek (ed.), *Multinationals as Mutual Invaders* (New York: St Martin's Press).

Rybczunski, T. (1955), 'Factor endowment and relative commodity prices', *Economica NS*, vol. 22, no. 4, pp. 336–41.

Schmalensee, R. (1988), 'Industrial economics: an overview', *Economic Journal*, vol. 98, no.392, pp. 643–81.

Sherman, R. (1974), *The Economics of Industry* (Boston: Little, Brown).

Steedman, I. (1979), *Fundamental Issues in Trade Theory* (New York: St Martin's Press).

Stern, R. (1976), 'Some evidence on the factor content of West Germany's foreign trade', *Journal of Political Economy*, vol. 84, no. 1, pp. 131-41.

Stern, R., and Maskus, K. (1981), 'Determinants of the structure of US foreign trade, 1958-1976', *Journal of International Economics*, vol. 11, pp. 207–24.

Sveikauskas, L. (1983), 'Science and technology in US foreign trade', *Economic Journal*, vol. 93, no. 30, pp. 542–54.

Tamor, K. (1987), 'An empirical examination of the factor endowments hypothesis', *Canadian Journal of Economics*, vol. 20, no. 2, pp. 387–98.

Theil, H. (1967), *Economics and Information Theory* (Amsterdam: North-Holland).

Theil, H. (1971), *Principles of Econometrics* (New York: John Wiley).

Toh, K. (1982), 'A cross-section analysis of intra-industry trade in US manufacturing industries', *Weltwirtschaftliches Archiv*, vol. 118, no. 2, pp. 218–301.

Tuong H., and Yeats, A. (1980), 'On factor proportions as a guide to the future composition of developing country exports', *Journal of Development Economics*, vol 7, no. 4, pp. 521–37.

UNESCO, *Statistical Yearbook*, various issues (Paris).

UNIDO (1981), *World Industry in 1980*, Sales no. E.81.II.B.3 (New York: United Nations).

UNIDO (1985), *Industry in the 1980s, Structural Change and Interdependence*, Sales no. E.85.II.B.8. (New York: United Nations).

UNIDO (1986), *International Comparative Advantage in Manufacturing*, Sales no. E.85.II.B.9 (Vienna: UNIDO).

UNIDO (1989), 'An Inventory of Industrial Statistics: UNIDO Data Base, 1989', PPD. 113 (Vienna: UNIDO).

United Nations, *Monthly Bulletin of Statistics*, various issues (New York).

United Nations, *Yearbook of International Trade Statistics*, various issues (New York).

United Nations, *Yearbook of National Accounts Statistics*, vol. II, various issues (New York).

US Department of Commerce, Bureau of the Census (1984), *Census of Manufactures 1982* (Washington, DC).

Vanek, J. (1968), 'The factor proportions theory: the N-factor case', *Kyklos*, vol. 21, no. 4, pp. 749–55.
Verdoorn, P. (1960), 'The intra-bloc trade of Benelux', in E. A. G. Robinson (ed.), *Economic Consequences of the Size of Nations* (London: Macmillan), pp. 291-329.
Vernon, R. (1966), 'International investment and international trade in the product cycle', *Quarterly Journal of Economics*, vol. 80, no. 2, pp. 190–207.

World Bank (1976), *World Tables 1976* (Baltimore and London: Johns Hopkins University Press).
World Bank (1987), *World Tables 1987*, vols I and II (draft edition) (Washington, DC).

Author Index

Agarwal, V. 135
Agmon, T. 172
Aho, C. 27
Aquino, A. 30
Auquier, A. 138
Aw, B. 101
Ayler, J. 141

Bailey, E. 141
Balassa, B. 74, 95, 113, 136
Baldwin, R. 110, 174
Batchelor, R. 36
Bauwens, L. 136
Bayard, T. 27
Bowden, R. 95, 112
Bowen, H. 27, 74, 92, 101, 113
Bradford, C. 6, 44
Branson, W. 6, 73
Buckley, P. 175

Casson, M. 175
Caves, R. 141, 144
Chilas, J. 43
Cline, R. 6, 27
Cowhey, P. 159
Curry, B. 143

Das, S. 139
Davies, S. 159
Deardorff, A. 3, 67, 71–2, 91, 94–5, 112–13, 116, 179, 182
Dixit, A. 70–1, 91, 93, 113, 138–9, 155–6, 159
Dollar, D. 111
Dornbusch, R. 133
Dunning, J. 173–4, 176

Ethier, W. 73, 92, 184

Falvey, R. 167
Flam, H. 167–8, 171
Friedlander, A. 141

George, K. 143
Gleijser, H. 138
Gray, P. 161
Griliches, Z. 141
Grubel, H. 61, 160

Hamilton, C. 113
Helpman, E. 92, 114, 127–8, 159, 167–8, 171
Hirsch, S. 43
Howe, W. 144
Huang, W. 136
Hufbauer, G. 43, 126, 141–2, 159, 192
Hutchinson, M. 133
Hymer, S. 175

ILO 188
IMF 134

Jacquemin, A. 138, 159
Jones, R. 94, 113

Khalizadeh-Shirazi, J. 141
Kindleberger, C. 175
Kojima, K. 175
Krueger, A. 103, 113
Krugman, P. 4, 6–8, 114, 127, 138, 159–60
Kumps, M. 159

Lancaster, K. 129
Lary, H. 52, 112
Lawrence, C. 35
Leamer, E. 74–6, 92, 101, 113, 136, 185
Leontief, W. 73, 92
Linder, S. 129
Lloyd, P. 61, 160
Loertscher, R. 136
Long, E. 159

Machlup, F. 35
Major, R. 36
Markusen, J. 135, 173
Maskus, K. 110
McGee, J. 141
McMeekin, G. 113
Meller, P. 159
Michaely, M. 7
Monoyios, N. 73
Morgan, A. 36
Mueller, J. 143

Neary, P. 95, 113
Negishi, T. 138
Norman, V. 70–1, 91, 95, 113, 138–9, 159

Obstfeld, M. 133
OECD 112
Ohlin, B. 138
Owen, N. 143

Petit, J. 138
Piggott, C. 133
Porter, M. 141
Posner, M. 109

Ranis, G. 44
Ringstad, V. 141
Roskamp, K. 113
Rugman, A. 173

Scheinkman, J. 94
Schmalensee, R. 140
Sherman, R. 144
Steedman, I. 92
Stern, R. 110
Sveikauskas, L. 74, 92

Svensson, L. 113

Tamor, K. 136
Theil, H. 159
Toh, K. 162
Tuong, H. 52

UNESCO 188
UNIDO 43, 95, 177, 187
United Nations 190

Vanek, J. 92
Verdoorn, R. 68
Vernon, R. 110

Williamson, P. 144
Winkler, D. 135
Wolter, F. 136
World Bank 188

Yeats, A. 52

Subject Index

Note: References to figures are in *italics*

Argentina 55, 80, 191
Australia 49, 55
Austria 86
autarky
  prices 72, 182
  state of 5, 74
average income, impact on IIT Table 7.3, 130,
  Table B9
average-cost curve 140

Belgium 89, 104, 113, 188
beta coefficient 116, 185
beverages 25, 95, 148, 151
'bloc' hypothesis
  formulation 103
  test of 104–7
Brazil 41, 43, 92, 191

Canada 49, 92, 166
capital goods, IIT in 65
chemicals 22, 25, 67, 95, 98, 120–2, 135, 145, 148,
  151, 171, 173
Chile 43, 191
clothing 22, 98, 121, 145, 151, 171
Colombia 55
commodity composites
  see composite commodities
composite commodities 113
cone of diversification 136
consistency of structural change 32–3, 55
consumer goods, IIT in 65, 67
consumer preferences 127, 158
convergence of industry structure 27
cost of technology transfer 111
country groupings 5–6, Table B2
country similarity
  empirical measurement 129
  in per capita income 126
  in size 126
country-similarity hypothesis 63

Dominican Republic 106

economies of scale
  and technological development 141
  external to the firm 155, 158
  importance for international trade 138–9
  internal to the firm 159
economies of scope 141
Egypt 80, 86, 92, 190
electrical machinery 22, 25, 27, 65, 67, 113, 121,
  145, 153, 171
employment entropy measure 143, Table 8.3
entry barriers 148, 153

factor abundance
  approach 6
  empirical indicators 75, Table 5.3
  physical definition 74
  price definition 74
factor abundance impact on trade
  general 116
  of physical capital 120
  of semi-skilled labour 121, 122
  of skilled labour 121
  of unskilled labour 122
factor abundance proposition
  contributions of various factors 125
  commodity version 91–2, 183
  correlation form 123
  empirical validation 122–3
  factor content version 92
  'strong' version 8, 72
  'weak' version 8, 72, 92, 123, 183
factor endowment regressions 115
factor endowments
  differences 76, Table 5.1
  dispersion 80, Table 5.2
factor input requirements 33, 82, 93, 136, 191–2
factor intensities
  average 95, Tables 6.1, B5–B8
  cross-country variation 98, Table 6.3
factor intensity rankings
  concordance 101, Table 6.4
  reversals 101
factor intensity reversals 93–4, 113
factor orientation 115–16, Table 7.1, 123, Table
  7.2, 184
factor prices
  convergence 90

223

factor prices (*cont.*)
  equalization 90
factor shares 94, 123
factor specificity 88
factor-input ratios 94–5, 112
foreign direct investment
  as a substitute for trade 173
  industry-cycle approach 175
  internalization theory 175
  intra-industry 173
  OLI paradigm 176
  product-cycle approach 174–5
  'unbundling' of 112
Finland 166
food products 25, 148, 151
footwear 22, 98, 121, 145, 151, 153
France 49, 63, 166
furniture 67, 98, 148

Germany, Federal Republic 33, 49, 63, 110, 166
glass products 145, 148, 151, 171
Greece 86, 104, 166
growth
  of exports of manufactures 36, Table 3.1
  of GDP 36, Table 3.1
  of total exports 36, Table 3.1
Grubel–Lloyd measure, of IIT 61, Table 4.1

H–O goods
  capital-intensive 82, 91, Table B4
  labour-intensive 82, Table B4
H–O model
  assumptions 7
  deviations from assumptions 137
  generalized version 71–2
homothetic preferences, assumption 70
Hong Kong 52, 80, 86, 92, 105, 191
human-capital endowments, estimation
  methods 75
human-capital intensity 98

IIT intensity 164, 166, Table 9.2
increasing returns
  see economies of scale
India 33, 76, 86, 105
Indonesia 80, 105, 107, 190
industrial concentration
  and country size 153, Table 8.4
  and level of industrial development 151, 153,
    Table 8.4
industrial output
  growth 25, 27
  structure 25
industry
  definition 4–5
  high-growth 33, Table B3
  low-growth 33, Table B3
international economics
  monetary side 131
  real side 131

international movement
  of capital 133–4
  of labour 134–5
intra-firm IIT 60
intra-industry trade
  and factor abundance 167
  and industrial concentration 162–3, Table 9.1
  and product differentiation 162, Table 9.1
  and quality difference 167–9, Table 9.3
  and scale economies 162, Table 9.1
  level 128–9, Table 7.3
  measurement problems 161
  product pattern 65, Table 4.3
  various types 59–60
iron and steel 22, 25, 95, 98, 120–2, 171
Israel 104, 166
Italy 49, 85

Japan 25, 27, 33, 41, 49, 52, 63, 69, 80, 85, 113,
  125, 166, 175

Kendall's coefficient of concordance 27, Table
  2.5
Korea, Republic of 41, 80, 105

labour migration
  see international movement of labour
leather products 98, 122
Leontief paradox 92, 109–10

Malaysia 41, 80, 86, 108, 190
market power 139, 142–3
market structure, relationship with trade 138–9
metal products 22, 27, 98, 144, 151
Mexico 86, 191
mineral products 145, 156
minimum efficient scale 139
monopolistic competition
  and industrial concentration 163
  Chamberlinian 7
  in the new models of trade 127, 139
multinational corporations
  and IIT 60
  and the technology gap 110

net exports vector 115
New Zealand 49, 104, 166
non-comparative-advantage trade 162, 164
non-electrical machinery 22, 67, 98, 120–1, 151,
  171
non-ferrous metals 22, 95, 98
Norway 49, 92

Pakistan 33, 41, 92, 105, 190
paper products 22, 98, 148, 153, 171
Peru 55, 191
petroleum products 95, 98, 145, 148, 151
petroleum refining 22, 25, 38, 95, 98
Philippines 86, 92, 108
physical capital, measurement problems 73

physical-capital endowments, estimation
    methods 74
physical–capital intensity 95
plastic materials 65, 67
plastic products 121, 144–5, 153, 171
Portugal 80
pottery 98, 121, 153
preference-similarity theory 126
preference diversity 127
printing and publishing 151
product cycle, stages 44–6
product-cycle goods Table B4
product differentiation
    horizontal 144
    technological 145
    vertical 144–5
professional and scientific equipment 121, 153

reallocation of resources, between industries
    88
resource distribution vector 115
revealed comparative advantage 104, Table 6.5,
    Table 6.6, 164
Ricardian goods 43, Table B4
rubber products 145, 151, 171
Rybczynski relationship 103

scale economies
    see economies of scale
semi-skilled labour
    contribution to H-O relationship 125
    empirical measure 75
similarity in country size, impact on IIT 129,
    Tables 7.3, B9
similarity in income levels, impact on IIT 129,
    Table 7.3, B9
Singapore 41, 52, 80, 190
size elasticities, empirical measurement 145,
    Table 8.1, 148
skill classes 74
skill differentials 73
skilled labour, empirical measure 75
Spain 166

specialization
    complete global 103
    inter-industrial 5, Table 2.6
    intra-industrial 4
specific factors, effects on trade patterns 90
specific factors model 88–91
Standard International Trade Classification 4
structural adjustment, implications of IIT for 59
structural change
    indices 32, Table 2.8, 55, Table 3.9
    international measure 30, Table 2.7
Sweden 191

technological advantage 109
technology gap 109-10
technology transfer package 111
textiles 22, 25, 98, 121–2, 145
Thailand 41, 86, 92, 108, 190
tobacco 25, 95, 148, 151
trade barriers, removal of 37
trade in manufactures, definition 46
trade overlap 60–1
trade patterns
    for H-O goods 49, 3.1, 3.2
    for product-cycle goods 49, 3.1, 3.2
    for Ricardian goods 49, 3.1, 3.2
transport equipment 22, 25, 95, 98, 120
Tunisia 108, 190
Turkey 33, 86
two-way trade
    see intra-industry trade

United Kingdom 41, 52, 63, 166
unskilled labour, empirical measure 75
Uruguay 80, 86
United States 27, 33, 41, 43, 49, 52, 63, 76, 80,
    92, 110, 123, 134, 166

Venezuela 92, 191

wood products 151, 153

Yugoslavia 85, 105

RADIO LIFE

DEREK B. MILLER

RADIO LIFE

Jo Fletcher

BOOKS

First published in Great Britain in 2021 by

Jo Fletcher Books
an imprint of
Quercus Editions Ltd
Carmelite House
50 Victoria Embankment
London EC4Y 0DZ

An Hachette UK company

A CIP catalogue record for this book is available
from the British Library

HB ISBN 978 1 52940 858 4
TPB ISBN 978 1 52940 859 1
EBOOK ISBN 978 1 52940 860 7

10 9 8 7 6 5 4 3 2 1

Typeset by CC Book Production
Printed and bound in Great Britain by Clays Ltd, Elcograf S.p.A.

MIX
Paper from
responsible sources
FSC® C104740

Papers used by Quercus Editions Ltd are from well-managed forests
and other responsible sources.

For my daughter

The Ancients decided that the earth was no longer safe for their Knowledge and so they put it all in the sky and hid it away in the clouds. But the sun considered the sky her own domain and so she scorched the clouds and burned them off. After that, no Knowledge could rain down on the people of the earth. Their memories grew weak, the land grew dry and in the cold they had to start again learning to make fire from sticks.

Children's Fable. Central Archive,
Arts & Literature, Oral History,
Class 3 Knowledge, The Commonwealth.

CONTENTS

I
PARADISO
1

II
PURGATORIO
113

III
INFERNO
325

IV
LEAVING
401

V
LATER
443

I
PARADISO

TRACOLLO

Two riders trace the ridge of the sand sea, miles from the Commonwealth and the protecting walls of the Stadium. They are unhurried. It is the *oscuridad*, when the sun falls below the horizon and the line separating the land from heaven vanishes. The dry season has begun and the temperature drops with the sun. Later, crystals of ice will form into fields of broken glass at night, their edges cutting the bitter Chinook winds.

Night comes. The riders and their mounts are silhouetted: blackened against a sky that is alive with colour. They cover their faces with scarves as the winds pick up and the shimmering green streaks of the night appear above the remaining line of day. No one living remembers darkness to the nights here. Black skies of white stars are only known by stories and songs.

To their right, below and far into the Empty Quarter, a sand pillar forms in the wind. And another. They dance together, and the riders stop to look. The fine golden grains capture the night: greens and violets and blues that reach upwards as if to offer a gift to the gods. Beyond the shimmering dance, far off and familiar, six Gone World towers rise, all straight lines

3

and crisp angles. From here, their surfaces blot out the stars; they are conspicuous by what they hide.

The horses are relaxed, experienced. They know this route and have not been ridden hard today. The habits of nightfall are familiar: they will be fed soon and afterwards, silence will envelope them. Stillness is bred into their line.

The shorter of the two riders takes the lead when the sand pillars settle and the moment has passed. She turns them off the road and towards a depression where they will hide them for the night. The horses descend slowly, stepping cautiously. They are laden, but the burden is fair and balanced for speed. The woman's horse carries more because she weighs less. On the side of her mount is a long rifle with scope and bipod. On his, a long lance with small levers built into the grip and a short carbine. In his boot there is a knife.

It is flat at the bottom of the ravine where the woman halts to look back. She cannot see the Gone World or the High Road from here, which means neither can see her. Away to the south is a long stretch of land, but there are no roads there and few reasons for travellers to cross it. She clicks her tongue once and the man scans the horizon. In agreement, he nods.

Together they dismount. The man ties his horse to a dried-out bush and scratches the animal behind the ear. From the back of the woman's horse he removes a canvas sack from which he pulls out a black triangular object made of a matte fabric that absorbs light and reflects none. Releasing a small catch at one corner, he flicks the triangle forward and – with a cough – a dome appears that is large enough for two adults to rest in.

The woman ties her horse beside his before unstrapping her rifle and a small backpack and disappearing into the tent. The man takes one last look at the undulating green lights of the night sky. Away from the fires of the Stadium, their colours are more vibrant and pleasing. A moment later he follows her inside.

The woman has already set up a small stove no larger than a palm that creates heat but no light, and is warming spiced beans and stalks of green onion with slices of carrot. She cuts two modest portions of dried beef and places them over the plant-food to soften. The two riders sit cross-legged over the stove warming their hands. The fabric of the tent allows them to see out, though it mutes the colours. The food, the tent and their bodies quickly warm. She turns down the heat, which will linger.

The man uses his boot knife to divide and distribute the portions onto two small steel plates. He hands her the better share, for she has not been eating enough lately. She pushes it back but he ignores her and eats his own portion.

They share a litre of water and drink it all.

Soon, he sleeps, while she leaves the tent and keeps watch outside. There is little to see but the sky – there are few animals this far from the wadi running beneath The Crossing, and those that scurry through the Gone World sleep at night too. Only big-eyed birds and flying mice hunt in the dark.

There was a time, when the woman was young, when the bandit trade was heavy. Now the Big Road is secured by the Dragoons and the Commonwealth controls outwards from the Flats beyond the AIRBUS to the edge of The Crossing. But tonight they both feel an unease in the air and so they take greater precautions, because tonight is unique: the man's lance is full with all six flags. It is the first time a Raider had returned with this much bounty in almost twenty years.

*

The deep night arrives while she is on guard. The horses have stopped stirring and the moon has sunk below the ridge that shields them from the road, creating a thin line of pearl-white along the edge of the dunes under the autumnal sky.

Into the quiet, but heard clearly by the woman, there is a sharp but distant explosion. Experienced and careful, she edges up the ridge to bring the Gone World towers into view. A light – maybe a fire? – burns through a glittering window. Two more small explosions follow: she sees them before they reach her ears.

The horses stir.

After a pause there is a low, heavy rumble that grows.

She brings the rifle into position, but does not look through the scope; instead, she looks over it for the wider view. She digs her right hand into the dirt, looking for a hard surface that might carry the vibrations. There is a heavy rock and she feels how it shakes as though from the Earth's core. The sound is so low and deep it is more like a feeling: a heartache or nostalgia. It is nothing she has heard before but the longer it lasts, the more confident she becomes of her supposition.

She knows what it is.

When she is certain it is over and she has stopped counting the length of the rumble, she returns to the dome where he is already awake and sitting.

The man cannot see his wife's expression but he understands her body movements and the nuance of her breath. They have almost thirty years together, and one daughter. They are the most decorated Raiders of the Commonwealth. Much passes unspoken between them.

'What was it?' he asks; his voice barely a sigh.

'A Tracollo.'

The man shifts onto his elbow. He rubs his eyes and allows

himself an understanding smile: he slept. She did not. Their days have been very long. The desert can provide dreams either way.

'It must have been something else,' he says gently.

She allows him a moment to invent what else it could have been. She is patient and watches him fail as he tests each possible explanation against his wife's experience and intelligence.

When they both sense his failure and his smile vanishes, she speaks again. 'It made the ground shake – even at this distance. I counted thirty-five seconds. I think a whole tower went down.'

The man sits, his legs crossed. 'The last Tracollo was Lilly's and that was fifty-four years ago. The chances of one actually falling after all this time are . . .'

'The same as they were then,' she says. 'No one knows why that one fell,' she adds, adjusting her rifle, 'but this time, it was helped. There were three smaller detonations before the collapse.'

The woman places her hand on the earth. The vibrations in the rock and sand are gone but it makes her feel closer to the proof. 'I think someone knocked it down.'

He considers the implications. 'You think someone else has figured out how to make explosives?' he asks. His grogginess shaken off, having forced himself back into the moment, he is alert now.

'It would change the balance,' she admits. 'Unless they found some. Which would be better, though still not good.'

'What time is it?' he asks.

'The moon is down.' The woman dons her wool cap again and twists the scarf around her face and neck. She opens the door to the dome and the tent fills with cold.

7

'I'll be glad to get back home,' the man says before she is gone.

'We may need to stay,' she replies. She grips her rifle and steps out.

The horses are awake now. She places a hand on her own mount's muzzle to calm him as she passes to climb the ridge.

At the top, as the Gone World comes into view, she opens the bipod, switches on her scope and resumes her prone firing position. The wind is low but constant and moving towards her. The scope measures it at 4.2 knots. She switches on the night vision and magnifies.

Tower three – the one people used to call Aladdin – is gone. In its place is a massive cone of debris that blots out the colours in the sky behind it.

She crawls forward a careful metre, which places her slightly higher on the ridge, giving her a better sight-line to the land where the towers emerge.

The towers are to their northeast. On her right, in the direction of The Crossing, fires are being lit. They are green through her scope, their centres burning white. Shadows are already on the move as the valley comes alive and she feels the energy of choices being made. Though her hand is steady, the images are out of range and so is the meaning of their movements.

She can only guess.

'Roamers,' she concludes flatly, knowing her voice will carry to her husband and no further. 'Too far away to see who they are. We might know them, we might not.'

Behind her she feels his hand gently squeeze her ankle. She turns.

His meaning is clear: *he is asking her to consider the wisdom of her action.* He will trust her judgement. But they are partners, and it is his job to force the question.

She does not crawl back down the hill and instead watches the fires approach the Gone World.

'The plume is enormous,' she says, describing what she sees. 'It's not like anything I've ever seen before. I can see four teams on their way over but my view is flat. I can only see left and right. Everything is too dark.' She pauses before adding, 'It's so dangerous these days with that tribe encamped on the Ridge.'

They are called the Keepers.

He does not know what they are keeping.

'Henry,' he says, 'come back. There's nothing we can do now.'

'They'll be pulling finds from the Trove, Graham. The last time there was a Tracollo, Lilly came back with the Harrington Box and changed everything. We need to know what's coming out of the depths.'

'We're carrying Full Flags, Henrietta – precisely because of the Harrington Box. We have no idea what value this already has. We can't risk what we have for the unknown.'

Henry tips her head towards the missing tower. 'That's the largest unknown we've ever seen.'

Graham nods. This is true.

They are talking too much, they know it, but the attention of the world is fixed elsewhere. Chatter in the night is now expected. The world adapts.

And this needs to be discussed.

Graham appeals to Henry's sense of history: 'When Lilly and Saavni and General Winters were kids, things were tougher and the Stadium unruly. We have systems now.'

'They didn't have a military force building up on Yellow Ridge back then either.'

He runs a hand over his face and does not answer her. His thin riding scarf is slack around his neck. After a moment, he nods again. This is also true.

9

Two Runners have gone missing since the Keepers arrived two moons ago. It is rumoured they were killed, but there are no bodies and no way to Attest. But the concern is mounting.

Henry waits for his answer. She knows what he knows; neither claims wisdom over the other. She does, however, tend to be the more convincing.

'Fine. We wait for now,' Graham says, a small concession. 'We'll visit the Tracollo in the morning, then The Crossing. Now, though, we wait,' he insists. 'And it's your turn to sleep.'

Henry watches the Roamers approach the plume of debris and imagines the shinies and Knowledge they will soon be pulling from the hidden depths of the Gone World.

It will be very hard to sleep.

BEAUTIFUL

Earlier that night and before the collapse, across the valley and on the flats above Yellow Ridge, a tent community is resting, cold under the green streaks of night. However vivid and inspiring, still the colours have turned grey for their leader since the Sickness arrived and his wife fell ill.

Don't sleep beside her, the sages advised. *You will become ill too, in the way that rot spreads through touching fruit.*

No, he said. *It doesn't work like that. And what would it matter if it did? The warmth of our bodies together is what life is for. Why forego what is good in the world only to have less of it for longer?*

Yes, they agreed. *That is why you are our leader.*

This was not why. He knew he had no wisdom, only conviction: one born from the momentum of an earlier decision that he cannot question because doing so would be a great undoing. But he does not correct them. Correcting them would turn their minds most unnaturally – the way that night birds turn their heads to look back. People are not meant to look back this way.

Their desert encampment has more than a hundred tents, grouped by extended family. There is room for many more, and

11

many more are coming. They are close to a cliff wall facing the Empty Quarter where water is most scarce but they have a well and purify what they draw using the sun's light in plastic bottles.

They can see The Crossing to their west; the Gone World is beyond, though everyone knows it lies beneath them too. There is a cliff and a drop to their west before the rolling sands begin. It is close, but not so close that the children risk falling. It is not far enough away, though, to sooth the fears of the mothers.

'You don't have children,' they say to him. 'You don't understand.'

No, he agrees. Not any more.

He has been awake beside his wife for hours. He often wakes this way now, his soul torn between wanting to watch her sleep and his body needing sleep itself. Being torn disrupts his peace and prevents him from existing fully in the moment, as is the way of their people. The Chinook winds warm what should be the icy desert floor, keeping the night dew on the sand from freezing. It arrives at his tent as a rippling breeze over the roof and threatens the sealed walls, turning the shaking home into a frightening song. Still, it is the permanent sound of change and there is a warmth – a certainty – to be gleaned in recognising how permanence and change are part of the same truth. His people do not see a contradiction in this but instead a poetry.

The Chinook. The wind carried its own name after the world was destroyed and whispered it into the ears of the people it found. How else would such an ancient word survive with no lips remaining to speak it?

*

Awake in the dark beside her, the Leader traces his wife's sleeping face with his fingers. He is gentle enough not to wake her. Later, he rests his hand on her chest and feels it rise and fall with each breath and the magic of living: the human heat that is warm but never burns. There on their bed he listens to her stir and like a child he plays the game of matching his own breathing with hers so he might feel what she feels. They are no match, though. He is so much larger, stronger, a model of health, with lungs that could hold a storm. His breath is too deep, too slow. The balance is forced: it cannot last, because all unnatural things are buried eventually. As the synchronicity is lost, the feeling of union passes and this stirs an emotion from a part of himself beyond his control.

In this way and that quickly – a grain of sand on a night wind – he is whisked away from serenity.

He knows this genie that is disrupting him; this curse. They call him *Time*. Time the Titan who is the enemy of Now. They battle, these two, in the legends of his tribe, a poetic battle that explains much to children and informs the talk of the people. Time's face, they explain, is never the same. He never stops moving. Wanting. Needing. Feeding. He circles as he hunts.

Now, Time's nemesis, does not move, but crouches on the earth, always present, always ready, prepared to be any and all things as circumstance demands. And the more Time prepares his attack, the more he circles his prey and clangs his armour and threatens and taunts, the calmer Now becomes. Now is steadfast in the only truth we can know for certain: I am here and here I am.

Poor Time, the lesser of the two Titans. Time cannot exist

13

in a single moment. Time can never be in one place. There is no rest for Time and so he is restless. Agitated, he lashes out where he can.

Tonight, Time is pressing on the Leader's mind, instilling an instant and complete understanding that the happiness he feels and the love he has for his wife is going to end. *Because life*, Time says, *is not the wind. It is not permanent.* 'It is mine,' he says.

Soon his wife's warmth will end and her breathing will stop. Knowing this splits him in two – here with her and also there after the end. It is in that glance back at himself from that other place that he becomes unmoored, because one part of himself leaves the here and now and becomes planted in the future. It is beyond painful because he knows that every moment they have left is precious. Most precious. This fills his chest with a terrible pressure that builds behind his eyes that distracts him and robs him of what is most dear – their final moments.

He is two men now, one looking back to the instruct the other:

Take it all in before it is too late, he tells himself. *Give all this a name. Place everything here in your mind. The texture of her skin. The curve where her nose meets her cheek, the exact shape of her eyebrow, because it will soon be gone like the billions of Ancients who are now dust and died in the Gone World at the height of a permanence they thought was theirs, only to be rent from his earth in a flash and their future obliterated. Will you choose to forget love?*

You know you won't. Because you remember her too.

Veronique.

The Rise. The land filling up and covering everything. Only the tops of the highest towers are left poking through. All those people who once breathed this same air – did Time not talk to them too?

Take it in, the voice says to him.

His wife stirs and he is back. He rolls her onto him so nothing is wasted. His beard becomes one with her hair. She inhales, and the pull freezes his chest. She exhales, and it burns. He cups her cheek in his palm where it was made to fit by Destiny. Her right hand finds his belly and rests there, fingers open. If only he could pour his own life into hers so they could share it evenly, divide it between them as rainwater drawn from a cistern.

'I don't want to go yet,' she whispers to him.

He did not realise she was awake.

'I don't want you to go at all,' he answers her.

'What if we're wrong? What if there is a cure but we've been headstrong by ignoring it? The Prophet arrived fifty years ago in the east and spoke of a world beneath the world. What if there are answers there we've ignored? What if there was a cure . . . before?'

'Your death saves us all,' he says by rote.

'How?' she asks, though she knows the answer. She likes his voice. She will listen to him saying anything.

'Trying to make the world better is what killed the Ancients. We accept the world as it is so that it will not die again, appreciate what we have so we don't lose more.'

He feels the crease of her smile on his breast.

'That's what we tell everyone,' she says.

'Because it's right,' he answers.

She does not reply but instead, she runs her hand around his chest, down his belly, running her fingernails along his soft penis.

15

'You're still beautiful,' she says. This may be her answer. It may not.

'I would take your place,' he says.

A puff of air through his chest hair. Her last laugh.

'Our brave leader.'

'I fear life without you more than death. Taking your place would be the coward's way, and I would take it.'

'There is no future,' she whispers, repeating their marriage vows. 'There is no past. Our words vanish as we say them. There is only now, and it is now we have each other, until that moment when we do not.'

Now it is his turn to smile.

'That is what we tell everyone,' he says.

He scratches her bare back until her breathing slows. It is laboured and heavy. The Sickness is a rapid and fading death. A few days. A week. They say it comes from deep beneath the towers of the Gone World where the bodies remain, the bones piled up. The Roamers and Explorers and bandits who would venture downwards either add to their number or bring it out fresh.

No one knows for sure.

Their blanket is made of sheep's wool, separate squares sewed together, given by a neighbouring clan. Each square is a picture or shape from everyday life. It is a worthy gift.

He folds the ragged edge so it does not disturb his wife's neck.

Twenty years of marriage. They are not meant to count them but they do.

For a time he looks at the ceiling of the tent and tries to feel, with every part of his body, the experience of her being there with him. It is a lie, he knows; this pretence of there being no past. And yet it works. Collective forgetting is possible because memory lives in talk, and talk lasts only as long as the wind. It is the personal forgetting that is harder, because that is written for ever on the soul. Silence erases one, but sometimes that only sharpens the other.

This life, this love, has left its mark on him, deeper than any wound, and what is theirs will become his alone once she is gone and he dons the white robe and red sash for his time of mourning. He will be expected to step forward into a new day and wordlessly carry the entirety of his wife's life inside him: her memories, her words, her face, her body, her ideas. Alone. Who else will know? Who else will remember?

There are others – more comforted spirits – who work to forget. They heal by unclenching their fists and allowing the sand to run through their fingers. But he is not such a man. Though he pretends, his faith in the teachings is not sure enough.

And so he tries to remember everything he can: is her breast warmer than her arm or are they the same? This is the heat of her.

When her head is below his chin and her leg curls over him, where does her bent knee touch his leg? This is the size of her.

When she relaxes her sleeping hand on his shoulder, how far apart are her fingers? Because this is the touch of her.

He feels the flutters of her eyelids on his chest. They blink, and blink again, faster now. He saw this before with their daughter. He breathes very deeply. He is not sure whether it is for both of them or simply out of fear.

'I can't see,' she says.

'I'm here.'

'Don't look,' she says. 'Don't look. I don't want you to remember this.'

Her eyes will be pale: a film of pearl across them that separates the world from her. Their daughter flailed when this happened. Five years old; she could not understand it. If she couldn't see her parents, she didn't believe they were there. Sound was not enough. Touch was not enough.

It is the light. We need the light.

Veronique was her name.

That was ten years ago.

She is here with them right now. His family is together. He knows this because he can smell her hair.

'Picture her,' he says to his wife. 'It is all you need to see now.'

'It is not our way.'

'Do it.'

Together they lie there, listening to the tent singing to them. She begins, slowly at first, and then faster and harder, to bang her head against his stomach as though she is trying to work her way into him so that he can absorb everything that she is and merge their lives together completely.

He accepts the pain until the line of her dignity is crossed. He clenches her head between his palms and stops her. But he does not look down.

'Don't let those people destroy the world again,' she pleads. 'They are going to make the same mistakes. You promised me when Veronique died – you promised that her death would save us all. Promise me now that you will protect what we still have, because it is too beautiful to lose. This life – it is all so beautiful.'

This is why he brought his people here. This was when their journey began; when their daughter died and they heard soon after a story about a people following the ways of the Ancients: a people committed to relearning all that was lost, all that led from peace to war, from life to death. That is when he knew what they had to do, what they needed to keep.

18

Her hand reaches up to find his face. She presses her palm against it, her fingertips closing his eyes so that, for a moment, all three of them can be as one.

'Too beautiful,' she says.

There is a deep tremor through the ground.

'It has already begun,' he promises. 'We are not strong enough yet to take their fortress and stop the madness, but we will be and soon. Tonight we committed – we announced ourselves. It was for you.'

With this, as much a gift as a curse, they fall asleep. Their remaining time together is both perfect and wasted.

He emerges in the morning naked and bathed in the orange light of dawn. A woman wraps a white robe around his shoulders and ties a red sash around his waist.

Barefoot, he walks the full distance through the camp to the edge of the cliff and seats himself on a rock. A silent crowd gathers around him and they join him facing east.

The painted greens of the Aurora lights have retreated and vanished behind the majesty of the dawn, each colour more vibrant than the spice at the southern markets or the blood that lingers on the butchers' blades.

His Deputy, expressionless, takes his hand in his own and washes it with water from an ancient bottle made of real glass. The water is cold and for a moment he resents it: the wet seems to be washing his wife's scent and touch from him – but this is the purpose. The cold is to shock him back to the world around, to stimulate an awareness of what is still here, including himself.

He takes the bottle from the Deputy's hand and drinks heavily. He is parched.

Together, the men and women and children of the encampment sit around him and watch the sun rise and the new day begin.

It is, as his wife said, beautiful.

THE HARD ROOM

Elimisha, daughter-of-Cara, wakes on a cold, polished floor in what might be morning. The act of drawing breath means she survived the chase, the explosions and even the collapse. It is too soon to even wonder how.

This cave smells of fine chalk and unwashed hair. Dust, older than memory, has settled on her brown skin the way ash from the night fires at the stadium falls on the arms and curly hair of her younger brother, to his endless delight.

She wrote his name on his forearm, and he looked up at his older sister – Elimisha! A Runner! – and walked away, proud and staring.

The written word: on their own flesh!

The floor tiles feel good against her cheek but are no distraction from the pain in her leg and hip, which does not throb from a single spot like a puncture wound but *pulses*. It feels like her heart is beating from her leg.

She reaches down. The blood is tacky and cool around her hip. This is better than wet and hot. There is no haemorrhage. She is not dying. Not yet, anyway. But she is damaged.

21

To calm her heart and slow the blood she tries to remember *how*, if not exactly *why*.

She had been slinking her way across the rooftops last night, moving through shadows, beneath downed girders and along troughs in the ruins to stay out of sight and ensure her Route remained secret. Thoughts running through her mind repeated: *I am an Archive Runner. I am the youngest Runner in twenty years. I am sixteen years old and proving what is possible.*

I am going to get this right.

True to Protocol, her black leather jacket had been zipped to the neck, her gloves fastened tightly, her sling-bag cinched over her left shoulder. She had already made her Knowledge drop at an Archive called Prydain and was on her way back via the Orange Route when she saw one of the tribesmen.

The Orange Route is a high run across the rooftops of the urbanscape. Her return was to be a night journey during a half-moon and she set out after a small meal of soft bread, dried meat and a full litre of water. Her mother had given her an apple too.

An apple: a loud, crunchy, shiny apple. If there was one thing she couldn't eat on an urban run it was an apple.

Mothers.

The Archive Chief had ordered her to drink the entire litre and watched her as she did. Now, lying on the floor, Elimisha understands the rule – in fact, she wishes she'd had even more to drink. She is thirsty.

Last night, the blues in the sky were deeper than she had seen in months, the fiery tips of purple more pronounced than she remembered. She would have stopped and taken in the beauty if she'd been allowed.

The Ghost Talkers like to read the sky as though it's a tome with stories of its own to tell. No one believes them, but everyone likes the tales. Strange that people whose minds are tilted off the True have the most amazing stories.

The view from the tops of the remaining buildings in the Gone World is the best. Much better than at home, where the fires that burn in the Stadium every night always block out the stars, hiding their light – other than that one spot behind the Stadium where the underground waters fall to the river below and roll out into the Western distance beyond the farming fields that feed the Commonwealth. And there is that time in spring, when the sun sets perfectly over the river as if falling into it: that moment when the great orange ball is cut in half by the horizon but is made whole by the waters below it.

It's always so crowded, though. It's not like anyone can enjoy it alone, not like on an urban run in the dead of night.

This was her tenth run: a milestone. It was a chance to prove to the High Command that their reluctance to trust younger Runners was ill-founded.

There was going to be cake.

Elimisha had been ordered by Lian, Chief Librarian of the Central Archive, to make the drop at Prydain and then work her way back as quietly as a shadow to make the Signal Mirror at dawn. There, she'd bounce the rising sun off the reflector and twist the blinders in the code that would announce her return. The Spotters would confirm her message and signal back her orders, then, after the shade fell over the entrance and everything in them disappeared into a shadow of black so intense that even the hunting birds above wouldn't see her go in, she'd make her way to one of the hidden tunnels.

She had made the Knowledge drop (as usual, with no idea

what was in the box she handed over) just as planned and was coming back, on her way to the Signal Mirror.

Elimisha heard the Tribesmen before she saw them.

Many tribes have passed through the region over the years. The old people, like Chief Lilly in Weapons and Communications, say they started coming when the Stadium began growing. They had talked about this when Elimisha did her apprenticeship there last month.

'When I was your age,' Lilly said, 'no one would to trek across the wastelands or the Empty Quarter just for water. People knew the Stadium was here. Some did come for trade, but there was little else in this region, because the Gone World had already been picked clean by previous generations and naturally, no one ventured inside the remaining towers because of the Sickness. Even now we're not really located conveniently between any two places. So if they come here at all, it's for us and The Crossing.

'As I assumed you learned in school,' she continued, while unwrapping a new package of ammunition, 'The Few arrived about a hundred years before I was born. They found the Stadium deserted but not gutted. It had power systems, high walls and fresh water, all encouraging them to stay. From them, a very small community grew. There was nothing else around the Stadium at the time. There was the Gone World and its towers, but there was no reason to go and visit other than to gawk and wonder at everything that had been before. Not much grew in the sands and there were few Finds of any value. The High Road didn't exist then.'

'So why did others start coming?' Elimisha asked. Traders had arrived that day with the ammunition that – fortuitously – had been set into plastic and the air sucked out by the Ancients.

Lilly had told her they did this to avoid corrosion, and that chemicals in the plastic preserved the bullets even across these hundreds of years. It was her theory that they'd done this deliberately during the final moments of their lives, knowing that ammunition rotted, and if they survived they were going to need it. But then they died so fast they couldn't use them. With so few people in the region, there is still ammunition to find; the problem has always been matching it to the weapons. Most of the numbers printed on them made no sense to them and even those that seemed to fit the gun barrels occasionally blew up or fired out wildly. Lilly used a carved-out stone box for a testing chamber, pulling a string tied to the trigger to avoid getting hands, fingers and faces blown off. Elimisha's job was to open the packages, load the weapons and – after Lilly had fired them – measure the clustering of the holes to see if the match and quality were both viable. Lilly insisted they always use three test shots. 'It's never unwise to measure well,' she explained.

They were firing .38 special ammunition from a Colt .357 Python and found that it worked. They had no idea what made the ammunition special and they didn't know what a Python was. Or a Colt, for that matter.

'We're still not entirely sure how The Few arrived in the first place,' Lilly said. 'We know there were thirty-eight of them, and they came from the north. According to the stories we've heard, they succeeded by marshalling the resources of the Stadium successfully and somehow avoiding the in-fighting and politics that ruined most small communities during the chaos after The Rise. When I was your age there were fewer than a hundred and eighty people in the Stadium. The next year, when I opened the Harrington Box, things really changed and now there are more than a thousand of us. Beyond the walls, tribes

25

and Roamers and Ghost Talkers and traders and Explorers and adventurers and . . . oh . . . all sorts – they pass through now, partly because of The Crossing. But these people?' Lilly had said, 'who just arrived a few months ago? They're different.'

'How are they different?' Elimisha had asked.

'They won't talk. General Winters sent people there to open relations, but they didn't respond, and still don't. And they won't accept our offer to come and visit. So we watch each other and so far, we aren't learning much. But the tensions are growing. They appear to be hostile to Knowledge, but that's all we know.'

At seventy-one years old, Lilly's hair is still long and blonde and her eyes still the colour of heavy ice.

The reason Elimisha had heard the tribesmen before she saw them was because they were a clumsy people. The Runners had spread word of this when they met and this rather proved it. Stopping on a slab of concrete behind one of the steel fan-boxes on the roof, Elimisha closed her eyes to listen to the shuffle of the fools' feet in the fine-grain sand that settles up here on every flat surface; the fine-grain sand that shouts out the location of every foot-fall and records every step across its surface so that the experienced can know the size and weight and number and direction of all the fools who crossed there and didn't have the foresight or systems to mark their routes in advance – to give them names, to train their people, to maintain them unseen, keep their locations safe – so that no Runner of the Commonwealth would ever be a fool.

Imagine, she thought, *to just wander around with no training, no preparation, no Order of Silence to build and maintain their routes and set traps to protect them, no schools and sessions to train their people.*

'If you are not careful,' she had wanted to shout to her pursuer, 'you might find a soft patch on the roof, worn by centuries of sun and water and rot. If so, you'll have a nice drop into the world of Yesterday. You won't like it much, but there will be plenty of bones to keep yours company.'

In nine runs she had never been seen or followed. Now, though, she had. Why does bad luck align most closely with consequential moments?

When she stopped, he had stopped too. When she started moving again he gave chase and his footfalls were hard and long – a sprint. She did the same. And she was faster and better prepared.

Elimisha leaped onto stones and bricks and pipes that all absorbed her weight and didn't shift or speak or sing out below her feet. She sprang the way rabbits do, dodging to the sides, looking behind them, staying out of sight. This was her training, her strength, her speed, her cunning – and the reason she'd been entrusted as a Runner so young.

She was moving quickly and the breeze was hot. Breath control was part of her training too: in through the nose and out the mouth, keeping the rhythm like a song in her head. Watch the feet, hit the marks, pace it out, remember the route.

Around a square hunk of steel she glimpsed another of them – to the south, blocking another Route she was *not* on. That was when she'd become nervous. How did they know how to flank her from both sides unless they knew the Route she was running? But no one knew the Routes, not even the people at the Commonwealth – unless they were Runners, former Runners, Archive Chiefs or members of the Order. And the penalty for loose talk was severe. And if spies were caught? Death, and the bodies returned to their masters in pieces. That was how General Winters wanted it, especially these days. It was grisly but it appeared to be working.

If not spies, she wondered as she ran, *was it possible that these beasts had been watching them and actually learning? These people who are said to hate Knowledge itself?*

Did they see no contradiction in that?

Or did contradictions not even matter to them?

Two Runners had gone missing since this tribe had arrived. Elimisha wasn't supposed to know this but she did.

She sprinted across the surface of the rooftop towards the edge. Across from her was a taller building rising up eight storeys. There was a gap between the edge of this roof and the flat face of the building ahead: a two-metre jump. For them it would be a Black Jump – a jump into the unknown with no way to return; a full-on gamble with death.

Not for her, though. This was Marker Eighteen on the Orange Route. She had trained for this on the Green and had now run it nine previous times:

You plant your foot to the left of the orange marker and you hurl yourself towards the opposite wall. You meet the wall with your hands and your feet at the same time. There is nothing there: no foothold, no window. The surface is sheer. The force of your jump will plaster you against the wall for a brief moment. And then you will drop.

'Drop?' one of the other students had asked. He shouldn't have asked. He should have shut up and waited until the instructor was done. If he'd done that, he wouldn't have had to clean the horse stalls.

You will drop straight down if you meet the wall correctly. Trust the world's pull. It never fails.

She practised it on the Green of the Stadium a hundred times by leaping from a raised wooden platform and smashing herself against a wooden wall across from it. And then she dropped and learned to trust the Order.

Elimisha sprinted for it as the tribesmen closed in around her, close now, but behind her, the way trailing birds flock after a leader.

There it was, as promised: the marker, a pipe sticking out of the wall and painted orange. The Tribesmen would not be able to follow her even if they had the courage. This is what she was taught.

The one on her left had a gun. She could see he was pointing it as he ran, but he was too slow, she was too fast, and bullets are rare so no one practises. No one can hit a mark on the move.

Twenty metres.

Ten.

Why were they chasing her? What did they want? Her bag? Her body? Her death? The Knowledge in her mind? *Why?*

Elimisha adjusted her final strides so she could meet the edge of the roof to the left of the marker with her right leg, which was the stronger. Closer, closer, closer still . . . hop with the left, plant the right, and then *pop*.

Up and out.

She flew over the alley below and slapped the wall with hands and feet. The force – promised, predicted and practised – suspended her there as the tribesmen took aim and before they could shoot . . . she fell.

Exhausted and injured and thirsty, Elimisha pauses her recollection and raises her head from the tiled floor. She looks down, past her feet, to the massive door, now sealed shut and locking her in here: in this Hard Room; the kind that the Adamists insisted was real even if no one had seen one since Chief Lilly pulled her finds from one so long ago.

The door has a massive wheel in the centre. The seal around the door is black and as thick as a snake. There is a light on above it glowing red – a colour she has never seen from a bulb before. She tries to remember, through the pain, whether the room was red when she entered.

No. It was definitely black when she came in. When she had rushed down the stairs and thrown herself in here it had been as black as a grave. The door, then, had been open. Maybe the light came on when the blast sealed it shut behind her.

'The light,' she says through the pain. The words come back to her in an echo – not as an exclamation but as a question.

The light?

How can there be a light here?

If nothing had caught her, she would have dropped twenty metres to her death on the broken metal spikes and debris below. But this was no Black Jump.

'When you drop, you twist,' her instructor had said.

So drop and twist is what she did.

Down, down two metres until . . . *contact*. She landed with both feet on an extension bridge. *Clang, clang*, two steps and three, into the open window of the building she came from and out of the night air. She was suddenly into the forbidden world of the inner walls.

Once inside she found the promised white rope dangling from the ceiling. With two hands she grabbed it and pulled with all her might. The rope spun across a pulley and untied a knot that released the extension bridge so that it plummeted to the alley below.

Try what I did, she challenges her pursuers.

Elimisha paused to catch her breath. She had never been inside one of the buildings before. The other times she had stayed above. This part of the route was for emergencies. She was standing now where the Ancients used to live and work doing . . . what? The massive room around her held nothing – nothing on the walls, nothing to sit on. Not even a plastic bag. It had been scraped clean by time, like almost everything else.

She breathed in, tentative; worried for a moment about the Sickness in the lower chambers. Another breath, more deeply this time. It struck her that this room was mapped: The Commonwealth wouldn't have sent her here if it was dangerous to breathe.

She slowed her heart, regained her balance and confidence, and assessed.

From this angle there was nothing the Tribesmen above could do; there was no way to swing in after her.

What had followed her in, dangling down on a string, was some kind of white metal egg. It was much larger than a chicken's egg and had a pattern on its surface of cross-hatching. At its top was a silver tube of some kind. The tube displayed pulsing blue light that was speeding up.

They were swinging it.

When it was inside the room with her, they released it.

The first lesson she was taught as a cadet in the Agoge – when she was a little girl, only five years old – was this: *If you see something from the Gone World that is very very beautiful or very very ugly . . . DON'T TOUCH IT.*

Elimisha was five storeys above the sand of The Rise. In line with the Route, she was now supposed to go back up the stairs across from her on the left wall below the EXIT sign and return

31

to the roof, completing a loop and coming out behind her pursuers in a spot invisible to them.

Going *down* the stairway itself was forbidden because there was no exit downwards. There was also no light. There was less air and what air there was, was bad. *Buildings are tall coffins,* she'd been taught.

The egg blinked and it was extraordinarily beautiful, almost hypnotic.

Recovering her mind and remembering her training, she broke from its spell and ran for the stairwell and as soon as she did she heard another metallic thump-thump-thump coming down at her from above.

During her apprenticeship in Weapons and Communications, Elimisha had seen Ancient Tech, most of it grouped into a broad category of 'shinies' because no one knew what they were or what they did. Unlike the inanimate shinies in Lilly's workshop, these eggs had their own sources of electricity and had been thrown after her with malice.

Away was where she needed to be.

Down was the only real choice.

So against all Protocol, down into the stairwell she went; into the Hollows where no one went, not since Death himself took residence there, people said. He waited there with his long arms and strong claws to pull down the curious and foolhardy and the brave alike.

She flung herself over the bannister to a landing and then she did it again. Three steps and she was in the middle of the third flight of stairs downwards when an explosion detonated above her.

This was no small charge like she'd seen troops use as they

practised formation drills and defensive lines. This was no ammunition detonation from a gun. This was not a small blast from a pulse rifle. This was a fireball. Above her the air turned orange like the morning light and a heat pressed down as though the air itself were on fire. A cascade of flares and smouldering debris rained onto her shoulders and the heat poured over her.

She rolled down the stairs.

On her feet again, head hurting, and glad – *so glad* – she was encased in protective leather and a back-guard, per Protocol, she followed the stairs downwards by feel, downwards to where nothing yet burned, nothing was illuminated by the orange cloud rolling above.

Another explosion – and far above her came the sharp cadence of falling plaster and concrete that was joined by a tremor of deeper crashes as the primary structures of the building – for so many centuries tortured by the elements after whatever they had endured in the wars that once felled everything else – finally surrendered their integrity.

She jumped and jumped down again and again with one thought only: they want me dead.

Her run was vertical and off-route and unprepared. She was exploring now, not running. Throwing herself into the Black.

Elimisha put all her faith in the presumed symmetry of the building's architectural design, flinging herself from bannister to step to bannister to step, hoping with each irrevocable leap that the minds of the Ancients were consistent and logical and reasonable like the minds of her own people.

Her feet slapped the steps as she landed but she could barely hear them as her tumbling progress gained force and certainty.

From a pocket on her right leg Elimisha pulled a glowstick.

She cracked it open and the tunnel became greener than the night. There, at her foot on the landing between the two stair-wells, was the corpse of a man, skin shrivelled, one clawed hand still at his own throat, boots on his feet.

A smell was pouring down the staircase now; it rather than fire was making her cough. She was sure it was a kind of poison.

Down. Down further, past more bodies.

Was she breathing death itself?

The Urban Explorers and the Adamists would have known. They invited her to run the Off-Routes. The nut-jobs actually went *inside* sometimes. They were drawing new maps of the upper levels and the first ones below the ground of The Rise – eight floors deep. Teenagers were pretending they were Adam from half a century ago: the exiled Prophet who claimed to have drawn the Underworld and went crazy with what he saw.

No thank you.

And yet, there she was, with the bottom arriving up at her as she ran. The air was so thick and stale it was almost unbreath-able; she had to pull it into her lungs as an act of will.

Ahead, in the glimmering light from her glowstick, was the basement level. It was a generator room with antique machinery encased in sheet metal, thick pipes running over her head, back and forth through gaps in the walls.

The ceiling shook. A door ahead had the word STAFF on it. Elimisha slammed her shoulder into it and fell in past the carcase of an old rolling chair. The closet-like enclosure had an open door and nothing inside except more bones – not a complete skeleton, though. Something had dragged much of a person here, then eaten the pieces. There was nothing else left, though, both predator and prey long gone.

At first she thought she had reached a dead end. Spinning around, she checked to see if there was another way out, but

34

there wasn't. The STAFF door was the only one. Brushing falling plaster from her face, Elimisha spun around again, trying to find somewhere to go, and saw how the shaking had started to change the shape of the flat wall in front of her.

The green glow from her stick had been showing her a smooth, flat surface. As the shaking became more violent and the walls themselves trembled under the shifting weight of a million tonnes of stone and steel, the outline of a perfect black circle formed on the wall – a line at first, until, in an instant, the top-most edge crumbled, chipping a wedge from the green-glowing wall and giving away a blackness behind it that screamed out to her an invitation to *go*.

Elimisha dashed at the wall and curled her upper body into a tight ball as she whacked into it, sending plaster and grit exploding inwards, into a tunnel that was now the barrel of a gun shooting her as she ran as fast as she could, the cloud of debris building behind her as she ran.

After that she wasn't sure. The tunnel split at some point. At the end was a perfectly flat wall that was either the edge of her coffin or another paper-thin board. What she does remember is deciding that it didn't much matter how hard she hit it.

Elimisha rammed through that wall the way the Dragoons burst from the battle tunnels below the Stadium and out into the wastelands before the Gone World.

Free of the tunnel there was a room, but she had only a second to take it in and make a choice. One way was up: heavy industrial stairs of solid concrete invited her to run eighteen flights to the surface, which was impossible. The other way was *in*.

Smack in her way was the thickest door she had ever seen: much thicker than the primary doors to the Stadium leading into the Commonwealth, thicker than the secondary doors beyond the holding pit. Even in the Archives she had never seen pictures of anything like this, thicker than her forearm was long. It was also open – just wide enough for a girl to slip inside.

It sounded like the Hard Room Lilly had described to her once, but this one had no water, no dead, no bones.

She was barely inside when a blast of air from the collapsing building hurled her body into space. The Tracollo behind her had sounded like the world in its entirety was being cracked open and the demons of the dark had all screamed outwards from that hollow centre, shrieking in their collective fury as they celebrated their freedom in her deafened ears. Had the door not slammed shut behind her from the blasting wind, she is convinced she would now be dead.

The light above the closed and sealed door is red, which makes the blood in her leg harder to see. Easier is the pipe or rod or spike jabbed into her thigh. Reaching down, she can feel the tacky blood. There's no blood-spurt, though. When there's blood-spurt, people can bleed out and run dry like a pierced bag of water. That could still happen if she pulled on it, though. Maybe it will and maybe it won't. She's no doctor. She's just a Runner.

Tenth run and now this. It takes a coincidence to spoil a party, that's what the Raiders like to say.

This is not what Elimisha promised her mother. This is not what she expected from becoming a Runner.

She will not cry, though. She will remember her vows and the sequence of survival: Water – Food – Escape. Signal – Return – Rest. All of this, in that order. That is her training.

Now, though, all of that can wait. She's had water and she's not hungry so what she needs is rest. Now she needs to sleep and hope that, while dreaming, the air and the Sickness do not kill her while her eyes are closed.

THE CROSSING

Henry sleeps fitfully as Graham watches over them both for as long as he dares, knowing that if he lets her sleep too much he will have to endure a full day's ride with her eyes narrowed and her mood sullen. With the Tracollo pulling them one direction and the weight of their finds pulling them another, he knows it is already going to be a tough day.

'Henry?' he whispers to her from his perch on a rock, her rifle across his lap, the sun's reveal of the land still to come.

'I'm up,' she says, her voice muffled inside the dome. 'Are the Roamers still working?' she asks.

Graham powers the scope and takes aim at the activity around the Tracollo.

'Busy as bees,' he says quietly.

Henry rolls onto her back inside the tent and rubs her face.

With the arrival of dawn and good visibility over land – and the attention of the world elsewhere – they can risk more talk.

'What's a bee?' she asks, sitting up.

'The most industrious of all ancient creatures.'

'You're just saying the phrase backwards,' she says, calling his bluff and ready now to rise.

He smiles beyond the scope and says nothing.

With her right hand she grips the puller and slides it silently upwards, allowing fresh air into the dome. She is tired, but after motherhood, nothing feels truly tiring any more. Alessandra was a terrible sleeper as a baby. It wasn't until four months into it – child screaming, black circles for eyes, a far-away stare fixed to her face – that she chose to ignore all parenting advice and simply lock Alessandra's lips to her own nipple at night, which permitted them both to pass out. The girl grew strong and healthy and powerful and Henry pulled through it.

The pain of childbirth she barely remembers. The fatigue, though: that walked hard on the mind; it left tracks.

Henry shuffles out of the dome to a shrub to relieve herself before joining Graham at his perch. She takes her own rifle from his hands and peers at the activity.

'They're digging?'

'They seem to be hauling,' he tells her, 'and excavating. They've started sifting too. I figure the small Finds will go first to The Crossing – probably the least valuable, at least as far as anyone can tell. They'll make rumours about the better ones, let those stir, see what kind of interest develops and what else comes out of the hole before they share the good stuff.'

'No one knows what anything is,' Henry mutters. 'My parents used to do this – that's what brought us out to these parts in the first place.'

'I know,' he says, although Henry doesn't speak often of her parents. Their deaths were the reason she remained here, though – the reason the two of them met. The reason they have a daughter.

'You know more than me,' he says. 'I'm just piecing it together with words. Helps me, anyway.'

'I didn't mean to bark,' she says.

'You didn't.'

'It's going to take weeks for word to spread beyond the region. Unless,' Graham adds, 'it doesn't get out at all because of these Keepers.'

Henry lowers the rifle and looks with her naked eyes, but she can see nothing from here. 'Maybe there's something coming out that Lilly can use,' she says.

'Like what?'

'You should check her list. The things she wants are useless to everyone else.'

Hours later the white sun is a fist above the horizon, pale enough to stare at. They ride towards it as though it was singing to them. They try to look uninterested, riding slow, watching for people on the road, trying to take in the mood. In silence they share the same wonder that a sun so big doesn't warm the land even more.

In an hour they are on the High Road. It will be three more to The Crossing if they let the horses walk easy. Henry is curious about the Tracollo itself but Graham shakes off the idea like rainwater. One delay is enough, he says, and she knows he is right.

Henry is first to see the travellers moving towards them. With her right hand she detaches the scope from the rifle and puts the cup to her eye. Her crosshairs align to the chest of a child sitting between her parents, all riding atop a wagon pulled by two mules. Behind them are three other families on similar contraptions cobbled from Gone World kit. The last wagon is hauling a cistern. The vehicle shimmies to a rhythm Henry knows: those tyres are thicker; the mules are pulling harder.

'They're hauling water,' Henry says.

'Children?' Graham asks.

'Unfortunately.'

'Dream Walkers, all of them,' Graham said. 'Never going to learn.'

'Maybe we can turn their minds,' she says.

'How often does that happen?'

'Often enough to give worth to the trying.'

In the time it takes to walk once around the Stadium, they cross paths. Henry and a female driver raise their hands in greeting and the men raise palms in peace. The first family pulls the mules to stop and the caravan halts. The horses snort out a morning mist.

Beside the woman is a girl. She is well dressed and her big brown eyes are healthy. She does not smile, but her gaze on Henry and Graham is deep and curious.

'You've rolled in at a strange time,' Henry says. 'You've heard about the Tracollo.'

'Strange times,' says the woman, 'but that's no interest to us. We have what we need and we have little to trade.'

Graham indicates west where there is still a moon. 'You look to be going west. Out to the Commonwealth? Those are our people. You're welcome to visit. We trade in Knowledge, not only objects.'

'Have no interest in the Commonwealth,' says the man beside the woman. He is unarmed. He strikes Graham as too chipper to be wise.

'We have a daughter,' says Henry to the parents. 'We wouldn't be taking her out into the Empty Quarter, though.'

'We have seen the vision,' says the man, smiling, confirming Graham's hunch. 'We know about the city that survived The Rise. It is like a Crossing for the entire world. We're going

41

there. It's only thirty days past the Stadium and along your river.'

'There's no city,' says Graham. 'That's a bad story. We're from the Stadium and we know the land. There's nothing out there. Water's good for six days out: our turbines clean it and everyone's welcome to it beyond the walls. After that, it's undrinkable again because it picks up the poisons in the ground. The greenery dies off quickly and the animals stop coming. It's the hard end, an easy line to see. Our Raiders have crossed fourteen days past that into the wasteland, that's twenty days out. You need to carry a fortnight's worth of water to visit the nothing that's out there and a fortnight's water to get yourself back to the sweet stuff. That's a lot of hauling for an ugly journey.'

'You didn't hear me, brother,' says the man. His shirt is bright red. Graham thinks Henry could shoot him from a mile away. 'I said *thirty* days. Add a bit to those two fortnights and there you are.'

'On the way,' adds Graham, as though the man hadn't spoken, 'our people found nothing. No footprints, nothing dropped, no campsites, no old fires. There's nothing but hardpan and sand.'

'They must have come another way,' says the man who will not learn. 'We've got enough for thirty-five days.'

'You'll die. First the mules will drop dead, because the pulling gets tough once the road ends, and then the little ones, old ones, the men, and finally, the women. Women last longest because they need less food and water to travel. But they'll die alone and saddest.'

Some of this was untrue. The Commonwealth had set up depots with fresh water at five-day intervals along the river. Raiders – and members of the Order of Silence – stocked it for thirty days west to where the mountains began and water ran cleaner from the high peaks. Officially, it was for the benefit

42

of the Explorers and some Runners bringing Knowledge to far-off Archives, but whatever the real reasons, it was an order straight from High Command and had been for some forty years. These provisions were only needed, though, because the land was truly as Graham had described.

He was sure because he and Henry had both looked themselves.

'You haven't seen what we've seen,' said the soon-to-be-dead man, no longer smiling.

'Why not leave the kids at the Commonwealth?' said Henry, knowing where this was going. 'You're going to pass by the Stadium anyway. Find the city and then come back for the children later with your good news. We're more than eight hundred strong behind those walls – the most powerful city on Earth, as far as we know. Your kids will be happy as clams.'

'What's a clam?' asks the man.

'The happiest of all creatures,' says Graham.

'No, no. We need to find the Shining City together.'

'You should go north,' Graham says, as a last effort to redirect them. 'Long ago, when there were waters running past the forest, tens of thousands of bottles broke apart, maybe more. We don't know how it happened exactly but we think the bottles broke out of hundreds of those rectangular containers you see here and there. Time broke them up and the waters wore them down. Later, those water receded and now there is a lake of sea glass like nothing you've ever seen. As long as the Stadium, maybe even as wide. I like to imagine it goes down for ever. It shines in the day and glints like a dream at night: all reds and blues, purples and yellows, greens of every kind, and cloudy whites as soft as a morning kiss. Just up north, a mere nine days' ride from here. The children will never forget it. See it instead. Let it refresh you.'

43

The child looks to her father but he is shaking his head. 'Next time, Bee,' he says to her. 'Next time – on the way back.'

'If you change your mind,' says Henry, 'you go to the Stadium – unarmed – and tell them that you're the guests of Commander Wayworth. Our people will let you in and the girl can stay as long as she wants.'

'Your graciousness will be rewarded by the birds in the sky and the fish in the sea,' says the woman.

Raising their hands once again, the caravan makes its departure to the west following their own black shadows cast by the rising sun.

Three hours later, the sun is a copper orb that dries the land without warming it. The shrubs are thicker here on the path and the first greens supported by the under-earth water present as small, dark leaves on spindly plants in the lower valleys. Small birds of mottled browns zip through the canyons faster than arrows, collecting bugs in their bellies and beaks for return to their young. The people leave them in peace. They are too small to eat and killing for sport leads to vultures and things that bite.

Henry reads the movements and faces of travellers and Roamers the way that Scribes and Evaluators read the contents of the Harrington Box. She measures their numbers, the cadence of their horses, the levity of their talk, the expressions on their faces. The inexperienced show their moods in a constant waxing and waning of emotion but the weathered and rode-out tend to hold it all back. It's when those people crack that a sense of the day is revealed.

The news of the Tracollo has spread as they expected and as Henry and Graham approach The Crossing, they converge with others doing the same. Not as many as she would have thought, though. There is a heaviness marring the anticipation, and more here than a hunger for early pickings and new finds. It is something she cannot yet name, but her suspicions run to the Keepers.

Graham trots on ahead of her, joining a line of weary travellers who are in no mood for talk. They slump low on their mounts, eyes focused on the tails of the horses ahead. Henry, coming up slowly, examines the make of their cloth and the quality of their weapons to gauge the distance of their journey. They are from a colony to the southwest, before the Empty Quarter begins, a five-day ride off. They are smelters, known for metal work. They must have set off long before the Tracollo, but they do not appear elevated by the news, which is an oddity, because if nothing else, the finds can be turned into Raw.

She matches her speed with a man looking more alert than others.

'How's the journey?' she asks him.

Their metal stirrups are polished, but the leather on which they hang is cracked. His lips are cut. She hands him a bottle of water and he drinks heavily and hands it back.

'Long,' says the man, not looking at her.

'You're from the south. Did you bring seed for the trade?' she asks.

'The old breeds are failing,' says the man. 'The new breeds are failing. The ancient ones from the Troves bear fruit but no seed. We can't figure it out.'

'About fourteen days' ride to your south there's a gathering at—'

The man scratches at his beard and shakes his head low. White bits of skin emerge like a cloud of snow. 'Yeah, we know. Nothing new there either,' he says. 'They won't flower.

We've tried everything. No way to know if they're *Semilla solos* until it's too late.'

'What about the New World crops?'

'Nothing wrong with new seed. Problem is the soil. The two don't like each other any more. We've pulled too much of the same out of the ground and now it's all barren. We need something new or all of this' – he did not look around, did not wave a hand. His meaning was already clear – 'won't be here much longer.'

Henry is about to nudge her horse forward to reach Graham when the man lifts his head to her. 'You're Commonwealth folk.'

'Yes.'

'Collecting all those books, learning what the ancients knew. Following their footsteps, right to the grave.'

'Is that what people are saying?' Henry asks.

The man spits something to the ground. He looks forward again. 'Things are getting worse. May be it's not your fault,' he says, 'but you don't look like no solution neither.'

Graham has stopped where The Crossing appears through the mist that often rises from the wetland below it.

Henry pulls up beside him. It is always a sight, changing with the light of day and the seasons of the year.

Before it became known as The Crossing it used to be called the Bridge to Nowhere. A plush green river of trees and brush pass beneath a glimmering, pristine arching bridge that rises from the dirt and sand on one side, ascends seventy metres above the tallest trees below, runs more than fifteen hundred paces from start to finish and descends with perfect symmetry into a scrabble of rock on the far end. The bridge rises from nothing and arrives at nothing. The Rise buried the roads that must once have approached it, and it buried the river it once crossed too. Some ground water remains, though, flowing unseen and unheard, but close enough to the surface for the most stubborn of plants to drink what the people could not.

Outside the Gone World towers and the towering tail of the AIRBUS, the bridge is the only structure that survived whatever had made everything else fall.

The surface of the bridge is glass, rising as one sheet to the apex where it splits into two – each lane passing around a Pavilion at the top – and rejoins on the other side for the descent.

Most beasts are shy to make the climb until they grow used to the idea. Henry's own horse was brought here as a foal. The distance and the dry it hadn't minded so much. Not even the cold. Flying over a forest, though: that was something new.

Since Lilly, though, the Bridge has been called The Crossing: up one side, down the other. There's no turning back. You miss something, you go around again. Other rules include no loitering beyond the last light; no bedding down on The Crossing, even for the shopkeepers, and there's no violence in the Pavilion at the top which commands the most excellent view of the Territory. The penalties for breaking these rules are severe.

There is a queue to get onto The Crossing. Henry and Graham can see the Militia standing with sword, spear and rifle. When they reach the front, the man who greets them is as spindly as starving wheat; it exaggerates his height. His mouth is as thin as wire and his eyes and voice are lifeless from boredom. His skin is unusually pale for these parts. There's word of some fair people in the far north – more pink than brown, like Lilly – but few around here. Maybe he is from up there.

'You're new,' Graham says to him from atop his horse.

The man assesses Graham and Henry. He checks their raiments for evidence of origin and intention. New he may be, but he is clearly trained for the job.

'You're from the Commonwealth,' he concludes.

'Yes,' says Henry.

'Royalty,' he mutters.

'What's coming in from the Tracollo?' Graham asks.

'Raw and shinies. A few Indies.' A line is forming behind the Raiders but the toll-taker is unhurried. 'Nothing an adult hasn't seen before. Those giant glass windows, though: those are going to be serious for building materials. A new village is going to rise out of those. What are you trading?'

'Knowledge,' answers Henry. 'Any books come in?'

The man snorts at the word 'books'. He's heard the word, but has no use for it. Literacy for his line died when there was nothing left to read, it never having occurred to his people to write something new.

Graham moves on. 'It should be busier. It should look like black birds on kill, but it doesn't.'

'May be too soon,' he says. 'Takes time for word to travel.'

'So be it,' Graham says, 'but this is thin. This is like any other day.'

'They say the Tracollo has released the Sickness into the air,' the man says.

'Well, you look fit as a fiddle, so . . . that can't be right.'

'What's a fiddle?'

Henry gives Graham a look.

'Who knows?' Graham tries to make Henry smile with some sleight of hand. 'Something at the peak of health.'

'I'm not that healthy.'

'At least you haven't lost your sense of humour.'

'If not the Sickness,' he added, not understanding Graham, 'it might be the new tribe. There are tents in the eastern cliffs before the Sands begin, a lot of them now. Largest colony I've ever seen outside your walls – four hundred and growing, they say. Those people don't smile. That might have something to do with it. But *quién sabe por qué sucede algo*,' he says.

'We don't speak that,' Henry says.

'It means . . . who knows why anything happens.'

'I took you for the north,' Graham says, 'not south.'

The man doesn't reply to that. He has one more question. He speaks low. 'Is it true that you have Big Electricity at the Commonwealth?'

At this Graham laughs. 'Oh yes,' he says, becoming serious again. He leans forward on his horse and whispers, 'We grab the lightning from the clouds when it rains. And we capture it in barrels.'

'Okay,' says the tall man.

'And later, we fill all the Gone World shinies with power and they talk to each other and come to life and reveal their secrets to us.'

'You can go on up.' He signals the Militia to let them pass, and preferably soon.

'And a cure for the Sickness.' Graham chuckles. 'We think it involves fruit.'

Henry spurs her horse onto the glass surface of The Crossing. The horse has been here before and understands it can walk across. Other animals, not so well trained or experienced, have been known to buck or refuse. There are stables for their use – the price for ignorance, as always, is high.

Their horses fall into step. A man with a wide broom cleans the bridge beside them. Children to their left are standing around a large pot where a man stirs smoking red nuts that

49

release an aroma that helps mask the horse manure and travel smells.

Henry shakes her head at him in judgement for his performance.

'You kill a rumour with sarcasm,' Graham says, 'not denial.'

'You killed it,' Henry says.

They don't ride far. Graham dismounts by a cluttered hut on his left, on the northern side of the bridge. The southeasterly sun lights it, making its drab colours more welcoming.

Three strong men are moving both Finds and Raw to a container beside the hut. They are sorting them, but their criteria is confusing. Outside the canvas door to the tent is a table, behind which sits a woman with a face lined like an old plum. She is short, with glassy eyes that are too pale for her dark skin. She is expressionless as Graham approaches.

'Good morning,' he says.

'Same to you,' she answers.

'You're new too.'

'I'm old,' she says.

'What have they pulled?'

'It's early. It's going to be weeks or more before they get to the bottom of it, assuming they don't come up with green skin and breath like death.' Her voice has gravel in it. Her teeth are bad but her skin is clear. 'So far there's a lot of Raw, usual stuff. Some shinies. Nothing that does anything, though; it's all a bunch of useless Deps. Go on in. First sale of the day is good luck.'

'The machines – they're inside?'

'Same price as the Raw now. They don't do nothing, like I said.'

'Why bother separating them out?'

'Habit.' She nods towards the three strong men. 'If I tell

50

them to stop separating I'll never get them to start again. You manage your affairs and I'll manage mine, handsome.'

Graham glances at Henry and steps into the dark of the storage shed.

THE FIND

Graham has been inside the room of corrugated steel metal before. Every few months, on a whim, he passes by the stalls that stockpile junk so that he can check through for possible spare parts. There is seldom much to find, even though there is plenty stacked into piles. Raw, even out here in the desert, is easy enough to come by. The challenge is finding what you're looking for.

The odds today are higher because there's more of it. The men have been hauling loads, leaving behind their scent. The room holds the heat and Graham quickly removes his jacket, scarf and hat before cracking his neck and stretching. There is a pile in front of him larger than he is tall. The light inside is poor, the bright glare from the doorway behind him putting the machines in his own shadow.

Graham wipes his face in preparation for the pain yet to come. The left side of the room is only too familiar. Unbeknownst to the shopkeeper, over the months and years he's been scratching small hatch-marks on the units he's already examined. So that's about fifty units he doesn't need to eviscerate.

Leaving, perhaps, another hundred still to go.

What might have been order when the men started to stack the new Finds is now a system of consolidated chaos. Shelves along the walls hold a variety of machines with buttons and knobs and keys, thin sheets of glass and tiny switches. There are sometimes words or letters beside, on top or underneath them. ON and OFF are common. Words of no discernible meaning like TREMBLE or BASS are painted white above controls. There are combinations of letters that have meant nothing to people for generations – EKG, or Highland HME109, QUINTON Q-STRESS, and AUX – COUPLING – FINE.

The rapid accumulation of new material has been hostile to the order of the shed. In only the one night and morning, the shelves have already been filled up and a large stack – a pyramid, really – has taken form in the middle of the tent.

Graham removes a small hand mirror from his jacket and reflects the light of the doorway onto the surfaces of the machines.

For more than ten minutes he searches for the words that Lilly once asked him to look for: BAND, MODE, TRANSCEIVER.

Nothing.

What he does come across is one that reads MOTOROLA.

He knew a girl named Motorola, from a smithing village. Nice name. A better week. He flips it over.

From his pouch he removes a folding tool that contains a series of heads which often match the bolts and screws on shinies. His tool says 'Leatherman' and it's one of his prize possessions. By keeping it well-lubricated with flower and herb oils and resisting the urge to sharpen it too often, he's found its head-shapes can open the vast majority of Gone World devices. Failing that, a rock usually does the trick.

This box has six screws that Alessandra – when she was five – called 'plus screws' on account of the shape. Graham used to tease her and insist they were X screws by rotating them, but Alessandra was insistent and would rotate them back, still arguing. One day, Alessandra removed one of her father's tools from the Leatherman and showed him how the shape was indeed arranged like a plus and not an X by virtue of its alignment to the hilt. By rotating the screw to match the tool she proved her point and Graham conceded his.

He then tickled her until she was blue.

Most screws are brittle and break when he rotates the heads, or else the screws are held fast in place by a red crust. In this case, the screws are strong and silver and do not break. With some insistence Graham is able to make them surrender their grip, allowing the tops to twist out into gleaming spiral spikes that he briefly admires before tossing them to the ground.

After wiping his nose, he eases off the plate and a cloud of fine dust floats into his face, which he blows away. The innards are beyond comprehension and the letters and numbers inside – although easy enough for the literate to read – do not otherwise convey any meaning.

In Weapons and Communications, Lilly has entire teams trying simply to find patterns in old tech in the hopes that an understanding will naturally evolve.

'Differentiate among things that are different,' she would often say. 'Before the Harrington Box, we never considered how much Knowledge might exist, how much we might be missing by not thinking widely, or how much we could still lose if we didn't pay attention to every category of importance. Once we found that children's game and considered the implications, everything changed. If nothing else, it's why we have our agenda now. We have things we want to learn and missions to learn them.'

To some extent this has worked. From as far back as he can remember, Lilly has been classifying shinies as *Indies* or *Deps* based on the first, global distinction: Indies – or *Independents* – are Gone World artefacts that do something independently: a knife that cuts; an axe that hacks; a glowstick that illuminates; the massive water-spun turbines below the Stadium that generate power. Lilly includes objects or machines that use electricity.

When he heard this thirty years ago, during his own apprenticeship with her, he asked the obvious question: *Independent of what?*

'Yes,' Lilly had said, liking his mind immediately, 'that's the question. Independent of what, or Dependent on what? Because I'm certain that most objects are dependent on something we can't see, hear, feel, or perhaps even imagine. But whatever it was, it was real and it permeated everything, and most Indies were eventually upgraded and replaced by Deps that – I have to suppose – worked better, when they worked at all.'

'I'm not really getting this,' Graham had said. They were at her work desk. They were always at her wide stainless steel and very cluttered work desk.

'Here's an example of a Dep.' She showed it to him: a beautiful hand-held object of opaque glass that gently curved to fit the hand. There was a sleek silver button on the side and nothing else.

'The Stadium, as you know, runs partly on Human Kinetic Power. So the more we bounce around on the Green and in the corridors, the more power we generate, which goes to the batteries, and when they are sufficiently charged, we get Big Electricity that we can use for any number of things: lighting, powering the pulse rifles, refrigeration, et cetera. This little thing seems to have a similar system inside it, so when we shake it for a few seconds it comes to life. But it doesn't *do* anything.'

She shook it and after a moment the shape of an apple appeared against the black. It was a lovely thing, and completely useless.

'It never moves beyond here. Almost every object we find has a related problem. Even ninety per cent of the refrigerators won't operate without completing that mysterious connection; they all remain dormant things. Whatever once gave them purpose or instruction isn't here anymore.'

Lilly's theory – which she maintains today – is that the world shared a kind of 'spiderweb' which once connected all Deps together in an elaborate system, and the reason they do nothing now is because that system either can't be reached or no longer exists. Most of the things that people used to do with Indies, Lilly believes, they eventually started doing with Deps. 'Books were once on paper, but after 2046 we can't find any more new books. Pictures were once on paper and those stopped too, but we can't find out which year. Music must be out there someplace,' she reasons, 'because it would be odd for a civilisation to evolve to the point where it could fly to the stars but then rejected all music. Even Moishe's electronic piano in the music room can record itself.'

So far, the search for books, photographs and music has been a failure, with not a single large trove found since the Harrington Box, only a few scraps here and there.

The object in front of Graham in the shed looks like an Indie, and once he blows off the dust, everything inside looks rather fresh.

He removes a small leather-bound notebook from his inside pocket and checks Lilly's wish-list.

It's always something with her. All the Raiders and Traders are slaves to her shopping lists in some ways.

From his backpack Graham removes a grey cloth bundle held together with a purple ribbon and unwraps it. At its centre are nine small objects Lilly has told him to find. One is a tiny glass tube with steel tips on either end. With one hand he holds up the mirror to reflect the sunlight from a roof hole into the device he's molesting and with his other he runs his fingers over the illuminated surfaces looking for a match.

He finds one – or something akin – between two U-shaped clamps on the green board. With his folding blade snapped into position he gently eases the tube from its fasteners and releases it. With his dirty fingertips he holds the two pieces up to the light and compares them. The new one has a tiny filament inside, like a thread. The one Lilly gave him, however, is different; its thread has snapped and curled.

Electricity, Graham knows, travels on roads – usually roads of metal, but water works too, as do some other substances. The broken thread in the old tube must be like a fallen bridge, not allowing the electricity to complete its journey. As they will be unable to fix the bridge, the tube itself needs to be replaced.

Graham rewraps the broken piece and walks out with the new one in his palm.

Henry is standing beside her horse. The sun is stronger now and the heat is coming, shining down through the dirty glass road to the green valley below her feet. The tallest trees do not reach this far up. It is the only place on Earth where people can see the top of a living tree. One could marvel at such a sight for a lifetime.

In an effort to look busy as she scans the crowd for danger,

Henry holds up a dress recovered from the Tracollo. It is blue with purple and yellow flowers. It has no arms and falls to her knees. It is in excellent shape – it even smells good. Clothing Troves are rare in this region, but they are very common elsewhere and there is a robust trade. Finding something that's nice, that fits, that's clean and that flatters the figure is never easy, and it seems to be harder for women.

'For me or Alessandra?' she asks Graham when he emerges, sweaty and dusty from the shed.

'You're the same size,' says the husband and father with the same lack of interest as every other husband and father.

'That's not the point.'

Graham leaves the argument to her and approaches the shopkeeper again.

'Find anything?' she asks, uninterested.

Graham holds up the tube.

The woman looks from the object to Graham.

'We charge by weight, handsome.'

Graham places the tube in his satchel and removes a small desert flower that he hands to the woman. Despite herself, she smiles.

Henry pays for the dress by teaching the woman how to make a knot for joining two ropes of different diameters together. The woman is instructed to perform it three times, which she does diligently. Once the Knowledge is transferred they agree the debt is settled and their trade-bond strong.

Together, she and Graham collect their mounts and continue their ascent of The Crossing towards the Pavilion. They walk slowly, leading the horses.

'What's your Find?' she asks.

'Something Lilly's been after.'

'Important?'

'Small,' he says.

The surface of the road is undulating, and it is not as slick as glass. There is a grip to it even when slippery and the horses, once accustomed to the walk, are surefooted.

Above them are wisps of white clouds in a soft blue sky.

At the top, they cross the Pavilion on the southern fork and pass it without entering. Henry mounts her horse again to gain vantage, to try to better understand the sullen mood of those assembled, all of whom should be more full of wonder and curiosity and attention than they are.

Graham watches her surveying the crowd in fine detail. Occasionally she smiles and waves to make it look as though her viewing has another purpose.

Her face is a smile but her eyes are not. Graham knows she does not like what she sees.

He mounts too, and keeping the reins at the withers, he presses the horse with his right foot, bringing the horses together for a more intimate talk.

'What?' he asks.

'The shopkeeper you charmed back there,' Henry says.

'What of her?'

'There's a tribesman talking to her.'

'So what?'

'So she's not smiling any more.'

'My charm doesn't work this far out.'

'I've spotted four others like him here. They're asking about us.'

'Everyone's interested in us. We're Commonwealth.'

'You're not seeing,' she says to him. 'Two explosions and then the Tracollo – and now they've sent their people here to learn from the movement on The Crossing. The people here sense it – a shift is happening. A new wind,' she concludes. 'We need to get back.'

Graham looks now with fresh eyes and sees that she is right.

This is why she carries the long rifle and he fights with a knife.

They alight from The Crossing on its eastern side and turn for the narrow northern road that circles back through the forest beneath the bridge. Meeting the High Road, they leave the activity behind them and head west in the direction of the Stadium. It is well past high noon and for a time they press the horses to a trot to cover ground, not sure if they are being pursued.

Henry gestures towards one of the break-off paths, a protected route to the tunnels, and Graham nods consent.

The land drops here and the rocks are brittle and larger and scattered about for no obvious reason, as if left behind by duelling giants. At a familiar boulder they turn off the path and direct the horses down a dried rill to a plain, where they slow their pace and let the beasts breathe out their hurry.

Graham is fussing with his lance again and Henry looks at him to examine the progress he hasn't made.

'You're working yourself up,' she observes.

'I told Lilly three times these new harnesses weren't working.'

'She'll sort them.'

'When?'

'Next time.'

Graham tries to fix what the entire Weapons and Communications Division has been unable to fix and fails. He's annoyed. 'I don't understand it,' he mutters. 'She's our greatest engineer and this is a stick on a hook.'

'She likes you. That's why she talks your ear off whenever you're there. When her team adjusts it you won't come back to fight with her as often or listen to her stories about the old days.'

Graham eyes his wife. 'Lilly is seventy-one years old.'

'She looks good, though.'

They stop in the shadow of the AIRBUS tail when Graham's horse grows twitchy. He and Henry check the ground for snakes or other causes, but they find nothing.

'It's something,' Graham concludes on instinct alone.

They share a litre of water before continuing. They are an hour out from the Stadium's first defences.

A shiver runs through the horses.

The sun is on its western arc. The road to The Crossing in the Gone World is far behind them. The horses know this route, although it is unmarked. By night, the Order will cover the trail and leave false markings to hide the Stadium's concealed entrances.

For now, remaining watchful, they keep moving. Silence is Protocol but Henry is thinking about Alessandra and wants to discuss their daughter before the return. She knows Alessandra is readying herself for a Choosing Walk. Graham took his when he was seventeen and returned to the Commonwealth within a year. Alessandra is still expecting to go, but for Henry, the Tracollo changes the calculation. Stadium-born Graham is wedded to the tradition. Henry, however, is Roamer-born and is not. She knows she must approach the topic gently:

'Benedicta,' Henrietta says, 'told me she brought in a Trove of three books two weeks ago. It's been keeping the Scribes busy. Lian actually smiled, I'm told.'

'Where had she been?'

'With the traders on the Golden Sea up north. Word coming down is that there are still Finds on the big waters to the northwest. They've been having luck with floaters and coastal drifters. The thinking is that containers get dislodged from the northern ice and they take long rides on the currents – that's when some come ashore.'

'Hmm,' says Graham, scanning the land for unwanted company. 'And there were books?'

'Picture books with hard covers. One of the books was about wine. Have you heard of that?'

He shakes his head.

'It's a dizzy drink made from grapes.'

'Oh,' Graham says, 'you mean *vin*.' He smiles at the memory. 'Thirty years ago there was a colony to the north. They spoke a language called *Français*. They called it *vin*. The kids would sneak into the storage rooms and steal the grape juice before the adults ruined it. They were nice people,' he says, 'but they hated speaking our language.'

'They didn't make it?'

'No. There's still an Abbey in the forest, though, past Sea Glass Lake, maybe another four days in. Almost no one knows about it and I haven't told many people back home. They're quiet folk with good humour. I knew a guy named Francis – I haven't seen him since those days. But no, that colony is gone.'

'This was during your Choosing Walk?'

'Yes.'

Henry knows this. She remembers his stories better than he does.

'I don't like the idea of Alessandra on a Choosing Walk, not these days,' she starts, arriving at the topic. 'We're not supposed to know this, but two Runners have gone missing.'

Graham says nothing.

'It's not a time for a Choosing Walk. This made sense back in the days when the Stadium was small and the world out here was empty, back when people needed to make a real choice to stay or go. It's a dated ritual now – especially for the young.'

'I don't think it is,' Graham says. 'The Commonwealth means more once you've chosen it. Just being born into something doesn't make it a choice. You were born a Roamer and you chose the Commonwealth. Now you're the best shooter and a decorated Raider. That matters.'

'Alessandra shouldn't be wandering the hardpan wondering where she belongs. She belongs at home. Exploring is a youthful conceit and I understand it, but she's ridden with us since she was five. She's seen more of this world than General Winters.'

'Alessandra may have something else in mind instead of a Choosing Walk. I'm not supposed to tell you.'

'You're not supposed to tell me what?'

There is a very distant bark of a dog. Henry's horse shakes its head.

Henry unhooks the leather stay holding her rifle in place.

Graham places the carbine around his shoulder and chambers a round. It is beyond instinct now.

'Definitely something,' he says.

ALAN FARMER

A lone figure on horseback charges across the untamed desert with the speed of a peregrine in stoop. He leans forward in the stirrups, whipping his horse's flanks with the reins. His lance is fastened tight to the left of his saddle and he carries no rifle, only an energy pistol in an ill-fitting holster across his chest that slaps against him to the beat of the stride. A hundred metres behind him and closing the gap are a dozen war dogs, their right sides painted blood-red, their left sides as yellow as an autumn leaf.

The man has seen this before. They belong to the Keepers; he once saw three bandits devoured by them. The dogs are fearless and experienced in downing a rider, and their trainers – Hunters – cannot be far behind. There is no fighting the dogs on account of their speed, their numbers and their indifference to deaths in their pack. They do not retreat if the battle is lost. Those who try, he believes, are killed to keep the line strong.

He whips the horse again and it keeps its speed up.

The man is tall. His skin has a pinkish tint that turns red when it burns from the sun. His hair is the colour of dry sand. His dark eyes squint into the wind as they tear.

When the dogs close to fifty metres he draws the pistol. He is a Raider for the Commonwealth, but he is no marksman. He twists, bouncing in his saddle, for the proper angle. He has no sure platform, no certainty in his shot – he is an archer on the sea taking aim at a bird. He will miss and he knows it.

With his thumb he presses the selector, then a second time for a scattering shot. When the dogs are clustered together enough, he fires.

An explosion of blue light draws out to a cone as quick as Ancient bullets. Three of them disappear in one animal, which tumbles to the earth, dead, and skids to a stop as the remaining pack grows even more ravenous in pursuit. The rider shoots twice more and misses both times. The pistol is spent.

He returns it to his holster, reaches down to the right side of the horse and removes a cloth bag. It is filled and folded like a parachute. The dogs are closer now. They are trained to bring a horse to a stop, to pull a rider to the ground, to rip that rider apart. He will not die by these beasts, whatever happens. There is another way.

Two dogs have broken off and are running beside him now on the path, while those in pursuit are forming a tight pack. He hurls the small sack behind him and faithful to Lilly's design, it opens in the wind, dropping dozens of sharpened jacks onto the ground.

One dog takes a wrong step, its paw immediately punctured, and falls back, but it is not enough.

The rider pulls his scarf across his mouth, reaches down and removes a canister from his bag. He pulls the pin and lowers his arm, trailing a poisonous green dust.

Two more dogs drop their chase and, falling to the ground, lie there writhing and scratching at their eyes and snouts, trying to get out whatever is already inside them. He throws the empty can at one of the dogs because he wants to.

The route becomes more complex as he twists and turns through large rocks and around brush and trees. He is not yet following a prescribed route maintained by the Order but is fighting to reach one, which will have snares and supports.

The dogs are more agile than his laden horse. Seeing they are gaining ground, he cuts loose his sleeping dome, his bedding and food – anything that might gain them a little extra speed. He has been a Raider for many years and knows this land. He is charging towards the boundary line of the Commonwealth's immediate domain. If he can make it, there will be support and defence. If not, he is on his own.

Behind him, beyond this first wave of dogs, he can hear the barking of a second pack, and behind them, as sure as the moon chases the sun, are the Hunters.

Ground and distance and time are his only allies and they are fast abandoning him.

Henrietta can finally see the mêlée through her scope. She has taken a prone position in the shadow of a rock and has magnified her sight to its greatest power. The rider is darting through the scree, hustling along off-route and trailing Lilly's countermeasures, but the second wave of dogs is in view from her angle. His efforts will not be enough to save him.

'That's Alan Farmer,' she says.

'It can't be him. He went south – he's been gone for months.'

'I'm looking right at him.'

Alan had Attested to their marriage vows. He was to care for Alessandra if both Henry and Graham fell.

'He's not going to make it,' Graham says. 'Not to the boundary.'

He is two kilometres away, if he were a bird, but weaving through the boulders, with the dogs at his heels, it is longer.

'We can help him,' she says, extending her bipod from the rifle stock. 'Set position. Light a flare. He'll see it and draw them towards us. I can clear the road. The closer they get, the easier the shots.'

'And once you do that and he passes us, the second wave will be on us and then the Hunters. You have five bullets in the gun. It won't be enough for both waves,' Graham says. 'We will not survive that. And we're carrying.'

Henry lowers her eyes from the scope. She knows her husband is right. She has one breath remaining before she has to say it aloud and she holds it as long as she can.

'He deserves to know why,' Henry says.

She swings into the saddle and, pulling taut the reins, yanks the horse into position. She spurs forward and together with Graham they ride for the higher ground on Yellow Ridge. The ascent is steep but with the sound of the dogs in their ears, the horses are eager for action and they rally for the climb.

Yellow Ridge forms a natural high wall half a mile long at the far end of the Stadium's patrolled domain. From there, the view is commanding in all directions: the Gone World's towers, The Crossing, the cliffs to the east, the Empty Quarter, the Stadium – Alan Farmer.

When she is certain that Alan can see them, she says to Graham, 'Fly the colours. Let him know.'

Graham removes the lance and with a gesture made fluid by repetition he flicks six small knobs on the pole and from it emerge, one below the next, six coloured triangles of blue, brown, green, pink, orange and yellow. From a pocket on the saddle he removes a small black stick that he strikes against his rifle; it bursts into light, glowing like a fallen star. He affixes it to the top of his lance and hoists it tall into the air with purpose and clarity: a sign to the valley below.

For Alan Farmer it becomes an understanding of why he is about to die.

Through his frozen tears, Alan Farmer sees his two oldest friends in the distance. Their poise and their proximity to one another reminds him that they are the only married couple in the history of the Commonwealth to both be Raiders. She is holding a rifle and he a glowing lance with six flags extended. It doesn't need the flare atop to draw his attention; the full flags do that. They are too far away to help and he knows it. And displaying the flags like that means that they know it too.

They look to him like the ancient gods everyone learned about from the Edward Gibbon book Lilly daughter-of-Rachael recovered against all odds from the Harrington Box half a century ago: gods who would stand on Mount Olympus and watch the fate of mortals from high above, with pity, but also with purpose.

Alan Farmer, awake to the truth, resigns himself to his fate and chooses to die fighting. He pulls up his horse, draws a short sword and hacks at the dogs. His last act will be to make time for Henrietta and Graham Wayworth to cross back into the Commonwealth's domain and protect the Knowledge they carry.

Henry watches Alan Farmer kill four dogs with his blade before a Hunter's bullet strikes him in the head. Every muscle falls and limp he slips from the saddle, sword still in hand as the dogs set to, tearing him apart.

'We have to go *now*, Henrietta!' yells Graham, not wanting to waste the time Alan has bought them.

Henry pulls her horse around and spurs it forward into a full gallop. Together they pound along the path in the direction of the Stadium, the second wave of dogs now over the far ridge and coming towards them as Graham had forewarned.

'Take point,' Henry calls out. 'We're close to the switch. You flip it and that'll give us the time we need.'

'To do what?' he asks, but she is gone.

Graham kicks his own ride into a hard gallop, riding upright, his head as level as a still lake. He angles his lance forward now, the flags slapping the stick in the heavy wind, and rotates the pole so that its small jutte arm faces outwards, ready to make the catch.

'Don't miss,' his wife yells to him from behind and so as not to lose focus, he tries to pretend he didn't hear her.

In his decades as a Raider Graham has thrown the switch twice. In practise, on the Green, he has made the catch a thousand times or more. His fellow Raiders would set up gauntlets on stadium grounds and the spectators would pour sand and dust, hurl old food and bang drums in odd rhythms to confound and unbalance the challengers, who had to fight the distractions and ensure speed and precision if they were to successfully trip the levers to activate the mechanisms that would let Lilly's deadly device halt their pursuing enemy.

But sport and combat are not the same. They train hard so war will be easy, but there is no pretending that the fake can ever replace the real.

Ahead on his left is the single ashen pole he has been looking for. It's hardened by tricks of fire and lacquered against the elements with pitch and tar. The pounding of the hooves is rhythmic. He finds the melody and levels the lance.

'Stay close,' he yells to her, knowing it is the only thing on her mind.

The dogs are close too. He hears the crack of Henry's rifle, followed by the squeals of a dying hound. His heart is pounding and it shouldn't be. He should be experienced enough now to stay calm in such moments. His family really is too emotional.

Graham flashes a look to check Henry's distance.

Two lengths.

One beat.

Close enough.

He knows the character of this horse across flat earth, knows how to measure distance as time.

He counts down from five.

At the mark he slams his lance into the weathered switch and feels the jolt through his arm and shoulder and back. The stick is cast forward and cracks to the earth in front of him, releasing a spring below ground and causing the earth behind them to release a hundred spikes in the direction of the dogs, each a metre long and – in a moment – a metre deep.

Six dogs are impaled on the weapon of Lilly's own ruthless design. The next are going too fast to stop and they leap over the front spikes to spear their soft underbellies on the next. Those of the second wave approaching the spikes are leaderless. They remain at the barrier, whimpering and barking.

Graham slows to a canter, waiting for Henry to catch up, but instead she dismounts quickly, landing on the ground in a crouch.

'What are you doing?'

Not answering him she scampers up a low rise on this side of the spikes and flicks open the bipod built into the stock of her rifle.

'They're out of range, Henry. The rifle's a hundred years older than the scope. Just because you can see—'

70

'I know what it can do,' she says quietly enough to silence her husband.

She sites them through the scope at nine hundred metres: the Hunters. These *Keepers*. Four of them – side by side – their robes not moving and hanging low.

There is no wind.

Henry Wayworth selects the figure second from the right for no particular reason, aims for the centre of mass, waits for the weaker of her two heartbeats to finish and squeezes the trigger.

There is a crack, a pause and a report from the answering rocks. The figure falls from his horse.

Graham watches. He cannot see the men from here, but he can see the shape slither off the horse and become dust. He looks to his wife. On her brow there is a twitch, a tiny crinkle along her scope-eye. He knows she is satisfied.

As Henry takes aim again, the three riders fall back, leaving the body. There is a distant whistle and the remaining dogs now retreat, returning to their masters.

Henrietta looks at Graham and sees herself in his gaze. 'What?' she asks.

'I don't know,' he says. 'Something.'

THE COMMONWEALTH

Alessandra is no stranger to the long absences of her parents. Her earliest Attested memory (by her father) is a moment when she was two years old and was brought to the top of the Stadium walls to sit with a Spotter and watch the arrival of her parents on horseback across the Flats. In one way it was an unremarkable image: two riders, side by side, crossing open terrain under an iron sky. But the meaning of that image changed for her over the years. It was only later that she learned that no one else's parents were both Raiders. No one else's parents formed a scouting team. No other scouting teams had two Raiders of such equal and high rank at the Commonwealth. Her parents, she learned, were special: not only because each was special, but because they were special *together*.

This, for Alessandra, was no surprise at all. *Obviously* her parents were special.

The hunger to be like them grew in her belly like a seed under the warm sun of admiration she saw from all the people. Her parents were smart and strong and brave and – she would also come to learn – rather attractive. Her mother's beauty emerged from her like a light. It wasn't the shape of her so much as the way she moved: a grace, a poise, a confidence. People watched her because they had to.

Her father had a charm, an easy way with people, a strong ear for listening and a soft way with words and humour. He was not strong in the way of the biggest soldiers or the blacksmiths or the heavy traders, but he was dexterous and surefooted and a brilliant rider; not the very best in the Stadium for speed and fighting, but one of the most experienced. Like her mother, Alessandra's father had seen every kind of terrain, weather, obstacle or danger. Being fast, he liked to say, means nothing for a man riding in the wrong direction.

Until she was five, the Stadium was her entire world, and it was enough. More than enough. At the centre of the Stadium was the Green, which for her was a world in itself. Soldiers practised there. The Ekklesia voted there. The Runners learned their routes; the Phalanx their formations; the Archers their instructions. At every full moon there was a party and a fire blazed in an enormous metal basin raised on a tripod. There was music and dancing and from the time she was ten, Moishe son-of-Tikvah played the electric piano from the centre of a half-shell stage made from the fuselage of a Gone World aircraft. The sound projected outwards and filled the night with melodies that parents had passed down to children through the ages and that Moishe turned into music.

Around the Green were the stands. There were once seats there, her mother once told her, but aside from those at the highest levels used by Spotters, they had been removed ages ago and their parts used for Raw, restitched or smelted, banged into new shapes or repurposed into something useful. They were long gone by the time she was five. Graham said that when his own parents were young almost everyone was forced to wear the fabrics from the seat cushions. 'They were awful and itchy,' her mother said, 'but they lasted for ever because the fabrics were cursed. When the trade routes intensified after Lilly found the Harrington Box, the arriving clothes were much, much better. The Gone World had vanished so quickly, and so few people remained, that there has always been enough clothing. The trick was finding it and trading it. They didn't have robust trade routes back then, so . . . it was seat fabrics.'

The Stadium's structure was filled with hundreds of rooms. Many on the second and third levels were now homes, while those above were for work. The ones underground were off-limits to those without business there but Alessandra knew what was down there because her parents told her things that other parents did not. The hydroponic farm with the constant electric lights was beneath them; the Weapons and Communications centres for research, testing and development; the storage rooms and stockpiles; the last of the Gone World fertilisers and seeds; the stables for the horses and some of the animal farming along or beneath the northern sections.

Above it all was the Snake Tower: wide at the bottom, it tapered towards the top where it met the glass viewing stand where the High Command kept watch over the flats in front of the main gates and the hard-scrabble land flanking it to the north and south. Only the cliffs and the waterfall and the river were out of sight from the tower.

Alessandra did not stay five. As she grew in stature she grew in ambition too. 'One day,' she thought to herself, 'I'll be elected to the High Command, or else I'll rise through the ranks of the military to General and sit there without needing a vote.' Other times – before she grew impatient and adventurous – she would imagine herself Chief of the Archive with Scribes and Evaluators working for her; Runners under her command and the secrets of the off-site Archives tucked away deep into her mind. Yes, there was also the third pillar of the community, the Ekklesia, with its Mayor and the daily runnings of the harvests and the waters, the turbines and the solar cells, the traders and market, the non-military education of the youth and the Attestation of all births and marriages and deaths and so on. But that was a bore. When Alessandra had turned sixteen the previous year and come of age to take a position supporting the Commonwealth, it became clear to her what she really wanted: to someday become Master of the Order of Silence.

No, the Order could cast no votes or tell any secrets, but they were the ones who knew *everything*. The Master of the Order was the spider at the centre of the web; the one who whispered in every ear and knew the secrets of all three pillars: the only one who saw it all.

That's what she really wanted. And being the only child in the Commonwealth whose parents were *both* senior Raiders? Whose mother had been born a Roamer and had only come to the Commonwealth as a teenager with her rifle slung over her shoulder? Whose father was both a ranking Soldier *and* a former Scribe who specialised in nature and science and was a close personal friend of Chief Lilly, daughter-of-Rachael?

Alessandra drew a picture in the sand with a stick once to imagine how the Order was the seeing-eye at the secret centre of the Commonwealth; there in the middle of the triangle made of the Ekklesia, the Archive and the Military.

Yeah. My chances are good.

According to a Spotter named Calvin, both Henry and Graham Wayworth have been seen approaching The Stadium with a full Dragoon escort.

Running across the Green now, Alessandra dodges Archers starting to take formation for some reason and ducks into the shadows of the East Gate, through the doors to the Ring Road inside the structure – now illuminated by a nearly full moon through the glass ceiling – and to the brass plaque by the Inner Walls, which is as close as she can get to the entrance.

'How close are they?' she asks one of the engineers standing by the receiving table.

The girl is only a few years older than Alessandra. She vaguely recalls her name is Clover. She might be wrong, though.

'Close,' said Clover.

Alessandra taps her right foot.

The giant portal here does not open to the outside world but instead leads to an ante-chamber with a locking system designed by Lilly years ago. The inner doors can't open until the outer door is closed. There is room for exactly one Phalanx of ten-by-ten men and women at a time to leave or re-enter. Rumour was that Lilly had also designed an override mechanism because 'she doesn't like to box herself in' and that General Winters could order it, but no one knew for certain. Rumours were popular with Alessandra's crowd.

'Close' feels very far away.

The first time she left the Stadium was when she was five. She still remembers that feeling now: of entering a world without walls.

At seventeen now and looking back, she might have viewed it the other way around: as having *left* a world *with* walls, but that wasn't how it had felt. It hadn't felt like an escape because the Stadium was never a prison. For that reason, the doors were not an exit but an entrance – and outside was the *everything*.

In the midst of it, on her own horse – her legs spread wide just to stay on top of it – the world was vast and expansive and unbounded. When she was little, her father would toss her into the air and she would feel the tickle in her stomach as she soared upwards. That wasn't what she loved most, though.

It was the moment of suspension: the moment when she was free of all weight and all constraints, taller than the tallest man, lighter than the smallest bird.

A breath of pure existence.

This was her favourite feeling. Her friends – especially her girl-friends – talked all the time about falling in love. Alessandra had never been in love (not really – she'd kissed a few boys, but that was only the hunger mixed with curiosity and a salty dash of boredom). If love was really something special, it was going to have to be better than flying. It would have to be better than looking back at the perfect whites and glass surfaces and steel struts of the Stadium as the horse took to a trot, leaving it all behind.

Love would have to be better than sneaking out of the Stadium on dark nights to explore the Gone World with her friends in the Urban Explorers.

Love was going to have to be pretty damn great.

Until it proved itself? No interest.

'When you say "close",' Alessandra says to Clover, 'do you mean close enough that I should be standing here like an idiot waiting for them, or close as in . . . probably sometime today?'

'I really don't know, Alessandra. I'm not in the Snake Tower. I'm standing here next to you.'

When she was five and she finally did go out to see the tail of the AIRBUS extending into the sky and visit the perfect arch of The Crossing over the river of trees below, she did return to the Stadium later. She must have done – she's here now. But it's funny that she can't remember that. It's almost as though she left a piece of herself behind out there and ever since, has been trying to re-unite with it.

Henry and Graham are close.

They trot their horses to the edge of the Flats where six members of the Dragoons have joined them and are now accompanying them to the gate: an honour escort, one for each flag they fly.

From the outside, the Stadium is still. There are no guards, no traders, no movement. General Winters has locked it down. Though the glass of the Snake Tower is tinted and dark, both Henry and Graham know they are being watched on entry. No one under twenty-five years old has any memory of Raiders returning with six flags unfurled. It is a sight and an accomplishment – and one that holds absolutely no interest or joy for either of them; not after watching Alan's death.

Henry and Graham dismount and lead the horses between the widening gap between the massive portals that open outwards and soon close, enveloping them in the safety of the Stadium's defences.

When the ante-chamber portals open, Alessandra jogs to her mother first. They touch each other's faces as Henry's mount shakes off the battle. It is clear to Alessandra from the sheen of their coats and the quivering of their muscles that the horses have seen action in the last few hours. That means her parents have as well.

'What happened?' Alessandra asks her father, who hands the reins to a stable hand but doesn't send him off quite yet.

'A lot,' he says, dusting off the Gone World from his clothes as though it were possible.

Without her noticing, Alessandra runs her thumb across the muzzle of her mother's rifle and finds the black powder of a recent shot.

*

Around them, the Stadium is whirling with activity and talk. The Tracollo was seen by everyone and Henry and Graham are the first to return to the Stadium since it happened. The excitement is palpable.

Graham unhooks his carbine from his saddle and puts it on the engineer's table where Henry is now placing her Remington, then waves off the stable hand.

The Engineers are staring at Graham's lance.

'Snap out of it, kids. We've had a day already,' he says, removing his gloves and tossing them into his sack.

The older of the two – a young man named Sorel – speaks as though to the lance: 'You are requested in the Central Archive,' he says.

'We know the drill,' Graham says.

'No, Commander, immediately.'

Immediately?

'Says who?'

'Chief Archivist Lian,' says the Engineer.

'Well. That puts the flame out, doesn't it?' Graham says quietly to Henry.

Henry isn't listening; she has matters of her own to address. 'You're new to this, right?' she says to Clover, who is now receiving her weapon. 'I remember you from hydroponics.'

'Yes, Commander. I'm with the Quartermaster now.'

'Let me answer your unspoken questions. This is a Remington 700 M24 SWS. It could be two hundred, three hundred, maybe even four hundred years old – we have no idea. No, we don't know what those words or numbers mean, and no, there are no others like it, although surely, at some point, there were many. It was discovered by my grandfather seventy years ago in a heavy sealed black box in a mountain cave under a pile of bones. It was used by him, then by my father. When he died, it became mine. It is the most precise long-distance shooter anyone alive has ever seen, by far. That includes the pulse weapons, which have no meaningful range. The Quartermaster knows this gun and has the cleaning kit. I fired it today. I want him to clean it,' she says, holding it up, 'thoroughly and gently. I want it treated like it's the last rifle of its kind on Earth.'

Clover looks timid before the challenge and therefore nothing like Alessandra, who from the youngest age feared nothing. It was not a trait either Henry or Graham encouraged, but it was nothing they were able to break.

'It *is* the last rifle of its kind on Earth,' said Clover.

'Now you're getting it,' Henry says. 'Off you go.'

Graham had wanted to bring Henry home right after the Tracollo. It had been a sight, to be sure, watching that plume blot out the night sky. Returning, though, had looked to be the wiser course, whereas following Henry's thoughts had seemed – in that moment, at least – the better one. Had they come back then, however, it was possible that the Tribesmen would never have followed them to The Crossing, and perhaps they would not have stumbled on Alan. Perhaps he would still be alive.

And what did they accomplish?

He slips his hands into his pockets and feels the cloth with the tiny tube wrapped in it.

Our one and only prize.

'Dad?' Alessandra says, shaking him back to the present.

'What?'

'Are you going to tell me what happened?'

Graham is honestly not sure.

Three Youth Platoons are in training around them. The youngest – the *tirones*, or basic trainees, aged nine to twelve – are standing in formation and taking instruction on core skills.

Three of them are wearing a red cross, the ancient symbol of health. Their tunics are painted in horse blood. If they are allowed to wear the cross it means they have already been tested for fear and been found steadfast and level.

His daughter used to wear that tunic when she was smaller.

'There was a Tracollo,' he says, hands on his hips, not sure what he has the energy to explain. He wants to bath and shave and put on clean clothes; to remove the road and the rough from his body and hair, ears and eyes. Once he is sorted and centred, he will gratefully spend as much time with his daughter as she needs to understand what has just happened out there. For now, though, his mind is still beyond the walls and he is being summoned to a Sharing that he is in neither the mood nor the spirit to attend.

'Is that all?' Alessandra asks. 'Shouldn't that be exciting?'

'There's more.'

'You were gone for two weeks. The Aladdin Tower has . . . vanished into the earth . . . and you came back with full flags and a foul mood. Mum also fired her rifle.'

'Yes.'

'At what?'

There is a second Platoon training now: the *paidiskoi*. The twelve- to fifteen-year-olds are grappling today. Most are bloodied. They think they are being taught to fight, but in fact the lesson is in the silent suffering of pain. For the Raider, for the Scout, for the Messenger, for the Soldier, endurance and countenance are paramount. The weak or timid are not sorted out from the strong; instead, they are teamed with them so they can become influenced. In war, no one can sit anything out. Alessandra had been near the top of her class. He'd hated seeing her bloodied when she came home at night, but the training only encouraged her.

This was different, though. She'd known Alan since she was born.

The Time Keepers were bringing out oils for the fires. Soon they would be lit and the crier would announce the hour.

Big Electricity? Graham had wanted to answer the toll-taker at The Crossing. *We have more electricity than you could possibly imagine: enough to light a Gone World tower. Enough to turn night into day and make the Stadium glow like a fallen moon. But we light fires with citrus oils and alcohols to pretend we are weak. And so the influence of The Few remains and we choose secrecy and silence and lies over power and truth.*

It is no wonder to Graham that Lilly was removed from the High Command and censured to be merely a station Chief. She was too outspoken, too certain. Too influential.

'Where are you supposed to be?' he asks her. 'Aren't you supposed to be over there?' he asked, pointing at the oldest training group, the would-be Runners, Spotters and Messengers.

'I'm with Lilly this session, Dad. I'm an apprentice now – I have been since the spot opened two months ago. You know this.'

'Right,' he says, his mind a cloud. 'Lilly.'

He reaches into his jacket and withdraws the cloth with the new glass tube and the old one. He hands it to Alessandra. 'Bring this to her. It's something she asked for.'

'What is it?'

'I don't know, something from her list. It might have come from the Tracollo – it came from The Crossing, anyway.'

'Dad,' she tried again, sliding the cloth package into her pocket and trying to get her father to focus. 'What *happened*?'

'The tower was knocked down from the inside using some kind of explosives. We don't know why, but we suspect it was the Keepers. We visited The Crossing in the morning to listen and learn. We were followed after we descended, and somehow or other the Keepers caught up to Alan Farmer rather than us. He was coming back this way at the same time. He didn't make it.'

'He . . . *what?*'

'Alan's dead. We'll send a team out to recover his body in the morning. I'm sorry I can't be more kind about this now. I've been summoned and my mind isn't clear. Go to Lilly. Perform your duties – and don't forget to give her the shiny. We'll meet in the evening, all of us, your mother too. We'll talk more after a rest, after I'm clean and I've had food and water.'

Graham made three strides before turning back and said, almost as an afterthought, 'It's good to see you.'

Alessandra stood on the Green, shocked by the news that a man who was effectively her uncle is now dead, killed by the new tribe in the hills. Another part of her, however, is angry, and has no intention of meeting her absent parents for dinner. If they can be gone for two weeks and ignore her like this on her return, they can wait a little longer for her company.

That is when she sees Naomi.

Naomi is the driving force behind the Urban Explorers these days. The group has been around since the first days of the Adam Map, when Lilly's own Tracollo went down. The High Command have been trying to stop the teenagers from sneaking out at night and exploring the Gone World, but there have always been too many tunnels, too many tiny breaks in the structures to keep people from slipping away. As magnificent as it is, the Stadium is hundreds of years old, not the flawless jewel it pretends to be.

'I heard,' said Naomi.

She was dressed in her Runner's gear: tight leather trousers with padding in the hips and protection in the knees, with a close-fitting black leather jacket to help her become one with the shadows as well as protecting her on slides and falls.

'Are we going?' Alessandra asks.

'No,' said Naomi.

'No. The most interesting thing to happen in half a century and . . . *no*?'

'Winters is going to lock everything down.'

'So what?' We can get out—'

'The problem has never been getting out, Alessandra. The problem is getting back in again without being shot. We've got Spotters, snipers, patrols, sealed tunnels. We can't do it.'

'For how long?'

Naomi shook her head.

Henry and Graham Wayworth enter the Central Archive. The enormous room is three levels down on the western wall, with natural lighting from tall, narrow windows. Absent any proof, it is the held opinion that awards were once presented here. The room provokes a sense of occasion.

Now, its walls are covered in books and boxes, artefacts and art. There are tables for study and for the Scribes and Evaluators. In the middle of the room is the largest table; the Raiders seat themselves here to await the Chief Evaluators.

'Do you think they know about Alan?' Henry asks.

'If they do, I plan on behaving very badly,' Graham says.

'They'll look to me to stop you,' Henry retorts.

'They don't know you as well as I do.'

'No. They don't.'

At the centre of the table is the symbol of the Commonwealth, fashioned from Lilly's first pull from the box: a circle divided into six symmetrical triangles, each one representing a division of Knowledge. Graham's pole flags have been placed on the Evaluators' side of the table in front of their respective chairs, waiting for their occupants.

In the four corners of the room are the customary Guards from the Order of Silence, draped in ornamental cloth. They are as still as statues, witnesses to the exchange. They have taken vows of secrecy and the penalty is ostracism or death.

Graham ignores them, which is easy to do as they don't move or speak, and places his feet on the stone table.

'There's a start,' says his wife.

'I haven't bathed, I haven't eaten, Alan's dead. You killed somebody. I handled things badly with Alessandra. And I really need to—'

The six Evaluators walk into the room from their antechamber.

Graham removes his feet from the table and stands with Henry.

Chief Lian is short. She may be over sixty but her thick hair is still black. Her eyes taper at the sides more than most. She pronounces words too well. She wears the green robes of the Chief Evaluator for Science and Nature and she is also wearing the iron seal of the Commonwealth around her neck, denoting her role as Chief Archivist – the position Lilly invented and held until she was ousted for deciding, after five years of playing with the library's structure, that the system found in the game was all wrong and they needed to re-build everything from the ground up.

'One hundred and twelve years ago to our counting,' Lian recites, 'the Stadium was discovered by the wandering Few. Finding fresh water and power, high walls and no people, they entered the Stadium without resistance. With wisdom and hard work, they reinforced the walls, organised themselves and managed their relationships, forming the foundation for—'

'Alan Farmer is dead,' Graham blurts out.

Lian turns to him. 'We know.'

'Why are we here?'

'We'll be brief,' Lian says. 'The High Command insisted you join a Sharing immediately.'

Henry raised a finger. 'The High Command asked us to come here, not to go there?'

'Yes,' says Lian.

'Why?'

'I didn't ask.'

'You're the Archive's representative on the High Command—'

'And so the judgement was mine to make. May we continue, Commander?'

'This speech is falling on the informed,' Graham says.

'It is our way, Commander. We recite to remember, not to learn. Afterwards . . . we'll be brief.'

'Let me help,' says Graham, more weary than defiant. 'I remember the destruction of the Gone World as though I was there. I remember the warring times that followed and the songs that warn us of the choices that led to it. I remember the first Tracollo, and how Lilly rescued the box from Cardo at the Pavilion and outsmarted everyone by opening it. I remember finding the books and photographs and a child's board game that Colonel Harrington, knowing that the end of the world was coming, packed away. I remember that it was Lilly's idea – as a teenager – to use the categories of *Trivial Pursuit* to structure our libraries and research agendas that we've continued to support by Spade, Raid or Trade.

'I remember too,' Graham went on, 'that Lilly was removed from her role as Archive Chief when she suggested that the categories and tokens weren't good enough and we needed to think of Knowledge in a new way – that maybe a children's game was a nice place to start but a bad place to end. And I can't help but think – on this day of days – that if we had listened to her, Alan might still be alive because Henry and I would have made a number of different decisions, given that the flags we flew all overlap and, frankly, don't matter. So forgive me for not wanting to hear the story again as it makes me extremely angry.'

'No,' Lian says with controlled voice, 'the world is not only these categories. All systems are imperfect. But the Game and its colours did something more important than give us boxes for new finds. They served – and continue to serve – to remind us of how much there is to know and that we must seek it rather than merely stumble upon it. Do you think it's a fluke, Commander, that we're the only colony which is fully literate? The only one with an Archive? The only one with a thriving and secure population, excellent health, a powerful military and a busy trade? The fact is, Commander, if we weren't using these categories we would be using others. Your job would have been the same, whatever flags you were flying. You should know that.'

Graham does not reply.

'General Winters is locking down the Stadium,' Lian announces, 'and putting the Archers on alert. She is sealing off the tunnels until we have better assessed the threats from the Keepers. While we are here, let's take inventory on what you collected out there. We'll begin with my own field of Science and Nature.' She reaches forward, places three fingers on the green flag and slides it onto the seal in the table covering the space. 'Share.'

Graham reaches down into his brown canvas pouch and

removes a bundle of cloth that he rests gently into the table. The evaluators all crane forward to see better.

Undramatically – because Graham is no master at the stone face – he whips off the layers of cloth to reveal . . . a device.

From the perspective of the evaluators and the Chief, it is round and red, set on tiny black pegs, and has two yellow bells on top with an arching steel handle connecting them.

'Before I turn it around, I remind you to see it for what it can do, not for what it is.'

Graham rotated it to face the evaluators.

It was Chief Lian who read out loud the words printed on the clock's face: 'Mickey Mouse?' she said, incredulously.

'Yes,' said Graham, 'and if you look closely at the bottom it also reads, "Walt Disney Production" – we don't know what that means, though it does sound like a workshop and the first is perhaps a name. Below it says, "U.S.A." which is the United States of America, which is where we think we are. Or what this place used to be, at any rate. If so, it's come quite far through time, if not distance.'

'I see,' said Lian, sitting back.

'It's a working clock, Chief, and while I don't know how accurate it is, I'm sure Lilly can find out by testing against the water-drop method, the sun dial and perhaps her star charts. We have a full moon – or almost – and she has excellent records of when the moon passes in front of various stars at this time of year.'

Lian hands the floor over to a kindly man a little older than Graham with naturally dark skin, eyes of hazel-green and a very short grey beard. He cuts an authoritative stance in his purple sash. He smiles at Henry as he uses three fingers to slide the brown flag of Art and Literature onto the seal. 'Share, Commander.'

Henry reaches into her satchel and removes a document on actual paper. 'This is also a material acquisition.'

All the Evaluators strain forward again, this time to read the unfamiliar words: *BWV 988 Aria.*

'That's music,' says Chief Koro.

'Yes,' says Henry.

'So it's for Moishe, then. We'll have him Attest, see if there's anything to it. We'll have the Scribes copy it in the—'

The doors to the Archive open with a rattling of armour and a barrage of footsteps. Henry and Graham turn to see General Winters, Javier son-of-Carmen, Chief of the Dragoons, and Birch. Along with Lian, that made four of the five members of the High Command.

Unlike everyone else at the Stadium, Birch has no matronymic that names her mother, nor has she earned or adopted a Trade Name for continuing a line of work into a third generation. Instead, she assumed a new name with her new position and in doing so shed her old identity.

Birch is the Master of the Order of Silence.

Birch is slender, and strong. She sits herself beside Graham at the table and crosses her legs. Her long hair the burnt red of cooling embers is braided back. Her complexion is unusually smooth for someone her age who has lived so much of her life on the road. Like most at the Stadium – Lilly being the most obvious exception – her skin browns rather than reddens in the sun. She wears a sleek black suit of leather, like a Runner's, but finer. Like Henry, Birch is in her late forties. Her green eyes are very observant. She nods to the two Raiders, who nod back.

Neither Winters nor Javier are so polite.

As Winters waves her hand, five of the Evaluators stand and take their leave of the meeting: this is no longer a Sharing but a Counsel. The guards leave too, closing the doors behind them.

Together the Wayworths sit and wait for Winters to begin, but she is not the one to speak first.

'When do we attack?' Henry asks.

'We don't,' says Winters, leaning back in the elegant chair of twisted steel.

'Why on earth not?' Henry says.

'There are more coming.'

Graham places his hand on Henry's thigh under the table. Winters has a tendency to talk too much; the trick is letting her, and that requires restraint.

Henry, responding, is motionless and as they'd hoped, Winters fills the space.

'Some of our Explorers go further than we admit. One has come back from the far east – I won't say how far, but far enough to witness a gathering of these Keepers. They are coming here. What we see on Yellow Ridge is only a wave. We could attack now and kill them off, but then we'll have to contend with both the numbers and the wrath of the coming thousand.'

'*A thousand?*' It is Graham this time. 'I've never seen a tribe with a thousand people – we're eight hundred and we're the largest I've ever encountered in thirty years in the wilderness.'

'We're sure of the numbers.'

'How do they feed a thousand moving people?'

'There's plentiful hunting a month out to the east and there's the forest to the north. They salt the meat. You know this,' says Winters.

'Yes, but—'

'They spread out, and they move food and water forward via a system of relays that travel faster than the advancing groups, back and forth, like blood cells through the body. The Keepers slow their march to align with the flow of resources. It is very slow progress, but it's also stable and it works. They also trade.'

'They'd have to be spread out over a hundred miles or more like a line of insects.'

'I don't understand,' Henry interrupts. 'So what are we waiting for?'

'For them to gather and, if we're lucky, attack us *en masse* so we can end them all at once. We'd be too thin to attack their line. We don't have the numbers to fight in the field like that.'

Henry turns to Birch, who has not so much as blinked her eyes.

'Do you agree with this?'

'It is not the place of the Order to—'

'Oh, spare me. Do you agree with this or not? Because I'll share a better idea.'

'Commander,' says Winters, 'it's not your place to lecture the High—'

'We attack the group on Yellow Ridge. We set up a fortress using those unbreakable windows from the felled tower and we launch a series of Dragoon attacks into the on-coming line of Keepers. They'll never have the numbers to counter us because we won't give them time to assemble. We'll be dug in like Romans and they'll exhaust themselves: a thin line of ants crashing against a mighty wall. And if we need to, we'll set up two more positions – maybe take over The Crossing and use the Pavilion at the top as a staging ground. We can pull them into a death triangle and winnow down their numbers until they give up or they don't exist any more.'

Two oil lamps burn out simultaneously, turning the chamber as sombre as the mood. Graham watches the remaining torches flicker in Henry's soft brown eyes. They are warm and kind and therefore seductive. He learned long ago not to read faces but actions because of how easily faces can deceive.

There are children on Yellow Ridge. She and Graham have both seen them.

'Birch,' Graham says very softly, breaking the darkness, 'The Order may be prevented from providing answers and solutions, but it is encouraged to ask questions. What question is on your mind?'

Birch looks at Graham. It is strange to him that her face has remained so youthful and untroubled, given the secrets she carries and the power she commands. Lilly doesn't like Birch's firm adherence to the rules; she feels that she's owed a personal loyalty, having founded the Order itself. But Graham has always been impressed with Birch. Everything seems to work when she's in charge and she can, with a few words, change the direction of the High Command in a moment. Silence does have a power of its own.

'What I would like to know,' Birch says, turning from Graham to General Winters, 'is what they want.'

RADIO

Alessandra makes her way to Lilly's workshop through the U-Ring below the main concourse. Natural light reflects down through the mirrors illuminating the curved walls and the glistening floor. On her left is the famous *Joy Is Power* indicator, showing the Stadium's reserves of electricity generated by walking back and forth on the Green and in the stands and along the Rings at all levels. How the floors turn their own movements into energy is one of Lilly's research projects. Alessandra has never seen the levels exceed fifteen per cent; right now they're registering eight per cent. Lilly says it's because the Stadium was designed for more people and more activity.

'We pulled more than 60,000 seats during the Great Conversion,' she once explained. Our permanent population is less than eight hundred and even with the Green full on Trade Day, we are seldom more than fifteen hundred. To me, it's a wonder we get to fifteen per cent at all. Maybe the Ancients combined the measures with the Turbines and solar, and obviously we use far less electricity than they did but I don't know. The place didn't come with a manual like your mother's rifle, unfortunately.'

Two guards, a man and a woman, are standing on either side of the Weapons and Communications Research Centre. Alessandra knows them both by name, but chit-chat is frowned upon while they are working.

'Can I come in?' she asks the man.

'You left. Are you expected back?'

'I have a delivery from my father and yes.'

Without turning, the man raps four times on the door to announce it is about to be officially opened. He then pauses, waits for two knocks in return and then swings it wide.

Lilly is facing away from the door. Her long pale yellow hair is tied back in a tail this evening to keep it out of the way. She sits on a tall stool over an elevated work bench of thick wood, a rare material here. She prefers it because it's a poor conductor of electricity compared to the metal desk and because – in her words – it has 'character'.

She never needs to turn around to know who's entered the room and Alessandra has never managed to figure out her trick. A mirror or reflection, she once figured, but that isn't it. Without turning, Lilly raises her right hand into the air and with two fingers, draws Alessandra into the room as though on a string.

Across the room to the right are two other apprentices, Simone and Bruno. Simone is a few years older than Alessandra, with black hair, like her own, and soft brown eyes. She is a little buxom and would make a terrible Runner; it is probably a good choice for her to remain here in a job where she'll be seated.

Bruno is more of a mystery. Like a dozen or more children, he was left here by his parents, who never returned for him. He was a teenager then – fifteen, best as Alessandra can remember, and too old for the Agoge, but in the past five years he has worked his way through the lower coursework. The Stadium is the only colony that demands literacy, and those who join late find learning the hardest, but Bruno learned quickly, and demonstrated an uncanny skill for solving problems with his hands. Lilly has some hope for his development as an engineer if he can learn the maths.

'Come in, Alessandra. I figured you'd come.'

Lilly is leaning over a massive hand-drawn map of the world, or at least as best anyone can imagine it. The full list of country names learned from Trivial Pursuit is on a piece of paper, along with names pulled from books and other found scraps. Lilly is convinced that the names and borders of countries changed over time and because the names – Russia, China, United States, India, Namibia, Czechoslovakia, Mesopotamia – don't have dates attached, she has been trying to figure out which of these names and locations existed last, immediately before The Rise. She says it is mostly a hobby because it has no practical importance, seeing as most of these places are too inaccessible ever to get to.

'I thought I'd be seeing you. I heard your parents are back and carrying.'

'They're in a Sharing now,' Alessandra says, plopping down on a cushion in a plastic chair beside Lilly's desk. 'Alan Farmer was killed.'

'I heard about that too. I'm sorry. I know he was very close to your family.'

'My dad's oldest friend, I think.'

'Yes, he was. They were very disruptive in the Agoge when they were young. Alan was studious – and he was also a brilliant Runner. I took him for a future Evaluator in Arts and Literature. It was his idea that different styles and designs come from different periods of time. His theory was that people are influenced and inspired by what they see; that they try to emulate it and improvise. Once he came up with that idea, I started looking at things a bit differently, examining the idea that classification systems don't only vary according to inherent differences, but also change through time based on new needs and new questions. Anyway, he had a real gift. His death is a loss. How's your father?'

'We barely spoke. He's unsettled,' Alessandra says.

She removes the small bundle from her pocket and places it on Lilly's map over a place she calls *Africa*.

'That is an ugly bit of cloth. I don't want it.'

'There's something inside it from Dad. He said it was on your list.'

Lilly peels it apart to reveal the broken tube and after that, the perfect and matching one.'

'Well, now. That is a surprise. Where did he get this?'

'He said they went to The Crossing after the Tracollo. I'm guessing it was from there but they were out for weeks, so I don't know for certain.'

Lilly holds the tube up to the light and examines the filament. 'This might work.'

'What is it?' Alessandra asks, not terribly interested.

'It's called a fuse. All electrical devices,' she explains, turning around to face Alessandra and crossing her legs as she does, 'have to run at a very specific level of power appropriate to their needs. This clever solution right here burns out first if the power is too high. A fuse is like a little soldier who sacrifices himself to save the rest. That's a lot of nobility in something so modest. This one is from my HAM radio. It burned out a while back – actually, must be close to fifteen years now. I used to show it to all the schoolchildren when they visited the different units. They loved it when a voice came through. I used to rush the classes down here whenever we came across something.'

Alessandra glances up at Bruno. He's rather handsome, although he's too calm and his mood is always quiet. There is little about him that invites conversation or engagement. He has the long, lean body of a male Runner – maybe even a Raider, if he stays with it and can learn to talk to people. She's seen him running laps on the Green and practising with the soldiers; if he's worked his way into Weapons and Communications he must have a brain too.

He looks up at her and she turns back to Lilly.

'Well, let's plug it in and see if anything interesting happens,' Lilly says.

Alessandra stands and follows her to a closet door. When Lilly opens it, she studies it as if it were a Trove – which it is, basically. Inside are dozens of devices, each squatting in its own organised space. The smaller objects are stacked on high, the heavy ones are lower. Rectangular and drab, sometimes curved and reflective, each item looks distinct and important here, which Alessandra always finds somewhat odd because they are also the kinds of machines that are thrown into piles on The Crossing and sold as Raw so crafters and blacksmiths can strip them and turn their pieces into something new and useful.

Lilly points to one at knee-level on the right. 'Get that for me – mind, it's heavy. There's a microphone at the end of the coiled rope. It doesn't work but I don't want to make it worse.'

Alessandra hoists the machine over to the work table, then Lilly redirects her to a low writer's desk in the corner of the room. Lilly pushes it back a few centimetres into a usable position before attaching the long black cord to a socket in the wall. She flicks a switch on the radio – and nothing happens.

'Open it. The tools are over there,' she says, pointing to a wall where every tool has a place. 'I take it your father showed you how to do it.'

Simone has stopped working. Unlike Bruno's lean physique, Simone is full-figured and curvaceous, her eyes bright and her silence always ready to be interrupted. Alessandra can't see exactly what she was doing but it looked like some advanced maths in relation to the tunnels that ran outwards from the Stadium to various points in the Territory. The tunnel map was among the most guarded secrets at the Commonwealth. If Simone had clearance from the High Command to work on that, she must be higher up than Alessandra had always assumed. She might even be part of the Urban Explorers. But Alessandra was part of that group herself; she'd made more than thirty sorties into the Gone World so she figured she would have heard if Simone was too.

'Are you almost done?' Lilly asks.

'Almost.' Alessandra looks around inside the box with the thousand wires, searching for some kind of slot or sleeve where it might go, like a sheath for a blade, but there was nothing but a manic tangle of shinies and snakes.

'I probably am, but I don't know where it goes,' she admits.

Lilly leans over her shoulder and points to two U-shaped clips on the hard plastic board. Alessandra places the new fuse into position and gently pushes until the machine pulls it into place with a *snap*.

'Turn it on, Wayworth.'

Alessandra presses the little black square button and the radio comes to life. The glass panels glow opaque white and night-sky green. The machine itself makes a terrible squealing sound.

*

Lilly is lithe. Despite her years, she is both dexterous and strong, although with her hips she doesn't like bending much. She began as a blacksmith and there is a memory of that power remaining in her body. She pulls her stool over to the table with the radio, sits and crosses her legs, then begins to adjust the dials.

Alessandra watches Lilly's thick black boots bounce at the end of her jeans. She's over seventy but she's fit. Her mum's jokes about her flirtation with her father don't look so harmless from this angle.

'It's okay, you two. I know you can't focus. Come on over,' she tells Simone and Bruno, who make no pretence of hesitation.

They stare at the device, which is an extraordinary thing. It is a black box, but on one face it has a screen that is illuminated in colours, lines and numbers with words and letters like ATT, HOLD, LEVEL, TIME, EXDP/SET. Other parts light up TUNE, TX, LSB, FIL2, VFO A 1 and more. Outside the colourful window are buttons and knobs that are equally mystical: Power, Transmit, Tuner, Vox/BK-IN, P-AMP/ATT, Notch, NB and NR, Menu, Function, M. Scope and still more.

'What is this and why is it interesting?' Lilly asks with a smile, knowing that – for these youngsters – the answer is *nothing*. 'It's called a HAM Radio. We don't know what HAM means so I simply call it a radio. It can send our voices out into the world using radio waves, and it can receive the radio waves – and therefore voices – of other people using their own radios. What that means is that we could, in theory, actually talk to people who are far away.'

'How . . . ?' Simone starts, but Lilly raises a hand to stop her.

'Hold off for a moment. Already, of course, we have a technique for talking to people far away. We use Signal Mirrors to bounce the light of the sun using codes. We use drums. We use smoke signals. We leave message drops – we have a lot of ways to keep in touch. What I'm talking about here is actual *conversation* with people who are hundreds, even thousands of kilometres away.'

'That's miraculous,' says Bruno.

'I don't know why you say that. The Ancients built those towers in the Gone World. This is hardly more impressive. And we know from the Trivial Pursuit answers that people have been to the moon several times; that an international space station circles the Earth – or at least it once did – and that we even tried to get to Mars. Pity about the outcome.

'The radio has six primary parts,' she continues, 'the power supply, which is why I have it plugged into the wall. The transceiver, which selects the frequencies we use to send and receive. The antenna tuner – which I don't entirely understand – the microphone – which lets us talk, and the speaker,' she says, tapping the black grille, 'which lets us listen. As it happens, our microphone is broken because it was submerged in water for three hundred years, which explains the colour and shape, but I like to leave it there because it completes the look.'

Lilly manually advanced through several bands, letting the apprentices listen for themselves.

'It worked for thirty-nine years and then it blew its fuse. It took me a solid decade to get my head around the basics. As we've discussed during your Induction Lecture, we have two main sections in Weapons and Communications – and don't say weapons and communications. We have – Simone?'

'Engineering and Reverse Engineering.'

'Right. And what's the difference?'

'In Engineering, we're trying to solve problems. In Reverse Engineering, we're trying to solve mysteries. The main one being, how did other people solve *their* problems and what can we learn from that.'

'Good,' says Lilly, 'and now explain it in your own words. You need to understand the intuition behind it.'

'Well,' said Simone, happy to be talking and not working alone with a taciturn Bruno, 'in Engineering, we talk to High Command or the Archive or the Order and find out what problems they're having. Like, how to grow food using less soil, or how to predict weather patterns, or how to build armour into the jackets that the Runners wear so they can come back uninjured after leaping around on rooftops. In Reverse Engineering . . .' she began, but Lilly interrupted her.

'And what's the first thing we do when we face a new problem?'

'Talk to Reverse Engineering.'

'Why?'

'Because maybe they've already learned things that could solve the problem and we can use those.'

'Exactly. Because we don't innovate and create for fun: we do it because we need to, and we've learned some humility over the years. The Ancients had space ships and global communications and weapons we can't imagine, so if we can find out how they solved problems, we do that first. Failing that, we put our heads together and do it ourselves. Reverse Engineering is trying to learn the mysteries of the Ancients by taking things apart, coming up with new ideas, new explanations, new possibilities. The more the Archive grows, the greater the chances of solving those mysteries faster, and the greater the likelihood of solving our problems sooner. That's why Knowledge is power: because the more you know, the more you can do. Now, Alessandra,' Lilly said, turning to her youngest apprentice, 'how else does this section learn beyond engineering new solutions or learning old ones from Reverse Engineering or the Archive?'

'From the outside. By building the Archive itself. Raid, Trade, and Spade.'

'That's our catchy phrase for the children to memorise, but what does it actually mean?'

'Raiders learn from engagement with other people – peacefully if possible, forcefully if necessary. Traders exchange our Knowledge for new Knowledge to create Trade Bonds. And Spaders dig it out of the Gone World with, you know, spades.'

'If this radio were able to talk to other radios,' Lilly says, turning back to the matter at hand, 'we'd be able to find other people – far-off people – and trade without risk. We could learn without effort. We could create trade bonds with people all over, wherever they were. Like tightening a weave in fabric, the world would draw close and rise again with the Commonwealth and the Archive at the centre. That little fuse your dad found,' Lilly said, 'makes it all possible.'

'But we can't talk to anyone,' Bruno says, 'can we? I mean, can the Knowledge from the Archive get out?'

'No, we can only listen. We'll never fix this one. It's dead. But it's not impossible we might find a new microphone somewhere. Unfortunately, we haven't yet.'

'And,' asks Bruno, 'in those thirty-nine years, how many times have you heard other people?'

Yes. That was always the crux of it.

'Seven times.'

'That's . . . not many . . .'

'No,' Lilly admits. 'And those times I did hear people, they spoke in languages I didn't know and we'll never be able to learn. They also didn't last long because the signals were very weak and eventually I lost them. For another radio to work, the person would have to be in a place with the right kind and enough electricity. They'd need a perfectly working radio – preserved, somehow, for hundreds of years without rot – and they would need to know how to operate it, which is not obvious. It took me ages, for example, to learn that I needed to cut and adjust an antenna and mount it on the Stadium roof and then receive signals appropriate to that antenna. That took me seven years – and I'm very smart. It was even longer before I started to understand the basic theory of how radio signals bounce off the atmosphere to reach other radios. They might even bounce off the moon, but that's just an idea I have. There's a relationship between radio signals and how they travel during the day versus the night. Reception was always better at night. Since the main difference between day and night is the sun – and therefore light and temperature – I think that the sun plays a role in radio transmission too. This has been a Reverse Engineering agenda for decades. But I simply don't have enough information to build a good understanding. Radio aren't like guns: they weren't built to be used by just anyone. There was a lot of learning needed, and now that learning is gone. So it's an Indie that's dependent on Knowledge itself. It's quite a thing.'

Alessandra doesn't take her eyes off the strange numbers and words. She listens to the squelching tones that sound like animals approaching one another – shoulders up, eyes low, danger in every step.

'So this radio. It could help the Commonwealth grow and learn more and make us more like the Ancients,' Bruno concluded, 'but probably won't?'

This is what Lilly brought back from the first Tracollo, thought Alessandra, a device that could possibly unify and connect the entire world and find people thousands of miles away – connecting them like one family, one Commonwealth.

And the Box with its books and games and children's entertainment. Lilly did all that.

And the mysterious White Board that in half a century did nothing and guarded all its secrets. Something Lilly took on impulse.

Lilly did all of this when she was Alessandra's own age: seventeen. She did all this without ever having had a father and only a year after her mother was murdered on the High Road. Lilly herself barely made it back alive after a gun battle.

And what was Alessandra doing? *Nothing.* Not making a name for herself. Not standing out meaningfully in any way. She was the daughter of the Wayworths, but she had yet to earn the name on her own.

'You brought all of this back from The Crossing,' she said.

'It wasn't The Crossing back then. It was called the Bridge to Nowhere. But yes,' Lilly said, 'this and the Box and the White Board were recovered from the first Tracollo. Not the one that fell straight down, of course. That buried everything beneath it. This was from Tower Two when it fell over and cracked open. That's how people started exploring below.'

'Why didn't they die from the Sickness?' Bruno asks.

'They did,' Lilly said, 'but not immediately. They made pulls first.'

For fifty years she's been telling this story.

Yes, the Roamers made Pulls that I found at the bridge.

No, I don't know where they came from. Inside, I suppose.

Yes, I did manage to open the Box. I can't tell you how. It's a guarded secret, I'm sorry.

Yes, Cardo and two thugs did try to rape me in the Pavilion when I came for the Box. I blasted my way out with my mother's Python.

The Sickness? Yes, thousands of bodies inside the Tower. You go in, you die.

But these were lies.

All lies.

Lies she told at the beginning – lies she continues to tell now. Lies that needed to be protected and repeated so that the Truth would never be learned and the Commonwealth would always be safe.

Lies that led Lilly to found the Order of Silence; that placed Saavni in charge.

Lies which only Birch knows to be untrue now – Birch, and whomever she has chosen to tell.

BWV 988

Graham and Henry sit together outside at the edge of the Green looking at the two bonfires and the rows of kneeling archers awaiting orders that will likely not come tonight. Henry has been on sniper duty for extended periods before; she knows how tiring the experience can be. It's the concentration and immobility that slow time – that, and the isolation. With no one to talk to it can be taxing. For the archers, though, it's even worse: you stare at your own foot until Anoushka tells you otherwise.

But none of that is her problem now.

Technically, Graham's mood isn't her problem either, but that she can do something about.

'At least you peed,' she says.

He smiles only a little and doesn't look away from the bonfire.

'Go on, complain. I want you to.'

'I'm not entirely sure what we're doing here,' he admits.

'Surviving.'

'That's a pat answer for the feeble.'

'We live long and we live well compared to everyone else in the known world. That's not enough?'

106

Graham looks up at the night sky. The colours are not as intense from inside the Stadium. There is too much light thrown up by the oil lamps and the bonfires, and the presence of all the people gathered there distracts from his pleasure in the natural beauty.

'I think I became a Raider to get outside the walls,' he says. 'Sometimes I find it ironic that you started life there and then decided to come in.'

'You need a new *Seeing*,' Henry says.

'Is that a Roamer word?'

'Yes. Well, no – it's the same word, but it has a different meaning to us. You don't know this?'

'Maybe? I forget.'

'The Roamers believe that everything is in motion: people, places, ideas, time . . . everything. Change is therefore constant and a fact and any effort to resist it is unnatural. We didn't roam simply because we couldn't settle down, we roamed to be at one with the natural movement of life. I was brought up that way. We did talk about this.'

'Not for twenty years. Tell me again.'

Henry rubs her hands in the cold. 'As one moves – through space, time, ideas – there are Crossings.'

Graham removes his scarf and wraps it around Henry's hands. The warmth from his neck is still in the cloth.

'Crossings happen in their own way. They might be planned but we usually refer to them as something unexpected. Like you finding that glass tube. Each Crossing creates an opportunity for a Union. A Union is when some kind of bond – a connection – occurs during The Crossing. Usually it's with another person or an object. If it's with another person, you both have to want the Union. If it's a thing . . . obviously it's just you.'

'So they can be rejected?'

'Oh yes. We have Crossings that don't result in Unions all the time. People and things pass by each other constantly. Those aren't Crossings. Crossings are when a bond is suggested. A face across the room who could become a lover or new friend. Maybe an object that seems to speak to you. In those cases, a Union is either agreed or rejected. A Seeing is when we Cross another way of understanding and embrace it. We don't always agree with it or make it our own, but we take it in. To Cross something that results in a new Seeing is a rare and special thing. It often requires courage and wisdom and an open heart to allow ourselves to be moved into that other place. A Union gives us more than we had before. A Seeing makes us more than we were before. One of the reasons I was attracted to the Commonwealth when my parents died is because Lilly's idea of building the Archive promised new Unions and new Seeings. And she was going to seek them out – not rely on fate or luck, but create an agenda to bring them to us.'

'And you think,' concludes Graham, 'that I need a new Seeing?'

'I think your understanding of our life needs to be refreshed.'

'You make me happy,' he said.

'I know,' she replied.

Inside the Stadium of the Commonwealth, behind a wooden door as polished and refined as a rifle stock, there is a music room. The room is draped with rugs to absorb sound and moisture. Hanging on the walls and touched by only a few are instruments: some are made of wood and string, others are brass and ornate and they all have voices, even though few have names because they have long since been lost. Many are warped or damaged beyond repair and though their shapes look simple enough, no crafter has ever come close to recreating them.

108

In the centre of the room stands the electric piano. It has eighty-eight keys – fifty-two white and thirty-six black. It has no strings to break or wood to warp, so its tone and action remain perfect. And the Stadium has electricity enough to power it.

Moishe son-of-Tikvah plays the piano. He is thirty-four years old and works by day as a foreman on construction projects. For military service he is part of a Phalanx, but the Evaluators have spoken to Winters because they do not want his unique hands to see war.

When he was six years old he was tested for aptitude like all children entering the Agoge. He was found to have a rare and native understanding of the patterns that create harmonies. He was initially taught to play by the two pianists of the Commonwealth and was then allowed to learn on his own.

He was both dexterous and studious and by the age of twelve there was no new music to teach him, the library having been exhausted. Instead, he was left to create his own, so he took it upon himself to gather the oldest people together and ask them to share any songs they knew – from their travels, from their parents, from their grandparents, from their dreams.

He transcribed them into music that the Scribes copied and had the Runners hide.

At formal events and rare informal evenings he entertains in the Great Hall. He also teaches students. To support the Central Archive, he responds to requests from the Chief Evaluator for Art and Literature. It's not often that he is called to this task, but he welcomes it every time.

He was called tonight.

In his chamber, where he lives alone but pines for Anoushka – who said last month they were finished, but he is not so sure – Moishe bathes and scrubs his hands red in preparation for visiting the Music Room. When he arrives he removes his shoes at the entrance and dons his waiting slippers. He arrives at the piano rested and clean and pristine.

He sits himself on the bench.

The piano is white. He has been told it draws power from the walls and possibly his own movements. How it works matters less to him than what it does.

To the far left of the piano, above the keys, there is a button as clear as glass. He presses it and it glows blue, signalling the instrument's readiness to obey.

The new documents retrieved from the Trove have already been positioned on the piano. He studies them, touching nothing. The paper is old but not the oldest he has seen; it's unfaded, not yellowed or rimmed with crust.

He can read the language at the top of the page. He recognises the name of the composer, a strange name that no one else has.

The letters and numbers *BWV 988 Aria* mean nothing to him.

For a moment he sits with the notes.

The room has one hundred and fifty seats, arranged like an amphitheatre, a semi-circle around the piano, which sits on the stage. The sound in here is excellent, but it changes when the room is filled.

For no reason he looks up and notices two figures seated at the back.

He squints and after a moment, recognises their faces. The Commanders.

He waves once and Graham lifts his hand.

Moishe looks down at the sheet music again and forgets the audience. He has a job to do and they, of all people, will not interrupt.

Beyond English, Français and Español, music is the only

other language he knows to have survived. Moishe does not find this surprising because, to him, it is the language of the angels and if only one language was going to survive The Rise and the emptying of the world, surely it would be music. It will be the language spoken by the dead so that no one will ever be alone in heaven.

There is a logic to every piece of music, however modest or complex. This one has no time signature, so he has to reach out with his heart beyond four hundred, even six hundred years, to understand the feeling that this person – this *Bach* – might have wanted him to feel.

BWV 988. The Goldberg Variations.

Reading before he plays, he sees that the notes are very simple at first. After several measures they grow sophisticated. It suggests the need for an emotional maturity from the very first note, otherwise the integrity will be compromised.

He starts to play and quickly stops. *Too fast.* He slows down, much slower: slow, the way a drop of water falls from an icicle after a thaw. He needs to reach across the boundary separating this moment from centuries before the entire destruction of the Gone World to find the emotion that this composer was feeling when he penned the notes.

Once Moishe finds a balance between melody and moment and mood, he plays again.

These two notes, with rests; a pause, three more, like pebbles dropping into water together, and then six that are given space to breath, separate from one another, but reaching – calling out; carrying the sensation forward.

Moishe plays the aria for three minutes. After three minutes he lifts his shaking hands from the piano and weeps.

II

PURGATORIO

HELLO

Time is hard to judge underground. Three weeks? A month? More?

When she first woke on the floor and opened her eyes, there was a warm red light in a sea of chalky air. She exhaled and her breath formed in front of her: a cone of white against the smooth surface of the floor, blowing off the dust of centuries. The pain in her leg did not radiate outwards from the stick that was jutting into it, instead, it caused her entire body to throb. She could feel the blood pulsing in her neck – in fact, every inch of her was pulsing.

Slowly, she reached for the black strap of the sling-bag, intent on pulling it over her resting head and gently – very, very gently, so as not to alert her own pain – sliding the strap out from beneath her to get access to the material within.

The effort didn't go unpunished. The pain was horrible. Alone, under a million pounds of rubble, she screamed.

Inside the bag was a triangular bandage in a small pouch marked with a red cross on a white background. She opened it, rolled it from the end until it became long and tight, and then she bent it into a circle and weaved it around itself to become a *doughnut* – a term everyone used and no one could define, but it had come to mean this. She placed the doughnut around the stick embedded in her leg. She'd been taught never to pull out something that was impaling the flesh as it might be what's keeping the rest of the blood in. Comforted by the knowledge that if she were going to bleed out it would have happened while she slept, she pressed another bandage to her leg, applying pressure to the wound.

Her trainer on the Green had told her that many of these kits with red crosses had been found in Troves, not just all over the Territory but beyond, in almost every ancient vehicle, in every tower, on every boat or building. The Ancients, Elimisha had decided long ago, were accident-prone and eventually they succumbed. The end.

That was her theory, anyway.

The air smelled bad but it didn't make her cough. Lying there on her back, in the quiet, she wondered whether the Sickness might already be inside her.

This room – this tomb – was unlike any place she had ever been. There was a silence here that was deeper and more perfect than any she had ever imagined. Growing up with two brothers and her mother in their small apartment, noise was constant. Inside the Stadium's rooms and halls, there were always footsteps and shouting voices and the racket of objects being pushed or pulled around. Out in the Gone World, when she was on a Run and alone, the sounds were smaller but intensified: her footsteps on the sand, or the soles of her shoes grinding over a rock; bugs and lizards speaking in the night, the distant cries of Traders or Roamers – sometimes even singing and music.

And the wind: always the wind.

Here there was nothing. No sound. No movement. She was the only living thing.

Elimisha pushed away the fear and the memory of last night's events and visualised sitting up, then standing. She pictured this with the same attention to detail that she used to perform her visualisation of Routes. Eventually – for reasons as mysterious as life itself – the repetitions passed from her mind to her body, and once in her body they became actions she couldn't refuse. In this way, Elimisha rose to her feet.

On her left was the massive door that had slammed shut behind her with the blast. Between here and there, hanging on the wall, was a red and glass box and inside the box was a long, useful-looking axe. Elimisha removed it from under the glass. It was far too short to use as a crutch, so she propped it against the wall before dragging herself to the door. On it was a central wheel she understood to be the lock. She turned it and to her delight, found that it spun easily.

Lefty loosey, righty tighty.

It spun left until it clanked to a halt. She'd seen no hinges, but knowing the door opened outwards, she pushed with all her weight and what little strength she had, leaning into it as though it were an argument, holding the pressure until the pain made her stop. Nothing had even *suggested* movement. This was no more a door now than a painting of a door on the side of a mountain of solid rock. It was going nowhere. Something bigger than her was blocking her exit and unless the world shifted again of its own volition, she needed to find another way out.

Turning to explore her own coffin, Elimisha began to walk.

Step after laborious step, she hobbled her way through the ancient bomb shelter, every part of it as perfect and unravaged by time as the best parts of the Stadium. It was not a familiar place, though: the Stadium had curves and lifts, and unbreakable windows which captured the best of the light. The minds

117

who designed it were obviously trying to create something of majesty, of souring inspiration and technological acumen. This place was all angles and straight lines, a temporary shelter from the forces of death: a hard place.

At the end of the hall was a T-junction and a door that read STORAGE.

To her left was a long corridor. Though far away, she could make out the word on that door too: COMMUNICATIONS. This gave her a destination.

As she trudged towards it, she passed another door on her right inscribed with the words CONTROL ROOM. She tried the handle and found it unlocked, but it was heavy and set on two sizable hinges. Pressing the handle downwards, she pushed it open and it yielded.

Inside was another red bulb inside a cage above the door. The room was filled with machinery and unlike in the hall, she heard a very subtle but clear *hum*. Elimisha poked her head in. The ground was dry, there were no footprints and the smell was the same musty scent as the rest of the dungeon. Not seeing any reason not to, she stepped inside to take a look around.

To her right was a cabinet made of sheet metal. The door had a small metal handle but no lock; pressing a silver button with her thumb opened it. Swinging the doors wide revealed three large machines with knobs, lights and gauges, all dimly illuminated. She had never seen machines quite like this before, although the style was reminiscent of others she'd seen in Lilly's closet in Weapons and Communications. They also looked like the piles of Raw she'd seen at The Crossing.

There were labels reading PRIMARY. RESERVE. FILTERS.

The gauge on the PRIMARY machine was measuring available power of eight per cent, and it was holding steady. Beside it, someone has written graffiti like at the Stadium:

Without power . . . it is just a cave.

There was a series of switches directing power to each room, all set to the OFF position. She had seen switches like this before; Lilly called them circuit breakers. It was possible that they had been in the ON position before a surge of some kind knocked them out.

Elimisha pressed all of them upwards. She heard a number of *clicks* . . . there was a flicker of light, another, a pause, and a burst of continuous white light shone from three long bulbs mounted along the top of the wall as the entire shelter came to life. Elimisha closed her eyes for a moment of respite from the pain and to celebrate a moment of good news.

The RESERVE unit's white needle was pressed flat to zero and the FILTERS light was off. Beside them were two buttons, one red, the other green.

She pressed the green button and immediately a whirling sound began, accompanied by a puff of air from a large vent on the wall. A second unit kicked into action, pulling the dust from the air.

Light. Heat. Air.

For twenty minutes Elimisha sat watching her situation improve. She had learned from Lilly how filters were used to clean water back at the Stadium so she surmised these filters were making the air fresher by removing particulates. What she didn't know was whether the machine was pulling out the bad air and pushing in fresh air from the outside or if it was simply recirculating the air that was there already. Was she breathing clean air, or simply fresher versions of the Sickness?

Whatever the truth, it hardly mattered at the moment: she was locked inside and had to breathe.

Looking down at herself in the bright light, she also accepted that she needed to clean herself off and change out of these clothes.

Eat. Drink. Heal.

Elimisha leaned over and pressed her hands to her knees, feeling the cool breeze from the wind-machine against her thick curls. If she could know for a fact that it wasn't poison she could enjoy it. In that moment, though, her ambivalence would have to do.

Strange there would be still be power here.

Her sciences classes at the Agoge had taught her the rudiments of how batteries work. Power goes in, it is stored ('by magic', everyone would joke) and is released to power systems later. How much later? No one knows because the engineers refuse to run down the batteries at the Stadium. What if they never charged again?

It was Lilly, though, who had stared at the brass plaque at the Stadium entrance and wondered what it had meant by 'kinetic power'.

Along with Edward Gibbon's abridged *Rise and Fall of the Roman Empire*, and – of course – *The Complete Calvin and Hobbes*, the Harrington Box that Lilly had recovered contained mostly books written by the Greeks. One book – *The History of the Peloponnesian War* by Thucydides – was written with their own language on the left page and the original Greek on the right. Gibbon, in talking about Latin, had explained how languages evolved and borrowed terms and built new words on others. Lilly had considered this important and she set a team to work on it. Elimisha had found the whole idea quite boring until Lilly explained that the word *kinetic* on the brass plaque might come from the Greek word *kinetikos*, which meant 'movement or putting in motion'. 'Could it be,' Lilly had asked, 'that the

Stadium is partly powered by motion inside it, and that motion is somehow captured and stored in batteries – like rainwater in cisterns – so that it can be re-directed later? When I was about your age, I invented a way to move water from the waterfalls into the well inside the Stadium walls using a kind of screw and a road for the water. Turns out the Romans did too – they called it an aqueduct – so I might not have been the first but I was in good company. What you need to understand,' Lilly said to her, 'is that the world of the Ancients – not the Classicists, like the Greeks and Romans, but *our* Ancients – needed tremendous amounts of power. They had Big Electricity. The biggest. The plaque gives us three sources: the sun, the flow of the water through the turbines and human kinetic power. I think that movement itself can create power. Why not?'

Elimisha looked down at her feet. If the world here caught no sun and no water flowed and no people walked, the bunker probably couldn't produce power. But . . . the earth had shaken. Could the fall of a building have been enough to wake the lights and charge the batteries?

She couldn't know. It was, as her science teacher called it, 'a hypothesis'. But if it was true, it meant that the eight per cent was only going to go down because there was no way to charge the batteries again, and at that point the lights would go out, the air would stop circulating and the heaters would cool. The deeper you go, she knew, the colder it gets – maybe not to freezing, but cold enough, in the dark, to feel like it.

It was going to be a terrible way to die.

What Elimisha thought of, in those early days, was how she could have been with her mother and brothers in their home instead of here in this bunker. Kuende, fourteen always studious; Jabiri – the jokester – seventeen, smart, though undisciplined.

He's a year older and is supposed to be the big brother, but Elimisha has been his guide since their father died and their mother fell into a sea of tears and wasn't able to reach the shore for two years.

On her feet again, her leg still burning, Elimisha flicked on the lighting for the remaining rooms and set herself to the task of taking inventory while searching for another exit.

The storage room had the kinds of cans she'd seen in the Archive Museum.

'*Don't open, don't eat,*' the Curator had warned them.

She was not going to touch those.

There was also rice.

She has been told that dry rice can last a thousand years and stay safe to eat. Traders bring the Stadium occasional shipments, so she knows how to prepare it if the stoves are willing to heat and there's any water to use. If she doesn't die down here from the Sickness – or some other illness – she'll have enough food to last months at least. Although what she would be waiting for, she has no idea.

And how long will that eight per cent last? She'd need to measure the drop and calculate it, and for that she'd need a way to tell time.

Maybe something would come up.

In the mess hall she found a jar filled with a viscous brown liquid that moved slowly when she tilted it, much like the tree sap that can be boiled down into a sweet soup that everyone loves – a rare delicacy from the forests between the Commonwealth and the small colony of Anchorpoint. She unscrewed the top and risked a sniff. It smelled wonderful. She dipped in a finger and tasted it. A surge of contentment started at the sides of her tongue, rushed down her neck and seeped into the core of her body – all the way down to her leg, where the happiness was defeated.

She tasted it again and the decided that if the goo *did* eventually kill her it would be better than freezing to death in the dark.

Beyond the control room, towards the communications room, was an empty sleeping chamber with three sets of bunk beds and two sheet-metal closets on the back wall, one between each set of beds. A thin vent on the ceiling continued to blow cool fresh air. Elimisha walked to the closet, running a hand across the woollen blanket on a lower bunk. A small cloud of dust rose from it as her fingers left grooves in the fabric.

The closets there had no locks. Inside were six full-body suits of a material she has never seen before, thick like Runners' leather but lighter and more supple, and cobalt-blue like the tips of the sky fires at night before they reached the green swirls. Each suit was edged in silver. Under the lights from above, they shimmered the way algae does in the moonlight by the edge of the river at the Frontier Command – the spot where the water becomes undrinkable, at the western-most edge of the Domain. She had been there once with her father. He ran his fingers through the algae, making dark rivers, and smiled.

The suits were hanging neatly on hooks. They all looked immaculate – and clean, which was enticing, particularly given her bloodied and filthy condition.

She removed one from a hanger and held it up in front of her to check for size. Unlike most ancient clothing, this one had no labels inside. The only marking was a vertical stripe on the right arm running down from the shoulder. It read 'Haptic Command Gear – HCG®' in red lettering.

Three of the suits were too big and three were huge. Elimisha flung one of the smaller ones over her shoulder and left the room to finish her tour.

The toilets were clean, if covered in the same layer of dust as everything else.

There was toilet paper rather than water and cloths.

All the bulbs worked in the halls and rooms.

As she mapped her surroundings and acclimatised herself, she ran her hands along the walls. She had been taught in the Agoge that Knowledge enters the body through all the senses: the Runner must be keenly aware of the wind on her cheek, the slickness of surfaces, the smell of animals or fires, the changing of the light, all of this at all times. The world is talking, she was told. It is your *duty* to listen.

The paint – the colour of nothing – chipped off into tiny flakes as she drew a line waist-high with barely a touch. The walls were drier than the bones of the dead. She rubbed her fingers together and the flakes fell to the floor as gently as a dusting of snow during an autumn flurry. She wondered whether they might also be soft. Whether, for example, an axe could make a hole in them to the outside.

A question for later.

Leaving the mess hall at the far end behind her, she proceeded at her own pace to the communications room. The shower was calling to her and she was hoping there was water. But for now, the beckoning promise of a human voice was more profound.

What she found instead were human eyes.

In Elimisha's mind, any *communications* room was really a *Weapons and Communications Research and Development Section*: a place run by a Chief, staffed by up to a dozen engineers and hosting ten or even a dozen apprentices. It was a place with thousands of tiny shinies lying around, rifle barrels being matched (or not) to ammunition, orders for repairs or creations being listed for the blacksmiths and messengers running back and forth to the Central Archive with questions for the Librarians or answers from them (usually: *No Idea*).

It wasn't like that in Lilly's private office, of course: that was hers only, with a workbench, a few chairs and a second table for a few invited others to join her. But the main room was all movement and metal.

This room was nothing like that.

After the door finished creaking open it revealed a small, austere work space: a place a Scribe might work, one who needed to be alone to copy a complex diagram from a paper no one understood. The U-Ring had some rooms like that, mostly cleared-out former closets, rooms without windows – rooms no one was ever meant to remain inside for very long. The kind of places the Urban Explorers would occasionally use for meetings in the middle of the night because they were unguarded and unwatched.

The only furniture was a wide table of sheet metal no better in quality than the best smelters could make today. In front of that was a chair with a woven fabric on the backrest and five wheels down below. It reminded her of the fancy chairs she had seen once in the Snake Tower when her class toured it. On the far wall, across the desk, was a calendar that said *Pirelli*. On the bottom portion was a grid for the days of the month for the year 2097. Above it was the most captivating – but also the most confusing – photograph of a woman Elimisha had ever seen.

This photograph was black and white, unlike most of the photographs in the Museum. The woman, who looked to be in her late teens or early twenties, was quite like her friend

Gina, with strangely pale skin and straight black hair. She was standing in a room with white walls and a window behind her and all she wore were thin black panties and a Runner's leather jacket. But it was the strangest jacket imaginable. There were steel studs sticking out everywhere. There was no armour on the shoulders or elbows and if she raised the collar and zipped it to the top to protect her against extreme conditions, the studs would have pressed against her chest!

It was madness.

Elimisha couldn't see her breasts, but she could glimpse enough of her neck and torso and thighs to know that she was beautiful and sexy but she was also very weak. It was a strange combination, like nothing she had seen before. Though her skin was lovely and her eyes deep and tender, she looked like someone recovering from a long illness. There was no muscle to her; no sense of power; no promise of speed or endurance. Her beauty, such as it was, came from her poise and grace and the way the light and shadows played on her skin. How, though, she wondered, could someone so thin and weak have such wonderful skin and be wearing a Runner's jacket? It made no sense. You're either healthy or you're not. And when you're not, your skin doesn't look like that! Or your eyes. And who'd be feeling sexy during such an intense recovery?

Elimisha couldn't imagine what kind of life would have led that woman to a moment where she'd have chosen to be photographed for eternity in a condition like that.

And yet, there she was: an actual *Ancient*. A real person. A young and pretty woman in a stupid jacket, dead now hundreds of years: Elimisha's only company in the cave.

Or maybe there are eleven more girls in the calendar? Yet another question for later.

Elimisha saw the girl first because of her eyes; because of

126

their warmth and soul. What she should have noticed – as an Archive Runner for the Commonwealth with a hole in her leg and a job to do and vows to keep – was the radio.

Elimisha hadn't even been born yet when Lilly's radio had stopped working, but her mother had heard it in Lilly's workshop. She'd been touring the Commonwealth with her class, learning about the work of the different sections and meeting all the Chiefs. They even got to try their hands at the tasks that animated the Commonwealth into a community.

That day, her mother had told her, they'd been extremely lucky because one of Lilly's engineers had discovered a voice, which was very, very rare. It was even rarer for the signal to be strong. Unfortunately, they couldn't understand whoever was speaking. Many languages existed across the world long ago, Lilly had explained; we knew about Greek and Latin, and Français and Español, but there used to be many more, maybe dozens – maybe thousands! – she had joked.

The fact that they had been able to listen to one of them that day on the radio was proof that people still existed far away and that was enough to stretch the mind beyond the edges of the known world and hint that it was bigger than they had thought.

They listened for almost an hour as the man talked and talked, all by himself, telling a story in a language no one there could identify, let alone understand. More and more people packed themselves into the workshop so they could hear the voice. Before that day, no one there had ever heard a person who was not in the same room. It was a lifetime of inspiration.

Elimisha's mother had asked if they could talk back to him, but all they could do was listen for now.

'Someday we'll find another,' Lilly had said.

Another what? Person? Microphone? Source of inspiration? She didn't know.

They listened to the same voice at the same time of night for the next three days. At the end the man said a final word – *sayonara* – and never spoke again. The word became used at the Stadium, wistfully, for final goodbyes. Maybe that was even what the man had meant.

This box in the bunker was clearly a radio. It was a similar size, with a large glass display illuminating numbers and words. More telling, of course, was the black cable that ran from a port on its face to a free-standing microphone covered in the same black steel mesh as Lilly's broken one.

What intrigued Elimisha wasn't the details of the radio itself (Lilly's was far too complicated to understand at all, let alone to use as a basis for differentiation) but how it was placed on the desk. It looked as if it had purposefully been pushed over to the side of the table and angled towards the operator to make room for a White Board – the same device that Lilly had brought back from her Tracollo.

That's what everyone called it, anyway, although it wasn't really a board. It was actually an elegant, lightweight angled wedge set on a curvaceous steel trellis that was polished more finely than the Stadium's main kitchen. On the taller part, at the back, was a curious bulge in the centre, like the top of an egg. Other than that – nothing. No buttons, no lights, no writing.

When Elimisha had asked Lilly about it during her apprenticeship, the Chief had said, 'I don't know. It seemed important at the time and it wasn't heavy so I put it in my backpack and brought it home. Since then I have learned nothing. I have no idea what it does and I never will.'

Surrender was so uncharacteristic of the Chief that Elimisha never mentioned it again.

She did, in secret, go back and look at it from time to time – furtively, as if it were a crime – she would run her hands over its perfect and inviting surface, wondering about it.

It was, after all, the only thing in the known world to have ever defeated Lilly daughter-of-Rachael.

This one looked almost identical to Lilly's except for the letters *HCG®* and the phrases *ISO Compliant* and *Made in Brazil* perfectly etched into the side.

All of which were meaningless to her.

She touched it and it did nothing.

What Elimisha wanted to do was finish her tour of the facility, clean herself up and change into the new clothes she had found that would be so much better than her own blood-soaked, filthy rags, and to drink three litres of water to replenish the blood she'd lost.

Before leaving the room, though, she pressed the long grey transmission bar and said . . . nothing.

She didn't know what she should say. Lilly's radio hadn't worked in twenty years and they'd never heard a voice in English. No one would be listening.

And yet . . . Her mother had listened to that man – her whole class, everyone crammed into the big workshop – had heard his last stories and thoughts and feelings. They might not have understood a word he said but they had been witnesses to his life – so far away, 'so lonely,' said her mother. Without a word coming back to him, with no proof that anyone could hear him, he spoke all the same. And because of that subtle act of faith – that gentle gesture – he had filled the hearts of hundreds of people with warmth and the promise of limitless possibility.

Buried beneath the earth with a calendar girl and a radio, could Elimisha do any less?

First, however, a shower.

There were still a few rooms Elimisha had not explored but the physical desire to be *well* exceeded curiosity. Leaving the comms room, she returned to the mess hall and kitchen and dragged herself down it, leaving more tracks and stirring up more dust. Hopefully, the filters would remove it.

Before the kitchen were the toilets and adjacent to them, the shower room, and next to that, first on her left after a storage closet, was the infirmary, marked with the ubiquitous red cross.

The lights were on in there too and aside from some broken glass from jars that had fallen during the rumble, everything inside was pristine. The kit contained the usual bandages, some medication she'd been warned – like every child – to *never, ever, ever put inside you*, as well as several bottles of liquid she decided to treat like medication. There was also – there it was – a needle and thread.

This was not for sewing clothing. This was for sewing humans.

Next to the needle and thread, in the same plastic wrap, were scissors, tweezers and various antiseptic liquids, almost everything she needed to remove the spike from her leg and stitch it up. The only thing missing was courage.

Sitting on the operating table, Elimisha cut the leather down to the puncture wound and then laid herself down and, as gently as she could, wiggled out of the trousers. The process took minutes, the anticipation of pain almost as bad as the pain itself.

She cut off her underwear too, then threw her jacket and shirt into the corner. The heaters had brought the room to a comfortable temperature but she was still shivering.

The mirror over the sink was clouded and for a moment she preferred it that way, but soon she became angry at herself for her gloomy mood and weakness. She rolled herself off the table, managed the three steps to the mirror and then swiped away the layer to reveal the truth of herself. Her skin was darker than late autumn leaves and her eyes were the colour of healthy earth. She was thin, but she was strong and had the same 'charmingly round face' and big brown eyes that everyone called 'friendly'.

Her hair, however, was a total nightmare and she was of a mind to take the scissors and teach it a lesson.

'Traitor,' she scolded, and in doing so, heard her own voice for the first time in days.

She tried the faucet below the mirror. A strange sound from deep in the wall answered her call for water: a *tha-thump, tha-thump, tha-thump* that soon brought out a splatter of brownish goo, then brown ooze, followed by brown water and then actual clear water.

The cool stream felt wonderful on her hands and wrists. If it was drinkable she'd be able to eat the rice by soaking it. If the stove worked, she'd even have hot food.

There was an argument for pulling out the metal rod now and stitching herself up before the shower, but another – and better one, to her mind – was being as clean as possible before messing around with an open wound.

Like the faucet, the shower worked. She found soap, or a gelatinous lump that used to be soap, in a box under the sink. It still smelled better than she did, so she spread it all over her body and through her hair. Though she tried to keep her leg away from the water, her wound still burned. Washing around it, Elimisha pictured every kind of result from pulling it out. Maybe the end was as smooth and rounded as this end was – but what if it was more like a Sagittari's arrow? What if it was buried deep in the meat of her thigh and pulling it out would mean ripping through her muscles?

The thought of it almost made her throw up.

Her training had insisted that she learn pain. Forced marches, sleep deprivation and hand-fighting until brutal defeat were all considered necessary to know the extent of what the body can endure so the mind doesn't flinch before reaching it – but this was something else. What if the wound was infected and the whole leg was growing infected because it was covered in some kind of sickness? And right that very minute, while she deliberated and prevaricated and talked herself out of action because she was afraid and feeling weak and alone and scared and naked under a billion barrels of stone and rock, with the front door sealed tighter than a Ghost Talker's mind, it was festering and seething in there, growing black and—

She pulled it out and screamed, falling to the floor in agony.

With her good leg, Elimisha pushed herself back against the wall and watched the blood ooze out and mix with the water and run down the drain to a spot even deeper into the world than she was now.

She reached up, smacked the button and stopped the water. Reaching over, she grabbed a four-hundred-year-old fluffy white towel and pressed it into the wound. The blood soaked in, but it wasn't pulsing, which meant the metal rod hadn't hit the artery, and in this way Elimisha learned that she wasn't going to bleed out naked and wet on the cold tiles of the shower in that place Adam had called (so long ago) 'the world beneath the world beneath the world'.

Over the next hour she suffered one pain after another.

Rising to her feet.

132

Stitching the wound closed with the sewing kit from the infirmary.

Dressing it.

Dressing herself.

Elimisha slowly pulled on the smaller of the HCG suits. As she gently squeezed the zip and pulled it up over her chest to form a V under her neck, the entire suit – as though it had a mind of its own – shrank to fit around her, as though the air had been sucked out and the cloth constricted.

As a test, she unzipped it – and it expanded again.

She zipped it up and it constricted.

She unzipped it and the suit expanded.

She did this five more times because it was *fantastic*.

After a final adjustment of the steel zip, Elimisha padded down the fabric on her hips as a habit and felt pockets, which turned out to have a very lightweight pair of eyeglasses in one side and a thin pair of gloves in the other.

Elimisha had seen glasses before; they were readily available in the Territory, but most of the time they were broken or too scratched to use. Those which bent images to make them closer were beloved and collected. The ones which bent images to make them further away were often traded. The glasses with darkened lenses were coveted by the Dragoons, Spotters, Archers, Runners, Raiders and anyone who fought in the bright light that reflected off the sands or winter snow. The last type, like these, were the most common, but did nothing at all. However, they were thin, lightweight and almost impossible to break and so they were often worn by horse riders because they kept their eyes safe from debris and wind at speed. Smelters and blacksmiths and builders also liked them as eye protection – and girls with long hair liked them to hold back their tresses.

Elimisha slipped them on to see what kind these were and

was unsurprised to find that they did nothing; no change to the colour, no distortion to the shape of the world.

Why they would be in a pocket for use of people wearing this fabulous suit, she couldn't guess.

Elimisha placed them on top of her head to keep her fully-frizzed hair out of her eyes as she hobbled her way to the communications room.

Settling herself down in the chair opposite the White Board and radio, she could feel that this chair had been a throne of power: a place where someone had sat (or had planned to sit) and talk to people all over the world.

Now, Elimisha was the Queen.

With the glasses on her head for a crown, she donned her gloves too, and like the suit, when she pulled the small zip at the base of her thumb back to the wrist, each one shrank around her hands until it was a second skin. They were so comfortable that she decided to leave them.

The radio, helpfully, had a toggle switch marked ON above and OFF beneath. Without a word or some histrionic gesture she flicked it upwards.

She was queen of a kingdom that might only be discovered, someday, by spade.

Her mother had said Lilly's radio hissed and made noises, 'like a snake strangling another snake.' Elimisha – lowering her eyebrows – had said that if one snake did that to another it would surely be a silent affair, but her mother had raised her hands up beside her face, opened her eyes wide and started chasing Elimisha out the apartment and down the hallway as Elimisha – a little pedantically, in retrospect – called out, 'Snakes don't have hands either.'

Her mother did, though, and they could tickle you until the air was gone.

This one didn't make any noises.

It didn't have any hands, either, so maybe it was working; it just wasn't receiving any signals.

Reaching over with her left hand, she depressed the long grey bar and said, 'Um . . . hello?'

The left side of the screen flickered when she spoke, creating small green hills that receded into the line like a horizon.

'Can anyone hear me?' she said, and watched the hills rise up again.

'Ahhhh!' she yelled this time, and the green bars filled the screen briefly.

Huh.

It wasn't an obvious conclusion, but it looked as though the machine was drawing the sound of her voice. Why it would do this, she wasn't sure, but it suggested that the microphone was working. Otherwise, how else would it know what to draw?

There was no sound, though, no reply. No response. No man in a foreign language to keep her company.

Elimisha placed her right hand on the White Board in front of her and ran her fingers back and forth, the way she often did at Weapons and Communications.

'Hello, hello?' she said after the pressing the button. 'I'm very interesting to talk to. If you're not sure and feeling shy, you really ought to reach out and give it a try.'

Did that rhyme?

Was she rhyming?

She did that to put the boys to bed when they were feeling rambunctious, but this was a sign of mental exhaustion. Her trainers had said this sort of thing would happen – not the rhyming, per se; that was her own madness. But starting to get punchy; to get giggly; to lose perspective; to fail to prioritise and follow one's fancies rather than needs. Fatigue does this and so does dehydration or hunger. The body needs, so you must provide. That's why every Runner, on arriving at a hidden Archive, is immediately interviewed by the Chief and asked the same Protocol questions: Are you injured? Are you in need of water or food? Nothing else matters until these problems are sorted.

Maybe her mind was trying to tell her to sleep as she'd had plenty to drink and the sweet amber was still coursing through her brain – that and a bit of dried meat from her backpack.

Nodding her head, agreeing with herself, the glasses slipped from her hair onto her nose.

A charged sensation pulsed through her entire body, starting simultaneously at the tips of her gloved fingers and the collar around her neck and then shooting up her arms and down her torso, meeting at her chest and flowing all the way down to her ankles where the HCG suit stopped.

It felt like sliding into a pool of water. Her entire body came to life. The sensation was so unexpected, so novel – so titillating – her attention would have been swept away, had something even more startling not happened in the same moment: through the lenses and floating above the White Board was a perfect sphere of what she later learned to be Planet Earth.

As the sphere spun, a gentle breeze seemed to come off it, registering on every nerve of her body.

Beneath the image, the White Board changed shape and a keyboard rose out of the material. Each key was embossed with a letter and some had words like DELETE, CLEAR and END. Above the keyboard, on the remaining surface, were instruments: a clock (15:12), a thermometer (19 degrees C) and a calendar with a year and a date that her mind was unable to register.

Through tiny speakers in her glasses came the soothing voice of a disembodied man.

'Hello,' it began.

LOCKDOWN

In Lilly's view, the Stadium really should have had a party. Over the years she has neglected too many opportunities to celebrate the small accomplishments and so they slipped by unnoticed. Other Chiefs from other sections often make efforts, and the High Command itself occasionally calls for an event when Raiders return with notable Finds. There are festivities when babies are born and named; weddings announced and performed; new Learnings shared by the Evaluators; new stories performed by returning Explorers. Even the turning seasons have their moments. Life is made joyful when effort is applied. Lilly, however, has never quite developed the knack, even when finding a matching fuse for the radio and making it work again should have been ample cause for celebration.

The Commonwealth is two weeks into General Winter's Level One Lockdown and Lilly is alone in her office. It is close to moon-high and Mickey Mouse – looking rather excited about it – insists it is 11:16 p.m. Which it might be. Lilly hasn't bothered testing the clock yet. For the moment she's happy with the company. Mickey is smiling at her and she rather likes it.

'Fancy a drink?' she says to him.

Last autumn Lilly had scored ten bottles of bourbon that were no less than three hundred years old. Traders had brought them in. She'd told them it was lizard poison.

'Do you plan on poisoning many lizards?' she'd asked.

They admitted to having no such plans.

'I'll trade you for a bag of apples, then? With the seeds.'

Too often the Ancient drinks are spoiled, but from time to time – like this time – the bottles had been found in the ideal conditions: dark and cool and underground. Anything called wine or *vin* or *vino* was best left untouched after so much time, but the same could not be said for Kentucky bourbon.

Very smooth.

'*L'Chaim*,' she says to Mickey, using a toast she learned from her mother from a language no one can even identify, let alone speak: *To Life.*

Lilly listens to the radio and it crackles, a static that makes no sense to her.

If the radio signals were plentiful and crashing into one another, perhaps they would sound like paper tearing, but that isn't happening. So what is it, then?

She imagines it as the sound of the universe itself.

Breathing.

According to news from High Command, several Runners have now been listed as missing. The Keepers are building forces on the Yellow Ridge to the east and trade has radically slowed at The Crossing. Food convoys from the forests continue to come in and the Commonwealth continues to send fresh water to wells in the territory as part of the peace strategy for the region (keep them calm, make them dependent on us). But it is a painfully dull time too. During Lockdown, no new traders may enter, no new faces can come in. No unnecessary Runs are made and Explorers requesting entry from signal mirrors or smoke or drums are denied or else told to wait for a critical mass, when they'll be allowed in all at once under heavy guard. Soldiers are placed among the out-wall farms along the river, while the Archers remain at the ready – and bored.

She turns the large black dial very, very, very slowly.

The radio says nothing.

She sips her bourbon.

Lilly should have hosted a party down here. Well, not in her personal office, but perhaps in one of the main work-rooms, after moving out anything that might accidentally kill someone. That was the challenge with hosting parties here. She could have made a speech, told a few more lies about the good old days, made a toast (not with the bourbon, obviously, that's another secret of hers) and then struck up the band for some dancing and frivolity while she ostentatiously flipped the switch on the radio and brought it to life.

A new era! A chance to listen to the voices of the world yet again!

Of course it would all be theatre. Seven voices in fifty-four years – counting the down-time when the radio didn't work at all – is hardly cause for real celebration, but that's rather the point, isn't it? We *create* causes for celebration. They don't exist by themselves.

Why do we need to say goodbye to the last falling leaf from the one tree that stands by the Southern Pass? Or light up the darkest night or dance on the evening of the longest day? We don't, really, except for the need to demarcate time, to foster goodwill in the community, to raise people's spirits and rejoice in the continued success of our existence.

So, put another way: every reason.

Mickey Mouse ticks away. What had been a satisfying sound at first has started to become relentless, like time is pursuing her rather than accompanying her.

140

Mickey has survived wars, famines and floods, but Lilly might be his last stop.

The radio has a scale of bands. Lilly has never understood them, not by a long shot, but having always found the voices at night-time rather than during the day, and always below 'twenty metres' on the dial, she has never bothered to poke around the higher frequencies.

Now, filled with Kentucky-distilled enthusiasm and for want of anything better to do, Lilly presses the button which makes the radio seek through the higher frequencies, all the way past forty metres – and that is when she hears a voice.

The radio locks onto the transmission and the entire screen lights up with new words, new numbers, new colours, none of which interests her right now because beyond the lights *there is a voice.*

A woman's voice, soft but strong, clear and close, is speaking in their shared language. Although Lilly's speaker is poor, choosing to crackle and distort the words, the voice sounds youthful and full of urgency.

. . . wish I could tell you where I am and what's around. But I can't. I also wish I could see the sun. Or feel the wind or even the rain. Though in a weird way I can see them whenever I want even though they aren't real.

There is a long pause and Lilly reaches for the radio, wondering if she's lost the signal but she hasn't:

I've never talked so much in my whole life without someone speaking back. It's like . . . talking to an Otis Shaft. Dropping words into the Black and – well, I know you can't drop words but – it feels like you can. Like you can toss them in and watch them fall and try and fill up the whole of the world from the bottom up but the words are

141

insubstantial so they can't fill. They aren't dirt and rock. They never help the world rise.

The thing is, I don't know if I'm even reaching anyone. Are you there? I don't know. I may only be talking to myself. I have so much to tell you – so many things, if you only knew . . . Well, I can't talk about that. I can't even talk about what I can't talk about. Those are the rules! Those are the vows!

There is another silence and this time Lilly closes her eyes, still listening:

If you're out there and you have a radio too, please talk to me. Please? I haven't talked to someone real in so long. It's so strange having a conversation with something that . . . well . . . I can't explain it. Something that talks back but isn't there. It's not really something you can imagine. I'm going to work on the hole now, trying to make it bigger. I'll be back tonight at eight o'clock with my evening programme where I'll read you a poem that used to be very popular. Poems – let me touch this, here – right, so, poems are 'compositions in verse'. I think that means songs without music. I'm not sure yet. But they used to be popular and they're short, so let the Scribes know they won't be here all night.

Okay. Enough for now. Talk to you at eight o'clock, everyone.

The talking ends. Lilly stands and straightens her jacket. Placing her reading glasses in her pocket she walks out the office room and into the main workshop. Bruno and Simone are disassembling a Dep and trying to find patterns in the maker's use of the small black chips mounted to the green boards. Letters, numbers, dimensions, anything. It is a fruitless task and Lilly knows it but that is part of the apprenticeship: learning to dive into deep water and manage the frustration, fear and failure.

She examines their faces for any emotion at all.

They are hard to read.

'What did you hear?' she blurts out.

The two look at each other. Four senior engineers at the far end of the room turn. They had barely heard her question, let alone the radio, but now they are interested. There is a chance – however remote – that Lilly is going to kill someone. It has happened before and they like to be on their toes.

'What do you mean?' asks Simone.

'For the last period of time. Hear anything unusual?'

'No.'

Lilly could see that Bruno hadn't either, but unlike Simone – who looks baffled by the question – Bruno is curious.

'What could we have heard?' he asks.

'A lot of angry language,' Lilly lied. 'I dropped something I've been working on for a while and I think I embarrassed myself. You're saying I didn't?'

'What did you say?' shouts Chaudhary from across the room, which makes two other men laugh and one woman smile.

'Come here and I'll act it out for you,' Lilly replies.

Chaudhary raised his hands in self-defence and everyone laughs again.

'Clear the room, everyone,' Lilly orders.

There is confusion for the moment and Lilly repeats her words. She isn't joking. 'No one comes back until I send for you. Consider it a vacation.'

It is Bruno who asks, 'What's a vacation?'

Everyone waits for the answer.

'Go,' Lilly says. 'Learn the answer elsewhere. Out you go.'

When the room is clear, Lilly walks to the front door too and – on checking that the hall is clear – says (very quietly, to one of the two guards), 'No one – not General Winters, not a commanding officer, not a child who forgot something – goes inside. Only me and whoever is standing next to me. Double the guard and keep this silent. Go.'

Leaving the two burly men behind her, Lilly walks off towards the Snake Tower in search of Birch.

At a distance, Bruno follows.

Lilly has forgotten it's day-time. Back when the radio last worked, she always used to listen at night. As she struts down the U-Ring towards the central staircase to the Green above, the sun's presentation is a harsh reminder of the years that have passed, apparently overnight.

The stairs don't help either. When she was young she would take them two at a time, running up them as smoothly as a young horse prancing up a hill. Now she has to hold the bannister. There is still strength in her legs but she is prone to spells of dizziness. She despises them because they make her feel weak, although her mind is stronger than ever.

And her will.

Time is an unjust thing. She concedes that she's probably not the first to notice this.

A senior Runner named Calliope bounds down the stairs and is about to pass Lilly when she is stopped by an outstretched hand. Calliope had been poached by the Order two years ago; her job as a Runner, Lilly knows, is only a cover. When she was younger, it was Attested that the girl had snuck into a bandit camp four kilometres to the northeast, off the High Road, and – singlehandedly – cut free three children who had been abducted and were going to be sold for the usual purposes. Following a path known to the Urban Explorers through one of the Commonwealth's tunnels, she had led the pursuing bandits into a trap, impaling them all on Riser Sticks. Those children are all members of the Commonwealth now. Calliope is on her way up. She was nineteen then. What is she now? Twenty-six? Lilly can't remember. What's getting lost for her as she ages is chronology. She remembers everything, but she can't always place the events in time. Maybe it's because the order of events was never what was important about them.

Calliope is very tall and has the biggest head of pitch-black curly hair in the Commonwealth. It sits on her head like a helmet and while she complains about it being unruly and regularly threatens to cut it off, there is no one who isn't mesmerised by it. Most women with her colouring have soft brown eyes. Hers are green. If she doesn't become General one day it will only be because she is so distractingly attractive.

'Chief?' she says, looking at Lilly's hand on her arm. 'Are you okay?'

'Of course I'm okay. Where's Master Birch?'

'I wouldn't know that, Chief.'

'Of course not. You're a Runner. How could you possibly know where the Master of the Order of Silence is right now?'

Lilly waits until the stairway is momentarily clear. 'It's pressing.'

Calliope checks the surroundings for eyes and ears and seeing none, she whispers, 'The Map Room.'

Lilly has one more question: 'Is anyone . . . unaccounted for? Outside the walls?'

'Chief, please don't ask me to break my vows.'

'Is it a worthwhile question I should ask someone else?'

Calliope hesitates and then says, 'Yes.'

Lilly releases her arm.

Out in the burning light of the day, Lilly walks through the archers on her way to the Thunder Room. It was renamed the Map Room years ago when the Order took it over, but Lilly's

145

mind and memory started long before both and she has never made the adjustment to the new name. After all, it was only forty years ago the change was made.

On her way, she considers her theory: someone from the Commonwealth is trapped nearby with a radio. She has been for weeks, maybe months.

This is both near-impossible and also entirely plausible. To know which is correct, Lilly will need to tell the truth about events from fifty-four years ago, and Birch will have to break her silence. One way or another, it is going to be an interesting conversation.

The Thunder Room is reached down a staircase carved into the rock from a passage that descends from the main foyer by the West Gate. It is unlike any other room in the Stadium and no one knows its original function. The most commonly accepted suggestions are 'pleasure' and 'art' because the design is brilliant, fascinating and mad.

The two guards with pulse rifles standing at the top of passage make it one of the most secure positions inside the Commonwealth. There is a sniper on the roof with a clear shot as well.

'Tell her I'm here, it's important, I need to come down and everyone else needs to go away.'

The High Command can issue such orders to the guards.

Lilly cannot. Not any more.

The guard follows her instruction anyway.

Lilly waits, turning her face to the sun as she hears the guard descend the three hundred narrow steps – steps she will eventually have to climb again.

The tunnel is a little wider than the shoulders of a large man and has only just enough headroom to accommodate the same. There are no lights or torches in the stairway, only a glow from the bottom.

The man is gone long enough for the sun to leave its burn on her cheeks.

Hearing his footsteps close, she turns and he nods once.

At the bottom Lilly passes through an ante-chamber lined with benches on either side. Beyond this is a heavy cast-iron door that is open but can be closed and sealed. Around the edges of the door are mystical creatures – women with the tails of fish, men with the bodies of horses, lizards with wings, dogs with multiple heads, all in stories learned from the Harrington Box.

The chamber beyond the door is round and enormous. The ceiling, carved from the rock itself, is a dome as smooth as glass. The walls, however, are rough and unfinished. The circular wooden table that goes around the entire room has a gap for the doorway itself. Facing due west is the only window, which extends from floor to the edge of the ceiling and curves with the room, offering a shimmering view of the inside of the waterfall, capturing the undulating lights of the setting sun and, at night, the greens and blues of the sky. The mornings here are dark.

The colours dance across the polished surfaces of the room and across the large round table in the middle where Birch is standing with her arms crossed. Whoever had been here before is gone and whatever she had been doing before has been put away.

A guard closes the iron portals, sealing them in.

The faintest whispers cross the curved ceiling and fall like winter snow into the ears of a listener on the other side. There is a science to the movement of the waves that Lilly can observe but not understand. What matters is that the room demands subtlety and welcomes secrets. Speak too loud and the result is thunder.

'Chief Lilly,' says Birch.

'Master Birch.'

'Apparently we have to talk? Urgently?'

'Yes. I'm going to sit,' Lilly says, not waiting for an invitation.

The curved bench that circles the table is fixed in place. It is not especially comfortable, but it will have to do. Leaning forward, Lilly realises she hasn't been here in decades. Despite it now being called the Map Room, it looks exactly the same. She figures the maps must be hidden.

Birch sits across from her. Though the distance is unusually wide, the sound travels across the ceiling. Their conversation is hushed.

'You know I got the radio working again,' Lilly says. 'Graham came back with a fuse. He decided to check an old Indie that reminded him of a girl from . . . well, it doesn't matter. Anyway, I've been playing it since he and Henrietta got back, but heard nothing, as expected. Less than an hour ago I decided to swing over to the most fruitless part of the frequency spectrum. I've never heard a thing over there. This time I heard a voice.'

Birch has woven her fingers together on the table as she listens. Now she opens them slightly to demonstrate dramatic enthusiasm as best she understands it.

'That's nice,' she says. 'It'll inspire the youth. I don't see,' she adds, 'how that's urgent.'

'No. You're not following. I heard a voice in *our* language. It was strong and clear, which suggests it is close – maybe very close. It also sounded . . . youthful.'

'That's certainly much more interesting,' says Birch, 'but I still don't—'

'I think she's one of ours. I think she's trapped in a room

with a radio, a room that somehow or other has electricity and has had it for at least a few weeks. And if it has been weeks, it means she has food and water to keep her strong enough to be coherent and focused. What I think . . . Master Birch . . . is that one of your people – or maybe one of the missing Runners – is at the bottom of a tower in a bomb shelter. I also think I know who it is. If you don't confirm it, I can always ask her mother.'

Birch does not stare at Lilly but instead looks at the centre of the table itself. She sits silently for a long time before saying, 'Tell me more.'

Lilly is not a huge fan of Birch's and hasn't been for years. Lilly helped found the Order with her friend Saavni, who was the first Master. Lilly served afterwards until she became a member of the High Command, at which time Birch took over. Nine years ago, however, Winters had Lilly step down for being too 'forthcoming' with her own opinions on military matters. Lilly had never found military affairs especially complicated and had been rather quick to say so. As best she could tell, almost all military actions came down to erecting barriers or overcoming them through superior positioning, movement, manoeuvre, intelligence, command and communications. At least, that was the framework she'd built over the years and it appeared to work better than the Trivial Pursuit categories did for the Archive. The fact that Winters refused to learn from Lilly and found her to be a threat rather than a support came down to temperament and, in Lilly's view, Birch ought to know that. As personal differences amounted to nothing, in essence, Birch should have had the wit to continue to keep Lilly fully abreast of circumstances, thus ensuring that Weapons and Communications could be better prepared to deal with Winter's inevitable blunders – because, in Lilly's mind, these *were* inevitable, and on the way, and all for the same reason:

she was arrogant and refused to listen carefully. If she did that with Lilly, Lilly was certain she would do that with an enemy. And then what?

And yet, Birch did listen. Whatever her flaws in loyalty to Lilly, they were not flaws in reasoning or loyalty to the Commonwealth, and for this, Lilly was prepared to talk to her. Also, she couldn't do what needed to be done without Birch.

'I caught the last few minutes of her talk. She was speaking outwardly, not to another person but into the world, hoping to be heard. The girl said she was trapped. She longed for the sun and wind. She said, 'I can see them whenever I want, but they aren't real.'

'What does that mean?' Birch asks. 'A picture?'

'I have a theory. Let me go on. She also mentioned an Otis Shaft. That was the term she used. Now . . . I know these exist in places other than the nearby Gone World and our towers. They probably exist in whichever towers remain all across the world. But I don't think everyone calls them that. Henrietta Wayworth told us that the Roamers call them "elevators", which makes sense because it has the same root as "elevate" or "to go up". What matters is that within the small space of our territory, different groups use different words for the same object. This girl used ours.'

'Do you have notes?' Birch asks.

'Of course not. You think I would risk writing all this down?'

Birches blinks very slowly, waiting for Lilly to finish her explanation.

'The girl also used the phrase "into the Black". Our Runners talk about Black Jumps, so the Black is usually the unknown or else the darkness into which we don't go because of the Sickness or whatever. She also mentioned The Rise, which is especially telling, I think, because you and I both know that

The Rise is an entirely local matter. In other places – far-off but charted – the land has dropped or the waters have come in or else receded, making the land today unlike the land of the Ancients. So if this girl talks about The Rise, she is probably talking about here. Have I made my case?'

'Almost,' Birch admits.

'She said she can't tell us where she is. And I got to thinking . . . *why not?* Why not tell us where she is so we can rescue her? If she's trapped, doesn't she want to get out? When she mentioned "vows", however, it became obvious. She can't give away her position without breaking her vow.'

'Why not?' Birch queried. 'I can see the risk in being captured by someone else, but that's a danger, not a breaking of a vow.'

'She's sitting on a Trove,' Lilly says, pointing a finger for emphasis. 'If she's a Runner, she has taken a vow to protect information in motion. If she's a Chief, she has a vow to protect information at rest. If she's a Runner sitting on a massive Trove of new Knowledge she will not surrender it to save her own life. That's a vow.'

For the first time, Birch's face shows an expression. If Lilly is reading it correctly – across a twenty-foot-wide table in a room lit only with natural light cast through a waterfall – it is incredulity.

'Have you been drinking the lizard poison?'

'It isn't lizard poison, it's Kentucky bourbon.'

'I don't know what that is.'

'No you don't and you won't find out until I start liking you better. And the answer, incidentally, is "yes" and "probably not enough".'

'Runners,' Birch says, ignoring the bourbon discussion, 'only carry Knowledge which is already safe within the Central Archive. We don't ask them to surrender their lives for simple

151

copies, even if the copy is important; a weapon design, a map or a medical procedure. Almost all Knowledge, as you very well know – because you designed it this way, Chief – is stored at more than one site. Runners don't surrender their lives for copies. Members of the Order might, conceivably, make a sacrifice to defend a Route or a Commonwealth secret or an entire Archive, but the circumstances would have to be . . . extreme. I don't see why a trapped girl would risk a slow death in a Hard Room simply to protect a new Trove.'

'What if it's not only a new Trove? What if it's *the Trove*?'

'I don't know what that means either,' Birch says.

'She was looking up the meaning of the word "poem". That's neither here nor there, but as she did, she said, "Let me touch this here". Does that mean anything to you?'

'No.'

'What about the cloud?'

'In the sky?'

'The information cloud.'

'Chief,' says Birch, her defences now breaking down, 'I have no idea what you're talking about. It isn't completely impossible that a member of the Commonwealth is trapped with a radio and a Trove of books. It's fantastical, but not impossible. I'm not ready to Attest to any of your claims yet. If it were true I'd be prepared to say, yes, rescuing her and having a second radio and a new microphone certainly would be valuable and we can take that to Winters to plan an operation, assuming we know where to look. Any Trove is important. But . . . *clouds*, Chief?'

'We cannot take this to Winters because she won't believe us and she'll shut us down before we start. Listen carefully, Birch. There's a children's story – a fable – my mother told me. I was maybe eight. She learned it from her grandmother, making the story almost a hundred years old, at least. It goes like this: way back when, the Ancients decided that the earth was no longer safe for their Knowledge and so they put everything they knew in the sky and hid it away in clouds. But the sun considered the sky her own domain and so she scorched the clouds and burned them off. After that, no Knowledge could rain down on the people of the earth. Their memories grew weak, the land grew dry and cold and the people had to start from the beginning. "Making fire from sticks" was the phrase she used.'

'We are ignorant and the land is dry,' Birch said, not accepting Lilly's analysis. 'So the storyteller created a fable filled with Knowledge and water and a nice metaphor about rain and clouds to link them together. It's a perfectly serviceable fable, Chief. Beyond that . . .'

'You're a fine thinker, Penelope, and you always have been. But ever since you were a little girl you have refused to make the creative leaps that are necessary for greatness. The problem isn't your mind; it's your personality. You just don't like being wrong, so you plan everything out and play it safe. Of course you became the Master of the Order of Silence! But take it from me: solutions are often on the far side of prolific failure. If we don't risk making a creative leap in the face of this radio transmission now – if we don't consider the massive implications of what it could mean – it will seal our fate because every risk we take in the future will be the product of our cowardice and lack of imagination now. I believe – although I might be wrong, Master Birch – that sixteen-year-old Elimisha daughter-of-Cara is trapped in a nearby but undiscovered room where she has found a portal to the greatest repository of Knowledge in the history of human civilisation. I think Elimisha has discovered the internet.'

From her bag Lilly removes three objects: the White Board

and two devices that look like pulse pistols without barrels. 'And to help you understand my conviction, I'm going to tell you a story that you have never heard before because no one has ever heard it. This is the story of how the first Tracollo really happened, where the Harrington Box was really found, and how I got it open. And perhaps most importantly,' Lilly says, tapping the White Board, 'where I found this and what I think it is.'

FIFTY-FOUR YEARS AGO

Lilly's mother, Rachael, once told her that she'd been named for a flower that used to grow in this part of the world, long before The Rise, 'Long before the deserts rolled in,' Rachael said, 'and the forests died and the sand piled at the base of the towers in the Gone World – a place where the urbanscape glowed so brightly with Big Electricity that the lights would reflect from the clouds at night. The people there,' said Rachael, her hand on Lilly's chest at bedtime, Lilly smiling at the dreamy possibility of it all, 'numbered in millions and when they wanted to leave they travelled in flying ships that zipped through the air faster than birds. And oh, the food there!' Rachael would roll her eyes in ecstasy, which always made Lilly giggle. 'It was so plentiful they would only eat half of what they were given and then just . . . throw it away! And then they'd take a nap on the table and snore.'

And they would laugh and laugh and laugh.

'Was I really named for a flower?' Lilly asked her when she was seven and getting serious. It had always been only the two of them. Her father wasn't a factor.

'Yes. They say it was pretty, but no one knows. We only have the word now, not the memory. But I knew you would be pretty and I liked the sound of it. We take what we know and use it to make what we can. For example,' she told Lilly, 'I knew all about love, so I took all the love I had and I made you. What I didn't know when I made you,' said Lilly's mother, 'was that you would be so smart.'

Ten years later and motherless after the ambush, Lilly stood at the blacksmith's forge where she'd been all morning. She did not feel like a flower and she wasn't feeling so smart either. Her rare and strange yellow hair was matted with black soot from the smith's furnace and her muscular arms were browned and glistening from two hot months under the summer sun. Lunch-break was coming soon, though not soon enough, but the restlessness inside her was not caused by the heat or hunger.

Today was the one-year anniversary of her mother's murder by bandits on the High Road outside the Stadium walls. She chose this apprenticeship with the blacksmith so she could learn to make weapons: the swords and shields and arrows and pikes that already armed the community – but not only those. She wanted to make the ones she had created in her head.

Lilly's imagination was alive with the possibilities of defending the Stadium, but the adults around her were too sunk into habit and complacency to see either the need or possibility. The anger was building inside her like filling a well that had no overflow. Today of all days it was too much. She needed someone to take it out on and there was only one person around.

'I'm not making another damn bucket. I know how to make buckets. I have mastered the bucket. This is an apprenticeship, not a punishment. I want to move on.'

Luther Blacksmith, the Forge Master and Weapons Chief, was a giant brown-skinned man who towered above Lilly. His blue eyes were weary from contending with Lilly's constant disappointment. He knew, however, what day it was and understood the cause of her impatience. He knew the shape of the story: a trading mission to a northern colony that was attacked. Lilly was the only one who made it back to the Stadium, and only after shooting her way out with her mother's own gun.

Lilly had always been a brilliant student but now, with her mother gone, she was sharp and dangerous like the end of a spear; all of her weight – all of her mind and emotion – was pressing down on that one point. Luther accepted her grief and pain, but it was her hunger that worried him. He didn't know what she wasn't willing to do in light of what she'd suffered.

Or not do.

Making buckets had felt like a good idea at the time. It wasn't any more.

Still, it's what the Council had ordered.

'It's what the Council ordered,' he said to her. 'They want forty buckets. We make the buckets.'

Lilly couldn't remember how long it had been since the Crier had announced the hour. The sun's heat was a hammer, making the surface of the courtyard an anvil. She looked up at the sun and considered its distance to the Stadium wall. Once it passed over, the shade would fall here and she would feel a little better.

'We need a better way of measuring time,' she said.

Here we go again, thought the Master Blacksmith. He said nothing. He was in no mood to antagonise her.

'We know the ancients had ways to do it,' Lilly said. 'We know what they measured too. Seconds, minutes, hours, days, weeks, months, years. What we don't know is how they did it. Now we use a stick and a shadow or else watch sand fall through a glass.'

'Stick and shadow work fine,' Luther attempted.

'Not when it's cloudy,' Lilly said.

'Not when it's cloudy,' he conceded.

'Or at night.'

'No. Not at night either.'

'Or when you're away from the stick and the markers that actually tell the time.'

'I suppose not.'

'Hard to argue that it works fine if it works less than half the time.'

'And yet we carry on.'

Luther turned back to work. He struck his hammer on the thin metal in his tongs and then tapped the edge of the anvil in a constant rhythm that was so fluid it became musical. Not all the raw metal from the finds was equally good for casting or re-shaping, but this one was curving nicely. He took pleasure in watching the ends gently turn towards one another like new friends.

'I'm guessing this is why the Ancients built time machines that ran on electricity,' said Lilly.

'I suppose that's true,' he said, only half paying attention.

'Hundreds of years later we can't make new ones or fix the old ones. Doesn't that anger you? That we're weak and stupid compared to them?'

'No,' said Luther.

'Why not?'

'Because we're alive and happy and they're neither.'

'I'm not happy. And my mother's not alive,' Lilly said. 'And I think it's because we're weak and stupid.'

Luther did not reply.

No one had assaulted the Stadium in numbers in more than a hundred years. There had been skirmishes beyond the walls that killed a dozen or so a year, of course, but nothing in numbers. There were bandits and wandering tribes; Roamers and Ghost Talkers. There were some distant colonies with whom they traded and sometimes people's tempers flared and blades were pulled. But on the whole, there weren't enough people left alive for a proper war. Luther considered this to be a product of the Stadium's philosophy: silence and secrecy. Don't make yourself a target and don't become one.

The population of the Stadium was under two hundred souls.

In Lilly's view, however, it was only a matter of time before the Stadium would fall. Her mother's death had proved that to her. She could feel a stirring in the winds and she knew in her bones that a day of reckoning was coming, so they needed to prepare. The outside world was growing more dangerous and more daring. If the Council of The Few chose stagnation as a strategy for survival it would mean death. Only relentless, unerring and attentive progress would save them. If the Council of The Few didn't have the brains to lead them in that direction, Lilly was going to grow up and do it herself.

'When are we going to start making new things, Chief?' Lilly asked him.

Luther's arm and hammer were swinging to a rhythm now. Twenty years of body memory, arm and hammer worked as a single machine, a beat as steady as a horse in canter. He ignored her, knowing his silence would be heard as an invitation to speak. Then again, so would any of his words. So he saved the words.

'I'm talking about things that don't exist yet,' she went on, 'or maybe things that once did exist but don't any more. Things like this,' she said, picking up a mystery object from beneath a work bench and handing it to Luther, who stopped hammering with a sigh and accepted it only because rejecting it would have required words.

'Guess what it is,' Lilly said with a smile.

It looked like an enormous fish hook with a small steel ring at the end.

'It's an enormous fish hook with a small steel ring at the end,' he said.

'No. Use your imagination. Picture a rope tied into the ring. What could you use it for?'

Luther didn't like using his imagination. When he did the pieces never lined up the way two pieces of metal lined up. The metal he could bend gracefully. The ideas came out twisted and misaligned.

'I'd rather not.'

'Please.'

He took it. Turned it around.

'We could . . . sit on the walls and dangle it over the edge and catch giant desert monster fish.'

'Desert monster fish?'

'You told me to use my imagination. You understand the danger now?'

'If you hold the rope,' she said, demonstrating, 'you swing this around so you feel the force of the spin in your hand and at the right moment you release it into the air and it flies up along the wall and hooks itself on! And then you can climb up! It's a climbing hook. Get it?'

'Why wouldn't I take the stairs?'

'Maybe our enemies are on the stairs and we want to encircle them, so one team scales the wall while the other fights from below. Then we pinch them like tongs. See?'

Luther's mighty shoulders dropped. He raised his hand and made a fist against the sky. The sun was two fist-lengths from the wall. Two fists was the same as for ever with Lilly around.

160

'You can break for lunch,' he said. The sun wasn't in charge of her apprenticeship, he reminded himself. He was.

She stood her ground.

'The Council,' he said in a last-ditch effort to talk sense into her, 'wants buckets so we can carry more water from the clean part of the river at the base of the falls back into the Stadium at the top of the falls. It isn't weapons work, but it's helpful. Why don't you want to be helpful, Lilly? Isn't that why you chose to be a blacksmith for your apprenticeship?'

'Helpful? Yes – and I could be so much more helpful if they let me invent better ways of doing things. The Stadium could grow bigger and better and smarter and . . .'

'Safer?' Luther offered.

'Yes! I'm going to learn everything there is to know and I'm going to make us more powerful than everyone else in the world. You watch me.'

Lilly looked at Luther to see if her appeal had meant anything to him. Disappointed, she tossed the poker to the ground and looked into his enormous, passive face.

'Who even built this place?' she asked, sounding resigned to the need for this conversation. 'The plaque on the wall says *Olympic Stadium*. What does that *mean*?'

Lilly was referring to the brass plaque on the outer wall by the Main Gate:

> Olympic Stadium MMXCVI [2096]
> Bicentennial Summer Olympics
> In Accordance with the Kyoto Treaty of 2085,
> this Stadium produces zero carbon emissions
> through its use of Circular Energy powered by
> solar, hydrodynamic and human-kinetic force.

'Two-zero-nine-six looks like a year,' Lilly said, 'because two-zero-eight-five is being used like a year in the sentence and we know that a treaty is an agreement. So they built this Stadium to fulfil an agreement. To do . . . what? Who was Kyoto? Why did they name a treaty after her? If there were Summer Olympics, does that mean there were Winter Olympics too? Does that mean there's another Stadium out there that's for the winter? Maybe it's also full of people. Maybe it's closer than we think. Maybe it's just beyond the desert—'

'There's nothing beyond the desert.'

'If we go west, where The Few came from, legend says we hit a massive ocean.'

He was ready for her to stop talking now.

'Can we stop talking now?'

'For God's sake, Luther! What happened to the Old World? And what's going to happen next? What if the same event is going to happen again, the way the sun passes overhead every day and we're unprepared but could be prepared if we only knew more? Are we really going to just sit here and wait for it while making buckets?'

'Stop,' Luther said to her. 'Enough. Something terrible happened to you, Lilly. It's put smoke in your eyes and now all you see is fire. But the fire is inside you. *You* are what's changing and I'm not going to help you set us all ablaze. You have to control it. You think we need to protect ourselves from the world. Right now, child, the world may need to protect itself from you. So go, don't come back until you're calm. That's an order.'

'Yes, sir.'

'Chief. Yes, Chief. I'm a Chief. Now go.'

As Luther started hammering away again, a commotion formed at the Main Gate and four soldiers armed with pikes and swords – and one with a pulse rifle – ran to the gate to take up position. The pike soldiers stood to either side of the gate and the rifleman knelt behind a waist-high boulder they'd dragged in long ago for this purpose.

The gate opened and Saavni ran in.

Saavni was Lilly's age, with raven-black hair, soft brown eyes and the build of a warrior. They'd come up together in school and were friends. Saavni wasn't inventive like Lilly, but she was extremely resourceful, didn't like fools and had an adventurous streak Lilly admired.

Saavni ran straight past the guards to Lilly, who was sitting under the shade of a tarp and drinking warm water from a tall bottle. She couldn't imagine why her friend was in such a rush.

'Adam,' Saavni said, doubling over at the waist to catch her breath when she arrived. 'He finally did it.'

Adam was Lilly's slightly younger cousin. She didn't like him very much.

'Did what?' Lilly asked.

'He made a Black Jump, Lilly. In the Gone World. He's . . . gone.'

Lilly stood there, incredulous. Adam was fifteen and, in her view, a little stupid. Where Lilly was beautiful and powerful and smart, Adam was feckless and skinny and strange. It wasn't that he was bent like the Ghost Talkers, it was more like his mind was weak and the more he tried to be like other people, the more strange he became.

'What happened?' she whispered. Luther was banging away at his metal and had no interest in Lilly's conversation, but she didn't want him to hear. Lilly knew the power of loose words; how rumours could turn the whole world against people. Secrecy was better, certainly where Adam was concerned.

'You won't get angry?' Saavni asked, keeping her own voice low.

'I really don't know.'

'We slipped out again.'

'I figured.'

'There were four of us at first – me, Verena, Sheku and Reed. Adam heard and wanted to come.'

'Because of Verena. But she's not interested in Adam, trust me.'

'I know,' said Saavni, standing up now and reaching for Lilly's bottle of water. She drank half of it before putting it back on the wooden ledge. 'But he wanted to come and we couldn't stop him, so . . . well, he came. We left with a band of Traders this morning when they opened the gate, then we hooked up with an encampment of Roamers down at the edge of the Gone World—'

'That's dangerous,' Lilly pointed out. 'Bandits often dress as Roamers and the Roamers can be foul-tempered and unpredictable when things aren't going well for them.'

'In this case, they gave us lunch in trade for carrot seed.'

'Roamers don't plant seeds.'

'No, they *trade* them,' said Saavni, irritated and wanting to get on with her story. 'So we finished and we slipped into the Federal Building through the gap in the fourth window on the south side – you know the one. So we're messing around in there a floor down and Reed dares Adam to go down three levels to see the first skeletons because we know Adam hasn't taken the Dare of the Steps before. Three levels down, though—'

'It starts getting dark because you're under the sand at that point,' said Lilly, arms now crossed.

'Well . . . Sheku went four down but he came back up all freaked out saying that the bodies had all fallen head-downwards right on the stairs, just like the old people said because – you know.'

'The Sickness.'

'Anyway, we all went down to see, but we didn't go any further because we didn't want to die. But this time,' Saavni continued, her tone saying that Lilly really needed to stop inter-rupting, 'we used mirrors to bring down as much light as we could – you know how at a click after Sun-High the light hits the stair shaft at the perfect angle? So with the mirrors we could reflect down five, even six levels and see much more. Anyway, we could see the Otis Shaft doors were open down there, and then Reed – because he's an asshole, he really is – dared Adam to go down. Of course Adam looked at Verena, because he always does, and she immediately told him not to, and she said it was time to head home because the sun would close the light window soon, but instead of going back up, your idiot cousin jumped off the edge onto that metal rope that hangs down and just . . . he just slid into the Black. Lilly,' said Saavni, her voice shaking a little, 'he's gone.'

'When?' Lilly asked.

'I rode here straight away. The horse is drinking now.'

'You're coming with me,' Lilly said, grabbing Saavni by her lavender shirt and pulling her across the courtyard.

'Where are we going?'

'Storage on level five and then back to that tower to find Adam.'

'It'll be dark—'

'That's why we're thinking ahead and taking what we need to make light.'

Lilly pulled Saavni by the sleeve of her fancy new shirt straight through the corn, spelt and wheat fields, past the row of berries and herbs and into the South Gate at the far end of the court-yard.

'I just got this!' yelled Saavni.

'The world is full clothing. I only have one cousin.'

'You don't even like him!'

'That's not the point,' Lilly said, pushing her down the stair-case to the lower level.

At the southern end of the Ring Road inside the Stadium, an inexperienced guard named Wax armed with a short spear stood looking bored in front of the storage room he was ostensibly guarding (from what, Lilly had no idea).

'I'm with Weapons,' Lilly said. 'I need . . . stuff. Get out of the way, Wax.'

The guard looked at the dirtiest girl he had ever seen. He looked at her blackened hands and face and her angry blue eyes. He wasn't sure whether this was what blacksmiths looked like, but he was pretty sure it was what they smelled like.

Lilly something, right? He'd seen her around. Her hair was weird. The sooner she went away the better.

'Okay,' he said, unmoving and unmoved.

Lilly pushed past him into the room.

It was dark inside, with only the light from the doorway illuminating the goods stacked on the shelves.

'What are you looking for?' Saavni asked her.

'Here they are,' Lilly said in reply, opening a coarse canvas bag. Inside were two cardboard boxes. One of them was open, which was no surprise because she'd been the one to open it a few weeks ago when she'd been in here rummaging around for interesting things to take back to Luther. What she'd found had been as close to magic as anything she had ever seen, which was why she'd kept it to herself and hadn't told Luther. She'd made a mistake, however. Aunt Sarah had invited her

166

to dinner and with so little else to talk about she'd let slip the news of her secret stash. Adam had heard. What she hadn't appreciated was that he actually been *listening*.

'You'll never guess what I found after a trade,' she'd said. And then she showed her aunt.

Stupid. You don't *share* secrets. You *keep* them.

The open box was still there and untouched and the identical second box was there too, but not the third, because Adam had taken it.

'Little shit,' Lilly said, picking out both boxes. 'He was *planning* to do it. He didn't jump on impulse, Saavni. He planned on making a Black Jump.'

'Lilly,' said Saavni, who had no idea why they were in that storage room, 'what are we doing?'

'Gearing up for the urbanscape. Now go and get that rope.' She pointed. 'And those knives. And that leather jacket and those gloves, and that bottle too – we're going to need water.' As Saavni did as she was bidden, Lilly glanced at the door to make sure Wax hadn't suddenly developed an interest in anything, then lowered herself to the floor, rolled onto her back and slid herself under the steel shelf at the far end of the room.

The black bag was still where she'd hidden it. She pressed it to her nose to smell the fresh oils inside. She jiggled it and felt around. Everything was there.

When she re-emerged, Saavni was looking down at her, those brown eyes curious, the lustrous eyebrows raised.

'It'll all make sense later,' Lilly promised her, adding, 'I'm not going nuts.'

Saavni frowned. 'What are nuts?'

'I don't know,' said Lilly. 'But if you put them together, they can replace your mind and it's apparently not good.'

Saavni wasn't interested in old words like Lilly was. What Saavni was interested in was Lilly's intentions. 'We're not seriously going after him, are we?'

'We're going to see if he fell and whether we can get him back. More than that,' she said, 'I don't know.'

The sun was still high in the sky when Lilly and Saanvi slipped out of the Stadium through a gap in the wall at the north end, not far from Luther and the furnace. Saavni's horse, Costello, was tethered to a smooth, weather-beaten log down on the flats below the Main Gate. It was possible a spotter on the tower, high up on the rising oval of the Stadium, was watching them even now, but Lilly didn't care. Unlike Saavni, Lilly didn't have parents any more. The worst that could happen was that rumours would spread about Adam being gone, so better for her to be seen trying to save him than not.

Saavni held the reins and Lilly sat behind her. They were both experienced in the saddle, but Saavni had taken to racing when she was twelve and she was now the best rider of their generation, such as it was given there were only thirty-five of them, so the climb to the top was limited. Saavni pressed them across the rocky and hilly expanse and out into the flatter desert beyond as Lilly sat behind and opened the black bag which contained her Colt .357.

Pulse weapons were extremely rare but they were also incredibly durable. When placed in their charging cradles under the Stadium, where The Few had first found them hundreds of years ago, the Stadium's Big Electricity recharged them, the green lights climbing up the spine of the magazine proving their worth. Whether dropped, smashed, submerged in water or frozen in ice, the pulse weapons could still be relied on for a hundred bursts to stun an enemy or thirty bursts to blow a hole in their chests or knock their heads clean off at two hundred metres. They had forty weapons, and each weapon had three magazines, making the Stadium the most powerful military force in the known world. With the Stadium walls rising protectively around them, General Mino thought they were invincible.

Lilly knew otherwise.

Less rare, however, were guns. Guns were everywhere: pistols and semi-automatics, short barrels and long ones. At the age of fourteen, Lilly had taken it on herself to start collecting pieces of them, oiling them, assembling the ones that looked as if they fit together best. The ancient six-shooters were the least complicated and therefore the most reliable. Hers was a Colt Python .357 and unlike the vast majority of guns left in the world, hers had bullets.

Luther had told her that most of the ammunition had probably been used during the Unspeakable Years after the Gone World fell and before the Long Quiet started, which was when The Few stumbled on the Stadium and created 'this paradise', as he called it. Today, most of the ammunition that anyone finds and trades is corroded or rusted or cracked or won't explode. And the ammunition that does work almost never matches any of the guns that work.

Fingers or whole hands have been blown off trying to match ammunition to guns, and after a while someone decided precautions had better be taken.

'Every so often,' Luther told Lilly, 'you come across some boxes where the owners had put them in special bags that somehow had all the air sucked out of them. If those wrapped bullets were kept in a cool place, they can still shoot today, even after hundreds of years. Sometimes we found giant depots of them. We think they might have come from an army.'

Lilly's mother Rachael had collected fifty rounds that looked good for her Colt. Lilly herself had found almost a dozen more once she learned what to look for in size and markings.

Now, Lilly checked the cylinder. There were three live rounds still inside. The other three she had fired at her mother's killers. She had no memory of whether the bullets had found their marks. She removed the spent shells and pocketed them, then carefully reloaded.

Lilly and Saavni approached the landmark near the end of the Gone World's territory: the tail end of an airship or a spaceship, entire and unmolested, that rose at a slant thirty metres into the raw blue sky.

AIRBUS.

There was no debris around it.

People said that whatever kind of machine it was had been eaten whole by the rising earth and that inside – like in the towers – was Sickness. The teachers said it had floated in silt and wet sand in the same way that sinking boats point skywards, until, somehow, the thick waters had become hardened earth and all that had been moving came to rest. The curious had looked into the glass windows to see the bones fastened tight into seats by straps around their torsos. Some had fallen apart, heads rolling off and disappearing into the dark where the windows were covered.

The world was full of Raw. No one needed the metal. Better to have a landmark in this barren place.

*

Seven towers rose out of the desert sands. Tumbleweed and brush had collected into massive piles on the eastern side, from where the wind came most often in the evenings. People considered that proof that the deserts went on for ever.

Each building had a name. This one was called The Federal on account of the words etched into the stone at the top. The other towers were higher than this one, which rose eight levels up from what was now the ground.

The rest of the Gone World was wiped out or buried. Whatever happened here, long ago, had happened fast.

Saavni dismounted and tied the horse to a pole jutting out of the ground. Lilly followed her as she led the way through one of the windows that had been destroyed when something fell from the sky, crashed through the floor and disappeared into the dark below. All the other windows on all the other buildings were intact. They were tough things: impossible to remove, except for this one, impossible to break.

Inside was the usual assortment of steel chairs and desks, drawings on the walls and the smell of urine that Lilly was convinced would last for ever if it soaked into concrete.

She followed Saavni down the stairs into the ever-darkening passage until they were on the fifth floor. It was widely known that the old Ground Level was eight floors down.

'The next one,' said Saavni, stepping over bones.

Lilly reached into her pouch and removed one of the sticks. She tore open the paper covering with her teeth, and then snapped the short stick so the tubes inside broke.

She shook it.

The entire staircase burst into a greenish-yellow glow. Saavni backed away from Lilly's glowing hands until her back was against a wall.

'It's not dangerous,' Lilly said.

'It's burning.'

'It isn't hot.'

'How can something be burning and not be hot?'

'I don't think it's burning. I think two different liquids mixed together when I snapped it. When they came together, they made light. Someday I'm going to find out how it works. There is an answer to everything.'

'It's like magic.'

'That word is death because it's where questions end. Now, where's Adam?'

Saavni led her to the Otis Shaft.

Lilly had never seen the doors fully opened before – no one had. Everyone knew the shaft was there because they'd pried the doors open just enough to look. But Saavni was right: now the doors were wide open, revealing a tunnel dropping straight down into nothing.

'We thought of tossing a torch down,' Saavni said, 'but the wind would have put it out as it fell and we didn't have oils.'

'Adam!' Lilly yelled as loudly as possible.

There was no response except from her own voice returning to her.

Lilly tossed the glow stick into the shaft and watched it drop sixty feet until it was nothing but a tiny green square, smaller than her thumb.

Saavni hung her head over the edge and looked down.

'Lilly . . . he's gone. He's really gone.'

The next day, back at the Stadium, Lilly went down to the inner ring, circled it underground until she arrived at the Western

Window overlooking the clean river that flowed out from under the Stadium, and made for Adam's apartment.

Lilly's Aunt Sarah and Uncle Grayson slept in two rooms behind a small plaque that said 'Equipment'. She knocked, entered and found Sarah there.

She told her what had happened to Adam.

For an hour, Sarah wept and talked, saying again and again that something like this had been inevitable because Adam wasn't right in his head. He was prone to being impulsive; to falling for ideas and for love and for excitement too easily. He was never a thoughtful boy, never cautious enough. 'Not long for this world,' she told Lilly.

When her breath returned, Lilly left her there with the truth and the consequences.

With no solutions and nothing else to do or say, Lilly returned to the forge with Luther and tried to be a comfort to her aunt and uncle as they had tried to be a comfort to her when Rachael was murdered.

For eight days word spread throughout the community about the loss.

On the ninth day, Adam returned.

Lilly was alone at her favourite spot behind the Stadium near the waterfall. There was a rocky ledge beneath the Western Window that was close enough to the wall itself that no one could see her when she sat there. Her favourite time of day was sunset. The orange ball would hang over the river, and in the reflection, there would be two suns. As it sank it would touch itself, merge, then become a perfect circle before falling into the river and vanishing. This is where Lilly would sit to think of her mother and try and imagine what her father might have looked like. Her mother had raven-black hair and fair skin – so how did she get cursed with hair so yellow? Did her father have yellow hair too? What would that even look like on a man? How could he have been attractive enough to find love with her mother?

Lilly never had got around to asking and now she'd never know.

As the sun burned below the water and the sky turned to purple, Adam turned the corner on the ledge.

At first it was only a figure; no one she knew. She looked and tried to determine who it was. The idea of Adam came to her before the truth of him. It felt as though the ghost of him was – in that moment – taking possession of whoever the person might have been. This is the way Ghost Talkers have explained themselves in the past. How spirits of the dead possess the bodies of the living for brief moments and a wall between worlds falls away. This version of Adam, in front of her, was skinnier than ever. His eyes were vacant and his skin pale. His hands were covered in caked blood and dirt. The shoes and clothes he wore – the same ones he'd been wearing the day he took the Black Jump – were filthy, as though he had been walking in mud.

The same shoes and clothes?

This must be how it happens, she had thought, *how the Ghost Talking begins for some people. Thousands, millions, billions – all dead below the sands and the waters. It is impossible for so many people not to hear their voices, their screams, their longing and their pain. Ghost Talkers are to be feared because they have lost their minds, but pitied too, and comforted, if they can be. They are often the kinder souls: the ones who cannot push back the emptiness of the entire world.*

Until that moment, Lilly had never thought of herself as one of them.

When Adam started walking closer it was affirmed to her that she was not.

They were the same shoes and the same clothes on the same boy.

Adam – *alive* – walked closer to her but did not speak. He did not smile or show any joy in having seen her or in having been seen. He stopped when he was close enough for Lilly to smell him, to know he was a person and not a vision, and when he did, he raised his right hand and showed three fingers together. Then he rotated his hand so they were horizontal.

'There are three worlds,' he said as though he were speaking from the grave. 'The world we see. The world buried by the sand. And a third world: a world below their world. And they are all connected.'

Adam turned and walked back the way he'd come as the waterfall continued to crash below them.

Lilly sat trying to recover from the shock of seeing him. When the moment had passed, she sprang to her feet and quickly navigated the rocky ledge to where it widened and met the flatter land on the northern end, then ran up to the Western Gate to get back inside the Ring Road.

In the cool of the Stadium, Adam was nowhere to be seen.

Without considering the implications, Lilly sprinted for her aunt and uncle's home, burst into their rooms without knocking and found her Aunt Sarah sitting on the edge of the bed in a kind of trance.

She was wearing a lovely orange dress with flowers that must have grown somewhere before The Rise. Lilly vaguely remembered seeing it on the rack on the last Trade Day a month before.

She wore no shoes. Her feet were flat on the floor and her hands were in her lap.

'Aunt Sarah?'

'Hello, Lilly.'

It occurred to her only in that moment not to ask the question she wanted to ask. Some part of her still thought Adam's appearance might have been a kind of vision.

'How are you?' she asked instead.

'Adam's alive,' Sarah said, Attesting.

'Yeah. He just found me on the ledge by the waterfall.'

'Something's wrong with him,' Sarah said.

'What do you think is wrong with him?' Lilly asked.

'I think,' said her Aunt Sarah, 'that the boy I raised is gone.'

'Where did he go, Aunt Sarah?'

'He's . . . away.'

Lilly had heard this phrase used for men or women whose minds were for ever broken by circumstance or pain. That hadn't been what Lilly meant, though.

'But . . . where is he?'

'The Thunder Room,' she said, still looking forward at the wall, her hands still resting on her lap as though movement were superfluous. 'He said he was working down there.'

Lilly left Sarah sitting on the bed in her flower-covered dress and went to find her crazy cousin.

Lilly ran, across the Green, though the harvest, past friends and old people, to the staircase no one used because it led to a room that served no purpose; a room that once-seen was ignored. Some said it had a strange power, an odd energy. They didn't like the way sound moved in there. It wasn't natural.

Of course Adam went there.

It was growing dark. The purples and greens of the sky were

not entirely visible as the last rays of the orange light fought to remain. The water outside the giant window – almost silent, as the Ancients had evidently wanted it – shimmered against the walls and across their faces.

Adam had lit two torches and placed them on the massive table.

He stood there drawing.

Lilly watched her cousin, who looked more like a shadow than a boy. His arm moved frantically and his concentration was intense. He had not even looked up when Lilly entered the room.

She had never known him to draw – he had never been one for the arts or other creative pursuits. He was in his last year of studies and hadn't excelled at much. For his apprenticeship he was thinking about farming because he liked the smell of fresh earth and watching things grow. Lilly had told him it was a good idea.

'What are you doing?' she asked him now.

'I'm drawing the world below the world that's below our world,' he said, wide-eyed. 'It's all connected. I have to draw the routes before I forget them.'

Lilly stepped closer to the table. He had somehow acquired a giant white sheet from one of the storage rooms and a vat of purple dye that some traders had made from cabbage, beets, flowers and oils. Using a medium-sized brush of wood and horsehair, he was drawing curves and lines and circles: squares that connected to other squares; what seemed to be steps leading upwards or downwards. He scribbled notes in places – words that made no sense, a grammar that didn't exist. He was drawing as though the lines were there already and all he had to do was copy over them to reach the other side of his mania.

'What is that?'

'The map of the underworld. Like I said.'

'Adam. How are you alive?'

'I brought the glowsticks. Each one lasts half a day. Two a day. Nine days. Eighteen sticks. I'd brought twenty. I was lucky to find the exit. Very lucky. Had to keep moving. Keep going. Stay away from the silent people. Watching me. All the time. Still too. Very still. I painted my name on one of them. *Adam Was Here.* Like on the walls in the Gone World. Tell us they once lived. Ghosts now. Bones. Dust. All the dead. They were all there. Now only their names are here. Our names too. We use their names. Our names are their names – living names of dead people. I used my blood because there was no ink. That will never go away now. He'll always remember me, standing there like that on his chest. *Bam!* Thought he could scare me but I showed him. I found the Hard Room – found all the Hard Rooms. Tunnels behind the walls. Sneaky tunnels. Most of them hidden. Not all, though. Some gave up their secrets to time and so I found the pattern. So much water down there. So much stick and rot. I'll never stop smelling it. Little dead children skulls. They don't float. You step on their heads and they're slippery so you fall and then you get angry so you reach down and find out what it was. It was a baby! Someone's baby! Slippery baby skulls in the green light with those big black eyes. "Hello, Adam!" They didn't talk – that was me. Nine days alone but it felt like months. No windows or light. I found a dry room, had a nice bed. I slept there. I wanted to go up and I found a staircase but I wasn't done. I have to make the map. The map is going to make me famous. The map is going to make them stop laughing at me. This,' Adam said, looking up at her for the first time, 'this is going to be my legacy. No one's going to pick on me any more. "Why aren't you more like your cousin Lilly?" everyone asks. "She's so beautiful. She's so smart. You're not beautiful or smart," they say to me. But I know things no one knows. My map – the Adam Map – this is the truth of things.'

He put down the paint brush and stood upright. He placed his three fingers together again.

Adam's words were only whispered but in that room, they thundered in her ears, travelling across the slick ceiling like ripples on the water and then dropping onto her like a storm. No one used this room because of that. It was impossible to be here when different people were speaking, making teamwork maddening and – who works alone? The passage down was too narrow to carry large objects and the stairs were too long for heavy ones to make their way back up.

Lilly became keenly aware she was watching a madman draw a map of nothing for no one. It frightened her.

'Adam, I'm sorry you went down there. Obviously, you saw some terrible things. You clearly haven't eaten anything proper in a week and you haven't bathed either. I'm sure you were lost and it's a miracle you found a way out. But what you're saying makes no sense. And no one,' Lilly said, pointing to the drawing, 'can memorise that much information while moving around underground in the dark. I have an exceptionally good memory, Adam, and I wouldn't be able to do it. That map doesn't mean anything. You need to stop now and get well.'

Adam put down the brush and pointed at her. 'You don't believe me, but I have proof! I have proof!' From beneath the giant table, Adam pulled up a bag of green fabric, unzipped it and removed two objects that at first looked like guns.

These were the objects that Lilly had placed on the table for Birch to see.

Back then, Lilly continued to explain, she had studied them as she walked closer to him.

The artefacts didn't look like guns so much as rifle receivers: there were grips and guards, but no barrels or stocks. The one in his left hand said PRIME and the one in his right hand said ACTIVATE. The triggers inside the guards were long and red, as though two or even three fingers would be needed to pull them. Each was covered by a plastic guard and at the bottom of each guard was a kind of safety device so that it would be impossible to pull the triggers by accident.

'What are those?' Lilly asked.

'Proof.'

'Of what?'

'That I was there!'

'They watched you go down, Adam – they can all Attest to the fact that you were there. It's the other craziness that's the issue.'

'It's proof the underworld exists, that I found the Hard Rooms. That I found a new world – an old world – a new old world!'

'You have a couple of broken guns and a bent head. These prove nothing. You could have found them anywhere. There's shit everywhere. You can't pick this world clean, there's so much junk and so few people.'

'They were in a special cabinet marked DANGER. WARNING.'

'Guns are dangerous. You were warned. So what?' She took the objects from Adam's hands. They looked like any other bit of Gone World junk, albeit shinier and cleaner. Nothing they found ever did anything, nothing ever worked – nothing except knives and hammers and other simple tools. Even objects that had been found in the most perfect condition, things that lit up when given electricity from the Stadium, did absolutely nothing. It was like they were waiting for something, something that never came.

Lilly flicked off the safeties and placed her hands on the triggers.

'They're for you,' Adam said. 'You're the inventor, Lilly. You are the creator. Use them. Make something!'

Lilly pointed them towards the staircase on the off-chance they were loaded and might discharge – though without a hole for a pulse or a bullet she couldn't imagine how. With a pitying look at Adam, Lilly pulled the triggers at the same time.

Nothing happened.

Convinced nothing ever would, she placed them on the table and looked up at Adam, ready to berate him, when she stopped and gripped the edge of the table because the earth beneath them, in that moment, began to rumble.

When Lilly caused the tower in the Gone World to fall by activating the fail-safe detonation using Adam's Finds, the depths were cracked open to the light and a wonderment rose like a plume over the Territory.

At the time she didn't know why the Ancients would build a mechanism to kill themselves and bring a tower down. That she would learn later.

After the earth shook, Lilly went running up the steps like an athlete and shot out onto the Green. She sprinted to the upper wall, following the eyes of others who were also watching in disbelief as the smoke blocked the green swirls in the night sky. They stood in silence.

To Lilly, it looked as though the spirits of the dead had been freed from their unholy prison and let loose into a world already vanquished and parched.

When the sky was fully black and green and there was nothing new to see from this distance, Lilly returned to the Thunder Room. She collected the trigger-machines and walked as quickly as possible to her hiding spot in the storage room. Pushing aside the stone, she hid the evidence of her actions even though she didn't understand them.

A Scout named Amelia Stone was sent by the Council to view the wreckage. She reported back two days later that the activity around the site was like 'maggots to meat'. Desperate hands had been carried there by worn feet to arrive in droves searching for something of worth in the rubble.

Word of her briefing got out. The population was smaller then, and secrets even harder to keep.

They learned that there had been two buildings of similar size. The first, Amelia explained, had fallen inwards and down, straight into the hole, as if the very foundations had been destroyed. There was speculation about whether the ground-water might have weakened the lower levels, causing the collapse. They had seen the results of erosion before.

Why now? was the most common question

Why not now? was the most common reply.

Any 'now' would have evoked the same question.

This thinking satisfied many.

But the shape of the fall – to fall inwards and down and not tip over – what does that?

Nothing does that.

And so some remained unsatisfied.

The building beside it also collapsed, but not in the same way.

The rumbling and destruction of the next-door tower weakened its upper floors but not the lower ones. As the first fell, pieces broke off and battered the other, shattering what most had considered unbreakable windows. As a flower bends towards the sun, so the standing tower had bent towards the falling one until it too tumbled over and exposed its innards to the new.

That was the tower that beckoned the adventurous, its gaping hole now exposed to the world like an animal whose stomach had been ripped open by a giant claw.

Stairs, said Amelia, lead the intrepid into the dark.

Working at ground level for the next few days, scavengers pulled silver-streaked, gleaming objects from the building. Everyone called them 'shinies'. They were beautiful things that had once done something but no longer did. Without names or known purposes, the people of the Territory would ascribe new value to them.

At first there were fights among the Roamers and Traders, bandits and local tribes, which included attempts to cordon off the hole and claim it, but that proved impossible because those who tried – those who placed themselves between the hole and the angry mob – soon ended up skewered or down the hole themselves.

People made pulls: chairs and desks, pencils and paper that was miraculously white and still dry. Artefacts with numbers and words etched into metals, clothing that hadn't rotted or dissolved.

They took anything that could serve a purpose, even if that purpose was only to wave something unknown around so the traders could convince the gullible of its worth.

This lasted until a new whisper came on the wind, the rumour that there had been something foul in the air down below. A smell. A stench. Bodies. Something that had killed people at the bottom of the building. The deeper they ventured, the more bodies they found. It was not only the existence of the dead that mattered: that had been expected, because the remains of the Ancients were everywhere. The sun had bleached bones by the billions.

What had surprised the spelunkers was the sheer number of bodies. 'Piles of them,' Amelia reported. And more: most had died with their heads downwards in the stairwells. 'Something killed them as they walked,' everyone noted, but not bullets or blasts; not falling rocks from above; not maniacal gangs of murders or man-eaters. These people had died on the move and in mid-breath.

What does that? people wondered.

A *Sickness*, they surmised.

There were children's stories and songs and poems and folk art about a great sickness that had wiped out the Ancients. Could this be the proof?

There was sickness in the world now, too; death that came from nowhere and could not be named or stopped. Maybe it was the same; maybe not. Maybe it was the same, only weaker after centuries had passed. Maybe the living were more immune than the Ancients had been. Maybe that was why people now survived.

Maybe. Maybe. Maybe.

It was just words. There was no way to Attest.

However, the Tracollo confirmed what everyone knew: the Gone World was deep and dangerous.

'This is the wisdom that's passing from voice to voice now,' Amelia explained. 'People are thinking that the Sickness had become trapped inside the buildings with the unbreakable windows. Now that the buildings have come down, the air has escaped like a breath that's come out of the earth. No one,' she said, 'is going to the bottom except dogs. They're being sent down to see if the air is safe – to see if monsters are down there.' She laughed. 'People are discovering that the dogs have no reason to go down the stairs, so they have to be encouraged. People have been dropping food in to make the dogs follow, but the dogs decided they weren't that hungry.

'Then they started throwing small animals down there, critters the dogs liked to hunt. I guess they thought the prey would run deeper on its own and the dogs would follow. It took a while for people to start thinking more clearly. After all, what does it prove if a dog does not return?'

Nothing.

It proves nothing and wastes dogs.

Lilly already had her proof. Adam had gone all the way to the bottom and survived there for nine days. His mind was going, yes, but his breathing was fine. His colour was normal. His hands didn't shake.

Adam might have been crazy but he wasn't sick.

This was Lilly's first secret; her first proof that the truth of a thing and the story about it can diverge so forcefully. The question in her mind was whether to bring the truth and story back into alignment or ... *perhaps* ... continue to set them apart.

Was it bad for the Territory to stay away from the depths? If there were secrets down there, might they not be better protected by silence or lies than truth?

Lilly hungered to go and see what Adam might have seen, to grab her glowsticks and explore the subterranean spaces. She might have controlled this burning need if Amelia hadn't told the Council about the box.

*

'I heard about it at the Tracollo,' she had reported (and her report had leaked out). 'Later, I saw it for myself at the Bridge to Nowhere, which is where it is now; in the possession of a crazy-ass Roamer named Cardo. It's a storage chest of some kind. He claims he pulled it from the lowest level – a Hard Room filled with water and the dead. I'm not sure it's true,' she'd added. 'He has muscles like a horse and a brain to match. He's the kind who aggrandises himself. Word is that he carried it out on his shoulder by himself, hitched it to a horse and dragged it to the Bridge to Nowhere. No one believes he went to the bottom and came back with only a box, but no one wants to tell him that either.

'I went there and saw it myself,' Amelia said. 'It's silver, like the best and shiniest metal. There's not a blemish on it. It's large enough for a child to curl up inside with the lid closed. Cardo has hauled the box to the top of the bridge inside the Pavilion like a trophy. I was there in time for the show because once he had an audience, he pulled out a big knife and started going at it. At first he tried to chisel into the lock – which was no kind of lock I've ever seen before – but that didn't work. Then he tried going after the hinges, but the metal was too strong. That led to him smashing it with a giant hammer. He didn't even dent the thing. At that point, the crowd started muttering, so he tried anything he could get his hands on. He bashed it with rocks, mashed it with his rifle stock, but *nothing* worked.'

She took a swig of water to wet her throat before resuming her story. 'It was kind of a joke at first. All the biggest men took a try, and there was a woman there with a pistol – she shot the lock but it only left a scar. Cardo was getting frustrated because he's that kind of animal. He offered a reward for anyone who could open it, so for the next few hours, practically everyone there had a go. When that didn't work, he raised the stakes: he offered a slice of whatever was inside, but that didn't make any difference. That damned box was sealed tight. It was all becoming a bit manic because now the box was hurting his pride – people were starting to laugh at him.'

Amanda looked around at her audience. 'Turns out, Cardo's cleverer than people give him credit for. He sensed the change in the crowd, so he turned it into theatre. He dragged the chest up to the highest spot on the bridge, and the crowd was getting into a real frenzy, placing bets on whether he would really chuck it off, and if it would break open if he did. He took off his shirt and waved it like a great flag, then he hefted the box and hurled it over the edge – and down it went, crashing into the ground . . . and *nothing happened*.

'It sat there, unbeaten, unopened. The betting ended because everyone had learned the lesson. The chest had won.

'Everyone became pretty moody after that,' Amelia said. 'People began swearing about the Ancients, cursing them for being unwilling to surrender even a few of their secrets to the living. What right did they have to take everything to the grave? Last I heard, Cardo had retrieved the chest and is now trying to sell it. Problem is, there are no takers, because word had got round about its invincibility. I left him imbibing a dizzy drink with his men.'

When Lilly heard this she knew she had to have the box. And she had to hurry. Amelia thought the story ended there, but Lilly knew better. That box was going to become a symbol soon: a totem of invisibility or something. Someone would want it.

The next day was warm, the skies blue. She rose early and found Amelia on guard duty at the top of the Stadium wall facing east, over the gully and towards Yellow Ridge. She was alone and looking through her binoculars, her pulse rifle resting against the wall. There was no activity below.

Lilly skipped the preliminaries. 'I want it,' she announced. 'I want that box.'

'It's indestructible and it's locked. It's useless, Lilly.' Amelia was ten years older. They knew each by name and family.

'Anything indestructible,' Lilly said, 'must have been made that way for a reason. It's locked because it's useful, and it's heavy because it's filled. Whatever's locked in an indestructible box, hidden at the bottom of the Gone World and unfound for hundreds of years must be interesting. Very interesting. I want it.'

'It's locked, Lilly,' Amelia repeated, 'and I watched a hundred people try to open it in every conceivable way. You'll never be able to open it.'

'I'll be able to.'

'What makes you think you can when no one else could?' she asked, lowering the binoculars and staring at Lilly. 'What are you going to do that everyone else in the Territory hasn't done?'

'What they should have been doing all along if they were half as smart as I am.'

'Oh yeah?' Amelia said, 'and what's that?'

'I'm going to find the key,' Lilly said.

Lilly set out in the afternoon with a box of glowsticks, her Colt Python revolver, enough food and water for three days, and Saavni's horse.

She crossed the deep gullies and rifts below the Stadium

that had been formed by waters flowing across them for decades or longer. Luther had crafted leather guards for the war horses to wear on their legs, protection against all the sticks and spikes and discarded raw they had to trot through day after day.

For five hours she rode alone and undisturbed, her gun at the ready. She passed the time humming to herself and counting the plastic bags that were for ever blowing in from the east and sticking to the browning shrubs. Some of them bore the most exotic words and pictures.

As she hummed, she considered her options. She had set off like a gunslinger into the wild, not knowing if her plan to find that key had any merit, but in that saddle, moving with the gait of the horse, hours with only vigilance and quiet, she had time to think.

Where was the key?

It was clear from Amelia's story that Cardo didn't have it, and by her reckoning no one was looking for it, so the pressure was off in that regard. Still, though. Where on this earth was she headed?

Down didn't feel like enough to go on.

Lilly considered the objects the Stadium's people had found and recovered from the desert sands over the decades, and also those that had washed against the walls as the traders lapped at the gates and left behind their wares.

She rolled her ideas around for hours, welded them together and pulled them apart. She looked at the bridle on the horse and the saddle; the hanging stirrups and her own position as a rider: it was all working together to make it possible for her to get from where she was to where she needed to be. Each object wasn't simply an achievement or solitary instrument; everything supported the other parts so that, through a kind of teamwork, they could form a machine – a system where every part needed each other to make something happen.

As more hours passed it became Lilly's conclusion that the triumvirate of box, owner and key formed a distinct system. If that was so, it stood to reason that they would not have been far away from one another during the cataclysm that set the world asunder. The box had been moved to the bridge, but the owner and its key had not.

She knew the rumour of where the box came from so all she needed to do was find its owner. Amelie might not have been convinced by Cardo's story, that he'd gone all the way down into the waters of the lowest levels, but after listening to Adam's ramblings in the Thunder Room, Lilly was.

And that meant finding this so-called Hard Room he'd talked about. She'd have to go straight down the stairs to the very bottom. That was the kind of linear thinking a man like Cardo would have: bigger, stronger, faster, further. Fighting, drinking, fucking. If he couldn't climb to the top he'd prove his worth by going to the bottom.

What else?

When she stopped for the night the wind was heavy with the fine grains picked up from the Empty Quarter to the east; it left golden shadows in the folds of their clothing. Above, a vulture gawked while soaring on a tuft of rising air in front of her. It twisted left, swirling upwards, and turned in search of whatever was not there.

Lilly camped but slept little. In the desert her mind turned to danger. The danger made her angry and it flamed the hatred in her heart. It was her character that forged the anger into courage.

*

Lilly slept and dreamed of throwing her wall-climbing hook to the sky and pulling down the secrets of the Ancients as the floodwaters rushed through the wadis and bathed her dry and battered feet.

The sun rose yellow and dull behind a haze of dust. When she had come for Adam, this dead place had been unmoving. Now there was life everywhere. The scavenging may have slowed but in the glow of the dawn, Traders and Spaders were still sifting through rubble for shinies and raw, their mood and voices tempered, their expectations low. They knew – because everyone did – that the bones of former treasure had been picked clean over the centuries and long before the Stadium rose as a colony.

That truth, however much it was known and accepted, was not enough to stop more than three dozen people from working away, each hoping to find an object that would change their destinies.

Lilly sat and watched to sense the patterns. She looked to see if anyone emerged wet from the depths, but no one did. Hers was a race that would not be won with speed alone and she knew it.

At midday, when people stopped to eat, Roamers set a camp on the edge of the second building. They were not possessive of the site and they paid her little attention. They ate their food sitting in a circle and watching a young girl dance to total silence in the middle. The girl was graceful, and the more her own dance turned inwards and soulful, the more graceful and beautiful it became.

The arduous work of removing the debris from the staircases had been accomplished, allowing the bright sun of day to shine into the lower remains of the tower. Lilly had never seen a building sliced in half – no one had. She had not known about the thick steel tubing inside the walls or the way the electric wiring had been thoughtfully placed throughout, creating a kind of mechanical organism. Simply studying the subject from above would be a worthy way to spend months and she planned to recommend it when she returned.

Lilly turned from the hole and approached the Roamers. She opened her palms and walked forward as though pushing an invisible wall, a common gesture on the road. A woman from the circle stood up. She was heavy in the hips and her face was wrinkled from years under the sun. Her dirty hair was light brown in colour. She was probably in her fifties and looked as though she had few reasons left to smile and wanted that known. She raised her hands in the same manner. They did not touch.

'I'm from the Stadium. You know us?' Lilly said, letting her hands fall to her sides.

'We know you,' the woman said, lowering her own hands. She wore oiled leather britches and a brightly coloured green jacket that was hard to come by but favoured when it was found because it sealed against rain and wind and sand. 'I wouldn't have taken you for Stadium Folk,' she said. 'They keep quiet in there. You're not a quiet one. I've never seen anyone watch the world louder than you. You've got a growling hunger in you, girl. There's something you want.'

'And what's wrong with that?'

'The Ancients were hungry too. They made all this and got so hungry they tried to gobble everything up. Everything gobbled them up instead,' she said, nodding at the earth.

'We don't know what happened to them,' Lilly said.

'We sure do. They died.'

'How do you get into it?'

192

The woman looked at a red rope that was tied securely to a girder that ended in a coil on the stairway landing.

Lilly followed her eyes.

'People here want to make some pulls,' the woman said, brushing her dirty hair from her face. 'I think you want something else. What is it?'

'I'm curious, that's all.'

'Curiosity killed the cat,' the woman said.

'What's a cat?'

'Something dead because it tried to learn too much.'

'The cat probably asked the wrong questions,' Lilly said.

Even with the structural damage, sunlight did not penetrate the stairwell more than five storeys. Making her way down and down and further down – more stairs than anyone had ever walked in living memory – she also learned that there was no respite from the dust she was pulling into her lungs and that clung to the sweat on her face. She wrapped a scarf around her nose and mouth, but it did nothing to shield her from the smell of the stairwell: chalk and smoke and the sweat of locals.

On each landing she found the embers of fires that had been recently lit to illuminate the path of the workers excavating and scavenging for finds. Doors on each landing had been propped open and the scuffmarks through the dust were testimony for what had been dragged and hauled up into the daylight for the first time in centuries.

Eight floors down she came to a door that opened into the grandest lobby she had ever seen. The floor was a material she would later learn to be *marble*. There were mirrors rising to the ceiling and magnificent lamps that hung low and glittered. The chairs were stylish and they all matched one another: a stunning combination of aesthetic perfection, harmony and balance. This was a place to feel at rest and greet old friends or meet new ones. To share the news. To rejoice in life. This was the old level of the earth. Eight floors down.

She closed the double doors and descended further, cracking a glowstick to light her way.

The deeper she went, the more skeletons she saw.

The final flights scared and disheartened her. There were more bodies, more dead, the pelvic and femur bones pointing downwards like the rumours had claimed. Skulls had rolled. These people had not been shot or stabbed; no arrows pierced them. They were not dismembered by explosions and they had not suffocated while sitting on the ground, for surely their positions would have been more varied.

A sickness? Maybe. But it was no natural sickness; nothing natural could kill a person as fast as a bullet. Whatever had done this was something *un*natural; unnatural – and no longer here.

The temptation towards fear, though, was great. The need for answers can outweigh one's capacity for reason; such is the urgency of Knowledge. Lilly had sympathy for this.

But little time – because she wasn't dead, and neither was Adam.

The deeper she went, the worse the stench grew. Below the Gone World's 'ground' level, the air became sticky and damp. By the time she reached the bottom, she was standing on skeletons and wading through water that came up to her thighs. It was much colder than she had expected – it felt like bathing below the waterfall in autumn, not freezing but bitterly cold.

At the bottom she pushed through the water down a long corridor, her feet slipping off the bones of the long-dead, making her way towards a thick metal door that was wide enough ajar for a giant man carrying a box to walk through.

Lilly's heart raced and her breathing was laboured. It was easy to understand how Adam's fears might have manifested in a place like this, sending him running home with tales of ghosts and souls trapped in the walls. It was easy to imagine him getting lost on the way back up, too. Adam hadn't fallen into the *Tracollo* (that was the word used by the Roamers). He'd made a Black Jump down an Otis Shaft, so who knew where he'd ended up? There were so many doors into so much darkness.

In the Hard Room, the walls were thicker than any she'd seen before. Once-locked doors were now open and room after room contained machines no one had bothered hauling up. Storage shelves were now empty, as were massive barrels that might once have been filled with water. It was a *shelter*: a place to live, a safe zone of some kind. It had been set up at the bottom of the building, so she reasoned that people would have been fleeing here to escape danger from above, maybe far above. Maybe planes really did fly – her mother had not been lying. And after all, Lilly had seen the tail of the AIRBUS. Did those same planes carry weapons? Were they once weapons of war? They would have been formidable things. And if every building had such a room as this, the threat must have been palpable and real.

She spat out the dead and raised her scarf.

Instead of sorting through the detritus in the sleeping quarters or the kitchen, she passed them over for an open door that read *Communications*. Whatever had not dissolved into the water over hundreds of years was under it or floating on it. The stench was burning her nose and the back of her throat and she was starting to feel the depth of the earth and the weight of the building and the deepness of the darkness on her mind. The skeletons she had tried not to think about now moved and reanimated in the rippling green light all around her.

Eye sockets seemed to be watching her. She wanted to get out – but she would not go without her prize.

Every step she took moved the putrid waters, moved the light, moved the shadows.

She breathed through her mouth and tried to focus on the task.

How had Cardo found the box? It must have been under the water. The crazy bastard must have been wading through it and kicked it.

I'm one to talk, she thought.

A dog barked somewhere. It was in the building that was pitch-black. It was lost. It was best not to think about it.

Lilly was starting to panic. Water dripped from the ceilings and objects long stationary were now knocking against the walls, pushed by the ripples that she left in her wake, every one sounding like a person who was going to close the door and lock her in, turning this treasure Trove into a tomb. She too would die here. She too would dissolve into the water and her bones would become like all the other bones and she would be as forgotten as each one of the Ancients.

That was when she saw the desk. The image seared into her mind, where it would stay for fifty-four years, long enough for her to be able to recount it in perfect detail to Birch, Master of the Order of Silence, who would be born more than a decade later.

The water was making an island for the dead man whose upper body rested on the flat desk as though he had died from exhaustion, even after making it to dry land. His head rested on his arms in permanent sleep. He wore a kind of suit she had never seen before. The colour was indeterminate because of the green glow of the stick, but the letters on the shoulder patch were clear: HCG®.

It was not a word, and the letters and symbol meant nothing.

Unlike the scraps of cloth that clung to the shelves and floated around her, his suit was intact, holding in place all his bones except his head.

On the desk, directly in front of him, was a perfectly smooth rectangular surface raised up on an elegant steel trellis. Unlike the desk beneath it, which was flat, this was angled gently towards him. Though everything was the colour of her glow-stick, Lilly knew that its surface was perfect and uniformly flat. Later, when she removed it to the surface, she would learn it was white. There was not a stain on it or a discolouration. There was also no mark, no word and no button. The only interruption to its paper-smooth surface and character was a black glass eye encased in metal and centred on the edge of the board at the far end which appeared to be looking at the corpse.

Lilly rubbed her hand over the surface. She wasn't sure whether it was her imagination but it felt as though tiny grains of sand, infinitely smaller than those in the desert, gently rippled like water as she moved her hand across the surface.

Whatever this thing was or whatever had been on it, Lilly knew only that it had been the centre of this man's attention in his final moments – and it must therefore be very, very important.

The only other object on the desk was a metal platform, to the left of the board with the glass eye, and on top of that was a more familiar-looking electronic box with the equally familiar – if otherwise meaningless – words above the various knobs and buttons that adorned its face: LOADING, PLATE, PRE-SELECTOR, MODE, GAIN.

Lilly had seen some metal boxes like this in storage at the Stadium and a few others brought in by traders in their wagons. Those at the Stadium did nothing and there was little market for new ones that came in. Often, the sheet-metal backs would be removed and given over to the blacksmiths to cut or re-cast into arrow heads, knives or spear-tips, among other things.

What made this box different from all the others she'd seen was a black coiled rope that ran from a silver hole in the front and disappeared under the water.

Lilly pulled at the submerged cord until she felt it snag. Undeterred, she yanked harder until the resistance gave way and up came the man's boney hand. It was clutching some kind of black device with a button on it.

Using both of her hands, she snapped off his bones and removed the little box.

Lilly looked around again to see if she had missed anything. She reached down into the frigid, stinking, poisonous water and felt around, but there was nothing. She tried with her feet as well, and then surrendered.

The board was remarkably light. If it had commanded the Ancients' attention at the very end, it deserved hers too, and so did the other thing he'd been clutching. Like the stirrups and reins and saddle, like the box and key and user, this had all comprised a system too, once: man, flat-board and cord-box. It was a solution to a question she would need to discover.

Quickly now, because her eyes were hurting and her lungs were aching and she wanted to scream but didn't dare because of what it might awaken down here, Lilly unslung the pack and tossed out the water, the food, the knife and the change of clothes to make room. She knew very little about electricity, but she did know that objects that used it didn't like water. There was no telling whether the water used to be higher and had already ruined everything. If she had more time she could check the walls for marks, but her claustrophobia was growing. She needed to get out of here.

With some strain, because it was much heavier than it looked, she managed to fit the machine and the flat-board into her backpack.

After pulling it back on, she turned her attention to the man. She pulled him backwards until that the front of his suit was visible. There was a name tag in a reflective material on his chest that read HARRINGTON.

There were stripes on his shoulders indicating a high military rank.

The suit was made of some sort of iridescent material that didn't feel like any fabric she had ever touched before. The long zipper on the front was partly opened near the collar. Lilly pulled it down, exposing the remains of his torso.

Around his spine was a necklace.

On the necklace was a key.

She pulled it off him, placed it over her own head and made for the exit.

The Bridge to Nowhere appeared to Lilly through the mist rising from the wetlands below it. She had ridden here with her mother more than once, just to gawk at it. It rose from sand, arched over a patch of woodland made green by freshwater hidden far beneath, and returned to the sand again. It was stupendous, awe-inspiring and utterly useless.

Children liked walking on it and looking down through the glass.

Horses did not.

In the past few days, since the towers had fallen, something had changed. Because of the many pulls and the desires of the Roamers and Traders to profit from them, small stands and shops had started to pop up on the bridge. At first, Lilly could see, it was to become more visible to the shoppers, to literally lift themselves above the competition. That, unsurprisingly, became a competition in itself, with new shops rising to higher ground up the bridge.

But that was not without its own problems. Why go up so high when you can stay at the bottom? The shopkeepers at the higher ends solved this by encouraging traders to take a journey all across the bridge.

'*Rise wanting. Return flaunting!*' they advertised.

It was weak talk, but this was not Lilly's business.

She spurred Costello on and together they made the climb up the glass surface, passing over the trees to the Pavilion at the top, where she heard male voices yelling and laughing, where her box was waiting for her.

As she rode she considered the finds and the offers around her. Some of this must have come from the Tracollo. The rest? Maybe the prospect of a market alone had attracted the sellers. Though her mind was firmly fixed on her mission, Lilly could not help but look at the finer things and think of her mother. The magnificent clothes and stitching from the old fabrics, the brightly coloured wires and cables, the mirrors and carpets, polished stone building materials, even the occasional bicycle. One man had set up a table selling children's toys, including plush pillows shaped like magical animals that had no names.

Everything around her was a clue to what the world of the

Ancients might have been like and what might have led to their destruction. And no one here cared at all.

'You there,' shouted a brave man willing to talk to someone as filthy as Lilly, 'come see this.' He held up a small object.

His smile was warming so she approached.

'It comes from a fabled lake in the north, before you reach the forest. It's bottle glass,' said the bearded man with a smile. 'Worn down by sand and time. All the rough edges are gone, nothing left but the pure fact of the thing. A rounded beauty alone in a cold world. Each one the same; each one unique. Each a soul,' said the man, 'just like us.'

Lilly's horse didn't care for the glass. It bayed and snorted. Lilly, however, loved it.

'I'll trade one for an idea,' Lilly said.

'What kind of idea?' asked the man.

'A way for you to sell more.'

'You'll have to risk telling me first.'

'I choose to trust you,' said Lilly.

'Well, have at it then, young thinker.'

'They're beautiful, but in a pocket no one can enjoy them. Take some thin Raw and wrap it around the glass. And then hang it from a string so it can be a necklace,' she said, thinking of Harrington and his key. 'Match the right colour of glass with the right person's skin. And keep a mirror here,' Lilly added, 'so people can look at themselves.'

The seller laughed, delighted. 'It's a deal. What colour for a fine mind that needs a shower?'

'Blue, please. I dream of big water.'

The bridge road divided as she approached the apex, the two arms gently wrapping around the Pavilion and then rejoining on the other side.

Her parents had taken her there once when she was eleven. A circular viewing station had windows all around. The gap that opened from the splitting lanes became a free drop into woodland. There was no other way to die like this in the territory.

Some, it was said, had chosen this death for themselves.

On the flat in front of the northern door were four tethered horses. Lilly had been expecting more activity; surely the box was a draw? It was when she saw the thick smear of blood leading from the door of the Pavilion to the far edge of the bridge where someone had been hurled off that the limited gathering made more sense.

Lilly looked more closely at the horses for signs of who might be inside. One of them had a harness with two long metal tubes holding a cloth that was folded cleverly to create a stretcher. The fabric held the outline of a box like a footprint in the sand.

Lilly removed her backpack and left it on her horse. There was a risk it might be stolen, but that was minor compared to her need to be fast once inside.

She slipped her Colt into the back of her waistband.

With a deep breath, she stepped inside.

For the past half-century, the story Lilly told was one of self-defence and attempted rape. She was attacked, she shot her way out of it and left behind three dead men, two of whom were at least double her weight. She returned with the box and became a hero when she opened it 'with the key Cardo had been hiding'.

Why had he hidden it?

No one knew. Lilly speculated it was to draw attention to himself. The unopened box gave him power. An open box? Merely the contents.

It sounded reasonable and with no one to Attest, it became the truth.

'What I want to tell you,' Lilly says to Birch in the Map Room, decades later and in a whisper that hugs the ceiling like a lover, 'is what really happened. I want to tell you,' she says, 'because it explains why I told no one that the Sickness wasn't real. Why I told no one about the flat-board – the White Board – and its relationship to the radio. Why I never told anyone that it was me who knocked down the towers using the detonators that Adam brought back from the underworld. Why all of this convinced me to found the Order of Silence and ask Saavni to run it.'

Birch says nothing.

'There were three men,' Lilly says. 'One was Cardo – I knew him at once from Amelia's description. The other two I didn't know. Cardo was wearing a shirt, but he had ink drawings all over his muscles and there were scars on his face. His head was shaved and he wore rings on his fingers. I didn't recognise the tribal markings, but I did recognise the box he had his feet on.

'The man on his left was long and lean, like he didn't eat enough. His teeth were bad and one of his eyes had clouded over. He was chewing dried meat with his mouth open when I walked in. The other was hunched over with his elbows on his knees. He had a sword across his thighs.

'I had wanted to buy the box and I said as much. "I heard it's for sale," I said to Cardo. "What do you want for it?" This is part of the story I always told and all of that was true. But here's where I lied. The story everyone knows is that Cardo looked me over and started to laugh. He said I was the dirtiest whore he'd ever seen and he wasn't sure he wanted to put his dick in me, but he'd be willing to try. He stood up and adjusted a big knife he had sheathed on his belt. He put a foot on the box.

'"For this box?" he said, "we'll bend you over it four times, twice for me, and once each for them. For that I'll give you the box. We'll be done by . . . tomorrow night. I'll even feed you between now and then. You'll need your strength." He laughed and they laughed, as you'd expect. He told me I should consider myself lucky, because he was the bravest man in the territory. He'd been to the underworld, he said, he'd gone where no one had been in hundreds of years, because he had the biggest balls on Earth.

'I told him that I was from the Stadium – that we have seed and clothes and tools and water and maybe even a horse. I said the box was useless to him and he was in no position to drive the price because there were no other buyers. I asked if he was going to continue to act like a fool or whether he wanted a deal.

'Cardo laughed at me. That's the story I always told. But that isn't what happened. Instead of attacking me, he laughed and then he pushed the chest over to me and said, "Have it. My gift. I don't need it because I know the secret."

'"What secret?" I asked, and he said he had been down to the very bottom – he had touched the waters of death and swum in them. He said he pulled the box from a dragon made of water and bone and here he was, alive to tell the tale. Others might doubt it but he knew the truth.

'I thought that was going to be it, but then he surprised me because he put the ideas together. He said, "You know what that means, don't you? It means there is no Sickness. It means that whatever killed the Ancients is long gone and whatever else is down there is mine. I am going to be the King of the Underworld. I am going to put together a crew of the strongest men and we are going to make the greatest pulls the world has ever known. I am going to control the world beneath the world." He actually used the same phrase that Adam had.

'At first I didn't know why he was telling me this – why share your secret? And then I realised it was because I was a girl. Maybe he thought I was weak, or maybe he was going to kill me and he needed to brag to someone before he did because it was in his nature. But in that moment I had my understanding: I realised that the one thing bigger than walls or weapons or inventions is Knowledge. You see, Birch? The one with the Knowledge is the one with the power. Down below – unreachable until the Tracollo, unapproachable because of the story of the Sickness – was the last undiscovered country we could reach. Since then our Explorers and members of the Order have gone further and mapped more, but at the time this was the next frontier. The only thing keeping people from invading that place and learning its secrets and finding its Troves was that story.

'Once I realised that, I knew what I had to do. I pulled out my Python and I shot Cardo right between the eyes. His two idiots stood up and reached for their guns but I dropped them before they stepped. I left with the box. I told everyone they'd gone mad with the Sickness – that they were foaming at the mouth, that when they'd made a move to rape and kill me I had no choice. No one questioned it for a second. I was a hero when I got back.

'I look back now,' Lilly says, concluding her story, 'and wonder how I was so brazen. Anyway, it all amounts to this: the tunnels are real. The Sickness is not. Consider it, Birch! All the books, all the music, all the pictures – they're all gone. Either the Gone World decided they didn't need them any more, or they put them out of our reach. I simply cannot accept that they chose a life without them – not with everything they accomplished. So if they put it all beyond our reach, it either still exists or it does not. There is no alternative. If it does exist, even a fraction of it, there will be enough to jump the Central Archive ahead by a thousand years.

'It is entirely possible that Elimisha has found a room like mine but better preserved. She has a radio and I'll bet you she has a White Board. I think the books and the music and the pictures are in the White Board. Or . . . or it's a door to find them. I don't know. It's all part of a system that we can't even imagine – and God knows I've tried. But if that little girl can make Knowledge rain down from the clouds it will change . . . *everything*.'

During the time Lilly has been recounting her tale and admitting her secrets, the sun has set and the Map Room has become dark. The waterfall behind the window has nearly vanished; now the torches reflect off the perfect surface. Without a word, Birch stands and walks to the northern edge of the window. She reaches into a simple wooden box and removes four more torches for the walls.

Though Lilly's story has been long, she feels a tremendous sense of urgency to make decisions and get moving. They need to find this girl before the Keepers gather, control the Gone World and deny them access to everything they have been working and fighting and dying to achieve since the Harrington Box was first opened and the Great Books were revealed, setting them on a course to ensure that the Knowledge of the world would never again be forgotten.

It is agony watching Birch drag the torch stands to the giant table, place them, try to light them, fail, try lighting them again, and finally sitting down again. It is all Lilly could do not to scream at her.

When Birch finally settles, she reaches beneath the table and – to Lilly's surprise – removes two enormous scrolls as well as an open wooden box filled with fist-sized stones.

With an expertise born of repetition, she unrolls the first map and places the stones on the corners to keep it open. Satisfied with the placement, she does the same for the second map, placing it directly to the side. From Lilly's angle and distance she cannot see what they are, but one looks more like art and the other like a technical or schematic drawing of a machine.

Still standing, Birch, the third Master of the Order of Silence, says to Lilly, 'I'm forbidden to tell you any of this. If you repeat any of this, one or both of us will die.

'This,' she says, placing her hand on the artistic scroll, 'is the Adam Map. Saavni found it and hid it away. I don't know why she didn't tell you but my team discovered it inside this desk about six years ago. And this,' she says, placing her hand on the second map, 'is what we have learned in those six years by studying the Adam Map for clues and using those clues to explore the Gone World. Because you're right: there is no Sickness. Saavni knew it, you knew it, I know it. We have perpetuated your first lie to keep people out, because Adam was also right. There is a world beneath the world, and a world beneath that too. The Rise is eight storeys high. But we all failed to imagine what should have been obvious from the start: that most buildings are less than eight storeys tall and are still there, buried entirely below the sands. And most of them have multi-storey basements.

'And there's more. You and Cardo went straight down and straight back up. Adam, though, stayed down there. What he learned, and what we now know, is that all the buildings are connected.

'The Ancients,' she continued, 'knew the world was going to end, so they set about building a vast underground network so they could be safe from what they foresaw as the danger. They didn't have much time so the tunnels are rough. Also, it turns out that they were wrong about their odds and solutions. Something killed them that they hadn't been expecting. So the catacombs remain: tunnels connect all the Gone World buildings together – or most of them, anyway – and the network is vast, but very, very hard to map.'

'He wasn't insane?' Lilly asks.

'I don't think that's the question, Chief,' says Birch. 'You were there and looked him in the eyes. Only you can Attest. What I know is that sixty per cent of this map has proved sufficiently accurate to guide us, or at least orient us towards passages that we might not have found on our own. He was down there only nine days, so the space he mapped out is limited compared to what the Order has subsequently explored and noted. But he got us thinking about how things were laid out, not only where they went. As for the other forty per cent: the rest is either too poorly drawn, incorrectly remembered, or . . . yes, he made it up. What he saw broke him and threatened the cohesion of the Commonwealth. That's why he was sent away to the east.'

'Do we know what happened to him?' Lilly asked.

'No, but there were rumours that he survived for many years, spreading his stories. And there is still a contingent of thinkers who believe that we should have killed him immediately rather than let him spread loose talk across the deserts. But this was long ago, Lilly; long before my time.

'Something else,' Birch says, turning back to matters at hand. 'Three Runners are missing and one of them is Elimisha. She was supposed to Signal from Blue Crest the night of the

Tracollo. Henrietta Wayworth insists that she heard three explosions before the Tracollo. No one can Attest but I believe her. Elimisha was on the Orange Route which crossed that tower. It is possible she went down – and it is possible she survived.'

'Are you telling me that we know where she is?'

'No, we never found a Hard Room under that tower. But we do know' – she points at the technical map – 'that the Ancients sealed some tunnel entrances or hid them, while leaving others exposed and clearly marked. We're not entirely sure why, but from uniforms and the linkages between hidden rooms and passages, we think there might have been a military logic to it.'

'Are we going to go find that girl and the internet or not, Birch? Because if we're not, I need you to tell me so I can lie to your face, tell you that I understand, and then find a way to do it myself. Because I'm not leaving this one to the amateurs.'

'We're going.'

'I didn't mean me. I'm seventy-one years old. Getting back up those damn stairs is probably going to kill me. You need someone young and strong and fast and willing to sneak out of here against the Lockdown Protocol, and it ought to be someone Elimisha knows and trusts for about a hundred different reasons. It also needs to be someone we can trust; someone who knows the route and has a mind for improvisation. I'd say a member of the Order, but I worry that if anyone gets caught they'll have to answer to General Winters and implicate you and we want to avoid that. This place isn't as big or secretive as we'd like to think it is. So who does that leave?'

'We need an outlaw.'

'What does that mean?' Lilly asks.

'I'm thinking Wayworth.'

'Henry or Graham? Because while Graham is a pain in my ass he's not exactly—'

'We need one of the kids from the Urban Explorers,' explains Birch. 'I'm thinking Alessandra.'

MISSION

Alessandra Wayworth stands in front the radio at eight o'clock the next morning, eyes wide and staring at the colours flickering on the front panel as her friend Elimisha talks about plants. She listens under the strictest rules – from both Lilly *and* the Master of the Order of Silence – to say *absolutely nothing*.

Birch has never spoken to Alessandra directly. Being approached by her and told to 'follow me' is like learning that God knows your name and wants a word in private.

As Alessandra listens, Birch, in her usual black leather, is leaning back against the table, her arms folded.

Lilly is sitting with her legs crossed, sipping hot water with a twist of lemon. She is refreshed from a night's deep sleep and watches Alessandra's face as Simone and Bruno are entrusted with writing down everything Elimisha says, no matter how little sense it makes.

Photosynthesis can be represented using a chemical equation. The overall balanced equation is $6CO_2 + 6H_2O$ which yields $C_6H_{12}O_6 + 6O_2$. As everyone listening knows: CO_2 = carbon dioxide, H2O = water; C6H12O6 = glucose. O2 = dioxygen. I'm joking, as no one knows this, but you'll have to hear me now so that we can all make sense of it later. All I can promise is that it's important for learning how to start growing new crops out there. Now, let's touch on the word glucose this time to see what that is. *[Pause]*. I'm thinking that I should have started reading inorganic chemistry first and then moved to organic chemistry but if I did that I probably should have backed up all the way to basic chemistry and biology, at which point, where are we? Might as well just do the whole curriculum. Which is what I'm reading: The High School Curriculum for . . . let me see . . . Cape Elizabeth High School in Maine, whatever and wherever that might be, last updated in 2085. Which is older than the Pirelli calendar, but that's another conversation. What did I say I was going to look up? Oh yeah. Glucose.

Lilly turns down the volume and snaps her fingers to get Bruno's and Simone's shared attention.

'I need the room, please.'

'But . . .we'll miss stuff,' says Simone.

'Yes.'

'If we miss it, it'll be gone for ever. We'll be letting Knowledge slip through our fingers like—'

'Like sand falling back into the desert. I know the metaphor,' Lilly says. 'You'll make an excellent Evaluator someday, Simone. In the meantime, I'm willing to sacrifice a little Knowledge for a bit of privacy. Okay? Now, get out. Both of you. And you,' she says, raising her chin to indicate Alessandra, 'you stay.'

After Bruno and Simone have left the room, Birch checks the door to ensure it is properly closed. Elimisha continues to talk utter nonsense as Lilly turns down the volume and directs Alessandra into a chair across from her.

212

Sitting, she continues to stare at the radio as though it were a fire.

'What do you think?' Lilly asks her.

'What?'

'That,' Lilly says. 'What do you think about that?'

'What do I think?'

'Snap out of it,' Birch says.

'Yes, Master Birch. I'm sorry.'

Lilly tries to soften her tone. 'We asked you in here because we need your help and we think you can handle it. But you look like you've hit your head on a rock. Can you focus?'

'Yes, Ma'am.'

'Chief,' Lilly corrects her.

'Yes, Chief.'

'Do you recognise that voice,' Lilly asks again.

'Yes, but . . . it's impossible.'

'Who is it?'

'Elimisha. She's a year younger than me but . . . you know . . . she's good. Fast. Smart. Strong. Likes rules. Maybe too much. Where is she? How did she get a radio? Is she in the Stadium someplace? Is this a test?'

'It's a mission,' Birch corrects her, resuming her cross-armed pose by the desk again. 'What I'm going to tell you is only known to me and Chief Lilly. No one else knows and no one else *can* know. Not your parents, not General Winters, not members of the Order. Are you still a member of the Urban Explorers?'

'I . . . um . . .'

'It's a yes or no question, Alessandra. You'll want to answer truthfully here,' Lilly says.

'Yes, Chief. I mean . . . yes I am, Chief.'

'Do you consider yourself an Adamist?' Birch asks.

'Well . . . no. Not really. I think some people have gone a

little crazy with those old stories. Everyone knows it's D3 down there so there's a limit to how far we go. I do think there's more to explore, like the Adamists do, so rather than go down, what I like to do is go up. There's a break in the northeast window of Landmark Five Tower and if you step off the Green Route at Marker Eighteen there's a staircase to the right and the thirteenth floor is wild! I don't what those Ancients were doing in there but—'

'We know,' Birch says.

'I don't. What does D3 mean?' Lilly asks.

'Dangerous, Dark and Dead,' Alessandra answers.

'We want you to find Elimisha,' Birch says, impatient with the chatter. 'Wherever she is, she's trapped with enough food and water to keep her alive; enough electricity to power the radio and – how do I explain this? – a very special kind of Archive that we want to retrieve.'

Alessandra looks at Birch, who hasn't moved and still wears no expression. She isn't entirely sure what's being asked of her. 'Me?'

'Yes.'

'Um . . . why?'

'Because,' says Birch, uncrossing her arms and gripping the table on either side of her, 'we don't want anyone to know we're looking for her. Which means if you're caught, you will lie. To everyone. We have confidence in your ability to get the job done and keep your mouth shut. Are we wrong?'

They are not wrong, but Alessandra has questions. She has never been in a room with people like this before. Yes, she's known Lilly since she was a little girl, but this is no social call. She has always thought her experiences in the Urban Explorers would get her into trouble some day, maybe even prevent her from rising through the ranks. It never crossed her mind that the Master of the Order of Silence might be watching the Urbanists for talent.

Thinking about it, though, it makes some sense. The Order needs people who don't fit into the system perfectly – the sort who can not only follow routes like Runners, but can also build routes from their imaginations. They need people who have a different kind of personality and character: the sort who want to push beyond the boundaries, not merely follow the rules.

Wow!

Alessandra looks at Birch. She is unable to suppress her own conclusion: 'You protect the Urbanists from the Military so you can find people for the Order! I cannot believe this – you've been watching us the *whole* time? It's a kind of test, isn't it? To see who to take in? It makes total sense now.'

'We also watch to make sure you don't get yourselves killed. There was no Order when Adam made his Black Jump,' Lilly says. 'I founded the Order afterwards.'

Can we get back to the topic, please?' Birch asks.

'Why don't you send the Dragoons and secure the site and just dig her out?' Alessandra asks, but as she finishes her question, she realises she isn't sure she's supposed to ask anything. Are there rules she doesn't know about?

How could she know?

'Alessandra,' says Birch, 'I'm going to answer your question and after that, we're going to work on the assumption that Chief Lilly and I have thought through the problem with more information than you have, and that we're coming to you for this solution already wise to our choices. Okay?'

'Yes, Master Birch.'

'Last night,' she says, 'I sent someone to the tower. There

is no way to get to Elimisha from there. We have to come at her from other passages from other entrances. If we secure those sites now, it will notify the Keepers that something is happening, and that might encourage them to attack – so if that's the case, we'll need to divert more troops away from the Stadium to fight or to cover the retreat if we're severely outnumbered. Both are bad options. Secrecy and stealth and quiet are all better strategies. We have selected you for reasons that we think are well-considered. So that's all you need to know about it. You either accept this mission or you don't. We don't want your opinion. Now choose.'

'I'm in.'

'You are going to enter through the Open Tower. That's the one that only partially collapsed beside the first Tracollo from fifty years ago, which we call Tracollo One or T1. At the bottom of the Open Tower building—'

'Bottom?'

'*Listen*. At the bottom of that building there is a passage that was built along the ancient power line that connects all the buildings in the city to the original electric grid. T1 is six hundred metres away from T2, which is where we suspect Elimisha is trapped.' Birch raised a hand to ward off Alessandra's potentially pedantic objection. 'We understand that T2 did not cave in completely like T1. We don't care. We call it T2 anyway. Now. I will talk you through the details in the Map Room. Assuming you find her – and this is the part you need to remember even if it makes no sense to you – you need to confirm whether or not the internet is real. If it is, ideally, you should bring it out with you. We don't know how big it is, or how heavy, or how it works, so if you can't bring it out for any reason, we're going to need to secure it in place. This is what you have to tell us on the radio, and if that's the case, we'll secure the site and come and get you. But we'd rather you escape unnoticed with it. You should probably bring a bag.'

'Do not leave the internet unsecured. Do you understand?' Lilly added.

'I honestly don't know,' Alessandra says.

In the workshop, Bruno and Simone are sitting together at their usual bench. Eight other engineers are busy stitching together a new type of balloon for hot air invented by a man called Foggy. Almost as old as Lilly, he is one of their cleverest inventors. Noting that hot air rises and having proved it through a series of tests, he now has a plan to heat the air inside very thin sealed bags that will make them rise far beyond the height of the Snake Tower. Using three different balloons secured to strings, he wants to create a coded language based on their relative heights. Low-high-low could mean 'enter through the East Gate' for Explorers, Traders, Runners, Raiders and others working the Territory, whereas high-high-low could mean 'hold position and wait for an escort' or whatever High Command preferred. The messages are unimportant now. The issue is the engineering. He needs to figure out how to raise and sustain the balloons. Everyone is very enthusiastic about the idea, but they haven't yet solved the problems. This is currently absorbing all his attention, as Simone complains to Bruno while Bruno himself is straining to hear what's happening on the other side of the door.

'You heard what she said a few weeks ago,' Simone whispers, not even pretending to work. 'Seven voices over half a century and never in our own language and always a weak signal at night. Here it is, a voice, early in a work day with the sun up and it's loud and clear *and* in the Common tongue. And then Master Birch shows up? And we actually *stop* securing the new Knowledge so they can have some privacy? What kind of insanity is this?'

She looks at Bruno for an answer.

Lana, one of the young Engineers, suggests that maybe the airbags would rise if Foggy were to talk into them for a while, which makes everyone laugh.

None of them are at all interested in whatever's happening in Lilly's office; only the apprentices are ensnared.

'Why did they let us in?' Bruno asks.

'To write it all down. Obviously. Lilly's hand cramps up if she writes too—'

'No, that's not what I meant – why let us know all this is happening?'

'Why not?'

'The radio is working and it's saying incredibly complicated things about important subjects like how plants turn sunlight into energy – but we don't even have a research plan on that topic, and neither does the Food Centre. And then Master Birch arrives? And some kid? Who's the kid?'

'Alessandra Wayworth.'

'Wayworth as in . . . daughter of the Raiders?'

'That's the one.'

'Is she famous for something?'

'No,' says Simone, 'but her parents are legends. Maybe she's going to share a secret with them.'

'Why not invite them directly?'

'I don't know, Bruno,' Simone says, annoyed now. 'None of that is our business, is it?'

The door opens and Alessandra is the first to leave the room. Birch follows and together they exit Weapons and Communications. With Lilly's office door left open, everyone can hear Lilly turn the volume back up on the radio. The girl is still talking:

—since glucose is a basic necessity of many organisms, a correct understanding of its chemical makeup and structure contributed greatly to a general advancement in organic chemistry. This understanding occurred largely as a result of the investigations of Emil Fischer, a German chemist who received the 1902 Nobel Prize in Chemistry for his findings. I don't know about all of you, but I want to know what the Nobel Prize is. So let's take a little journey over there. Poke!

'I need to use the toilet,' Bruno says, removing his apron and placing it on the table. 'Good luck, Simone.'

'With what?'

'Everything,' he says.

BLACK JUMP

Four hours later, as the day approaches sun-high, Alessandra squats low in a wind-carved valley among three of the tallest of the remaining fourteen towers. There is no breeze now and the sand is motionless. There are, however, sounds.

Sound carries well here in the Gone World but sourcing them is nearly impossible. So many surfaces are smooth that sound ricochets the way a stone skips on water, bouncing off the windows, the solar glass, the steel and the struts.

She was taught by her parents to trust the *existence* of noises but not their perceived directions. That was when she was a little girl, maybe six or seven, when her parents had introduced her to the mysteries and unique qualities of the desert and the Gone World.

Animal cries, hoofbeats, weapons-fire, birds, people talking – these things are real and give you information. But where they are? What direction? How far away? There is no telling, so play it safe, be slow. Running, they had told her, is how we attract the young into the glamour of the work – although most Running is slower than walking.

Creeping, really.

No one would sign up to be a Creeper, though. *Might as well call us bugs.*

It is hard for Alessandra not to pull back from the reality of what she is doing and fill her own head with trivialities. Her father always said that repetition – of routes, of fighting, of running and jumping, of multiplication tables or signal codes – moves Knowledge 'from outside to the inside', until it is no longer simply Knowledge but part of us; like the food we eat and the light that passes into our eyes.

'So when you're doing something very familiar,' he had said, smiling, 'it tends to leave the mind free to wander. It's not necessarily a bad thing. But don't lose your purpose.'

This from a man who could sit speechless in a saddle for a month – with even the horse standing stock-still.

Obedient to her first mission as a Member of the Order (which she thinks she is now, but was too afraid to ask as Birch led her to the tunnel that let her slip out under the noses of the Commonwealth's Spotters), Alessandra is staying low and quiet as she makes her way to the first Tracollo, hoping no one is there. It is on the far side of four low buildings only three to five storeys high that rise out of the earth.

'No one will be there,' Birch had said.

'How do you know?'

'Because the Order has made sure they would be too afraid.'

There are birds in the sky today below the wispy clouds far above. They pass in a V-formation travelling westwards. Nothing obstructs their path.

The air looks bluer up there. Cooler. Fresher.

Better.

*

When Lilly's Tracollo fell and the second tower snapped in two, the otherwise pristine desert floor became littered with the debris of ten storeys of building. *There are surely other dead cities, she was taught, and it may be that the land there did not rise. We simply don't know. If the land did not rise, we can wonder what their own streets and High Roads might have looked like. What kinds of animals or vehicles might have wended their way through the towers in those Gone Worlds. What else might have lived or worked or remained there. But for us, here in our Territory? Between the sealed towers is only sand and the few plants that grow in it. Here are tiny animals that the birds prey on and we occasionally put into soup. But when the Big Tower snapped, it splashed its insides and outsides across the desert floor like a person throwing Raw and shinies out of a bucket.*

The Order created routes through the debris. The one that passed the first Tracollo was called the Purple Route. It led to an Archive in the deep forest to the north called *Narnia* after a book found there in a Trove. However, this time Alessandra has only three hundred metres left to travel.

Checking her lines, listening to movements and hearing only a distant rattling of metal, she sprints for a cave created by a plank of concrete falling across the pile of a rubble. They call it Marker Nine. In the back, tucked in the corner beneath a half-clothed skeleton covered in ragged cloths, are two litres of fresh water and a flare. Or that's what Runners are taught, at least.

Each of Alessandra's steps falls on an object: a rock, a piece of fallen metal, a half-buried wheel that was once carried in on a tide. When she reaches the cave she has left nothing behind, not a single footprint – which is helpful, because around the Tracollo comes a column of men moving in her direction.

They march three abreast and are led by a man of average

height but very strong build. Their clothes do not match; they are wearing nothing that clearly distinguishes them from any other tribe or clan or community or colony. No headdresses, no jewellery, no paint or piercings or colours. What does distinguish them, however, is this discipline.

Armed with swords and spears, bows and arrows and the occasional rifle, the men all walk softly and in rhythm with one another. They do not talk, cough, sneeze or spit. They flow, the way smoke flows from under a door, following one another the way one ripple in a puddle follows another.

Alessandra backs further into the darkness of the ruins. From an external zipped pouch in her sling-bag, she withdraws a thin fabric the colour of the sand and dirt and covers herself with it as she drops slowly to a prone position and becomes part of the earth in a place where no one would bother to step. From here, and in this way, she waits.

One of the men in the column closest to her breaks from formation and walks directly towards her.

Alessandra cannot lay any flatter. She cannot retreat into the dark of her cave any further and the small exit at the far back behind the skeleton is narrow.

The man stops less than a metre in front of her. The weave of this fabric lets her see out enough to realise that the man could bring his sword down on her head in a flash and she will not have time to know she is dead.

She holds her breath and waits for discovery.

Alessandra once saw a column of men. She was ten and at the top of the Snake Tower above the Stadium. She stood between her parents and watched a thousand souls – not Roamers, but people they had never seen before – pass the flats before the Commonwealth gates and, without a sound, move onwards.

'They are disciplined,' said her mother. 'We are lucky this time. Disciplined men are hard to fight. That's why we are disciplined too.'

It was the first time she had ever seen the Stadium prepare for war. But there was no war, only a Crossing, her mother had said: the brush of one tribe against another with no Union made and nothing exchanged, nothing left behind but disturbances in the sand when they were gone.

It had been, however, a sight to see, with fires on poles and the horses pulling the long trains of gear behind them.

Together, they watched the procession.

After a time, Henry muttered to herself.

'What?' Alessandra said.

'Men,' she repeated.

'What about them?'

'In some tribes it is only the men who fight. You see them?' She had pointed. 'The women are with the children in the middle.'

'Why?'

'We're not sure.'

*

It is not a sword that presses down on her covered head; it is something worse.

A heavy, acrid stream of urine hits the ground in front of her, splashing onto the fabric all around her. As he pisses he sways and, to pass the time, draws pictograms. Quickly bored of that, he adjusts his aim and blasts the top of her head.

The sounds of it – dampened, lower, with a richer splash and a pleasing gurgle from the fabric – clearly appeals to him, so he keeps at it, drilling a nice dent into whatever he thinks he's pissing on which is, in fact, at the exact spot where the two halves of Alessandra's skull are welded together.

The fabric becomes so soaked that the warm liquid flows through the stitching down into her hair, around her forehead and into her eyes, stinging them, then down further still around her nose where the rivulets gather and then drip off from the inner edges of her nostrils.

She has to open her mouth to breathe. The wet stings her lips.

He must be draining his own bodyweight of water.

Alessandra wants to take her boot knife and slice off his hose, but drawing blood would draw attention and get her captured and killed, or worse.

When he is finished he splashes the remains everywhere like a battle-dog shaking itself after a rain. He stomps his right boot three times before he spins in the sopping dust and returns to the line.

Angry, stinking and disgusted, she distracts herself by counting the rows as they pass. The foot soldiers are followed by cavalry. She estimates the number of horses. With a Runner's eye for detail she notes the weaponry. Under explicit instructions from her trainers and her parents alike, she looks for Gone World firearms and explosive weapons.

There are few, but the few are noteworthy.

In all she counts sixty rows but the smell and her disgust and her immobility may have thrown her off her concentration. Maybe there are more. Or fewer. Three columns gives her 180 troops, though. Enough to take command of the entire urbanscape if they want to.

When the men and horses and dogs have passed she continues to wait until the dust settles and the sounds have moved off.

*

Alessandra tilts her head so the remaining urine runs off the side of the fabric before removing the cloth altogether. She decides to abandon it. It might be washable but the memory will be a permanent stain. Out in the sunlight again, she notes that she is coated in filth from face to foot and utterly disgusting.

For a moment, Alessandra looks around. Behind her is an army only she has seen, an army that is marching towards the Stadium. Ahead of her is a pit into darkness and her first mission as a member of the Order: to locate Elimisha, communicate the status of the internet back to Lilly via radio, and secure the Trove one way or another.

While doing that she'll rescue Elimisha and report back on that army too.

There is a low route to the first Tracollo from here but Alessandra has opted for a high one of her own design. Armies don't always march together. Sometimes they come in waves, she's been told, and sometimes troops arrive late to guard the back. Better not to remain here among the snakes and brittle grass. Better to take to the sky with the birds instead.

Leaving the cave behind, Alessandra darts to the narrow alley between the two buildings and wedges herself into the gap. After flipping her pack around to her chest, she presses her back to one side and her feet on the other. This is why there is armour against her back. This is why her boots stick and her gloves are thick.

She slides up and then walks her feet. Practised in this manoeuvre, Alessandra can cover one metre in ten seconds. At twenty metres there is a ladder she has been told is secure which will take her directly to the roof. The door up there is locked and cannot be opened (they've tried with everything but explosives, which they can't risk) but it joins the Green Route at Marker Nineteen and from there she'll be on safe ground.

She needs two hundred seconds or three minutes and twenty seconds to reach the ladder. It is a long time to be exposed, but the passage is rarely trafficked and when it is – who would look up?

Reaching up, finally, Alessandra grabs the ladder with both hands and lets her feet slip. She dangles there by her two gloved hands, almost sixty feet up, but not for long because she needs to turn around. Taking a deep breath, she releases one hand and pivots her entire body so she is facing the building she is attached to. As quickly as she can, she replaces her hand on the bar, flips her other hand around and using her feet to help, muscles her way up three cross-bars on the ladder until her feet finally find purchase and she is safely on.

Three more metres up she reaches the top of the building and takes a breath. Her trainer has instructed her to always pause when there is a safe moment and bring the heart rate back down.

Deep breaths.

The body wants air.

At the corner of the building there is a mythical stone creature with wings, much like one of the beasts on the iron door leading into the Map Room. Together, Alessandra and the flying dog stare over the rooftop's iron edge at the distant marauders, who continue to march on.

She strains her eyes against the glare off the smooth sands and glass towers. The sun is high and ignites the alluvial plain beyond the edge of the urbanscape.

*

She leaves her rooftop friend with a pat on its stone head and meets up with the Green Route marker. All Runners have been warned that rooftops can become soft – people have been known to fall in. That's one of the reasons the Order establishes routes to follow. In this case, discreet nails have been placed into the roof, then hammered over and made to look unremarkable, giving Alessandra a path to follow across the building.

At the far corner there is another steel ladder that drops all the way to the ground. Quietly, so not to draw attention, she glides down to the risen earth, where she stops at the bottom, drops to a knee and takes a long pull from her canteen.

Not far – maybe the distance of a rock thrown by a strong boy – is the hull of a boat gleaming a lunar white. Its top third sits perfectly on the ground, turning it into a hut. The rest is below the sands of The Rise like the AIRBUS and so much else.

Alessandra meanders slowly to the boat's hull, knowing that motion attracts attention and a person sprinting is a sight to turn any head. Once there she takes shelter from any prying eyes. The stink of her hair is worse now that she's been sweating.

The entrance to the underworld is close.

When Alessandra was ten years old, her mother woke her long after moon-high on a winter night and told her to dress for the cold. Her entire class was going on a march. She wasn't prepared, but she had been raised to always be ready to flee or fight. It had been freezing. She and her classmates walked in disciplined silence. They walked for two full days with only brief stops to rest and eat during the night between. Their socks became wet and their feet swelled and their bellies begged for the unleavened bread they knew the Officers carried in their packs, but the walk taught them to suffer and to know and appreciate when they were not suffering. *This is a life of continuous readiness and warfare*, it was explained. There were other lessons:

- *The Knowledge will not keep itself safe.*
- *The Stadium is only a home.*
- *Only the Commonwealth is eternal.*
- *Socks can be replaced.*

If there were others, Alessandra cannot remember them now.

A wind is picking up. It is channelled between the buildings into a chilling blast. In her boat, a coolness finds the edges of her damp clothing. Moving again will restore warmth.

Dogs begin to bark. It's hard to know their direction and what happened with Alan Farmer means they might not be wild. Alessandra smells ripe and is upwind: she needs to get underground.

Where the tower broke in two, all those decades ago, there are still jagged edges of shattered windows. The sun, far across the southern sky, reflects its daylight through them, casting rainbows on the sands in front of her. A slat from the roof makes a ramp to the lip of the building where Alessandra is expecting a red rope that she can take down to the staircase inside.

She can't see anyone, and there are no dogs, despite what she's hearing.

Sometimes, she thinks, Runners run.

After checking that her sling-bag is secure, leather boots zipped to the top and gloves snapped tight, she sprints like a stallion across the sands to the remains of the Mutual Building. Committed, she locks her vision on the distant DANGER symbol on the ramp, willing herself towards it as though it were pulling her. Alessandra is as tall as her mother and her stride is long and powerful.

'Poise' her father calls it: a body sleek by form, her tied-back black hair streaming behind her as she runs.

Flat here, the ground. Why the ancients built their towers so far apart from one another in some places and so close in others has never made sense to her. There was usually so much pattern to their thinking when she looks at what they once made; what they once did.

Card number one hundred and forty-four of Trivial Pursuit *asks, 'What planet did the* Mariner *spacecraft visit?'*

Answer: Venus.

The Ancients had reached another *planet.*

She ran as though the world burned around her. As though fire itself was chasing her. Alessandra Wayworth, Runner of the Commonwealth, Member of the Order of Silence.

Two horsemen in black burst over a hill two hundred metres behind her. They are riding side by side. Between them is a net.

On the Green, Alessandra can cross a hundred metres in the time a water-filled jug takes to drop from the top of the flagpole to when it snags on the rope, inches from the ground. She is the second fastest woman and the eighth fastest person overall at the Stadium. The memory in her bones lets her measure the distance from here to ramp on the Mutual Building while her instincts do the maths based on the speed of her pursuers.

She isn't going to make it.

*

Alessandra slides to a stop, pulls Lilly's Python from the chest holster as fast as she can – but before she can pull the trigger, there is a crashing sound and both horsemen and their mounts disappear into a hole that their own weight and motion have created, breaking through whatever had been making this part of the Gone World flat for hundreds of years.

Twenty metres away, in a cloud of dust, the riders are . . . gone.

She hears the thud of their bodies hitting something below. The horses start baying and screaming; their legs and bodies are surely broken. What has become of the men she can't say.

For a moment Alessandra is alone.

She stands there knowing she is now supposed to go to the ramp, swing down the rope and into the gaping hole of the Mutual Building. The world – the Fates, the Gods, the Ghosts of the Ancients, the Values that whisper their promises and warnings into the ears of the people – all agree that she should exploit her dumb luck and get going.

But the blackness of the hole in front of her calls out. She has to look.

How can she not look? It pulls at her. Just a look – a glance to know what's down there, what no one has seen in living memory. Hers could be the first eyes—

Slowly, as if approaching a scared animal, Alessandra walks across the flat surface she now understands to be the roof of some buried building.

At the edge, she cannot see inside. The angle of the sun is all wrong and what light does try and penetrate the hole – a hole jagged with glass and steel struts – is captured by the dust and sand that takes hold of the light and refuses to let it pass.

With one flare she could see it all.

These are Alessandra's thoughts – until three more riders

231

turn the far corner of the Mutual Building, denying her access to the ramp and her rope and her Mission.

These riders have no net. They have intention in their eyes.

When one of them raises a rifle to his shoulder, Alessandra looks down into the swirling dust below her. Thinking of Elimisha and the internet and her mission and her parents, she makes the Black Jump.

MUSIC

When Elimisha saw the Earth spinning in front of her above the White Board she became breathless. She had never seen the Earth before and yet, as though awaking an ancient memory, she knew instantly what it was: a child returning to a lost home. There was a terror in seeing a physical object hovering in front of her but the fear was calmed by the tranquillity of the scene itself. The Earth rotated, unique and whole, leading Elimisha away from loneliness and outwards towards wonder.

As she looked and watched it slowly moving, she remembered that she had heard something too – a greeting.

'*Hello,*' a voice had said. '*How may I help you?*'

'Hello?' Elimisha says softly, looking past the sphere to the girl on the wall and after, to the open door behind her.

'Hello, how may I help you?' it repeats.

This is a man's voice. He is an adult. His voice is deep and comforting, like listening to her father when the lights are out and the bonfire on the Green flickers over the ceiling in her bedroom.

'Where are you?' she asks.

'Right here,' he answers.

'Right . . . where?'

'With you, to assist you.'

'Assist me with what?'

'Whatever you need.'

Elimisha removes the glasses. The Earth disappears.

'Can you still hear me?' she asks the voice, testing an idea that the glasses and the voice are connected, just as the images and the glasses surely are.

There is no answer.

Her trainers would tell her to breathe and control her fear. Her mother would tell her to steel her heart and remain brave. Chief Lilly would tell her to reason through the problem. 'Ask a question, think of a possible answer and then *try and prove yourself wrong*. If you fail to prove yourself wrong, it does not mean you are right. It means your confidence in your answer has gone up. That's all. Only when no one can prove you wrong can you be properly confident. But even then, you must hold onto the possibility that you might still be wrong. Why? Because maybe no one can find the flaw in your reasoning. Maybe you've reached the edge of your capacity for logic but . . . sadly . . . not the end of logic itself. Maybe, simply put, you don't know *how* to prove yourself wrong.'

This, she admitted to herself, did not sound simple. In fact, engineering logic and science were rather complicated.

'Welcome to Weapons and Communications,' had been Chief Lilly's response.

Willing to test her idea further, Elimisha repositions the glasses on her ears and nose and speaks. 'Is this is a radio?'

'The object to your left is an ICOM HAM radio, circa—'

'So . . . *you're* not a radio? That's a radio. What are you?'

'I am an artificial intelligence entity rooted in a Prometheus system, tasked with providing knowledge and services.'

'And you're . . . here with me?'

'Yes.'

'You're not a person?'

'I am an artificial intelligence entity.'

'How can someone be artificially intelligent? Doesn't that mean stupid?'

'In this case it means inorganic.'

'You're inorganically intelligent?'

'Yes.'

Elimisha could tell that Lilly – if she were standing over her shoulder – would not be impressed with Elimisha's line of questioning. She would be directing her to get focused. *Get to what matters*, she would be saying.

'Can you hurt me?'

'No.'

'Do you want to hurt me, whether or not you can?'

'I am tasked with providing knowledge and services. I have no motive or capacity to cause you deliberate harm.'

'What about unintentional harm?'

'I cannot fully anticipate the consequences of providing you with requested knowledge or services.'

'So you can partially anticipate it?'

'Some images, video, music and information have been known to widely cause distress or be age-inappropriate. As I get to know you, the better I can provide you with knowledge and services that will not likely cause harm, if that is the setting you prefer. However, the consequences of learning cannot be predicted. Will you permit me to learn your preferences?'

'Yes. What's a video?'

'A moving image.'

'How can you move an image?'

'By taking hundreds, thousands, millions or billions of images and displaying them at a frame rate that exceeds the human eye's capacity to distinguish one from another as separate images, thereby creating the illusion of motion.'

'Show me a video.'

'Of what?'

'Something interesting.'

'I don't know your preferences well enough to anticipate your interests. Would you like to start a new profile that allows me to learn your interests and preferences?'

'Sure.'

'Would you like me to restrict harmful content as I come to determine it?'

'No.

'What is your name?'

'Elimisha.'

'Elimisha. Swahili for "educate", to be a giver of knowledge.'

'What's Swahili?'

'Swahili, also known as Kiswahili, is a Bantu language and the first language of the Swahili people. It is commonly spoken in the African Great Lakes region and in other parts of eastern and southeastern Africa, including Kenya, Tanzania, Uganda, Rwanda, Burundi, some parts of Malawi, Somalia, Zambia, Mozambique and the Democratic Republic of the Congo, also called the DRC. At its height, it was spoken by tens of millions of people.'

Elimisha knows what a language is and she knows what a lake is. Beyond that, none of the words mean anything. However, that isn't the interesting part.

'How do you know all that? And so quickly?' Elimisha asks, continuing to watch the Earth spin and realising it must be a 'video'.

'My systems have access to numerous archives and can access them rapidly.'

'You're a Librarian?'

There is a pause before the Prometheus system says, 'Yes.'

'How big is your Archive?'

'Approximately one hundred and forty exabytes. Unfortunately, access is currently limited because of severe damage to the sub-oceanic cables, wide-spread hub- and storage-failures and the inaccessibility of the satellite networks.'

'Uh huh. So . . . it's big but used to be bigger?'

'Yes.'

'Bigger than the Central Archive at the Commonwealth?'

'I have no information on that facility.'

'What's in your Archive?'

'Everything.'

'Let me ask it differently,' Elimisha says to the globe, for lack of anything else to look at. 'We classify knowledge into geography, entertainment, history, arts and literature, science and nature and sports and leisure. Do you have information on all those things?'

'Yes.'

'So you have six flags on . . . everything.'

'Images, videos, books, music—'

'Wait,' Elimisha says, 'you have music?'

The voice of Lilly – over her shoulder – tries to get a word in again to redirect her to what's essential but this time Elimisha is not interested and pushes her away. She wants to know this.

'I have more than one hundred million songs dating from Édouard-Léon Scott de Martinville's performance of "Au clair de la lune" in 1860, through Riddhi Chakma's *Hip-Hop Renaissance Volume Four* uploaded from Bogra, Bangladesh in—'

'Okay, okay,' Elimisha says, overwhelmed by the words, the speed, the spans of time, the new names, the foreign languages, the presence of a disembodied voice – and the dawning understanding that here, with a White Board and a pair of glasses and her Haptic Command Gear, is a gateway to an Archive that has no walls, no shelves, no Librarians, no paper or boxes or towering ceilings, no Scribes or Evaluators or Archivists or Runners. An Archive that appears to have no limits.

Elimisha removes the glasses for a moment and rubs her face.

She pushes her curls out of her way and replaces the glasses, telling herself, *Get a grip on yourself.*

The building, she knows, has solar windows like the Stadium. One of the questions at Weapons and Communications, when she apprenticed there, was why had the Towers no electricity if they could create it from the sun? Surely the power goes into a battery made of water, like it does at the Stadium, right? But clearly not, because the intact towers were dark inside. Perhaps all the lights were broken? But that seemed unlikely, when the illumination panels at the Stadium still worked.

Foggy, one of the senior Engineers, had a theory that the building didn't generate electricity for itself, like the Stadium did. Maybe it contributed to powering everything and used only a bit of what it produced for itself. In that case, maybe the tall towers are all part of something broken; they collect electricity but have no means of sending it to its final destination.

Foggy said the answers would lie underground, in some kind of physical connections between or among the buildings. Lilly agreed and said it was a pity, therefore, that no one would ever learn the answer.

Except this 'Prometheus system': this still worked.

'Why are you working when everything else is broken?' Elimisha asks.

'Because I was designed to survive,' it says.

For several moments Elimisha sits and watches the Earth. She had no idea it was covered by so much water; that there were so many stretches of land unconnected to others. The top had a little snow and the bottom had a lot. Many sections were beige like the desert but other parts were green. The scale was beyond her comprehension. The atmosphere was so thin.

From her perspective – out in space, where she sits – there are no people. If she were to move closer she would find some, those in the Territory, at least, and a few in the northern forest and maybe out at the colony at Anchorpoint where the Traders go to collect salt and whatever might have washed ashore this year. But Anchorpoint is a month's journey to the northwest and no one really knows how far the waters stretch.

Looking at the planet, it occurs to her that she has no idea where they actually live – which part of this sphere is hers. She is tempted to ask, but the solitude is playing on her mind more heavily than the expanse in front of her.

'You said you had music. I want to hear some.'

'What music would you like to hear?'

Elimisha had never heard music that wasn't being played or sung directly in front of her by musicians. The very notion that she could listen to it in their absence was wild. She had heard music echoing down corridors, though, and she had heard it come through her window from the Green when she wasn't looking. Maybe it would be best to think of it like that.

'What music did other people request?' Elimisha asks.

'When and where?' asks the Prometheus system, always aiming towards precision.

'How about here, at the end. What music did people want to hear when everything was . . . ending?'

Instead of an answer using words, a gentle piano chord fills her ears, a sound Moishe might create. That chord rings and is soon followed by four other notes rising up a scale as though climbing a short hill together. The final note plays again – and a second piano plays two soft accompanying notes as though it were a bird song in the background. When they fade, the chords walk back down the hill to rejoin the first. It is when that note repeats and steps away from the little hill that Elimisha feels she has been invited into a melody she has never heard before. Inside the doorway of that new experience is a chorus of men's voices that rise up behind the gentle piano, making way for the warmest, most gentle, most kind singing voice that Elimisha has ever heard. He sings to her and to all the people who are facing death. After a gentle introduction, the man's voice blows through Elimisha's soul like the white light of eternity and tears race from her eyes as her chest constricts and he croons, '*Lean on me . . .*'

For the next four minutes she is exposed to poetry, rhythm, tenderness, love, pain, memory, hope and the terrible and vast expanse between what was lost and what little remains.

As Bill Withers' voice sings out the last notes, Elimisha stands, picks up the axe, drags it down the corridor and beats the concrete wall beside the blast door, trying to get out with everything that is trapped inside until she collapses into a sweaty heap and sobs.

Over the next two weeks Elimisha gains a rudimentary under-standing of the White Board and the glasses and suit; of nanotechnology and how the nanites of the White Board are taking their commands from her operator cues, creating tactile surfaces that allow her to type or steer or feel or use tools that were faster by hand than voice. She comes to see how the arti-ficial intelligence listens and learns from her; mimics her use of terms, metaphors and analogies to help her better accom-plish her tasks in the most natural ways. The disembodied man's voice speaking to her learns her accent and inflections and comes to feel like a companion sent directly from the Commonwealth to rescue her.

In the morning she rises and exercises and beats at the hole, trying to get out. After that, she showers and eats. Once her body is calm and her mind clear, she sits down with the internet and explores.

One afternoon she flies like a bird across the Mediterranean Sea, south of Piraeus in Greece, to where Sparta's and Athen's forces had once clashed. She watches a re-enactment of the battle as though she is hanging over it one minute and in the fray itself the next. Another day she strolls through the Louvre, circa 2051, on a five-hour tour guided by the profes-sional curator who speaks Elimisha's language but with the most delicate of accents. Jumping to 2073, she enjoys a laser-light show of the Pyramids at Giza celebrating the hundredth anniversary of *The Dark Side of the Moon*, a record album by a rock and roll band called Pink Floyd.

She drives a car at Le Mans; SCUBA-dives in the Comoros Islands before the coral reefs died; goes sky-diving over Shanghai; sits at a clam shack on the coast of Maine watching the Atlantic Ocean lapping the craggy rocks as the light fades behind her, then sees that same sun set into the Pacific Ocean between the twin rocks at Rockaway Beach in Oregon.

There is nothing she cannot experience with the internet and the Haptic Command Suit, no place she can't go ... no place except home.

'Do you know another way out of here?' she asks it.

No.

'Why can't you contact people for me?' she asks later.

Because there is no one else using the system.

'If you were designed to survive, why isn't anyone else here?'

Because, it explains, *people were not.*

After days of this, days of deep loneliness and fear and occasional bouts of hopelessness, she would sometimes close her eyes and tell the computer to put her on top of a mountain above a forest and then feel the air all over her body and pretend she was outside and free.

Eventually, her spelunking through the Archive led her to wonder about how it had all ended. The man's voice answered her simply, because the greatest mystery in the world now was no mystery at all when it happened. With time to learn the new vocabulary, Elimisha came to a basic understanding: On November 19, 2097, at 08:02 UTC, a single if extraordinary flare from the sun knocked out a network of mission-critical orbiting satellites, cutting off vital communications and data systems and setting the world ablaze with geopolitical recriminations. Governments and corporations were quick to accuse one another of capitalising on the flare's unbalancing effects. A century's mismanagement of diplomatic relations and multilateral processes, and the de facto abandonment of global institutions – all designed to prevent and manage catastrophic destruction – had left the planet fragile. Accusations quickly escalated into military actions which fuelled reprisals until one state – arguing that a first strike was the only rational response left – unleashed a bio-engineered nanotech weapon that targeted people with specific genetic markers. The victimised countries promptly launched coordinated nuclear strikes on the antagonist, obliterating the population and triggering a programmed retaliation from sea- and space-based weapons. The biogenetic weapon – which had never been fully tested – quickly mutated and spread from the targeted population to everyone else on Earth.

Forests decayed into deserts and land gave way to waters. Particulates from the bombings transformed the night skies from black to green.

Everything that had once been connected now stood alone.

They called it the Solar War. Less than twenty-four hours into the crisis it became clear that it was going to threaten all life on Earth. The military in this part of the world started rapidly carving out emergency tunnel systems to link buildings and utilities below-ground, in case large populations needed to move into conjoined shelters. Robotic excavation was advanced at this time, Elimisha learned, and commercial androids were immediately re-tasked, becoming efficient digging machines – until they too fell apart.

In the expectation of biohazards and contamination, bunkers were fitted with fail-safe devices to seal in the affected and destroy the bunkers so that others might live.

How anyone survived at all, Elimisha didn't know. The records stopped.

What Elimisha does know is that she is trapped, alone, and now responsible for the greatest repository of Knowledge in the history of human civilisation.

*

243

This is a Trove: Knowledge at rest. One way or another, she is duty-bound to protect it. Looking at the radio, she decides that if she can't get out, at least some of the Knowledge can.

ADAM WAS HERE

A Black Jump is the worst of all choices that comes at the end of all the worst outcomes because the only time a Runner faces a Black Jump is when everything meant to support her in the field – the educators, the Agoge, the trainers, the Order of Silence, the military troops – has failed. A Black Jump is literally a jump into the unknown. It can go down for ever, or end in anything – water, rubble, spikes . . . It is an act of utter desperation, which is everything the Commonwealth is structured to avoid.

Alessandra has no time to think about any of this as she jumps into the dark pit.

She falls in preparation of a drop that will last for ever. If she lands at all, she will need to buckle her legs and roll out of it. Arms crossed as if in death, she lets the air out of her lungs and tries not to scream or close her eyes.

But she does both.

Down . . .

A five-metre fall ends on something soft and forgiving.

Knees bent, her legs absorb the hit and Alessandra rolls off the dead horse onto a floor made of stone. In the room now, not above it, she can see. What's hard is breathing.

The dust is chalk-white and blacks out her view in most directions.

Head still dizzy, she crawls back to the horse and pulls Lilly's revolver out of its pouch. It has three green markers for sighting: when she aligns the two in the back with the one in the front they form a perfect line showing her that she has taken aim.

Her mother is the expert shot but it was her father who taught her to fight in enclosed spaces. *Lean into the fight*, he would say.

Gun up, Alessandra quiets her breathing and tries to calm her heart, which is still pounding from the fear of the jump. Time isn't making sense any more; she cannot tell if she's been down here ten seconds or two minutes. She isn't sure what's still in motion from the drop and what motion belongs to something else – something with motive.

There is a noise to her right that is terrifyingly close.

Figuring *everything* is hostile, she twists to her right, throws her back against the soft stomach of the horse and fires.

The bullet blows a hole in the other horse's head. The flash from the barrel lights up a man on his knees, one hand closing around a fallen rifle.

She shoots twice more and the report is absorbed into the vastness of the building, a room as large as the Sharing Room in the Central Archive.

That's three bullets fired. Three more in the cylinder. She *must* keep track. But that's not all: now she has to move.

Positions, her father had explained, *get used up, just like ammunition. People make the mistake of getting too comfortable when things are working out. If you're firing from an exposed position, change it up. Especially in the dark, because of the muzzle flash.*

His advice saves her life. She rolls away and takes to a prone position by the second dead horse as three bullets riddle her old position. The man has not only missed his mark, he has also given away his own position in the dust. Alessandra kills him with one shot.

That's it. Two men on two horses. They're all that's down here. *Not up there, though.*

As fast as possible, she scampers away from the dead all around her to look for a staircase to take her down, because there is no point in even trying to get back up, not with an army wanting her dead.

Knowing other men will soon be looking down – and maybe with those flash-bombs her mother had said preceded Elimisha's Tracollo – Alessandra hustles to the edge of the room, away from the hole in the roof.

This is some kind of great hall or maybe a party room. Her back is pressed against a tall glass wall that looks out onto dirt and sand. In front of her is a fountain with a spiralling sheet-metal sculpture adorning the centre. At the centre of the wall to her right is a wide, elegant staircase going down, and in her liner pocket is the map of how to get from Lilly's Tracollo to Elimisha's.

Though it is only a guess, she is pretty sure that the journey from one to the other passes through this building, and if it does, the answer lies beneath.

As Alessandra stands and runs across the polished, perfect but dust-coated floor to the staircase – and, hopefully, the resumption of her Mission – three men emerge at the rim of the hole above. As one of them tosses down a rope, Alessandra disappears down the stairs, taking them two at a time into the unknown.

*

The Harrington Box has a book of ancient Greek myths. One of them tells the story of the Labyrinth at Knossos. As Alessandra descends into the black without a light, trusting that the stairs will go on and on and that the directions she memorised from Birch are correct, she finds herself thinking about Theseus.

In the introduction to that story, it says the word for a ball of yarn in Middle English was *clewe*. Later, as the years passed and language changed, the spelling became clew, losing its final 'e'. The homophone was clue, and, 'Today,' said the book, 'we use *clues* likes balls of yarn in the labyrinth at Knossos to find our way through the maze of our mysteries.'

The lesson for that day at the Agoge had been that the current world is always built on the foundations of the past and that civilisation rises, layer on layer, to new possibilities: word building on word, story on story, but constructed less like a tower and more like a mountain. 'What is built,' said the teacher, 'cannot be so easily destroyed.'

There are skeletons and bodies as she arrives at the bottom. Water has collected there and she hesitates before accepting that she has to step in.

When she does, her foot slips on a femur and she falls into the black water and rises freezing and cursing and angry. Very angry.

It is too much. She removes a glowstick from her jacket and cracks it, revealing a massive puddle or water reservoir. The room is long and rectangular, with a hallway on her right and a series of doors to her left. There are pictures on the walls, abstract images that may have once been considered 'art'. A thick algae has grown up the walls and over the surfaces of tables.

Glowstick up, the pistol and its remaining bullets pointing

ahead, she whispers to the dead around her, 'There had better be a fucking tunnel down here.'

The switch-backs of the stairs disoriented her but she is reasonably certain she's moving westwards now, back in the direction of Elimisha's new Tracollo. As she walks, Alessandra looks for an Order Marker called Albert Wormwood, the name of an artist carved into a brass plaque under one of the paintings on her right – and she finds it.

Yes.

If she had reached the first Tracollo, headed to the bottom and followed Birch's instructions, she would have passed through here. So she is back *en route*.

The surface of the water is covered in dust. It doesn't move like water as she walks through it; it is more like a giant bed-sheet roiling up and down with the wind.

Theseus was looking for a Monster. Alessandra is hoping to avoid them.

The recent collapse, she tells herself, shook up the nearby structures and weakened the glass ceiling that the riders fell through. It was dumb luck – or, seen another way, it was the inevitable result of the Gone World falling in on itself and being attacked with explosives. Of course it was weakened. What else?

Alessandra follows the route in her head. She follows trust: trust in Adam and his map. Trust in Birch. Trust in Lilly. Trust in her own memory. Trust that the ground has not shifted under her feet – beneath the water – yet again.

Moving through a series of open doors, past old machines that were once used for washing clothes, she arrives at a wall with a hole in it that is shaped like a coffin with rounded edges. This is not something that was part of the building when it was erected; it was added later. It appears to have been blasted out, or somehow carved. Though different in shape and texture, it reminds her of the tunnels beneath the Stadium used by Soldiers and Traders and Runners.

Alessandra follows the water into it, running her fingers along the wall as much for support as to connect to something beyond her own fears.

At almost the same instant, she hears two distinct sounds from opposite directions. The first, ahead of her, is a whistle: air is passing through a small opening with enough force to leave a note. There is also a kind of throbbing. It is even and – if the idea isn't too preposterous to consider – actually sounds like drum beats.

The second sound is footfalls on the stairs behind her. The bastards are still coming for her.

Being inside the tunnel is a risk; maybe an unacceptable one. Behind her are Keepers and ahead of her is – *what*? It's impossible to know. She could back out and stand her ground, try and fight but she doesn't know how many are coming. Sound, she well knows, can be deceptive. Or she can continue and hope for the best.

Back to trust again.

A black cable appears on the ceiling, running away from her. It's held in place by U-shaped clamps hammered into the stone at regular intervals. The Ancients not only dug this tunnel but ran electricity through it.

It must go someplace, she reasons. *There has to be something ahead.*

Alessandra commits to going there – but not with the glow-stick. That only makes her a target. There are four more in her sling-bag, so she tosses it behind her into the water and walks on.

They'll still know she's in the tunnel, but when they're standing over the green glow, *they* will be the targets.

The water behind her is illuminated. The first feet splash to-

250

wards the glowstick. Ahead of her is the black shape of the
tunnel itself, where the sound grows louder and louder as she
rushes forward. There is no way it could be but – if she had to
put a name to it – she would have to call the sound . . . *music*.

And in that music is a man's voice telling her to 'stay alive'.

Alessandra moves as fast as she can in the dim light until a
shape begins to take form in front of her.

It is a half-naked, fully-grown man with steel claws for hands.

SPY

Bruno is not an experienced rider. When he was a child he occasionally rode in front of his mother during their long journey from the East, but that only acquainted him with the challenges of being in a saddle. Speed, command, pursuit – these were not his special skills. When Alessandra stole out of the eastern-most tunnel he was able to follow her because they were both on foot. After several kilometres, in the burn of the late morning, she met her contact, Aaron son-of-Shauna, a horse wrangler for the Dragoons, who placed her on a horse used by the Order. He'd seen this one in action before. It was scared of nothing. As she rode off, Aaron and his horse were left behind.

Not being observed in the exit tunnel had been hard enough. He'd had to hide in the shadows, then jog across the desert to make up for the time he'd lost. But fighting Aaron for his own horse was harder. Although he was a Keeper by birth and belief, Bruno had grown soft during his ten years at the Stadium. It turned out apprenticeships with the farmers and Scribes and archers and Chief Lilly had done little to teach him how to walk into a fight.

Luckily for him, Aaron was no better.

'Bruno?' he'd asked, seeing him approach. 'What are you doing here?'

There was an answer – one that no one had suspected and he'd had to keep to himself for year after painful year as he waited for the rest of his people and the Leader himself to arrive – but it was not, even now, an answer he wanted to share.

He walked up to Aaron and said, 'I need your horse. There's something Alessandra forgot. I'm to give it to her.'

Turned out Aaron wasn't quite as gullible as all that. He started, 'I have my orders from—'

So Bruno struck him with a rock on the side of his head, dropping him to the earth with one blow, where the blood ran thick into the sand. It should have been easier. His heart shouldn't have raced the way it did and there should have been no hesitation or guilt. But there was, and that was because the softness of the Commonwealth had entered him. So much talk about the past and what used to be there and so much more about the future and what should come next . . . it was spreading him thin, making him lose focus, allowing Time to play on his mind.

Aaron lay on the ground. Whether he was dead or not was of little significance. Bruno needed the horse to confirm Alessandra's destination, which was the one part of the story he wasn't able to guess. He'd been able to piece things together well enough to know that now was the time for him to report back for the final time. The radio worked again and Lilly had heard something she considered so secret that she needed to see the Master of the Order of Silence rather than General Winters. It was something so important that she needed to recruit someone who was outside the chain of command. It was something so urgent that Alessandra daughter-of-Henrietta needed to leave immediately. And it was all because of a voice on the radio that was close and sitting on a Trove that could 'change everything'.

The return of Alessandra's parents flying all six flags had been a spectacle, one that Bruno had thought significant, but still he had stayed. It had been a good decision to wait and see if any more came out of the ground. Apparently, the single fuse mattered a great deal more than the flags.

On horseback, following Alessandra, he is finally free. This is the end of his time as a spy – no more pretending to be an Urban Explorer so he can sneak off with information for his people while the others break minor rules and try to add lines to a nearly worthless map to test their own mettle.

No more lies. No more deception. No more pretence of helping these people bring back the horrors that killed so many people.

They were not *bad* people. Some were good and kind. But they were misguided, and as the Leader always said, 'Our mercy is their greatest weapon.'

It became clear after half a day tracking Alessandra that her destination was the first hole in the ground that went to the bottom. What wasn't clear to Bruno was why Alessandra was going to look in that hole for the voice on the radio – but the Leader might know the answer and that was enough for now.

An hour ago he broke off his tracking and headed to Yellow Ridge to meet his people.

Now, he rides up to greet them.

The camp at Yellow Ridge has massively expanded since last Bruno visited, four months ago. The tents are spread out and wide enough for four soldiers to engage on any avenue as needed. There is no effort being made to hide their positions, but fortifications have been built using Raw to protect it in case the Stadium becomes expeditionary. Bruno himself has carried the message that an attack here is unlikely. It runs against the General's character and her beliefs that the Stadium is smart and the barbarians are fools and will eventually break themselves against the walls the way birds fly into the windows of the towers and never learn.

Still in his mourning robe, the Leader walks to greet him as he dismounts. He will hand the horse over to the *caballero* later. For now, holding the reins steadies him. It is quite a moment, knowing he is back for good, that he has decided for the second time in his life to turn away from everything he knows for a cause greater than himself.

'How are you?' the Leader asks him.

'I'm well,' Bruno reports, wiping his face with the clean cloth handed to him by a child he doesn't know. 'I have no injuries. I'm shaky, though, and emotional. I have important news. Because of this news and how I left, I won't be able to return to them. I am here now.'

'I see,' the Leader replies. A crowd has gathered around them and the Leader makes no effort to send them away. What Bruno has to tell him privately will come later. For now, they are all one.

'Tell us: in all those years, have they changed you?' the Leader asks him.

The horse snorts and pulls on the reins. Bruno calms it with a touch. 'Yes,' he admits. 'They think differently about so much that the only way to stay present within myself was not to fight the ways I was changing. I found pleasure in their rituals and their company. I found loneliness too. I grew from being a boy of seventeen to a man of twenty-seven. These were important years. There was love and loss during that time too. Coming back is . . . wonderful, and also painful.'

The people listen. Some nod.

'There are good people there,' he says, repeating himself to explain it better. 'Some are kind and funny – I was in love with a girl for three years. Some are cruel, they would walk over the bleeding to serve themselves. In this way they are like all other people: no better and no worse. They are systematic and imaginative and I admire that. They have a hunger for happiness and rejoicing that I will be sad to see end because there isn't enough of it.'

'Have they convinced you of their way?' the Leader asks him.

Bruno, having anticipated this question, nods, acknowledging it, then shakes his head as an answer.

'No, Leader. They accumulate knowledge believing that it will teach them how the Gone World ended so that the same mistakes might not be made. But really, they hoard what they learn and don't become any wiser. They speak about the Gone World constantly, but they don't humble themselves to what they don't know; they simply keep pressing and pushing for more, as though their own ability to ask questions is enough reason for answering them. It never occurs to them that their path might lead to the same weapons, the same relationships, the same errors, the same consequences as those they fear. I think this is because they lack humility. They are arrogant and single-minded and have organised themselves to go only one direction without questioning whether they should be going anywhere at all. They cannot stand aside from themselves and see what they are doing and imagine the harm it may bring.'

'This direction they are going,' the Leader asks, 'does it follow the Ancients or does it lead another way?'

'Their future seems to be the world's past. If they are taking their learning in another direction, I don't know what it is. As best I can tell, they don't know either. They simply press on. A horse with no reins.'

'And we know where that road leads,' he says.

'Yes, Leader.'

'You feel sorry for them?'

'Yes.'

'We're stopping them, Bruno, not punishing them. If words were enough, we would use them.'

'Have we had those words yet, Leader?'

'What do you mean?'

'Is there no last conversation to be had? One final chance to stop what comes next?'

'Their Archive is a seed,' the Leader says, 'that will grow into the plant that strangles the life out of the world. Surely it needs to be stopped now.'

'Yes, of course,' Bruno concedes. 'But what if they could be convinced?'

'Come back to the tent. We can discuss the rest with the Deputy. Take your time,' he adds. 'There is no rush.'

The Leader turns to go, but Bruno stops him with a hand on his arm.

'Actually, there is,' Bruno corrects him. 'Time presents itself again, Leader. There's a girl travelling through the desert. I think I know where she's going but I don't know why.'

He speaks of the radio and Alessandra and the voice and the Trove, trying to explain Lilly's insistence that this changes everything, though he can't find the meaning in her phrase. He tells the Leader about Master Birch being consulted and the girl's secret departure, speculating that Alessandra is going underground to find the source of the radio.

'The bottom can't be reached,' the Leader says. 'There is Sickness there. They're looking in the wrong place.'

'There are those who believe that tunnels connect the deepest places in the Gone World, Leader. Alessandra might be trying to use them to reach her destination even though it's buried.'

'What about the Sickness?' the Leader asks.

Bruno knows that the Leader's daughter died from illness, and the wife too, a most generous and kind woman with a beauty that could break a young man's heart. So he tries to phrase his idea as gently as possible. 'Perhaps the Sickness of the world now is not the same as the one that killed the Ancients,' he says. 'Perhaps,' he says, not looking the Leader in the eye for fear of causing him unnecessary pain, 'there is only a Sickness above the ground, although most of the dead are beneath.'

The Leader knows his people killed two Runners and he had thought the third was killed in the building's collapse. Perhaps she survived – and if she did, he knows where she is, although getting there is another matter.

'We have troops coming here from the north, but they don't know the Territory. I'll send men,' the Leader concludes.

'They'll need a net,' says Bruno.

STAYING ALIVE

The Librarian provides Elimisha with almost three hundred and fifty years of recorded music, including pieces written much earlier and recorded centuries later, which amounts to a thousand years or more of musical exploration – almost none of which she'll hear before she dies down here and all of which will be buried unheard if she does.

Once again, per her daily routine, she stands in front of the hole with her axe, sweat from an hour's work dripping down her skin and her eyes shining with determination and hostility. She pulls the axe back with her gloved hands and yet again lets the blade hack into the chalky concrete in time to the beat of her latest musical selection, 'You Make Me Feel Like Dancing' by one Leo Sayer.

Despite the Librarian's protestations about limited access and the destruction or inaccessibility of many mirrored sites and data centres, there are a dozen-times-a-dozen lifetimes of music for her to listen to and even after taking an eight-hour music-appreciation course (she should have slept, she knows it, but it's so hard to rest with so much to learn at her fingertips) she doesn't entirely understand how one era of music differs

259

from another. What she does understand is that the beat really picks up in the 1960s and then it all gets 'funky' in the 1970s.

And funky is good.

From then on the beat never really stops. She's been trying to take it in order but it's been too much.

When the Librarian offered to 'curate a playlist to her interests' and she said, 'Sure—' it asked what kind of mood she was in. Elimisha didn't know what kind of mood she was in other than bitter, angry, resentful, self-destructive, hopeful, overwhelmed, sad and dutiful – for which there seemed to be no single word – so it asked her what she planned to do while listening.

'I'm going to break out of a bomb shelter with an axe.'

So the Librarian made a playlist for that.

What she has learned – and is now the only person in the world to know this – is that if you're trying to chop your way through a four-hundred-year-old wall, music by the following people and bands really helps: ABBA, Lenny Kravitz, Gin Wigmore, Beyoncé, Stevie Wonder, Kool & the Gang, Aretha Franklin, David Bowie, New Order, and her favourites so far – The Bee Gees.

'Stayin' Alive' is what she listens to most often.

As Elimisha hammers away to the dulcet wailings of Barry, Robin and Maurice Gibb, two gunshots pop from the direction of the kitchen, followed by a woman's scream, an explosion and a massive crashing sound from inside the kitchen itself.

'Librarian, turn off the music,' she instructs, lowering the axe and looking back at the T-junction. She knows that she heard something, but after a month alone underground she isn't sure that what she heard was real. There is always a chance she is losing her mind.

There is nothing – not a sound . . . at least, not until she hears someone kick a pot across the concrete floor of the kitchen and swear like a drunk Dragoon at the midsummer party.

Axe tight in her grip, Elimisha limps to the corner of the hall that splits to the kitchen on her right and the Communications Room far down the hall to the left.

If this is a hallucination, she thinks, *it is so obvious as to be trite.* 'I can't get out so my brain has made another door. Obviously. And the person in the kitchen is going to be a version of me. I wonder if anyone's studied dreams before? I'll bet someone has.'

Her hands throb to the beat of her heart inside her leather gloves. Her muscles twitch from an hour hitting the wall.

Axe in hand, leg dragging, she limps to the kitchen door, pausing every now and then to listen for any sounds; any confirmation.

Quietly, and with minimal pressure, Elimisha presses down on the handle to unlatch the door and with a gentle hand she pushes it open – to find a young woman with a pistol standing in front of her over a dead body.

Elimisha isn't sure if the vision is real. The girl is wearing a Runner's uniform and looks to be her age. Her face is red with blood and her eyes are fierce.

She looks familiar. She sort of looks like the girl in the Pirelli calendar if the girl in the Pirelli calendar was muscular and bathed in blood and pointing a gun at her chest.

The girl raises the gun at Elimisha and shouts, 'Drop the stick! Now!'

Elimisha looks at the girl, who doesn't fire. Her reactions and her eyes and her speech and that gun – she admits to herself – are awfully life-like for a hallucination.

'Are you real?' she asks.

'Am I what?'

The girl really does look familiar. She both is and isn't a version of Elimisha herself: same Runner gear, same age, almost the same height, but lighter skin and her hair is much, much filthier. Whatever issues Elimisha might have been having with her curls earlier, they are long gone.

She may not be a ghost after all.

'Who the fuck are you and how did you get in here?' she asks.

'I'm Alessandra Wayworth, Archive Runner for the Commonwealth.'

Elimisha knows the name – she knows such a girl – but she isn't at all sure that the beast in front of her is really Alessandra Wayworth. But that's only of passing interest compared to her second question.

'How did you get in here?'

'The . . . tunnel,' Alessandra says, looking back the way she'd come in.

The metal shelf with the poisonous canned foods has been pushed over to reveal a tunnel. It is crude, the edges rough, but the dimensions are perfect: a passage out carved by a machine.

'Elimisha,' says Alessandra, 'you know me. Can you put down the axe, please?'

Elimisha grips her axe tighter. 'Are you real?' she asks again.

'I was sent to find you. I was followed. They tossed some of those little bombs after me – the ones they must have used on you. The tunnel collapsed behind me, so now I'm stuck in here with you. I assume we're stuck?'

The look Elimisha gives her removes any doubt.

'Is this an Archive?' Alessandra asks, because she was instructed to ask.

'Yes,' Elimisha answers, lowering the axe as Alessandra lowers the gun.

'Is anyone else here?'

'Not . . . exactly,' she answers.

'We heard you on the radio. That's how we found you.'

'You heard me?'

'You were talking about plants.'

'Why didn't you answer me?'

'Lilly's microphone doesn't work.'

'Who did you kill?' Elimisha says, looking down at the body below Alessandra and realising she probably should have asked about this earlier but – when? Everything feels equally important at this point and the dead can wait.

'Don't worry about him. How big's the Trove, Chief?'

'Chief?'

'This is an Archive at rest and you're securing it, right?'

'I guess so. Yes.'

'Then you're the Chief, Chief.'

Chief Elimisha releases her axe and feels a buzzing, prickly sensation in her palm as her fingers finally unclench. On instinct, after years of drilling, she looks at the Runner on the floor and asks, 'Do you need food, water or medical attention?'

Through the damp, the grime, the smell of gunpowder and urine, Alessandra hears the words of order and structure come from a girl even more trapped and scared than she is and begins to laugh.

Elimisha, hearing her, begins, slowly at first, to laugh too. And once the emotion fills her chest, she starts to cry. The muscles in her shoulders seem to collapse like a falling tower and she drops the axe as she sobs.

Alessandra rushes over to embrace her.

Behind Alessandra and in front of Elimisha is the half-naked and well-shot-up body of the claw-man. Alessandra not only hit him twice but also stabbed him through the neck with a dagger.

He's lying on his back.

Elimisha, calmer now, wipes her face and stands to examine the body.

'It was dark and I was very scared,' Alessandra says from behind her. 'Those guys were coming up fast behind me and this guy was about five metres from me. I fired. I think that's why they stopped following me and chucked in the grenades instead.'

The body looks like a man in his thirties, with skin like Alessandra's – what people at the Stadium call *leaf-brown* – and eyes much darker than Elimisha's. They stare, wide-eyed and open, at the ceiling above him.

He isn't a person, though. It never was.

He – it – is dressed in workman's overalls, unsnapped to reveal a bare, hairless chest of fine but not unusual definition. He wears thick leather boots. Instead of hands attached to the wrists, there are thick metal claws with blunted ends. Alessandra is examining them closely as Elimisha tentatively pokes the chest with her finger. There is some kind of dried blood on the chest, but not splattered from the shot. It looks more like a decoration, as though it was painted on for some reason. The blood has flaked off, so Elimisha is having trouble finding meaning in it.

'The shape of these claws are the same shape as the tunnel texture. I think this thing carved the tunnels out somehow,' Alessandra says.

Elimisha can now see that the blood on the chest is definitely writing of some kind. Alessandra steps over the body and straddles it for a clearer view. The writing is very old and very smeared and what is left has turned to a blackened crust. Once her eyes see the words, though, there is no mistaking the message.

'It says "Adam was here",' Elimisha says.

'Oh,' says Alessandra, 'you're right – it does. I see it now.'

'Adam was Lilly's cousin. This is the proof! The tunnels are real! The Adamists were right.'

Alessandra stops looking at the claws and gives Elimisha a pathetic look. 'I just came out of the tunnels. The *tunnels* are the proof that the tunnels are real. Not the graffiti.'

'That's . . . also true.'

'Master Birch already briefed me on this. That's how I found you – and why we're not dead from the Sickness.'

'Why aren't we dead from the Sickness?' Elimisha asks.

'There isn't any.'

'Oh . . . no, there is. Or there was. There's no question about it. I've seen them – in the Inferno Room.'

'The what?'

'I don't want to talk about it,' she says, walking over to the tunnel and starting to crawl inside.

'You can't get out that way. They collapsed the tunnel.' Alessandra sticks a finger into the hole she made between the claw-man's eyes. 'So amazing.'

'What the hell is it?' Elimisha asks.

'It's a machine shaped like a person. Maybe it was meant to act like one too.' Alessandra looks up. 'Maybe these are the ghosts everyone talks about.' She raises one of the legs. 'It once walked around – look, see? The boot's soles are worn down. Maybe it kept walking after everyone died, the way some machines kept going. Are you okay?'

'You just stuck your finger into its brain.'

'It's . . . a machine.' Alessandra taps its bare eyeballs. 'See?' She sticks her fingers up its nose. 'It's a thing. A weird thing. But a thing. What happened to your leg?'

Elimisha looks from the claw-man to her leg. Her bandage

265

is hidden by the Haptic Command Gear but the limp is too obvious to hide when she moves.

'Got hurt.'

The mechanical doll-thing at Elimisha's feet looks forbidding. As it was never alive she is not sure it can ever be dead, either. It seems to be looking towards a sky none of them will see again if they can't find a way out.

'Too bad I shot it,' Alessandra says. 'It's a tunnel-maker – maybe it could have tunnelled us out of here. Where's the Trove?'

'What?'

'The Trove you found – that you were reading from. It's the internet, right? Master Birch and Chief Lilly want to know if it's small enough that we can take it with us.'

'We can't get out at all.'

'We'll get out somehow. They know where we are. Or they will once I tell them over the radio. That still works, right?'

'Yeah.'

'Is there something else I can wear? I've been in water and . . .' She winces.

'You can take a warm shower and then put on the Haptic Command Gear. I'm wearing a small. You might need a medium.'

'Looks like it was made for you.'

This makes Elimisha smile. She points Alessandra to the showers and fitting room as she bends down to start cleaning up.

Alessandra leaves the messy kitchen and walks down the long hall as instructed, looking for the showers. There is a room marked 'Habitat'. She opens the door and goes inside.

There are no showers.

The lights are off in the room but a red bulb is glowing brightly, casting a bloody hue over four skeletal remains. One

– an adult – is crouched over a desk on the right side of the room. In the bones of his hands are two devices that look like the grips of guns. Between them, under the head, is a book. The three other bodies are against the far wall directly in front of her on the floor. The one in the middle had been an adult. She sits bolt upright, the empty sockets of her skull staring at Alessandra, but whether in plea or accusation, she can't tell. But in her stomach she feels it's about fairness and unfairness, sorrow and pain, the eternity of the space between love and emptiness.

The woman's arms are around the two smaller bodies. Their skulls are resting on the remains of her lap.

Alessandra backs towards the wall.

'They came here to be safe,' Elimisha says, behind her now. They thought this place could protect them. But it wasn't built for what killed them.'

In sight of the four skeletons, Elimisha tells Alessandra a story that she has now memorised by rote:

'There was a historian in 2099 who wrote a retrospective on the century. Dr Antonio Molinari. He said that a global collapse was coming because the institutions which gave peace its structure were being eroded by neglect and malevolence. He predicted that as the institutions were dismantled, civilisation's resilience would be too, until we finally became fragile enough that even tiny events could cascade into Armageddon. He called that cascading process a *Tracollo*. A collapse. It's from a language that used to be called Italian.

'Years later there was very bad space weather and Earth was caught in its path. There was a Coronal Mass Ejection, a massive one, so enormous that the flare charged the particles

267

throughout interplanetary space and changed the night skies from black to green. At that time, the entire world was electronically connected but politically divided. So when the Sun took out the satellite systems around the world and fried the grid, which is what they called the connectivity, everyone blamed each other. It was like their emotions caught fire.'

Alessandra stands there, watching the dead. She has seen bones before, hundreds of them, but never a family, never resting in their moment of death. And Elimisha's vocabulary is almost incomprehensible. *Italian? Armageddon? Particles?*

Elimisha continues as though in a trance, 'The damage wasn't irreparable. There was terrible data loss and many dependent systems failed, but it was hardly the end of the world. The trouble was, countries started accusing each other of using the disaster to gain advantage over one another – small misunderstandings led to big attacks, which led to a series of regional wars. An untested and unstoppable biological weapon was mated to nanotechnology and it spread, killing people almost immediately. The heavily populated centres went down first, then some of the bioweapon bled into the food supply, causing genetic-level damage. No one knew how to turn it off.

'They had a few days' warning. They didn't know exactly what was happening, so they prepared tunnels and shelters and evacuation plans. They put fail-safes in the biggest buildings so they could be destroyed if the virus – or whatever it was – got in. It was the only way they knew to isolate it. They put military personnel in charge, believing they had the discipline necessary to do what might be needed when the time came. Colonel Harrington was one of them, but he didn't do it. So was he,' Elimisha says, pointing at the dead man at the desk, 'and he couldn't do it either. How do you murder your own family?'

'Not everyone died,' Alessandra says, looking around the red room. 'We're here.'

'A few turned out to be immune. Others were isolated and they outlived the bugs. This was more than three hundred years ago. I've been eating rice and bee honey. I read about some archaeologists who found honey from Ancient Egypt three thousand years old. They said it tasted exactly the same.'

'Are you okay?' Alessandra asks.

'That's the first time I've ever told that story to someone else. I've been practising it over and over and over, in case I'm the only thing that gets out of here and I have to recount it. No one would be able to Attest, but soon you'll see the proof too, and then you can Attest, and because we both saw the same thing and our reputations are—'

'How do you know all this?' Alessandra interrupts.

'Go and shower. Put on the Haptic Command Gear. Make sure you bring the gloves and the glasses from the belt. After that, I'll show you the Archive. When you see it,' she adds, 'try not to freak out, okay?'

MISSING

It is a clear night. The view from the Crow's Nest at the top of the Eastern Wall is sublime. The wind has settled and if Henrietta were to make a shot from here it would travel the world as if pulled on a string.

She only lowers the scope from her right eye when the final rays have disappeared from the top of Yellow Ridge. Once the sun is gone Alessandra won't be able to use the Signal Mirror, and that means she isn't coming back tonight.

She turns to the Spotter whose position she'd taken. She can't quite bring his name to mind, although she knows it's something everyone else would remember. 'If she had signalled, which tunnel would have received her?' she asks him.

'I don't know, Commander,' says the young man, who has unusually long hair. 'I get the signal, I send a messenger to the Gatekeeper and he makes the choice depending on what else is happening out there. I only know once the messenger comes back. Then I can sometimes see what's happening, but usually not. We can only watch a small number of the entrances from here.'

'What happens now?' Henry asks.

'Alessandra was assigned a Signal Mirror by the Buried Clown near Blue Crest. A few weeks ago we cut off his hat, installed some flooring over the hollow parts and then mounted a new double mirror, so if she climbs the back of the Clown and removes the hat she can use it at sun-up and sun-down. It's interesting, because Weapons and Comms worked with the blacksmiths to create a latching system for the hat so when it gets windy—'

'So Alessandra has to sleep out there?'

'Yes, Commander.'

Henrietta looks through the scope again. The fires are burning with impunity over Yellow Ridge. If the brightness of the glow is any indication, their numbers are growing, but still Winters won't make a move; she continues to talk about the Battle of Cannae and how she's going to draw them down into a trap; how she's going to encircle and kill the barbarians.

Lilly, as usual, had been the one to speak up, reminding her that it was the barbarians – under Hannibal – who'd won that encounter. His strategy had been based on the Romans being arrogant.

That was the sort of thing that got her booted off the High Command. Now that she *was* off it, there was no stopping her.

'Calvin,' she said. 'Your name is Calvin, right?' that fact returning to her from nowhere.

'Yes, Commander.'

'Of Calvin and Hobbes fame, I presume?' Henry doesn't much care, but the silence is annoying her. Any distraction – even Calvin's mouth – is an improvement at this point.

'Yes, Commander. My parents were in their twenties when the High Command released parts of the Harrington Collection to the Museum. There was a lot of interesting stuff – you know, the Gibbon book, Thucydides, Homer – but just like everyone else, they really wanted to see the 200th anniversary edition of *The Complete Calvin and Hobbes*. The last one was published on 31 December 1995, so the 2095 edition is the one that Harrington packed away. You know all this, of course . . .' His voice trailed off.

'Tell me the story of your name, Calvin,' she says.

He looked relieved. The small talk comforted him as well. He'd never stood this close to someone so famous. 'Okay, so the four volumes amount to one thousand, four hundred and forty pages, and you remember how every day the Curator would turn a page in the glass box? That meant we could see two pages at a time – but it still took almost two years to see the whole thing. What was so interesting to my parents was how no one here at the Stadium had ever imagined telling stories with pictures before. Or imagined that written stories could be funny because we took every Find so seriously. My mother said that watching Calvin and his parents changed their entire world view.'

'Oh yeah?' Henry says. The sun has been replaced by Keeper fires now. Life with death.

'It made them think that maybe one kid would be enough.'

It was a good joke. Henry would have laughed had the mood been right. As it is, her mind is too far away.

Comedy wants intimacy, not distance. The sky here is too big to fill with laughter.

She returns her scope to its pouch and tries to calm herself with the view, although it is poor comfort, because without the scope everything – and Alessandra – is even further away.

It doesn't make sense. When Alessandra didn't show up at dinner, Graham was the first to say something was wrong. Without needing to discuss it out loud, they both went to find

Lian in the Central Archive. The soaring windows along the Southern Wall had been sealed tight and the lighting inside had been set low. She and four Scribes – two elder and two younger – were debating.

As they walked in, a younger scribe was saying, 'The lesson here couldn't be more clear. Thucydides said it directly: "The strong do what they can and the weak do what they must." This is how decisions are made, by seeing the world with clear eyes and making the reasoned choice. The Melians made the wrong choice and so they were defeated. It's a simple story about power.'

When the four scholars reached agreement, Lian had smiled. 'That is General Winter's reading of the conversation as well. It is not, however,' indicating Graham, 'his reading, as I recall. Commander Wayworth here used to be a Scribe long before becoming a Raider. Tell us your reading of the Melian Dialogue, Commander.'

'We're trying to find Alessandra.'

'I'm told she's on a Run. Tell us – while you're here.'

Henrietta crossed her arms. She knew Graham was powerless to resist sharing his minority views of the world. Hopefully, it wouldn't take long. It made no sense that Alessandra would be sent on a Run during a Lockdown. Something was off. Her ears heard Graham but she was watching Lian for clues.

'It is no surprise that the strong usually win over the weak,' Graham said, animated by this rare opportunity to share thoughts, not only information. 'In fact, it is so unsurprising one might wonder why someone as astute as Thucydides would bother writing it at all. That's when I realised it wasn't what he wrote – you see, the story isn't about Athens winning over a tiny island with a tiny military. It's about how Melos, even knowing they would lose, chose to fight anyway. *That's* what's interesting. If you want to win, by all means be stronger. But if you want to avoid war, being stronger isn't enough. You need to know how the other people think. That, in my view, is what Thucydides was trying to tell us. In my other readings – before I changed career paths – I was working on an unfinished theory that defies common sense and it's this: losers start wars. Consider the ones we know about in the twentieth century. Germany started and lost World War I. It started and lost World War II. North Korea attacked the south and lost. The Arabs attacked Israel three times and lost—'

'Japan attacked Russia and won in 1904,' Henry said, 'and North Vietnam attacked the South and won.'

The other Scribes stared at them, wide-eyed over their acumen.

'We've had these conversations before,' Henry explained.

'I'm not saying the losers always start the wars. I'm saying it happens so often that being stronger evidently doesn't stop others from attacking. In all my travels,' he went on, 'I have learned one thing: peace needs as much of a strategy as war. Given that we're the strongest in the Territory and clearly don't understand the Keepers, I think the conversation is relevant.'

Graham smiled the world's most undefeatable smile – a smile that Henry had to cut short.

'Lian, a moment, please?'

As Graham strutted among the Scribes, Lian walked over to join Henrietta in a private conversation.

'Commander?'

'Did you send her on the Run?'

'No. I was told by a messenger that she was out.'

'Sent by one of the other Evaluators?'

'I was busy and didn't ask. I'm sorry. It didn't seem

significant. We have Runners going out periodically throughout the week.'

'Not during a Lockdown Protocol.'

'No, I suppose not. Who was the messenger?'

'It was Eric son-of-Danielle. You're going to find out who sent the message?'

'Yes. My daughter's missing, allegedly outside the walls during a Lockdown – and that after three Runners have gone missing and Alan was murdered.'

'The boy is only ten, so don't bite his head off, okay? It wasn't his idea.'

Henrietta found Eric asleep in his parents' quarters. They were not pleased to see Commander Wayworth, but she outranked them.

The answer to her question was *Chief Lilly*.

LOVE

Seventy-one-year-old Lilly sleeps alone. It wasn't always this way. When she returned with the Harrington Box, she agreed to turn it over to the Council on the condition they made her Chief Archivist. This done, she was invited to join the Mid-Command where Section Chiefs gathered each month to coordinate action. Though only a teenager, she became a participant in government where the Chiefs educated each other and learned from each other and put their knowledge to the service of shared goals; turning existing conditions into preferred ones. It was at one such meeting in Lilly's mid-twenties that her relationship with Verena Roughsea deepened.

Verena was twenty-eight and a bit older and more experienced than Lilly. She came from a family of sea-dwellers who had journeyed inland to the Commonwealth for trade and met resistance on the Road. Her mother, like Lilly's own, had been killed, although that was where their similarities ended. Lilly's father had never been part of her life, whereas Verena's was worse than absent: he tried to sell her to the Stadium. But the Stadium back then did not buy children – not until later, when Lilly recommended they start so they could build their numbers without having to worry about spies.

Even without payment, the man left Verena there and never returned.

Five-year-old Verena was placed in the Agoge with the other orphans and rose through the ranks. By the time Lilly met her in her mid-twenties she had become a Chief of Movement, in charge of all transportation outside of military operations, all comings and goings, all horses and manner of motion. She worked for the Mayor and coordinated with High Command. In secret, she coordinated with Saavni in establishing the Order of Silence.

Lilly was attracted to Verena's confidence, her clarity of argument, the way she moved. Verena noticed and they become lovers. That lasted for four years, ending abruptly when Verena informed Lilly that she was leaving.

It had made no sense.

'Leaving . . . me?' Lilly had asked.

'Leaving the Stadium.'

'You mean the Commonwealth?'

Verena did not answer immediately. It was as though the two were not the same in her mind.

Lilly pressed her. 'You're leaving here with me in it?'

Verena had a tendency not to answer questions with an obvious answer. It was not a stance; she genuinely thought people spoke as a means of catching up rather than informing themselves.

'Leaving to go where?' Lilly asked, also ignoring her own question.

They had been in bed. They shared an apartment above Door 3, Section 2, Ring 8, which caught the morning light. The rays were sliding through the partly open slits of the shutters, across the blankets and Verena's sandy skin.

'I can't say. I've been asked to do something. The Commonwealth has secrets that run wider and deeper and . . . further . . . than even you know.'

'That's no surprise,' Lilly had said. 'Nor is it an explanation.'

Verena's calm voice sounded more like a teacher's than a lover's. Lilly hated it when she spoke like that. It was the only time she felt at a distance, and it was compounded by Lilly almost always being the smartest person in the room: she didn't like being condescended to and she felt condescended to now. She wasn't used to it.

Verena, however, was not in a conversation. She was imparting information. Lilly could hear the distance in her voice – a distance she often saw in Verena's eyes, learned from being an abandoned child who had had to make her own way. That distance, however, had closed dramatically and passionately and even comically during their time together. It was painful to see it return. It was a surprise to know that Verena had reserves of it that she could call upon when circumstances demanded.

They were beside each other in bed in gowns of soft cotton but Lilly heard Verena as though she were sending coded signals from a lamp on a ridge. As she spoke, explaining the facts but revealing nothing, Lilly remembers looking at Verena's shoulder and imagining it gone from her bed, the warmth removed, the dialogue of their love silenced.

'Will I ever see you again?' Lilly asked.

Verena paused too long to answer, which made it one.

Lilly stood, dressed and left the room.

Three days later Verena was gone.

Five years later there was a man. Lilly tried taking lovers pretending she was as bold as her mother while learning that she was not. Her courage was manifest in other ways. Her heart, however, needed protection. She settled into this truth of herself and both slowed and lowered expectations.

His name was Gideon and he was older, almost forty. He had a sharp mind and an easy way of talking. His humour was gentle and his manner quiet. She felt at ease in his presence and they became good friends. She fell into the rhythm of his company and decided she was better with it. They tried for children. There was a brief flowering but it lasted only two months and, in its course, went away.

The doctors and the healers sat with her. 'A water baby' was what they called it. She was instructed not to deny the sense of loss.

She did not deny it, but she could also not define it. She pictured a cloud – a smear, a distortion in the wind – that became a place for the person who might have been. A daughter, someone to talk to; someone to sit with without talking. That would never be.

She ended the relationship with Gideon, who was heartbroken, but did not resist. Three years later he met a woman named Jennifer, who already had a child.

Lilly was happy for them.

Two loves were enough for her. Later, and by her fifties, she was not beyond the reach of intimacy but her mind had been turned upwards and outwards, away from the body and more towards the stars. Some Evaluators say the peak for the creative mind – a mind like hers – is in the rich and imaginative period of one's thirties when there is both enough knowledge to work with and enough energy to use it. To this, Lilly only laughed louder than a hailstorm on the Stadium's roof and when she recovered, turned her still active mind to ever greater challenges.

*

279

She sleeps alone now, and lightly; that is a function of age and she accepts it. She does not feel it in her mind but she does in the bladder and so too in the patterns of restlessness without cause.

Tonight, though, the cause is external. There is a knock on the door and a rapid entrée even before her invitation to come in.

'Of course it's the two of you,' Lilly says, sitting up and rubbing her face. 'Is it morning?'

'Pre-dawn. Start talking,' Henrietta says.

Lilly looks at Graham, who does not come to her defence. There is no lightness to his mood.

The Wayworths. They form a phalanx around each other no matter the odds or circumstances.

'Close the door,' Lilly says.

Henrietta does as she's told and then crosses her arms to avoid strangling Lilly, which would be unproductive because that's where the knowledge is.

'She's working for Master Birch and the Order now. We sent her out to the Gone World. We heard a voice on the radio – thanks to Graham here – that I'm certain is Elimisha daughter-of-Cara. I believe she's sitting on a Trove important enough to affect the direction of the future. Given all Alessandra's personal skills, including but not limited to her speed, her brains, her judgement, her capacity to fight and improvise – not to mention her head being packed with seventeen years of information from the two of you that I'm absolutely certain you weren't supposed to tell her – she was without a doubt the best person for the job. Also, she's not technically a member of the Order yet, so Birch can look General Winters directly in the eye and say that no members of the Order are unaccounted for. Which will be necessary because Birch and I are running a conspiracy. Welcome to the revolution. May I put on some trousers, please?'

Lilly dresses and leads the anxious parents out of her apartment, through the Ring and down to her office. Yes, yes, they're nervous and worried for their daughter, but the question is whether she and Birch had been right to make the decision at all and if so, if they've chosen the best person. As the answer to both is affirmative and unequivocal, all that remains is dealing with the fallout.

Walking downstairs before sunrise is not a joy for her legs. Each day she works to strengthen them, climbing stairs and even jogging slowly around the Green, and as a consequence, each day her legs are both stronger and more sore, meaning that her efforts to walk better are preventing her from walking better – so whoever created the human body had done a terrible job and she wanted to have words.

It isn't as though Henry and Graham are the only concerned parents here. Elimisha has a mother too, and two siblings, both promising and who both adore their sister. But at least Cara has the good sense not to burst in demanding answers to decisions made long ago.

Everyone serves, Lilly thinks. *Everyone plays some part in the Stadium's survival, everyone plays some part in moving us forwards. Everyone has some role to play in learning, delivering, archiving and protecting the hard-won Knowledge of the Commonwealth so we can rebuild the world in the event of catastrophe, precisely what the Gone World never did. They went digital, the digital failed and now humanity knows nothing after The Rise except the scraps we reclaim from Spade, Raid and Trade. It all depends on Knowledge. How can you get anything done if you don't know how to do it?*

281

'What?' Graham asks as they approach the door to Weapons and Communications.

'What do you mean, "what"?'

'You were mumbling.'

Was she? Lilly does have a tendency to do so these days.

'I was talking to myself and I won't apologise for it. I'm interesting. Now get in there.'

Lilly had left explicit instructions for the radio to be attended at every waking moment and for the fewest number of people to know about it. Birch had asked Javier to place extra guards at the door, guards known to be especially discreet.

The limited personnel, unfortunately, meant extremely long working hours for both Simone and Bruno and Lilly was only half-surprised on entering to find Simone with her face down on the desk, sleeping soundly on the White Board that was continuing to do its characteristic 'nothing'.

'Morning,' Lilly says, touching Simone gently on the shoulder.

'Chief.'

'Where's your partner?'

'He's not here.'

'I see that. Where is he? I thought he was supposed to relieve you three hours after moon-high.'

'He hasn't been here since yesterday.'

Graham and Henrietta enter Lilly's office. Graham pours himself a dram of Lilly's Lizard Poison, knowing she can't say a word as this is only the first part of her punishment – the one he knows she doesn't think she deserves, and therefore isn't consulting her on the matter.

The radio is silent. It glows impressively but does nothing.

'When was the last time you saw him?' Lilly asks Simone.

Simone can sense the situation has changed – not only

because the Wayworths have entered the room but because Lilly is sounding concerned. This is rare.

'He said goodbye soon after you and Master Birch and Alessandra left the room. Is it okay that I'm saying this?' she asks, looking at Graham and Henrietta.

'What else did he say?'

'He said "good luck".'

'With what?'

'He said, "with everything".'

Lilly looks at Henrietta, who knows immediately what this means. Lilly, however, isn't willing to accept the unacceptable conclusion so readily.

'How did you vet him?' Graham asks.

'Usual channels. He'd been here for years – seven years. Ten years, maybe. I don't know.'

'He wasn't Stadium-born?' Henry says.

'Neither were you.'

'And yet it's relevant.'

Lilly looks into the blue glow of the radio for no other reason than to fix her eyes on something. Could she really have been duped by a spy? And Winters? And Birch? And Javier? And everyone else? This is a place of secrets and lies and she knows that because she has been the progenitor of much of it – but to be played? By a *child*? The implications were more than she could embrace. They went beyond her own pride.

'The Keepers would have had to drop off a teenager, alone, and leave him here for a decade of his adolescent life. A life that involved – well, *everything*. Growing up, love, sex, hate, fear, honour, courage, learning, studying, debating . . . everything. And through all of that, he would have had to keep his convictions that the Keepers are right and we are wrong. That's preposterous.'

'I think it's the correct conclusion,' says Henrietta.

'If it is,' says Graham, 'we have no idea how much or in what ways we've been compromised, and it underscores yet again that we know *nothing* about the enemy.' He restrains himself from mentioning Thucydides and the Melians.

'What do these animals believe that deserves greater loyalty than we do?' Lilly asks. 'Look around! We are the greatest civilisation—'

'Something,' Graham interjects, uninterested in Lilly's shock. 'They're loyal to something. A way of life, a belief, a philosophy. I don't know. What I do know is that you and Birch have a confession to make to Winters, right now. And Henry and I won't be there to hear it because we have other things to do. Tell me,' he says, leaning forwards, all gentleness in his voice gone, 'where's my daughter, Chief?'

CAPTURE

'Leader?' comes a small voice. It belongs to a girl of fourteen, a distant niece of some kind; it can be hard to keep track of them. Her name is Mora. She likes new clothing too much in his opinion, which he has kept to himself.

Is it dawn? Already? *These days are so full.*

He reaches out his hand in bed to wake his wife before remembering.

'Yes, Mora?' he answers.

'Word has come from the riders who were sent after the Runner.'

'Let them in.'

She is confused by his use of the plural but allows the single man inside.

The Leader sits up and pulls the tanned skin of a once-white sheep over his shoulders for warmth. There are other clothes – ancient clothes with vibrant colours – that work as well, but this one reminds him of other times.

His face drawn, he listens to the rider recount how two horses and two men fell into a new pit and how a girl in black leather bested them, shot them in the dark and disappeared into the depths.

The Leader resists the impulse to try rubbing life back into his face or else raise his voice.

'There is no way out,' says the man, certain everything will work out. 'We followed her down, despite the Sickness, and sealed off a tunnel she was inside. I think we got her, but if not . . . where can she go?'

'Why couldn't you catch a couple of girls?'

'They never misstep, Leader,' says the man, now on his knees. 'We don't understand it.'

How many days and weeks since he started this by dropping the first building? How many days since his wife's last breath? Already he cannot count them because the number speaks nothing to the feeling and therefore the truth. The Days of the Dead and the Days of the Living are not the same. For her – for their daughter – time slips away like rain from oiled leather. Counting their days, his wife and his daughter's, as though they were the same as his diminishes them all. He will count nothing and carry the weight, without number, alone.

The man continues to kneel, unable to answer the Leader's question.

His mother had told him that the Ancients had machines that could fly. She knew this because she had once seen a field of machines with wings, far away from here.

'Imagine it,' she had said. 'I was excited, but I didn't see any people to enjoy them. It is better to have the people without the machines than the machines without the people,' she explained. 'A kind of joy is lost and we don't deny that to ourselves. Flight! Like the birds! But in forsaking it, all other joys remain. Why? Because joy can only exist where there is life, and so life comes first. That is what we must keep. That is why we are called the Keepers.'

All the greatest virtues, she said, put the needs of others first. Loyalty and duty and sacrifice are greater than desire and passion and even wonder. *So we must choose. The soul only matures in the act of choosing,* his mother said. *The Ancients,* she explained, *either did not choose or they chose poorly. It is better to remove the temptation than to untangle the knot.*

Even now, he still dreams of flying.

Eyes closed, the Leader takes flight in his own imagination, not as a machine but as a bird. Beautiful and alive, he soars from the rock on which he sits and catches a thermal that hoists him far above the company behind him and outwards across the scrabble of the earth to the Gone World. With the eyes of a hunter he studies the ground so that he might understand the movements and meanings of everything below.

It is easy to feel the wind through his feathers when he closes his eyes. It is easy to sense the slight flutter in his belly when the wind changes and he drops unexpectedly before . . . tilting, ever so . . . he catches the edge of the wind-river that he rides to find that peace again; that necessary control.

Looking down, he can see the two Tracollos staring back up at him like black eyes gouged out of the earth: one from the time of his parents and one that his men created a month ago while chasing the curly-headed girl across the Gone World, the girl who slipped through his fingers as his wife slept beside him on her last night.

This is the wounded face of a dead city. Beneath it now are two girls who sit on a Trove that will raise the dead and kill them all over again.

And that needs to stop.

The longest tunnel out of the Stadium is known, sarcastically and without affection, as the *Funnel*. It begins in the site of the original Communications room at the northeast quad of the lowest Ring. That Comms room was looted long before The Few arrived and little more than the name on the door remained. The tunnel is the width of a narrow doorway and as tall as the tallest man with his arms outstretched. The edges are rough, chiselled and perfectly uniform. They were cut by a machine – the Order knows about the mechanical people with hands like claws. Beyond the edges of the shared maps, Explorers have reported on ravines full of them, lifeless as the day they were made. You enter the tunnel and travel two kilometres straight ahead. There is no turning back if others are following, and if anything – or anyone – has found the tunnel's exit and is coming, whoever is in the front will do the fighting until the end.

There is nothing fun about the Funnel.

The Order controls the access and generally Birch doesn't send Runners through it, or Explorers, or Traders, or anyone else with normal business outside the walls. She is too worried that the exit will eventually be spotted because wherever it had been intended to terminate, it now opens onto the side of a cliff that requires either a dexterous fifteen-metre climb to the surface or a ten-metre rappel to the bottom of a ravine that is too exposed for her liking; once inside it, there is too great a chance of being surrounded by an enemy from a superior and elevated position, especially if they choose to bring forces in from either side.

This morning, however, is an exception, and not only because she is pretty certain that Henrietta and Graham Wayworth will kill her and hide her body if she doesn't obey them and get them safely and undetected through the Commonwealth's perimeter to find their daughter.

The Funnel Room is now a storage space for winter gear, including blankets, sheets and outerwear for military and civilian personnel and equipment like shovels and torches and oils. The room is seldom visited and because the rattier blankets are stacked in front of the Funnel entrance, it is well hidden.

Birch closes the door behind them and turns on the electric lights.

'I obviously can't stop you, but are you sure about this?' she asks. 'Alessandra might be fine and we haven't heard anything on the radio yet.'

'Her mission was secret,' Graham says, 'and now, because of the spy, it's not. They will go looking for her and they probably know exactly where to start. The greatest chance of her completing her mission is for us to find her and escort her and the other girl – Elimisha – back here, or to take them elsewhere, to a safe location of our choosing.'

Birch does not answer. What he says is true, but she knows his motives are to protect his daughter. On the other hand, what difference does his motive make if the solution remains the same?

'Are you going to tell Winters?' Henry asks.

'Once you're long gone. In four or five hours, late morning, and by then I expect we'll hear something from Elimisha. Either she'll continue her regular pattern of Sharing on the radio or else she'll say or do something to signal that Alessandra is there and knows the plan. In any case, my hope is that you

289

two can get the girls back with the internet or as much of it as you can carry on foot.'

Graham tightens his empty backpack.

'If you make it back, you'll be the only team in history to return with all six flags twice.'

The two parents look at Birch, expressionless.

'Right. When you get out of the tunnel and start the Run, return the canvas blanks to their original position to cover the exit. The Yellow Route will give you access to the most direct path until it links with the Red. Send up one flare to signal return and three flares to request assistance. I'll be alerting Anoushka and the archers to your excursion, and Javier and the Dragoons as well. Try not to come back before I do.'

Birch hands them both a canteen of water. They each drink half.

'Godspeed,' she says as they disappear into the pitch-black of the Funnel.

Five hours later, Lilly ascends the Western Stairs to the ground-level ring, which she follows to the direct stairs leading to the Snake Tower. Two silent Praetorians permit her entrance to the ten gruelling flights of stairs she needs to mount.

She's not sure if Birch is already there, but she knows they are both are expected because Winters accepted Birch's request for a high-level meeting. *There is no way the conversation is going to go well*, she thinks as she walks up, holding onto the polished wooden bannister on the way. Winters is going to be angry that Birch and she made decisions without her; she's going to be testy over their evident insubordination, and if she didn't have a good sleep and a big breakfast, she'll use the occasion to chew them out in front of everyone else in a bid to reassert the authority she obviously doesn't have, because if she had it, Lilly and Birch would have gone to her in the first place.

Fucking politics.

According to some signs in the Control room, this place once had 'air-conditioning'. No one is certain what the phrase means, but if air can be conditioned in some way, it probably means the temperature can be altered. That means the Snake Tower staircase would be even cooler, which would have been nice.

Then again, if the elevator in the Otis Shaft was working she'd be able to ride up and down with a view. That would be even better.

Oh well.

No longer one for ceremony, Lilly is wearing baggy green cargo trousers, a black leather jacket and ancient Engineers' boots that buckle on the side. She carries a Leatherman like Graham (his gift to her for her sixtieth) in a pouch on her belt. After the sixth flight she slides her gold-rimmed sunglasses on top of her flaxen hair, the arms fitting tightly against her scalp inside the ponytail, and swears.

When she's finished, she returns the glasses to her face and continues humping her way up the stairs despite the pain in her hip.

Two Praetorians in black garb – the kind of guard who will kill you if General Winters orders it, no matter who you are – are stationed at the top of the stairs before the closed door. Their assault rifles glitter with the oils Lilly invented more than thirty years ago.

Lilly raises her invitation medallion and the faceless guard on the right reaches behind him to open the door for her.

*

The top of the Olympic Viewing Station – the Snake Tower –
is a half-moon with an unobstructed view of the entire Green
below. The glass windows are three metres high and angled
outwards at the top. A technology understood by no one,
including Lilly, dims the windows when the sun is at its peak.
When night comes it not only accommodates the few stars in
the sky but illuminates them.

Like The Crossing, the floor here is smoked glass – a glass
so strong bullets cannot break it and wars cannot damage it,
as is known from experience. From here the High Command
can view all 360 degrees of the Stadium Wall and its defences.
At this height, they can see the desert beyond Yellow Ridge
and to The Crossing; all the way to the hills where the Empty
Quarter begins and all life that drinks water ends.

Lilly, a bit winded, finds General Winters sitting beside her
assistant, who is placing small red bricks on a map on the table
in front of them. As Lilly walks closer, the numbers present
themselves and performing quick calculations in her head, she
realises that whatever she thought was happening beyond the
walls is not what she is looking at now.

'You have a thousand troops on that board,' Lilly says. 'That's
more than our entire population and a two-to-one battle ratio
against our professional soldiers. If they have explosives, it is
a game we could lose.'

'It's not a game,' Winters says.

Winters has her hair cut short now and, unlike Lilly, she has
grown a bit thick around the middle despite being four years
younger. To Lilly, this means she's expended more effort climbing
political ladders than actual ones. She is, objectively speaking,
a good engineer and a clear thinker, but her capacity to adapt
to circumstance has been always weak. Eyeing Winters and the
board at the same time, the mismatch is too stark to ignore.

Lilly scans the room for the first time and is shocked to see Henrietta Wayworth, her back to the proceedings, staring out the window, her best scope detached from its rifle and pressed to her eye. She is scanning the ridge for movement.

'Henry? Where's Graham?' Lilly asks.

Henry turns and there is fear in her eyes.

She has never seen Henry scared before.

Henry does not answer Lilly's question with words but instead crosses from the window to the war-board, reaches into a wooden box beside the Territory Map and removes a small blue block that she slams down in the centre of all the red ones.

'He's here,' Henry says.

Lilly spins to survey the room properly. Winters, her assistant (she can't remember his name), Javier, Henry, Birch (long leathered legs crossed on a red chair), Lian, and – ah, no, as usual, the Mayor is missing.

Lilly waits for Birch to say something, to take the lead and state what's already known, but she doesn't move, so Lilly has to assume the worst.

'Why?' she asks.

'He was captured. Giving me time to escape.'

'And you decided to come back here rather than continue on to your mission objective?'

'They were waiting. It was an ambush.'

A fast and brutal ambush that Henry does not want to relive right at this moment. They had left the ravine below the Funnel exit directly where the route begins, emerging between the skeletons of two Gone World land-vehicles. From there, the plan was to follow the wadi into the garden of towers and make their way to the first Tracollo, which was supposed to have been Alessandra's entry point to the underworld. Instead, ten horsemen came on them from two directions at once.

Graham was the first to react, flicking off the safety on his rifle, dropping to one knee and killing five men and a horse in two seconds. His magazine empty, he pulled his sword from Abraxas and charged into the other fighters, going for the horses' legs to drop the men and then cut them down.

'Run!' he yelled.

She knew why.

She had never left his side in a fight before, never abandoned him, and she was prepared to die to protect him. This was her one life and her one man and their Union was stronger than ever before because they had explored the very heights and depths of life together and there was no replacing or moving beyond what they had.

He would joke with her, 'You're supposed to be the Roamer – and unlike everyone else here, you're the one who stays.'

'I love you,' she said to him.

And instead of joking, his eyes filled with tears and he turned away.

He did not turn away now, though. He charged at the Keepers expecting death.

She would not have left his side even then but for their daughter, and for their vows to each other and to the Commonwealth. And the internet and what could change if they had it; change that he valued and trusted.

So she captured a horse from a fallen rider, turned it and left him.

Henrietta fired three flares into the sky once she was clear and a squad of twelve Dragoons dressed in the beige robes of battle came out to escort her home.

'Are those numbers real?' Lilly asks, pointing at the war-board and taking a seat at the table after hearing about the ambush.

'They're based on the Order's estimates,' Winters says. 'The numbers are a best-guess but the deployment patterns are certain. When I decided not to attack earlier, I did not anticipate force levels this high.'

She looks at Javier and he nods, admitting that he had been consulted on the decision.

'What do we know of their intentions?' Lilly asks.

'Nothing we can Attest to. However,' says Winters, her voice demonstrably losing interest in this casual conversation, and – because Lilly knows the move – putting her back in her place, 'we're fully prepared. Meanwhile,' Winters says, looking out of the window to where the problems are mounting, 'Master Birch has told me everything – about the girls and the Hard Room, the radio, the Trove, even this magical theory of yours about an Archive that can fit in a bag. You know it's ridiculous, right?'

'Either the Ancients stopped reading books, looking at pictures, listening to music and sharing information with one another or they stopped using Indie solutions,' Lilly says. 'There's no alternative logic. And if their technology moved on, some remnant of it has to exist. To find it, we would need a perfect alignment of electricity, portal, a way to—'

'Oh, spare us, Lilly,' Winters says. 'The girl found a Trove and some food and water and – by some miracle – there's a bit of electricity left to power the radio. I don't dismiss the importance of finding a second radio and I want to get it, but the rest is preposterous. And we have real problems outside the window. The only reason you're here is because I have an assignment for you and Birch.'

'An assignment,' says Lilly. Her voice is as flat as the land outside the walls.

'I need you and Master Birch to prepare The Drop.'

Lilly looks to the others for reactions but they are expressionless.

'Aside from all the challenges and risks, General, Commander Wayworth and I both think these people have access to explosives,' Lilly says. 'We think the Keepers used them to set off the Tracollo last month. Likewise, I'm told one of the Spotters saw flashes the other night.'

'When?' Henry asks.

Lilly raises a hand. She wants to get through this. 'The Stadium's defences,' she says to Birch and Javier, 'will be limited if the Keepers have acquired explosives, because the walls won't hold against them. Our entire defensive model – the one you and I designed together, Marsha – was based on the presumption we'd be facing bows and arrows and the occasional bullet shot from limited enemy forces who haven't read the military strategy of the Greeks and Romans like we have. In this case, we're looking at the greatest force we've ever seen, ever *heard* of, with discipline that appears to match our own, with the distinct possibility of explosives. The best way to win here is not to fight.'

'You'd have us surrender, Lilly?' Winters says, sarcastically.

'No,' Lilly says, barely containing her anger, 'I would give them a reason to go away.'

'And how would you propose to do that?' asks Javier, finally joining the conversation.

For years, Lilly didn't understand why Winters had elevated Javier to Chief of the Dragoons. He was, she would readily admit, the best rider in a generation. He had a masterful understanding of the training of horses and riders, crafting manoeuvres for mounted fighting and supporting the phalanx, and for setting relays to carry messages. But this was a kind of thinking that was close to the ground. He was a man who was at his best when his boots were dirty, not when he was a mile high in the Snake Tower, trying to use his imagination without the aid of his hands.

But at least he had the good sense to ask questions when he didn't know the answer.

'The missing piece in all of this,' Lilly says, addressing him directly, giving him the respect of her full attention, 'is that you don't create a tribe of thousands without something very significant at the centre holding them together. In my time as a Scribe, as an Evaluator, as an inventor, as someone who has read almost everything we have, I believe that nothing holds people together better than a shared idea: something so fundamental and explicable that people willingly gather around it because it feels right to them. They call themselves Keepers – so what are they Keeping? How are we a threat to that? Is there anything we can do about it? Our best military strategy right now is finding out how these people think and using that to encourage them to go away. I suggest we send someone over to talk to them. Or,' Lilly says as she stands and walks to the one blue wooden block in the middle of all the red ones, 'we use the man who's already there.

'Henry,' Lilly says, 'if we could get a message to him – your scope has a laser for marking and signalling, doesn't it? – perhaps if—'

'Our big idea,' interrupts Winters, 'was once your big idea, Chief. It's to overwhelm and kill our enemies with superior force and better weapons, thereby establishing our dominance of the territory. You know the stories of the dark years after The Rise. You know the fighting. The absence of mercy. The reason The Few took the risk to come this far into the desert. You and Master Birch will now go and prepare The Drop. We will lure the enemy onto the flats and then end it all in one strike. The survivors will tell the story for a generation.'

'The Drop,' Lilly says, in a very, very quiet voice, 'took nine years to build and fifteen years for everyone to forget we built it. Yellow Ridge is there because of all the earth we moved. General, what is the point of having the greatest Archive in the known world if we are so resistant to using that Knowledge to solve our problems?'

'My husband and my daughter are out there,' Henry says. She speaks softly, but her voice is crystal-clear.

'There's no reason to believe Alessandra is at any risk,' Javier tells her. 'She's probably well on the other side of the enemy force. Your husband is a legitimate concern, but for now I am more concerned for the rest of us. I suggest we mobilise the full civilian force. We number seven hundred at strength. With our walls and weaponry we have the advantage.'

'That includes children as young as ten,' Chief Lian says.

'Everyone has a role to play when our survival is threatened. That is what the Agoge teaches. There are tasks even for the children,' says Winters. 'The Stadium was designed to be defended.'

'The Stadium was designed to be a fucking sports arena.' Lilly sits back in her chair and folds her arms.

'But the Commonwealth,' says Lian, trying to calm them, 'is not the Stadium. The Commonwealth, I will remind everyone, was designed to survive with or without the Stadium. That is our Big Idea, General.'

There is a knock at the door. One guard draws a pulse weapon and takes position behind a thick metal barrier as high as a table with a slit in the middle for firing. The second guard opens the door.

A teenage boy with almond eyes and black hair like Lian's looks up at the unsmiling guard and hands him the black tablet book used for sending written messages around the Stadium.

'For Chief Lilly, Sir,' says the boy, backing away until he is standing outside the doorway.

Winters looks annoyed that Lilly is receiving mail in the Snake Tower but says nothing.

Lilly takes the tablet. The message in Simone's hand is admirably clear and brief. She reads it silently. When she is finished, she wipes the chalk away and closes the cover of the tablet.

Henry's eyes are burrowing into her and so Lilly turns to her first. 'Simone says that radio contact has resumed. There is a message here from both girls. They are trapped together, the Keepers know more or less where they are and I was right about the internet,' she says, not even bothering to turn to Winters to gloat.

'We need a new plan.'

RICHES

Graham's hands are bound in front of him as he sits cross-legged on the floor of a large tent on Yellow Ridge, surrounded by hundreds of Keepers, several of whom are his guards. He suffered only scrapes after Abraxas was knocked out from beneath him and he fought his way through a wall of Keepers with his shortsword before being tackled and bound, but he had given his wife what she needed: time.

The Keepers had encircled him, jumped him and pressed his face into the earth, his cheek flat against the fine-grained sand and white quartz, before being hauled to his feet by a mountain of a man.

They walked him through a camp that was orderly and clean and armed. Not a soldier made a sound, not a song, not a murmur.

He was brought to this tent, given water, which he drank, and then he waited.

After what may have been an hour, the tent flap is folded open and a man wearing a white robe and a red sash walks in. He is carrying two small folding stools. He is not mighty in appearance, nor scarred from battle, and there is a softness to his eyes that Graham reads as both sadness and resolve. He lifts his head and the soldiers around him back off but do not leave.

The man places the stools across from one another and sits in one. He motions for Graham to rise from the floor and use the other. He does and without words, they regard one another.

They sit in silence for a time, far longer than would be normal or expected at the Commonwealth, but Graham is widely travelled. Customs vary and he adapts; speaking first is rarely correct.

The soldiers behind Graham do not move. Their presence is calm. None are restless.

A woman enters, bearing an earthenware jug and two mis-matching cups. She pours water into both and holds them out. The Leader reaches for one and drinks, then nods for Graham to do the same. It is fresh and carries the slightest taste of apple. He drinks three cups.

'What's your name?' the Leader asks. His voice is husky and low. His accent is different from the Stadium-born. He has heard something similar once, to the east, months away from here.

'Graham Wayworth.'

'What does your name mean?'

'The first was chosen by my parents. I was named for a friend of my father's who's dead now. The second has been the name of my family for three generations. We are Trackers and Explorers and Raiders: it means that we are worthy to set the path, to find the way home.'

'That's a good name,' he says.

'What's yours?'

'I was born with one but I have none any more. It was used by my wife and my parents. It would have been used by my daughter if she had survived and carried it forward. Now I'm alone, but I have a role and a duty. I am Leader. My name and my role are one. What I am is who I am. What I was is forgotten because it no longer matters to the Now.'

'Who we were always matters in who we are,' Graham says, 'even if it is forgotten.'

The Leader looks at Graham intently, listening carefully. 'How?' he asks.

'In our language. Our dreams. Our decisions. In our values, our virtues, our vices. In our fears,' Graham says.

Two bowls of hot food arrive: the meat of a bird in broth with potatoes and onion. Two spoons are provided and at the Leader's gesture, they eat.

'The woman you were riding with. What is she to you?' the Leader asks.

'My wife. The mother of my daughter. My partner. My lover. My friend. She's a thinker and a warrior.'

'She survived the attack, I'm told,' he says. 'She was joined by your mounted forces and returned back to the walls.'

Graham eats to give his mouth something to do other than say what he feels.

'We have had little contact with your people,' the Leader says.

'From what we can see,' Graham says, 'you've had more than enough.'

'What are you doing in there?' the Leader asks.

'You've had your reports from your spies. Nothing that should bring us to war against each other,' Graham says.

'How do you know that?' the Leader asks.

'We solve mysteries and we solve problems. We learn. We recover Knowledge that was lost. We make things possible. We enrich our lives and the lives of others and we become better for it. We share a great deal of what we know. We have helped this Territory become what it is. We turned the Bridge to Nowhere into The Crossing and gave it worth. We provide clean drinking water to everyone who wants it. We are the centre of all regional trade. We are a force for peace in this Territory that was once barren or else full of bandits on the High Road. You should come and visit. See it for yourself,' Graham suggests, wiping his mouth and sitting back.

The Leader's face is placid. 'Life is not rich enough for you?' he asks. 'You need more? You'll find it in the past?'

He waves a hand and a young woman with far-away eyes places a small table no larger than a stool between them. On the table she places a bowl. From the bowl the Leader lifts a large flower, recently plucked. It is bright yellow at the centre and the dozens of small pedals around it are an unearthly pink, darkening into fuchsia. They grow off the cacti.

'This flower grows near the Stadium – and here, and under The Crossing. What richness of life can you not find within it? In the smile of a pretty girl? In the laughter of a child? In the muscles of a horse, the dancing pillars in the desert? How is all of this not enough for you?'

'It's a nice flower,' Graham says.

'The reason you're here is to give me some insight that will allow me to make a decision about the fate of your people. Answer my question.'

'The fate of my people,' Graham says, 'isn't your decision to make. It's ours. I suppose the fate of your people might be. But I warn you, we're prepared for war. And the woman who prepared us . . . not the General, the other one . . . well, she's got a mean streak.'

'Forget war,' the Leader says. 'Why isn't the world as it is enough for all of you? Why do you need more?'

'Because . . .' says Graham, not entirely understanding what

303

the Leader is asking. '. . . because there *is* more – much more, out there, buried in the sands, hidden in people's minds, hinted at in old songs, written on walls and scraps of paper. There was once a universe of unlimited human potential and creation. Humanity once travelled to other planets. We cured disease. We wrote music and stories, and . . . and the Commonwealth is recovering what we can, keeping it safe and using it to move forward.'

'But . . . why?'

'Why what?'

The Leader is a having a hard time making the man articulate his motivations. The frustration forces his mind to try something else. 'You are committed to finding and saving old knowledge. I understand this,' the Leader says. 'But my people look around at the world and know two things: the Ancients knew more than us. And that knowledge led to this,' he says, waving his hand. They are inside the tent but his gesture is perfectly clear to Graham. 'I tell my people,' he continues, as though talking to a child, 'if one thing leads to another, and that state of being is undesirable, don't do it. So we look at your actions and we look at what they will lead to and we say to ourselves, why would they destroy the world all over again? These people who consider themselves so learned? There is either something wrong with their minds, or with their souls.'

'Your premise is wrong,' says Graham, equally exasperated. 'Knowledge does not necessarily lead to the destruction of the world. Knowledge makes new things possible – not only objects and systems and solutions, but new kinds of happiness. New ways of *being*. New kinds of joy. It expands the very meaning of what it means to be alive. Don't you see? You don't see, do you?'

Graham leans forward on his stool. His hands remain bound because he is a killer, but the Leader does not break Graham's silence and does not hurry him into words. The guards, the girl – everyone is patient as Graham explores route after route, knowing this conversation is consequential.

He decides to speak about himself. 'A month ago – a moon ago – Henry and I returned to the Commonwealth from The Crossing with a piece of paper – well, three of them. It was sheet music for a piano. Sheet music teaches a person – if he can read the language – how to turn the instructions into sounds using an instrument. We have a man at the Commonwealth who can do this. He is very gifted. He doesn't only read, he listens with his whole heart. He seems to connect to the minds of the dead and he brings the truth of their experience back into the world for all of us. It's like watching the dead rise. The music was written by a man named Bach. When Moishe played that music, it was like . . . I remembered what it means to be alive. I remembered why I sacrifice. I remembered how much good there is and how much of an obligation we have to recover it. To make the world whole again.'

The Leader leans forward too. He looks at Graham. 'Why is that needed?' he asks.

'Why is what needed?'

'Piano music.'

'It's . . . beautiful,' says Graham. 'It is a testimony to what people can achieve – what we can be at our best. I'm guessing you've never heard piano music.'

'These feelings you describe, of feeling alive, knowing the value of living, finding again your purpose. I understand these feelings. I share them with you. But you are not explaining to me why you need this Bach music to feel it, why you cannot find it in a flower. You say the music is beautiful and I believe you. Perhaps I would even like the song myself. But how does the beauty of that song compare to a flower?'

305

'I don't know,' admits Graham.

'Or to that of your wife?'

'It depends on her mood, to be honest.'

For the first time, the Leader smiles. It is brief.

'My people see a flower growing on the side of a mountain and we find beauty there. We see the crystals of ice forming on the sands at night and we see beauty. We see the Auroras dance and the pillars form in the night winds and the children smile and the women flick their hair in the breeze and we see beauty. Maybe you do too. I am heartened that your people care about such things, and maybe there is still some hope for you. But unlike you, we are fulfilled, and in being fulfilled ... we harm nothing. We endanger nothing. We risk nothing. We live in the Now. You, however – your Commonwealth – you ignore the Now and live in both the past and the future. You chase after Ancient knowledge to create a new future that endangers us all.'

The Leader looks intently at Graham. He wants him to understand this. 'Whatever they knew – whatever is under the sand – is what destroyed the world. If you continue to learn, there is every reason to believe that you will do the same. And you risk this ... why? Because you cannot find enough beauty in a flower or a girl or a horse or a sunset. The restlessness of your spirit is what threatens to kill us all. Can you not see the foolishness in that? Why it needs to stop?'

Graham had been told these people did not care for Knowledge or ideas. It is dawning on him that everything he had heard was wrong. They care about both – they just think completely differently about them.

This man, this Leader, is forcing Graham to question what he has taken for granted since birth. The Harrington Box was opened before he was born. Lilly had already set their course.

Having never even grappled with his own beliefs, he is struggling now to build a convincing case for them. How can that be so? The Leader, though, is certainly right about one thing. It comes down to *life*.

'Some of the seeds aren't taking to the soil any more,' Graham says. 'If we understood the science of seeds, we might be able to fix that. What you're not accepting is that doing nothing also has risks. It is not the way of nature to remain stable and strong. Things fall apart unless we struggle to put them together. We swim forward at the Commonwealth because the current of the river is naturally against us. We learn to govern ourselves, to feed ourselves, to save ourselves from disease and discomfort. To build better defences and fight back against the decay all around us. You lost your family. We might have been able to help prevent that if we'd worked together. There's still time for others.'

'They died to save us all.'

Graham sits back. The pace is too fast. The ideas too rich. The Leader's pain too deep. Everything the man is saying is worthy of more discussion. But his philosophy is hardened by the loss of his family. To abandon it would be to admit that they might have lived. This is now a journey too far. If only they had all used their time more wisely.

'You are describing a world without change and without risk,' Graham says very quietly. 'But here it is the Roamers who are right. Everything changes and love itself is risk. You are trying to make the wind stop blowing, the children stop wondering, the eye stop seeing and the heart stop seeking. This ... this cannot be done. What you are choosing is not sustainable. Time will win because life itself *wants*. We have to submit and proceed wisely. Is this why you're called the Keepers? To keep things the same?'

'To keep us alive.' The Leader is unmoved. The distance is too great. He gestures to the people outside the tent. 'There are many people who choose life – many people willing to fight for life. More than you think. So that we might all live.'

'We're not your enemy,' Graham says.

'I believe you don't want to be, Graham Wayworth, but you are. And the truth is, you are also your own.'

VAULT

Alessandra and Elimisha sit together with their internet glasses, staring into the holograms and watching videos while sucking brown syrup off their fingers. A bluish tint reflects off both their glass lenses and their unblinking eyes as they twinkle with astonishment in a world so vast, so expansive, that all they can do is bounce from possibility to possibility without plan or direction – children in a room of toys, unleashed and unashamed.

They had started with the problem of the robot and asked the Librarian to explain it to them – but only after Alessandra had wanted to answer one question herself.

She'd stood over its body and hooked a finger in the waistband of its trousers.

'Wanna look?' she asked Elimisha.

'At what?'

'You know.'

'No.'

'You're not curious?'

'Not really, no.'

'I'm curious.'

'I'm not.'

'You're not curious. Have you ever . . . done it?'

'No. Have you?'

'Once,' Alessandra said. 'With Drake.'

'Son-of-Estelle?'

'Yeah.'

'Do you love him?'

'No. I was curious. I'm counting to three and then I'm looking.'

'This is pointless compared to what I'm about to show . . .'

'. . . two . . . one . . .'

Alessandra peeked but at an angle that make it impossible for Elimisha to see.

'Oh my God,' Alessandra says, appalled.

'What?'

'There are two of them!'

'Oh, bullshit.'

'You're right,' she said, whipping down the trousers to show a smooth, asexual surface. 'But I proved you *were* curious.'

Later, after Alessandra had settled into the shock of the internet and been coaxed back to normalcy after taking off her glasses and standing in the corner of the room for almost ten minutes, they learned about the *thing* Alessandra had killed.

What they learned was that the Ancients had committed themselves to the invention of many types of robots and humanic machines. And they also learned conclusively was that their own unit was really, *really* broken, and no amount of repair was going to get it to help them dig their way out of the bunker.

'You had to shoot it in the face?' Elimisha asked once the conclusion was clear.

'I really, really did,' said Alessandra.

*

310

For the morning broadcast, Elimisha decided that secrecy was useless now, so it was time for full disclosure. The Keepers knew where Elimisha was and they had chased Alessandra into a nearby basement too, so if they chose to dig them out, there would be nowhere to go. They'd have to stand and fight and – somehow – destroy the internet. Given that she had no idea how to do any of that, it was better to ask for help and hope that someone was listening.

'They'll be listening,' Alessandra said. 'They said so.'

After their morning session they lost themselves in the metaverse.

Together, side by side, they watched pictures in motion. They listened to music – at first, randomly, and then – once Alessandra had acclimated to music with a beat – 'pop charts'.

They looked at the world from above; from the windows of the Apollo missions, the International Space Station, the Marriott Space Hotel and eventually from the viewing windows at the top of Tranquillity Tower on the moon.

They had never known that the sky was black and the universe was filled with stars.

Alessandra took them car racing at Le Mans, but become more interested in the motorcycle racing at the Isle of Man TT. She watched from the eyes of Natalie Coin as she navigated curves at 300 kilometres an hour.

Elimisha wanted to go SCUBA diving. By the late twenty-first century most of the coral reefs had been either destroyed or were protected from human intrusion, but early HCG® IMAX dives had been recorded off Australia, in the Red Sea, and in specialty wreck dives including the 2046 sinking of India's Mysore guided-missile cruiser off the shallows of Goa.

At midday, they decided to visit their home. Neither had never seen the Stadium as it had been used during the Olympic

Games. Through the gear they heard the roar of the spectators and lived the experience of athletes who had recorded their every movement, experience and emotion in their Olympic-approved HCG® suits, allowing everyone in perpetuity to experience the events as they did.

On what is now the Green, Alessandra pole-vaulted with Miriam O'Conner, who won the gold medal for the United States, and Shira Voy, who took the silver for Canada. Elimisha pulled Alessandra into the modern pentathlon, a sport the Librarian told them was meant to replicate the skills of a cavalry officer behind enemy lines. Together they experienced the heartbreak of three-time champion Abigail Evans as her horse tumbled on the third jump, sending her flying from her saddle, breaking her left wrist and ending her Olympic dream.

Pushing away a bowl of rice in disgust, Elimisha is ready to make an announcement to everyone gathered: Alessandra, the Pirelli girl, all her friends on the other pages, the dead robot and all the Ancient spirits still trapped inside the internet.

'I'm making a copy of everything,' she says, tapping a small black box with a single glowing blue light. 'It's called a Quantum Drive. It's all going in *there*. Everything we see gets copied into the box. I'm Archiving. The Librarian explained how to do it, so ... it's happening now. I don't know how much, but we can put a lot of the internet into that box and then take the box with us to plug into another workstation even if it isn't connected to the internet. Lilly has one of these in her lab. I can't think of any reason it wouldn't work. At first I'm filling it with what I choose. Later, before we go, I'll instruct the Librarian to copy whatever it wants and fill the box. This,' she tells Alessandra, 'is now the Central Archive of the Commonwealth.'

Alessandra hasn't considered that.

'The invisible spiderweb that Lilly always suspected must have once held everything together is actually the internet. All the things that don't work? All the Deps? To be able to work, they needed to access the internet and they used to do that in a thousand different ways, like satellites and relay-stations. When it all went down the Deps lost their connections and became bricks.'

Alessandra's confusion is evident and Elimisha doesn't understand why at first. Then, 'You never apprenticed in Weapons and Comms, did you?'

'I just hung around there a lot because Lilly and my parents are friends,' Alessandra admits. 'I don't understand half of what you're saying.'

For a moment, during their lull, everything stops. They hear the thin hum of the generator and the wisps of air moving through the ducts. Instinctively, like any animal looking to escape, Alessandra turns to look at the door in to the hall that leads to the blast door or the kitchen tunnel.

There's no getting out. There's only being discovered by the Keepers or rescued by the Order. Until then, all they can do is sit.

'Want to see something cute?' she says to Alessandra, who at first doesn't hear her. Elimisha waits until she comes around.

'What?'

'Cute.'

'What does that mean?'

'It's a word describing lovable animals. It means you want squeeze them until they pop but you also don't want to hurt them. Apparently, you deal with the conflicting feelings by making little noises and shaking.'

Alessandra doesn't seem to care, but Elimisha has been through these moods with the internet too. It takes her on an extraordinary journey and she feels the escape – then she remembers she's trapped and all the Knowledge along with her and she returns to the desk feeling distant and moody and depressed.

'Here,' Elimisha says. 'Watch this.'

Waving her hands over the White Board like a magician, Elimisha loads a five-minute compilation reel of cats purring, eating, scratching, climbing trees, falling off tables, being startled by dogs, chasing mice, being chased by mice, sleeping on people's heads and being blow-dried.

'What are those?'

'Cats.'

'They're great,' Alessandra concludes.

'They really are.'

'What else is cute?' Alessandra asks.

Elimisha shows her:

> Raccoons
> Koala bears
> Pandas
> Ducklings
> Baby seals
> Kittens
> Ezo Momongas
> Baby snow weasels, and
> Puppies.
> Lots and lots of puppies.

A child of the desert, Alessandra is drawn to the polar bear cubs frolicking in the snow. 'Where did those live?' she asks.

'Svalbard, Norway,' comes the answer.

'Where's that?'

The Librarian provides a map and a location.

'Tell us about it,' Elimisha orders and a few minutes later the girls are looking at a rectangular structure built into the permafrost in Svalbard. At the top there is a square of broken crystals that glow in the night sky. There is writing on the side of the small building. The words are vitally important to the future of humanity, but there is one they don't know.

'What's a vault?' asks Alessandra.

PREPARATIONS

Lilly and Birch have work to do if The Drop is to be ready for a Keeper attack which could come at any time or never. Neither are convinced using the weapon is a wise idea, but they have been given their orders.

Birch descends the stairs from the Snake Tower with the agility of a teenager, barely making a sound as she skips from one step to the next. Lilly used to have better knees and hips, much like she had better patience, but as all are now wearing thin, she lands on each step with her black leather engineers' boots like she is crushing the skull of an enemy.

Birch stops on the fifth landing and waits for her.

'What are you looking at?' Lilly says.

'I can wait.'

'Kiss my ass.'

At the bottom Lilly follows Birch across the Green, where new battle preparations are underway. Anoushka is placing her archers in a new formation. The Spotters have fortified their locations with the shields that Lilly invented three decades ago: two equilateral triangles made of metal, joined at one edge to create a free-standing structure to deflect incoming weapons that can be rotated to accommodate the movements of battle. Pulse rifles are being distributed. The youngest children are herded indoors and moved into protected shelters in the lower ring.

Together, Lilly and Birch walk into the catacombs that are off-limits to all but the Order of Silence.

Lilly watches Birch as she follows her. Her leather trousers flatter her proportions as she walks. Lilly does not feel a longing for sex or affection any more, although she knows both men and women her age who do. What she does miss is the sense of longing, the hunger for contact. Something vital feels lost with it gone.

Is it odd to stare at someone's ass and think of yourself? *No*, she thinks, *it's normal*.

Is it strange to think about sex on the eve of battle?

Of course not. The mind turns to life when faced with death.

Question and answers. Questions and answers. The tide goes in, the tides goes out.

She wonders if the ocean is a real thing.

Birch stops and turns back to look at Lilly, as though sensing that her mind has drifted from their task.

'It's nothing. Keep moving,' Lilly says, waving her on.

They have entered the subterranean structures of the Flats through a blue door guarded by four silent Centurions. It is known as the Hollows. In three steps they have passed under the outer walls of the Stadium and into the Hollows covered – above – by the artificial earth Lilly created from pillars and wood, steel plates and unbreakable glass from the first Tracollo. This land was once a valley between the Stadium and the hills, but Lilly changed all that. What a project it was – and what

317

a passion for destruction she once possessed, so sure was she that safety could be achieved by strength.

She seldom visits the mechanical world in the Hollows these days. It is a vast, dark, empty space filled with high explosives tied to the load-bearing supports and buckets filled with sharp-edged shrapnel to rip apart the soft loins of anything above when the earth falls downwards.

There are a lot of bugs; a lot of snakes. It's damp, too.

Even if none of that were true, Lilly still wouldn't want to come here. This was the largest and most intense engineering project she ever oversaw; this now feels like a step back to an earlier period of her life when she was angrier and even more self-assured, and wildly creative but also misdirected. War destroys, she knows that, but it also creates.

The Drop was an impressive idea. She is just no longer sure it's a good one. What she has learned since then is that any weapon built will eventually be used. So yes, war creates, but it also creates destruction. It would be odd for the Ancients not to have learned this lesson too.

'Are we actually thinking of using this?' Lilly asks Birch.

When Birch turns, her look says it all.

'Don't you sweat in those things?' Lilly adds.

For the first time Lilly can recall, Birch smiles before turning back to one of the primary explosive chambers. She runs her fingers over it and holds up her hand, which is glistening in the light, demonstrating how damp everything is.

'There are redundancies in every fifth sector,' Lilly says, 'because I assumed a twenty-five per cent failure rate on detonation. The actual design needs only twenty per cent of the columns to blow up to kick off a cascading failure that will start at the centre and simultaneously work back to the Stadium walls and outwards. I assume we're within that margin?'

Birch slides her fingers along the wires that connect the charge to the main power grid. Lilly looks at them as well and sees them as an answer: every wire has been replaced over time and there are no discolourations.

'Why did you build this?' Birch asks. It is the first time that Lilly can recall her starting a conversation.

'To save us in case of a massive attack that we couldn't repel or outlast.'

'I think it was because of Verena,' Birch says.

'I hope you've enjoyed this conversation because now it's over.'

The ceiling here is wood covered by earth. Birch was a child during the construction, but she remembers the trees being brought in – more trees than she had ever seen. The smell was glorious.

Birch sits on a stack of planks and crosses her legs. Here, in the dim electric light, her eyes are a glistening brown and Lilly notes an unexpected softness to her face; she would not have expected that from one with such a solitary and hard life.

'I know that Verena left you to serve the Commonwealth,' Birch says. 'She didn't run. She didn't leave you.'

'I know that. I don't need you to tell me that.'

'This,' Birch says, opening a palm as though it could hold the entire Weapon, 'will not save us from what's out there. I actually think that even if the Keepers are defeated on the battlefield, they still might not be deterred from coming back.'

'That has crossed my mind as well,' Lilly says, hands in her pockets.

Birch still wants to talk, which surprises Lilly. The Drop, they both know, needs no preparation. You activate it or you don't. Lilly got the idea from Adam's detonators that set off the first Tracollo. Birch and her team have maintained it, and it is Birch alone who will start the detonation when so ordered by the Head of High Command, in this case, General Winters. That Birch wants to *chat* is a first for Lilly.

'Our assignment is to carry out the secret functions needed to sustain the systems of the Commonwealth. You know this: you started the Order with Master Saavni. But over the decades,' Birch says, 'we've had to become far more nuanced in learning how to go about doing it – and that nuance has not always received a welcoming ear from High Command. It sounds technical and unimportant, but it isn't. The Order doesn't simply wander through the world with cans of paint marking out routes and setting traps. That's the easy part. What's hard is learning how other tribes and clans and bands all use the land, where they go and don't go and why. Where and how they shelter. Where and how they travel and with what . . . with whom. We've learned that watching the daily habits of unfamiliar peoples teaches us a great deal about their life-and-death commitments. Our people are not only slipping between the rocks, Chief Lilly, they are slipping between ways of life. Once – in the days of The Few – those ways of life were far apart from one another. Today they are overlapping.' She places one hand partly over another. 'There are fewer spaces in between and someday, if the populations continue to grow, if the radios connect us, if our Knowledge changes the dynamics of time and space, we will be living on top of one another. And what was once a secondary function of the Order will become its primary goal: to understand the minds of others and prepare the way. I'm telling you this because I think a new era is beginning and I don't yet know what to do about it.'

This is the most Lilly has heard Birch say in one sitting.

'Winters won't be the solution,' Lilly says at last.

'She's your fault, you know.'

'I beg your pardon?'

'General Winters sees everything as attack and defence: barriers to erect or barriers to overcome. It is the mindset of a mechanic or an engineer. You are the one who set us on that path. Out of everything that could have been learned from the Harrington Box, you focused on machines, and everyone else followed along. General Winters rose through the ranks on the values you emphasised. You know that, right?'

'I was seventeen years old, Birch.'

'Not when you built this place. I was a child then. You stood on the walls like a queen directing the construction.'

'What's out there?' Lilly asks, moving away from the subject of her own complicity. 'What life-and-death commitments?'

'There is . . . passion,' says the Master. 'Tremendous passion, Lilly, that runs as deep as our own. Passion for what, I don't know, but for *something*. We've put up walls to keep ourselves in and others out. We collect Knowledge and hide it away. We're a powerful fortress, but we're not a movement. We collect, but we barely use – we barely even teach. The Keepers' message, compared to ours, is very simple: *we're alive and the Ancients are dead. Let's not make their mistakes.* And so their numbers are growing. It gives them something to live for . . . and, perhaps, to die for.'

'So we have a problem,' Lilly concludes.

Birch says nothing.

'Why doesn't the High Command know all this?'

'I told them. They think it's a military problem.'

'So what do we do?' Lilly asks.

'Find the internet,' Birch says, 'and take it away.'

'To where?'

'There's a place.'

A soldier dressed all in white enters the vast chamber. He calls to them and the echo repeats his words.

'The enemy has been spotted. Their advance has begun. You are ordered to take your posts.'

Graham Wayworth's captors have led him to the edge of Yellow Ridge and unbound his hands. He has been positioned to look down on the flats, where he will be allowed to witness the destruction of his home. If he fights, he will die, and if he runs, he will catch an arrow in the back.

The Leader rode beside him. Their conversation in the tent is over and there will be no returning to it. They stand there together now, overlooking the battlefield. The mounted troops and the infantry have moved to the edge of the Ridge.

War is imminent.

In the full light of the late morning Graham can see the entirety of the Stadium below. He is relieved to see that it has been locked down and they are ready. The Spotters in the Crow's Nest have been removed and placed behind their mobile barriers and the Mirror System and deflector plates are up. The Main Gate is sealed. The steel shutters on the windows and over the apartments on the far Western Ring are all closed to resist in-coming arrows and other missiles. The pikes have been raised from the underground chambers to repel any oncoming force who have the nerve to approach across the ground.

To the uninformed, it is a tortoise with its head pulled in.

To Graham, it is a cocked pistol waiting to discharge.

What is new is the flag hanging from the Snake Tower. It is as long as six tall men and as wide as three. It is noticeable from every angle of approach. The flag is as white as innocence; the symbol it carries is blacker than death.

It is the universal symbol of danger:

Graham turns to the Leader and says, 'They're ready. There is no way you're getting through that gate or over those walls.'

The Leader scans the valley and is satisfied. 'It's only a wall,' he replies.

'No, it's Lilly's wall. That makes it an instrument of death,' Graham says. 'She's the finest mechanical and strategic mind we've had in five generations and she had a rocky childhood and then a bad love life. You don't attack something like that. You run away from it.'

'You people have a colourful way of speaking.'

'You go there, you die.'

'You eat too much.'

'What?' Graham says, looking at his own stomach. 'No I don't. I'm no heavier than you are.'

'Your people: they bring in more food than they send out. Even with the farms down by the freshwater. If you don't trade for food, you starve. We have blocked your trade.' He points to the Stadium. 'They are already starving. It will take time, but eventually, they will have to leave.'

'We have stores of food. And we have tunnels that you can't imagine.'

'We know all this. Our spies have told us.'

'Yes, of course – but it doesn't matter. The form of warfare you're talking about is called "a siege". It can work, but it won't work on us.'

'It will.'

'We produce our own food, so below a certain population, we are sustainable.'

'You have no stomach for that amount of death, especially among the children. Our will is stronger.'

'Our tunnel system is secret and extensive. You don't know where they go and you can't block them. And so the siege will never work.'

'Yes, we do know where they go, and yes, it will.'

The Leader raises his hand. He extends his finger to the valley and the Flats and the place Graham calls home where right now his wife might well be watching him through her scope from the top of the Snake Tower with its blacked-out and one-way windows. 'We may not know where your tunnels come out,' the Leader says, 'but we know they all return to the same place. They all go there.' He points to the Stadium. 'You are going to destroy them all for us with your giant weapon. You are going to cut yourselves off from the food you need and you are going to starve or you are going to leave. Either way, with your numbers diminished, your people weak and your leaders weaker, your way of life will end. You will be stopped from gathering the knowledge that threatens the world. And even if some of you remain, your work – your path – will be over.'

III

INFERNO

GAMBIT

General Winters stands at the window of the Snake Tower holding Henry's scope in her hand. Henry is beside her. Lian has left to secure the Central Archive by hiding the most valuable books, paintings and scraps in hidden compartments, just in case the Stadium is overrun. Javier, as quiet and obedient as ever, joins Winters on her other side. Together they look down at the archers gathered in the rear quadrants of the Green and on the lower ridge of apartments, now emptied of non-fighters and under the command of the military.

'I don't see the Master Archer in position,' says Winters.

'She's scaling Ladder Six now, General.'

'Have the scouts reported in with enemy numbers?'

'They have, General.'

'And?'

'They estimate around a thousand. Maybe two hundred horses. A few hundred dogs.'

'How are they arrayed?'

'They aren't, General. We're anticipating a mad, savage rush down the hill.'

'And their armaments?'

'A few dozen rifles. Mostly we saw shortswords, bows and some lances on the horses. A few are on bicycles, which, given the flat terrain actually isn't a bad idea.'

'Won't help them.'

'No, General.'

'I see no reason to open the gates and take to the field yet. I say let them bash their heads against our walls until they're weak and close.'

'Unless they have explosives, General,' Henry reminds them.

'If we get a hint of any,' says Javier, 'we use The Drop. That's why Lilly built it. If they come down in a rush we can kill a thousand in an instant. Our Archers can take out the survivors from behind our walls. I say we send the Dragoons through the tunnels now, take a distant position behind them, and once we activate The Drop, we'll have the survivors surrounded. A hammer-and-anvil solution. This is what Hannibal did at Cannae, causing utter devastation. It will send a resounding message throughout the Territories about our power. We will then establish ourselves for what we really are: the dominant military force in the Territory.'

'Unless,' Henry says, 'we're not.'

Winters looks at Henry. 'What are you doing here?'

'You wanted to borrow my scope.'

'I can use mine now.'

'This is a sports centre, not a castle.'

'You're supposed to be in Sniper Location Echo. Once it begins, you kill the leadership on downwards, not just anyone. You are dismissed, Commander.'

Anoushka Sunrose, Master of Archers, reaches the crest of Ladder Six and slides onto the top of the stadium wall on her belly to avoid line-of-sight detection. She too is dressed in

328

armoured leather, like a Runner, but unlike the Runners, hers is brown from neck to ankle, lighter than her hair but darker than her eyes. She wriggles her way to the base of a giant pole angled outwards that extends high above her. The DANGER flag is at eye-level far behind her. She wonders whether it will prove to be a message the savages will heed or a target for them to shoot.

Anoushka is forty-two years old. Her face is long and thin, her hair is tied into a ball on the top of her head. The fingers on her right hand are hardened and rough from years pulling at bow strings. She was among the best of the Commonwealth archers and, as always happens with everyone truly good at something, she was promoted out of it and into management. Now, instead of her trusted weapon, she holds an ancient Indie compass with which to take bearings and a small red flag to issue orders.

She's facing an incoming army of a thousand with nothing but her opinions and she doesn't like it.

'You,' she says to a messenger, a boy of about twelve. This is his first proper job.

'Master?'

'Go down to the Green and find me a bow and a quiver of thirty arrows. Tell them it's for me. I want a good one. Go now.'

The wind at the top of wall is not the same as the breezes across the Green below or even the Flat beyond. She has discussed this problem with Lilly, explaining that arrows are subject to directional changes, especially on the return arch to the earth when they have lost most of their power. Lilly's solution was to place diaphanous fabric at key locations on the battlefield, best viewed from Anoushka's angle and not the enemy's, so she could better judge and direct the barrage.

The archers on the Green are blind to the enemy. It is Anoushka's eyes alone that will command three hundred bows.

Lying still and breathing calmly, she stays very low in the protection of the viewing wedge. The sun today has turned the Flat to a lovely gold. A pool of sunlight ripples over the long approach to Yellow Ridge. She hasn't seen Moishe in nine days – they had a fight and she stormed off, leaving him fragile. She did try to find him before her deployment to the wall but he had already been assigned to his Crash Team, ready to repair any breeches or weapons failures during the battle.

She hopes word has reached him.

Anoushka twists on her belly and slips to the edge so she can see her Deputy Master below. He is a first-generation sol-dier with eyes like a falcon. He's holding a long red pole and looking up at her from ten metres below. Around him is the Great Compass Ring. It is ten metres across and marks out 180 degrees of arc. She will take the bearings on her compass and share them with him. He will redirect the Company by angling the pole to the bearing, and three hundred archers will shift to mimic his gesture. They are a machine: together, they will own the air, so the sky can command the earth to cease all movement.

Henrietta Wayworth has assumed her position inside as a sharp-shooter. Her rifle scope is charged. She looks through it periodically, but prefers to watch the entire ridge with her naked eye to better appreciate the entirety of the problem. The scope only focuses more attention on a smaller part. With Alessandra and Graham both out there somewhere, looking through the scope feels like crawling under a rock.

She is lying on a metal table. A few small rags have been left there, at her instruction, so she can position the rifle at her cheek. The constant, annoying wind in her face from the hole in front of her dries her lips and eyes, but there is no real solution for this other than placing a piece of glass there until the battle begins. It's not a bad idea, but for now she'll suffer the breeze.

Henry hears the shuffle of feet behind her.

A ten-year-old girl has taken a position by the door like a tiny guard. This girl has fair skin, blue eyes and red hair, all of which is unusual enough to be memorable. She wears a bag with a red cross on it; it is packed with medical supplies. She is positioned here to be Henry's message-carrier but it looks like she's also being trained as a First Responder.

'You look familiar. What's your name?' Henry asks.

'Bee.'

'Do I know you?'

'At The Crossing you told my parents to bring me here when they went looking for the city to the west. I was sick so they did. They haven't come back.'

'You look better.'

'I am.'

'How are you doing?'

'I need to pee.'

'Everyone needs to pee during a war. No one ever talks about it.'

The girl looks scared and now Henry does vaguely remember her. It's not an unfamiliar story, nor even a sad one. Assuming she survives the war, she's better off here.

'Pee in the corner,' Henry tells her. 'I won't tell anyone.'

She turns back to the hole in the wall and looks out again, scanning the hill, waiting for the first indications of enemy action as Bee's urine hits the floor behind her with a force that threatens to leave a dent. This is the standard indignity of conflict. When civilisation breaks down, the bladders are always the first things to go.

Henry catches movement and re-activates the scope.

A shadow, a head, a torso arises as a phantom from the ridge. It is the only face she can see. She amplifies and across 1.2 kilometres of quivering air she is looking at the face of her husband. He is alive, and if the swagger of his body is an indication, he is unharmed. His hands, she can see, are not even bound. She can tell that he is looking directly at her, although he can't possibly see her.

He knows the battle flag is flying. He knows they have taken up war positions. He knows where she is stationed and he knows where to look. So he is looking at her, even if he cannot see her – because he knows that his wife can see him.

She zooms in as close as she can and points her rifle directly at his chest so she can read his lips and see his hands.

A man emerges and stands next to him. He is wearing a white robe and a red sash.

Henry activates the sighting-laser on her scope and takes a new aim at his hands. She taps out a coded message that flickers on his interlocked fingers resting by his groin. She tells him where Alessandra is – or might be. He's to get there if he can.

She repeats the message, and then repeats it again.

In the middle of the fourth attempt, Graham's hands move. He places the thumb of his right hand between his first two fingers. He then encloses his left hand around his right as though protecting the shape he formed. He whispers into the wind and hopes her eyes are sharp enough to read his gestures and words.

Protect the tunnels, he says. *Don't use The Drop.*

Acknowledged, she replies. *Alessandra?* she taps out.

He makes a face she knows only too well. It means, 'I'm working on it.'

'Bee,' Henry says in a soft voice so as not to frighten the child, 'go to the Snake Tower and tell General Winters I have contact with my husband. He is instructing us to protect the tunnels at all costs and not to use the weapon. Your message changes the course of our history. Do you understand what I've said?'

Bee repeats the message.

'Go now. And go very, very fast.'

As Bee rushes out the door, Henry moves the scope from Graham to the man in the white robe and red sash who is standing beside him. She moves her finger from the right side of the receiver to the trigger.

As she does, the man's hand points to the valley below and with that small gesture hundreds of troops rush over the edge of the ridge and charge screaming into the valley and onto the Flat, swords drawn, spears set and hate in their faces.

Henry gently squeezes the trigger and shoots the man beside Graham.

CROSSINGS

Above the Main Gate Anoushka watches the oncoming assault, dumbfounded by the numbers and the rage. The tribesmen and the horses and the dogs roll over the ridge and across the flats like a flood and there is no end to their numbers. She has seen battle before, but not like this.

The sounds issuing out of their throats are not the war-cries of beasts. There is an anger and a self-righteousness to those calls; a genuine and deep hatred of the Commonwealth that stuns her.

Under their feet and their hooves is a sound she has never heard – a sound that no one has ever heard: the rush of an army over the Hollows.

She looks up at the unbroken blue sky. It is clear of birds and undisturbed by the turmoil below. It is still peaceful there, but that will soon change, because the sky is her domain.

The Keepers cross into range, trampling the directional pole and its cloth to the ground, but it is no longer needed, because the dust kicked up by their many, many feet tells Anoushka everything she needs to set her archers loose.

Anoushka holds out her compass and points it in the direction of the stampede with the greatest concentration of enemy. She adjusts the mirror so she can better see the compass bearing and rotates the plastic glass until north is captured in the small arrow. They are coming down at forty-eight degrees east by northeast. With hand signals and her red flag, she relays the information to her Deputy Master, who takes the instruction and points the tip of his giant pole at the proper bearing on the giant compass at his feet.

Three hundred bodies shift their position to match his own.

Leaning back so she can meet his eyes, she slices her hand downwards, as though it were a sword upon a neck, and with the precision of an ancient machine, a volley of three hundred razor-sharp arrows meet the sky, forming a dark rainbow over the Stadium wall, and fall with wicked intent onto the heads and bodies and silenced throats of their attackers.

They re-notch and release a second volley.

Again iron meets flesh and again the foot soldiers wash over their own to press the assault.

As Anoushka prepares her fighters for a third round, she sees the first arrows coming back towards them from the oncoming Keepers. A quick sideways slash of her flag signals the danger and the waiting Phalanx and her Sagittaris raise their shields in defence.

A head pops up beside her from the top of the ladder: a certain piano player she recently broke up with. He is not supposed to be here.

'Have you abandoned your post?' she says to him, wishing she had said something different, but she didn't and she can't take it back.

Moishe smiles at her.

'I told you to stop smiling at me like that,' she says, unconvincingly.

Moishe only smiles at her more: a smile as incongruous to their relationship as it is to this moment of war and potential annihilation.

It is a smile she fears more than the barbarians on the Flat. It is a smile that speaks to the depth of his emotions, the taste of his lips, the kindness of his heart and the bliss she will fall into and never emerge if she accepts his love as completely as he is offering it. She fears it will confine her and this is not what she needs as a Master, as a soldier, as a woman. She needs to be elevated above it all. Bliss is not the motivation she needs.

The trouble is, he is offering her wings to soar above whatever is base and low in this world but she is too prideful to accept them – too worried that happiness will rob her of her ambition.

Which it might. Isn't all ambition driven by some discontent? Isn't that discontentment therefore needed? Doesn't it need to be nurtured? Happiness sounds stagnating to her. And this is a place of motion.

Maybe we'd be better off as Roamers.

Moishe is not smiling to distract her or trap her. He is smiling because he is happy to see her.

It's so linear it drives her nuts.

'Go and do your job!' she yells at him.

Scooting past her, he jogs along the wall. He's needed inside the Main Gate and this is the fastest way to get there . . . while passing Anoushka.

In the Snake Tower, the elevator opens and Javier wipes his face with a cloth as he approaches Winters.

'Report,' General Winters says, watching another volley of arrows and a lone figure running across the wall of the stadium in the direction of the Main Gate. She's not quite sure who it is. It might be the piano player.

'I've sent the divisions through the tunnels,' says Javier, 'and they're emerging at Lawson Point. They have orders to come back around once The Drop is activated.'

'So that's the last of the Keepers? Concentrating themselves on the Flats? You're behind them now?'

'Honestly, General, we don't know. Anoushka is giving them hell from above,' Javier says, 'but these numbers . . . we don't know how deep their line is. They're chopping through the pike barriers now and they're almost at the walls. We have no casualties and they're taking dozens but there is no let-up in their attack.'

'Do we have them surrounded or not?' Winters asks.

'Surrounded . . . yes. But that's not the issue,' Javier says, wiping his face for the umpteenth time. 'We don't have enough forces to press a rear attack. We are *massively* out-numbered, General, so we either commit to staying behind the walls and hope they don't have more explosives to punch through, or we take advantage of their concentration of forces out on the Flat, right now, and use The Drop. We can use the Dragoons to secure the perimeter and prevent any survivors from regrouping.'

Winters stares at the Flat. It is filled with the enemy and the walls still hold. If there are indeed more on the Ridge or beyond, they can bear witness to their brethren's folly.

Now is the time.

She sends Messenger Harishma to issue the order to Birch. She is thirteen, with very dark skin and the strong legs of an athlete or Dragoon. She has cut her hair short like a boy's and while too young to be a Runner, she wears a leather jacket like the uniform she soon hopes to don.

She is fast and, to her parents' consternation, fearless and ruthless. Nothing will stop her from delivering the message. This is why she is Winters' personal messenger.

Harishma flies down the Snake Tower steps until they connect with the central stairway. She swings around first one bannister and then another, practising the moves she has seen the Runners perform on the Green. As she whips around the second, she bashes into a slight girl who reeks of urine and is wearing a medic bag. She's seen this girl before: she's small and weak and her red hair makes her look like a freak.

'Watch where you're going, kid,' Harishma says as her shoulder checks the little girl, who falls backwards and bumps her head against the wall; her chin slams upwards and she bites her own lip and cheek, which start to bleed.

Harishma disappears into the basement through the tunnels and carries on to Birch, who is the warrior she will someday become.

Bee hoists herself up, blood on her lips, and hobbles outside to the Green. Her head throbs, and so does her ankle. The rounded bone on the side of it that has no name is hurting and she winces as she runs. As she passes through the archers, the buzz from the twanging strings reaches the same perfect pitch as the ringing in her ears; in that moment the world is in perfect harmony.

She reaches three soldiers manning the elevator to up the Snake Tower, the fastest way to General Winters.

'I have to use the elevator. I have a message for General

Winters from Commander Wayworth. It is very—' she starts, but that is all she can say because her last words become inaudible when suddenly the ground shakes, an explosion splits the air and a fire lights up the sky beyond the walls.

WAVES

The explosives ignite, but the land does not drop. It rises into the air, higher than the darkest ambitions of hell.

At the moment of the blast Henry had been acquiring a new target from her perch at Sniper Location Echo. In a harrowed breath, before the sound even reaches her ears, the vista before her eyes is replaced by blackened earth. That is the last she sees of anything before a shear of wind and debris rips through her viewing hole in the wall and tears open her left eye, which is unprotected by the scope.

In anger as much as pain, she drops the rifle, clutches her face and rolls off the table, landing hard on her left shoulder. As her head strikes the floor she knows that Bee has not delivered her message, that the tunnels Graham told her to protect are no more and everything is . . . somehow . . . lost.

Moishe's job had been to release the cables that dropped the weights and snapped shut the Jaw Gate that both rose up and slammed down outside so any breach would be impossible. For some reason, the mechanism was stuck and he needed to sort it out. The Main Gate was closed but the Jaw Gate was

340

impenetrable and needed to snap shut. Once there, he is to take shelter behind of one Lilly's triangular shields to effect the repair.

But he is too slow and he stands too tall. For one last time he extends his left arm and waves to her.

Anoushka watches as an enemy blade blown into the air by the force of the blast slices off Moishe's left hand at the wrist and sends him toppling over the wall and onto the Green below.

When Moishe opens his eyes he sees a beautiful little girl with hair like a sunset wearing a bag with a painted red cross. She has a touch of blood on her lower lip. Wordlessly, she is already applying a tourniquet to his stump. He stares into her perfect blue eyes as she performs her job. Blood sprays across her chest and neck as the veins on his arm are constricted by her twisting a stick in the bandage with all her might. She keeps going until the flow finally stops, then she ties the stick to his forearm, places a clean bandage on the stump and wraps it carefully.

When she is finished she sits and places her arm around him and pulls his head to her chest. 'Don't worry,' she says to him. 'I'll protect you.'

Graham crouches down beside the Leader, who was shot before The Drop was ignited. Though debris is raining down on them, Graham is unharmed by the blast. Rather than run or take advantage of the confusion, he drops to one knee and crouches by the Leader, who reaches up to grasp Graham's hand.

He will be dead soon and they both know it.

'Your wife?' the Leader asks about his chest wound.

'Yeah.'

'Mine would have done the same,' he says to Graham.

'I believe you,' Graham says.

The Leader's voice is raspy. Blood is trickling from his mouth. 'I am remembering my daughter and my wife. I dishonour them in my final moments by living in the past.'

'No you don't,' Graham says to him, 'because love is always in the Now.'

The Leader nods once, before he releases Graham's left hand and dies. When he does, Graham closes the man's eyes because that is the way of the Commonwealth. He sits beside the man's body and for a moment, wraps his arms around his own knees and surveys the carnage and catastrophe of their collective making.

Where once there was a cragged valley of rocks and brush that Lilly had turned into a flat, there is now a valley again: but this valley is filled with fire and smoke. Graham looks down on it like a premonition of what's to come. In the roiling black smoke, the closed gate flickers into view and then, like an apparition, it is gone again.

The danger flag still hangs from the Snake Tower.

The walls have held.

The fortress, such as it is, remains.

He watches as Anoushka's arrows fill the air again, even after that blast. Winters shows as little mercy for the enemy as she does understanding.

Bursts of sapphire-blue from pulse rifles fall like starlight into the remains below and Graham is filled with a terrible sense of lost possibility.

There is a canteen on the ground beside him. From habit he lifts it, opens it and drinks until it is it empty.

*

Graham turns away from it all and looks eastwards. The setting sun behind him turns the towers of the Gone World a fiery orange; further off, the rays are burning through The Crossing, turning it to a half-ring of crystal and fire.

Alessandra is out there and he is outside the walls, beyond the valley – even beyond the Keepers. This war is lost to them now and if he can anticipate Javier's moves, there are probably Dragoons circling around to the Ridge now. He doesn't want to be caught in the middle when that happens. If he can find a way to escape, he can start his search for his daughter and the internet and maybe do some good.

As he stares off into the distance, however, he sees a dust storm kicking up from the ground. It is not blowing in because the skies are clear; instead, it is coming up from the earth. It takes Graham almost a minute for his mind to allow him to see what his eyes are already staring at: a second wave.

Like the dogs that brought down Alan Farmer.

Before Graham can make his move to leave, the Deputy on his horse joins him beside the fallen Leader.

Looming over them both, the Deputy asks, 'Did you close his eyes?'

'Any reason to kill me will do. You don't have to start making things up.'

The Deputy dismounts and stands in front of Graham, albeit at a little distance. They do not speak for a time as the second wave comes into view.

'Only now are you starting to understand what we mean by sacrifice,' he says to Graham.

'You might be right,' he says. 'And yet, all of this . . . *all* of it' – he gestures in a half-hearted way – 'is purposeless. It all could have been avoided with a little wisdom. A little understanding.'

343

'Your tunnels are broken. The Stadium is cut off from its food and supplies. The people of the Territory will abandon this place and move north through the forests or south to the smaller colonies. Like a thousand others before you, your colony has failed. Your people are trapped by their own decisions.'

'Aren't we all,' Graham asks sarcastically.

'How did he die?' the Deputy asks Graham.

'My wife shot him. Maybe she'll kill you too.'

'Perhaps she will,' he says calmly.

'You people wrap words around fear and call it philosophy. If you want to know what probably destroyed the Gone World,' Graham says, 'that's a good bet.'

Birch and Lilly return to the Snake Tower without a new plan. They stand shoulder to shoulder with the rest, looking down at the pool of death below the fresh army on the Ridge up above.

Anoushka has also seen the new wave of troops, and when she did, she stopped her assault on the survivors in the pit. She did it for mercy. She did it to stop the provocation of the new troops. And most importantly, she did to save their arrows.

Inside the tower, the High Command viewed what everyone below was seeing. Winters spoke first: 'We defend the wall. We defend the Commonwealth until the end.'

It is Lian who speaks this time. She is, after all, the Evaluator. 'They tricked us into using The Drop, General. They concealed their second wave. They were willing to let the first thousand die as a gambit to destroy our tunnels and they have outsmarted us because we never thought anyone could do that.

We also thought that an army this size could never be raised against us. Now, if my sums are correct, we starve or we leave. Because they aren't going to attack.'

'Why won't they starve instead?' Winters asks.

'Because they can come and go as they like and we can't. There are outposts and smaller trade routes that will welcome their business, especially having lost ours. Simply put, they're free and we're trapped.'

'You're making all that up,' Winters says. 'Look at them: packs of wolves on a hill, ignorant, unlearned, disorganised – they'll attack us again and they'll crash against these walls and we'll burn them alive, this time with liquid fire from the parapets. You would have us think you know what they'll do, but all you're really telling us is what you would do.'

'I am making a reasoned argument with what we know. If we had more Knowledge, we could make better arguments. That's why we collect it,' Lian says, with a clear edge to her voice.

Lilly snorts.

Winters turns to her. 'What are you even doing here?'

'Thinking. I thought someone ought to.'

'As you consider the options, General,' says Birch, quickly, 'I will remind you that there are . . . alternatives. Grand alternatives that the Order of Silence spent many decades, at great cost, making possible.'

THE ASSIGNMENT

The detonation of The Drop rattles the bomb shelter and Elimisha and Alessandra both instinctively slip from their seats and hide under the table.

The shudder is not strong but they can feel it: a dusting from the ceiling, a rumble of shocks, followed by a groan as from the Earth's own pain.

'What was that?' Elimisha asks.

'I have no idea.'

'Are they trying to get in?'

'That wasn't close. It was far away and big,' Alessandra says.

'Another Tracollo?'

What else? they both think.

'How many bullets do you have left?' Elimisha asks.

'Three.'

Elimisha had asked the Librarian about guns and ammunition that might have been stored with them in the bunker. There had once been a dozen assault rifles and eleven pistols, not counting the one strapped to the waist of the skeleton in the other room – but those weapons hadn't been maintained in four hundred years and the stockpile of ammunition had suffered corrosion. The only active weapon is Alessandra's.

The lights flicker and then stabilise.

'Okay, okay,' Alessandra says aloud as an answer to the moment. Or possibly an appeal.

Neither one is inclined to crawl out from the meagre shelter of the sheet-metal table. They both know it offers no protection from a building falling on their heads, but as Runners they've both been taught to hide when the surroundings or the route become uncertain; to think it through, to adapt and innovate. This is all better accomplished while hiding in a small, dark place.

Has anyone *ever* had a good idea in a large and well-lit room?

'Okay. What are we supposed to do now?' Alessandra asks Elimisha forcefully, as though the question itself is a decision.

'We're going to prepare for Breach Protocol,' Elimisha says in a whisper.

'Like at the Stadium?'

'Yes.'

'How? I have three bullets and neither one of us has ever done this before.'

'You took Mr Whitaker's class on Stadium operations, didn't you? You're a year ahead of me.'

'Well . . . yeah. But he only explained them, he didn't tell us how to do them. And not in a bomb shelter.'

'The idea's the same,' Elimisha murmurs, her voice low. 'We need to secure the Knowledge and we need to prepare for the enemy to get in. We don't let the Knowledge fall into enemy hands: that's the first rule. Chief Lian is under orders to destroy the entire Central Archive if it's overrun – the rumour is that Lilly has filled the floor with explosives.'

347

'That's a myth,' Alessandra says firmly, but Elimisha is shaking her head.

'Why?' Elimisha says. 'It makes sense. If whoever's attacking us knew what the Stadium knows, they could become even more powerful. Plus, all the Knowledge stored there is saved elsewhere, which is the whole point of all this. Our problem is that – well, this *is* the Central Archive. So we need to do what Lian would do. We need to plan to break the internet in case they get in, and we need to take with us as much of it as we can when we get out.

'Up on the desk—' Elimisha starts to say, but Alessandra is a step ahead.

'Can we get out?'

Elimisha doesn't answer, which is the answer.

Choosing to go first, Alessandra slides out from under the desk and sits back on the chair, feeling better for it, if not safer. She reaches out her hand and helps Elimisha into the second chair.

Glasses on, Elimisha waves her hand over the White Board to activate it. She lifts the small black box with its curved edges, no markings and the one perpetually glowing blue light along the edge. She places it on the White Board and the nanites immediately reach for it and clamp down. The blue light begins to move back and forth, from edge to edge, as though it is looking at them.

'We'll need to work fast,' Elimisha says, her priorities now clear: 'Librarian? Copy all disco music to the drive.'

'Done,' came the voice through the glasses.

'What does it mean, "done"?' Alessandra asks, who heard it too.

'It means,' says Elimisha, 'it's done.'

'It didn't do anything.'

'You didn't *see* anything, but now all the disco music is in the box. So if we take the box with us, connect it to a functioning White Board and glasses that have electricity, we can listen to it, even if there's no connection to the internet. So if we're breached, we destroy the internet, grab the box and run.'

'What if the bad guys get the box?'

'Honestly? I don't think they'll know what it is and there's no obvious way for them to learn. I mean . . . Lilly still has no idea and she's been thinking about this for ever. There's no obvious reason to put the Quantum Drive on the White Board while wearing a pair of glasses, is there? Might as well put half a coconut on your head while wearing a raincoat.'

'Are you okay?'

'Not really! No!'

Alessandra decides not to poke her any more.

'You can tell it what to copy by just talking to it,' Elimisha explains. 'It seems to understand everything if you speak normally. I'm going to check the tunnel and the generators and stuff, see if I can find places for us to hide in case we're breached. I'm thinking that if we can't fight we might be able to hide and wait for them to go away, then follow them out afterwards.'

'The Commonwealth is coming for us,' Alessandra says. 'They got the message. I'm sure of it.'

Alessandra, now in charge of Archiving, tells the Librarian to play 'music that'll make me happy' as she sets about exploring the internet on her own, trying to find things to copy to the box.

Perhaps it would wiser to tell the system to make its own choices, but for the moment Alessandra doesn't like the idea of leaving everything to chance.

Aloud, but not necessarily to the Librarian, she adds, 'Okay, let's get this party started.'

When the music begins, Alessandra realises that the AI had combined her request with her encouragement to herself. A song called *Get the Party Started* begins with a girl giggling and then a thick, loud, pounding beat that Alessandra loves. The lyrics start: 'I'm coming up, so you better get this party started.'

Which is depressingly appropriate.

'Far out,' she mutters and wonders as she does whether that phrase too is new or old.

Connected to music and released from time and space and gravity, Alessandra engages the entire sensory experience of the HCG® system and glides and dips on a blanket of wind, rising and soaring through the remains of the internet. Much of it is down, but she has no sense of what is missing – only what is found.

Now she is a Runner through a library as vast as an artist's imagination and she can climb any surface, leap over any space and arrive anywhere she wants with just a wave of her hand or a click of the button that is projected into the air in front of her eyes.

Every time she jumps from a word to an object to an idea that lands in a place populated by a million souls who – somehow, out there – still exist, she feels as though she is leaping across stones a thousand metres in the air. She can start anywhere, go anyplace, linger or sprint. There are no set routes, because they form beneath her feet as she runs. There is no Order of Silence because there are no secrets. She is alive in the minds of every person who has ever been and created anything at all.

The sensation is utterly joyful – until it takes a turn.

Starting with a childish curiosity about the Olympics and

following connections almost randomly, she arrives at moments of horror:

Olympics – Greece – Mediterranean – Crete – Knossos – Labyrinth – Jorge Luis Borges – Geneva – United Nations – Universal Declaration of Human Rights – Nuremberg – Holocaust.

She arrives at a photo of a line of soldiers raising their rifles at a line of women holding babies beside a pit.

And then come the videos.

Alessandra removes her glasses.

The system resets so the Earth spins silently in space.

Graham does most of the cooking at home, leaving Henry and Alessandra in charge of the washing up. He takes a certain pleasure in varying their diet, surprising them with new foods to take their minds away from the dwindling options that are coming from the soil, and the women enjoy that. Sometimes they eat on the Stadium's wall, watching the sunlight. Sometimes, in the fair months, they cook down at the base of the waterfall. Most often, they sit at their little round table in their apartment on the ring, talking together.

Alessandra once came from a class where a Deputy Archivist had been lecturing on The Few. He talked about choice: the choice to venture out into the unknown, their luck in coming across a structure with power and fresh water and enough seclusion to fortify it before they were challenged and overwhelmed. He talked about how they faced internal threats too, and how discord or failure to compromise could have

351

weakened their early resolve. And he talked about how it was a near-miracle that The Few had been able to solidify their control over the territory before being attacked by wandering tribes or bandits or Roamers.

It was a cheery picture of their origins: the women who led them through foresight and cooperation, and the men who rose to the occasion.

Alessandra had been outside the walls with the Urban Explorers by then. She'd seen the devastation close up. Her parents had wanted her to know about it. Her mother in particular viewed the Commonwealth's Choosing Walk with suspicion; she always said it was designed to scare young people into returning, rather than equipping them with the resources needed to become independent and wise.

Alessandra, like all young people, was being trained and prepared for war, but no one ever explained to her why wars happened at all. And no one ever seemed to devote attention to preventing them, either.

'There aren't enough people left to worry about it,' was the pat answer.

'You told me,' Alessandra had said to her parents, 'that there's plenty of stuff out there – plenty of clothes, plenty of animals to hunt, more than enough places to make shelter, maybe not right around here in the desert, but out into the forests and where the Big Waters begin. So why do people fight?'

'Honour, interest and fear,' her father said, quoting Thucydides.

'Colonies or nations might fight for those reasons,' her mother had added. 'But people will fight for any reason.'

Courage regained and the glasses returned to her face, Alessandra braves the history and images of mass slaughter and genocide and slavery and terrorism and torture. She watches children taken from their parents and sold like animals into bondage and permanent misery; gas attacks and mechanised warfare; concentration camps and mass murder and gas chambers; planes used as missiles; cars used as battering rams against whole families; explosives dropped on food lines; chemical weapons dropped from aircraft over hospitals and schools; genetic marker-targeting with bioweapons for ethnic cleansing; the weaponisation of space and the Moon; the eradication of entire political parties – of entire *categories* of people.

So many categories of people, all attacking other categories. White and black. Jew and Gentile. Christian and Muslim. Democrat and Communist and Nazi. Japanese and Chinese and Korean and Philippine. Indian and Pakistani. Hutu and Tutsi. Turkish and Armenian. Catholic and Protestant.

Categories of people who don't exist any more.

She looks at the black box: a vehicle of remembrance.

Should we really remember everything? No matter the consequences? Won't that bring the categories back? – bring all of this back?

'Chief?' Alessandra yells.

'What?' Elimisha yells back from down the hall.

'Have you found . . . all this other stuff?' Alessandra shouts.

'What stuff?' Elimisha answers from another room.

'The . . . bad stuff.'

'There's a lot of that,' Elimisha shouts. 'A *lot*.'

'Should I save it?' Alessandra asks.

'Yes.'

'Have you been doing it?' Alessandra shouts.

'It hasn't been Breach Protocol yet, so . . . no, not yet. I only started copying things a few days ago and it's mostly been science and a lot of maps so we can start to grow new seed and discover and recover things that might still be out there. I only learned about the Quantum Drive just before you showed up.'

'Why should we copy the bad stuff?'

'It's Knowledge.'

'We're assuming all Knowledge is inherently good?' Alessandra asks. She is not certain Elimisha can hear her properly. 'Can you get in here? This feels important. I don't like yelling,' Alessandra yells.

As she waits, she copies across thousands of maps, hundreds of languages and dictionaries and translator tools and both high school and university courses in medicine, biology, chemistry and physics. She has just started collecting material on astronomy and cosmology when Elimisha arrives covered in a dust that changes her skin from its normal *bark-brown* to an eerie shade of grey.

'What have you been doing?'

'I was under the cabinets in the bedroom.'

'Why?'

'Looking for hidden passages and stuff.'

'The one with the dead people?'

'No. Obviously.'

'Maybe you should be looking in there.'

'I don't want to.'

'That's not a good plan, Chief,' then, 'Fine, I'll do it later,' Alessandra says, turning back to Quantum theory – whatever that is.

'Did you solve that problem?' Elimisha asks, plunking herself down into her chair again. Alessandra notices that Elimisha has changed the dressing on her leg. The wound has not become infected, which is very lucky, but she was impaled through the meat and neither girl thinks she'll ever walk properly again, let alone run or climb.

Neither mentions it.

'It doesn't make sense that all Knowledge is inherently good,' Alessandra says. 'Haven't you ever lied to anyone?'

'Not really.'

'Not your mum?'

'Well . . . her, obviously.'

'And the Urban Explorers? Every time we go out, we're lying. Turns out, by the way,' Alessandra says, 'that the Order of Silence is depending on us to break the rules and lie so it can find the best talent for the Order. It's weird, but I think lying and telling the truth and remembering and forgetting – they aren't all lined up and obvious like I thought before. I think it's more complicated than that. I'm thinking we might have to consciously decide what to put on the box and what not to.'

Elimisha shakes dust from her hair, creating a cloud they both brush away – ineffectually – by waving their hands around. 'You might be right, but I think that's for the Evaluators to figure out. Runners protect Knowledge in motion and the Archivist protects Knowledge at rest. The internet is all Knowledge at rest, so we protect it. When you copy things, you're like the Scribes. And when we carry the box, it's like we're Runners again. You see? We just need to do our jobs.'

Alessandra looks across the room to the Pirelli calendar girl in the leather jacket and no trousers. She never blinks. She never moves. She has no ideas, no opinions, no family, no history, no tastes, no needs, no desires, no friends, no decisions to make. She just fucking stands there . . . looking pretty, weak, and hungry.

'I'm sick of her,' Alessandra says.

'She's been there in the dark for more than four hundred years. Isn't that amazing?'

'I think that's long enough.' Alessandra stands up, walks over to the girl and turns the page. Next in line is another skinny, previously sick girl of about the same age with the same sad look on her face. This one wears a diaphanous cloth of some kind that's being caught by the wind as she walks barefoot across sand, her hair blowing in the breeze and her pale skin exposed to the harsh rays of the light.

'What the hell is it with these girls?' Alessandra asks.

'She's going to step on something,' Elimisha says. 'Barefoot in the sand? Can you even imagine?'

'That was before The Rise,' Alessandra says, trying to make sense of it. 'I'm sure there was less metal and stuff.'

'Yeah but still . . .'

They both look a moment longer.

'Under what circumstances does a woman wander around naked in the desert?' Elimisha wonders.

'Maybe she was attacked. You know the dangers.'

'She looks fine. There are no bruises. And the picture's kind of . . . pretty.'

'Ghost Talker?'

'That's all I can think of.'

Alessandra turns and looks back at Elimisha and the spinning Earth between them. 'Until you found all this, the only thing Evaluators did was determine whether something was true. They didn't decide whether it was valuable. We simply collected whatever we found and worried about whether it was valuable later.'

'What do you mean, valuable?'

'I mean,' Alessandra says, throwing up her hands, '*good* – I mean good for us. Like . . . the way food is good for us. Or

356

whether it's poison. We're putting Knowledge into ourselves and we're not wondering what might happen to us. Evaluators don't know how to do that. There was never enough to worry about it before. Now there is.'

'And?' Elimisha asks.

'And I'm saying maybe we shouldn't copy some of this. Secrets can be good.'

'I don't think that's our choice to make. I think it's a worthwhile question, but for the Commonwealth. For . . . you know . . . adults.'

Alessandra does not agree, not at all. 'Some of these ideas are crazy and dangerous. There are places where they used to take knives and cut off girls'—'

'I know. I know. I saw. I know . . .'

'Well,' says Alessandra, 'they don't do it any more, do they? And I really don't want to give them the idea. Do you?'

'Not really.'

'So let's not!'

Elimisha is unconvinced. 'If we don't remember, who will?'

'Maybe it would be better if we forgot,' Alessandra says, coming to the inevitable conclusion of her line of reasoning.

'Are you agreeing with the Keepers? Who tried to kill us?'

'The Keepers have some kind of philosophy,' says Alessandra. 'They don't actually know anything. I'm looking at real stuff that will actually hurt people. It's not the same thing.'

'You're still recommending that we throw out the past and lots of Knowledge. Like them, you're suggesting that we forget.'

'I guess I am. Yes.' Alessandra removes her glasses and starts to pull off the gloves. They fit snugly and it takes some time. 'You said the Gone World ended because people didn't trust each other when something bad happened, and they didn't have ways to work together to solve their problems. If that's true, it's not really about remembering or forgetting, is it? It's about how we work together with whatever we've got. If some Knowledge will make it harder to work together, I say we leave it out.'

'What if it's the opposite?' Elimisha says. 'What if knowing all that is what brings us all together? What if that's the proof we need to scare us into cooperation? Or what if there's something that seems useless or harmful now but in the end is what saves us all? Or, what if people already remember and we just don't know it? Then we'd be the ones to forget and they'd be the ones to remember and we're throwing out what we need the most! We can't know any of this just sitting here,' Elimisha says.

'People used to *own* other people!'

'Maybe, out there someplace, they still do. And maybe all the best reasons for not doing it are sitting right there!'

'I think the risk of doing harm is greater than the possibility of doing good. I say we copy the science and the great music and forget all the history and literature and religion and anything that makes people hate each other,' Alessandra concludes.

'All that stuff was supposed to make people love each other,' Elimisha whispers.

'And it didn't work – perhaps you've noticed!'

Elimisha isn't convinced. And she's the Chief. 'I think that if you bury the truth on purpose and someone finds out, there will be hell to pay. Copy it,' Elimisha says. 'That's an order.'

That night, Alessandra lies in her cot, unable to keep her eyes closed. She is picturing the family in the next room and feeling the weight of their presence. If she could be anywhere now it would be with her mother on the Western Wall, facing out over the river that gushes out from deep underground and meanders into the far distance where no one ever goes. She imagines that it was a big sky tonight, a night without clouds when the colours fade with a softness and warmth that is nothing like fire.

Like the presence of the family in the next room, though, Alessandra feels the presence of the Keeper army in the distance of her daydream. Watching the sun set is not enough. There is a danger lurking out there and she has to attend to it. It would be wishful to think their intention is to walk past on their way to another place like the troops she and her mother watched when she was little.

And yet that sound last night, the one that caused the ground to shake yet again . . .

Alessandra looks up at the mattress above her. There are hatch marks there that seem to move in the poor light; they are disturbing her vision and that's more than she can take, given the silence, the family, the Keepers.

She slips out of bed in search of a new mood.

Out in the hallway she stands in front of the door that hides the dead family inside. As she stares at it a thought occurs to her. She walks to the Communications Room and sits at the Throne. The system comes alive when she puts on the glasses.

The Librarian has told them about retinal scans and voice recognition passkeys, barriers that once prevented people from sitting down and simply using an access point like she is doing now. Knowing that the entire world was ending, a 'Presidential Executive Order', whatever that was, banned all barriers to general internet access in the final days. If that one last act of foresight hadn't happened centuries ago, she and Elimisha wouldn't have been able to use the internet and radio now. Not for the first time, she reflects on the impossibility of knowing how much is owed to the dead.

359

'Librarian?' Alessandra says, waking it.

'Yes, Alessandra?'

'Did you know the family inside this bunker?'

'Yes.'

'How long were they here before they died?'

'Four days.' It provides the date and local time.

'Is there a record of their experiences?'

'There is a video diary.'

'What's a diary?'

'A diary is a record of the creator's experiences, thoughts or attitudes, often produced daily and intended for means of catharsis or record-keeping. Diaries were historically produced in written form, but later were created using a variety of multi-media, including but not limited to audio or visual recordings, biometric data entry and automated or programmed self-surveillance.'

Alessandra doesn't know many of these words but she has grown used to that and is currently not in the mood to care. Every question is like a Black Jump into endless exploration on the internet; the only thing that breaks the fall is remembering why you asked in the first place.

'Can I see the last entry?'

The Librarian says yes and then produces it. As soon as it plays, Alessandra realises that she has made a mistake.

Replacing the spinning Earth is the face of a man, perhaps a little younger than her own father, with pinker skin. His face looks careworn and there is a tremendous anxiousness in his eyes. His hands are busy beyond the edges of her glasses. It is clear that he recorded this from the very seat where Alessandra is now sitting.

He has well-cut thick black hair and his eyes, a cold blue like deep ice, are as bright as her own when she looks into a mirror. The detail and texture of him are as real as looking into her father's face as he bends to kiss her goodnight. She is looking at an Ancient as though he is here, speaking directly to her from a seat across from her own.

He is afraid but controlled. She has never seen an adult so scared, but he is not a soldier now: he is a father.

'They say,' he begins in a weak voice – and his accent is much like her own – 'that the sub-sea conduits are being attacked and we could lose connections to Europe, Asia and Africa any time. The satellites are ... off-line. The solar flares and the EMP did a real job on them. After that, the suicide satellites moved into position beside mission-critical systems and self-de-structed, which took down almost everything else. The debris is in orbit, we're told, so they're predicting a cascade failure greater than anything we've ever seen. The whole civilian grid is going to be destroyed. The missiles have landed, but they weren't nuclear – not yet. I'm told they released a neurotoxin or possibly a nanotech bioweapon that kills ... immediately. I don't know if we'll be safer in here or not, but the kids feel better in the bedroom so we'll ride it out there. I brought a few books with me.'

The man rubs his face.

'I never read the classics – I wasn't interested. Now I feel like I want to be close to something eternal, something that's already lasted, so I know it will be here later too. We got so much wrong.'

There is another explosion in the video. It sounds like a heavy thud. Dust falls into his hair. 'I have to go. Abigail and William are scared. May the Lord have mercy on our souls and forgive our folly.'

The man stands and the screen becomes empty. Without Alessandra prompting it, the image changes and she is watching the family from inside the room where they are going to die. Alessandra watches the two children cowering under the arms of their mother. The man kisses and hugs them. He touches his wife, who says to him, 'Read to us. Anything.'

He sits at the desk and opens a book and says, 'This is the Longfellow translation of Dante.'

The woman is not listening to words, only to the sound of his voice and the heartbeats of her children.

> *Midway upon the journey of our life*
> *I found myself within a dark forest,*
> *For the straightforward pathway had been lost . . .*

The man reads as though getting the words out and into the air somehow matters, is somehow an act of necessity.

The children cry and with every subsequent shake, the dust falls from the ceiling. Alessandra listens to his words and, like the children, tries to be soothed by them. But they cannot because they are scared and young and she cannot because she knows how the story ends. As the man is compelled to read, she is equally compelled to listen. A bond – a duty – has been awakened in her that feels like it would be unholy to break. She must bear witness, even if doing so breaks her.

The language is opaque and much has been lost over the 1,200 years between the writer's own voice in the year 1300 and her own ears now, but there are moments of transparent understanding that flow into her; pure and complete:

> *Of those things only should one be afraid*
> *Which have the power of doing others harm;*
> *Of the rest, no; because they are not fearful.*

Soon after reading this verse a thunderous boom shakes the camera and, moments later, the children begin to cough, followed by the wife and then the man. A drop of blood flies from Abigail's mouth and the man becomes frantic as the woman tries to comfort her children while her own coughing becomes uncontrollable.

His hands shaking, the man removes a key from around his neck and opens a box from which he removes two yellow and red devices that look like the receivers of a rifle but without a stock or barrel. He breaks the seals on them as the little girl spits blood and the mother screams, her eyes darting to anything – *anything at all* – that might save them.

He holds the detonators, shaking from pain inside himself, one pain of the body and another of the soul. He is meant to squeeze the triggers and collapse the building to end the excruciating pain instantly, bringing forward the end that cannot be stopped. He turns and watches his children as blood trickles from down their eyes instead of tears and his wife clutches them to her breast in an effort to return them to the body that built them from the very stuff of her own; a body that was once a fortress that protected them.

Alessandra knows for a fact that the man cannot and did not pull those triggers, because she is sitting in the room that otherwise would have been rubble. She knows the children will cough themselves to death; a cough so violent she imagines their souls trying to escape their dying bodies to find new hosts.

All of this is coming next and it will happen before her eyes – across the centuries – and Alessandra starts to cough and gasp for breath too because she is so choked with fear and terror and empathy and love and she yells, 'Stop it! Turn it off!' and that fast – an eyeblink – the glasses return to the silent, distant spinning Earth. Four hundred years vanish in a heartbeat, leaving Alessandra rocking in her chair like a baby, with her head down between her knees in the hope that she can vomit this Knowledge out and it will become something separate from herself that she can wash away and forget.

'No,' she says to herself.

She *will* bear witness. She will Attest. She will be strong and see the past, but she will not pass on the sickness of *mind* that caused the Ancients to kill their own, to do this to one another *on purpose*. She will not leave these decisions up to Evaluators who might lack the empathy to know the pain of what they might cause.

He was unable to bring the building down and spare his family their excruciating deaths. So Alessandra, centuries later and in her own way, will do it for him.

When she has recovered, she orders the Librarian to find the bad memories that might already be on the Quantum Drive – the memories of human destruction and malfeasance and murder and inhumanity; the literature that made sense of them; the videos that documented them – and erase them all: the racism, the nationalism, the anti-Semitism, the sexism, the ideologies that would have separated the people at the Commonwealth into groups they have never even heard of and filled them with ideas they would never have dreamed on their own.

The Keepers are right about one thing . . . you can stop the plague, or you spread it, and Alessandra is not going to be the source of humanity's second Apocalypse.

Alessandra returns to her cot to sleep. The ticks on the mattress are still moving, but she no longer cares. She falls into a deep sleep and dreams of a kitten who walks, uncertainly, across a thick rope between two soaring building and – despite almost slipping off many times – successfully reaches the other side.

RESCUE

It is dark when Henry wakes on the cold slab of stone beneath her shooting perch at Sniper Location Echo. She does not realise how dark it is until her right eye adjusts to the moonlight streaming through the shooting window in the wall. With a shaking hand she reaches up to touch her left eye and feels thick blood caked all over her face. She cannot see the hand that probes her. It is only her right eye, the one that was protected by the shatter-proof scope, that can see the dust as it drifts across the moon light.

The girl – Bee – is not here. Henrietta is alone.

If the room is still, it is not silent. Wails of pain float through the air – not her own; they come from outside somewhere. The Flats, she assumes.

Henry too is in pain, but it is not unbearable. The debris that blasted through the window struck her face and her open eye, but the rest of her had been protected by the leather. There is no mirror, but she is certain the scratches and other wounds are deep.

There is a dull pain in her side from the fall off the table. Her ribs, perhaps. She is bruised too, but those will heal.

Henry braces against the table to push herself up. The dizziness compels her to hang onto the table leg. Feeling unsteady and light-headed, she finds a piece of cloth to cover her left eye, creating a patch.

The room smells like woodsmoke, rotten eggs and burning meat.

When she is ready she stands and looks outside to assess the battle.

It is night. Yellow Ridge is a black mound traced by a meandering line of orange torch fires stretching for miles, separating the black earth below from the white stars peeking out from the rising greens swirls of night above.

If every light is a soldier, there are *thousands* of them. Somehow The Drop did not kill them off. Henry wonders if Winters set it off too soon. Whatever the reason, an enormous, organised army awaits them at dawn.

Her rifle is on the table. She checks its condition. It is filthy and covered in grit and dust, but there are no scratches on the unbreakable crystal of the scope and nothing indicates that it can't fire again. She will have to test it later.

As the shock starts to wear off her eye socket starts pulsing with pain and she thinks of Graham and Alessandra.

Henrietta slings the rifle and hobbles to the doorway. She uses the walls for support and holds the bannister of the stairs on her way down. There is a long, torch-lit corridor full of people on missions to fulfil their tasks; they ignore her as she progresses gingerly. She is not the only one wounded and she is not requesting assistance.

When she breaks out into the Green the smell hits her harder. The Phalanx formations still stand and the Archers remain at their ready but there is an uneasy quiet and their formations look slack.

She grabs a Lieutenant Colonel she knows as he is walking by. He looks perturbed when he sees her.

'Rodriguez,' she says.

'What happened to your face?' he asks.

'Where's Winters? The High Command?' she says, ignoring his question.

'We're told they're building a new strategy.'

'What the hell does that mean?' Henry asks.

'It means the old one didn't work. That's what it means, Commander.' Rodriguez is old for his rank.

'And in the meantime?' she asks.

'We've been told to defend the walls at all cost until they get back with something better. So while we remain poised for battle waiting for the hammer to fall, the enemy is resting and sleeping and eating and gathering their strength for an attack that could come now or never.'

'Where are they building this new strategy? Up there?' she says, nodding towards the Snake Tower.

'The Map Room.'

Birch and the High Command hear a pounding at the door of the Map Room, which is rare because usually the guards restrain anyone from doing that, most often by killing them.

As that didn't happen, it means it is probably Henry Wayworth, because no one else would dare.

Except Lilly, of course. But she's already in the room.

Birch winces at the noise pounding her ears because of the domed shape of the ceiling. As quickly as possible she waves her hand and signals the guards at the door to open it before they all go deaf.

As expected, it is Henrietta – but the sight of her injuries holds Birch's tongue. Even Winters says nothing.

'What happened to your face?' Lilly says as she stands and moves across the room to meet her

'It's nothing.'

'Let me see it.'

Lilly removes Henry's makeshift dressing and stares into the frosty lens of what remains of the eye. She knows, having seen such wounds before, that it will never heal and Henry will never see through it again. 'I'll wrap it up so it doesn't get worse,' she says gently.

Henry looks into Lilly's face for an answer to her unspoken question and, reluctantly, finds it.

Birch looks at Winters for the right to continue and she nods, knowing that sending Henry away now is pointless.

Javier and Lian are there too, leaning over a very large map of the region.

'The situation,' explains Birch, 'is that we have food reserves for sixty days for seven hundred people, after which we starve. That's two months. By three months, we're dead and have lost the Stadium, unless we regain access to both the farmland by the river and a critical mass of trade supplies. We might do the first. We'll never do the second. The fact is, the Commonwealth is not sustainable if the Keepers maintain a siege with that new army. What I want to propose is a way that will possibly save the Stadium, will definitely save the Commonwealth and preserve our way of life, and should save most of the people. Despite this,' Birch adds, 'it will sound like failure.'

Winters places her hands on the table and slumps. When she saw the Keepers charge across the flat she had been certain the day was hers and the battle would become the poetry and fire-songs of the territory for decades to come. Now they're planning to flee and the fault is hers. She still doesn't know what she did wrong.

Lilly has her own thoughts on the matter but for a change, holds her opinion.

'Speak,' Winters says to Birch.

'I'll start with the Stadium. I suggest we take six hundred people away and leave a hundred behind to defend it. That would give them a year or more of food reserves. Not all our tunnels are down; those left will allow them to smuggle in smaller quantities, which might be enough, especially if we leave a contingent of the Order behind. We've not only been storing Knowledge: we've been packing away rice, dried meats, water, seed and more. The Few – long ago – were able to farm on the Green and with the pulse weapons and explosives and their training, we believe a small contingent of a hundred people can defend the walls even against these odds.'

'And where would these six hundred people go?' Javier asks.

'I'll get to that. But the first part of the plan is finding the girls and rescuing the internet.'

'You mean,' says Henry, 'rescuing the girls and finding the internet.'

'Yes. Of course,' says Birch, though her face says otherwise.

Using a detailed map of the Gone World buildings which Henry has never seen before, Birch explains how there is a good chance that the Otis Shaft in Elimisha's building, which goes all the way from ceiling to cellar, might still be accessible. The shafts, she says, are extremely durable because of their shape; they are often the last parts to fall. There is also an air vent, apparently, that might connect the Otis Shaft to the bunker, and with an extremely long rope . . .

Henry's face throbs and she's unable to focus on the details. Her eye pulses and burns with every beat of her heart as she fights back the dread that surrounds her like a black cloud of smoke, threatening to engulf her if she makes the mistake of thinking about it.

She needs to not think about it because Alessandra needs her, and so does her husband. So if there's a mission outside these walls to save them, she's going.

'I'd like to return to my question,' says Javier, less interested in the rescue plan than the entire crazy strategy itself. 'Move on to *where*? We've been here a hundred and fifty years because there's nowhere else *to* go.'

Birch looks to Winters for approval and she, in turn, looks non-committal about the release of their greatest secret and for which countless lives – Members of the Order, Explorers, Runners, Archivists, settlers, soldiers – have been lost or destroyed.

'I need verbal permission to release this information, General, so others can Attest.'

'Granted,' Winters says in a resigned tone.

'South,' Birch says. 'We will go very, very far south.'

'That's a Black Jump into nothing,' Javier says.

'What I'm going to tell you,' says Birch, 'is our most closely guarded secret. And Lilly . . . it is going to pain you.'

Birch instructs the assistants to make space for a second map to sit beside the detailed Territory map now at the centre of the table. 'The Commonwealth is larger than any of you know.

Our Stadium,' she says, trying not to be dramatic, 'is not the Commonwealth's only home. In fact, there are four hundred more souls who are part of the Commonwealth. They live in a Museum built by an architect of the mid-21st century named Emilio Rubinson. It is located in a mountain range in a place called Mexico in an area once called Veracruz.'

'What are you talking about?' Javier asks.

'Forty years ago an Explorer came back with news of a community who lived there. The path there was . . . perilous . . . and it took years to get there and back again. These Explorers became our first Cartographers. The Order of Silence got the idea of charting the coastlines from Card number 106 from the Trivial Pursuit deck.'

Lian, who long ago memorised them all, quotes, 'Which 16th century cartographer created a map designed to simplify navigation?'

'Right. We used it to build a route,' Birch says, moving on, 'which we now call the Blue Route. Originally, it started with a climb over the mountains. Our Explorer – David Shoreman – earned the trust of the Museum folk by teaching them how to stitch nets to guard against flying bugs, how to deliver babies more safely and how to clean water using recovered bottles and the light of the sun. The Museum language is called *Espanyol*, but many of them spoke ours too. A bond was formed and a relationship began. It turned out they had a small Trove of Knowledge there too and they were like-minded as to its value, but unlike us, they didn't have a Harrington Box and a Lilly to give that impulse some structure. We taught them our classification systems, Scribe processes and archiving solutions and they mirrored our efforts. We started to exchange Knowledge, which is why, fifty years ago, the Central Archive began growing so rapidly. It was too far away for our Runners, so we had the idea that the Museum should have their own Runners and Evaluators and Scribes and all the rest. Coordinating our efforts while keeping them completely secret meant they needed to meet us halfway and we each needed a liaison, a representative from here to live there, and one of their own to live here. At first we were the teachers, but that didn't last long and now their people know as much as ours, and in some subjects, more. Our treaty-bond commits us to helping one another. They are – and always have been – waiting for us. And we have been waiting for them. And now . . . now it's time to send our people there.'

'There's another Commonwealth?' Lian says, trying to draw out the logic of this.

'We like to think it's the other part of the same Commonwealth, Chief.'

Fifty years ago. Lilly does the maths in her head.

'Who did you send? This Liaison?' She doesn't really need to ask.

'Verena,' says Birch. 'But it wasn't me – it was before my time.'

Lilly does not move a muscle. She holds her face perfectly still. 'Is she . . . ?'

'She died two years ago.'

'How far away is it?' asks Javier, ignoring the drama.

'About two thousand five hundred kilometres,' says Birch, her voice flat.

'How would that even work?' Javier yells, opening his hands in appeal. 'We'd have to fight our way through barbarians from here to there and feed six hundred people, some old,

373

some young, some injured, some weak. We'd be a drawn-out line of exposed civilians, because we'd be leaving our best to defend the Stadium. It's a fool's plan. Exciting and bold, yes, but foolish.'

'In all our wanderings,' Birch says quietly, 'we have never come across a territory with more people than here. It's a dead world, Colonel. If we take to the road, we will be the most powerful army on it, even with only two hundred armed troops. All our children, our elderly, our infirm, are trained for war. We go slow, we keep the lines tight. We dig in and fortify when necessary. If these Keepers let us go, our chances are better out there than here because time is against us, Chief Javier. We need to prepare the departure while a team is finding the girls and the internet. I will be leading that team.'

'I'm going too,' Henry says.

'There's no sense in denying your condition—'

Henry ignores Birch. 'I'll meet you in the stables.'

As Birch and Henry walk towards the door, Lian moves back to study the map. It shows a coastline along an endless ocean stretching thousands of kilometres down a country that has no apparent end.

'Mercator,' she says to herself, running her fingers along the unbroken line as though it were the curve of a lover. 'Gerardus Mercator.'

On the way out of the Map Room, Birch takes Lilly by the arm.

'Get away from me,' Lilly whispers.

'There's a letter for you.'

'What letter?'

'I was only allowed to release it if the secret of the Museum became known. It's part of my—'

'What *goddamned* letter?'

'From Verena.'

DECOYS

When darkness falls, Graham watches the Keepers light torches all along the Ridge around him. It is an extraordinary display, given the scarcity of wood in these parts. At first Graham thinks the lights are a ritual, a ceremony for the dead below.

They are not.

Each Keeper is carrying two or three torches to exaggerate their numbers. They keep moving, on foot or by horse, handing them off to others, making it impossible for anyone at the Stadium to count them or track individual movements. It is, he can tell, both a practised dance and a sophisticated military manoeuvre. Graham is developing a grudging respect for these people, who are brave and self-sacrificing, if strong-headed and unyielding in their immutable beliefs.

The Deputy, who had left him unattended for hours, now returns on a horse, dismounts and stands beside him again.

'Are you going to bury him?' Graham asks.

'No.'

'You think so little of life?'

'We think that little of death.'

'How about,' Graham says, standing, 'I go home. And when I do, you all go home too. It's been a day. Let's be done with it.'

The man snorts like a hog.

'He was a better leader than you,' Graham says, resigned to what he knows must be done next and knowing it will have to be uncompromising and fast. 'He had questions. He *wondered*. He was pained by the cruelty of the choices he faced. There was a humanity to him. You, however, have no questions and so you'll never learn anything.' He tosses a pebble at another and hits it. 'I don't see you lasting long in this job.'

'He had no questions.'

'The bullet didn't kill him immediately,' Graham says, choosing his words carefully. 'His last words were about the memory of his wife and daughter. His final thoughts were of the past. He betrayed your religion and therefore all of you. He chose love. A bit late, if you ask me, but it was touching all the same. You should have been there.'

'You lie.'

For the first time Graham hears a tension in the man's voice. What he tells the Deputy is not what he believes in his heart, but there is work to be done and he is a Raider, not a diplomat. Now is the time to weaken his enemy because the chance for peace is as dead as the past.

Graham looks around and sees that for all the movement, all the activity, all the torches and preparedness, no one is paying any particular attention to them or their conversation. Which means the time is now.

He dusts off his boots and stands, brushing himself clean of the dust and the day. He steps to the old Leader's dead body and kneels down. With care, he unties the red sash and removes his white robe, which is red at the stomach with blood.

The Deputy, confused by this foreign ritual, stares on.

Graham, undressing the body, asks a question. 'There was a girl approaching the Gone World. What happened to her?'

'We buried her,' he says.

'That girl is my daughter,' says Graham, 'and she survived. Unlike you.' Without raising his voice or blinking, Graham shoves the long slender knife from his boot up through the man's chin and into his brain.

As the Deputy's hands reach instinctively to his own neck, Graham pulls him in close and eases them both gently to the ground. He does not say a word as they lock eyes, but he follows the Deputy's gaze until the distance is too great.

Alone with two bodies, Graham works quickly. He dons the white robe of the former leader and ties the red sash around his own waist, which covers much of the blood. He is hoping the darkness and the movement will cover the rest.

There is a hood, which he pulls over his head before mounting the Deputy's waiting horse. A touch of the heels spurs it to movement and together they gallop along the ridge in the direction of the Gone World where Alessandra – he can only hope – is still waiting.

The Tribesmen look at the determined rider racing across the Ridge. His robes are illuminated by the orange flames of their own torches. There were rumours among the newcomers of the Leader's death but they are people who have been taught to trust their eyes and there in front of them is the man himself.

As he rushes past them, his face and features are obscured by his mourning shroud but they recognise his body and the quality of his riding.

A lone figure in white, he bursts from their ranks on the Ridge and for reasons of his own, tears across the desert sands towards the Gone World, leaving a rippled cloud of spreading dust in the moonlight behind him.

The Spotters see the new movement on the Ridge.

Anoushka, below on the Green, is covered in Moishe's blood from carrying him on her own shoulders to the medical ward, where she had to leave him in the care of a child whose head barely reached Anoushka's own chest. Having returned to her post, she hears the rhythm of warning on the steel drums used by the Spotters to signal an enemy change of position.

She's heard it almost a dozen times already tonight, and while the Spotters are good at their jobs and ten of those times she's agreed with their assessments, the relentless pacing is wearing her down. She tries not to think of Moishe's missing hand, which is lying . . . somewhere. But to not think about it, she has to think about it first, making her curse her own mind.

Anoushka grips the sides of the ladder which will take her up to the top of the wall (for the twentieth time today, at least) but she pauses to lower her head, catch her breath, clear her mind and regain her focus.

They are saying there is something new to see. She needs to be able to see it.

Knowing she is alone and that her face is concealed in the dark, she allows herself a few precious moments to sob, then she shakes her head and breathes it off, steels her eyes and mounts the ladder.

Around her neck is one of the ten night-vision monoculars issued to the division Masters. She cradles it like a newborn as she climbs and crests the wall.

Lying flat on her stomach she turns on the Infrared

Illuminator and the night becomes hers to command. Each monocular bears the symbol of the inter-locking Olympic rings of the Stadium. They were found here by The Few. She was told they were for watching sporting events.

She and Moishe, two years older than her, are both Stadium-born. They didn't see each other as possible mates until about five years ago. They met as adults – with hearts equally open – one night after he finished playing his piano at a spring festival. She told him that he concentrated too hard when playing music. She hadn't yet realised that she was already jealous for his attention. This had made him laugh. It reminded him of a story his grandfather used to tell of a rabbi who would concentrate so intently that one time a bird passed over his head and burst into flames.

'What's a rabbi?' she asked.

He didn't know.

'What was he concentrating on?'

'You,' Moishe said. 'He just didn't know it yet.'

He told her that night that every song is a story that carries a promise of a resolution and a happy ending. He said his ear told this to the heart without it ever passing through the mind. It had learned that only recently and hadn't told anyone yet.

She was worried from the beginning that she might drown in the depths of him.

She places the monocular to her eye. The Keepers are not coming down the hill; instead, there is a figure in a bright white robe riding north on the ridge as though the horse's tail is on fire. She magnifies and presses the monocular against the pole for stability. She can see him riding towards the Gone World and counts twenty riders following him. She can't see his face but she is certain she has seen those robes before.

The Leader.

If the figure in white is the Leader of the enemy force and he is leaving the field of battle in a hurry, the High Command needs to know.

Anoushka's senior messenger is a lanky boy. Although he is fast and reliable, he is rubbery and his limbs flail as he bounces off the torch-lit tunnels below the Green. His arms whip around him after every turn and he skids around corners with the unpractised skill of a foal on blue ice.

When Birch finally sees the source of the commotion she wonders how he was chosen for the job at all. He would make a better decoy than a silent messenger – he wouldn't last long in the new job, but he'd be good at it until the end.

'Quiet,' Birch says to him when he comes into view.

She is clad in black leather, standing in the underground stables that were untouched by the blast. She is soothing a black horse that is calm already. She slips a shortsword into her backpack and a pistol into a holster at her side. Henry, beside her, is already mounted and she too is all in black. Her rifle is harnessed at her side and she is chewing dried meat, not having eaten in a day.

There is a new – and proper – patch on her eye. She is not the first to have lost one.

'From General Winters,' says the boy, talking to the dirt between his knees.

Birch and Henry say nothing.

'The enemy leader,' he announces, 'has taken a contingent of soldiers to the Gone World. About twenty of them are riding in his wake, moving fast. They're ten minutes ahead.'

'Where are they going?' Birch says.

'They ran off the Ridge in a hurry, making a straight line towards the urbanscape.'

'That doesn't make any sense. Who's the source?' Henry asks.

'Anoushka, Master of Archers.'

'She's very solid,' Birch says to Henry.

'General Winters thinks the Keepers know about . . . wherever it is you're going,' says the boy, panting and clueless.

'Leave,' Birch instructs the boy and in haste, he is gone.

Once the excitement leaves the room and no one is sucking the air out, they consider what they heard. Henry says, 'I put a bullet in the Leader's gut. I accept that Anoushka saw someone in a white robe, but it wasn't the man I shot.'

'Maybe it's the new one,' Birch says, mounting her horse and motioning for their escort team to prepare themselves.

'Not in the same white robe it's not. He was the only one wearing white.'

'Maybe it's the colour of leadership. The new one dresses like the old one?'

'Maybe,' Henry says.

'If they know about the radio or the internet, why not take a hundred troops and secure it? Why only twenty? They have people to spare and no counter-force in the Ridge,' Birch asks.

Henry considers Birch's question and, turning her horse towards the tunnel entrance off the stable says, 'We don't know. We don't have enough information.'

'That,' says Birch, 'is the correct answer.'

Henry and Birch wrap black scarves around their faces and ease their own horses down into the tunnel, where they fall into line with two columns of Dragoons dressed in black robes.

Each carries a lance that is long and heavy and rests on the shoulder of the rider in front.

The mission leader, at the front on the right, clicks his tongue once, twice, and on the third they all move in unison at a walk. The horses know the pattern; they are trained for this exit manoeuvre, which is known as a Cruel Birth. He clicks again and they all advance at a trot in the dark of the tunnel as the orange light of the Stadium's interior fades behind them and their own shadows ahead grow long and then faint and then vanish altogether.

Their speed rises to a canter, with less than a metre separating each one in the dark. They are moving fast, like a building wind. Henry is finding her right eye starting to tear, which it has never done before, and she realises she cannot judge distance any more, meaning that she will never be able to shoot properly without the scope's instruments to be her missing eye.

She concentrates, again, on her family.

The Dragoons ride to the sound of the hoofbeats and their own thighs slapping the saddles, the horses' breaths and their enormous lungs echoing out like thunderclaps.

'How's your face?' Birch, beside her, asks Henry as they gallop.

'What possible difference does it make?' Henry answers.

She can feel Birch continuing to look at her.

'What?' Henry asks.

'We're clear on the mission, right?'

Henry has no time to answer as the party rips through vines and a diaphanous gauze that conceals the exit.

Like a porcupine backing out of a cave at the speed of sound, the Dragoons – singly, on cue and dancing as one – lift their lances from the shoulder of the rider in front and hold them outwards.

In moments they encounter five enemy soldiers on patrol, drawn by the curious sound they could not locate or name; their lives immediately end, impaled by the Dragoons, leaving no witnesses to the midnight venture.

Moving fast as a unit, the columns break to the right in front of the two women, those who had been riding behind them joining their fellows.

The practised choreography means the two women are now riding to the left of the Dragoons.

'Make sure the Leader in white sees you and follows you,' Birch says to the mission leader, 'but don't make it too obvious.'

'Yes, Master,' he says.

'Godspeed,' she says to him as the columns peel away to the east and she and Henry veer away from them and set off clandestinely for the Gone World ahead.

BREACH

Elimisha rises early and looks at her sleeping friend on the facing cot. Alessandra is lying on her side with the pillow tucked comfortably beneath her head. To Elimisha, Alessandra looks much older than her seventeen years. She's more womanly than Elimisha feels. She doesn't have the same soft-edged, baby-smooth skin. Alessandra has a confidence and certainty and independence that Elimisha sees in people in their twenties or older.

Then again, maybe all girls think this about the other girl across the room.

When she stands to stretch she feels an immediate stabbing pain in her leg, which collapses beneath her, forcing her back to her cot. Blood has soaked through her sleeping gown and there is a tingle all the way down her leg to her feet. Something is really wrong and she has no idea what it is or what to do about it. At the Commonwealth, the doctor's usual advice is, 'Leave it alone and keep it clean and let the body do the work.' That's better advice than most people get at The Crossing but it doesn't always work.

It's not working now.

385

Elimisha struggles to her feet anyway and performs her morning routine. She checks the time with the Librarian. It is only 5:30 a.m.

Elimisha sits in the communications room with her morning tea, a drink she discovered here in the bunker and which has become a blessing. At this early hour she seldom broadcasts; in her view it is better to keep to a schedule. However, now that she knows the Stadium is listening, she figures everything has changed. It feels strange, speaking to a stranger in Weapons and Communications, but maybe it's no stranger than speaking into the void, which is what she was doing before.

Feeling lonely, the silence becoming too heavy, Elimisha pulls the microphone towards her, depresses the grey button and starts to talk:

'Good morning . . . Stadium. I know someone's there but I don't know who. I wish I knew what was going on out there. I feel like I'm trapped in that tent – do you know the story? It was a Commonwealth storyteller who wrote it. My father used to tell it to me – I was still pretty young when he died, so it always makes me a little sad, but I'm sad now, so maybe sharing it is what the sadness wants from me. I don't always know what the sadness wants. Anyway, it's called *Wilful Creatures*. That's what he used to call us, me and my brothers. Do they know I'm okay? Has anyone told them? And my mum? You need to tell them – they must be going crazy. Okay, so, there were once four children who lived in a tent in a deep forest. But the forest was so dangerous they weren't allowed to go out. So every night, when their parents fell asleep, they would each place their hands on a tent wall and together they would push it until the tent grew a bit bigger. And as the tent got bigger, more and more of the world started to grow inside it – more trees and animals and relics from the Gone World. Each morning the mother would wake and say, 'The world looks so much bigger today!' and the father would say, 'That's because the children are growing,' and this happened every day until the tent was as wide as the world itself and the children became adults, and there was nowhere else to go because the world was now full and endless. But that didn't matter because on the day that the world became whole and complete, a little tent appeared in the centre of *that* world and inside it was a family with four little children, fast asleep with their parents.'

Elimisha pours more tea.

'I didn't know if they were called Wilful Creatures because they tricked their parents, or because they had the will to change the world and explore it and make it bigger, or whether it was because it was somehow a story about how all of us will survive because life promises to start over even at the end. I like it, though, knowing that nothing really ends. I guess the big question is whether or not it repeats in an endless circle or whether that circle can be broken somehow. Who knows?'

She pictures her father kissing her on the forehead and both cheeks, the way he did every night, then calling for their mother to come in and do the same.

'Anyway,' she says, after another sip, 'I used to picture the trees growing inside the tent – and this is kind of funny actually, because—'

There is a *BANG* and Elimisha spins in her chair to look behind her. She hears bare feet slapping against the floor and knows it is Alessandra, but she is not running towards her. She's is running from the bedroom to someplace else.

She hears Alessandra scream, 'Get the gun – *get the gun!*'

Elimisha opens the desk drawer and removes the pistol. She

struggles to her feet and moves as quickly as pain allows down the corridor, listening to thumping and banging inside the kitchen.

When she arrives, she sees Alessandra in her nightgown holding up the axe and shaking.

A man's voice comes from inside the caved-in tunnel. It is eerily calm, the accent different from their own.

'We have already won the war. There is nothing you can do.'

'Fuck off!' yells Elimisha.

Alessandra looks at Elimisha and sees her holding the gun.

'Are there really no more weapons?' Alessandra asks.

'None that work, and bluffing won't work here,' she whispers

'We have to get out of here,' Alessandra whispers back.

'We have guns,' Elimisha yells at the man, bluffing. 'We're armed and we'll kill you all!'

Alessandra gives her a look.

Strong arms start swinging tools in the tunnel. Their progress is aggressive.

Elimisha grabs Alessandra and pulls her to the side and whispers, 'You have to hold them off. I have to destroy the internet.'

'Yeah, okay. Go fast.'

Elimisha pulls away but Alessandra doesn't let go. 'Wait – then what?'

'I don't know!'

Hopping down the hallway, her heart pounding with fear because they are trapped, Elimisha shouts, 'Librarian!'

'How can I assist you?'

'Can you destroy yourself?' she asks him.

'No,' the Librarian answers.

'If I break the White Board, is the internet broken?'

'No. The interface provides access to the internet. It is not synonymous with—'

'If I break the board, can I permanently prevent access to the internet?'

'Internet access can be restored by reconnecting another device capable of performing a handshake wi—'

'I don't know what a handshake is.'

'May I assist you in finding definitions for the term handshake?'

'I don't want to make the internet work. I make to break it!'

'Breaking the internet is a colloquial phrase from the first years of the twenty-first century meaning—'

Elimisha unplugs the Quantum Drive from the White Board and kicks the board from the table, smashing it on the floor. She drops her glasses too, smashes them and brushes the remains away from the desk so there's no obvious relationship among the pieces.

Alessandra appears at the doorway to the Communications Room. Her eyes are wide.

'Holy shit, what did you do?'

'I destroyed the only device with an interface that can perform a handshake with the internet.'

'You . . . what the fuck are you talking about?'

'I broke it. But it's still here, somehow. I don't know how it works!'

'They're going to get through,' Alessandra says. She is wearing her tight blue and gold HCG suit and her leather running boots now. The pistol is gripped in her right hand.

'Take this,' Elimisha says to her. She extends her hand with the Quantum Drive in it.

'What are you doing?'

'This is still an Archive and I'm still the Chief and you are still the Runner. We both have jobs to do and we both made vows. Put this in your bag and get away. If you can't get away, you must destroy it and everything on it. They don't know how many people are in here. We were stupid enough to yell at them so now they know there's at least one. I'll lure them down the hall and barricade myself in here. You'll hide in the hole in the kitchen and when they all pass you, you'll slip out after them with the Quantum Drive. You take the gun because . . . you know.'

'Elimisha—'

'You respond, "Yes, Chief!" That is your sworn duty. You are holding all six flags and the future of the world in your hand – literally. And,' she adds, for Alessandra's sake, 'they might capture me and not kill me. We don't know. So this is the only plan where we both might get out alive and save the Knowledge. Right? So let's go.'

Alessandra lifts her sling-bag from the floor, opens the main compartment and places the box in the middle of her rain gear for protection.

They both move back towards the hammering in the kitchen. The Keepers are not through yet, so there is still time for Elimisha's plan to work.

But when they pass the Control room, there is a new sound: a clattering of something heavy and metal hitting the floor from behind them; it's coming from inside the Inferno room.

'We're surrounded,' Elimisha says. 'Hurry – go and hide.'

Alessandra, though, freezes in place, whether from fear and indecision or because she knows – in some way that does not involve language or thought – that she is the one with the gun and the only one capable of fighting because of Elimisha's leg.

A person emerges from the Inferno room. That person is dressed in black and speaks in a soft and calm and female voice which is not supposed to be there. It says, 'I have a way out. We have to move fast.'

390

But Alessandra is so ramped up and tense she cannot make sense of the image or the words. She only knows that Elimisha had a plan, they are surrounded, and she needs to go and hide.

Aiming for the centre of mass, she shoots.

OUT

Alessandra's bullet hits Birch in the stomach.

Her hands drop to clutch the wound as she staggers back two steps before lowering herself to the floor and shaking her head.

All these years of sneaking around past enemies and trudging through dank tunnels only for this.

'I'm with the Commonwealth. Don't shoot me,' she says and, after inhaling for more breath, adds, 'again.'

'Who the hell are you,' Alessandra demands as the chipping of the walls starts behind her again. The woman's face is familiar but right now, at this very moment, nothing is familiar.

'I'm Master Birch. I'm here with your parents, Alessandra. Henry and Graham. It's a long story and we've had a very hard night. There's a vent near the ceiling that connects, eventually, with the Otis Shaft and comes out on the roof. There's a rope and your parents will pull you up. Hurry up. Please.'

'You need to go first,' Elimisha says. 'You *need* to go.'

'I can't leave you here,' she says to Elimisha.

'I'll come after you.'

'How?'

'Go,' Birch interjects. 'We'll find a way. Go – and leave the gun, please.'

The chiselling and hammering change their pitch. Rocks and concrete are breaking out and flying across the kitchen floor. The hole is getting bigger.

Alessandra grabs Elimisha by the arm one last time. 'There's something I need to tell you – something I did. Something you won't like. Something you told me not to do but I did it anyway and now I'm not sure because—'

'Tell me later.'

'I'm afraid you'll hate me.'

'I won't hate you. Go!'

'Yes, Chief,' is all she can say.

Alessandra hands Birch the gun and rushes into the room with the skeletons and the rope and the way out.

Elimisha helps Birch to her feet, both of them bracing against the wall for support. The bullet is a 9mm and it is lodged in her gut and though she is accustomed to pain from a life of constant exercise, training and war preparation, this one is debilitating because it is not only pain – it is injury.

The Inferno room is only a few metres down the hall. Birch pushes Elimisha inside the room she's been avoiding for more than a month. Birch herself stops in the doorway and leaning forward, takes aim down the hall.

With only a moment to talk before the Tribesmen breach into the kitchen and come looking for them, Birch asks, 'Is it real? The internet – is it here?'

'Yes, it's real.'

'Can I destroy it?'

'I've tried. It's . . . hidden. But we can't destroy it.'

'That's too bad,' Birch says as she sees the first man, holding a crossbow, turn the corner into the hall. She shoots him dead before his eyes can focus on what killed him.

'You need to get yourself out,' Birch says to her. 'I'll secure the site.'

Alessandra is long gone. Elimisha looks at the rope leading to the vent and the vertical shaft inside it.

'My leg—'

'I know. You're going to have to continue to do your best. You've done a very, very good job.'

Elimisha takes hold of the rope and yanks it. A moment later she feels it gently tug back and a man's voice, weak and far away, yells something but it is too distant for her to make out the words.

Gun in hand, Birch slides out of the Inferno room, focusing down the barrel and attuned to any new target, and hobbles forward into the Control room, where she closes the door behind her. She is looking to kill the power.

Once inside, Birch buckles at the waist for moment from the pain of the gunshot wound. She doesn't know enough about the insides of the human body to know what was hit, but she has seen enough injuries to know which are least likely to heal.

She breathes shallow to catch her breath and recover her anger, which is all that is going to help now.

Birch has spent a lifetime silently moving through tunnels. It is little surprise to her that she will die in one, although she never thought it would happen for being too quiet.

The control room is not unfamiliar. She's passed through rooms like this before. She reads the labels and signs and flicks everything that is in the *on* position to the *off*. The lights go out all around her and are replaced by the red emergency lamps.

She finds a switch to turn those off too, turning the shelter into a pit of black.

From her hip pocket she removes a night vision monocle, removes her boots, takes another breath and opens the door.

Bathed in the green light of her night sight, Birch sees three men standing back to back in the middle of the hall.

But not for long.

Birch was a member of the Urban Explorers at fifteen. She was approached by the Order at eighteen. 'We want you to use your Choosing Walk for something else,' they said to her. It was something never attempted by someone so young: a six-month Run due south, long past the end of the guarded Road.

The Blue Route, they called it, because, 'on it you will touch the sea and the sky'. She was told, 'At the end you will meet a man named José. You will exchange bags and then you will come back. You do this,' the bearded Explorer with the inked arms said to her, 'and we will welcome you to the Order. You have a week to decide.'

She kills the three men; two with the remaining bullets from Alessandra's gun and the third with a long, thin knife she'd received as a gift from Graham Wayworth long ago.

She's now out of bullets.

A thirst is building in Birch's mouth. She knows what it portends. Returning to the Inferno room, she steps in and closes the door behind her.

Elimisha is gone and up the shaft. Birch can hear banging inside it: the injured girl making her way up. Distantly, a man's voice – surely Commander Wayworth's? – is shouting something to her; his voice is too muffled for meaning.

For a pause – for a long, deep breath – Birch considers how to use her remaining time. More Keepers are coming and she cannot follow the girls.

She turns to the desk where a steel-backed chair is occupied by a dead man. His arms are splayed across it and his head rests on a book that does not interest her.

What does catch her attention are the two handles in his bony grips: ones which resemble what Lilly described to her in such detail.

'Oh, Lilly,' Birch says to herself.

She places the now useless gun on the table and pries the detonators from the skeleton's hands.

Birch stares at the door. It is only a matter of time. Pushing the corpse off the chair, Birch sits down, pushes the detonator safeties off and presses both pieces against her stomach to relieve the pain of the gunshot.

An internet of all remaining human Knowledge.

A Library of limitless wonder.

A chance to know everything humanity has learned until now, and to apply it to the challenges of the day for the betterment of the world.

To have had such a treasure and squandered it.

It would have been nice to grow old, Birch thinks as someone starts to pound against the door.

Graham sits in the sand, his feet hard against the edge of the concrete circle that leads down into the shaft. The Order poked a hole in the roof here – it drops down into the Otis Shaft – but the idea that anyone would have voluntarily gone into it strikes him as madness. Then again, he knows he's trying to adjust to more than forty years of believing that the depths will kill you with Sickness. It's like being told that urine tastes like lemon; the ears hear, but the mind rebels.

He wears riding gloves. Inside them he can feel that he's starting to bleed. An annoying wind has picked up and it's chucking sand against the right side of his face, which was covered by the hood but that's been blown off and there's no putting it back on without letting go and he can't do that because there's a girl dangling down there with a hole in her leg who is – he hopes – climbing as best she can, but he knows that he won't have the upper body strength to lift her, and he knows she can't climb the steel cables without the use of her legs, because her right leg can't wrap and pull, so for right now she's dead weight and he's hoping against hope that the rope won't snap because he has no idea how strong it is.

Alessandra is on the roof now and behind him, her feet also planted in the sand, also pulling. He can't see her but he can hear her grunting, giving everything she has.

And she must be exhausted.

He should be feeling much worse than he does, but he doesn't because despite all the odds – of escaping the Keepers, of anticipating the Dragoons' deployment, of riding them into an intercept and not getting killed by either the Keepers or his own people, of fighting his way through that and linking up with Master Birch and his wife at the rendezvous, of Birch saving Alessandra using maps that started with the Adamists and ended with his daughter climbing out of a pit of doom – he and his family are together again, with only Henry's eye as a casualty.

It's a serious casualty, but it's not life-threatening.

Graham heaves harder and he knows Alessandra is doing the same, but it's slow and he's not sure it's going to work.

'Henry, would you *please* get over here and help us?'

'No,' she says for the third time.

She is perched on a rock surveying the hills and the windows in the higher towers and the approaches to their position and the morning sky for birds that might signal ground movement. She is not losing her family again. They need her remaining eye and rifle more than her strength, which is limited now in any case.

Vows or no vows, this world can burn so long as the three of them ride it out together.

Alessandra's groans are unsettling Graham. His daughter's sounds have always unsettled his calm. When she was a baby, the slightest cough or sleepy moan used to have him on his feet; even before Henry woke up, his hands were inspecting her for rational discomforts before lifting her to provide irrational and unconditional love.

There is a thud: a deep, powerful, concussive thud.

'What was that?' Graham yells, turning to look at Henry.

Her face tells him that he already knows.

Graham lets go of the rope.

Spinning around, he grabs Alessandra's left foot and yanks it towards him and then, quickly, he falls on top of her to shield her from what comes next.

For a second – for a pause – Alessandra is apoplectic. She tries to prevent the rope from slipping back down but she can't; the weight is too much.

The pause – the paradise of not knowing the truth – ends when a flame bellows up and out into the orange morning, cuts through the rope in a flash, relieving Alessandra from bearing the full weight of her friend in her hands.

Her father is shielding her from the black ash and debris that rain down on his back and legs. Underneath him Alessandra is no longer struggling; her body is immobile and her eyes are fixed on the fire in the sky.

When the first stone sears through his jacket he decides he'd had enough. It's time to go.

Pulling his daughter to her feet, he grasps her chin and speaks to her unblinking, unbelieving eyes. 'We have to go. The roof could give way. There is nothing more we can do here.'

IV
LEAVING

SOJOURN

When Henrietta was a little girl and her parents died, the Roamers taught her a term for her state of mind: a *Sojourn*. The mind, they explained, tries to follow the dead by leaving the body behind. The body carries on doing what living things do, but it falls into a state much like the animals – proceeding, acting, functioning, but never speaking or thinking or reasoning in quite the same way. The mind of the person on a Sojourn lives in a perpetual state of wonderlessness, trying to follow the dead to where the living can't go. As a result, they become much like the dead.

In many ways, said the Roamers, the animals are better off because unlike the Sojourner, the animals can still feel a range of emotions from joy to fear, from excitement to malaise. But for the Sojourner who leaves the body behind – often to chase after a Union that has ended – there is no range of emotions, only a flatness to sound, a greyness to light and a coldness in the companionship of others. This was how Henry felt as the Roamers moved off, leaving her to guard the graves of her parents with her father's rifle, alone in the desert.

*

403

With the bunker destroyed and the Gone World on fire again, Alessandra rides on her mother's horse, clutching her sling-bag in her arms as though it were a baby. Henrietta can tell from Alessandra's body language that her own Sojourn has begun.

On the fifth day of riding north, away from the Gone World, away from the Keepers and The Crossing and the Commonwealth, Henry decides to unhook the clasp at the top of Alessandra's shoulder and free her trapped hair from beneath the strap of her sling-bag. When she does, Alessandra flinches as though struck. She hugs the bag tighter, pulling it to her chest. Henry opens her palms to signal calm and decides to leave well enough alone.

Even now Alessandra has not asked her mother about the eyepatch. That, to Henry, is proof of how far away her mind is.

At this distance from the war, there is no sense that the world is anything but peaceful and quiet and bright. Sea Glass Lake is less than a kilometre from the edge of the Great Forest and as they approach, it glitters its rainbow of colours, a vibrant and magic spectacle that has been a source of artistic and poetic inspiration to the Territory for generations.

Despite Henry's injury and general fatigue they have made good time, and without pressing their mounts or themselves. Henry and Graham decide to let the horses linger and graze. They are off the Road now, travelling mainly in the wadis and gullies and lowland to stay out of sight. They are nine days north of the Stadium. The trade road curved westwards three days earlier, and there are no paths here. The only reason to venture into the depths of the forest is to hunt for food or to collect wood. There are paths and better ways in than here but Graham has his reasons.

'Look,' the father says to the daughter.

Alessandra looks with her eyes but not her heart.

'We were here when you were nine,' he says. 'You must remember it. Tens of thousands – maybe hundreds of thousands – of bottles once broke here. Our best guess is that massive ships capsized, losing their cargo, and the unbroken bottles floated here when this area was full of water. They must have all fallen over that outcropping over there to the northeast, smashed at the base and then piled up, over and over and over again for – well, who knows. A long time. We think that the constant lap of those long-since-vanished waters wore the edges of the shards into gems and pebbles and now it's this glimmering sea of jewels. It's gorgeous by day, but we should stay and see it by moonlight too, when the reds are pulled back and only the greens and blues light up. It transforms from one place into another at night – and then when the dawn hits it, all the reds and oranges and yellows light up too, as if the sunlight were falling like raindrops. I just love this place.'

Graham looks at Henry after his speech. Though their eyes meet, they are seeing their daughter.

That night they pitch their black dome on the far side of the lake at the edge of the forest where an upturned boat hull rises like a hollow tombstone. They feed and water the horses and do the same to their daughter, who opens her mouth mechanically, an invalid willing to receive warm food. They put her to sleep in the dome clutching the bag the way she used to clutch the stuffed animal Graham gave her for her fourth birthday, acquired from a travelling craftsman with a gentle profession. He called it a *lion*.

'There were animals that looked like this?' Graham had asked him.

The craftsman had smiled and shrugged. 'Either that or someone out there has a wonderful imagination,' he had said.

At dawn the morning sun is warm and good and strikes their dome. Henry awakens first, flushed by the heat. She has never liked the weight of the dome air in the morning and so steps outside, letting Alessandra sleep on. There is a pleasant smell of grass and leaves here; a feeling of growth and life and water and the suggestion of far-away ice. Above, an arrow-head of seven birds pass in formation that is a song in routine.

She clicks her tongue twice and Graham appears from behind a small knoll with her rifle.

He silently shakes his head and she nods her own.

When they are close Graham removes Henry's patch and the gauze and inspects her face. 'No infection,' he says quietly, 'but no improvement.'

'The eye is dead,' she says.

'You look sexy with a scar,' he tells her.

'And an eye the colour of Sickness?'

'Patches can be very stylish.'

She grabs his nose and wiggles it.

'Where are you taking us?' she asks as he washes her face with a soft cloth and applies a new dressing.

'The Abbey, assuming it's still there. I told you about the colony that made the *vin* back when I was on my Choosing Walk. It isn't on a Commonwealth route and there's no trade road. Nothing crosses the forest there and there are no finds mapped nearby. If they're still there, they'll take us in and keep our secrets. We need to stop moving and rest someplace until Alessandra comes back to us.'

'What's an Abbey?'

'It's a place of solitude and reflection. Or if you're feeling

406

less generous, it's a place for misfit men to live together out of the reach of history.'

'What do they do there, these solitary misfits of yours?'

'Mostly they argue, do magic tricks and tell bad jokes.'

'So . . . your people,' Henry says.

'Exactly.'

ABBEY

Abbott Francis has his eye on Frere Jacob, who is finally coming around to hating rabbit soup. It has taken a long time and more trips to the outhouse than should naturally be required. Jacob had made the mistake of declaring his love and passion and commitment to rabbit soup one night, stating at the Big Table, 'I could live on nothing but rabbit soup!' Abbott Francis, in charge of the education and welfare of his Abbey companions, had said, 'and not by every word of God?'

'God,' answered Frere Jacob, 'in the few scripts we have to understand Him, never mentions rabbit soup. I am happy to include the words of God in my eating of soup,' he had boldly asserted, 'but I will not remove my soup from the words of God.'

And so Abbott Francis took Frere Jacob at his word and put him on a nothing-but-rabbit-soup-and-water diet until Jacob came around to admitting that he had probably overstepped a bit – but Jacob was a stubborn one and it was Francis' conclusion that Jacob was secretly hoping that his decimation of the local rabbit population would create a *fait accompli* and

God – in his wisdom and mercy – would remove the rabbit from his soup for him so that Jacob might save face and get on with eating other things.

By this point, however, he has come to realise that if God doesn't help him he'll have to relent and help himself by admitting that unreflective faith in anything which is not moderated by wisdom and reason is probably a bad idea, which, he has come around to realising, was probably the lesson the Abbott had wanted him to learn in the first place.

Abbott Francis didn't hear Jacob say these words, but he could see how he stirred his soup for a long, long time before putting more of it in his mouth, which was proof enough that *some* lesson had gone in.

As it happened, the Abbott didn't know much about God and wasn't really that interested anyway, because the few scraps they'd cobbled together from the Bible, from the New Testament, from the Talmud and the Koran seemed to have only thing in common: God didn't really want anything *from* us; he wanted things *for* us. And what he mainly wanted was peace and for people to be good to one another. Acts of harm or extreme were the general no-nos at the Abbey and failing a theology that was more sophisticated, that seemed a reasonable way to live.

The big surprise, over the years, was finding out how many people disagreed.

Meanwhile – because measurements can be helpful – Abbott Francis has started a count of how often Frere Jacob has taken to squatting and moaning in the poo-shed. His final analysis was that Jacob's pride was – literally – wearing him thin.

The Abbott knows he should call an end to all this and consider the lesson learned but . . . it's amusing. And how do you simply end something amusing in a world gone mad? It was a good question.

A question worthy of a glass bead.

Francis is at the Big Table this morning. He is playing a game of chess with Frere Vince when there is a knock on their heavy wooden door.

It is rare for someone to knock. The Brothers come and go, guests are accompanied and enemies usually walk right in.

The Abbott stands and, thinking twice on it, sits again. He has an ingrown toenail that's bothering him and pressure on it makes it worse. He knows he'll have to go after it with a sharp knife at some point but . . . better tomorrow.

Instead, he calls Jacob to go and answer it. Jacob is in the kitchen looking at his latest batch of soup. He has deliberately overcooked it as a means of punishing the rabbit – twice – for his own mistakes.

It is an unkind gesture towards everyone, including himself, and he's ashamed. Still, he's doing it anyway.

'*D'accord*,' he yells in response to the Abbott's request. After tossing his hand towel to the wooden cooking block, Jacob passes the long table and the Abbott and opens the unlocked door. Before his eyes is a sad family.

'*Je m'appelle Graham Wayworth*,' says the man. '*Je suis un ami du Frere Francis. Pouvons-nous entrer?*'

Despite the man's reprehensible pronunciation of the Français, he extends his arms to the woman with the wounded eye and the girl she's supporting and ushers them all in. Jacob is only twenty-two but he knows the ailment on the girl's face better than the mother's. He has seen it many times. She is *away*. It is not an uncommon state of mind here. Many people who come to the Abbey – for a day, for a lifetime – look like this on arrival. When Jacob was sixteen he became aware that his own father was *away* and would likely never return. That is when he decided to come here, to a place where people are always present.

'My wife and daughter don't speak the language. Can we use the Common?'

Brother Jacob hates the Common because it sounds as flat as a raccoon pelt and his own mouth doesn't like the shape of the sounds. But hospitality demands sacrifice, and many of the scripts about God they have found are in the Common. The general consensus is that it was written in this way so as not to overwhelm the reader with its beauty.

Jacob opens the door fully and the late-afternoon forest light floods the room and reveals the smiling Abbott, who has already recognised his old friend's voice.

Trying not to wince with discomfort, he embraces and kisses his old friend on either cheek, and Graham returns the gesture and sentiment.

'I said I would visit your Commonwealth. I didn't. I am ashamed and I apologise,' says the Abbott. 'It's just so . . . big.'

'I'm glad to see you all well,' Graham says. 'You look stronger and thinner. Younger. Doing absolutely nothing all day clearly agrees with you.'

'Everyone out there is in such a hurry, but I can't see where they're going,' he says.

The Abbott is tall, in his early sixties and has a broad chest. Wordlessly, he grasps Henry by both hands before he reaches out to Alessandra, whose hands are weak. Her eyes stay low.

'You are welcome here, daughter-of-Graham.'

Henry smiles at this. It has been a long time since she has heard anyone mention the name of the father. She knows it is a common practice in some places, but it makes no sense to her. It's a matter of logic: you always know who the mother is.

But . . . men.

Francis draws them all inside, closes the door and seats them at the table while gesturing for food and water.

'So,' Graham asks, 'have you figured out what religion you are yet?'

'Not quite,' Francis says. 'We only know about Catholics, Protestants, Jews and Muslims, although we suspect there are more. We like how the Catholics recognise sin and both enjoy and apologise for it. They're the most fun. The Protestants are less distracted by such things, which can be handy if you need to get anything done. The Jews ask the best questions and then search for answers with both passion and moral intent by arguing. It's most fun to be Jewish when we're drinking. Although being Catholic can be fun too. It's never fun being Protestant. And the Muslims, who don't drink so this is an issue, have the most wonderful way of breaking up the day into these segments of activity and then prayer and reflection, which seems wise and comforting and communal. Unfortunately, they wake up a bit early for our tastes.'

'So really, it's nothing but work around here,' Graham posits.

The Abbott uncrosses his arms and places his palms up towards Alessandra. 'And who is this powerful young woman?' he asks.

'Our daughter, Alessandra,' Graham says, introducing her formally, although he's already spoken her name. 'She fell into a hole with a friend. She came out alone.'

'I see,' says the Abbott, his thick leather boots scuffing against the wooden floor as he settles into a new position.

'You know about the war at the Stadium?' Graham asks.

412

'Yes – we've been tracking the troop levels and monitoring the traffic on the roads to see if they are putting up stops. So far it's clear, but it's only a matter of time before that ends. I heard about a weapon?'

'Yes. That was us.'

'I see,' he says.

'We had no idea a force this large existed,' Graham admits.

'I'm not surprised. With these Keepers there's a ... simplicity. *Look around at all the destruction*, they say. *The Ancients did this. The Commonwealth is the ally of the Ancients. Join us and resist a new destruction*. It is clear and noble, if misguided.'

'You've become better at our language,' Graham says.

'A necessary evil.'

'Are we safe here?'

The Abbott nods and smiles. 'We have more than enough food and water out in the forest. Fewer rabbits than before,' he says, raising his voice slightly, for some reason, 'but still more than enough. We stay quiet and there's nothing people can take from us they couldn't find elsewhere and at less risk. We're better armed than we look and we whisper it in our trades to make it well-known. We're safe, but we're hoping the mood of the world will change.'

'It is not only a passing mood, Francis.'

The Abbott looks at Graham. 'Can you still do the trick with the coin?'

Graham smiles. 'It's been a while.'

The Abbott digs into his right pocket and pulls out a coin that is silver on the outside and gold at the centre. On one side there is a bear on a rock with the words, 'Canada 2 Dollars.' It is worn from being frequently handled. He slaps it on the table and slides it across.

'That's my lucky coin. Keeps the bears away,' he says to Alessandra.

'There are no bears here, Francis,' says Graham.

'See? It's working.' He winks at Alessandra.

Graham picks it up and feels its weight. He then pinches it, shows it to everyone, and – quickly wringing his hands together – makes it vanish into the air.

The Abbott is delighted. 'Make it fall out of my nose.'

He does.

'That's true talent,' he says, pointing to Graham.

'I fear for you both,' Henry says.

'Stay as long as you need. Keep your weapons close. Avoid the soup.'

The Abbey comprises four buildings and there are no defensive walls, only a thin fence of wooden planks wired together to keep out the less motivated rodents. The living quarters, also made of wood, are adjacent to the stone-built Gathering House. The chapel is a library but one that would be unfamiliar to the Commonwealth, for nothing here is classified or coded, copied or formally studied. Instead, it is a place of curiosities and artefacts designed to stimulate imagination and evoke inspiration. They invent here, and create, and solve problems big and small. Unlike the Commonwealth they have no designs on perpetuity: life is for living and then it ends. All that matters here at the Abbey is trying to do good and be good and have a few drinks and laughs along the way. There is no agenda here beyond peace, but it is one they will fight to maintain.

That night Alessandra sleeps between her parents like a little girl. She twitches and calls out and mutters words that have no meaning to them.

414

During the following quiet days she walks in the forest around the Abbey, staring at the way the leaves are the subjects of the wind.

She goes nowhere without her sling-bag.

THE MUSIC MAN

On their twenty-second day at the Abbey, a strange man appears in the woods. Through the scope of Henry's rifle she can see he is unkempt, with a long beard and tattered clothes. His age is impossible to determine through the hat and hair and fabric. He drags behind him a small wagon that is painted on the sides with animals and musical instruments. His approach is slow and as subtle as a rockslide because the wagon is rickety and the man mutters to himself as he walks along the barely visible dirt path. If there is any deception here, then he is the distraction, so Henry scans the forest for danger.

She finds none.

Henry tracks him for another two hundred metres through the dense but thinning forest to the fence. On the way, humming a tune, he passes her unseen in her look-out perch. At the flimsy gate he stops as though it were the door to a house and taps. Receiving no reply, he loudly opens the gate, saunters into the perimeter, closes the gate behind the wagon once it is inside and proceeds to seat himself on a tree stump by the Gathering House door.

After sitting silently to catch his breath, he stands, straightens his jacket, brushes back his hair – which is no improvement – and knocks on the door. Henry watches all this from her position twenty metres away in a tree, her finger resting on the receiver and clear of the trigger.

The man waits patiently and after a time the door opens. The young Brother, Frere Jacob, smiles. Henry can hear their conversation, though she cannot understand the Français, which is both fluent and fast. Jacob looks calm and curious and eventually invites the man inside.

Henry shoulders her rifle, climbs down the tree and approaches the door to listen from the outside. She may not understand the language but heated words always freeze open hearts, whereas the sounds inside are doing quite the opposite.

She can hear men talking jovially to one another. She listens for several minutes, hearing three other Brothers joining them. Soon after, she is listening to the sound of mugs being clanked together, *spondees* spoken and libations drunk. They're having more fun inside than she is outside and at that point she suspends her suspicions and decides to join them.

The Brothers all fall silent when she enters the room – but it is not on her account. The man has started cranking a wheel on his strange wagon, and as he does, it starts to usher forth a song. It is nothing intricate, not like the layers of storytelling that come from Moishe's playing or from the orchestrations he arranges for the other musicians. This is delicate and gentle and solitary, sounding like a set of glasses being tapped by the tip of a metal prong, over and over. The notes dance and flow and overlap, their time apart separated into perfect beats: a melody, a child's song. To Henry, it sounds like rain falling on flowers from a dark but not foreboding sky. It lasts for some two minutes and ends on the note on which it began.

It leaves behind a silence as fresh as morning dew.

Henry is surprised but happy to see Alessandra standing in the corner.

The man, hatless now and largely bald, waves his hand and ushers Henry in as though she were a long and awaited friend. She cannot help but smile at this table of jolly folk who appear to have no other care in the world than camaraderie, and no inhibitions about a stranger arriving from a dense forest with music in tow in the midst of the war.

'*Et quel est ton nom, ma chere?*'

'I don't speak the Français,' Henrietta says apologetically. She cannot remember the last time she was in a room with only men. It feels almost comic. Is this what they do when women aren't around? What a nice thought. And would that it be true.

'Don't be shy,' he says in her language, in her accent. 'Tell me your name.'

'Henrietta,' she says. 'My father called me Henry.'

'He wanted a boy?' the man says.

'No. He wanted me. He said my name was too long and by making it shorter he could say it more times in a day.'

'To Henry's father and his love for his daughter,' he says, raising a glass, and all the men drink to her father and his love for his daughter and they continue to drink when the toast is done because no one reminds them to stop.

'You look handy,' the music man says to Henry a few moments later as conversations turn elsewhere and the drinking becomes a party that ignores them both. 'I wonder if you could help me fix a wheel.'

With Graham in the corner Henry decides the music man is no threat. She follows him to the wagon parked in the space between the table and the far window. There, he crouches down beside the hub at the centre of the back wheel. Using a metal spoon he'd taken from the table, he pries off the cap

418

and indicates what is beneath. 'Have you ever seen something like this? I'm hoping it's a conversation-starter,' he says, pointing to the seal of the Commonwealth and the six-wedged pie.

'Yes I have,' she says. 'I think I can help you.'

EVERYTHING

The forest is filled with bugs come dusk and the woods are full of crickets. The crickets are nice. The other bugs are not. The Brothers find the limits of their own mercy when the mosquitos arrive and the constant slapping occasionally synchronises into a rhythm and a pitiless song of death, but no one is listening.

Inside, Henry and Graham join the music man in the room Francis has prepared for him. The room contains a bed and a plastic chair, a wooden desk and a large bowl filled with fresh water for washing. Beside it there is an attractive blue glass bottle and a cup for drinking. On the bed itself is a white sheet and an itchy but warm blanket. All the Brothers sleep in similar rooms, with their own personal touches.

When the door closes, the man sits on the bed with one leg tucked underneath him and his back to the wall. In private he is less vivacious and theatrical. He has not changed out of his costume: this is work for him and it will not end until so ordered.

He motions for them to sit.

'You're from the Order?' Henry asks.

He speaks quietly, his accent changing back to their own. 'There are a range of solutions for moving unseen.'

'How did you find us?'

'We didn't. We're all looking everywhere. No one knows whether you've survived and if so, whether you've collected the Prize.'

'The Prize,' Graham repeats.

'That's what High Command is calling it.'

'What's happening at home?' Graham asks.

'I do have news. But before that,' he says, turning to Henry, 'where is the Master? She left with you.'

'Birch is dead,' Henry says. 'She saved my daughter and secured the Archive by setting off the explosion.'

The man says nothing, but by his expression, he knew her well.

There is a tap at the door. Henry stands and opens it to find Alessandra standing there clutching her bag.

'I asked her to come,' says the man. 'I told her who I am. You're most welcome, Archive Runner.'

Alessandra says nothing. He waves her in and she steps inside, closing the door carefully behind her. She does not sit, instead lingering by the entrance which is also an exit.

'When I left,' he says, anticipating their questions, 'nothing had changed. The stand-off continues. The enemy forces remain on the hills. Their numbers continue to swell. There is now discussion of whether or not to evoke the Walk. Much of that decision rests on what I learn from you. It is Winters' intention for the core military to stand their ground and hold the Stadium to the end, but she's prepared to evacuate the population if you have the Prize. Do you?'

Henry and Graham both know that Alessandra is the only

person alive with the answer to that question and she hasn't spoken since the explosion.

'What is your name?' Henry asks him.

'I don't need one,' he says. 'I know that you and Master Birch departed with the Dragoons. What happened after that? How did you all reunite?'

'Henry shot the Leader and I killed the Deputy,' says Graham. 'I escaped in the Leader's robes and a tribal force followed me, which I hadn't intended. They assumed I was him and so they followed. Apparently, I was spotted by the Stadium when Henry and Birch broke away from the Dragoons for their own mission. The platoon engaged the Keepers who were trailing me – luckily, they recognised me—'

'It wasn't luck,' Henry interrupts. 'I knew I hadn't missed my shot, so I told them to verify their targets because something strange was happening.'

'Oh,' Graham says to Henry. 'Thank you.'

'You're welcome, dear.'

'Henry and I stayed on the surface to secure the site and Birch went down to find the girl—'

'Chief,' says Alessandra.

Henry and Graham look at their daughter. It is the first word she's spoken since the fire on the mountain.

It is the man who engages her. 'Which Chief?'

'Chief Elimisha. The Archive was called The Inferno. It was named after a book by Dante. Elimisha was the youngest Chief of the Central Archive in the history of the Commonwealth.'

'We think,' Henry says, not entirely following Alessandra's reasoning, but also not wanting to contradict the first words she's spoken in weeks, 'that the Tribesmen set off explosives after beating us in a race to the Hard Room, which unfortunately took the lives of the Chief and the Master,' she says.

'That's not what happened,' Alessandra whispers.

The three adults wait for Alessandra to fill the space.

'It isn't called a Hard Room. It's called a bomb shelter. The bomb shelter was retro-fitted days before the Solar War with a connecting tunnel, provisions, communications, internet access and a safeguard mechanism. If it became contaminated, the officer-in-charge was to destroy it and everyone inside it to both stop the contagion and to end their suffering, because the survival rate was close to zero. Humanic robots were re-purposed to create subterranean passages between key nodes in the underground network following the electric grids to guide them from one building to another so that military and civilian personnel could work as a community during survival and restoration, but none of that worked because they didn't understand the kind of weapon that was unleashed. The sun only broke the world because the Ancients had made it so fragile. If they had made it more resilient to harm by working together, the solar flare would have been only a gentle blow. Instead, it set the tinderbox alight. The reason the world ended is because the Ancients didn't work together and trust each other. It was that simple, really.

'The tribesmen dug through to the Archive. We were fighting them off when Birch showed up behind me. I turned and shot her in the stomach. The Chief was already injured in the leg and there was no way the two of them could climb out. Elimisha ordered me up the shaft first and I went. She was supposed to follow me and Birch was going to stay behind to secure the Archive. She's the one who set off the explosions using the failsafe. She probably waited as long as she could to give Elimisha time, but she had to uphold her vows. It wasn't enough. I should have pulled harder.'

The adults are each beset by their own list of questions. It

423

is the man from the Order who speaks first: 'Why did Master Birch set off the fail-safe explosions?'

'To secure the Archive.'

'You said that, but a single Archive – even if it's a reasonably large or important Trove – isn't worth the death of a Master. Commander Wayworth could have cut the rope if they started to climb after—'

'It wasn't just "some Archive", okay? You're not *hearing* me. It was the *Primary* Archive of the Commonwealth. It was a gateway to the internet. It was ... *everything*. Maybe not everything-everything, but close enough, and more than we could ever have collected in ten million full-flag runs. The Harrington Box was a seed,' says Alessandra. 'The Inferno was the forest.'

'And Birch secured it at the cost of her life?' the man asked.

'Yes.'

'Well then,' says the man. 'I guess that's that.'

He places his floppy hat on his head and wipes his face with a cloth from his pocket. 'I'll need to fill my water bottles before I go. I need to get back and report to General Winters. They have some hard decisions to make,' he says, standing. He taps the music wagon a few times. 'I'm going to be sorry to leave this tranquillity behind. You can tell the Abbott it's a gift.

'You were very lucky,' the man says to Alessandra, 'to have touched an Archive like that. To have seen what no one else alive has ever seen and never will again. You and Chief Elimisha have solved two of the greatest mysteries we have: what happened to the world, and where did all the Knowledge go. Now we know, thanks to you both. You'll have to explain it to us a few times, I fear, because I didn't understand it all, but there's time. I'm sorry for the price. I understand why Master Birch and Chief Elimisha had to destroy it. It's a pity it's gone.'

'It's not gone,' Alessandra whispers.

'What?' her mother says.

'You can't destroy it. It's a global network, like roots under a massive tree. It once connected all the Deps together and worked like a Central Archive – one that anyone could visit from anywhere. But it was all dependent on the satellites that don't work any more. And all the information between continents that didn't use satellites passed through the sub-ocean cables, most of which have been cut. Much of the Knowledge is mirrored in data centres, but there's no way to know what exists on which continent or in which part of the network and what doesn't. The internet is still there, though. It's like . . . like the waters that run beneath the Gone World. Master Birch destroyed the only access point we know. We'll find another. That's what's next.'

Graham reaches for Alessandra's shoulder and touches her gently. 'The chances of finding one again are very, very low.'

'No they're not,' she says. 'I have the maps. It's all in here.'

Alessandra removes her sling-bag from her shoulder, unsnaps the end and unrolls the top. She extracts a piece of fabric that she places on the bed as carefully as if it were a tiny broken animal in need of care. She peels back the layers and there, in the middle, is a small black box with a blue domed glass and small holes on one side.

'What is that?' the man asks.

'It's . . . *everything*,' she says. 'Everything we could save, anyway.'

'Are you telling me,' says the man from the Order of Silence, 'that in this little box is an entire Archive?'

'I'm telling you,' says Alessandra, 'that this is the Central Archive of the Commonwealth. It's not the *entire* internet, but it's way more than you can possibly imagine. It'll take lifetimes upon lifetimes of Evaluators to even see it all.'

425

'Is there another copy of this?' says the man.

'No,' Alessandra says.

'So that . . . that is the most precious object on Earth?'

'Yes,' Alessandra says. She wraps it up and returns it to her sling-bag. None of the adults object. 'If we have electricity Lilly can access all of it with her White Board and some glasses.'

The music man looks at the Wayworths. Even before Alessandra was born, Henry and Graham were a formidable couple, with their skills, their uncanny connection to one another, Henry's Roamer background and Graham's strange calm and humour interlaced with a killer's skills. They were universally respected throughout the Commonwealth – and now their daughter is a legend in her own right. A girl who will need a long time to recover from what she has experienced, but one – if he is any judge – who is likely to rise to the High Command faster than any before her.

All of that, however, is for another day. For now, he has his orders. With the Prize secured, their path is clear.

'We have a long, long walk ahead of us,' he informs them.

CHICKEN

In the morning the Abbott sets out breakfast, even though it isn't his turn in the rotation. Guests are rare and he enjoys the rituals of hospitality. It is a pity that their offerings are not what they were only twenty years ago. Brother Hamon – torturer of plants *extraordinaire* – has been cutting stems and grafting them to others to create hybrids that he hopes will yield new food solutions. He has a wild theory that because important crops are no longer flowering and reproducing like before, small animals can no longer eat them, which means big animals can't eat the smaller ones, and somehow the entire world is a kind of enormous machine that is winding down because the smallest parts are broken. If he can grow a flower, he can change the future of the world.

Francis is not surprised Brother Hamon sees the world this way. He arrived with a heart so broken he has yet to even find the pieces, let alone reassemble them. The cause was a girl in a village to the east and months away by horse. He said he was so in love with her that every aspect of life, from eating and drinking to walking and breathing, were infused by an awareness of her spirit. It was as though she was a sea and his every gesture was a slow and deliberate journey inside her.

Worse still, she loved him too.

She died. Her death was as sudden as these things sometimes are.

He left and came to the Abbey, and fourteen years on, Abbott Francis still doesn't know her name. Even in death he doesn't want to share her, poor boy. Of course the world looks broken and slowing down. Of course a flower could fix it all. How could he see it otherwise?

The Abbott lays out dried meats, berries and a hardened flatbread they often eat with goat's milk cheese. Sometimes they are broken into small pieces and softened in whisked chicken eggs and cooked over a flame. Everything is better with salt, but that is hard to come by this far inland – and soon it will be impossible, on account of the war and the end of trading, at least for a while.

In time the other Brothers stumble in, eyes red and shoulders drooped after a night of too much happiness. (Does nature favour balance? Does the human body? Does justice and time and history? All good questions, all worthy of a new piece of sea glass. All worth remembering for later . . .) They sit at the table touching nothing until everyone has arrived. Brother Patel has a chicken joke he's been saving. The Abbott has begged him not to but the man is undeterred – he has apparently re-written the joke especially for his Commonwealth audience.

Abbott Francis retreats to the corner of the room for a moment once the table is set and takes in the full moment. It pleases him. He can hear his guests' voices from down the hall discussing the weather – a popular topic on a day of voyage. Graham has explained the situation, to a point. He will be sad to see them go, and so soon, when there are years of conversations yet to be had and entertainment for many nights. Too much passes too quickly and so much is left undone. At least, the Abbott thinks, he has been aware of this wistful truth and his heart has been open to the joy of the visit.

As Graham and his wife take their seats at the table, their shoulders are touched and patted by the hung-over Brothers. As Abbott Francis looks at them he has a powerful sense that the moment they are in is already behind them.

He looks around for the daughter, but she isn't there.

'You will love this joke,' Patel instructs his captives, pressing his palms downwards to keep the happiness that is at the centre of the Earth from erupting too quickly. 'Listen, listen,' he says, barely able to contain himself.

'A chicken walks into the Central Archive. He walks up to the Chief Archivist and says, "Buk." The Archivist looks at him and says, "You want a book?"

'"Buk."

'"Any book?"

'"Buk."

'So she gives the chicken a book and the chicken leaves.

'Later, the chicken returns. "Buk buk."

'"You want another book?" she asks.

'"Buk buk."

'So she gives the chicken another book and the chicken leaves. Later that same day the chicken returns for a third time. "Buk buk buk," it says.

'"You want a third book?"

'"Buk buk buk."

'"You read the other two?"

'"Buk buk buk."

'So the Archivist hands the chicken a third book, but this time,' Brother Patel chuckles, 'but this time,' he says, shaking as the best part approaches, 'she gets suspicious. So she follows the chicken out of the Archive, across the sands, through the Gone World, to a small pond at the edge of the forest, where the chicken swims up to a bullfrog on a lily pad. The chicken shows the bullfrog the book. And the bullfrog looks at it and croaks . . . "Read it."'

Everyone erupts in laughter except poor Brother Jacob. Confused, he shakes his head and says, 'Chickens can't swim,' at which point all order is lost.

Alessandra is outside the hall, walking along a worn footpath by the perimeter of the compound. The first leaves are beginning to fade and she stops beyond the Gathering House to admire them. The few trees inside the Stadium are all small and food-bearing. The surrounding desert turns no colours beyond what the sky offers and the air lacks the wild scents of the forest that have awakened parts of her that, until now, had not known they were sleeping.

Sensing movement, she turns her head, her hand moving to her knife before she sees Abbott Francis.

'Good morning,' he says. 'I missed you at breakfast. Walk with me?'

The grounds of the compound are well-manicured. As they walk, the path slowly transforms beneath her feet from dirt into an artful walkway of carefully laid flat rocks mixed increasingly with sea glass from the special lake. The closer Alessandra and the Abbott stroll to the centre of the compound, the more intricate and colourful the path becomes until, finally, they arrive at a well in the centre of a mosaic so vibrant and alive it looks like a star that has fallen to earth.

Five paths converge here, set with curved wooden benches that wrap around the well.

Francis invites her to sit down, then joins her.

'Did you build all this?'

'Me? No, of course not. I'm not that creative. Hundreds of people did this over decades. I did make two of the benches, though, and carried stones for the well. I worked on the roof of that one over there too.'

'No, I mean, did you start all of this?'

'Oh. Oh no, I'm the third Abbott. This is our seventy-fourth year here. We were once part of a large and glorious colony but we're all that remains. That's a story for another day. Next year we'll have a big party. I fear you're going to miss it.'

'Why are there no women here?' she asks him.

'I suppose,' he replies, 'that it would require an unusual kind of woman.'

'Unusual . . . how?'

'Unusual . . . weird. Men will often join a company of women, but women seldom choose to join a company of men – even if they're as charming as we are.'

'That's probably true.'

'Why,' he asks. 'Do you want to stay? You can, you know. You are welcome here.'

'No.' Alessandra taps her right foot. 'What do you do here? Other than eat and drink and laugh and argue?'

'There's more?'

'I mean . . . what's your purpose? Why live out here in the middle of nowhere all by yourselves?'

'Oh, right. You all have a grand purpose. It must be hard for someone as young as you to imagine a way of life that isn't directed towards something specific.'

Alessandra says nothing.

'Well . . .' he continues, trying to answer, 'I think it's pretty here. It's nicer than many other places I've been. I like it more than the desert. It's cooler in the summer and a bit warmer in the winter because of the trees as the winds don't much bother us. We don't get many bad people passing through because there's no reason to come here. The food's okay most of the time. If I become lonely for new faces I travel, but I always come back. But I don't think that's what you mean. You want to know if we have a grand purpose too.'

'Yes.'

'There are different ways to contribute to the world. One of the most important is to be the kind of person you wish there were more of. There's no telling what kind of effect that will have, but I can promise you that the only wrong answer is "none at all".'

Alessandra looks away from him to the ground.

'What happened to your friend?' he asks gently. 'The one who didn't come out of the hole with you?'

'I don't want to talk about it.'

'Tell me anyway. We have to be brave in the face of time and I don't think our paths are going to cross again. I can't promise that I'll hear you better, but no one else will hear you the same way.'

'She was hurt – she couldn't climb up the rope fast enough. I'm sure Master Birch waited as long as she could and I don't blame her. But it wasn't long enough.'

'You're not only grieving. You're carrying something. Do you blame yourself?'

'I could have pulled harder.'

'I don't think that's it. Your hands were bloodied when you arrived and so were your father's. Unless she was a metre from the top a little extra effort would have changed nothing. The guilt isn't from physical weakness; it's closer to your heart.'

'I lied to her.'

'I see.' There is no condemnation in his tone.

'There was something she thought was important to keep and I thought it was better to throw it away, so when she wasn't there, I did. She ordered me out of the bunker so I could save what I'd already destroyed. I feel like I . . . I don't know . . .'

'Like you betrayed her.'

She looks at her feet.

'What did you throw away?'

'Evil – knowledge about all kinds of evil things people did to each other in the past. There was a Trove – a very special kind of Trove. I only kept the good things.'

'Why did she want you to keep the evil?'

'She thought it was best to remember. She said that the past being buried is very different from burying the past.'

'How old was she?'

'Sixteen.'

'Sixteen,' Francis repeats.

Alessandra senses of the weight of Elimisha's words by studying the Abbott's face. Does that mean she was wrong?

'I did understand what she meant,' Alessandra explains. 'If we bury the truth on purpose it'll come back to haunt us somehow. But . . . we all have secrets, don't we? The Commonwealth has secrets. The Order of Silence has secrets. All the Archives in the Territory and beyond are secret. Survival of all human Knowledge is based on secrecy. I don't see why it's okay for those things to be secret and not some Knowledge about the past.'

She turns to the Abbott, wanting him to understand. Her voice cannot hide the depths of her appeal. 'The Ancients hated each other – they did awful, *awful* things to each other for reasons that don't matter any more. If we bring those memories back, people will feel shame and anger and want revenge.

Other people might start to adopt those words and categories and ideas and start to believe them. Remembering all that could be the reason for new wars, new evils. I realise what she said was important, but I don't see how Attesting to all that is necessarily better.'

'Do you think you did the right thing?' the Abbott asks her.

'I don't know – I thought so at the time, but now, out here in the woods, I wish we still had it so we could talk about it together. What do you think?' she asks him.

What does he think? It's a good question.

'I think,' he answers carefully, 'it's less important how much you know than what you choose to do with it. I've never entirely understood the Commonwealth's hunger for Knowledge. There does appear to be a greater emphasis on finding it and saving it than putting it to good use. I think many people share my confusion, and that's part of your problem.'

'Lilly says you can't get anything done unless you know how to do it.'

'That's reasonable,' the Abbott says, 'but it applies more to things than to people. If you want to get things done with people, you need to know their stories and what they learn from them. It's rather different.'

'My father,' Alessandra says, 'believes that art and music and stories all make us more connected to each other; they show us that we're not alone.'

'That's certainly true. But they also teach us how we're different from one another too. Understanding those differences and knowing how to manage them is better than pretending that we're all the same.'

'A lot of the differences I learned about from the Trove don't exist any more,' Alessandra says, digging the toe of her boot into the mosaic to see if any of the sea glass will move. It won't. The reflection from the sun is mesmerising. Sitting at the centre of all that color makes her feel like she's on a stage of some kind; it elevates her sense of purpose. It makes her want to talk, as though talking here will make the words and the lessons more lasting. She knows, even now, that she will never forget this feeling: the need to arrive at Truth.

'If the point of all this is to make life better for people,' Alessandra answers, 'we may need to forget things and start fresh.'

'That conclusion,' Francis says, 'would put you at odds with your entire culture.'

'I know.'

'And your parents.'

'I know.'

'You must feel quite alone.'

'Yes.'

'But not at peace with that reality.'

'I'm not sure I'm right. How can it be right to forget? To pretend massive things didn't happen to all those people? To simply wipe out their pain?'

'So if I understand correctly, you're conflicted because remembering might be a threat to the living but forgetting is a betrayal of the dead.'

She gazes at him. 'Yeah, I guess that's it.'

'Your pain is starting to take the form of a question. It's a question about your friend, but also a question about everyone else, above all, the Ancients. Can you hear it? If you can, you should voice it.'

Alessandra looks her hands. The ones which had been unable to hold the rope. 'What do we owe the dead?' she answers.

The Abbott pats her hand. He places a piece of blue sea glass in her palm. It is smooth and rounded, but for a chip in the clouded surface revealing a beautiful, watery interior. 'Take this,' he says. 'It's a tradition of ours. Once you come up with a good question, you take a glass stone and you hold it as a symbol of your question. When you feel you are ready to part with the question – because you've answered it, or outgrown it, or replaced it with a better one – you leave the stone in a special place of your choosing. Picking one up and letting one go are both acts of growth and wisdom.'

'Thank you.'

'We place our old questions in an empty lakebed. You might have passed it on the way here.'

Alessandra cracks a smile.

'Oh come on. That was better than the chicken joke. I know you heard it through the window.'

'I kind of liked the chicken joke.'

VERENA'S LETTER

Dear Lilly,

It is unlikely you will see this letter, but I have been assured that if the secret of the Southern Commonwealth is ever revealed the Order will hand it to you. The odds of that happening in both of our lifetimes is low. As I leave you the Stadium is secure and filled with a new structure and purpose and vision that we never had before. It was your courage, your Find, that unified us and strengthened us and gave us purpose. You should be proud of what you've created and what you have done for us all.

Unfortunately, what is best for the Commonwealth is worse for us and so we become victims of what we love most.

I'm writing this the night before I depart and I'm leaving it here with the Order because I'm not allowed to share this information beyond the Stadium's walls.

I'm in the Central Archive now and it's very late. I've been permitted three hours of solitary access because it's supposed to instil in me a sense of purpose and understanding about why I'm doing this.

The Archive is a special place at night. It feels like being inside the womb of civilisation itself. There is a sense of floating, like a baby, with everything we know about the world all around us. I felt both unborn and also the centre of the universe.

I have everything to explore and read and I'm allowed access to even the most fragile texts. But would you believe I'm spending the evening reading Calvin and Hobbes and writing to you?

I was once told that everything found in the Harrington Box was held in such awe that it took the Evaluators months to realise the comics were meant to be funny and it was okay for us all to laugh. It was interesting to learn that you can stare at something, even focus all your mind on it, and still not see it for what it is.

I don't want to know anything new before I leave. Instead, I want to revel, one last time, in a sense of home and domesticity: the very things, of course, I know I'll never have with you. I wish we could have had that, the two of us. We could have adopted a child, maybe two. Or one of us could have become pregnant. Probably you. I know there are some fine men you have your eyes on.

I imagine a life that is less ambitious, less curious and more contented. But still I go.

I have been asked to join the new High Command of the Southern Commonwealth as the liaison. If you are reading this, you'll know about the Museum already. Though I haven't seen it yet, I have to tell you that it is a remarkable thing. It is located in a place once called Mexico, in a region named Oaxaca. The people say there was a city with that name but it's long gone now. The people fled into the mountains to the east and took shelter at the Museum, much like The Few found the Stadium.

The population of the Museum is around ninety or so, I'm told. They have a festival that they insist dates back long before The Rise – what they call 'El Cambio', or the Change. The festival is a celebration called the Guelaguetza. Though the main languages there are Espanyol and our Common, which they call English (and I suppose we should too?), the word 'Guelaguetza' comes from another language called Zapotec. Apparently, cultures are built on the remains of other cultures, like ours

438

is built on The Rise. Even languages seem to lay one on top of another, influencing and enriching with new ideas and practices. (Oh, Lilly, there is so much to know!)

What is important about this festival – and may be essential to our survival – is that the word Guelaguetza evokes an ethos called the *obligación de la reciprocidad*: the obligation of reciprocity. They believe very deeply in the mutual and heartfelt exchange of gifts and services and blessings and it is this belief which has made their hearts open to exchanging with us. Our Explorers told them about our love for Knowledge and how The Crossing emerged as a place of exchange.

I've always thought of The Crossing as a very practical place, one driven by necessity, but they see it as a symbol and the more I think about it, picturing it in my mind rising from the sands and flying over an ancient river of green trees and grasses, only to descend back into the sands again, I can begin to see the beauty and romance of it the way they do. That eluded me before, and I think it's because I know what happened to you there, and what you did – what you had to do with Cardo and the others. I wasn't able to see past that history into what it has become. Again, Lilly, it's all because of you.

The Museum people feel that such a culture is like their own and that somehow our souls are already intertwined. They have a lovely way of talking, as though much of what comes from our minds is motivated first by the heart. I wonder if I will learn to see the world this way too. This sense of us being connected has made it easy to open relations with them and build trust. That trust, Lilly, will double the size of the known world. With this at stake, I have been asked to go there and oversee the progress of our friendship.

Can you think of anything more important, more vital? Even us?

The existence of the Southern Commonwealth is the greatest secret we possess. Should the Northern Command fall and the people need to flee, there is an escape route – we call it the Blue Route. It is the road I'm taking, in the company of an Explorer who knows it. I leave at dawn.

I will describe it to you, because if you are reading this, it is your future, and it will be hard.

Our Stadium, as you know, was once a major attraction for visitors. Years ago, The Few found boats behind the waterfall – this has been kept secret from everyone but the military. The hulls of these boats should have rotted over time, but they didn't because the material is particularly resilient. Visitors would ride these glass-roofed boats out from under the waterfall and tour the river which, I'm told, once looked and ran differently than it does today. The fifty boats are each named for a state in the United States (that's the region of the world where the Evaluators think we live now). Each can hold twenty people. Because of the flow of the river these days and the fact that the engines no longer work, any use of the boats would be a one-way journey, so they have been saved in case a mass evacuation is needed. The people will travel with the boats for about a month. The river water is undrinkable, but Explorers and members of the Order have created depots along the way with supplies and fresh water. This is one of the reasons we discourage talk about the Shining City and other myths to the west. The truth is, there are such cities but they're ruins and we don't want people stumbling on our caches in their search for them.

After a month you will reach mountains so high that they are capped with snow even in summer. You will leave the boats here because the waters now run too shallow. From there, you walk due west. The going will be hard and the young and old will suffer the most. Hunting will be plentiful. You'll find the hills teeming with deer, wild boar and jackrabbits. The Explorers say the ease of the hunt will be an indicator of your safety because only animals that know people are afraid of them.

There are fruits growing wild along the route; enough to sustain even a thousand people on the journey.

Eventually, I'm told, we will meet the ocean. This will be less like a body of water than it will an image of the sky having fallen to earth. I am looking forward to seeing it.

On the beach, which is much like a desert that touches the water, ancient

440

ships rest on their sides, half-buried in sand. Hundreds of massive containers rise from the shore, colourful monoliths or grave markers of giants or monsters who once roamed the coastline. There are carts and wheels, pipes and tubing, toys and artificial limbs – I am told to prepare myself for the thousands of human-like bodies that have washed to shore. Apparently, they are incredibly lifelike, with eyes staring blindly as if their attention has been seized and their minds are in rapture. They are robots or humanics, machines built to serve the Ancients which were made to look like them.

From there the route turns south and you will walk along the coast. Solar generators will purify drinking water, but now the problem of food will grow more acute. After that, it's too hard for me to explain. He tried to tell me what a selva is (in his language it means 'trees more dense than a wall'?) but that makes no sense to me.

What I do know is this: we join continents together, the north and the south – you and me.

I will not be allowed to write again because I cannot compromise the Secret. No information about us is allowed to flow north. I also think that you need to let me go. I know how you are: if we communicated in secret (I'm sure you'd find a way!), you would never move on with your life. All the same, I plan to keep a personal account of my experiences here as part of the Archive. My papers will be waiting for you when you arrive.

Dear Lilly, we have duties that are larger than our own lives: a commitment to keep the world and its memories alive, to solve the problems of the world with knowledge and passion and promise. Like you, I will keep my vows to the Commonwealth. I regret only that I did not make my own vows to you.

An artist here has written a poem for the children to memorise on the boats, before the Long Walk. It is sung to the same tune as the 'Season Song' – every child at the Stadium knows it. My heart is torn because I hope no child will ever have to learn it – but also that no child will ever forget it if they do.

As I think about it now, it is also my song to you.

We're taking a trip
We're going away
To find a new home
A place we will stay.

The walk will be hard
The walk will be far.
But we won't be alone
Whoever we are.

Remember the coast
Where water meets land
If I become lost
I will go there and stand.

And if it grows dark
I will be brave and be strong
I will scare off the monsters
Until help comes along.

I'll need water to drink
and food for my tummy
A safe place to sleep
So I can be comfy.

I might have to wait
Through sun and through snow
But I trust you will find me
Wherever I go.

Yours in love.
Verena

V
LATER

THE SONG OF US

When the refugees from the Stadium arrived, almost eighteen months later, they learned that the people of the Museum did not only celebrate the *Guelaguetza*, but also another festival called *Dia de la Asuncion de la Virgen Guadalupe*: a celebration for the goddess of life and nature.

A silver-haired woman of indeterminate age and excellent posture gathered them all into the field outside and addressed them in English. Everyone was acutely aware, after the Long Walk, that this was the largest gathering of people on this continent in four hundred years.

The woman's name was Gabriela deSoto. She had welcoming eyes.

'According to legend,' she started, 'a goddess was born, perfect and without sin, from the heart of the forest itself. Her kindness and beauty were so intense that the forest chose to give her a son so they could be happy together and her love could be directed to something good and outside herself. But sadly, the son grew heartsick when he became a man because he had no woman of his own to love, and for all the love he had for his mother, something inside him started to die.

445

'Guadalupe was rent by a pain inside her very soul because she had not imagined that their love would not be enough. The son chose to go away and wander the world in search of a wife. He was gone for ten years and every day Guadalupe's tears would water the earth. The flowers bloomed around her but gave her no comfort. After ten years, the son returned, as broken as his mother was elated. She sheltered him and protected him, fed him and loved him, but the space between them had become as wide as the distance between two oceans, for each was longing for a kind of love they could never have.

'Today,' she continued, 'the people of the Stadium have arrived, but our tears are not those of Guadalupe, but instead the tears of lovers who do finally meet, face to face, the authors of the poems that captured our hearts. Today is not a day of welcome or even new friends, but of unification and home-coming. This is not a new place, my friends, but the missing half of your own homes.'

As Gabriela deSoto had hoped, the hardened and weary refugees broke down and cried in their embrace, fulfilling the circle of love that poor Guadalupe had been denied.

There had been no Rise here, no deforestation, no heavy winds pushing up the sands like in Nevada, no floods leaving behind cargo planes and containers. Here, it was the sea levels which had risen, flooding the low-lying lands, and as the waters rose it felt as though the world had dropped.

El Cambio: The Change.

Lilly, by then, had a limp. She was gaunt from the irregular diet and too much stress on her ageing body. Slowly, painfully, she had walked more than two thousand kilometres over varied terrain. Once upon a time, the stairs of the Snake Tower had been a challenge – on the Blue Route, she had had to face mountains. What sustained her was the message she had received: that although Master Birch was dead, Alessandra and the Wayworths all lived, and so did the Prize, which would meet them in the south.

To lose Verena and then the Prize on account of being too weak, too old? That would have been too much. So Lilly walked.

She didn't know the word *tumour* yet but she felt that something was growing inside her. Having, so long ago, carried a water baby, she felt a change. Unlike that time – which had felt like life – this felt like death.

Three days after they had arrived and been embraced by the people of the Museum, Lilly met Alessandra in the oval 'gift shop'. With soaring ceiling and skylights and tall windows along a curved wall, it was an elegant – and empty – space. Alessandra, who had arrived with her parents four months earlier, had chosen it precisely because it was secluded and unused. This would be the new Communications Room.

When they embraced, Lilly felt frail and old to Alessandra.

Instead of asking about the Music Man, Master Birch and Chief Elimisha, though, Lilly went right to the point. Sitting herself on a white plastic chair, she said, 'Okay, show it to me.'

The Museum has a total floor area of over twenty thousand square metres, with over six thousand square metres of gallery suites for displays and exhibitions. Even with a thousand people inside, the Museum is mostly empty; quiet space is easy to find. The gift shop-turned-Comms is one of the many unused rooms that had long since been cleaned out by looters and abandoned by the community.

Still, it's clean.

'Once a year,' Alessandra tells Lilly while unpacking Lilly's

447

White Board and unfolding the Haptic Command Gear, 'the entire community sweeps and washes and dusts the whole place in preparation for yet another holiday. This one they call *Navidad*.'

'What does that mean?'

'Christmas.'

'Which is . . . what?'

'I don't know,' Alessandra admits. 'I haven't looked it up yet, but I know it's something to do with a virgin giving birth to the son of God in the desert and a man in a heavy winter coat who then shows up to give him gifts.'

'In the desert?'

'Yes. And the coat's red. With white trimming. And there are bells.'

'I don't care. Show me the Archive.'

Alessandra had carried it as though it were a newborn baby, with all the care of a mother holding the fate of the world. Now she extends her hands and allows Lilly to reach out and pick it up. 'Be careful,' she says.

'Well . . . obviously.' Lilly is gripping it carefully but tightly, as though it might be an object in a dream she can see but not grasp.

'It's so light,' she says.

'Knowledge doesn't weigh anything,' Alessandra explains.

'No, I suppose it doesn't.' Lilly's hands are shaking a little. She has stopped holding sharp objects due to this new affliction and has instead taken to barking commands to cover for her increasing palsy which she generally denies despite it being obvious. Seeing that Alessandra is nervous about it, she says, 'I won't drop it. My grip is good. The shaking is something else.'

'It doesn't seem worth the risk,' Alessandra whispers.

'It is,' says Lilly, 'because when you reach the end of your life and there's a chance to hold everything you earned – everything you sacrificed for – in the palm of your hand, you do it. And if you can let someone else do it, you do that too, especially when it's me saying I won't drop it. You're honestly telling me that this is a library?'

'Come,' Alessandra says, taking Lilly's other hand and pulling her up. 'I want to show you the world.'

The room Alessandra has picked for Lilly's journey into the Quantum Drive is the small unused office connected to the gift shop. This will be the new Central Archive. The room that the Museum now uses, she has decided, will be called the Library. Everyone will be able to access the Library. The Central Archive will be another matter. She – not Lian – will be the new Central Archivist.

And if the adults don't agree to this, she's decided, she will withhold the password protection she and the Librarian placed on it.

The password is Redemption. No one knows but her.

After showing Lilly the basic mechanics of the Haptic Command Gear, White Board and glasses, Alessandra leaves her to explore.

Lilly emerges from the secluded room thirty hours later, her eyes red from so many tears. Outside, in the jungle, the weather is hot and humid. Gabriela deSoto, the ruling Matriarch – who is slightly suspicious of Lilly, which Lilly considers an excellent instinct – says that summers are usually like this, and winters are very, very wet, which is, actually, a blessing because the rainwater is drinkable whereas the ground water can cause terrible pains in the stomach and even blindness.

Lilly has listened to these important facts with little interest and now, after her experience with the Quantum Drive, she has even less. She is not in charge here and will not live long enough to die by anything external. Her end, she knows, is already inside her. The Quantum Drive, however, is a new life.

When Lilly emerges from the new Central Archive, she finds in the new comms room reading a book he's found in the library. He isn't waiting for her, but is the first to see her.

'Welcome back,' he says to her as she stumbles out.

'Has Alessandra explained to you what's on that machine?' she asks.

'I'll have to look myself. I find it hard to imagine.'

'It's been said,' Lilly says, sitting down beside him on a rolling chair, 'that Paradise is our questions answered. Your daughter pulled Paradise from a place called Inferno.'

'She's a great kid,' Graham says.

'She has planted a seed that will restore civilisation itself.'

'That's great. I'll definitely take a look. Unfortunately, the suit Alessandra brought with her doesn't fit me. I think I'm a large.'

'You can use the glasses alone,' Lilly says, rubbing her eyes again. 'And I think we have a large in stock too.'

'I was making a joke.'

'Oh yes, I'd forgotten about your sense of humour. It turns out,' she says, thumbing over her shoulder, 'there used to be funnier people than you. They used to stand before an audience and tell humorous stories, sometimes for up to an hour. It was called "stand-up comedy" – although some were sitting down.'

'Uh huh.'

'Graham,' Lilly says, changing the subject, 'I know Gabriela deSoto is the Chief of the High Command here, which is fine, but she has a rather relaxed attitude towards security. In fact . . .

there's no security around here,' she says, waving her hands for emphasis. 'No procedures, no armed guards, no perimeter defences, no walls. It's like the early days before I found the Harrington Box and we got organised. I thought Verena would have locked this place down.'

'It's quite peaceful, Lilly. I rather like it.'

'It's great until all of a sudden it's not.'

'One could make a pretty strong argument,' he says, 'that this place is so nice and peaceful because of whatever it was Verena did. One thing I've learned is that there's always more going on than meets the eye. Have you, for example, actually talked to anyone yet?'

'I'll get around to it.'

'Uh huh,' he says again. 'Meanwhile, Chief, there's no one out there.' He puts the book down. 'We just walked a thousand miles and we saw barely anyone – a few colonies, the odd bandit. There's no force out in the woods here. The Museum is also armed and Gabriela has a Rapid Reaction Force – I've already talked to them. They're called *los Agradables* – the Agreeables. Isn't that great? They're sharp. I'm not worried.'

'Charming. Here's what we're really going to do,' Lilly says, forgetting that she's neither twenty-six nor in charge.

According to Lilly, the first task was to use the maps and schematics from the internet Find to help them locate more HAM Radios so they could establish communications with the Northern Command. The artificial intelligence known as the Librarian on the Quantum Drive helped them find locations where HAM radios were either once sold or repaired, or had been used in Mexico in the final years before *El Cambio*. Expeditions would be sent out to retrieve as many as possible – at least one and up to thirty; Lilly had plans. Using a term coined by Elimisha, these operations were to be called Discover and Recover, or D&R missions.

Second, but concurrent, was to find another empty Quantum Drive (or as many as possible) and copy the full contents of their own. The Commonwealth would still need Runners and it would still need off-site locations to store the Archives, but they probably wouldn't need Chiefs to command them any more, because the Archives could be hidden and also (they learned) password-protected, so the Quantum Drives would be worthless if found by anyone else. Each one would be a Harrington Box that was completely secured, even against people as smart as Lilly.

The new structure of society was already taking place in Lilly's mind. The pieces fit together with symmetry and purpose, designed to achieve a condition in the world that Lilly alone could see but everyone could be made to understand.

A fine piece of engineering.

It was not only the Quantum Drive that revitalised Lilly after the Long Walk and the growing awareness of her own limited time. It was the opportunity to *think* again. Here was the quickening in her chest she'd been missing; the sense of driving purpose that was nearly sexual in its capacity to fulfil.

Ah, to stop making buckets with Luther and imagine the unimaginable again: to go forth into the future with the confidence and clarity of youth.

Yes, this is what got her into trouble the first time: a supreme confidence in her own conclusions, driven in part by personal trauma. Then, it had been her mother. Now, to a lesser extent, it was the Long Walk and losing Verena a second time.

It was hard for her to learn from these lessons, though. Maybe if she knew how everyone on the continent east of Yellow Ridge had somehow heard about the Commonwealth and decided to hate it, she'd have a better grasp of what she'd done right or wrong. But that was an unanswerable mystery, at least for now. Perhaps, someday, if there was ever peace with those people and they could talk to one another in confidence about their mutual errors, she'd learn how word had travelled to them and prejudiced their minds against her and hers.

She was in the comms room explaining her master plan to Graham when the thought struck her: could it have been *Adam*?

They'd ostracised him even though he was only a boy, saying his visions and character were a disturbance to the peace. Even his mother, Lilly's aunt, hadn't been able to plead for him, for her argument had been based only on love, not reason. She'd had no argument left to make, which is why she'd left too.

Lilly had never heard from them again. She hadn't known where they went, until Birch told her that Adam had gone east, and that some of the Order had been concerned about his loose talk.

What if he had met people, Lilly wondered, *and what if these people had believed him? What if the Keepers believed him and learned of the Commonwealth and came to see the Commonwealth as a threat? What if* Adam *had created the Keepers?*

Could Adam, Verena and Lilly – all of them, and in their own ways – have started all this? Had the three of them been the cause that took fifty years to reach its effect? Had this drama always been destined to play out like a Greek tragedy?

'Lilly?'

The voice is familiar and calming and warm, a voice she knows and recognises and loves.

'Lilly? Have you finally snapped?'

Graham.

'Not yet.'

'You drifted off there.'

'I had an idea I've never had before. I don't know how it never occurred to me.'

'Something you want to share?'

'Graham . . . did you talk to them? The Keepers?'

Graham is still sitting with a leg crossed, his boot up on a chair. He no longer carries the knife, not since arriving here.

'Yes.'

'Do you know why they attacked us?'

Graham draws a deep breath of the lush air into his lungs, air filled with the smells of plants and rain and sunlight and life. He would hold it there for ever if he could, but each time he exhales it is an opportunity to draw it in again. It's strange the way this place has made him more sentimental.

'We all want things to be better, but we're all at odds on how to achieve it and that is a terrible, terrible pity.'

'How did they come to us, though? How did they gather such forces against us? What made it start?'

'I don't know. Why?'

'I think I might know,' Lilly says, 'and if I'm right – and I am beginning to suspect that I am – then I have seriously overestimated the power of walls and weapons and seriously underestimated the power of words.'

According to the Librarian of the Quantum Drive, the Museum was founded in 2048 with a grant from the Organisation of American States – the OAS – to celebrate one hundred years of regional solidarity. Inspired by Frank Gehry's Guggenheim Museum in Bilbao, Spain, the sweeping steel and glass building of irregular curves perches on the top of a glorious hill in the Sierra Madre of Oaxaca that faces east over the plains of Veracruz and out towards the Gulf of Mexico far beyond. Ground was not broken for construction, however, until 2069, because of tardy payments, new hostility towards multilateral cooperation, financial skimming, corruption and political backsliding.

Five years later, the Museum's basic structure and interior were completed, but at sixty per cent over budget, and almost immediately the project faltered and became a symbol of internecine conflict.

By 2080 the OAS was rendered irrelevant because of growing 'localisation', which was the term given to the revolt against globalisation, the counterforce that claimed to resist 'imperial homogenisation' and 'culturcide'. Countries and cultures wanted their own languages and religions and ways of life back. Cooperation was mistakenly thought to be antithetical to those goals.

The warm oak-panelled halls were never filled with the promised art, only with echoes and accusations. By the beginning of the Solar War, the Museum had been abandoned and forgotten.

But one piece had been installed, and here it remains, perfect and bright, even after all these centuries. The title of the exhibit, *The Sound of Us*, is carved into a brass plaque in Spanish, English, Portuguese and French, the four languages most prominent in the Americas. It is on display in a space inspired by – and larger than – something called the Turbine Hall at the Tate Modern Museum in London. It is a room for enormous installations, to support the expression of limitless imagination.

Ilimitada imaginación.
Imaginação ilimitada.

Imagination illimitée.

The first and only installation, as seen from the side, looks to be a massively tangled jumble of red tubes that begins at a single point near the floor on one side, rises to the ceiling, where the entanglement fills most of the hall, and then, at the far end, descends again to another single point.

As the spectator stands at the southern tip, however, the perspective changes and it becomes clear that the tangled tubes are an impressionistic but still discernible map of the entirety of the Americas, from Islote Águila in Chile all the way to Cape Columbia on Ellesmere Island in Canada at over 83 degrees north – a point even further north than the destination where Alessandra has argued that a D&R must be sent: Svalbard, Norway.

The long red tube that meets the viewer is a mouthpiece.

'Speak,' says the plaque in four languages, 'and become *The Sound of Us.*'

And so the child – it's so often a child – says something into the open end, something simple, even trite.

'¡Hola!'

The enthusiasm of that greeting enters the tubes made of aluminium and carbon fibre and travels to the far end – but not in a straight line, and nor does it travel only once. Instead, the message splits thirty-five times, staggering and cutting, colliding and harmonising so that the sound, symbolically passing through all thirty-five states, becomes a kind of music.

When Lilly was young and opened the Harrington Box and shocked the people of the Stadium into action by announcing that never again would the world be darkened by ignorance and superstition, she was driven – she knows now – by fear. The death of her mother had been the prime mover and she was the turbine that turned that experience into a new energy.

Here, among the Mexicans of Oaxaca and high up on a hill that was once inland and overlooking the plains of Veracruz (which have long-since vanished under the water, making the Sierra Madres a coastal mountain range now), no one is driven by fear any more.

They had been rent from their homes and set out on a journey – an Exodus – that should have broken their spirit and made them bitter, but instead they walked the devastated lands and found them empty: a world bereft and in need of husbandry and hope and possibility.

And when they arrived, they met a people who believed in that already, and in their hearts, without ever having had to make that same arduous trek.

So when Lilly sat with Graham and Henry and Gabriela deSoto and a lovely man named Don Carlo (who sported a stylish, close-ly-cropped grey beard and had almost black eyes), she pitched her plan and they heard it with new ears, for by then, they too had spent days on the Quantum Drive, following their own curiosities into stories and pictures, emotions and recriminations about how foolish – how *damned* foolish – mankind was.

When Lilly explains the plan, it comes out more . . . *technical* . . . than she had planned. But she is far too excited to filter her thoughts. She feels forty years younger, with the energy of a stallion.

They sit at the table Lilly has had hauled into the gift shop – which she has renamed the Communications Room, leaving out any reference to weapons. This, she explains, is going to be the hub for a new global network of communications. This is where the Commonwealth will steer the fate of humanity.

Gabriela and Don Carlo both speak English. The kind of English Lilly is now speaking – having spent weeks in dialogue with the Librarian – makes no sense to anyone. Her enthusiasm, however, speaks volumes:

'Understanding challenges of propagation for the HAM radios is going to be a major problem if we want to start getting positive reception at serious distances on a stable basis,' Lilly sort-of explains. 'What we need, but don't have access to, is solar flare activity and information on background x-ray flux. The thing is, the green skies that we are all accustomed to, especially in Northern Command, are caused by charged particles in the Earth's upper atmosphere interacting with the Earth's natural magnetic field lines. What happens is, HAM radio signals scatter off these particles, greatly enhancing propagation on the VHF and UHF radio bands – the truth is, it was sheer dumb luck that I had tuned the Stadium's radio to an F-layer frequency, which is what allowed long-distance signals to better refract off the ionosphere, especially at night. That's how we first managed to hear those distant voices. Dumb luck, though,' she concedes, assuming anyone is understanding her, 'isn't a strategy. So what I'm proposing is that we fill this room with radios using the information that the Librarian has given us on where we might find them using our new D&R teams, and then I suggest we train up our Explorers into a new class of traveller we'll call Engineers. They'll need to have the skills of Runners and the minds of Scribes. I want these people to position and build and maintain as needed a set of relay-stations at various intervals all across the Americas – and beyond the Americas, if we can get there. Those radio signals I caught over the last fifty years? Now I know how the radio works, we're going to look for them. And we're going to learn their languages. It turns out that "*Sayonara*" is Japanese – it actually means goodbye. No more messing around: I want the song of us to be heard *everywhere*.

'And once that's done, I want to talk about boats, because Alessandra Wayworth – now Commander Wayworth, because apparently we need three of those – has plans that involve a small island in the heart of the Arctic Circle.'

SVALBARD

Seven months later, Lilly sits in her wheelchair in front of Workstation Three in the Communications Room, having displaced Maria Consuela Lopez (despite Maria being their best Radio Operator). The tumour in her spine is growing larger and there is constant discomfort, which gets worse when she's immobile too long. The Southerners – with a more caustic wit than their northern compatriots – have dubbed her wiggling and adjusting movements as *baile del Diablo*, or the Devil's dance, but there's little she can do about it. There might be only one Commonwealth connecting two continents now, but there's definitely more than one sense of humour.

Lilly doesn't care about any of this at the moment for she is growing extremely impatient. 'Would it kill your daughter to send us a message?'

'She's busy, Lilly,' Graham says, trying to calm her down as one might a child.

Alessandra is on an ice-breaker in the Greenland Sea, latitude seventy-eight degrees north and approaching their final destination. She is leading the first intercontinental Discover &

460

Recover in the Commonwealth's history. It will also be among the most important, if she's successful.

Everyone is waiting to find out the results and Lilly's anxiety is palpable. Those gathered know she doesn't have time for these long pauses any more and Lilly's heart – say those who knew Verena well and loved her and drank with her and cried with her and have heard a thousand stories about Lilly long before the woman herself arrived – has done too much waiting.

Su corazon. Everything is about the heart with these people. Lilly rather likes it.

This gathering and the interminable quiet are the results of Alessandra and Elimisha's experience in the bunker where they discovered that baby polar bears are cute and followed that sentiment to the discovery of the vault – a discovery which set the Wayworths in motion again. Henry and Graham took to the land, and Alessandra made preparations for the sea.

The Quantum Drive possessed a detailed roster of all the markets, stores and warehouses that once sold or repaired VHF and HF radios in Mexico City, which was northwest of the Museum, and Guatemala City, to the southeast, which meant the expeditions would know where to look within a few metres – or at least, they would once they'd all learned to read maps.

Guatemala City was, at the time of the Librarian's last update, 1,500 metres above sea level, and Mexico City was over 2,200. Each, they hoped, a fantastic sprawling metropolis in some state of disrepair with treasure waiting to be claimed.

Henry and Graham led separate and parallel D&R teams of twenty: Graham went to Mexico City; Henry to Guatemala City.

The expeditions both took three months.

Each city was a jungle now, with towers rising out of the green the way the Gone World rose from the sands.

The teams each established two tower-top signal relays and returned with nineteen radios between them.

That left Alessandra's project by sea.

As her parents ventured out into the unknown jungles, Alessandra's team made for the waters to the east, coming from the Sierra Madres and into the state of Veracruz, where the Atlantic Ocean had long since inundated the city of Heroica Veracruz, scattering its memories across the western world on the North Atlantic gyre, the currents of the Gulf Stream.

Lilly and Alessandra were both counting on the Mexican government's long-term preparations for climate change at the Veracruz Shipyard, which had been built in 1982, then considerably updated and expanded in 2051 by a Dutch architectural firm specialising in industrial off-shore projects for facilities that had once been coastal or inland. As it was Mexico's first heavy naval construction centre, the D&R teams considered the Floating Veracruz Shipyard the most likely place to still possess open-water craft able to take them north – that's as long as they'd not otherwise been sunk, stolen, vandalised or wrecked.

Alessandra's first dictate as a D&R commander was that everyone on her team learn how to swim. No one from the Stadium could and only a few from the Museum knew how. Alessandra had had to get video instructions from the Quantum Drive. The transition from classroom to open water had not been smooth.

They found the shipyard one and a half kilometres out at sea. The inland waters lapped against vegetation rather than sand and beyond was nothing but flotsam; most of it plastic bottles that had still not broken down and sunk below the surface. Sea Glass Lake was a glittering and serendipitous jewel forged in the unwitting fires of a catastrophe. This was the opposite: a floating mass of colorless filth caused by the apathy of inhumanity.

There would be no swimming through it, even if they could have managed the distance in the open ocean, which none of them could. After two weeks of searching, the team unearthed an 'unsinkable' Boston Whaler with a Unibond hull construction (according to the Librarian), sitting on a pile of rust that must once have been a carrier. The building housing it was now so covered in vines and hemmed in by trees that it took four days of chopping and hauling before they could extract the boat and pull it onto the main path that was once a road. After that they were able to lift it on steel wheels and a trellis.

It took another week for it to touch water.

And a day of rowing back and forth to move them with all their gear to the flotilla.

Their efforts, however, were not wasted, for there, dry-docked on the shipyard, was the very thing they'd been seeking: a Littoral Combat Ship, a near-shore vessel with open-water capabilities. It was the most sophisticated piece of engineering anyone had ever seen: built late in the twenty-first century for the Mexican Navy, it had survived not just the war, but also the rising acidity levels of the Gulf, because it had been stored in a wrapper the Librarian called 'Time Capsule Technology' designed to keep unused ships in pristine condition prior to deployment.

Alessandra named the ship the *Saavni* after the first Master of the Order of Silence.

The inexperienced crew focused their attention on learning the basics, especially propulsion and piloting, and tried their best to touch nothing else. Many of the systems were dependent on satellites and connectivity, none of which functioned, but the ship's electrical generators were powered by wave motion, each wave striking the hull turned into the electricity that turned the engines and propelled them forwards.

Below decks, they found ten pulse rifles similar to those at the Stadium.

Alessandra assigned one of the older men to be pilot. He was about the same age as her parents, with the scars and lines on his face to prove it. When he asked why he was being given that assignment, Alessandra told him she liked his name.

Everyone called him *Suerte*: Lucky.

He considered that an excellent reason.

They installed one of Lilly's radios and stocked up with provisions and finally, after months of preparation, they set sail for the north.

They followed the coast of Yucatan to the Cuban archipelago and from there, turned northwards to Florida, enjoying a lively debate on whether to retain the classical names or to respect the new ones they learned from the locals watching in awe and wonder as the Corvette glided past their simple dwellings.

In South Carolina, they met natives who fired at them as they sailed past. Alessandra ordered them into deeper waters.

Lucky piloted their ship successfully to the Norfolk Navy Yard, where they expected to find armaments and a possible settlement. They found nothing but destruction.

*

464

They docked the *Saavni* in Canada, because they now needed a craft that could handle more than the coast and more than mere cold.

They needed an icebreaker.

Despite the unimaginable levels of detail provided by the Librarian, no one really knew what awaited them. The Knowledge they had was four hundred years old, and as everyone agreed: *things change.*

Alessandra knew it was a gamble travelling to St John's in Newfoundland in search of the new boat, but Canada had maintained superb public records of the Coast Guard's actions and responses to climate change and war right up until the end. When the waters started rising in Labrador, the Canadian Coast Guard had, at considerable expense, started a new programme they called *Longevity*, futureproofing ships and facilities as best they could and dry-docking its fleet in newly built berths. The result was that her D&R team soon found her a new ship – an electrically powered Arctic 8 Icebreaker – in excellent condition.

Knowing that a single error – a single unnecessary risk – could doom the mission, it took them twelve days to figure out how to get it down from its perch and into the water.

The crossing from St John's to Ikerasassuaq at the southern tip of Greenland forced them into the Labrador Sea, the first stretch of open water they had ever faced – which made them the first humans to be surrounded by nothing but water since the Solar War.

They had to fight the southeasterly Baffin Currents dropping down the Canadian coast, then the East Greenland currents pushing them westwards as they tried to make for land.

It wasn't just the ocean causing problems. Even though they grew accustomed to the twenty-four-hour sun, the eternal light

465

during the night-time confused them, filling them all with a restless energy that sapped them by day. Their skin darkened and their faces grew weathered. Their constantly squinting eyes were wrinkling on even the youngest crew members.

When they saw the coast of Svalbard they stood on the deck and cried.

Their approach to the island was the last Lilly heard of their location. Their lack of contact may have been due to the radio's signal being hard to maintain. Or maybe they sank. Or perhaps Alessandra was busy as a Captain and Commander of a mission.

Her theory, which she shared with Graham and Henry in the Comms room with dozens of others gathered around, was that Alessandra was a twenty-one-year-old former Urban Explorer and all-around pain-in-the-ass who couldn't be bothered to share what she was seeing at the moment.

In the Communications room, the windows are open and everyone is silent. The wind through the palm trees sounds like rain.

It is too much for Lilly, who starts barking orders to the operators. 'Give me a global radio check.'

Japanese, French, Mandarin, Spanish, English and German are spoken simultaneously into the radios, and each uplink transmission is followed by a brief pause before the foreign operators respond – and when those voices reassemble, they become a global *Song of Us*, filling the oval room with a cacophony of sound the likes of which the world has not heard since the fall of the Tower of Babel.

Each Radio Operator, trained to hear ambient noise as the enemy, wants to use headphones to avoid this din, but on this day Lilly has forbidden their use. She wants to hear the answers, even if she can't understand them; she wants to hear the world talk and answer back, to feel their voices in her chest.

'Maybe,' Lilly hears Graham say to her, 'we should play that song she wanted to hear? We come up on the hour in two minutes. Maybe it'll get her attention. What do you say?'

Lilly sniffs.

Commander Alessandra Wayworth, Captain of the Commonwealth Icebreaker *Elimisha*, stands at the prow in her red parka and stares ahead over the waters to the snow-capped mountains. Her glacier glasses are tight around her eyes. It is bright, but there is less ice than expected. The *Elimisha*'s electrical propulsion system offers maximum torque from one knot, which proved a blessing when they encountered an expanse of deep ice that had broken free of Greenland's glaciers and they'd had no way to avoid it, so had had no choice but to barrel through it. Now the *Elimisha* is cruising at ten knots through thin plates of floating ice that are no threat to the boat or her now-experienced team.

There are fair skies and visibility is excellent. The air smells like the colour of the sky.

Approaching the inlet that should take them to the vault, Alessandra turns backwards and uses her walkie-talkie to speak with the command deck above. 'Why am I not hearing anything?'

Lucky's voice crackles over the intercom. 'I think Southern Command is expecting you to call in.'

Abril has joined her at the prow. She is ten years older, and

Museum-born. Alessandra chose her as much for her glowing and optimistic personality as for her engineering prowess and problem-solving skills. She is taller than Alessandra and her black hair is long and tied at the back. Her smile is expansive, her enthusiasm contagious. She smiles out over the sea.

Lucky says, 'I lost the signal, Commander. I'm switching to the secondary band.'

'Pipe it through the speakers if you get it. It's coming up on thirteen hundred hours and they promised me a song. I don't want to miss it.'

Moments before the hour Lucky announces he has made contact again, and through the loudspeakers mounted to the deck, Alessandra hears Lucky's intercom being dragged across the table to the HAM radio's small speaker.

A woman's voice – more beautiful than any voice that has sung out over the waters of the Northern Hemisphere since *El Cambio* – starts her song with a simple hum before telling a story of defeat and love and loyalty as a man returns to Georgia on a midnight train.

The ten men and four women under Alessandra's command join Gladys Knight and the Pips sing 'He's leavin' . . .' as the ice-breaker glides east-northeast into the Isfjorden on the western coast of Svalbard, Norway.

The black rock to the south welcomes them like an out-stretched hand. The land is utterly bare, like it was at home when she was young, but this is a new, treeless tundra and not a desert.

'Two hundred years of recorded music before the Change,' says Abril, 'and the nineteen seventies are still the best.'

'Is that true for Spanish music too?' Alessandra asks.

'Oh, yes. I still have so much to listen to, but that is what moves me the most. That and the twenty fifties, because there was a roots revival then as the world tried to turn back the clocks and recover their national souls. It might have been a bad time for politics but it was wonderful for music.'

Abril has two younger sisters and a younger brother. She talks about them constantly. She tells Alessandra that she reminds her of her youngest sister in disposition but her brother in the heaviness behind her eyes. He fought against the Hidalgos fifteen years ago, experiencing terrible things, but he doesn't talk about it. Alessandra should meet him – *Do you like boys? You do? This could be good, then.*

Abril stops talking and squints ahead as the boat slows. Lucky is keeping them in the centre of the inlet. The sonar is working, but their maps are dated and they have learned that flotsam tends to collect in natural harbours like the one they're approaching, so they slow to two knots.

'Lucky,' Alessandra says, once the song ends, 'tell Lilly where we are. I suspect she's driving everyone crazy back there. I can't make that joke last for ever.'

Their electric engine is silent. They have the waves, and the birds and the wind for accompaniment when the song ends. Abril points to the right and those on deck turn to see, floating in the water near shore, the sterns of seven boats bobbing like dabbling gadwalls. The crew has come across this before, in Maine and Halifax: boats chained to piers now submerged, their hulls floating ever-upwards towards freedom. They are perches for seabirds, and serve as rough measures of rising sea-levels.

The hulls clap together as the *Elimisha* approaches: a waiting audience for their arrival.

'From the position of the boats, I suspect the water here has risen by two or three metres at the most,' Abril says, analytically. 'That's nothing. They say the vault's one hundred and thirty metres up the mountain. It should still be okay.'

When Lilly's voice bellows out of the *Elimisha*'s speakers, it is somehow lower, deeper and louder than in person, despite being nine thousand kilometres away.

'So have you found it yet or what? Over.'

Alessandra waves off the question and Lucky knows he's to take such calls himself, and privately, until there's something to report, which is much like being instructed to throw his body on a grenade.

'She's become more formal,' Abril murmurs to Alessandra as the boat rounds another twenty degrees to the northeast.

'Yeah,' Alessandra says. '" Over" was a nice touch—'

Lucky blows the horn. Condensed air is sent screaming out across the waters as an announcement, a declaration, a warning: *We are here.*

One of the D&R team, a young man in a purple knit hat, shouts as he sees the vault and its distinctive crystalline sculpture facing them like a signal mirror. It is halfway up the sloping crest of the mountain, bright and vibrant against the black volcanic shale that surrounds it.

As they draw closer to their destination, the rest of the vault entrance rises out of the ground, exposing the horizontal striations of the venting below and – when they are close enough to make out details – the twin doors themselves. The structure is as much a sculpture as it is the entrance to a facility. It was built as a beacon to travellers; now it is a clarion call for rebirth.

'When I lived in the desert at the Stadium,' Alessandra says to Abril over the sound of the wind, 'we could see the Gone World from the tops of the walls. At sunset the light would—'

But she stops suddenly, because there, on the black shale, drawn by Lucky's horn rather than repulsed by it, is a powder-white bear cub with eyes as big and black as rare pearls.

Everyone on board points and – for reasons Alessandra cannot understand – all the Museum-born wave at it.

'What is that?' Abril asks, her voice filled with excitement.

'An *is bjørn*,' Alessandra says. 'A polar bear cub.'

'It's so . . .'

'Cute.'

'You have seen one before?'

'Don't pet it.'

Abril raises binoculars to look more closely at the bear, but Alessandra gently nudges her back to the Vault.

'*Si, claro*,' Abril says.

'The doors?' Alessandra asks.

'They are closed.'

'Check again.'

'They are closed.'

'That could be the angle. They might be—'

'*Están cerrados. Absolutamente.*'

'We've come a long way,' Alessandra says, 'and someone could have looted it since then.'

Abril lowers the binoculars and gives Alessandra a hard look.

'Fine,' Alessandra says. 'If you're positive, I'll be positive.'

Everyone except for Lucky, who has volunteered to remain on board and man the radio, proceeds to the shore in two heavy rubber dinghies. On landfall, their boots crunch on the shale; they climb up to a road and follow it as it winds up the hill.

They walk in the grooves of tyre tracks that have hardened in the mud like the footprints of dinosaurs.

Seen from the side, the entrance to the vault is not a rectangular monolith but slopes downwards at the back, descending into the earth as though it were the top of a sunken building like those of the Gone World. The face is only four metres tall but, alone against the black rock and against the blue sky like this, it towers in their imagination.

They have talked about it for so long: to see it in person is nothing short of a miracle.

There is a sign on the right side of the building. What they notice first is four words next to an abstract symbol – a black crescent encircling or maybe protecting a blue orb of sky. Beneath it is a single green leaf. Perhaps the black is the darkness and seclusion of the island – which sits 78 degrees north inside the Arctic Circle – and the daylight is a future hope; the leaf the promise? Alessandra is no Evaluator; this is not her concern. Only the words matter:

Svalbard Global Seed Vault

Together, and stationing no guard outside, they cross a small footbridge to the heavy steel doors.

The polar bear cub has been met by a parent. They sit together, two hundred metres to the north, watching these creatures that walk on two legs and travel in packs.

It is Abril who steps to the front, past her Captain and her mates, to place her two palms against the door before turning and smiling at everyone.

'*Ahora*,' she says, all business now. 'Who has the key?'

*

At the Museum, the radio comes to life with a crackle and Lucky's voice, a resonant baritone that could sing duets with thunderclouds, fills the Comms room.

'We've found the vault,' he says in his heavily accented English.

He's speaking English for Lilly's benefit, only it isn't beneficial because Lilly knows he would have said more if he'd been speaking in his native Spanish. She has come to find the Museum-born loquacious and she'd been counting on getting more information.

But apparently that isn't how it works.

She has come to the grudging conclusion that people are harder to reverse-engineer than objects.

'I'm going to hang that guy by his feet like a . . . a . . . what the hell are they called?'

'A piñata,' comes a woman's voice from the back of the room.

'Right. One of those.' She's ranting, she knows that. She's old and – on balance – she's possibly saved more lives than she's taken (although the numbers are big on both sides), so no one interrupts. 'Of course they found it,' she says. 'I want to know if it's intact and full. There should be millions of seeds there, matched to their originating countries all over the world. It was once the largest gene bank on the planet and I need to know if it still is. If this works, the potential for ecosystem restoration, food cultivation, medicinal research—'

'Lilly,' says Henry, gently, 'in your condition, you can either yell and drop dead immediately or wait quietly for the answer and die later. Your heart can't take it. You can't do both.'

'It's always *el corazon* around here, isn't it? Fine. I'll quiet down.'

But she doesn't. Lilly has no idea how to shut up and the learning curve looks too steep.

'They said,' she continues, 'that the vault was designed to be fail-safe – but nothing's fail-safe. *Everything* fails – our

473

imaginations fail; our memories; our patience. You can't separate out the human condition from engineering. That's why the term "futureproof" is preposterous.'

'Alessandra's not answering,' Graham tells her, 'because she knows you're probably acting this way and she's enjoying every moment of it even if she can't hear it.'

'You're probably right,' Lilly says, realising she's been played.

'Chief?' says Maria Consuela Lopez, who has resumed her position at the radio now that Graham has physically rolled Lilly away from it. 'General Anoushka at Northern Command is requesting an update.'

'Tell her she'll know when everyone else knows.'

'Yes, Chief, she figured you'd say that. But I've been asked to remind you that today is her wedding day with Moishe and she would consider this a special gift.'

'They're in,' says Lucky through the radio.

'Tell the General that they're in and to stand by and shut up, I don't care what day it is.'

No one speaks. Birds are calling to one another and the wind blows through the palms outside the windows. The light flickering through their enormous fronds makes the room feel overgrown with life. It is impossible to stop thinking of seeds.

'They're passing through a kind of tunnel,' Lucky reports. 'They're on a walkie-talkie so I'm losing reception as they get further into the mountain. I'm moving the *Elimisha* closer for better line-of-sight. Stand by.'

Despite now having access to the exact time of day, Lilly continues to watch Mickey Mouse instead. She has discovered that digital clocks are better for knowing the exact time, but analogue clocks are better for understanding the relative passage of time. Waiting is not a digital activity.

Mickey's hand moves three excruciating minutes before there is another human sound.

It is Lucky again. 'They say the storage room is filled with plastic boxes, just like in the pictures. We're opening them.

'There are . . . seeds. Many, many, *many* seeds, We will have some inventory to take, but Abril is giving me the thumbs-up from the entrance to the Vault. It all looks intact, Chief.'

A roar of clapping begins spontaneously. Lilly waits for the emotions to settle and for all eyes and ears to return to her, ready for the command they have all been waiting for her to issue.

A dozen lands are waiting for the results of the expedition; partners who will meet the Commonwealth Global Explorers in harbours along the European and African coasts first, and then, after Alessandra and her crew return and a new team takes their place, they will try and make the trip to Asia, where other colonies will invite them to port. There are seventeen in all: the entirety of the known world. Maybe fifty thousand souls.

Out there, in the darkness and the silence, there are more.

Their stories are all different – but their hunger is all the same, because the Roamers back in the desert were right: there is a sickness living in the soil, which is transmitted to people through contaminated water and foods. This sickness once decimated cultivated crops, forcing people back to hunting or migrating.

It is Lilly's theory that returning uncontaminated seeds with the capacity to germinate to their original lands will help revitalise their native soils, allowing people to repossess the land again and take root.

Time will tell.

A stretch of time that will, unfortunately, be measured in years and possibly decades; far more time than Lilly has. When the answer is revealed and the first grains are milled, the first bread baked and then broken in a *fiesta*, she'll be in the ground beside Verena.

And yet, for Lilly, it is enough to have made it this far in only one lifetime. It is a journey that began with her mother's murder and has resulted in the unification of the world.

There's still work to do. General Anoushka says the Keepers remain, but they know nothing about Southern Command. Just as the Commonwealth was blind to the build-up of the Keepers forces and the depth of their philosophy and conviction, so too are the Keepers ignorant about the Commonwealth as an intercontinental learning machine and a hub for the dissemination and accumulation of Knowledge and rebirth.

In this way, they have already won, because now it is the Keepers who are contained behind their walls of ignorance and the Commonwealth which is free to move and grow. In time, the Commonwealth will encircle them.

And if they can find another direct connection to the internet itself?

That is only a matter of time.

Lilly and Gabriela deSoto, Henry and Graham – they all know that there is now a chance to rebuild what was lost. Doing it the right way will require someone better than her: someone who can rise above her own fears and not be driven by them. Someone like the girl she used to be.

After opening the Harrington Box, Lilly found a card inside the Thucydides book. Somehow – in a story now lost to time – the book had travelled west from the Boston Public Library on the East Coast. Maybe Colonel Harrington had expected to return it some day – or maybe he knew he never could. Either way, written on the card was the sentence Lilly had used to name the Commonwealth and craft the foundations of their culture: one she has since learned was once etched in stone across the frieze of the Boston Public Library, a building long-since submerged under the cold waters of the Atlantic:

The Commonwealth requires the education of the people as the safe-guard of order and liberty, said the card, *free to all*.

So young, Lilly had thought it meant the education to build walls, build weapons, build power. She hadn't then understood that what the Commonwealth really required was the wisdom to govern itself that could only come from universal education.

That was why it was 'free to all' – because only the educated can work wisely together.

She had helped build the Commonwealth on a misinterpretation of an ancient text, and in doing so had had to watch it fall. Now, however, she is going to get it right.

Lilly snaps her fingers to command the attention of the radio operators. All eyes turn to her, ready to begin a spirited journey into a better future.

'Begin The Crossing,' she says.

ACKNOWLEDGEMENTS AND DENIALS

Not enough people helped me in the writing of this book.

Oh, sure. I know the convention. I'm supposed to wax on about the vast number of people without whom none of this would be possible, but the simple fact is that a little more help would have been great. From whom, you ask? Well, off the top of my head: urban planners, environmental-change modellers, metallurgists, stadium designers, horse wranglers, pole-vaulters, technology futurists, spelunkers, musicologists, bunker designers, and would it have killed someone to bring me a cup of coffee with some of Lilly's lizard poison in it once in a while? I mean, honestly, sometimes I wonder why I bother.

Despite having been abandoned by academia and the entire engineering community, I will admit that the people at Janklow and Nesbit – especially Rebecca Carter – once again set the standards for excellence by connecting me with the world's greatest publisher of science fiction, Jo Fletcher (who should also be able to snap her fingers for coffee, but I digress). JFB at Quercus and Hachette has been a God-send as I ventured forth from literary fiction and into science fiction. Thanks for believing in me and helping make this possible.

Meanwhile: thank you Dr Jennifer Milliken, Dr Una McCormack and Dr Bernard Finel, who provided wonderful ideas and insights on early drafts. Obviously, any gross errors in the manuscript are theirs and folks should contact them directly. Cut out the middle-man, that's what I say.

Thanks to Nicola Howell Hawley for creating the map of the Commonwealth and the Territory.

I listened to many versions of the *Goldberg Variations* while writing this. The one that moved me most for the chapter on Moishe was the interpretation by Simone Dinnerstein.

The graffiti in Elimisha's bunker – 'Without power . . . it is just a cave' – is taken from a stencil inside NORAD at the Cheyenne Mountain Facility.

The line: 'If it's very very beautiful, or very very ugly, don't touch it' was uttered by Dive Master A. Sami E. Samaco when I earned my PADI Open Water Diver certification in Bahrain in 1999. Is that great or what?

The conversation between Birch and Lilly in the Hollows was inspired by – and one sentence taken directly from – Daniel J. Boorstin's introduction to Edward Gibbon's *The Decline and Fall of the Roman Empire* ('The daily habits of remote and unfamiliar peoples help us understand their life-and-death commitments'). I have a Ph.D. in international relations and spent more than a decade with the UN working on issues of local knowledge and designing cooperative solutions to complex problems and security challenges with communities. Needless to say, I agree with Boorstin. Also worth reading in this regard are Jerome Bruner's *Jerusalem Lectures*; Clifford Geertz's *Local Knowledge*; and Adda B. Bozeman's *Political Culture in International History*.

Graham's interpretation of the Melian Dialogue is my own. The Neo-realists really screwed that one up, in my opinion, but I'm too busy to write the peer-reviewed article debunking them. I am available for lectures, however.

The chicken joke was adapted from Garrison Keillor's *Pretty Good Joke Book*. I'm not going to say that I improved upon it because . . . that's unnecessary. I will, however, mention that I'm not mentioning it.

This book owes a debt to Walter Miller Jr.'s *A Canticle for Leibowitz* (1959). The abbey is an homage to Miller's own, and my Francis is a second chance for Miller's hapless one who met such a poor fate ('eat, eat!'). I consider *Radio Life* (and what I hope to be the subsequent series) to be in *direct* conversation with that 1959 novel on whether or not we are doomed to repeat our own mistakes. I also hope to contribute something of value to that conversation.

This book also owes a distant but real debt to the song *Telegraph Road* by Dire Straits. If this story had an origin, it might have been that song, which I first heard when I was sixteen.

Radio Life is dedicated to my daughter Clara who inspired, one way or another, every brilliant, bold, wilful, adventurous, thoughtful, curious, ass-kicking warrior-poet in this story; you inspired those women, Clara, because you inspire me. I am so lucky to be your Dad.

Derek B. Miller,
Oslo, Norway,
August, 2020

Derek Miller was born in Boston, Massachusetts and grew up in New England. He did his Master's in National Security at Washington DC's Georgetown University, then studied at The Hebrew University in Israel and St Catherine's, Oxford before completing his Ph.D. in International Relations at the Graduate Institute in Geneva. Before becoming a full-time novelist, he worked all over the world for a variety of organisations, including the United Nations. His first novel, *Norwegian by Night*, won the CWA John Creasey Dagger and was an *Economist* best novel of the year; subsequent crime novels *The Girl in Green* and *American by Day* were both shortlisted for the CWA Gold Dagger. *How to Find Your Way in the Dark*, an American mid-century epic, is due out in 2021. *Radio Life*, his first science fiction novel, inspired by his love for the classic *A Canticle for Liebowitz* by Walter M. Miller (no relation!), shares a grand if troubled vision about the role of knowledge and wisdom at the heart of any of our possible futures. He lives in Oslo, Norway, with his wife and children.

Our Child of Two Worlds

ALSO BY STEPHEN COX

Our Child of the Stars

Our Child of Two Worlds

Stephen Cox

Jo Fletcher
BOOKS

First published in Great Britain in 2022 by

Jo Fletcher Books
an imprint of Quercus Editions Ltd
Carmelite House
50 Victoria Embankment
London EC4Y 0DZ

An Hachette UK company

A CIP catalogue record for this book is available
from the British Library

HB ISBN 978 1 78747 162 7
TPB ISBN 978 1 78747 161 0

10 9 8 7 6 5 4 3 2 1

Typeset by CC Book Production
Printed and bound in Great Britain by Clays Ltd, Elcograf S.p.A.

Papers used by Jo Fletcher are from well-managed forests and other responsible sources.

To Sarah, of course

CHAPTER I

Amber County,
the first week of November 1971

Cory ran through the woods, kicking dry leaves, wanting everything. He wanted so-much to laugh with the joy of it, but he needed all his breath to run. At his heels bounded Meteor, grey shaggy curls and cheerful barks, in case any living thing could not guess they were coming. Dogs were such good friends. Close behind, Chuck and Bonnie ran too, his truest human friends, and behind them, the whoops and calls and crashing noises of the rest of the gang. Counting to two hundred might not have been enough . . . The teenagers had longer legs, and this race would not last much longer.

Run Cory run. His tentacles tasted the air, to enjoy the damp kicked up under the leaves, the faint trace of a male fox, the dog scent that was not Meteor. Among friends he ran tail out, signalling enthusiasm. Cory felt the touch of cold in the air and enjoyed how November light was lower; he saw the trees that day by day were shedding their leaves, their glory of gold and flame. Cory felt the solemn presence of each tree, he felt as well as heard the startled birds rising and the little lives scuttering to hide.

Cory-wants-it-all-all-all. How good to have older children to play with, and a dry day of running and talking and kind games. Soon Thanksgiving and rain and snow and dark, Dad's birthday and Christmas . . . Cory loved First Harbour, his home-world of eternal gentle summer, but Earth seasons were glorious.

The narrow way twisted and turned through oak, maple, and ash. Cory knew it well now, but still felt ahead with his mind. A big shame that the woods behind his house, the woods beyond the Fence, had been spoiled. There were too often people watching for him – people who called for him, or chanted strange songs, or lit fires where they shouldn't. All the fuss scared away the animals.

In those woods, people left tripwires to set off cameras, thinking Cory was silly enough not to feel the tripwire – or pools of stuff so he would leave footprints. People pinned envelopes in clear plastic bags to trees; the letters begged, and threatened, and asked, and sometimes had money. Cory never opened them; the grown-ups took them and dealt with them. People knowing about Cory spoiled having fun. The rough scrubland below was spoiled too, with its tents and trailers and wandering snoopers, the smell of latrines and coarse smoke. If he was spotted, people would come running. Crowds would soon gather, even if he hid straight away. Groups of humans could seem friendly but be wild in their enthusiasm, unpredictable, dangerous . . .

Better the grown-ups drive him here, a short way northwest, to be free in the woods where he was not known to go.

Chuck's hand on Cory's shoulder, a sign to stop. Cory and Chuck and Bonnie panted, just a little, and heard the racket move closer. Meteor barked three times from the sheer joy of the splendid game, telling everyone where they were. No more kicking up a trail. It was time to make the teenagers work for their victory.

Cory ruffled Meteor's head with a four-fingered hand. 'Quiet.' His splendid striped ears sought to find the exact approach of the chasers. Cory's friends knew to grab him, and Cory hid all four of them. No living thing would notice them. Step by careful step, Cory led them off the trail, weaving through bushes and trunks. The teenage friends would overshoot. But they were smart – Zach and Simon would be grown-ups soon – and they had played this game before.

Hiding was almost cheating, but a minute or two did not count. The plan was to find an unmarked way down to Butler's Folly, the long-closed mill that was now a riot of creepers through empty windows. Emblazoned with old signs and new that warned children not to enter and not to play, it was a castle of secrets by an overgrown creek. They had watched lizards warm themselves on summer days and fireflies dance brilliant green messages on summer nights. Dancing all-together to the radio, teenagers and kids as friends. Zach had fallen off the wall and gained a most exciting scar.

The wind changed and Cory smelled smoke, heard the whining roar of some machine, a double note. Something about that noise tugged at his stomach, brought a touch of fear. But up above were the Ship's machines, its flying hands and eyes; somewhere nearby would be the Ship itself, resolute to protect him.

As they walked, he felt his friends grow solemn. The noise grew, and the smell. Animals hid in fear, birds flew . . .

'A dozen or more humans ahead, Little Frog,' said the Ship, through the silver communicator on Cory's wrist. 'Gene and Molly have not arrived yet. Be careful.'

Earth was a planet of many dangers. Cory was always careful. A little further and they would see . . .

Cory stopped, his friends too, and stared. Their castle of brick and stone was changed, there was a fence, and a giant pile of long drainpipe. Great stupid machines were grubbing up the bushes, destroying the picnic places hidden from the road. Places where Cory had watched frogs spawning and wild bees bumble in the flowers. Where they had harvested berries and wormy apples from abandoned trees, where they had photographed the eerie beauty of fungi. A tree crashed somewhere near. And there were fires, men were feeding them with damp branches, throwing up smoke.

There stood Zach and Simon Robertson, and VJ, Bonnie's cousin, watching. Distracted, Cory realised the teenagers had cheated – divided their number and sent one party by the other, shorter track. Admiration for their boldness outstripped his outrage, but the whine of chainsaws, the rumble of a truck, filled his head.

Humans found it hard to talk hidden. Cory pulled his friends down and unhid them.

'What are they doing?' Cory said.

'Dad said the Mill was sold again,' Chuck said, his face still summer brown with freckles.

Bonnie had that frown, that chewed lip, that meant someone

4

was going to get told off. 'We should go and find out.' Even in dungarees to run in the woods, she tied a bright red cloth in her hair. 'They're going to reopen the State Park. Where the Meteor fell. I bet it's something to do with that.'

'We're not supposed to play here anyway,' said Chuck.

Bonnie clicked her tongue. 'You're *scared*, Charles Henderson.'

And so Chuck and Bonnie walked towards the nearest men, waving the teens to come too. Cory and Meteor would go crouching, hidden, to listen. Cory must be careful. Already too many people knew about his clever hiding with his mind; it had been an accident that the Robertsons had found out, and that day of emergencies when VJ had. But everything Cory did or could do was news. It brought reporters and Trouble, and Mom said things were best with a Quiet Life.

The man in charge wore a hard hat, in case a tree fell on him. He was not the kind of bossy human that made him angry at kids.

'You kids need to stay away.' He gestured at the teenagers, now ambling towards them too. 'Tell your friends.'

'What's happening, sir?' asked Chuck.

'Twenty-four vacation apartments, four houses and a fancy restaurant – so all this has to be cleared.' He waved, to left, to right, as if he could wave away the old mill, old trees, the foxes and raccoons, the birds. Wave away the crisp leaves and the smell of fall. 'Our boss's after the rest of the land too.'

'What about the trees?' Bonnie asked.

The man looked puzzled, then laughed. 'Plenty of trees left. Even if he logs right up to the ridge. We have to move real quick, the weather won't hold off long.'

5

The smoke stung Cory's eyes, bringing tears. Bringing memories too, of those first days on Earth. Amber Grove had burned, and Molly, his Earth-mother, had shed tears from emotion; one of a hundred strange things. He remembered the humans' dreams of that time, of fire and smoke and destruction.

'Now, you need to stay away. We're going to be spraying, to make it easier to clear.'

'What kind of spray?' Bonnie asked.

The man shrugged. 'Army stuff, does all the work for us. Kills every plant it touches, works like a charm. As good as burning it off and works in the damp. We're putting in drains too.'

That was the ponds with their frogs and dragonflies gone too.

Bonnie steamed, getting herself boiling hot, ready to argue. Chuck grabbed Bonnie's arm, and the whole gang walked two hundred yards to the edge of the woods. Cory was trying to see in his mind, the trees gone, the land poisoned. It brought up other images, bad ones. Memories of lessons on his home-world.

'I guess if he owns the land, we can't stop him.' *How can you own land? It's like owning sunlight.*

The humans argued. 'There's plenty of other places. Millions of trees.'

'We should start a protest.' That was Bonnie.

'Who'd care? If it was nearer town maybe . . .'

'Everyone's always protesting. My dad says we need more jobs in the town. New buildings are good.'

Cory was silent. Birds nested in the cracks in the walls. Cory remembered the drum of woodpeckers, the curious work of the ants. There would be living things ready for the sleep of

6

winter, who would have to find new places. The squirrels' caches of food would be lost.

Cory gave the *tock-tock-tock* of frustration. 'Humans must do something. Yes-they-must.' They all fell silent.

'Burning trees and seabirds all covered in oil.' He had seen it on TV, thick tarry oil choking the birds and killing the fish. 'Rivers so poisoned even water burns. What Army spray do to the animals? To people?'

Talk properly, Cory. The teens teased him if he did not, like they made jokes about his birth name meaning Little Glowing Blue Frog. He was angry enough not to care.

'It's kind of sad,' Chuck agreed.

Humans were so stupid. Soon, Zach and Simon could be ordered to be soldiers, sent to kill or be killed in a land far away, a vast murdering that had been happening since they were babies. They each promised Cory they would not go to the stupid war; they would hide or go to Canada.

The humans, the rest of Cory's gang, were silent. They must feel his alarm, his fear, his anger pouring out of him. They were his friends, good people.

'Your folks are here,' Simon said. And yes, up the road came the baby-blue camper van. Dad and Mom and Baby Fleur, his sweet human sister.

'We could go further down, by the creek,' Zach suggested. Zach and VJ liked each other but there was some big horrible human thing. VJ was dark like Bonnie and Zach was paler like Chuck. Because of that and only that, some people didn't like them hanging out. Cory felt cross enough to pull his ears off sometimes, humans were so weird.

'If you don't protest, I will,' Bonnie said, and everyone knew she meant it.

Supper was tuna with macaroni and cheese. Mom put a little hot spice in, which Cory liked. The radio played 'Have You Ever Seen the Rain?'

Mom and Dad were not agreeing with him, and he suddenly had no appetite. Meteor gnawed at her rubber bone.

Mom held Fleur sleeping and ate one handed with a fork. Under her eyes was dark; Fleur woke often in the night. 'Cory, if you write to the paper, it will create a massive row. You know we've got to keep a low profile.'

Cory had written one letter, to the *Hermes*, about the poor fish dying in the lakes to the north. The *Hermes* now sold a hundred thousand copies each week round the world, because Cory had made Amber Grove famous. The Great Lakes had been there for millions of years and then humans came and used them to dump poison. Cory's letter about pollution had brought all the TV crews to the bottom of the road where the barrier was. Two trucks of workers had come from the power-plants in the north, and Mom and Dad had four of them to drink coffee while Cory hid on the stairs.

'Do you want the plant closed? How will we feed our families?'

So many people had come to town, to protest or to support him. Senators had come from Washington to ask Cory to endorse their ideas for new laws. Grown-ups said that the tall one, Muskie from Maine, might be the next President.

'One little letter . . .'

'Remember the beef letter?' Dad said.

Those schoolchildren in Houston had asked why Cory didn't eat meat. All he did was just explain. Ranchers came all the way from Texas with a TV crew to offer everyone in Amber Grove free steaks from poor, gentle, murdered cows. Founders Green was a barbecue for two days, stinking of burned flesh. It was called a 'stunt' and it made the town cross for weeks.

'What is the point of being famous?' Cory moaned.

'Maybe it would be better if we weren't,' said Dad, trying not to yawn. 'But you know why it happened, and we can't get the milk back in the bottle. I'm sorry Cory, you know there are people who want us to go. You want to stay near your friends, don't you?'

'Yes of course yes.'

Cory guessed what his Earth-father was about to say.

Grown-ups were so predictable. Dad said, 'Cory, maybe someone else should lead the fight.'

Cory gave a massive fed up noise. Cory kept telling humans his Excellent Plan, but they weren't listening. His people survived the Times of Hunger, had healed the Poisoned Land. His people must come now and get the humans to listen.

'Cory, don't sulk,' said Mom.

'Not sulking.' He ate tuna from duty, his mind elsewhere.

Cory's people must come right now. 927 days since he had landed on Earth. The colony starship *Dancer on the Waves* had been destroyed by the vicious snake machines. Yet it sent messenger ships forward and back, many months to have reached old home, and the colony-world which was to be his home. Many-many months for more starships to be prepared and to come and rescue him.

9

They had not come. As ever his terrible fear, colder than any ice, that they were not coming. That the messengers had been destroyed, and his people did not know he was here. Or that his whole people had been attacked by the predator snakes, and they were too busy fighting to send a starship for one little boy. This nightmare idea was a big hole that could swallow him up.

Dad put his big human hand on Cory's. They must feel his sadness. He loved his human family and his friends, but he wanted the smell of his own people, the oneness of the lodge, the dreaming-together. He touched his communicator. How he missed his mother who died saving him . . . The device held her dying words left in love. How sweet and painful they were. Everyone on the ship but him had died.

Cory saw his sorrow on Gene and Molly's faces. Dad took Fleur, and Molly held out her arms. His human parents held him in love.

That evening, in Cory's bedroom, Dad yawned and played a new song, a silly one about Cory with a chorus about his scrapbook in four volumes: 'All The Places I Want to See'. Then he sang old favourites, slow songs for sleep. Cory did not ask for more; he was impatient to sleep, to dream, to recharge for the next day. In the dark, sleep came, his swift and reliable friend.

Cory went swimming in his dreams, down through the top layer where humans dreamed, down through memories and stories and music, down down down to the cool dark layer where his people should be dreaming with him. Of course, it was empty and lifeless, as it had been every night on Earth. Even if he had been a solo, sailing the Northern Ocean of his home-world, he would have known others dreamed far from him.

He had loving family and friends and yet how alone he was.

Then: a spark. Something astonishing in the emptiness. He swam towards it, a tiny bright fleck like a lightning bug. It flickered and moved. This was new; he had to chase it with all his dream muscles not to lose it.

Somehow – he just knew – it was a dreaming-together . . . yet one he could not join. It was so fragile, so far and yet he knew it was of his people.

It took so much effort to focus. Yet he was closer to it now. It was like looking at a dream through a pinhole. Yes, it *was* a dreaming-together, sixteens of his people in an *open dream* he could join. To be on the edge of it and, for moments, touching it, was a moment of yearning so strong it was pain. He could not tell what was him, and what was them. A few moments of joining, then it was gone.

He called out, here I am, here I am. In vain.

There were healthy dreams and unhealthy. They did not follow day logic, and every child knew that sometimes dreams showed you things you wanted rather than things as they were.

Yet his birth-mother told him the old saying: what comes in the dreaming-together is true.

Cory swam on in darkness, looking and listening, feeling and smelling for the others. He swam longer than was wise or restful, chasing hope until the dawn, until he could dream no more.

For when his people came, all would be well.

CHAPTER 2

An unexpected caller

Far too early, Molly sat in the big chair by the bedroom window. Fleur, blue-eyed and born with a little fuzz of Gene's black hair, snoozed innocent and well fed on the breast. Fleur was perfect, she was beautiful, and she was as persistent as a jackhammer ripping up the road.

Fleur had woken twice in the night, that Molly remembered. Dimly she thought Gene had gone to the baby too, then retreated to the spare room.

There was a relentlessness to it; how shallow sleep was when you had an ear open for the hungry cry. Molly wondered if she could catch another hour before Cory bounced in for a talk. Or stay in the chair, rather than risk waking Fleur when she tried to put her in the crib.

A call of nature decided it. With care, Molly moved Fleur to a shoulder and stood. She walked to the sunshine yellow crib and, heart melting, put Fleur into it. John had made that stout wooden crib for his son Gene; it had come to them when

13

Molly was first pregnant, beautifully restored. After the miscarriage, Molly had kept it as a sign of hope amid despair. Gene had made the mobile of yellow birds and pink clouds, and Eva knitted the blanket.

Books talked about making a routine, but Molly kept telling everyone, 'Fleur hasn't read the books.' It wasn't helpful that everyone was so ready to give unwanted, contradictory advice, particularly once she said she was breastfeeding.

Molly went to the bathroom and, as she left, tuned in to a noise downstairs: a raised voice, hooting and trilling. Two voices in fact: Cory and the Ship. She went down the stairs, feeling cranky and straining not to take it out on her son.

In the kitchen, Cory was cross, *tock-tock-tocking* in frustration and interrupting the Ship. He strode up and down, talking into the silver bracelet. His tentacles emphasised the swoops and trills of his voice, his ears twitched and his tail lashed. A bowl of oatmeal steamed; he'd fixed his own breakfast, and Meteor was slavering at her toy. Both alien voices fell silent.

'Cory, look at the time. You might wake Fleur.'

'Morning Mom. Ship is being oh-so-very-annoying.'

'Well, argue outside or not at all.'

It was a school day, and Cory would be happy and off her hands in a while. How often she pushed him away because of Fleur. Going to Amber Middle School was impossible – the school would be deluged with gawking tourists outside, maybe a lunatic with a gun – but the School Board supported an ad-hoc school sometimes as big as twelve students. World-famous academics begged to teach there.

'Well, I'd like to go back to bed, sweetie-pie,' she said. 'But if it won't wait . . .'

'Should wait for Dad, tell both of you. Don't want to wait.' He sat and grabbed a spoon of raisins. 'My people are coming.' Said with all the certainty he might declare a sunset beautiful or point to magnetic north.

Cory said that often, but as hope, not this blunt certainty. And Molly felt many things. Heaven knows the world needed the purples, as a wake-up call to humanity. Humans needed allies against the snakes. Cory needed his people too – she knew that – and yet what she felt prickled at her eyes and turned down her mouth. A feeling of loss swept in, swamping the things she should feel. *What if his people take him back?*

She filled the kettle, trying to hide it. No time for tears. 'Well, that's wonderful, Cory. When will they be here?'

Cory didn't answer. She looked, and he was eating, staring into the bowl as if it could give an answer.

'Ship says no messages. Network always listening out for them. There are beacons.'

Barely awake, she couldn't understand. 'So how do you know?'

'I dreamed it. A splendid dreaming-together, sixteens of my people . . .'

Gene had taken pages of notes on Cory's extraordinary dreaming, how the purples shared their dreams and guided them. It seemed to knit their whole society together. Cory took her silence as invitation to give a longwinded description, but for all his superlatives, it sounded like moonshine: something and nothing.

He was waiting for her response. She sipped coffee,

15

remembered a discussion of a month ago and said, 'So how close are your people? How soon before we'll meet them?'

His ears dipped; a bit defensive. 'Don't know.'

'I can't remember, did you dream with your dads on your moon?'

Ears down a little more. 'Much too far, everyone knows that.'

Be gentle. 'So, Cory, if your moon was too far, that means your people would have to be really close. They'd have to be here on Earth . . .'

'*Tock-tock-tock* Ship says I am wrong.' Cory gave that odd shiver of the head which served as his eye-rolling protest. 'Even little child of my people knows what is made up in a dream. First-graders. A proper dreaming-together. I wish-dream all the time. I know the difference.'

'Who knows? Let's hope they come soon. Let's hope they can tell us how long they will be.' She felt the insincerity behind her words.

Cory trilled an emphatic statement, then said, 'Whatever comes in the dreaming-together is true. It would be nice to be believed.' He leaped up. 'I will take Meteor for her run. Meteor is always interested.'

How painful when you disappoint your child. Two and a half years since Cory arrived. Molly had named him and saved him. But where were his people?

What if his people take him away? What if they don't come, and the snakes destroy us all?

When Gene came down, holding Fleur freshly diapered, he found Molly sobbing.

★

16

Evening, and Molly sat at peace in the big chair by the bedroom window. She had the drapes a few inches apart, so she could watch the sky. The Ship could be anywhere, but she liked to think it hung over the town, guarding them directly. Molly had always enjoyed watching the sky, but since Cory came, she had new reasons. New hopes and new fears. But right now, all that was far away. A nap, then a wonderful coffee with her soulmates Janice and Diane, a chance every day to talk about other things. Mrs Robinson had dropped off supper. Molly felt safe and well . . .

The guitar next door had stopped. Gene sneaked his head through the door.

'Need anything, Molly-Moo?'

'Just you.' The six huge blue correspondence folders on the other chair almost glared at her. But she didn't have to be the mother of the most famous boy in the world every minute of the day. Publishers had sent Gene another crate of space stories too.

'He's still cross with us about the dream,' Gene said, coming in. 'He's going to try to have it again.' He put down a brown square parcel on the table, proofs of the new guidebook for Amber County.

'The Ship is sure it couldn't be true.'

'Sure,' Gene said.

Molly stood, pulled the drapes together and embraced him. How sweet his kiss, tasting of mint, and how her body remembered. He knew how to hold her. That hand stroked where her back ached sometimes. In other times that could have been a pass . . .

17

'I'd like to,' she said, meaning it.

'But not tonight? That's okay.'

They sat on the bed, his arm round her shoulders, cherishing their time alone.

'The book is there,' Gene said. 'Bit more on the last film, then that's done.'

Gene could no longer work at the library; he'd be mobbed by tourists and reporters. Nowadays, he was finishing films for the new Visitor Centre. But the eternal question hung in the air: what then?

Molly knew where he was headed, and she didn't want the conversation. 'Can we not talk about this now?'

He shrugged. 'Just, I can write songs anywhere. We may not have long before his people turn up. Cory sure wants to see more of Earth. We could make a plan.'

Molly had joked that Gene would have kept the family travelling until she went into labour, on a boat, or up some glacier in Alaska. He frowned, but it was not much of an exaggeration; it was Molly who had insisted they come home, to have their baby with Dr Jarman and Rosa Pearce, to be surrounded by her friends – people she liked and trusted. For her, two months on the road had been more than enough. Too many false alarms and the odd real danger, too many demands for their time, too many hasty departures and unfamiliar beds. Day by day, great or good, the travelling had palled. For her but not for him.

She used her discouraging sigh, but Gene was picking up strength.

'Cory wants everything. Our time on the road just fed his appetite. We're not locked up, let's show him a bit more. Take a month or two. The Grand Canyon, Yellowstone, the Rockies. The West Coast, right up into Canada.'

This tired her. 'We can decide later.'

'We were going to travel, when we got together. We talked all the time. You were keen, we were going to cross the country . . .' Gene was in his stride. 'People travel with babies. People say they can be easier to handle when younger. We don't have to worry about trains and planes, the Ship will fly us. It could bring us home in an hour or two if we needed.'

She didn't want to discuss this. Was that so hard to understand? 'I get airsick.' The Ship had never let them inside. The three times it had flown them, their vehicle had been gripped to its hull with metal tentacles.

'It would give us something to look forward to. Say, skip the West. We could go to Europe.' He clearly thought this was a winning card. 'All those galleries and museums, old castles and so on. Great hiking.'

'Of course, that would be great.' She could fake enthusiasm but didn't. 'A motor tour, like an ordinary family. Two adults, two kids, a dog . . . followed by half the world's press and a spaceship as big as the White House. Let's talk after Christmas.'

He was frowning now. 'Don't you feel cooped up? You can't even go for a walk without having Cory along to hide you. Being everyone's business?'

They both hated it, all of it, the trucks of mail and not daring to open a newspaper. Hiding behind the alien Fence to have some privacy, stopping everyone telling them what latest nonsense was in the press. The threats, the adoration, the endless attempts to use them for this or that. These were twisted,

19

troubled times. To Molly, it was such a gamble they would be safer anywhere else.

Gene fell silent, looking at Fleur for long minutes. For all his fretting, he was a good father.

'After Christmas,' she said, reaching for her book. If he wouldn't take a hint.

'You promise we'll go?'

'I'll promise we'll discuss it, after Christmas.'

'I think if we moved, for the summer, we'd have a month or two before anyone figured it out. Wouldn't it be great to feel free? Maybe one of the other families would come too. The kids would entertain themselves and we'd have babysitting on tap. We'd feel freer than we are now.'

He wouldn't give it a rest. He'd ruined the mood. She snapped, 'You're kidding. You know what it was like.'

'We're young,' he pleaded.

'I'm tired, Gene. I'm going to the other room. If Fleur wakes, feed her yourself.'

She stood, and after a moment, he stood up. 'Fine,' he snapped and walked out.

It took an hour for her to feel she might have handled it better. Then forty-five minutes when pride prevented her making the first move. She was getting ready for bed when he reappeared, looking rueful.

'Of course, it can wait,' Gene said.

'Write it in your diary,' she said, kissing him. 'We'll talk after Christmas.'

'When you want to.'

'Let's go to bed,' she said.

The conversation was gentle, about shared joys, shared frustrations. To their surprise, desire came, and they made the old moves, slow and gentle. Physically it was still awkward for her, but still, it was a blessing, a healing, a renewal of vows.

Molly woke with a start from the deepest of sleeps. For a few moments she did not know where she was. An Army cell? That place they'd stayed in Vermont? No, she was home in her own bed, Gene still snoring, her sidelight still on. It was the phone ringing.

She made her way down the stairs, in the half light from the landing. The clock said half past eleven, and the latest ex-directory number was top secret, only for people they trusted. Lifting the handset, she said through a mouth thick with sleep, 'Molly Myers.'

'It's Selena.'

Molly wasn't expecting her sister. There was something odd in the voice, some note of strain.

'Hi, are you okay?'

'Yes, I'm fine.' No, Molly decided, she wasn't. 'Look, M, this is short notice, but could we drop by? Would you mind?'

Drop by? The way Molly liked to drive, Indianapolis was two days away. 'Uh . . . yes, I guess. When were you thinking?' She grabbed at the calendar. 'Next week might be—'

'Well, we're in this motel. Not very clean, to be honest, and the lock on the door's broken. And the man at the desk is a creepy brute. I've had to put the bed against the door. So we could be at yours by suppertime? I have the boys with me.'

'Right. Sel, it's almost midnight.'

A long silence. 'Oh, okay. Sorry. We're in some creepy two-bit place in Ohio, like one of those awful slasher stories. I know it's short notice. I'll find somewhere to stay.'

'We'll put you up,' Molly said, then regretted it. How many to cook for? How many beds? Perhaps Mrs Hardesty could help. 'Is Mason with you?'

'No, he's busy.'

Molly paused, trying to hear under the words, wondering if Selena would say more. Once the sisters had been so close.

'I have to go. Suppertime at yours.'

'Call me when you're at Bradleyburg. It's complicated, getting here without a fuss.'

'Speak soon, Sis.'

And she was gone.

Molly hung up. They still sent diligent Christmas cards, and Molly sent athletic Connor and bookish Rory money for birthdays – but, for years now, the sisters had been so distant. Each happily pretended that they meant vague promises that 'next year, you really must come for Thanksgiving', but somehow it never happened.

Through childhood, Selena had been younger Molly's best friend, role model, confidante. By her teens, however, for her own survival, Selena had become their mother's enforcer, the good girl, the example. Selena had conformed, Molly had rebelled, and they had grown apart. And yet when Selena married Mason, the dullest man in Indianapolis, a tearful Selena had whispered in Molly's ear, 'You soon, Molly. You'll be away from them too, and free.'

Molly, half asleep, was still holding the calendar. She hung it back on the wall.

She had tried to like Mason for her sister's sake. Old-fashioned Catholic, and that hearty patriotic Rotarian Elk can-do attitude, she could live with. But he was a defence contractor in an Army town – when Cory came, they had to keep him secret. She could not have risked Mason learning about Cory.

Then Cory had become the most famous boy in the world. Selena and Mason had been interrogated by the FBI, so Molly had called Selena, dreading it, feeling the need to apologise. Her sister had been shocked, confused, and to Molly's astonishment, hurt. 'You should have told us,' she'd said. 'I would have understood. Of course, I would have helped you hide him.'

Molly fumbled and said, 'Oh, I knew you would. But Mason . . .'

'Mason would have kept his mouth shut, if he knew what was good for him,' Selena said, with a sharpness that had surprised her.

And now her sister was coming.

It was not quite a meteor, but Selena's call was the order of things turned upside down.

CHAPTER 3

A sister arrives

In the kitchen, Gene rolled his eyes at the news that Selena was coming and poured coffee in silence, without even a gruff, 'Fine!' Cory was ebullient, delighted with the announcement of new children. He rattled off questions about Rory and Connor but, as the distant aunt, Molly mostly didn't know the answers.

'Why didn't you take me to see them?'

'That's grown-ups making things complicated,' she said. There was no point her fretting over what might be wrong; in a few hours, she'd meet her sister and find out.

When the story of Cory had broken, the press had swamped Selena too. There'd been photos of the O'Regans taken in the street and a lot of unpleasant speculation. The Myers were safe in Crooked Street, but when they left it, the world felt like a goldfish bowl.

Molly did not want the press nosing into her family business.

Six months on, the Myers and their friends realised most of the press were just doing their job, and the majority could

25

be pleasant about it. There was a quiet compromise. Mostly, the big newspapers and TV people kept away from Crooked Street. The deal was, Mayor Rourke or Dr Jarman dropped by Francine's diner every so often, to chat to the press who hogged the upstairs room. Once a month, the Myers would agree to some brief photo-call, to keep the beast at bay. Those photographers were polite and respectful. Yet there were dozens of stringers and freelancers in town, and dozens of townsfolk who would sell the Myers out for a cheque. And all the ways the Myers could drive out were watched by freelance photographers on motorbikes.

Of course, Cory could hide, but that brought its own problems. There was far too much gossip in town about strange occurrences and the woods being haunted. Roy heard people talking in bars. 'But he'd gone!' they'd say. 'Disappeared! Do you think he can turn into a squirrel?'

'Nah, it's like that TV show, you know, the space transporter.'

Hints about Cory's power crept into those wilder magazines that printed anything they were told about the Myers. They got it wrong, of course. Cory did not become invisible, he became *ignored*, *overlooked* – but a camera had no mind to be confused. It was inevitable that, sooner or later, someone would get a photograph or film of him and work out his hiding and they would all be less safe.

The Ship could send drones to knock a photographer off their bike, or cloud their film with a careful dose of X-rays, or blow out the tyres on a TV truck – but it would only create a new story, and editorials raging about attacks on the press.

26

The Ship had shown restraint but, if something worried it – 'an assassin might pretend to be a photographer, Mrs Myers' – it would act without discussion.

Evening promised rain. Selena called from a phone box in Bradleyburg, childish voices squabbling nearby.

'Venneman's Diner, a mile out of town towards Amber Grove,' Molly said. 'You can't miss it.' The place had doubled in size since the Meteor fell.

Selena snapped, 'Shut it, kids!' at her children, then whispered, 'I think he's following me.'

Molly's world skipped a beat. 'Who?' There was clearly something wrong.

'You know who.'

Mason? 'Tell Mrs Venneman a nurse sent you. She'll let you park out back.'

'Not you? A nurse?'

'Sel, who knows who'll be listening? A nurse.' It was a standard procedure and Mrs Venneman's discretion could be relied on.

There was a new urgency now, and Molly set up their best double-bluff game, with two cars. At the junction was a metal, human-made gate and two National Guardsmen waited day or night in their little wooden hut. A phone call and she knew exactly who was waiting, two motorbikes, Mr and Mrs Repent-Ye!, the man in the Stetson and the three hippie jugglers. The TV van had gone at sunset.

Gene had sighed, and now took Cory and Fleur for a random drive in the old Ford. With Cory visible in the window, giving a cheeky wave before ducking down, the photographers would assume that was their best story. Meanwhile, Molly would be in the back of Mrs Robertson's car, following ten minutes later. Mrs Robertson was a new friend by necessity, an eager conspirator among the neighbours. Molly lay in the back, while Mrs Robertson drove and gave a running commentary.

'It worked; they've all gone after Cory.'

Molly fingered the communicator. She hated it – the Ship used it to listen in on conversations – but she might need its help.

As Mrs Robertson drove Molly to the rendezvous, rain speckled the car windows. The diner was busy, bright light spilling across the parking lot, and Molly steeled herself for people recognising her, even under a headscarf and wearing her ugly disguise glasses.

She saw Selena at once. Far from parking discreetly out back, she was right under the light in the front parking lot. She sat on the front of her car, smoking, in one of those modern transparent raincoats. Anyone driving in would see her.

Molly got out of the car and trotted over. Selena dropped the butt and stubbed it out. She held out her arms for an awkward embrace, trying to smile. Selena was adept at make-up, but her face was in the light. There was a dark bruise around her left eye, and Molly could not shield her shock.

Selena embraced her anyway, holding her for a long time.

'What in the name of heaven——?'

'Mommy had an *accident*, falling down the stairs, and we don't have to talk about it,' Selena said.

Molly felt an old, protective anger bubbling up. 'Mommy's sister doesn't believe a damn word of it. Was it Mason? Who's following you?'

28

Selena shrugged, breaking the embrace. Molly studied her face. The last time they'd met, Selena had looked the younger. Now, there was strain and sorrow, and not enough sleep.

'You're going to get wet here,' Molly said.

'The air's fresh, and the boys are dozing at last. They couldn't sleep last night in that horrible place, such nightmares . . . It's been hell. Mason talked such garbage about you and your boy. It's good to see you, Sis.' Selena swallowed, holding something back. 'Look, this might be more than a day or two. If you can't—'

'Stay as long as you need. Mrs Hardesty lets the house next door. I checked and it's free for the next few days. Or Dr Jarman could put you up . . . His place is huge, a mansion out of town with a wall round the grounds. Cory loves it. You have to tell me what happened.'

Selena put her hand over her eyes and began to cry.

'Safe sounds good. M, it's such a mess. You were right all along.'

Molly held her, and knew the interrogation had to wait. Practical things – showers, food, beds. And Molly wanted to look at that bruise.

By Crooked Street, the rain was drumming on the car roof. Molly bustled Selena and the sleepy boys into her house. Gene was waiting, and his special polite expression vanished when he saw Selena's face. He looked at Molly and she frowned back.

'Grab the bags, Gene.'

'We're eating in the big room, just for space,' Gene said.

Cory had a cloth over his arm like a waiter, ears perked up

with anticipation. The boys stopped, so suddenly that Molly bumped them. Every child on Earth knew what he looked like.

Selena went straight up to Cory, saying, 'Well, I'm your special auntie. It's such a pleasure to meet you.' Cory accepted the embrace, his tentacles tapping Selena's right unbruised cheek.

'Sorry you are hurt,' Cory said, and she said, 'That's kind. It's fine.'

People often said that there was something about meeting Cory for real that went beyond what you expected. Just how much his tentacles moved, the mobility of his strange striped ears, the faint *otherness* of his smell.

'Say hello to Cory,' said Selena to her boys, with a little edge to her voice. 'We talked about this.'

Many kids loved Cory at first sight, but a fair number were wary, like the brothers. Connor and Rory were quiet, anxious and exhausted. They stared at Cory as he tried to engage them in cheery conversation about his toys and games.

Gene produced his near approximation to Molly's fish cakes. It turned out the boys hated fish. He suggested yesterday's lentil bake, which produced raised eyebrows from Selena, as if he had suggested moonshine.

'We've got beans, cheese and bread.' Grilled cheese got a cautious nod.

Selena took fish cakes from politeness and tried hard not to stare at Cory eating. Just sometimes, he forgot and used his tentacles to taste a sauce or pick up a carrot stick. On autopilot Selena took out a cigarette, a lighter, then carefully put them down, remembering. Mostly she ate the fancy salad, made to

Janice's famous recipe, and bread. Amber Grove had its own honest-to-goodness bakery again.

Cory tried to keep up the conversation, rattling off a long list of exciting things to do, questions about Indianapolis, and a plan for Connor and Rory to meet his friends. All this produced sullen silence from the boys, ferocious looks and *tuts* at them from Selena. Cory's dismay was obvious. The adults, meanwhile, made conversation, avoiding the discussion they wanted to have. Selena had no interest in music; current affairs and religion were out, so Molly ended up telling light stories about the changes to Amber Grove.

As soon as he could, Gene told the boys, 'We should get ice-cream and go to where you're staying next door. Why don't we make up a den there, for sleeping?' That produced polite nods.

The moment Gene had all three boys out of the house, Molly said, 'How often has Mason hit you?'

'He'll come after me,' Selena said, gazing into the distance. 'He says I'm too ill to look after the boys, that I'm an unfit mother.' Her voice broke a little. 'He knows the judge . . .'

Molly touched her hand. 'Nonsense.' The way Selena was staring into nothing, she guessed she was on some medication. 'How often, Sel?'

'Three times. He hit me three times, the kids a couple. This time, I'd warned him, if he hit the kids again . . . He was so angry . . . He said I'd never see them again.'

'No one knows you are here; if he does come, he won't find you. Sheriff Olsen won't take any nonsense. We know a great lawyer, we'll protect you.' There was a nasty story about Olsen, and what he thought about wife-beaters. The vengeful half of Molly almost approved.

Selena's grip tightened. 'I haven't got anyone else. We were at a party, and I realised – all my friends were the wives of his friends, his colleagues. Our lawyer, our doctor, our neighbours are all friends of his. It's like they all came out of a box. These Hoosiers all stick together. Not like *your* friends, Molly. Real friends.' A sob, and Selena blurted out, 'He betrayed me with other women. I want a divorce.'

Molly blinked, because Selena's Catholicism ran very deep. Selena saw the Church as a harbour against life's storms, not an arm of their mother's power. Florida had not mellowed that poisonous icy woman, whose lies about Molly had gone around the world. Their mother would turn on Selena too.

'Well, let's keep you and the boys safe . . .'

'Oh, the boys. Mason's such a brute, the things he said to them. *I was going to leave them. I was lying.* Sorry M, I'm in pieces. I have to smoke.'

A disgusting habit, but they threw on coats and went out to the porch. The rain wanted to remind her, it was November and real cold was coming.

Selena pointed at the Fence – elegant, silver, alien – and the gate in it that let you out, to go down Crooked Street. The Ship had made the homes at the top of the hill safe, but visibly different. Somehow, the Fence could watch, deter or repel attack.

'It's like something from one of those films.'

'Well, people are far too nosy.'

'I'm not surprised. Little Cory doesn't really have a nose, though, does he?' There was an odd note to her laughter.

Molly quelled her anger. By now, she should be immune to the tactless things people said.

Selena went on, 'He was a real charmer at supper. Really trying to make friends. Such an amazing thing you did, Molly. You're so brave. And Gene, I'm sorry he doesn't like me. He's a real gentleman.'

'Of course he likes you,' Molly lied.

'Mason knows the judge. He says he going to take my boys away. That crew of his, they always back him up. And the priest.'

Molly couldn't claim to be a lawyer, but nurses did see the seedier side of life. 'He's trying to scare you,' she said. 'Even in Indiana, they're not going to take kids from their mother and give them to a violent man.'

'He'll say I'm sick in the head — that I don't know what's true or false.'

'Well, we'll prove he's lying. I should examine you, the bruises and so on.'

'No.' She stubbed the cigarette out under the porch rail, out of sight. 'Thank you.'

Molly suppressed her irritation; she would always know the burn was there. 'For court, I meant.'

'I'll think about it tomorrow. At least the judge is a human being.'

Where did that come from?

'I mean, what happens when Cory's people come?' Selena waved at the sky. 'I've thought about this a lot. It must worry you. His kind will want him back.'

Molly's tears prickled, out of nowhere. Suppose tonight was

the night. The Ship would chime through the bracelet when the purple starships were here – and everything would change. She'd fought these thoughts off many times.

Selena carried on, not looking at Molly, 'An American kid, stranded on some savage island, in the middle of the ocean. We'd take them back, wouldn't we? Well, they'll see us as painted savages, with bones in their noses. You won't have any choice.'

Gene would say, 'We don't know that.' Gene wouldn't talk about what it meant for their family. 'Two civilisations meet. It'll be as big as the day we tamed fire. It's bigger than one family. It won't be up to us what happens.' Gene loved and needed Cory as much as she did – but he was also sure the purples would need an Embassy, probably in space.

Molly trotted out the ready answer. 'We'll cross that bridge when they come. If the adults have half Cory's compassion, they'll figure something out.'

Selena frowned a little, then silence fell between them.

Pulling out another cigarette, Selena said, 'I mean, we'll just be brutes to them, won't we? Animals. And people are best with their own. Boys grow up, and he can't date a human.'

Molly always changed the subject. She hated to think how alone Cory might be when he was older. And some people had dirty minds. She hated the sordid, unnecessary speculation and sneers.

Cory had made Molly a mother. Cory had changed her life, and Gene's, beyond imagining. She had fought and lied and run, risked everything for him, and Gene too. Everything Cory taught her about his people, everything he said about his world where no one was left behind, told her that the purples would want him back.

Yet Molly's heart burned with a mother's heresy. What better claim did the purples have?

'Will you pray with me?' Selena asked, putting the cigarette unlit in her pocket. Molly tried not to sigh.

A thought kept coming, something she had not said aloud. Yes, his people would come. Yes, they would change everything and humanity would have to adapt. But Cory was her son, and she would keep him. She would not let strangers take Fleur, so why should her son be any different? She believed in Gene's steadfast courage and love. He would stand by her side.

Molly closed her eyes, shutting out Selena's words and the complex feelings they threw up. She made Cory a silent promise.

Let your people come, with all their power and wisdom. Whatever they think, I am your mother and I will keep you. My cause is just. Cory, I swear I will not give you up without a fight.

The wind roared in the trees and the rain rattled on the roof of their home. Applause.

CHAPTER 4

The next few days

The first night, Molly heard movement around the house and found Selena had let herself in. Wrapped up in a blanket, her sister smoked in her kitchen and stared into the trees. It had taken Molly nearly an hour to convince Selena there were often people in the woods. The Fence kept them well back from the house; it was best just to ignore them.

The next morning, Molly got the boys fed and washed with no sign of Selena. Connor and Rory were polite to Molly, talked to each other, but were wary of Cory, as though he was a growling dog. Cory was quiet, talking to Meteor in alien.

Gene leaned his head to Molly's. 'He tried to be friendly in their dreams and it freaked them out.'

It was like the Eversons at number 7, all over again. Or that family further down the road, who'd asked them to leave. She'd told Cory not to do it, but it was hard for him to accept it.

Selena floated in with an eerie chemical calm, fully dressed and made up. She had always chased fashion more than Molly ever

37

did. Their guest embraced her sons, gave Cory a pat, cooed at the baby, and took black, sweet coffee. Molly got straight to it, there were decisions to be made, but her sister waved them away. Selena must speak to a lawyer, and Molly would call the Sheriff if she wouldn't. Selena was vague. Then, as if it was a minor thing, she said, 'I'll need to borrow some money. I spent every cent on gas.'

Molly was shocked. 'Don't you have money of your own?'

'Mason didn't want me to work. I've got my jewellery though. We could pawn it.'

There wasn't a pawnshop in town, not officially, though Molly knew who to ask. Gene said, without hesitation, 'No, let us help you out.'

After a long pause, Selena said, 'We don't need charity.'

'Helping family isn't charity,' Gene said, frowning, jaw clenched.

'It could be a loan,' Molly said.

The night before, Selena had refused to be examined by Molly, or Dr Jarman. Now Molly launched into extolling Rosa Jarman − once her boss and now her friend − her long nursing experience, her absolute discretion, and as an aside, her unbendable Catholic faith. That did produce a reaction.

'I'm fine,' Selena said, fumbling in her purse. 'But if you want me to, I don't mind. She must look at the boys too. I'm going for a cigarette.'

Molly called Rosa at once. Then she had to take Cory in her arms and reassure him again he hadn't done anything wrong.

'*Why-γγγ* they don't like me? So many bad feelings.'

'Well, it happens with children on Earth too. And it's all difficult for them . . .'

'I will try harder, share dreams with them tonight.'

'No, Cory!' She was sharper than she intended, and he cringed. 'Cory, that's not working.'

'Most excellent way to know people better.'

'Yes, it's wonderful, sometimes. But they don't like it.' She spoke from bitter experience. It was so natural to him; he still couldn't accept he'd done the wrong thing.

Eventually, Rosa came, examined the boys and spent an hour with Selena. Then she slipped away, leaving Molly a note to come around tomorrow. An annoying little mystery.

The next day, 'Meteor Day' played on the radio, sad and eerie. Simon and Garfunkel had not been there, none of those who sang about it had been.

At breakfast, Molly brightly suggested going to the Jarmans'. 'Lots of running around room. The hot tub . . .'

Molly made the call to the National Guard, pleasant men who the street kept friendly with an endless succession of lunches, baked goods and coffee. To a man, they adored Cory and, from kindness, hid their guns from him.

'Car just turned up, Mrs Myers. Not one of the regulars. A blue Oldsmobile.'

Her stomach turned. 'Indiana plates?'

'I'll just wander over, friendly-like, and explain the ordinance.' Mayor Rourke and the Sheriff made sure there was no parking anywhere near the junction. The TV people had to pay one of the neighbours a fortune to park.

Ten minutes later, the National Guard said, 'He drove off. One of the photographers asked who he was, pushy, of course, and the guy in the car didn't like it.'

'Let's go,' Molly said.

The Jarman place always had its press too, a little campsite of tents and trailers and TV trucks. There was little point in playing games. Molly squeezed everyone into the camper and drove, followed by the relentless motorbikes. At least there was no Oldsmobile.

Molly saw the familiar turning.

'Wasn't there some trouble here?' Selena said.

Molly shuddered. The Chicago Mob had tried to seize Cory, one evening in spring, just about here. Four cars of armed gangsters and a waiting helicopter. Cory had hidden the Myers, slipping them through the attack. Then the Ship had arrived at inhuman speed, full of fury and vengeance . . .

'Tell you later,' Molly said.

By agreement, Dr Jarman offered the tour to the O'Regans, while Rosa admired Fleur and took Molly to a warmed greenhouse, full of fresh herbs, just one of the many homely touches she had added to the house.

Molly's first question sounded foolish as she said it. 'Did Sel say why she didn't let me examine her?'

Rosa looked grim. 'She's ashamed that you were right about Mason and she doesn't want to discuss it with you. But the good Lord help me, if I see that man, I will take a scourge of thorns to him.'

'Mason might be here.' Molly explained about the blue Oldsmobile, then said, 'How bad was it?'

Rosa said, 'Face, arms. A punch in the stomach. I think two or three times in the last few weeks. Worse than the kids.

Nothing broken.' Then she went quiet. Rosa was not one for more words than was needed.

'I didn't take to the man, but I never thought he would be violent,' Molly prompted.

'Men are barely above the beasts.'

'Well, doesn't she need to report it, or . . . something?'

'She'll talk when she wants to.' Rosa touched the modest crucifix round her neck. 'And she's not well. She promised to talk to Edgar about her medication. I'll hold her to it.'

Molly was about to form the next question, but Rosa wasn't done.

'He told the boys that Cory's people worship the devil – what a wicked liar.'

'*What?*'

'Selena let slip that she might come here, and he started throwing all sorts of abuse around. She's worried the boys heard that. Maybe I should ask Father Dolan over.'

'He still after baptising Cory?'

'Oh, the bishop is even keener. The moment the Holy Father gives the word.' Their eyes met and Rosa smiled. 'I said you were a hard case, but I'd work on you.'

'Thanks.'

Rosa picked up her gardening gloves. 'Let me know how we can help.'

'I need a walk.' Molly checked Fleur and took her outside in the stroller, if only to clear her head. Somewhere, children were whooping and a dog barking – but Selena was sitting on the long porch, sobbing, while Dr Jarman kept a paternal hand on her shoulder.

41

'M, I saw someone, in the bushes.' She waved towards the tangled trees. 'He had a camera.'

Dr Jarman caught Molly's worried gaze and gave a slight shake of the head. People were always trying to get over the wall, whether after Cory or Dr Jarman's priceless knowledge of him, so the place was now a fortress. There was vicious barbed wire on top of the wall, and alarms. The Ship stationed spies to keep a watch out, keen to protect the human doctor it most trusted if Cory was sick or injured.

Jarman took other precautions too. 'I'll get Reuben to let the dogs out.' Reuben was a veteran of Korea and a man of few words – groundskeeper, security and driver in one. There were six black German Shepherds that you could not mistake for pets. 'They'll find if anyone is there, two minutes flat.'

'I did see something, I did,' Selena said.

Molly nodded – but, half an hour later, neither the unsmiling Reuben nor his eager canine crew had found even a twig out of place.

Back in Crooked Street, the kids and Gene were upstairs playing a chess tournament and Connor had discovered a use for Cory, who was a fair player.

In the big room, Molly tried to get Selena interested in the endless correspondence files, if only to distract her, but Selena was too tearful today. It didn't help that there had been people crashing around in the woods last night, drunks calling for Cory to fly out and talk to them.

'Those men – Mason paid them,' she repeated.

'Oh, Sel, they come all the time. Bachelor parties last time, can you imagine?' Molly picked up the letter, fretting about Roy Disney, who had said he would close the theme park for the day if Cory came, and promised no press.

'Sel, your doctor. Have you said that sometimes . . . ?' *You see things.*

'Oh, *doctors*.' She gave a dismissive wave. 'He was a friend of Mason's. These Hoosiers all stick together.'

The phone was ringing. Molly welcomed the interruption, but when she lifted the receiver, the Guardsman told her, 'Mrs Myers, Johan at the end of the road. That blue Oldsmobile is back. I walked over and warned him about the parking and the guy in it gave me his card. He's a lawyer. Indiana licence plate. I wrote it down.'

An Indianapolis address. The scribbled phone number of a hotel in Bradleyburg. Molly wrote them down on autopilot.

'Thank you,' she said. 'What did he look like?'

Fair, so not Mason. About his age, though. A bit nervous, but having press hovering nearby while an armed man asked you your business might do that.

'Thank you, Johan. Call Sheriff Olsen please and tell him the guy has been hanging around. I'll call our lawyer.'

Selena was in the hall, listening. 'He's come, hasn't he?'

'His lawyer. I'll call him – deny you're even here.'

'Get the Ship to scare him.'

Molly was tempted, but said, 'We can't do that. Look, I'm going to call this guy. It might get unpleasant.' She wanted Gene there and Selena not listening in, but if she went into the upstairs bedroom, Selena might listen on the extension.

★

43

'This is Molly Myers.' Gene stood by the phone, while Selena was in the Hardesty house with the kids.

'Thank you so much for calling.' He had a pleasant, professional manner.

'I don't know why an Indiana lawyer wants me to call him.'

'Your sister, Selena. Has she been in touch?' Molly strained to hear; you could sometimes tell if someone else was by the phone. A slight intake of breath, perhaps; some microscopic sign.

'We spoke in September; I had a card in October. Is she all right?'

'She's not with you? The children?'

'Heavens, no. What gave you that idea?'

'Well, she's disappeared, with her children. I'm a friend of her husband. Mr O'Regan noticed that she took a detailed road map of New York State and two containers of gasoline from the garage. And you have been much more in touch in recent months.'

How subtle the change to a gentle interrogation. But Molly had been grilled by the FBI and the Army. 'That's odd. I can't account for that. I haven't seen her for years. We spoke on the phone, I guess two or three times – you know, after it all came out. We're not close.'

'Mr O'Regan wants to know that Selena and the children are safe. Mrs O'Regan has been unwell. She talked a lot about you, recently.'

Gene was scowling, but Molly touched his lips with a finger. *Stay out of it.*

'Well, I hope she's okay.' Molly wanted them to show their hand.

44

'So, I guess Mrs Venneman was mistaken? You know Venneman's Diner on the Amber Grove Road? She says there was a woman, with two children in the car, waiting outside for a while. We had a bit of luck – young Henry Venneman is one of those harmless oddballs: he collects and remembers licence plate numbers. Astonishing.' A careful pause. 'So it *was* Mrs O'Regan's car.'

Molly was shocked. She'd failed. She should have spoken to Mrs Venneman. *Don't be distracted*, she told herself. Deny it. Say they helped Selena go to Canada. And yes, she thought, straining to hear again, there *was* someone else on the lawyer's phone.

'It's not the only sighting,' the lawyer said, while Molly firmed up a Canada story.

Another voice came on the line. Mason said urgently, 'Molly, I just need to know the kids are okay.'

Brute.

'You're getting no help from me,' she said, icy and certain.

'Molly, I swear, I just need to talk.' He sounded hurt, desperate.

You told lies about my son.

'Mason, keep out of this,' the lawyer said.

Molly used her voice of steel. 'We've spoken, Mason. She's safe, she is well away from here, and I want her to talk to the cops. She's getting a lawyer. Men like you should be in prison.'

'We can fix this,' Mason said.

But his friend took back control of the conversation. 'Mrs O'Regan will not be talking to the cops. We're concerned for her and the children. We don't want this in the press. Can you imagine?'

If it's a threat, thought Molly, *it's very skilfully done.*

45

'We know lots of journalists,' she said. 'Anything with my name on it will be on the front pages. Maybe Sel should get a court order, give an interview to the Indiana papers, see if your church and colleagues like the wife-beating marriage-breaker.' Molly would rather make her sister drink battery acid than risk telling the press her personal life, but Mason didn't need to know that.

'What has Selena told you? About the cheques? About the . . . accident. Is she listening in?'

Gene was miming cutting his throat, hanging up the phone.

'You daren't go to the press, or the cops either,' Molly said.

The lawyer paused and she imagined a hand over the phone, some hasty conversation.

'Mrs Myers, Selena stabbed my client with a carving knife. Fortunately, it was only the arm; she was aiming for his body, but he defended himself. Mr O'Regan wants to keep the family together. He won't press charges. She took the children from his mother's house under false pretences and disappeared. Mr O'Regan then discovered she'd stolen cheques from the business chequebook and forged his signature to cash two of them. That's his company's money, Mrs Myers. He'll cover every cent, but the company might take a less lenient view.'

Gene rolled his eyes and Molly felt the world shift under her feet. If Selena had just done as Molly told her, Mrs Venneman would have said nothing.

Selena lied to you about the money. The gas.

'She's not herself,' Mason said. 'I know we've had problems, but I'm worried about her. About the kids. If she loses her temper again . . .'

Molly knew she should not engage anymore, but . . . 'You slept with other women,' she said.

The lawyer said something. Mason said, 'I haven't been a perfect husband. I need to make things right.'

He was pleading; he even sounded ashamed. Certainly, it was no denial.

Gene took the receiver from Molly's hand and hung up. 'Holy cow,' he said.

'It might not be true,' she said, not even convincing herself. Of course a woman might grab something to defend herself. And stealing money to keep her kids safe . . .

'Do you think she did stab him?'

'He hit her, Gene. We can see the bruises. The kids say so too.'

'Whatever happened was at night,' said Gene. 'She has the family temper; she's always struck me as that calm mountain that's really a seething volcano. Remember the prom story you told me a dozen times?'

'Yes.' Maybe Selena did have money and gas to get to the Myers place. Or maybe it really was bank fraud. Molly herself had lied, robbed and broken the law for Cory. What would she have done without friends, or family, or Gene? Suddenly, all of Selena's fears made perfect sense.

Gene looked at her, concerned, and Molly felt gratitude and warmth. Thank goodness Team Myers was so strong.

They needed Selena to tell the full story.

'What are our options?' she asked.

CHAPTER 5

New York City, that week

In the TV studio's waiting room, Dr Pfeiffer pretended to read the newspaper, so he had an excuse not to talk to the other guest. The tweed-jacketed academic espoused the sour slops of left-liberal thought and Pfeiffer had clashed with him before. The third guest, Augustus Mablethorpe, was an English author, unfamiliar, and late.

Pfeiffer once had his pick of the best TV programmes, the best channels. Back then, he would have laughed at a call from *Debate with Dempsey*. People clamoured for Pfeiffer's fiery opinions and his willingness to take on his opponents. He had all but spoken for the Administration. But now that he was the 'controversial, disgraced' former advisor to the President, he took what opportunities he could get, even this second-rate mud-wrestling match.

They had the *Vigilant* among the papers. He made a point never to read it.

The President had appointed his secret enquiry, to blame

Pfeiffer for the imprisonment and mistreatment of the Myers, but Pfeiffer had fought it. A great enthusiast of the Xerox machine, he had kept files on the scientific scandals of two Presidents, worse things than even the most paranoid pot-raddled hippy could imagine. The nastiest, juiciest story of all had shocked Pfeiffer to the core as a citizen, a doctor and a scientist. Even now, he shuddered to think of it. His blackmail worked, but it had been a poor victory. The vague report exonerating Pfeiffer had been universally derided. He had walked free, but his reputation was stained and diminished.

When would this programme get going? He had an important appointment this evening, and the producer had promised them they would be done in time.

He flicked through another paper. Governor Wallace had made another speech, whipping up his followers against Cory. Or more precisely, against some great danger talking to the purples might pose. Wallace was a demagogue, and a smart one. He might run for the Democratic nomination, to poison the water, to strengthen the racist, segregationist powers in the party. Behind him marched shadowy forces who had bombed churches and synagogues. Liberals forgot that in the Fifties, Pfeiffer had poured scorn on the so-called science behind racism, so Wallace's people saw Pfeiffer as part of a sinister leftist world conspiracy. But at least being smeared as a Jewish Communist made a change from being hated by liberals as a fascist warmonger.

Here was Mablethorpe, the third guest, one of those very long, angular Englishmen, arrogant enough to patronise a Boston blueblood, and whose voice conveyed mediaeval court-yards and bad drains.

50

'Dr Pfeiffer.' He held out a long bony hand. 'As our civilisation *gasps its last*, we men of learning are reduced to entertaining the mob like trained monkeys.'

Pfeiffer shook his hand and wondered what the man could possibly have to say that was so interesting. Pfeiffer felt a stirring in his stomach, a tightness in the throat: symptoms of 'fight or flight'. Just as the boxer or the airline pilot feels those nerves and uses them, he expected them before a debate.

They were hurried under the brilliant lights of the studio. Their host, Dempsey, a famous war reporter brought low by alimony and drink, shunned a first name. It was the four easy chairs format, so difficult to know exactly how to sit. Mablethorpe opted for folding himself into his seat; it looked both peculiar and uncomfortable.

The programme was live but transmitted with a small delay in case someone used bad language. They were introduced, and the host went straight into the discussion. 'Dr Pfeiffer – I don't see how the purples coming will make ten cents' difference to Joe Public.'

Ah, an easy shot. 'This is one of the most profound moments in our history. What we already know today should change us. Another intelligent species exists. Like us, they are social, they write and use mathematics, and they base their civilisation on science. If this tiny corner of the galaxy has at least two such species, we know there must be many more. The purples show us what we might be. They have made astonishing advances – thinking machines like the Ship, faster-than-light travel that takes us far beyond Einstein; they have medicine, communications and technologies we can only dream of. But we are not

51

a simple people who can only gape at magical wonders. We need not be natives on the shore willing to sell our land for a fist of beads.'

The leftist was already twitching to leap in. Pfeiffer disapproved of long hair on men in principle, but on anyone over twenty-five it looked ridiculous.

His next example might be misunderstood, but it was important. 'In the middle of the nineteenth century, Japan was backwards, feudal, using swords and horses. However, they opened themselves to the world and made the crucial decision to learn. In two generations, they were an industrial society. They beat Russia, a major power, in a modern war. In another generation, they posed a serious threat to the United States.'

The leftist was sitting up, but Pfeiffer just raised his voice and sped up. 'Now, that was very different. But America should be the smartest and hardest-working country in the world. Let's commit ourselves to partnership with the purples and Western freedom – Western science – will solve many of the world's deepest problems. The greatest days of America lie ahead of us. We can stand proudly beside them as leaders of humanity, a great civilisation.'

Dempsey made a gesture and the leftist broke in, 'Emmanuel, you miss the point. It's telling that you talk about winning wars. Cory's people have no war, no poverty, no famine, no violent crime, no racial prejudice. You claim we're the most advanced civilisation on this planet? A few stops from here on the subway, children go to bed hungry and suffer diseases the rich have not suffered for fifty years. Innocent people are daily shot in the street. Yet we have the wealth to fight endless wars and to topple elected leaders in other countries. Cory sees this and he calls us out. He shows the horror we should feel. That's the real challenge to America today. A moral challenge . . .'

He was in the pulpit and away. It was a decaffein-ated Communism, without the brutal discipline that made Communism dangerous. But these were new times and America might require difficult alliances. The sinister snakes would slaughter free and enslaved nations together.

The Englishman coughed. 'Oh, dear, oh dear,' he said, pulling faces as his hands writhed together. 'Of course, I am no *expert* on the wonders of science like Dr Pfeiffer. But isn't it far more likely that this child is a *hoax*? We are being *gulled*, gentlemen, dear viewers at home, for some *nefarious* purpose. *Non sunt multiplicanda entia sine necessitate*, after all.' Mablethorpe looked smug.

For a moment, Pfeiffer was without words, furious that his time was being so wasted. But his blood was up, and he was ready to fight. 'Occam's razor is a prejudice, not a principle,' he said, jabbing his finger at the man. 'Samples of Cory's blood and cells were examined by twelve scientists from six different countries. No serious scientist disputes that Cory Myers is from a different species. No other Earthly species has his form of DNA, no Earthly creature absorbs oxygen in the same way . . .'

The leftist looked bewildered. 'The family gave a televised press conference,' he said to the Englishman. 'There were two hundred journalists there. The Ship flew over Washington. Use your eyes, man.'

Pfeiffer nodded vigorously, welcoming any ally against this nonsense.

Their host sat back, gloating.

Mablethorpe waved a hand, brushing away these points like someone dismissing a bad smell. 'A hoax.'

Pfeiffer said, 'Three more proofs. His immune system—'

'Oh Dr Pfeiffer, I would never *dream* of suggesting this was a *poorly constructed* hoax. It's clearly required a vast amount of time and money, and no doubt the best brains in America colluding. It's a *magnificent* achievement, the very Manhattan Project of fraud. But let's tug at the green curtain, shall we?'

Pfeiffer reined in his temper. There was a jug of water beside him and he imagined the man getting it in the face . . .

Mablethorpe continued, 'The child is seen, sometimes, but mostly *hidden away*, appearing and vanishing like dear Saint Anthony. So convenient. The *Ship* has not been examined by all these independent experts, has it? Dear viewers at home, our civilisation is rotting from within. You can smell the gangrene, the barbarians are at the gates and cruel tyrannies across the world wait to finish us off. And the President of the United States of America appears on TV with a *carnival sideshow* – a children's comic-book character. Who benefits?'

Pfeiffer felt his temper building again. This man was calling him a liar. 'I've studied Cory – I've talked to the Ship, many times. Scientists I know and trust have worked with me to examine alien artefacts—'

'And it is all *magnificent*, Dr Pfeiffer. I don't know if he is a puppet or something you grew in the laboratory. But why, Dr Pfeiffer, why? Who pays you? Surely there are *limits* even to your greed and ambition?'

Cory stirred up many things. There were those who used

54

his childish hopes to back up their own political views, those terrified and gullible over contact with another species, those who longed to give up their freedom. Those who believed this was just the latest wonder and TV would find something better in a month. Pfeiffer had a special loathing for educated people who chose not to believe hard facts. Even worse were those who denied objective truth just for the joy of argument.

'We are faced with a new threat to our civilisation, our entire species. The Russians were attacked by another hostile force . . .'

Mablethorpe twisted his body and made more idiotic grimaces. 'Oh, now we trust the barbarian hordes of Muscovy and the Great Helmsman of Peking?'

Pfeiffer was treading a careful path. He loathed the Soviet Union, and the man who ruled China was probably worse, certainly less rational. Yet faced with an attack from space, the USA, the USSR and China might have no choice but to work together.

Did the smirking Englishman believe any of what he said? He was a brilliant, slippery eel in an argument and apparently quite willing to fuel paranoia.

'If these purples really exist, we should ask the Cherokee and the Sioux what the friendship of a great civilisation is like. Ask the first Tasmanians. Our future may be in alien museums, our cities the ruins their tourists may visit. Beggars for scraps at their table, "*all as one with Nineveh and Tyre*".'

The long, sorry argument was over. As the cameras stopped rolling, the Englishman smiled at Pfeiffer and said, 'Well, Dr Pfeiffer, I do feel we gave the soap companies their money's worth. Let us plot a rematch, shall we? I know a bar with genuine Scotch not a block from here.'

Pfeiffer brushed away the bony hand, ignored the leftist, and nodded at the host because he wanted his fee.

In the lobby of the TV studio, some bright-eyed young man said, 'A car, Dr Pfeiffer?'

'No. I have other plans.' He did not want to keep the Six waiting.

'Your friend is here.'

Abe Kaplan of the *Vigilant* had appeared in the lobby. The worst journalist on the most hostile of the big newspapers, he had been out of the country when Cory was unveiled to the world. He had been chasing the story ever since. The Myers hated him as much as Pfeiffer did.

'He's a journalist. Call security.' Pfeiffer knew he'd squeaked it. At all costs, Kaplan must not know where he was going.

The studio man looked a little flustered. Kaplan, piggy-eyed, took the opportunity to get close, exuding a great wave of peppermint mouthwash and carbolic soap. The coat was foreign-cut, expensive, and in need of a clean.

'Dr Pfeiffer, I only need a few minutes.' That grating voice.

'Go to hell,' Pfeiffer said. 'I have nothing to say to you.'

'I'm close, Dr Pfeiffer, so close. And how I write it, how you come out of it, will matter.'

'Call security!'

The studio man held up his hands. 'It's only the lobby.'

Kaplan was taller and ten years younger. Pfeiffer could not outrun him, but neither did he want to talk. He considered going back into the building. But he needed to get to his appointment. It would be a disaster if this journalist found out about the Six, even though those great men never met without an innocent explanation.

'Three minutes.'

'Five.'

Pfeiffer dragged Kaplan over to the window – outside, November rain was bouncing ankle-high – and said, 'I've told you before, I have nothing to say to you.'

'Cory Myers can do things with his mind, extraordinary things. You were by the lake when the Myers were arrested. Soldiers were seriously harmed, picking up two peace campaigners and a little boy. Perhaps they have some alien weapon, but I think it is Cory himself.'

Pfeiffer had indeed been there, had experienced the attack, and he tried not to show his shudder. *Cory spun nightmares, monsters from his mind, a great fear gripping armed men and rendering them helpless . . . three soldiers screaming, unable to breathe . . .*

'Huh!'

'Those soldiers have been moved like pieces on a board. The Army brought down a wall of silence. I've been digging for six months and I think the rumours are true. I'm so close. What was the plan? To use the country's favourite child as a weapon? To hide what his people can do? It is all realpolitik now, isn't it? I heard you just now. Our enemies' enemies are our friends.'

'That's all nonsense.'

'Dr Pfeiffer, will you stake your professional reputation, and tell me on the record, that what is claimed of Cory is impossible?'

It was a trap. Because the rumours *were* true, because the

Government had used everything within its power to suppress it. Because, if Pfeiffer confirmed that story, he might end up in jail.

'I have nothing to say to you.' He put on his hat and undid the snap on his umbrella. He was going to get wet. And he was never sure if the FBI were following him.

'I know it's his mind. This time a year ago, three thugs tried to kidnap him. They were arrested and disappeared. The government drops a hint it's witness protection. I have highly placed sources in the Five Families, the New York Mob. They're scared, Dr Pfeiffer. Our local capos have ordered "hands off" the Myers, on pain of ending up buried under a freeway. They're fighting a turf war with those Chicago goons to protect him. It's the kid that frightens them, not that lunatic spaceship.'

'Our time is up.'

'You'll come out of it badly. Everyone will rake over the other allegations. The first story sets the tone.'

'No one who reads your paper matters. It's yellow journalism with a bigger dictionary.'

Kaplan snarled his smile. 'And how can he hide, Dr Pfeiffer? How do the family keep disappearing?'

'Our time is up.' Pfeiffer turned and trotted back towards the elevators. The studio flunky was there, watching the confrontation.

'I want a car.'

'I have one waiting. It will be here in two minutes.'

The flunky helped Pfeiffer into the sleek car. Pfeiffer gave a downtown address, but a block later told the driver, 'I'm going to get out at the next corner.'

Pfeiffer went through the smoky bar, not his kind of place, but it was easy to walk past the restroom with his hat on. The jukebox played that sentimental dross you heard everywhere that month, 'Will You Still Love Me When the Purples Come?' There was a man with a cheroot at the rear fire-door. He said nothing, just stepped aside to let Pfeiffer through and slammed the door behind him.

At the end of the alley was a taxi. The driver said, 'I'm waiting for someone, Mac.'

Pfeiffer gave the password – 'Valley Forge, please' – and the man leaped into action, gunning the engine and shooting off the moment Pfeiffer shut the door. A second car appeared behind them, with no job but to block the way to anyone following. Whizzing through dark streets, Pfeiffer tried to steady his breathing, and pushed Kaplan from his mind. He would soon be in the presence of the Six.

Pfeiffer mulled the great question. When the purples came, who would they negotiate with? Would they share their true wealth, their scientific knowledge? Faced with all the countries of the world, the tyrannies, the chaotic and backward former colonies, the faded glories of Europe – surely, logic dictated they should side with the States. In truth, they would probably be guided by the boy. But that was why it was so important the family listened to a realist: someone who understood the balance of power.

Let the purples come before the snakes. He saw in his mind's eye New York, Boston, Washington in flames, and shuddered. The decisions that would have to be made.

The boy was the key. It had taken months, but despite the

mishaps of the past, Mrs Myers had finally met with Pfeiffer, so he still had an opening of sorts to the family. Precious Cory, the key to the power of the Ship and the trump card for when his people came.

Kaplan might turn the public against the boy, but he had not published his story in all these months so he clearly couldn't prove anything.

The Six met in houses and clubs that smelled of money and power. Round the table sat moguls dealing with aircraft and cars and shipping, oil and mines. Markham, self-appointed chairman, the brash industrialist whose empire helped build the defence of America's interests on Earth and in space. There were two rival banking empires, newspaper tycoons who gave Pfeiffer a column, a voice – and Overton, the pharmaceutical king who funded Pfeiffer's research. They were the resources and power he needed, now the government was closed to him: odd allies but needs must. He waited in the car, finishing his line of thought.

Pfeiffer had exaggerated his power and influence when he'd been courting Mrs Myers, and likewise exaggerated his rapport with Mrs Myers to the Six, all part of the necessary game. When the purple aliens came, he needed to be in those first conversations, to ensure the aliens had a sound, rational guide, not be led astray by the childish filth of the anti-war demonstrators, the simple slogans of the Communists, or even the profitable nonsense of Madison Avenue.

The Six liked to think they could buy anything they wanted, including him. But he had things they could not buy, and he would not be used.

Pfeiffer would play a clever game. He would be there when history was made; he would make the mocking papers eat their words. He would have his revenge on that unprincipled crook in the White House. He would mediate between the two worlds, and his would be the name people remembered: not ambassador to a mere country.

Pfeiffer would be ambassador to a whole civilisation — Ambassador to the Stars.

CHAPTER 6

Stick out your thumb

In the Hardesty place, Gene was playing the guitar to the boys, in the big room with the door shut against the shouting. Cory's ears were right down and his body shaking. Rory and Connor were silent, pale and shut down. Selena and Molly were arguing. It started in the kitchen, but it was getting louder. They were in the hall outside.

At least the boys were a little more used to Cory now; Rosa's pet priest had spoken to them and Gene was starting to get to know them.

'Okay, we'll *pack and go*.'

Gene gave the boys a smile he didn't feel and said, 'I'll be back in a moment.'

He opened the door to look. Molly stood blocking the way out of the house, Selena held her suitcase. Each sister glanced at him but didn't stop.

'Get out of my way,' Selena ordered.

Molly was in full flow. You sure could see the family

resemblance: the mouth, the eyes, the shape of the chin. The temper.

'Selena, it's a simple question. It's not about the money, it's about lying to us.'

'You believe *him*, not me. I don't have *anyone else*. I don't have *anywhere to go*. Keep your stinking money.'

'I believe you,' Molly was saying, 'I believe he's a violent man. We're glad we can help. Can't you see you were wrong, though? We deserved to know—'

'Have you ever been scared for your life? Really scared?'

Yes, we have. We've been chased by the Army. Gene slipped into the hall, between them, closing the door. 'Molly, Selena, can we keep it down? The neighbours . . .'

Molly glared at him. 'I can handle it.'

'I guess Gene thinks adultery is just dandy,' Selena said. 'Fine, I'll take the boys and go.'

'Don't be ridiculous,' said Molly.

'Get out of the way,' Selena said to Gene.

'If everyone calmed down . . .' he said, hands up.

'I can handle it, Gene.'

'I want my boys. Out of the way.'

'They're playing with Cory. Let's just all calm down and . . .'

Selena swung the suitcase at him, the metal corner catching his knee in a jab of pain.

He cussed – wow, it hurt – and Molly snapped, 'Put it down.'

Selena came right up to him, in his face. She smelled of forbidden smoke. 'Get them out of there. We're going.'

'Put the case down,' he said, 'and everyone take a few deep breaths . . .'

Selena roared, stepped back, and swung the case back for a second, two-handed blow. Her keys clattered to the floor.

Molly huffed, like he'd done something wrong. 'Gene!' She stepped in, to ruin Selena's swing, and the suitcase fell too.

Selena's face fell into sadness. The fight went out of her.

'Let me see my kids.' It was more of a wail than a roar. Molly put her hand to Selena's shoulder; she shook it off, but no one was shouting anymore.

'You're not helping, I've got this,' Molly said, and seething, Gene walked away.

Rosa wouldn't put up with these tantrums. Go stay with her.

That night, in his own house, Gene finished changing Fleur, Little Boo, in the trance of the midnight parent. Molly had gone into urgent labour at the Jarmans' wedding: a frightening couple of hours. Gene had stared into Fleur's face and fallen in love . . . but love can mean heavy lifting.

At last, glorious sleep beckoned. Then Gene heard a clink, someone or something downstairs.

He grabbed his communicator, in case help was needed. Then he went to the dark top of the stairs one careful step at a time, ready to shout, or call the Ship.

Someone was crying, whimpering. He turned on the light.

Selena was in nightgown and bathrobe, in a huddle by the front door. She was trying to cry quietly. *Give some people a key and you're never rid of them.*

Gene came down the stairs, moving steadily, so as not to spook her. The knee ached at each step.

'He's out there,' she whispered.

'Who?' Gene realised that was a stupid question.

'Mason. And I left the boys next door. Suppose he takes the boys?' She put a frozen hand to his.

She wasn't well. 'Sel, the Ship will tell us if there's anything out there bigger than a squirrel.'

'He's out there.' She scrambled to her feet, sobbing, distraught. 'I'm sorry . . . I'm sorry about everything. He's come for me. He'll be armed.'

'You're okay. He can't be—'

'I did stab him, Gene. I just grabbed the knife . . .'

'Okay.'

She was barefoot, crazy in this weather. 'Let's look together, and check your boys are okay.' He raised his communicator to his mouth.

'Any trouble, Ship?'

'There's nothing, Mr Myers,' the Ship replied.

Gene threw his thickest coat round her shoulders – the cold was bitter now – and grabbed the summer coat for himself. She pulled on Molly's gardening boots. He walked Selena back, she took his arm, playing with the big flashlight's beam here and there. Two of the drones whirred overhead, hard to see against the night sky.

'I don't like them,' she said, looking up.

Gene only grunted. It was the price they paid.

The door was shut, and she fumbled for the key. 'I can't believe I left the boys,' she said.

'They're fine kids.'

She gave him a grateful smile. 'You have such a way with them. Fleur is so lucky.'

Wary of flattery, Gene said nothing. He got his key and let them in. 'No harm done. Shall I just look round?'

'Both of you are right. I think I'm seeing things,' Selena said, her face full of fear and grief. 'Isn't that terrible? How can anyone trust me?'

'You're safe with us.'

'Thank you.' She got out a cigarette, offered him one. He felt a need so strong he could taste it. Maybe smoke just one, to build rapport.

But before he could give in to the urge, she had pulled it away. 'Oh, sorry. Molly would kill me, seducing you into wicked ways.'

They both smiled.

Those long, difficult years for the Myers; the death, depression, the alcohol-soaked rift in their marriage – and where had Selena been? What help had she offered her sister? Gene could think of nothing. But she was family, and the right thing to do was the right thing to do.

'I'd like to travel when I'm well,' she said. 'See the West. M and I thought Hawaii was so exotic, we used to cut out pictures and hide them.'

He blinked, had Molly been venting about him to Selena? Her eyes were soft, there was no malice there. She said, 'It's hard, the first year with a baby. Molly . . . she'll come around.'

Gene thought about California; it was just his opening bid. He was worried his deepest dreams would scare Molly off completely . . . but he couldn't let go of them.

★

Two days later, they closed the library early. Gene was back to give his feedback on the last film for the Visitor Centre. The film people, Mayor Rourke, and some other worthies watched in the library basement. Cory wanted a little time alone, and after Selena's latest drama, her latest weeping three ring circus of an apology, Gene knew how he felt. Gene had given Cory the keys and let him go explore.

Rourke worked the projector himself. The latest film: the fauna and flora, the sights and the hikes of the area. Gene hated seeing himself on screen, and thought his presentation was wooden. But Rourke clapped, and the film people looked very pleased with themselves.

They looked at him.

'It's okay,' he said, wanting rid of it.

The Mayor beamed. 'Gene, you're a natural teacher. You're no Hollywood actor, but you know your stuff. It really made me want to go hiking, with a bird book in hand.'

'Well, if it does the job,' Gene said. There was another film, of course, about Meteor Day, the relevant sights, how the town had rebuilt; the way the Army had fenced off Two Mile Lake and footage of the Ship. Gene had refused to be in that one. And, finally, one careful film about Cory, mostly clips from newsreels and interviews with their friends. A famous scientist took down the sceptics using simple words and a kind tone.

The town had changed more since the Meteor than it had since the railroad came. Now, you might hear that the Prime Minister of India had turned up in a motorcade, wanting to meet the Myers. Like most VIPs, all she got was her photo in front of the Meteor fragment on Founders Green.

Gene gave his thank-yous and disappeared upstairs to the long room where the archives brooded, and where Cory would be waiting. There was a stack of new books and Cory's telescope, but no friendly greeting. Then Gene looked behind the shelves and found Cory wrapped in a blanket, asleep.

There was something beautiful in seeing a child in healthy sleep. Gene put on the old-fashioned Sam Spade hat Molly had bought him and sat looking out at the town. The lights were going on and the sky was darkening, and he felt Amber Grove close round him like a trap. That scene in *Pinocchio* where the whale swallows the ship.

His best friend Roy had warned him that the new baby would suck up time and sleep. It wasn't unusual that Molly wanted a padded fortress, a hand-picked world of people she trusted. It was not surprising that she wanted no more adventures, no part of his daydreams. But he was beating his wings against the bars.

He'd talked often about travel with Molly, those first years they were together. Then, the spring the Meteor came, she'd said yes to a trip to the West Coast. He knew it was her peace offering but she'd managed to smile about it. He'd hoped it would heal them. Then the Meteor came and there was no trip. And now she had rewritten history, forgetting that she'd meant it.

Those months on the road had smelled of sweat and dope and incense and too long in a car. Gene had talked to real artists, rolling stones, free spirits, doers and thinkers from all over the country, people who'd encouraged his music, talked of new chances and new sights. He had seen the possibilities – he could see them right now.

Their name could open extraordinary doors.

Cory muttered something and stretched extravagantly, like a cat. Then his eyes opened, and he did his curious yawn.

'Good dreams?' Gene said.

'Looking for my people,' Cory said. 'I want them to come and fix everything.'

Gene wanted them to come too. He feared they wouldn't – but, whatever happened, he would keep Cory safe and well as long as he could.

The snakes were implacable enemies of life itself. The chaos of Meteor Day would be as nothing if they returned.

One of Roy's men ran Gene and Cory home. At the bottom of Crooked Street there were floodlights, two TV trucks parked illegally, perhaps a dozen photographers: the whole circus. One of the Olsen cousins, in uniform, was arguing with a TV presenter next to someone on a motorbike.

Almost by instinct, Gene pulled Cory down. The communicator trilled and Cory began talking to the Ship. The National Guard swung open the barrier and the truck went up and through the Fence. Who knew what had brought the media this night?

Molly met them at the door. 'There've been some explosions in Australia,' she said as they went in.

The fact the press had come to the Myers was ominous. Gene saw that the phone receiver was droning, off the hook.

'Ship says go inside,' Cory said.

They sat round the kitchen table, Fleur asleep in her basket, Cory playing with Meteor and listening. Gene was astonished at how dry his mouth felt. 'What's going on?' he asked the Ship.

'The Australian authorities have announced a nuclear accident in a remote part of their country,' the Ship said, 'an accident involving an experimental bomb. They are trying to explain away fallout reaching deep into the desert interior. There was a snake landing – a small one – and they began assembling some form of structure. The Australian authorities sent three planes to observe what looked like some unexplained phenomena. The snakes destroyed all three – but not before a clear description was radioed back.'

Gene gripped Molly's hands. Her eyes closed, she swallowed, and Cory sent out his own cold fragments of frightened dreams. Fear rose again, familiar and heart-breaking.

'The authorities wanted it dealt with, so I obliged. The threat is removed.'

'Is that all of them?' The Ship and its Network were for ever searching the skies and the surface of the planet for intruders.

'There has been nothing since the deep Atlantic episode in July. Two weeks ago, a single snake vessel landed in a remote part of the Himalayas. I watched it closely, but it was largely inert: I suspect a monitoring station. The political situation there – the war between India and Pakistan, tensions with China – is complex even by human standards. I have taken advice from Professor Zarin in Moscow and others. I find the Chinese government opaque to deal with.'

Gene asked, 'How much does the world know?'

'Australia? There was a French documentary crew filming wildlife in the region. French television is reporting "extraordinary revelations", so I think the crew has evaded the authorities.'

'How could they land on Earth?' Molly pleaded. 'You said the Network was fool-proof.'

71

'They did not fool me for long and I will increase my vigilance. Mrs Myers, these are small-scale intrusions. The Himalaya outpost will be no more within the hour.'

Gene thought the Ship sounded sure of itself – but it was not all-powerful, nor was it infallible.

'The fallout,' Gene said, thinking of invisible poison on a desert wind; the clean snows of the mountains turned to a dangerous rain.

Molly gripped his hand tighter. They had marched to ban the bomb, had won an end to the tests that poisoned children. But the snakes brought closer a time when the weapons might be used in large numbers.

'The authorities are moving swiftly. They understand what they need to do to protect human health.'

'My people need to come,' Cory moaned.

The adults' eyes met, and they exchanged worried smiles.

'Of course, they'll come,' Molly said. 'The Ship will keep us all safe until they do.'

The next day, Olsen and his deputies were busy clearing yet more members of the press from the bottom of Crooked Street. Cory went over to his friends, and Gene phoned his father. They assumed any phones in Crooked Street would be tapped, so anything really secret they did in code, or from phone boxes or friends of friends' houses. Of course, people with two alien communicators could talk to each other without human snooping – but then the Ship listened in.

The phone rang and rang; perhaps John had forgotten the arrangement and was out doing stuff on the farm. *Overdoing* it.

Then a breathless voice answered, 'John Myers.'

'Hiding any symptoms?' Gene opened. John's 'indigestion' had been getting worse for months, until Molly had searched his bathroom cabinet and found his angina medication.

John had been brazen: *Nothing for you to fuss about.*

'Hah.' Today, John's breathing was heavy. Had he jogged back to the house? 'Red needed a second opinion on something. Your mother is with the church ladies. How's your new houseguest?'

'She'd try the patience of a mountain.'

John laughed. 'That was one of your grandpa's,' he said. 'Molly told Eva, you're wanting to up sticks and go wandering.'

'Yeah. It's not like Molly should be surprised. We talked about travelling at our engagement party.'

'Remember that summer when Grandpa and I took you out to see shooting stars?' Gene did; there had been many such summer nights. Grandpa had said, if Gene got straight As in his tests, he'd get a telescope. His grandpa had showed him the moons of Jupiter and the rings of Saturn and told him with love and care about life.

John's breathing was better now. 'You and he were chatting away, and that night, he told me, "That boy won't stay on the farm." Your mother and I knew that too. We figured it would be college and then away. Picking apples would never be enough, not for you.'

'I loved the farm. You didn't want me to go, but you wanted me to know I could.'

'You were a loud-mouthed know-it-all at eighteen. You still are.'

Gene laughed. Some kids knew their future was set in stone, following their parents, perhaps going to fight for Uncle Sam in some mysterious war or other. Some marched to a different drum. Gene had always thought the future would be astounding. He read about computers and space flight and revolutions in clean power, agriculture, and medicine, and how the world could be changed, for good or for ill.

John said, 'Bill Burrowes and I have been talking for a long time. Someone will have to manage the old place when I'm gone and we all know it's going to be Red Burrowes, not you. I called to say, don't worry about us. You and Molly do what you need to do.'

'Molly and I don't agree what we need to do.'

'You know she's a keeper. A man would be a sheer fool to throw a woman like that away.'

As if he would. Yet, Gene thought, his father would not be here for ever to say annoying things.

'I don't plan to.'

After the call, Gene wanted to be on the farm, to talk to his father face to face. All those dreams he used to have – and here he was, a librarian without a real job, in a pleasant backwater, not so far away from his parents. He had many blessings to count – but, in his heart, he knew he had far further to go.

Molly thought his dream was California, or Europe, even. His need was bigger and brighter than that; California was just what he could ask for.

The Ship wouldn't let humans inside it, but when the purples came, there would be other choices. Maybe they would take him to visit Mars and Jupiter and Saturn. Once those planets would have satisfied him, but now . . . that was just Earth's back yard. Gene imagined even bigger.

Gene wanted to see so much more than the wonders of Earth. The future had hit them like an avalanche. Who else deserved to return with Cory to the purple home-world? Gene knew the purple home-world night and day – from Cory's dreams and from Cory's long enthusiastic descriptions. He wanted to be the first human to breathe those strange, perfumed winds; explore the myriad islands and the vast artificial lagoons where the purples farmed the sea; those teeming green cities, full of music and dancing. He wanted to see silver boats and towns in space, a moon even more magnificent than Earth's, and meet a people wise and humane, a people who had found a kinder path, who would teach and inspire him.

How he wanted to hear a new music, new stories, and help bring humans and purples together. Of course, he'd be bringing the best of Earth to show them – and of course, with Molly by his side.

If he could only enchant Molly with the idea, all her worries about what might happen would melt away. He needed to share the adventure with her. No dream without her was worth having. The purples would save Earth, Crooked Street – and Amber Grove would always be there. But they were young, and this was a chance that four billion people could only dream of.

Now, when Gene looked at the sky, in his mind he stuck out his thumb. With guitar and a few bags, the Myers family would hitch a lift to the stars.

75

CHAPTER 7

A stand-off

Two days later, the news was full of the snakes in Australia. Molly had seen the snakes in Cory's dreams, with mouths of fire soaring through the skies like jet planes, turning at sickening, inhuman speed. The French wildlife researchers' film showed enough to be eerie, but not enough to convince the sceptics.

Selena was a little like those sceptics – thinking only of her own dilemmas, she waved away the snakes, politics, the war.

Together in Selena's bedroom, Molly held her hands. 'He can't come here. He won't come here. But we ought to make decisions . . .'

'Not now.'

'We could file the divorce papers.'

'Not now, M. Can't you just make him go away? Get the Ship to blow his car up, or something?'

Molly imagined the great silver machine hanging over Bradleyburg. That was the last thing they needed, even though she was so angry with Mason, with the abuse, and the lies he had told his boys about Cory.

'I don't feel well. I don't feel like *me*,' Selena cried.

Mason's lawyer had sent a long careful letter, urging a meeting. Selena had used the Myers' lawyer to send an undiplomatic reply. Mason could file criminal charges, she explained, but so could she. Gene thought Mason would have to go home eventually – surely his employer wouldn't give him weeks off just to chase his family?

It stuck in Molly's craw, but she decided that the best thing might be if both sides kept quiet about the assault. A sort of nuclear stand-off. Mason could admit adultery; Selena and the kids could stay in New York. They could compromise with a legal separation . . .

Yet a thought always persisted, nagging at Molly: would *she* walk away from her kids? *Ever? No*, she thought, *not even faced with a whole civilisation who wanted him back*. Mason might be just as resolute.

'Maybe I should talk to him,' Molly said.

'You take good care of me,' Selena said. Molly took that as a yes.

Molly was not surprised that Mason refused to come to Amber Grove, where Sheriff Olsen walked the streets. A controversial figure, the press had talked a lot about the Sheriff and the tales that surrounded him. It had been Olsen, of all people, who had found Cory and his dying mother, who had helped Dr Jarman and the Myers keep him a secret.

If the meeting had to be in Bradleyburg, Molly wanted to meet somewhere that was safe and private, but that could become public if they needed. She traded a favour. Bradley's Stores agreed to close the coffee shop an hour early, and make sure the window blind was down. It would be private enough, but if she screamed, there would be people around. The Myers knew the unknown way out of that building, so even if they ended up surrounded by press, they had options.

The temptation was always to take Cory into any tricky situation, her much-loved *Get out of jail free* card, but it just would not be fair to have him listen to what would be a disturbing adult conversation. Cory would be with Reuben in the getaway car and they would all be wearing those irritating, invaluable, communicators.

November fell on Bradleyburg's familiar streets like a dark blanket. The town didn't accept being overshadowed by its smaller neighbour and fought hard for its share of visitors' dollars. Molly wore a wig, tinted glasses and headscarf, and did what she could for Gene with a scarf, a borrowed coat and a logger's hat.

They slipped into the building through the staff entrance, where they were met by the manager, who took them through. They were there first. Molly sat where she had once drunk a painful coffee while deceiving Dr Pfeiffer, while the manager applied himself to a big ledger. She took slow sips, thinking the coffee at Francine's was better and half the price.

A few minutes later, Mason and the lawyer appeared. Mason wore his coat awkwardly, for his right arm was in a sling. The lawyer carried an attaché case.

'Molly, Gene,' Mason said. He had one of those bland, square, handsome faces. Molly felt a tremor of revulsion at the feeling that a man who'd hurt a woman was walking the streets free and respectable. She wanted him punished.

As they'd agreed, the Sheriff of Bradleyburg was there, a big, grey-haired barrel of a man.

'There's going to be no unpleasantness,' he said. 'I'm going to have a cup of coffee in that corner.'

Gene shrugged. 'No wife-beaters this side of the table,' he said.

Mason sat, wincing, and the lawyer frowned.

Molly folded her arms and wondered how bad the knife wound really was. With any luck it had got infected.

'How is she?' Mason asked. 'And the kids?'

'Fine,' Molly said. 'But let's skip the chat.'

The lawyer produced a document. 'Mr O'Regan still wants to try for a reconciliation. If there is a temporary period of separation . . .'

'Mason has been violent to Selena and the kids. There will be no reconciliation,' Molly said, although she had no specific instructions from Selena, except to get Mason to go away. 'We have a very detailed affidavit.'

'Well, Mr O'Regan could make the same claim.'

'Self-defence, a desperate act against a violent man.'

'The children need their father.'

'He'll need to move state, then. They're not going back. It will take a great deal before Selena even considers letting him near them.'

'Dragging this into the courts will hurt everyone. "He said, she said" . . .'

'Let justice be done, though the heavens fall,' quoted Gene.

Mason shifted and winced. His body language said he wouldn't let his lawyer speak for him much longer.

'Mr O'Regan's employers might insist on pressing charges.'

'Mr O'Regan's employers might never find her.'

Mason leaped in. 'Look, Molly – of course, you take her side. But, you do understand, I can't give up my kids? I must know they're safe – that she's safe too.'

'You should have thought of that,' Molly snapped.

'She's not well – the way she went for me. She just goes off into these dazes. She lets pots boil over. She might hurt the kids . . . not meaning to, but a fire or something . . .'

Molly had been wondering how well Selena would manage on her own. But that was irrelevant. Her sister wasn't on her own. The lawyer was staring at her, as though he could read her mind.

'We can mend this. The marriage vows . . .'

'She shouldn't be shackled to a dangerous man,' Gene said. He'd never liked Selena, but he was on her side.

'How's the Church with the adultery, the beating her up?' said Molly, wanting to make him squirm, to realise what a public struggle would be like.

She was surprised to see shame, guilt, on his face.

Mason said, 'Our priest told me to find her and make it right. He wants an update.'

The lawyer looked uncomfortable, and Gene was about to weigh into Mason, which was deserved but wouldn't get them anywhere.

'Go home,' Molly said. 'Take the pressure off Selena. The kids can be in school, they're making friends . . .'

Mason frowned, leaned a little forward. The eerie restraint was slipping. Something was burning in him. 'I need to see them now. I'm their father—'

The kitchen door opened, and everyone looked around.

Sheriff Olsen, bare-headed, nodded and walked over to the table. 'Bodge,' he called, 'we must surely owe you dinner.'

'Lars.' The big man was rising from his. 'You should come to ours. Well, I have an errand.'

The manager of the shop had speedily closed his ledger and was heading out. A play was unfolding which Molly didn't understand.

Bodge was speaking as if in court. 'Nothing is going to happen here to disturb the peace of the county. I am right outside the door.'

'Of course not,' Olsen said.

Bodge headed to the door.

'You have no jurisdiction here,' the lawyer told Olsen, a little too fast and high to be commanding.

Olsen slapped his chest. 'I'm not wearing a badge. Bodge and I know the boundary to the inch. He's said it: no disturbing the peace here. I've just come to see my friends the Myers.'

'You're no stranger to either side of the law,' the lawyer said.

Mason was glaring at Olsen, weighing him up.

Gene had a reassuring hand on Molly's thigh. Had he expected the Sheriff?

'This is a friendly discussion.' Keeping his voice level and calm, Olsen said, 'Mrs O'Regan doesn't want you around and I think that's a good place to start.'

'You can't keep me from my kids,' Mason said.

'Well, courts, that sort of thing – I mean, I haven't seen any evidence. I'm keeping an open mind on who started this fight, a big man who played football at college, or a housewife. Maybe we should ask my old friend the judge.'

'I'm not scared of you.'

Olsen's face did not change. 'Maybe you should be – afraid of the law, anyway. Mind you, the law doesn't always find the culprit. This guy I knew, a big drunk old farmer, he used to knock his wife around. She was a slip of a thing, half his weight. He hurt the kids too. Honey, the woman, was too frightened to testify – well, she was almost a kid herself. My wife spent an evening trying. There was nothing I could do.'

'This is hardly relevant,' said the lawyer.

That awful story. They said Olsen and three of his deputies had jumped the man – and, at that point, imagination took over, with lurid versions about what had been said and done. Olsen never denied the story; he'd just smile and refuse to discuss it at all.

'Anyway – strangest thing – the man fell off the barn roof one day, broke his leg and changed his mind in hospital. You could hardly believe it. Never climb on a roof drunk, Mr O'Regan.'

'Don't you threaten me,' said Mason, and there it was: the pretence was off. Mason was dangerous, and angry.

The lawyer looked at Olsen like he was a seventeen-foot-long crocodile.

'Lay a finger on my client, and you'll rot in jail,' the lawyer said.

'I'm not having a brute like you harassing a scared woman, O'Regan. Go to the press, go to the courts, and things will get nasty. There'll be a lot of mud your kids will hear. One step into Amber County, and I swear on the Good Book, the law will protect her.'

Almost on cue, almost as though he had been listening, the other Sheriff swept in.

'Lars,' said Bodge.

'I'm finished here,' Olsen said. Olsen: the man who had saved Cory twice. He was part of their circle, this flawed, dangerous man.

'Your threats don't frighten me,' Mason said.

Olsen grinned. 'I haven't made any threats, Mr O'Regan. Just offered neighbourly advice. You'd sure know if I'd used a threat.'

That evening, while Molly was reading to Cory in bed, he asked, 'Will Bad Man Mason stay away?'

'We hope so. And we can hide Selena and the boys if not.'

'Good.' Cory sighed, his copy of a human sigh. 'My people need to come very soon. I cannot find them again in dreams. Cory is despondent.'

'They'll come,' Molly said. Finding-in-dreams had come to nothing, as the Ship had warned. How much he must want his people, heart and body and soul. She understood how he must be feeling, because that was how she badly she wanted him.

'And they will sort this world out and then we can go to my home-world. Dad says all the Myers can go together.'

Odd, she thought. She wondered just what Gene had said. 'Well, sweetie-pie, I don't know that's going to happen.'

'Dad says we must go and see home-world. He promised. Big

adventure, chance-of-a-lifetime. You must come too, Mom.'
Cory looked anxious. 'All the excitement, all the people. First
humans coming to First Harbour . . .'

It made her crazy, Gene promising things he could not
deliver.

'Well, we can talk about everything when they come, can't
we.'

It wasn't the answer Cory wanted. He grew sadder. 'Mom
does not want to go,' he said.

'Cory, Grandpa and Grandma might not be well enough . . .'

'Huh. My people have much better medicine than humans.
Can bring everyone. I so love Earth, but I want to go home.'
Then, wailing, 'So fed up with being solo – being castaway
orphan. Being the only one.'

What could she say? What could she do? She kissed him and
said, 'We'll work something out. It would be such an adventure.
And Cory, you are not alone.'

'Don't leave me, Mom. Everyone left me. Everyone died.'

She sang to him, knowing she had disappointed him. He
closed both sets of eyelids, and turned on his side to sleep –
and, all the while, she told herself, Gene would not have
promised . . .

Molly slipped into the big room, where Gene was staring at
music sheets like they could bite. 'He's asleep,' she said.

'Great,' Gene said. 'I can't pretend this garbage is going anywhere.' He got up to embrace her.

'He was talking,' Molly ventured, 'about when his people
come.'

'They'd better come,' Gene said. 'Snakes landing – we need

their help. This is such small stuff, much smaller than Pevek. I wonder if they're testing us?'

Maybe, but she had to settle this first. 'It sounded . . .' Now it felt petty. 'He was saying, we ought to go with him, go home with him.'

Gene looked at her — and she realised that she had been a fool. The man who still read those stupid books wanted to go into space. Of course he did.

'It might be an idea,' he said.

She felt hot. *Keep calm, Molly.* 'You want to go — you promised Cory we'd go. Was that smart?'

'Molly-moo, just think: who else is going to have the chance? They're not going to be flying tourist trips on Pan Am, not for a while.' He was trying to persuade her, as if this were a fortnight vacation.

'I mean, it's dangerous,' she countered. 'Space — the snakes — alien diseases. And years of our lives? And why would they want us? We'd be alone.' The purples were not human, and humans would not fit into their world. Humans lacked the alien lodges, the communion of dreams. Humanity was more violent and savage than the purples had ever been.

'Not for ever,' Gene said, still trying to manage her. 'I mean, we'd really have to like the place to stay. But, you know, they'll sure set up an embassy here, so we'll need a human one there. Why shouldn't we go, for a while? We're family.'

'Yes, *family*. You'd leave your *parents*?'

Gene took her hands and she shrugged him off.

He looked wounded. 'Well, they might need persuading at first. But I'm sure the purple doctors will help them . . .'

86

Molly felt her anger rise. 'It would mean leaving our friends – bringing up Fleur without human doctors? Without other human children?'

'Maybe we'd take the whole gang. Crooked Street and all.'

She couldn't tell if that was a joke. An hour ago, she'd assumed talk of him going to the home-world was a pipe dream.

'Are you on drugs? The whole idea is *insane*.'

'So is adopting an alien. We made a success of that.' He was getting angry too, and louder.

'I'm telling Cory I won't go.' She went louder still.

'You're being ridiculous. He wants his mom, his sister. What are you going to do, refuse to let him go? Tell the purple civilisation to take a hike?'

It hung in the air for a moment. There was a moment where she could have dodged it, but the time was right. He needed to know.

'I'm not giving him up, Gene.' She stood up. 'We've suffered enough. His place is here, with us. Earth is his home now. The purples will have to live with it.'

He gasped. 'You are *out of your mind*.'

The tiredness, the strain of Selena and Mason, feeling surrounded, with so little safety. The trip west had been just a cover for this – this *betrayal*.

Molly lost her temper. 'I *won't* go,' she snapped. 'And you – you're going to abandon us? Leave Fleur? What kind of a man are you, breaking up the family?'

'Molly, that's not fair. You've just told me you want to pick a fight with a whole species – and I'm the one being crazy?'

'You're selfish. Reckless, thoughtless, dangerous! I won't do it, Gene, I won't. You're not going to run away from us. You're not going to leave the kids without a father. You're not one of those men.'

'It'll destroy him. What if he wants to go?'

'You'll wreck everything if you run away. I might lose both of you.'

'We'll sure lose him if we don't. You're being *impossible*.' He pushed past her and strode through the door, slamming it behind him like an Olympic sport.

You'll wake the baby.

Too late. Upstairs, Fleur wailed.

CHAPTER 8

The Jarman place

Molly sat in a bedroom at the rambling, half-empty Jarman place. Selena was standing by the window, where she could look out, hopefully without being seen. There was noise from the woods, a motorbike on one of the trails.

'It's not him,' Selena said. 'He checked out of the hotel – went back to Indiana.'

'He did. There are people out there – Press, Meteornauts, protestors. But he's gone.' That's what the two Sheriffs thought was more likely than not.

Selena sighed, turned away and walked to the bed. She sat.

'Thanksgiving together at last,' she said. 'This is what it took.'

Humour was good.

Molly said, 'That's right.' There was a lot to do that week. She was hoping all her family and friends could be together. Would John and Eva make it to the Jarmans'? Eva said John needed some more tests. Or would the Myers go to the farm?

Gene wanted to go and bring his parents back; it made her anxious, but it also made sense.

'I'm not one to put my nose in where not wanted,' Selena said, 'but I'm sorry if I've caused trouble between you and Gene.'

'No, not really.' And she found herself confiding in Selena.

But Selena was gentle in her criticism of Gene. 'I see why he's feeling wanderlust. Men feel so pinned down when the baby comes – pushed away. But he's too good a man to let you down . . . You'll figure it out.'

Well! Selena siding with Gene.

'How about *me*? I feel *pinned down* sometimes. I'm a good nurse – I'd like to go back to work. With Cory, now the baby . . .'

There was a muffled noise, a vibration. It took her some moments to realise that it was the communicator, tucked into a pocket. The Ship had turned it on remotely, which she hated. So rude, breaking into a personal conversation.

She talked into the machine. 'Ship, it's not a good time.'

'Mrs Myers, please find Mr Myers. It's urgent and I want to brief you two together. You and only you.'

Selena was staring.

'I won't be long.' Molly went into the corridor and hollered for Gene.

The two of them sat in an unused guest room, Fleur bright-eyed on Molly's lap, listening as the Ship brought them bad news. 'NASA has confirmed that it has lost contact with *Mariner 9*. The probe broke off transmission.'

The unmanned space mission to Mars.

Molly felt the earth lurch under her. She looked at Gene. From his face, he'd had the same thought. The tragedy of last year's Moon landing – the deaths of the two astronauts in *Eagle* – had been the first snake attack. She could think of other reasons why *Mariner 9* might have stopped transmitting – equipment failure, or a meteorite. After all, *Mariner 8* had failed on take-off. But perhaps it was something else.

'It is fruitless to speculate,' the Ship said. 'I will treat this investigation as a priority.'

Gene said, 'The Russians also have probes headed to Mars.'

'I'm aware.'

'Ship . . .' This sounded stupid, so she tried to make it less so. 'Ship, we do rely on you.'

'Of course, I have remotes I can use. However, I will still need to be in the vicinity of the planet.'

Molly rocked Fleur a little, singing to her, but it was not Fleur who needed reassuring. When she found Cory to tell him, his shiver filled the room. Her argument that *Mariner* might have been hit by a rock, or just suffered some malfunction, did not reassure him.

They heard nothing from the Ship until the following evening, when Cory was asleep. The Myers were preparing for bed when the Ship spoke from the communicator without warning, 'Set up the viewing disc and inform me when you are done.'

When they had unfolded the flat black disc about two feet across, on which the Ship could project images, the Ship said without preamble, 'The *Mariner 9* spacecraft was destroyed by snake action.'

91

Molly felt her stomach jump. Gene took her hand.

'It might have been an automatic reaction by a single snake machine, or it might have been a patrol. Therefore, I investigated Mars.'

The disc leaped into life. Moving pictures showed fast flight above a lifeless surface of rocks and desert, a few drifting patches of dust, and above a sky of murky pink, blue only around the low sun. No plants, no water, no glint of metal. Ahead reared a mountain, a vast cone, and from its flank rose a spume of smoke or dust. Perhaps it was a volcano – did they have those on Mars?

Answering their unspoken question, the Ship said, 'Olympus Mons, the largest mountain on the planet. That plume is a snake excavation.'

Molly felt her heart race as the perspective suddenly shifted. Three silver flames hurtled towards the camera with familiar speed. The unseen device carrying the camera speeded up, rose further from the surface and began a series of stomach-turning evasive manoeuvres. Then the Ship replaced that image with the planet Mars, half in shadow, against a field of stars.

Molly felt nothing but dread.

'They detected my remote. Every time they detect my presence, they attack it. The area was once volcanic, indicating rich mineral resources.'

'Get to the point,' Gene said.

'They are building a production complex like the one on Pevek, from which I deduce they will be building more machines, and more facilities. Even if humans learn of the activity, they are decades off sending a spacecraft, and it will take years to get there. And anything they do send will be swatted from existence: like pitting a child's kite against a military helicopter. However, this does appear to be the snakes' only active complex. They may have inactive facilities elsewhere. I continue my investigations.'

'So what do we do?' Molly wondered.

'Well, to be clear, if they send a scouting party to Earth, I will destroy it. The Russians have given me some of their ridiculous number of fission-fusion weapons, and I have my own resources. Maybe, deterred here, they have lost interest. But maybe they wish to come again, this time in force. The longer we wait, the more resources they will have.'

The Ship stopped a moment, a very human pause. 'The worst-case scenario is that they could build tens of thousands, then millions of machines, all capable of space flight, strategy and attack. They could set up a diffuse production system across the surface, which would be much more difficult to attack, and muster an army far beyond any response I could give, with or without assistance. Fission-fusion weapons are not ineffective, but the snakes will surely find ways to disable the primitive human missiles that deliver them. The war would spread to Earth itself. You can imagine the consequences.'

Gene said, 'Cory's people might come first.'

If they were coming at all . . .

'My analysis is speculative but gloomy. The builders rescue individuals at the most extreme cost. Also, the circumstances under which the colony ship was destroyed surely requires a mission. The builders have not come, which after all this time causes me a high level of concern. The two most probable

93

solutions: they do not know where we are, or the builder civilisation is under too great a threat to come.'

A moment, then it said, 'My responsibility is to Cory, not the Earth. I wish to take Cory, put him in suspended animation and hide him.'

Molly bit her cheek, trying to hold herself together.

'No,' Gene said.

'Only Cory can make that decision. What will help him make it is this: humans are cellular beings. It would not be difficult to test the apparatus on humans; the builders have used it to transport a wide variety of animal specimens to other planets. Obviously with sentients, even minor brain damage must be avoided. I propose to make some urgent experiments, starting with low-sentience mammals, then moving onto humans. If the tests are successful, I might be able to place you, perhaps a dozen humans, all in suspended animation and hide them . . .'

'*Experiments?*' Gene's voice rose. 'We can't have you experimenting on humans—'

'Be logical. Cory will ask me if the machines are safe for you, and I cannot answer that question without experimentation. Assuming the system works, in two months I could place Cory and your immediate social group outside danger.'

Molly was speechless. The world would be left vulnerable to an implacable enemy. The snakes were metal bacteria, breeding and breeding until they could invade: sentient missiles which could make more missiles – and decide when to attack. And the Ship wanted to run away?

'So we nuke them,' said Gene, looking sick. 'Or you help humans build better rockets.' They had met marching for peace — how Molly had loved his passion for peace! — yet here they were, with the survival of Earth at stake and no good answers other than extreme violence.

'My pilot instructed me not to pass technology to humans. That order proves very unhelpful, but I must be clear: my priority is to save Cory, not the defence of the Earth. I regret this.' The machine managed to sound sorry.

Billions of lives.

Molly had never seen Gene grimmer. 'There must be another option.'

'We will need to discuss my plan with Cory, and I need your cooperation, since otherwise you will confuse him.'

'Suppose he refuses. What would you do then?'

'If I cannot hide Cory, then we must remove the threat while it is still contained. That will mean acting now to destroy the base.'

'How?' Gene said.

'Clearly it will be well defended. It is a complex problem. I rescued three major propulsion units from the main vessel. I have repaired them. They could approach the machine nest at very high speeds and be detonated. Other devices would follow them in to confuse and deflect the inevitable attack. One well-placed detonation of this scale could destroy the production facility and most of the robots, perhaps all. The probes and I would follow behind to carry out such further tidying up as necessary.'

Molly was feeling sick to her stomach, thinking of Dr King, all the petitions and letters she'd written, all the songs they'd sung. *Give peace a chance.* She fervently believed in peaceful ends and peaceful means because the human heart could be reached, human beings could be redeemed. There was no heart in a machine to change.

The Ship had learned persuasive intonation. 'They killed four thousand builders in an unprovoked attack. Many human casualties in Pevek. Mrs Myers, even this option poses its difficulties. I am risking mechanisms I cannot rebuild. I will have fewer resources after the attack.'

'But if the attack succeeds, that protects the Earth,' Gene said. 'Maybe. At least, it buys us time. And these things aren't people.' He looked at Molly. 'It's a sort of violent disarmament. Blowing up guns.' He'd used that argument before.

'I prefer evasion,' said the Ship. 'Advise me how to find volunteers, so that I can test suspended animation on humans.'

'We ought to call the President,' Gene said.

'I am not willing to have my freedom to act constrained,' the Ship said. 'Given these facts, the authorities' only logical move would be to force me to protect Earth. To do this, they have an even bigger incentive to capture Cory. That is unacceptable, and a distraction from what I need to do. Tell the government and I will have to fly Cory and you three somewhere beyond their reach.'

'Where?' Molly asked.

'An island, warm, with suitable dwellings and supplies. There are no other inhabitants.'

The humans digested that.

Gene said, 'We need to think about this – how we tell Cory . . . *what* we tell him.'

'Either option requires a quick decision. I am happy to answer further questions. I am making necessary preparations for either plan. The Soviets tell me they have lost contact with both their space probes. They are less easy to stall than the US government. They may go public. They see the Western powers as complacent about snake attack.'

The communicator fell silent.

How do you have that discussion with a child?

It was a restless night, filled with doom-laden dreams. Whenever Molly settled, Gene woke her, getting up to scribble thoughts on paper.

At breakfast, Cory was silent.

'Bad dreams,' he said at last.

'Okay,' Gene said, and set out the situation, as fairly as he could. Each revelation chilled the room until they were all shivering. Molly breastfed Fleur, stroking her cheek to stop her sleeping on the nipple. She said little. This was too much responsibility, even for someone as bright as Cory.

Cory sank his head in his hands. 'Mom, Dad, we can't run away, we just-can't leave and let everyone be attacked. Can't find my people in dreams. Maybe not coming soon. Maybe . . . maybe Cory wrong . . .'

Molly hugged him. She felt ill, thinking about an army which could grow faster than Earth could respond, a nuclear war fought not between people, but between humans and alien machines, machines which didn't need air or water or food, their soldiers without fear or morals, who couldn't be frightened or converted.

'So we tell the Ship to destroy the snakes,' Gene said. 'It's very clever, and if it doesn't get all of them, then we can discuss what we do.'

If the mission failed, then the world would have to work together; there'd be no other option.

It was Cory who spoke to the Ship. 'No running away, no hiding for us. Save Earth, keep yourself safe.'

The Ship didn't trust their friends either. They gathered at the Jarman place on the evening of the attack, listening to the wind outside while a fire blazed inside. Molly imagined death coming down from the sky, robot snakes landing on Founders Green, mushroom clouds rising on every horizon.

What do you do on the day which might be the end of the world? They'd settled for a vague message to their friends. 'You are packed and ready to go, aren't you? We haven't asked for months. Just in case you need to . . .'

Fleur slept, against her warm body. Gene's arm was around her, and Cory snuggled between them like a penguin chick. The dog gnawed at some old bone.

'There have always been predators.' Cory shivered. 'Things that ate us. We had to be better at hiding and scaring. We had to be smarter.'

Being a mother, Molly thought, *there is always something to fear, always something to hope for – and always some things you just don't know. Children think you are in control, and on your first day you learn you're not.*

Her amazing son kissed her hand and they gazed together into a dark sky and a hidden future.

'This is the Ship. I am moving into position at very high speed, following the other devices. It will take one direct hit to destroy the nest.'

The Ship chimed, bells and flutes, then added a few words in Cory's language.

'Hunting song,' Cory said. 'About . . . hunting sea beasts that kill.'

Molly had seen the monsters in Cory's dreams. The snakes were worse. She closed her eyes and breathed, in and out, in and out, asking the unfeeling universe for success.

'I am meeting defensive action and in force. I was wise to use remotes near Mars.'

'We don't need a commentary,' Molly said.

How foolish that sounded aloud.

The Ship ignored her and carried on, 'I have detonated the first missile, sacrificing it to clear the approach.'

Two left.

'My remotes are suffering significant losses – but so are they. I am making progress. The second missile is largely past their defences.'

A pause. 'A partial hit. The missile deviated off-course and exploded early. I cannot be sure I have done enough damage.'

'They've got some defence you don't know about?' Gene asked.

'The third missile is on track. Yes, some form of interference, but I am switching systems. On track.'

Gene was clutching Molly's hand so hard it hurt.

The machine made a deep ringing gong. 'I have made a direct hit. The facility is destroyed.'

The Ship began to chant.

'Hunting song,' Cory said.

'Harpoons hit home
our aim was true
have slain the demon
killer of the people
monster in the dark
harpoon hit home
big feasting tonight.'

Odd, that Cory's people of old ate the clawed sea monsters, but practical, since they had killed them for self-defence.

Gene breathed out a little more. 'Ship, how many probes survived? Are you damaged?'

Cory's language trilled out of the communicator.

Cory's fear raised the hairs on Molly's skin and stopped the breath in her throat.

'Ship, are you there?'

'This is unfortunate,' the Ship said. 'The nest was destroyed, but I am under attack. There is a substantial craft approaching at very high speed, surrounded by smaller craft. An effective ambush. My detection systems are inadequate.'

'Ship,' Molly said, 'whatever happens, we need you. Don't take risks. Run away. We need you back here. You're our last hope, to help us defend, to explain . . .'

Cory spoke in his own language, and the machine answered in kind.

Then it spoke English. No emotion, just a little emphasis in the sentences. 'No time, Mrs Myers. This vessel is faster than I am. This has been a significant misjudgement. It has a faster-than-light capacity, and they are preparing to use it. If they

100

wish, they can flee – and disappear from my reach. Maybe to alert others or build a fleet somewhere else, too big for me to defeat.'

'My people are coming!' Cory said.

'It would be better to have reliable evidence,' the Ship said.

Cory gave the Ship an order, shrill and angry.

Molly's skin crawled as she felt his fear.

'This is a threat to Earth, and to the builder home-world. I will act to fulfil the mission.'

Gene said, 'Ship, retreat. Regroup . . .'

It almost sounded gentle. 'Today, I may outgun them. In a month I won't. In six months, they could destroy the Earth with impunity. I must strike this formation and detonate my engines. It should be highly effective. If I am to be destroyed, at least I will take the danger to Cory with me.'

Cory fluted.

'I'm afraid I'm not going to do that, Cory. No time to debate, Mrs Myers. I leave you the mission. Keep Cory safe.'

Molly felt a great wash of horror from Cory. Meteor whined.

The Ship was chanting again.

'Hoo-hoo,' Cory said. 'Song means . . .

> '*I have mission*
> *to protect the lodge*
> *a sacred trust*
> *protect the young*
> *prepare my weapon*
> *protect the lodge . . .*'

Cory spoke to it, sharply, and the Ship answered in a few crisp syllables. Then there was silence.

'Disobeyed.' Cory moaned. 'Bad-brave-naughty Ship.'

A minute or so later, the communicator crackled static and fell silent.

The Myers were too stunned to act. Fear hung around the room like mourning clothes in an old photograph. Fleur woke up, grizzling, so Molly sat in the big chair and fed her. Gene sat on the bed, his face drawn, his arm around Cory. Every few minutes, intense coldness came off him, making Molly's skin crawl and her heart jump. Gene winced, and each time, Fleur stopped sucking and opened her mouth to wail. Molly couldn't tell where her son's sadness and confusion ended and hers began.

It can't be good to have Fleur near Cory in this state. It can't be good to leave Cory alone.

What were they going to do? Surely, as soon as the authorities knew, they would send soldiers to protect the Myers.

Her son wailed. 'Ship . . . Ship protected us in all ways and now Ship is gooone! *Hoo-hoo-hoo.* What if more snakes come?' Then he babbled in his own impenetrable language.

'Cory, it will be all right,' Gene said, the parent's hopeful lie.

Molly's communicator was dead. A sudden thought struck her: what would happen if the Ship's defences in Amber Grove went down with it? Gene's anxious eyes met hers. There was no book in any library for any of this. They needed information from Cory, but he was in no state to talk calmly.

Was the Network, the Ship's eyes and ears in space, still working?

'Everyone dead and now Ship gooone. *Hoo-hoo-hoo.* If anything breaks, I may not be able to repair it.'

Gene said, 'Perhaps we should hit the hay, Big Stuff. Your mutt will miss you.'

Cory had a hand to his head. 'What-are-we going-to-do?'

'Hot milk,' Gene ordered and led Cory from the room.

Molly looked at Fleur dozing on the breast and a weird fear gripped her, a dreadful idea that kept swimming up. She became paralysed with the choice facing them.

An hour later, Gene came back. He looked gaunt, like someone human had died, as he went over to the crib, and peeked in. Fleur was deeply asleep, a little bundle in pink. He touched her ear with a finger, as gentle as the thought of a kiss.

'He's going to chase up his people in his dreams. I just hope . . . I just hope they're coming.'

She rose and put her arm round his waist; instinctively, his arm went around her shoulder.

'We have to run,' she said. 'The Army. The Mob. The press. We have to tell our friends.' She looked down on her daughter and wondered what world she had brought her into. 'Do you think Cory . . . the sadness . . . do you think it will hurt her?'

'He's a great big brother. She's lucky. But it sure couldn't hurt just to . . . you know, avoid her being around his nightmares.'

Gene bent down to kiss her, but Molly was numb.

The Ship felt no need to respond to humans unless it wanted to. Its absence would not be noticed at once. But *Mariner 9* had gone. The Administration and the Russians would have suspicions within a day, at most. They had so little time.

Molly knew this would be a time of parting, a time of loss.

It was a bitter truth — their friends and family would seek the Governor's protection. Gene and Molly had their own plan, which was very different.

Molly made the decision. 'We've got to wake our friends.'

CHAPTER 9

Interstellar space

Thirty days into its mission, *Kites at Dusk* cruised through the brilliant sea of stars. It sang a duet with its sibling ship, *Repurpose Snakes as Dung Buckets*, the other half of the mission. Machine minds searched in every direction for the predators, the snakes, the enemies of life.

Thunder Over Mountains came into the feeding place, where he was hit by a symphony of smells, feelings and sound. He picked up the strong scent of four-spice, stirring his memories of beach feasts under the stars with a whole theme of briny sea mollusc notes. And, of course, he smelled the crew and felt traces of their emotions – the notes of anxiety and confinement. Barely thirty days from home, the mission just underway, and fear was growing. It muted his hunger. The first step of the mission was Waystation Jewel, and who knew if it would be there when they arrived? Out there among the stars were the metal predators, the destroyers of the colony-world . . .

The hymn of resistance was like a meditation.

We will make those predators our prey.

Crew were crammed sharing-elbows-and-tails in the feeding stations. Thunder took the food of the day and took the next free seat. He bent his face down to the plate of six-molluscs and land-kelp, savouring before tasting. An impromptu group was trying a joining song, and there was an orchestra of talk.

'Vat food,' said a crewmate he did not know well – a healer-leader. One of his fellow pattern-bridgers joined them.

'Few of us can tell the difference,' Thunder said. Planet-dwellers were always ready to complain about everything. Perhaps they used that to relieve the tension of things they could not change. The starship was less comfortable than he wanted, but what did they expect? The thing he missed to the point of pain was the children back home, those enjoyable, unpredictable hours on the children's roster. All-had-decided, it was now too dangerous to take children to the stars, or to risk conceiving in flight. It was one of a thousand costs of the Hardening.

The screens in the feeding place showed the stars as if to say, look, out there is real. A warning chime meant the ship would soon slip into other-space, to move faster than light. The pictures of stars would disappear and be replaced with reassuring clouds, forests and seas. The unease of being in other-space rather than true-space was almost entirely psychological yet Thunder still felt the difference.

The snake machines, the destroyers-of-life, could not attack in other-space as far as anyone knew. Therefore, it should be by far the more reassuring part of the journey. Some things are not governed by reason alone.

'Thunder wants to find *Dancer on the Waves*,' said his close-colleague.

Part of the mission was to seek out the lost starships, the unexplained losses since the coming of the destroyers. The lost colony ship was of course, the mystery of mysteries. Thunder would make the old discussion as short as he could.

'Is there hope?' the healer asked, a ritual.

'There is always hope,' Thunder said. Yes, the ship and its crew could survive out of contact for years. But there was not an atom of evidence where it was.

Some of the space to be searched for *Dancer* lay in space long conceded to the snakes. If it was there . . . many said there was no hope.

'Seeking the colony ship is little better than walking on the floor of the lagoon, hoping to tread on a particular thorn-fish,' Thunder said. How he wished that was not true.

'Choices must be made,' another said. 'Harder choices than we have known. Why devote any time to it?'

Thunder sent a glance at his lodge-mate: *be silent.*

But the healer gave her own answer. 'Dreaming-between-the-stars may find any of the lost vessels. If enough of the crew live and dream-together . . . if they are within the range . . .'

'. . . then we may yet find *Dancer* by chance, looking for the others.'

For Thunder, faint hope had been replaced with an obsession. He used it to mask his distress, his self-criticism. His unease at dreaming-between-the-stars, the dangerous and unreliable last chance.

The healer turned to Thunder. 'Are you on the search rosters?'

107

Thunder did not answer. He wasn't.

'Help us look,' the healer said, with enthusiasm. 'What is your lodge position?'

'Anchor, by choice.'

'We need strong anchors. And you are a patterner, a bridger-between by profession, which is a most excellent combination. The dreaming is hard, and not without risk. The more widely we share the burden—'

'The time may come but it is not now.'

He must be polite, so he lowered his mouth to the food and began tentacle feeding. The healer did the same to her last scraps. No offence taken.

Thunder would have his medicinal dose of privacy soon, a precious time to be alone. He almost envied the ship's handful of solos, whose cells were in odd corners of the great ship, allowing them respite from other people. A long and dangerous mission would send more solo. It might push one or two to the sickness-that-kills.

Thunder missed Spinning Disc, his wounded love. It had been the most unhappy of departures, almost a physical pain, as he headed to the stars. He was taking the hunt to the destroyers-of-life. And yet, he wanted others to take the risk of dreaming. Guilt nagged at him.

In the privacy cell, he called up the machine memory of Pilot, his old friend, the mother of his son Little Glowing Blue Frog. He watched scenes of them both, with the little one growing from a cub playing in water, to the splendid child doing the Pioneer dances with such joy for life. These visuals brought love and pain, just like the day the starship *Dancer on the Waves* had embarked for the stars. What a time of hope that had been, a new world for the people. No starship had been lost in twenty-seven years and only two in the sixty-four years before that. Thunder had been in the crowd, echoing the sounds and movements of those leaving. It was a moment of pride for the whole people. But, at that very moment, the snakes had been amassing around the colony-world. Unknown to all, they were only forty days from the home-world.

How Thunder missed Pilot and their son. All had sung their death-praises without the bodies, but how he resented not knowing the means of their death. From the faint fractions of chances, he conjured up the idea that *Dancer* might have survived. Or that Pilot and Little Frog were in suspended animation, hidden from the snakes. It was the most fanciful idea. He almost longed for this dreadful hope to finally die, just so that he could walk on.

He enjoyed the children of the space habitats. But Little Frog was different. Attentive fatherhood had never been the agreement. Sometimes he had skipped a chance to talk to Little Frog. He knew each occasion he had missed, and the boy, warned, was not unduly hurt. Now each time felt a wasted opportunity. He had a dangerous fantasy, that he would find Pilot and their son, and they would be in one lodge for ever.

The healer had sent him a message he did not want to hear. *We need strong anchors, holders-within. Share the burden.*

Mind amplification was respectable, in the hands of the cautious mind-healers. But the fringes of the field were full of risk-lovers, wild speculators and obsessives, making attempts to unite unnatural numbers in a dream, or to send dreams beyond their usual range. The tales of disaster were not exaggerated. Those in such experiments had been damaged in the nine senses, or driven to the sickness-that-kills. Worst of all, whole lodges had been dream-burned, frightening isolation from the-all. Before Thunder was born, all-had-decided on a strict prohibition.

Then the destroyers came, and the unthinkable had become thinkable, to save the people and their planet. Despite the-all-had-forbidden, it emerged that shocking experiments had continued, and now dreaming-between-the-stars was a tool, however flawed, to link the people across the vastness of space. Perhaps it could transmit a little knowledge faster than the snakes could – and any edge in the struggle to survive, no matter how desperate, could be considered.

That did not mean he wanted to take the risk. Even the training unnerved him. Dreaming-between-the-stars produced phantoms from children's tales, things that could not be explained.

Privacy time was over. He would search for lost ships using intellect instead, piecing together probability and clues.

Outside their private place was a crew-friend, hopping from one foot to another, eager to pass on every rumour and gossip.

'The dreamers—'

'Yes?'

'They found a person. A single dreamer, frightened and alone.'

'Impossible,' he said, and felt foolish. Dreaming-between-the-stars was new, but already the people knew that it could not always be relied on. What, less than sixteen days ago, there'd been the same claim of a finding a solo. Some in the dream had not been convinced; most now said it was a phantom.

'Do we have anything personal? Any idea of where?'

'Very little. A brief contact – terrified, calling for help, alone. Those in that other dream think it's the same person. The sceptics last time now think it is a true dreaming.'

Who dreams alone when they can dream together?

'They must try again,' he said, a torrent of feelings bubbling up. This was nothing. It was probably nothing.

It might be one of the crew of *Dancer on the Waves*. It might be Pilot, or Little Frog.

Terrified. Alone. Needing help.

'What did they sense of the dreamer?'

His friend knew what he was thinking and took his hand. 'They said, it might well be a child.'

He knew the odds against, yet the hope blazed up and burned until it hurt inside him.

Terrified. Alone. Needing help.

CHAPTER 10

Midnight

Gene and Molly were all but packed. Molly looked round the safe, familiar bedroom, a world she was about to lose for the second time. She wiped her eyes. 'I'm going to wake Selena.'

'Jeez.' Gene scowled and looked at his watch. 'Let's just go. We haven't got time.'

'She might want to come.'

'Tough. You saw the weather forecast.'

'Don't you think she deserves to decide?'

Gene slammed his case shut and snarled, 'How long will Big Sis take to get ready? Two hours? She likes the Jarmans, she sure needs professional help, she's safe enough with them.'

Molly knew all this. 'Don't be like that. I'm all she's got.'

'She'll slow us up. She'll sure be pissed with you when she finds out, but let her.'

Downstairs, her friends were debating how long to give the Myers before they called Governor Rockefeller and put their own protection plan in motion. From that first argument here, all those months ago, to Diane's birthday only a month ago, the same decision stood. John and Eva had made the same choice, and indeed, their health made it inevitable.

Molly tried not to see the split as a betrayal. Gene and Molly just didn't trust the billionaire Governor, they couldn't. The President held the only prize the man could not buy – anointment as the President's preferred successor.

Molly wanted the same as Gene. 'I agree she should stay. But we need to persuade her – not run away.'

'Disappearance Inc might not take her.'

'Uh . . . I warned Pierre we might be two cars, six people, and a dog.'

Gene grabbed the cases. 'Your sister will screw everything up. I'll look round Cory's room again.'

Disappearance Inc was a quixotic network, an Underground Railroad for those strange times. They moved people and hid them, and they'd never lost a client. It had been Pierre from the network Carol and Storm had turned to, to hide the Myers at Christmas.

Molly woke Selena, deep in a medicated sleep, and it was ten confused minutes or more before Selena truly grasped the danger. Then, she was terrified.

She gripped Molly's hands, like she was drowning. 'I want to go with you,' she said. 'Where are we going?'

'To stay with friends. People who have done this before. Sel, you'd be so much better off staying . . .'

Selena's eyes filled with tears, and the lamentations began, just as Gene predicted.

'I don't understand, M. If it's not safe, why aren't the others going with you . . . Why aren't Rosa and Dr Jarman coming . . . ?'

Gene left and came back with Rosa, to argue Selena out of it, and tapped his watch again. The minutes ticked on, two persuading against one, then Dr Jarman came looking like a bear shaken awake from hibernation. It was three arguing against one. Selena, sick and frightened, proved to have a backbone of steel.

'Molly, I'll take my chances with you.'

Gene broke the impasse. 'Selena, can you be outside and ready in forty minutes? We'll all help.'

'Yes. Yes. *Thank you*.'

'For the record, I think this is dangerous and dumb.'

'Taking Cory away from the best medicine humanity can offer him? That's dangerous,' said Jarman. 'Even now . . .'

'We've planned this,' Molly snapped. The little voice that said *stay with Jarman* used that argument. But they had enough alien drugs for decades and the machines that synthesised his blood. Molly had the book listing everything they knew, and Disappearance Inc included at least one doctor.

No time for long goodbyes as the first flakes of snow started to fall. They'd need to borrow two cars. Selena was compliant, not arguing long over anything. They dressed Connor and Rory, ignoring sleepy protests, and put them under blankets in the back of one car. The Myers loaded Cory into the other, the blue Chrysler, and he went straight back to sleep. It was closer to an hour, but they were ready.

All their friends stood solemnly, for the last embraces.

115

Dr Jarman and Rosa, who had fought to save Cory's life, Roy, who could have betrayed them and who had been the most loyal of all. Janice and Diane, who understood her.

No light came from the media shanty town, or the scattered tents of those who waited for reasons of their own. Gene drove out of the gate, followed by Serena. Reuben drove a Jeep behind them, ready to frustrate any followers.

'Your sister drives like a nun to a funeral,' Gene snapped, and Molly's heart was close to breaking. No one followed, and after a few miles, Reuben flashed his headlights in farewell. They were on their own.

They reached a summer place, a house deep in the woods, one of several they'd been offered if they needed. After a few brief hours sleep, Molly woke in an unfamiliar bed, barely knowing what day it was. She fed Fleur while Gene snored on, oblivious. Thank goodness Gene had agreed to halt there, when neither of them were really fit to drive.

Long before they returned to Amber Grove, Gene and Molly knew they needed a plan. They had been bombarded with offers of sanctuary, at a time when they didn't need them, everyone from Robin Heights, Michigan (population 1011) to a hundred different nations – and the New York Mob.

Carol and Storm had introduced them to Disappearance Inc in New York. The Myers liked them, and Cory trusted them. They had a twelve-year flawless track record, and from the advice offered, they understood how the FBI worked, how to move money, how to get false papers. It was run on idealism, on pay what you can.

Gene and Fleur slept on, and Molly went into the kitchen, to find Cory cooking his own oatmeal. From the smell, Cory had fed Meteor sardines and bread rather than open the emergency dog food.

Tick tock tick tock. Who buys a clock that loud?

Cory moved the oatmeal off the hotplate and went into her arms for a hug.

Molly wanted to say it would be all right – it's the parent's job to reassure the child – but she could not bring herself to say it. They needed to be lost to the world before the authorities acted. She held him as if to stop him flying away. There was grief and fear in him, but something like hope too.

After a long hug, there came a sigh. 'Thank goodness my people are coming,' he said.

'Oh,' she said, not thinking much of it. 'Did you get a message?'

'A dreaming-together.' He broke the embrace to gaze into her face. '*Definitely* a dreaming-together. My people, Cory is just so sure. In a starship.' A beat, then, 'Well, what else could it be? Impossible not to be a starship. I was having a nightmare, so I went into dreaming-together layer and there it was. Little and bright and far away. But I joined it. Real deal.'

She could hear Gene's voice in her head. *It sure sounds like wish fulfilment to me.* The night that the Ship, Cory's protector and confidante, was destroyed, he dreamed of rescue.

'What happened? Did they speak?'

'They are looking for me. They called out to me; they're coming.' He was holding her again. 'Mom needs to believe me.'

It seemed safe to say, 'I hope they are coming. You know we don't understand dreaming.'

'Cory needs to find them again. Make sure they know where I am. Make sure the message vessel got through.'

'You do that,' she said, full of emotion, fearing for her family, for the Earth – needing the purples to come, and trying to ignore that stab of fear that they would take Cory away if they did. She thought of all the times Cory had come into her dreams, full of feelings and colour and smells.

'Let's have breakfast.'

Tick tock tick tock.

The children had argued and gone to different rooms. The adults sat in the kitchen, almost too warm now, with a large map in front of them. Selena was in talking waxwork mode, only half there.

'We've spent a lot of time thinking about vanishing,' Gene said. He couldn't stop touching his face, where he had shaved down to a moustache. Their experiments last spring convinced him that it disguised him more than being either clean-shaven or having a beard.

'Option one is Canada,' he said. 'Then anywhere in the world. Our friends can get us across the border without any fuss.'

Selena didn't react. Gene went on, 'Well, we have plenty of Cory supporters in the west . . .'

'Honolulu,' Selena said, smiling at Molly. That brought back memories of so long ago. The sisters' code word for travel and adventure. 'You know so many people. Could we hide in Hawaii?'

Molly could see Gene's mind whirl. He grinned. 'Why not?'

'But it's not a plan,' Molly said. They'd had offers from the

West Coast. Some of the people seemed very loose-lipped. Pierre would not fly them that far.

'Let's just get somewhere safe, just for now,' she said.

Gene gave her a glare. *Don't be difficult.* 'Well, now we're safe to drive, we need to get moving. The weather forecast is trouble.'

Molly nodded. 'If we rendezvous with Pierre, we can review the options.'

'One Molly one vote,' Gene grunted.

Molly gritted her teeth.

Selena drained her coffee. 'The sooner we get out of the state, the better. I've no doubt Mason will be back.'

Gene hated the moustache. Molly thought it was rather dashing. A brief bedroom thought, a touch of joy when the world was so dark. Molly called the message service again, left another message. A few hours without an answer, it didn't mean anything.

CHAPTER 11

Heading east

The sky threatened snow as Gene pulled into a gas station. Despite Selena, they were making fair time. While Molly went to the payphone, Gene stretched his back facing away from the road and the station, hoping Selena and her boys would not take too long in the bathroom. Cory hid and took himself and Meteor behind some bushes for a comfort break.

Up above them hung a big billboard for *Supper Out of This World*. It was a brilliant poster campaign, but it still drove Gene crazy. Sailor's Knot implied the Myers endorsed their tinned tuna, though in reality it was all Madison Avenue flimflam.

Molly caught Selena outside the bathroom; they chatted, just a few sentences, then Molly walked over frowning. 'The kids are fine. I left another message.'

A big 'what if' hung in the air.

Dr Jarman was right, Gene thought. They really should go west. More options if Cory was sick. Pierre could get them to a plane west if not fly them himself.

'Let's keep going,' Molly said. 'I'll take a turn at the wheel and we'll find somewhere the kids can run around for a bit.'

Back in the car, they hit the road again working their way through small towns, stretches of ugly urban sprawl and long stretches of farm and woodland, Selena following. On the back seat, Cory was silent, lost in his own thoughts. The radio burbled.

Soon the road was running alongside the sluggish grey river. A sign said, *Old Watermill Museum*. In the parking lot were two school buses and a car. *Nope*.

A mile further on, the land climbed and a historic bridge of green iron crossed the river, perhaps twenty feet above the water. The water was narrower here and faster. This side of the river, there was a picnic area.

'No one picnicking today,' Molly said, turning into it. Nor was there anyone in sight. A hut for refreshments was shuttered and the bathroom locked behind a metal grille.

'Meteor needs a big bathroom break,' Cory announced – by which he meant that *he* wanted a run as much as the dog.

Gene needed fresh air too, and a walk to unknot his neck and shoulders. As he got out of the car and Molly started fussing Fleur, the wind rustled in the trees. No birds sang.

Gene cast his eyes around the picnic site. They were in clear sight of the road from here; they really shouldn't linger.

Molly is wrong about the West Coast crew, he thought as he took a few steps, putting the walkie talkie in his pocket. But you had to tread carefully to win an argument with her in her dark, unpleasant moods. Right now, Cory's health would be the doubt in her mind.

Cory's waterproof was deliberately two sizes too big, so the hood pretty much hid he was an alien, although those paying attention might wonder at his movements.

'Let's look at the river,' Gene said, and without waiting for an answer, took Cory and Meteor along the path. Frozen mud sometimes cracked underfoot, it was treacherous. There was a shallow route down.

'Gene, don't go too far!' Molly called. She was already deep in some conference with her sister – probably plotting to out-vote him on where they would go. Pierre had a plane, anything was possible.

'Throw sticks in river,' Cory said.

'You're a great swimmer, Cory,' said Gene when they reached the swift river's edge, 'but don't get too close. Keep Meteor away too. If she falls in, it would be real dangerous to rescue her.'

'Cory is not some reckless little kid.'

'It's my job to worry about bad things.'

'Grown-up job on my planet too,' said Cory. 'Sorry, my *other* planet too.'

It was worse when he corrected himself.

There was frozen mud under the thin snow, but they were wearing boots and there were rails by the steps. Cory had his walking stick and from time to time, Gene grabbed hold of branches. It wasn't too bad. Meteor, of course, would be filthy by the end of it – but Meteor sucked up mud like a magnet; she could get dirty running across a dry lawn in summer.

Gene checked his watch. Five minutes by the river, then back.

Time to have the argument.

They heard voices ahead. Emerging back onto the riverside, the path ran under the bridge. Up ahead were four boys, who stopped to look at him. Three teens, not fully grown, and the fourth a kid . . .

The smallest had his hands tied behind him; his face and clothes were smeared with mud. Despite the bitter cold, he wore neither coat nor hat. When he met Gene's eyes, Gene saw he was gagged.

An old memory of terror and humiliation hit Gene: two kids forcing Gene to his knees, stuffing underwear inside his mouth. Old fears and new fury rising inside him, he left caution behind.

'What the hell is going on?' he said in his most adult voice. The three older kids were aged between fourteen and sixteen, all shorter than Gene, and none had the fuller jaws of adult men. Two looked defiant, but the third in a red wool hat showed shame, turning away from Gene's gaze.

'Just a game, mister,' said the tallest, the broadest, the leader.

Part of Gene's mind had to worry about Cory, but he had that odd sensation he sometimes felt, like a silent note, that Cory must have hidden. 'Well, he doesn't want to play anymore. Let him go.' It was an adult order, uncompromising. No 'boys will be boys' here. His most shameful memories were times when he'd let things happen to others. The power of the bully lay in the failure of men who stood by when these things happened.

Yet they had numbers, one was holding a stick, and Gene had Cory to protect.

'Shame if he fell in,' said the leader. His bovine, cruel face stirred more memories.

Yes, thought Gene, *they probably could shove their victim off the bank.*

After all, his hands were tied. Gene could swim, but that would be a tricky rescue, and dangerous for sure. It was a clever, nasty threat.

'You'll go to jail,' Gene said, every ounce the strong adult in charge. 'The most trouble you'll ever have been in.'

Gene was getting through to Red Hat, who was looking shaken.

'Let's leave him, just go,' Red Hat said. 'Sorry, mister, we'll get back.'

'You fag,' said the leader. 'I knew you were a fucking girl.'

The two teens were standing tall – and a fresh anger rose in Gene. He wished he had his own stick to use as a weapon. He moved a few steps towards them.

'You, in the red hat. Help the kid further away from the water and we'll say no more about it. Your friends aren't stupid, they realise they're in big trouble. They'll decide to be smart too.'

Gene saw the bullies' eyes dart behind him, saw one of them mouth a word – and he heard Cory screech – a noise which you knew no human throat could make. *Crack* – there was someone else behind him, and to the right.

'You stupid fuck,' said the head bully.

A splitting pain lanced across the side of Gene's head. He staggered, lost his footing, plunged down onto the ground, all the breath knocked out of him.

Nothing quite made sense. Time slowed as he fell. Gene was sliding, trying to grab something, but his hands only found frozen mud. There was some thorny bush; he caught hold of it and came to a painful, twisted stop.

Somehow, he was wet and close to blacking out.

Cory's power flooded out, all bitter fear and anger . . .

Cory unhid, and Meteor began a furious barking. Cory was so-scared and he felt his power rise in him. Four bullies — although one looked sorry. His beloved Earth-father slid closer to the river. The walkie talkie was in his pocket, so Cory could not even call for help. *Shouting might bring others*, Cory thought — but the Bad Almost Man who threw the big chunk of wood had seen Cory and was coming towards him.

He must control his power. He squatted to grab Meteor, who wanted to bite the youth.

Dad was big and heavy — how would he get him up the slope?

Everyone he loved on the great starship had died. *Everyone.* He had lost his protector, the Ship. He ought to hide Dad and wait for Mom, but Cory felt his power surging, demanding he use it. He hated what it did to humans, but this fright and anger would not let him hide. It would not be stopped.

Cory screamed an order at the humans, then realised it was in the people's language; they would not understand — but he was losing control. He had to warn them, he had to. 'STOP!' he screamed. 'Run-away bad people! Run-away before Cory hurts you!'

'Grab the freak,' the head bully shouted, starting to come forward. The youth closest was more scared of furious Meteor than Cory.

His fear and anger fed the power, and it was stronger than he was. He saw the boy's face twist, and Meteor began to whine.

He wrestled to control it. Cory would only scare the almost-adults — he wouldn't hurt them. They would run away.

A nightmare came and the power took it. In the cold polar seas of his home-world, the second most deadly predator floated, waiting for its prey. A translucent blue thing, spineless and brainless, the size of a table, it dragged behind it a hundred stinging cords which carried a paralysing venom. You could not hide from it, for it had no brain to confuse, and its response to being scared just made it all the more dangerous. It unfurled its webs of death and paralysed you, then it would surround you, summoning others of its sort to digest you. Cory made the venom-web and sent it out into the human minds.

The nearest bully froze, feeling the dream burn his skin with cold, then slow his breathing.

'Jesus Christ!' he gasped, before he began to choke. The stench of urine rose in the air as he fell into a mass of thorns, so Cory focused on the other two, who screamed and skidded away.

The sorry-now teen in the red hat was dragging the little kid to safety.

Threatening a little kid? Nothing like this could happen on his planet.

Cory wanted to stop. Cory wanted to and run and check his Earth Dad was breathing, but his fear now rode him, a useless fear.

The Bad Almost Man who threw the stick was now thrashing in the mud, having a fit like poor Meteor had, the leader was kneeling, his hands to his own throat. The fastest runner was furthest away, he too tripped and fell.

Meteor was whining in fear, and it was only then that Cory

127

realised he must rein back the dream, stop them thinking that their muscles were not working. Cory the Monster might kill them.

Cory fought his power for control.

Selena was smoking and half watching Connor and Rory as they stomped about, when Molly heard the screech from the riverside.

Cory's in danger.

Selena dropped the cigarette, her eyes wide. Molly froze for a second – then thrust Fleur towards her sister. 'Take the baby,' she said.

She could see a car coming up the road from the mill, slow even for this weather.

As she slipped and slithered down to the river, she felt the dreadful, familiar cold of something big and dangerous touch her mind. Cory was using his horrific power.

'Sweetie-pie,' she called out, not daring to use his name, 'Mom's coming!'

Molly fell, a hard fall, and she was muddy now. Getting to her feet, she came face to face with a teen in a red hat, struggling to untie a younger boy.

He looked at her, and said, 'It wasn't me. You with Cory Myers? He tried to help us—'

She pushed past him and there they were: Gene, on hands and knees, and two teens lying flat, stunned or dead, she couldn't tell. Cory, hood back and visible, stood quivering, trying to bring his power under control.

She enfolded her son in her arms, whispering words of love,

and got a strong sense of the thing he was creating: a cold death for a cold day.

Bit by bit, Cory got control, and the thing faded.

There was blood on Gene's hands, his temple. He managed, 'The kids — the kids first.'

She rushed to check the teenagers. Neither was conscious, but one had a strong pulse, almost racing. The other was sluggish and weak. Not much she could do. Stay? Leave? Get help.

A nurse does the job and has the heebie-jeebies later, Molly told herself. Cory was squatting, drained and shaking, his arms around Meteor. She flipped his hood up to hide him, *oh, sweetie-pie*, and went to examine Gene.

'Get away, get away!' Gene muttered, holding a hand to a wound to the forehead. A hefty chunk of wood had blood on it. Molly tried to look at Gene's pupils, but he was fighting his way onto shaky legs.

What had happened? The first boy said Cory had tried to save them.

Selena appeared, with Fleur strapped to her back, walking stick in one hand and a tyre iron in the other. In her wake came Rory, clutching Connor's arm, both scared and open-mouthed.

'What happened?' Selena hissed. 'There's a car — people.'

In her hurry, Molly hadn't brought the first-aid kit. *You fool.* 'Gene, we need to get back to the car.'

'What happened?' her sister said. 'We felt something.'

'Sel, I need your help, to get them up to the car. I might have something for the teens.'

Connor lifted Meteor, inert. Gene put his arm round Molly, and Cory could just about stumble along.

At the top of the track, a man stood, bald, and round-faced, deeply worried. He was wearing big square glasses, slipping out of fashion, square glasses for a square guy.

'What happened?' he asked.

'My husband fell. There are a couple of sick teens – I think the kids had some sort of fit,' Molly improvised. *Both at once? You need something better.*

'Maybe they use drugs?' she suggested. After all, half the country was frightened of what the other half was taking.

Selena was staring at Cory.

The man blinked. 'I'm Hamish Van-Buren-like-the-President – I'm running a school trip. We're missing some boys – they must have snuck away. Have you seen any others?'

'I'm not sure. My husband's had a bad fall. You should go check on the two back there.'

Connor put Meteor down and both Selena's kids moved away, staring at Cory. The teacher stared too. Cory's face was buried in the dog's flank; he might just pass for human if he didn't look up or speak.

'This all feels wrong,' the man said. Molly saw red hat and the younger kids, over closer to the road. Witnesses. Waving at the school bus.

'I've got to get a first-aid kit,' Molly said, walking Gene past the man. There was another woman by an unknown car.

'So these kids are sick or hurt . . . your husband is hurt . . . what happened?' said Van Buren.

Molly took a breath. He was asking reasonable questions. 'I told you.'

The man gasped. 'Where's your son gone? He's vanished. The dog too – they were right there.'

Frightened, Cory must have hidden; she hadn't noticed.

'You need to go get your kids.' What if they were getting worse?

They had to leave. Molly got Gene into the car, where he sat like a cartoon drunk. She sensed Cory was near, in the car. She put Fleur in her travelling seat. Selena was at the door of her car, talking to her kids inside it . . . then she looked up and stared.

'Where's your son gone?' the man said. 'What's going on?'

'I don't know what you're talking about.'

'I saw who he is,' the man said, almost a whisper. 'I saw.'

'We'll call for an ambulance . . .'

'We can drive the kids to the hospital quicker than the ambulance will come. Was there a fight? They weren't exactly angels.'

Molly looked up and saw Selena coming towards her, looking frightened and angry. 'We have to go, Sel.'

'Not unless you explain *that*,' Selena snapped. 'My kids played with it.'

Now Molly had a new terror: there were a hundred things her sister might say, none of them helpful.

'Sel, come on, I'll explain. It's not like you think.'

Selena was in full flow now. 'They kept telling me – they got these odd feelings. Maybe Mason was right. Maybe he is *dangerous*.'

It was like watching a car crash. Her sister was about to betray her. She had to be brutal. 'You know you see things,' Molly said. 'You need to take your medication.'

'What happened to those boys, Molly?'

Van Buren was watching this exchange. 'Mrs Myers, did Cory hurt them? Everyone says he's such a gentle child.'

Molly couldn't see how to win him over, she couldn't help the bullies, and she needed to go.

'My husband needs medical attention,' Molly said, shutting the rear door. Van Buren was looking at their licence plate. Gene was struggling with the seatbelt.

Selena just needed to get behind the wheel and follow Molly to safety – but instead, she stood by Molly as she got into the driver's seat.

Selena gripped her by the arm. 'I trusted you,' her sister said, tears in her eyes.

'Follow us, if you have any sense.'

'You need to stay,' Van Buren said to Molly.

Molly revved the engine. 'Stand back, Sel.' She looked for the safest way out of the parking lot. She remembered the thugs Cory had struck down, all those months ago, the soldiers by the lake when the Myers had been captured. Some people were still suffering, all these months afterwards.

Tears prickled in her eyes as she gunned the engine. Sounding the horn, and making it clear she was not going to stop, she forced the car forward. Van Buren and Selena got out of her way and, with the engine still roaring, she headed for the turning. Out on the open road, she drove as fast as she dared, trying to remember the map in her head, glancing in the mirror from time to time to see if Selena was following. She was not.

Cory unhid and wailed, an alien sound that was just how she

felt: scared and angry and frightened, and deep in the biggest mess imaginable.

Meteor whimpered, Fleur mewed a little and Gene groaned.

How long before there was a story on the wires? Molly wondered, *with police cars looking for them? How long before people wondered about the silence from the Ship?*

CHAPTER 12

Boston, that afternoon

Dr Pfeiffer glared at the principal, and she looked back across the desk as if he was something she had trodden on.

Pfeiffer's wife had insisted that she do the talking and he was close to boiling over, but he had promised Rachael not to be tactless.

'Our girls must have been provoked.' Rachael was trying to keep her tone polite, but there were red spots on her cheeks. She might be about to do the unheard-of thing and lose her temper in public.

'I'm afraid that although we teach our pupils how to behave, we can't stop them having opinions. Dr Pfeiffer, you are a public figure, and a controversial one.'

'Your pupils need to read the newspapers with more care,' Rachael said.

Pfeiffer held one of his hands with the other, and squeezed it, an old trick to stop him lifting the jabbing spear of his accusing finger and launching into an attack. This woman was daring to look down on him. He had wanted to threaten the school lawyers, call the last of his friends in high places, but Rachael had given a firm no to that. This was for them to sort out.

The principal adopted a smug, self-satisfied smile. 'I accept your daughters were provoked, and you may rest assured that all those involved will be punished. However, the first to use force must be punished more. The suspension stands. Of course,' she added smoothly, 'you always have the option to move the children, if you find us unsatisfactory.'

'They are extremely bright girls and if their attention has slipped, it is because they are being bullied,' Rachael said, her voice just a little higher-pitched.

His wife had lost her temper perhaps four times in her life, and he knew she was close to it now.

'Excuses are easy,' the principal said. 'All things being equal, I think we should leave it there.'

They rose in icy politeness, and left.

'I'll take the girls to my mother's,' said Rachael. 'We'll probably stay the night.'

'Thank you. They'll like that.' His girls had stood up for him against their classmates. For most people, Dr Pfeiffer was the cold-blooded creature who had imprisoned the Myers, and who had somehow escaped justice. When the slanders reached into the schoolroom, his daughters had fought back. He felt rage and embarrassment at his lack of power. They might have to change school, but you never knew if it would solve the problems.

'You could come too,' she said, and he was tempted. His mother-in-law still thought he was a great man, a good choice for her daughter.

'I'm sorry,' he said with regret, 'but I do have to work. Perhaps tomorrow.'

He had disappointed her; he could see it on her face. 'You know, Emmanuel, you really do pick the wrong fights. You could just avoid arguments and concentrate on your research – your *real* work. Those insights on the immune system are so enormously promising.'

Pfeiffer wasn't sure. What if Cory's people came? What if he saw that great encounter only from the sidelines, as a third-choice pick for the chat shows? The *Post* had called him a 'former scientist' last week. *Him!* His work for Overton might produce powerful, plentiful drugs against some of the world's deadliest killers, five, ten years down the line; that would silence those who said he had abandoned science for power. But would it be enough?

Rachael was troubled. He had married the brightest and best of his female students, and she had brought him happiness, a joy that was more than just intellect. Age and motherhood might show on her face now, but she was still a beautiful woman.

He kissed her. 'I will try to set the girls an example.'

'It's not for me to tell you what to do.'

That's what she said on the rare occasions when she told him what to do, and he knew he should heed her.

'Tell the girls I owe them a treat, very soon.'

Pfeiffer came home as it grew dark. The maid was at the dentist, so Pfeiffer was alone in the brownstone, dealing with correspondence and the proofs of his latest article. The air was filled with Schubert, Mendelssohn, Mahler.

It was well into the evening. The phone rang, and as he

answered it, the tape machine whirred into action; he wasn't
having the police denying he had been threatened anymore.

'Yes?'

The man asked to speak to room 231.

Pfeiffer replied, 'I'm sorry, this is a private residence.'

The man apologised crisply and rang off.

It was his last source in the Administration, a simple code:
very urgent, call within half an hour if you can. Phone number
two.

Pfeiffer threw on coat, hat, boots and went into the night.
Winter was cold and dreary and that was the reality of it. Calls
from his source were never social, never trivial. It might be
good news, or bad.

Loyal friends of Rachael's lived a few doors down. Impressed
that they knew someone important enough to be bugged, they
had given Pfeiffer a key to the basement apartment, with its
own phone line, for occasions just like this. As soon as he had
let himself in, he called his source.

'Have you heard the news?' the source asked.

'I've been working.'

'There's been an incident with the boy. It's crazy here, like
someone set fire to the place. The Ship's been silent for days.
It's not responding to messages.'

That was hardly unusual; the Ship could and did ignore
humans for weeks on end. 'Get to the point. What about Cory?
Is he hurt?'

'Local police say he attacked a couple of teens. Or they
attacked him. They're sick — you know, the mind stuff.'

Pfeiffer felt his stomach roil at the thought of Cory in danger.

Cory's powers revealed to an ignorant world – oh, the President would surely grab the Myers . . .

'The Ship would be all over that—?'

'There's no reaction – nothing at all. We kept asking if it had checked out the *Mariner* fiasco, but it didn't even reply. Now this fight with Cory—'

'Is he all right? The Myers?'

'Well, they were away before the local police arrived this morning. We only found out an hour before the press got onto it.'

Pfeiffer groaned. The boy was in danger, his whereabouts unknown . . .

But his contact was still speaking. 'So now the FBI are in charge, and everyone is shouting at everyone else to put the milk back in the bottle.'

'What about the Ship?'

'Well, that's the strange thing about this fight: there've been no sightings of any drones, or the Ship. And the Russians have lost two Mars probes too. We heard that . . . *very* unofficially – so the Secretary of Defense decided to poke the Ship.'

When the Administration wanted a response – to see if the Ship was still there, for example – they flew a helicopter or light aircraft into Amber County. The Ship always responded to that, fast and angry, warning the plane, local air traffic control and the Administration that any aircraft over Amber Grove better turn away or it might be destroyed.

'They flew a plane right over Crooked Street, there and back – there was a recorded warning in English. But nothing from the Ship.'

There are two possible explanations, Pfeiffer thought. *Either the Ship is damaged, or it is out of range. And either is a disaster.* Pfeiffer felt his stomach churn. *The boy must be kept safe – and we cannot lose the Ship's vigilance against the snakes.*

And yet . . . perhaps this was a door opening?

'We've closed local airspace, claiming we're a plane down. They're hinting it was one of the Ship's drones. And they're reaching out to the Myers and their friends to offer them protection.'

'Public opinion may turn against them, if the world knows what the boy can do. This is all very dangerous.'

'The Administration understands this is important. They'll put up with noise if they have the boy.'

Pfeiffer asked more questions, all the while scrawling notes on his pad:

Call the Myers, offer help.
Call Rachael, warn her I might be away.
Call the Six.

As soon as his source hung up, Pfeiffer called the Myers and left a message. Then he had an urgent decision to make: should he alert all the Six, or talk to his ally Overton first? It took only moments to decide: *Overton.* Day or night, one of his staff would answer, and they would wake Overton if needed.

Overton, the great philanthropist, was such a different animal from the others. They had dined alone in his New York mansion three times, the last only a week ago. Overton spoke often about the meeting of civilisations, and how the knowledge the aliens would bring should be used to relieve suffering. He came alive talking about the science labs and student scholarships and libraries he had funded in the South.

The others invited Pfeiffer to dinner for power or money or information, but Overton wanted to know what kind of man Pfeiffer was. Now, when Pfeiffer called and explained the situation, his voice was brisk and alert.

'Very grave,' said Overton. 'The Administration assume the Myers will make other plans. The President is such a curious soul: half giant, half pygmy. And, of course, they will only be one of many after the Myers. Which is why you and I have a different plan.'

'We have discussed this in principle,' Pfeiffer said, suddenly very cautious. His mouth was going dry.

'I must commend you, Dr Pfeiffer. Your plans for the sanctuary we made for the Six were meticulous. So, I prepared another one: all the laboratories and precautions you could desire, expert staff standing by. Neither the world nor the Six will ever find it. The future of mankind requires us to take command. We will offer the Myers the hand of friendship. Markham and the others, we don't need them.'

'We go it alone?'

Markham was the self-appointed leader, a man who thought the President weak. The other four were cut from the same cloth: men who expected to get their own way. Men who would not appreciate betrayal over Cory, the great prize.

'Of course, we will play along, feed them misinformation and when the time comes, I will sweep them out of the way. That will be my job, Dr Pfeiffer, you may leave that to me.

You will keep the boy and his family well. But this is no time for faint hearts. Are you with me, Emmanuel? Are we brothers in this noble cause?'

It felt like a long pause, as if he were waiting on the school diving board while other children were laughing at his cowardice, his flabby body.

Pfeiffer took a breath, gripped his courage and jumped.

'Yes, of course.'

CHAPTER 13

Choosing a sanctuary

Molly had to stop the car, to feed the baby, to check Gene again. She pulled up a side track and hoped no one would want to use it. Gene was woozy, but his pupils reacted fine to the flashlight. He could tell four fingers from two. You heard these awful stories of someone getting a blow to the head and walking off, perfectly normally, and dying from a brain bleed a few hours later. Pierre needed to get them somewhere where Gene could get an X-ray — but somewhere they would not be in danger.

She hid the bandage as best as she could and helped him change his blood-smeared coat. He winced as he moved.

Cory and the dog dozed, and that was probably good. Molly didn't have the full story and what anyone else might know. Fleur was unsettled but got to work at the breast. And it was then Molly gave in and cried, sobbing for ten minutes or more.

It all felt so hopeless, but she needed to keep going. She needed to try Pierre again, get a message to her friends. Change the licence plates and dig out the false papers. Once they had fled into the night, smeared as spies. Now they would call her son a monster, an attacker of children.

Everyone knew what they looked like. Everyone would be after them.

She dried her eyes; she must look a sight . . .

'What's the plan?' Gene said, slow but making sense. He leaned over, cussing as he moved, and gave her a hug.

'Next phone, I'll try Pierre again.'

'I missed . . . what happened to Big Sis?'

'She stayed behind,' Molly said, feeling a new lurch of fear. *Had Selena heard anything about their escape plan?* 'Heaven knows what she'll say.'

'We gotta find a hole and hide,' Gene said. 'I sure hope she gets away. And keeps her mouth shut.'

Molly checked her own clothes for blood and changed the plates, refusing Gene's offer of help.

Twenty minutes further down the road, a one-street settlement with a phone booth. If it wasn't for smoking chimneys, the place could have been dead. She got out of the car, notebook in hand . . . it was cold . . . dialled the number, and to her relief, a familiar voice answered on the fourth ring.

'*Allo?*'

'Pierre, it's Molly.'

A car passed; for a moment she thought it was Van Buren . . . She was seeing enemies in every passer-by.

'No, this is Anton.' His cousin, also part of the network. 'Pierre is heading south. I can radio him. What's up?'

She gave the shortest possible summary.

'*Merde.* Where are you, exactly?'

She talked, looking back to see if anyone had stopped or was looking.

Molly called three other numbers, left messages. The telephone tree would be activated, her friends and her family would have some warning of this disaster.

How cold she felt, how defeated by it. They had a long way to travel. She got back into the car, where Gene gazed at Fleur. He held the baby upright, which she seemed to like.

'Little Boo just gave me the coolest smile. She's going to break hearts.'

'How's the head?'

'Like a truck fell on it.'

'Pierre is coming. We just need to get to the rendezvous, then make plans.'

'No chance of going west?'

She wanted to find the deepest hole she could, with people she trusted. Who knew how long they would have to get away?

Molly started the car. 'Let's get to the rendezvous.'

Winter sun broke through over the deserted showground, the acres of land used for parking. Molly parked out of sight of the access road. The scatter of snow could not hide the fly-tip here, as high as her chin. A broken-down car, tyres, bottles, mattresses. Signs of a fire. Humans were filthy.

They stayed in the car to keep warm and Gene ebbed in and out of wakefulness. Molly peered at her watch. She thought for the first time, soon she might need glasses. Like her mother.

Winter made this a desolate place. Tattered posters talked of a motorbike exhibition, the Fall Fair. Different hands had sprayed on a fence. *JESUS SAVES. END THE WAR. SC loves SJ*, whoever they were. Graffiti was ugly. It was an eerie place where once was light and noise and fireworks and cotton candy.

It felt like a cold hand on her heart. She gasped, what unearthly danger was this.

Hoo hoo hoo. A yelp from the dog. Then she realised Cory was climbing through to sit on her lap, and his fear and misery filled the car.

He'd grown since he first came to Earth, but they found a way for him to cuddle her.

'Cory hurt those almost-men. Those teens. I hurt them. They're going to die yes-they-are.'

'They won't,' she said. Cory just spoke aloud her fear, because . . . because she knew from the thugs, from the soldiers by the lake . . . Cory's power had come close to killing before.

'The doctors will check them out. They'll be fine.'

'C-c-cory is a MONSTER.'

'We're all monsters some of the time. People will understand . . . you were trying to help.'

'Mom is just saying that.'

It was the strangest thing imaginable . . . how many people had taken to the Myers as symbols . . . of hope, of change, or American can-do. People said the free, loving spirit that had arisen in the Sixties had been dying. They said, Cory had given hope wings again.

'Pierre's coming – remember Pierre? – and he's going to take us somewhere safe. We need to check Dad's head.'

'Will Chuck and Bonnie and VJ and all the others come now?'

146

'Maybe later. Other children stay there sometimes. No promises.'

A big truck drove into the fairground, it flashed its headlights at them and came closer. The driver jumped down from the cab – short, burly, and she recognised the way he moved. Pierre dressed like a lumberjack and knew planes, boats and anything on wheels.

Molly got out of the car, she could have hugged him with relief, but she didn't know him that well. He stank of coarse tobacco.

'We need to move,' Pierre said. 'We haven't heard anything on the radio, but surely soon – the cops, the Feds, the press. So, where do you want to go?'

'Halcyon, for now.' The strange old house on the Maine coast, where Disappearance Inc had begun.

Pierre produced two metal ramps, and Molly drove the Chrysler into the truck, an anxious, awkward manoeuvre. Molly recoiled from the smell of smoke. No choice but for them all to clamber into the cab, which had a little sleeping area. Two bunks, but too short for Gene lying down and too narrow for him curled up. Cory and the dog took one, and Molly would ride up front.

They had left the state when the first story broke. 'We are hearing reports of an incident involving the Myers family. It appears Gene Myers and two local teenagers were injured. The situation appears very confused, with some witnesses saying Cory Myers was attacked.'

People saw the Myers as they wanted. Who would be more dangerous, those whose hopes had been dashed – or those who had from the beginning seen him as ugly and sinister?

Everyone knew what they looked like. Everyone would be after them.

It was dark and snow speckled the windscreen as they entered Maine. The cabin was stifling hot, the smoke had given her a cough, and Pierre kept talking in fast French into one radio.

The founders of Disappearance Inc, Val and Lloyd, had been so reassuring and felt so trustworthy. But Pierre said they'd been on a lifetime cruise in the Caribbean and this week Lloyd fell ill.

Pierre drove, stifling a yawn. Snow fell into a grey sea. The long curve of Mourning Gull Bay, Halcyon at the south tip, the town at the foot of a green mountain at the north end. The house was set back from the road and well above it, more run down than she had thought, and those odd turrets.

Molly had been wooed by the idea of Halcyon. They'd been shown pictures of an arty summer group dining al fresco, lit with lanterns, boats on a gentle blue ocean. Grim, cold, this felt very different. No other guests, no welcoming hosts.

Pierre backed the truck into the courtyard. She was dog tired and didn't fancy getting the car out of the truck. Here came a vast bearded giant of a man, who must be Joel the handyman.

'Rooms warming. There's food.'

'Bed first, I think.'

Meteor was subdued, Cory sleepy still . . . how his power drained him. Molly carried Fleur into a warm cluttered hallway which overwhelmed the senses. Bright ceramic plates – a narwhal tusk, ships in bottles – seascape paintings and clocks and barometers. Gene followed, Cory over his shoulder. 'I can manage, I can manage.'

Even Meteor, who loved sniffing round new places, was subdued. Joel called, 'Up the stairs, second right.'

A pleasant room with two beds and a crib. Some curious paintings, their meanings not obvious to a tired glance. Even here, all her fears gathered to berate her. But it was a fresh-made bed and it called to her. A sleep, a bath, and fresh clothes and she would feel better.

Gene settled sleepy Cory under a blanket. Then Gene glared at her, red-eyed and angry.

'It's a catastrophe,' Gene said. 'Your sister's fault, slowing us up. We'd have been an hour or two ahead. None of this would have happened.'

'Don't be like that.' Not now, not this.

'I said she would slow us up. Then she turned on us. Right now she'll be talking to the Feds. Did you tell her where this place is?'

Sel might talk. What would she say? Molly feared they had mentioned Maine, the coast.

'Maybe we should have told her about Cory's power.' Molly didn't want the argument. She felt so betrayed by Selena – why didn't he understand how she felt?

'We should have left her behind. I should have insisted, we should have gone to Canada, and then headed west.'

Molly was close to snapping. 'You agreed. To her coming, to Halcyon, to everything. You didn't have to wander off, and get into danger, like a stupid ten-year-old.'

'You just like your own way.'

'Picking a fight. How's that keeping a low profile?'

'The kid might have drowned.'

Molly grabbed her bag, said, 'Time for you to be the adult,' and walked out. She was sobbing, rage and fear alike. In the bathroom, she locked the door, and jammed a chair under the handle.

Everything had gone wrong.

CHAPTER 14

Halcyon, the next day

Cory was working on his eulogy for the Ship in Molly's room, while Meteor recovered from her bath in front of the radiator. The Ship had been a person, if a strange one. It changed its mind, it had a temper and a sense of humour. It seemed a little odd to Molly that the purples did not see their thinking machines as people; they had no rituals to mourn them. Cory wanted to anyway and Molly told him he could. She hoped it would help her sad, lonely little boy.

Molly tried to read a book. Gene had gone for a walk without asking her, so now she was worried he would be seen. Their descriptions would be everywhere. Joel hollered, it was Carol Longman on the phone and Molly went downstairs.

Joel had been called up, he had faced the tribunal, and they denied his right of conscientious objection. He had walked to Halcyon four summers ago and he had worked there ever since.

'Carol? Are you at the office?'

151

For security, no one was supposed to phone Halcyon from any phone they used regularly.

'No, of course not. Have you seen the news?' From the voice, it wasn't good.

'We're having a news-free day.'

'Abe Kaplan's done it. He's scooped everyone with the army story.'

Molly felt hollow. Could things be any worse?

'Headline: Cory Myers Put Soldiers in Hospital. Administration Lied. Kaplan's stood everything up, when the Army attacked us, the long-term damage for two of the soldiers, the cover-up. He's got quotes from the families. And he's done a long story on those thugs too, and how they just vanished into the prison system. He has a source in the Mob. Dr Jarman and Sheriff Olsen are in the firing line for holding one of the thugs so long on the Psych ward.'

Molly couldn't say a word.

Carol said, 'I guess a couple of his contacts went on the record after . . . you know, the bridge incident. Kaplan's mostly after the Administration.'

'I guess it was always going to come out,' Molly said, numbed at the thought of how bad it was. This was just gas on the flames.

'It's hell here. Everyone is saying the government hid the truth, *Witness* hid it – that I lied. I'll never win a Pulitzer, not the way people are going for me. My editor won't even let me defend myself. He says other people need to write our rebuttal.'

'We're not doing an interview,' Molly said firmly, upset that Carol hadn't asked how they were doing. 'Cory's distraught – we all are. It's a disaster.'

Carol's tone changed. 'Here's me talking about my problems. Well, I'm coming down with Storm and we'd love to see the little fellow. You might like the company. Of course, no interview yet.'

'We'd like to see you,' Molly said. Gene might talk to Storm. 'Although it's not a good time.'

'Tell me the facts. Oh, Dahlia Diamond called me. She has the mother of the boy Cory defended going on her show tonight. Dahlia wants to make sure you watch it. She's fishing for an interview, of course.'

Dahlia Diamond was a real force of nature. 'She can't have an interview either. I've got to go. Love to Storm.'

Molly hung up and tried to find a dry tissue. On her way back upstairs, she heard the bedroom door close.

She opened it and said, 'Cory Myers, listening to private conversations again.'

'It was about me and not good,' Cory said. 'What is it?'

She told him, as gently as she could. He wailed, and she felt his huge sorrow.

The armchair was big enough for Molly to hold a sad and lonely Cory, who huddled into her.

'No children here, no one to play with,' Cory said wistfully. He depended on company.

'You have Meteor and the cats to play with. And Carol and Storm are coming.' That got a twitch of a reaction. 'And Joel gives great piggybacks.'

'No one will like me anymore, not even Bonnie, or Chuck or Zack or Simon or VJ.'

Cory's sorrow filled the room and Molly felt like she could drown in it.

'Of course your friends still love you. They know the truth.'
She cuddled him, trying to work out what to say. 'People will
calm down,' she said. 'People will think it through. The little
boy's mother is defending you.'

'That is a very good thing.'

Molly felt drained, like she could wrap herself in a quilt and
sleep for a week. Even disturbed sleep was better than this. But
Cory needed her. *Keep him busy*, she told herself, *give him other
things to think about*.

'When will my people come?' he wailed. 'Then they can take
everyone nice in Crooked Street and John and Eva to home-
world and my people can fix John's heart and Eva's lungs. And
defend the Earth.'

'Well, when they come, things will be better.'

I will not give you up.

'Mom, you will come to my home-world? You do *want* to
come?'

How difficult it is to lie to a beloved child.

She equivocated. 'It would be a big adventure, but right now,
my head is too full to think.'

Cory turned his face up to her, his big violet eyes filling her
with his grief. 'So truly Mom doesn't want to go. Mom wants
to leave me – because I am *monster*—'

He howled, and she held him tighter.

'Oh Cory, but this is the truth: I want to be with you and
be your mom. That's what matters. When your people come,
we'll do the best we can.'

How could she argue they were his best family if humanity
rejected him?

'Will only Dad come?'

'She kissed her son rather than answer and his smell brought back so many good times, even when they were hidden from the world. They had been so fearful, starting at shadows, lying to friends; few days passed without lies and anxiety and false alarms. And yet now it felt like life had been simpler then.

'Cory needs you *both*.'

Molly knew that, and Gene knew that too. They'd thrown those words back and forth, over the divide: *the kids need both of us*.

It was true.

The next day, it snowed. Storm and Carol had made slow progress; they'd broken their journey overnight and finally arrived mid-morning. Gene helped Storm get bags and a load of box files out of the Jeep.

'Notes for the book,' Carol said, handing him the typewriter.

Gene, Storm and Cory had disappeared to run the dog or chop wood or something, while Molly made coffee in that big kitchen. The journalist was at her most tactful, keen to get a consistent story. Gene had written notes, even a sketch map, and Cory agreed it. Molly passed all this on.

Carol flipped back through the notes. 'This fits with what the little kid and his mother said to Dahlia.'

'I can barely talk about this to you, let alone the world.' Molly stirred her cup.

'It must be unbearable.'

'What's going to happen?'

'Congressional hearings. The police, of course. There's a

155

rumour the teen's family will sue. The Administration – who knows?'

Carol was soon pounding away at her faithful typewriter, filling the room with its clatter.

Molly was left looking at a rip in Gene's pants, thinking he could sew up his own damn clothes if he went on being like this.

She turned on the radio to hear, 'The latest development in the Myers case is an intervention by Governor Wallace. Speaking on a campaign tour of the western states, Governor Wallace led his remarks with a comment on the story.'

The voice was familiar. 'I have long warned you that those crooks in the Administration were lying about the Myers. I always said the purples might be dangerous. If one boy can cause this much harm, what will a giant fleet of their starships do? The Myers lied, the liberal media hid the truth and even now they are trying to play all this down. Your President lied to you. Things will be very different when there's a decent man in the White House. We should reopen Alcatraz, just for the Myers.'

Molly felt the world closing in. So much of the country was angry and disillusioned. Surely all these frightened, disappointed people would not turn to Wallace?

Gene had no encouragement to offer, no reassurance – just silence and distance, now that they were sleeping apart. The music he played was loud and angry, or so gloomy that it dragged her deeper into sadness. Each day he withdrew a little more. He took to going off on long solitary walks among the pines, brushing off her concerns. What if he fell, or was caught?

It was Gene's job to be strong when she was not, Gene's job to help her – and yet it seemed he had nothing to give.

The Russians wanted to put nuclear weapons in space, to defend the Earth. A hard-fought peace treaty would have to be revised. The President was being attacked from left and right. He would meet the Russian leader; he had a plan. The world was losing its mind.

That night was the first of the burnings. The TV cameras showed a churchy crowd with their children, throwing Cory masks, the comics, the clothes into a blazing fire, faces twisted in hate, while some prim woman was spouting lies.

The next day, Storm and Carol played *Tiles* with Cory, using the alien board game to keep him occupied. Molly was out of sorts with Carol, who'd suggested she speak to Dr O'Brien, the Disappearance Inc doctor.

Carol had been almost pushy. 'All this, and the baby too . . . it can't do any harm.'

'I can manage,' Molly snapped. Fleur was a bright spot, not a burden, even though sometimes when she picked her up, she felt drained of hope. O'Brien and his wife were true believers in Cory. Carol was a friend and meant well, but what gave her the idea she needed to talk to a doctor?

Gene had not spoken to her since 6 a.m., when he'd asked where Fleur's ointment had got to. She thought she should make the effort and went looking for him, finally coming across him on a window-seat in a sea-facing room. A few old books sat on the table. The room was chilly and he was wearing his heavy coat. The frowning weather matched his face.

'The truth is out there,' he said to the window. 'Cory was

trying to save lives, but people don't care. They just swallow what they're told.'

'Some people care,' Molly said, running her hands through his hair. At least he didn't brush her aside. The Myers' refusal to return and face the authorities was putting their allies in real difficulty. Flight meant guilt.

In private, via Dr Jarman's father-in-law, the Administration had offered options aplenty: clever, unscrupulous, two-faced options that all came down to trusting the President's word. They would recognise Cory as an Ambassador, they said, and hide him behind diplomatic immunity.

'Humanity sure doesn't deserve him,' Gene said. 'Even the snakes can make governments work together. When the machines come, they'll rip us apart.'

Molly couldn't think of an answer. He might explode or stop talking altogether.

'The purples are coming,' she said, as if saying so would make it true.

He sighed, and she picked up the books he'd been reading: one was about an Arctic explorer, and others covered nineteenth-century expeditions in the Pacific. 'Any good?'

'Yeah, kinda.' He sat up a little, with a touch of energy. 'You know, these men who went out there, left their wives back home. I bet it was rough.' He tapped the explorer's book. 'Yet this guy had six kids – he sent his kids letters while he was on his travels. They had a good marriage.'

'Did they ask the women? In those days, the wife just had to take it.'

'They've printed a couple of her letters – they're wonderful, you can really hear her voice. Of course, it was rough.'

He took her hands. His were so cold; he must have been here for ages.

'And sometimes people came to the New World and brought their kids over when they were settled. So, one of us could go with Cory – not for ever, just to settle him in. He's a child of Earth too, so a link home might be useful. The whole world would benefit.' Gene hesitated before he carried on, 'Walking under other stars – smelling other winds. We'd be able to let humanity know what it's like out there. Governments sent pilots barely able to string sentences together into space. They should have sent poets and musicians. I could do the world a favour, going with them.'

There was nothing Molly could say. She just stayed silent.

'You won't go, and you don't want me to.' At least it was gently said.

Molly whispered, 'The purples will like somewhere warm, with water. I think humanity could find the purples a nice island. They could have a proper base, a settlement. They could bring their children. Or one of their cities in space. There would be no need for Cory to go.'

The silence grew between them.

'Imagine Fleur growing up with no father,' she said at last. 'I think John and Eva are putting on a brave face about John's health. He's getting worse, and Eva too.'

Gene's face tensed and she squeezed his hand.

'Dad wouldn't want us chained to the bedside. And besides, the purples will cure him in five minutes when they come.'

159

'Or they won't.' She gazed at his face for some sign of change, some sign she was getting through.

He turned away. 'I knew you'd say no. The spring after you lost the baby, I was wrong to take no for an answer then. Travelling would have helped me, for sure – helped both of us.'

I lost the baby? Molly thought. A wave of sadness and anger swelled. We *lost her.* She should have lashed out at that, told him the truth – that when you travel, you take your misery with you – but, instead of anger, tears came at the casual way he had brought the death up – the way he was rewriting history.

'The purples will take Cory,' he said. 'So it's a clear choice: we go with them, or we lose him. Why would they hang around?'

The purples will find a world divided, Molly thought, *and the louder half will be hating her little boy*. How could a couple divided fight against that? When had Gene become so hard and selfish?

Molly got up, mumbled some excuse, and left him.

In the sitting room, Carol had two papers to show her: the local, and the *New York Times*.

'No,' Molly said, 'it's all lies. I don't care.'

Carol sighed, just a little. 'People are calling in sightings of Cory.'

'Yes, that happens . . .'

'It's on purpose,' Carol said, 'to slow the police up: hundreds of thousands of people, all over the country, every day. The FBI are tearing their hair out. The student radio station in Portland has been closed down. That's happened in other places too – because they keep giving out the numbers on air.'

Molly dared to take the newspaper and read it. There was something called 'The People's Committee to Defend Cory Myers' – already claiming 'State spokesmen' in twenty-nine states. Strange times. For a moment it lifted her spirits. There was hope, here – hope in the idea that people were protecting Cory for who he was, for what he stood for just by being him.

Then she turned the page, read about those who envied and admired Cory for his power and wanted it for themselves. Those who wanted that power used against the country's enemies. Those who thought what happened by the river was funny. . .

And a cold hand gripped her heart.

CHAPTER 15

Dealing with humans, December

In the high tower room, Cory was dancing to the radio, lost in the music. *Leap and swirl, stomp and jump,* the sort of dance you could not do near the gramophone. Singing without words.

'I'm not like anybody else.'

Meteor was trying to dance too, following him around the room.

Faithful Meteor.

He danced so he did not have to think, so that he was simply an instrument played by the music. But the programme ended, and then it was just humans talking. *Talk, talk talk.* He turned it off and tried holding back the fear.

Look at the view, he told himself. He sat by the rattling window and Meteor came and pushed his way on to the seat next to him. The ocean at Mourning Gull Bay was very fine, with big sea waves driven by cold winds crashing onto the shore. He remembered the storms on his own planet, and the warm rain lashing warm oceans. Even the salt of the ocean tasted

163

different. But Cory must not think about his home-world for sixteen of minutes.

Humans called it the Glad Game.

Snow was good, and Christmas was coming, and the cats liked him. Most cats didn't. It was strange to have a house so big with so few people in it.

Further round the bay was the harbour, where the houses huddled low against the wind. There was an island, with its green mountain he wanted to climb. Little human water ships. He imagined the bay in spring or summer, all the sails dancing in the warm breeze. Cory liked the angry sea and the strange sandy beaches and the grim grey rocks looked very fine to scramble up. He liked the hardy trees that stayed green in winter, whose needles smelled of Christmas in his hands. Those trees were often hard to climb. On Earth, some animals hid in sleep from the cold; he could feel their lives so tiny and slow, like suspended animation. He wondered sometimes about the poor dead Ship's offer, how it would have felt to sleep, hidden in some crevice of the Moon. And there were still seabirds who had not fled south for winter, herring gulls with their raucous calls. He had yet to see a Mourning gull.

How he mourned the Ship, which had been his guardian, teacher and companion, now gone. The Network in the sky which should warn of alien attack did not reply to him. Everyone wanted to know whether there were snakes out there, how they could be detected. But Cory didn't know.

His communicator held personal memories but it had lost its English and couldn't call another device. Out there were mobs of angry humans, searching for him. And his Earth Mom and his Earth Dad dreamed of darkness and danger and loss; he found little consolation there. When he listened to the bitter-sweet recording of his first mother's voice, it just reminded him that the snakes had won.

His people had not come, even in his dreams. The together-dream, that little flicker of light, was not to be found, though he sought it every night. But as the weeks passed, he believed that the starship the dreamers were on was getting closer. He refused to believe it was the sadness and his imagination seeking hope. That voice had to be ignored.

Be here, Cory. Enjoy here. Play the Glad Game and the bad things would hurt a little less. He missed his friends so much.

The post had come and that was very fine. His friends wrote twice a week, Bonnie sending long letters full of indignation, and the names of all the people in town who believed him, and Chuck shorter ones. They sent comics too. The Robertson teens had a wild sense of humour which made Mom make a sour face, and their dog Isaac wrote to Meteor – funny letters with little drawings explaining life from the dog's viewpoint. Cory and Mom replied on Meteor's behalf; they were fun letters to write. Eva always wrote to Cory, and John scrawled lines on the end.

He wanted them all here.

Fleur was good; she was trying to pick her head off the ground like the babies of his home-world. Cory thought Fleur recognised him now. He would hold her and sing her the songs the big children sing to the little ones, and tell her stories she was too young to understand. It was sad for Fleur to have only one brother in the lodge, so he must be all the children for her.

How sweet Fleur's dreams tasted, like soft little sketches of light: a world of feeding and warmth and Mom. No stories, though; she was not yet the pilot of her dream.

Sometimes Dad and Cory camped up here in the high room together, with the heater glowing and quilts piled over the zipped-together sleeping bags. Meteor had her own special blanket. Mom didn't come; she slept with Fleur in their bedroom. She never said so, but Cory knew she was worried in case his bad dreams hurt his sister. That made Cory very sad, almost ill-and-sad, because babies need to be given other dreams to grow. But he knew that not all his dreams were healthy.

The snakes had won again.

The Glad Game stopped working and here came the fear and the cold, rushing in like a raging sea, and Cory was not strong enough to hold it back. Meteor whined and retreated to the door.

The bell went *clong-clong-clong*, one two three, and that meant Cory must come down at once – but only a small part of him heard it; the rest was lost in the storm as Cory's fear and sadness poured out from him and vanished through walls and ceiling and floor.

His power had come, unasked and uncontrolled, with no enemy to fight.

That evening, Cory woke to shouting, indistinct at first, then loud enough to hear through the walls.

'*Quit your nagging.*' That was Gene.

'*I can't take this. Not another moment.*'

'*It was a fucking suggestion, not a fucking order.*'

The music suddenly went louder, then there was a screech that meant a precious record, one of Halcyon's library of music, had been scratched.

SLAM!

That was a door crashing shut like a big exploding firework.

Long ago, Gene and Molly had been very careful explaining divorce to him. They had expected it to be a strange idea to him, but of course people might find they were no longer suited. Yes, it was unhappy and a bad thing to rush separation until you were sure, but there was no need to hurt each other. Back home, the whole lodge – perhaps two lodges – would be around them, awake and asleep, helping them to separate in a caring and loving way. But humans could not do that.

Crooked Street had been like a lodge.

The shouting and the fear got inside him. He couldn't bear that his parents were quarrelling when he needed them together. He hated the episodes when his fear grew out of control.

He was in the waking world now. *Annoying.* Perhaps he should update the Plan on how to sort the Earth out. All the stupid things humans did, which they would have to stop when his people came. The Aral Sea was disappearing, a *whole* sea, and all the birds and fish that relied on it.

He would spend half an hour putting the Earth right—

There was a crash from outside, and he heard Dad swearing.

He opened the door onto the narrow wooden stairs and saw his Earth-father trying to get up; he had fallen coming up the stairs.

'I thought you'd be in bed, Big Stuff.' Dad was slurring a

little. He hung onto the banister, moving as though his body wasn't quite listening. Maybe he had banged his head again.

Cory's tentacles tasted the air: cigarette smoke, and wine, which looked like juice but was not for children. Carol and Storm drank most nights, but they took care to hide it from Mom. Alcohol made Mom very sad and ill and she didn't drink it anymore. But two days ago, Dad had made a pro-dig-ious mess being sick in the bathroom.

'You'll wake Fleur up,' Cory said now.

'Don't look disapproving. I'm . . . I was going to tell your mom I'm sorry — sorry for the shouting. But she's locked the door. It's my room too.'

Cory was trying to decide how he felt, but he already knew that. He felt tired and small and sad. It was always better to sleep with someone, and he did have Meteor.

'You're drunk,' he announced. 'You need to find a bucket.' He was just trying to be practical, but his dad took it as rejection.

'Okay, I guess I screwed up. I'll sleep somewhere else.'

Dad turned around, his body doing its best to balance. 'We both love you,' he said. Then he made a worrying climb down the stairs, limbs askew like a toddler.

Suppose the Bad Men came and Dad was drunk — how would they get away?

'Molly? Please?'

Cory shut his own door and prepared himself and Meteor for bed. *Humans!*

CHAPTER 16

Halcyon, two days after Christmas

Cory loved it when the sun shone. The sky today was bluer and colder than any he had seen before. It made the ice sparkle. Christmas had been exciting, with presents from his friends, but it was mostly over – and here he was, stuck hiding in a house with the same few people. Cory was fed up with trying to entertain his parents – cheering them up felt harder than lifting them in body – but at least this morning there was the exciting expedition to look forward to.

Joel and Storm took turns going to check the unused houses. There were five in the area, all closed up for winter. The people of Halcyon checked that no one had broken in or set fire to anything.

Cory didn't understand why someone would burn a house someone else used. The hobos he did understand – people who liked to wander and to be alone, like some solos of his own world, those who did not want a lodge.

Joel's car-truck-whatever was huge and black. He called it

the Beast. Cory put Meteor under her blanket on the back seat and they drove up the trail together, taking the back way out. The Beast made fierce animal noises getting up slopes and fighting the ice.

Cory must look for the tracks of the big-footed hares, who turned white for winter. Sometimes, Joel said, where there were hares, there were lynx, a sort of fierce hunting cat. Cory wanted to see a lynx, even though it was bad news for the hares. All the animals for miles around would spot Meteor, unless Cory hid her.

'Do you get many break-ins?' Storm asked.

'Teens for a dare. Hobos — it's a hard time to be on the road.'

Joel marched around each house, looking for damage. Then they went in to see that the heat was on very low, and that no pipes had burst.

The third place, a very fine little house in grey stone and painted wood, was surrounded by snow-covered trees. It was quiet everywhere, except for them.

Joel did his checking walk around the outside of the house, looking for leaks.

'Can't be more than a mile from the road,' Storm said. 'Oh, there's been visitors.'

There was garbage scattered around the back doorstep, tins and packets.

'Racoons,' said Joel. That was obvious, from the tracks.

'So, a detective story, who brought the garbage for them to get into?'

There were no footprints, but it had snowed yesterday. Cory closed his eyes to concentrate, to listen and to feel out with his mind. Ah – there *was* something here: two somethings, and they were under the house. Only raccoons after all.

Then Cory felt something else: a human, frightened and alone. His mind followed the feelings up to the top of the house. He focused: not a large human.

He should tell Storm – but then he thought of Bonnie and Chuck, and how good it was to have friends. Perhaps the scared-alone person needed a friend.

Cory looked down, so Storm could not see his indecision. 'Two small things under house. Raccoons maybe.' In his back-pack, he had a bar of chocolate he'd been given for Christmas and the pastry he hadn't eaten at breakfast. 'Go into house. We should go into the house.'

Five steps led up to a tiny porch. Storm pulled off a glove and bent over, feeling under the steps.

'The key's gone,' she said. 'Our visitor might still be around.'

'Cory go. I will go, hidden. No danger if I go.'

Storm felt unsure, her face looked unsure. Inside her coat was the walkie talkie; in her coat pocket was the big heavy flare gun. 'Suppose it's some drunk with a stick?'

Cory pleaded his case. 'I can walk in darkness. I can hide. I can smell if someone there.' *So many things humans cannot do.* 'I will be most extra careful.'

Storm smiled. 'Okay.'

This was what he wanted: an adventure. He hid himself and slipped through the door. It was cold, but warmer than outside. It smelled as all these locked-up places did. Looking for big bear traps, he stalked through the rooms. It was clear that someone had been in the kitchen, where the plates had been rinsed but only camping clean. He smelled a human – sweat and dirt and soap – and something else, a nasty smell like rotting food.

Up the stairs he went, because the human had not moved.

'Cory, what's going on?' Storm called from downstairs.

Cory stayed hidden as he stepped through one of the bedroom doors, because this was certainly *the* room. The bed had been disturbed. The closet door was closed. He felt with his mind and knew the human was in the closet. The human was frightened, and sad or ill or hungry, or all of these. It was shivering, a child, frightened and alone.

He took off his backpack and found the chocolate and the pastry. Then, putting them down by the closet door, he unhid himself and whispered, 'Here's food. I'm a friend. Do you want help?'

Nothing happened, except that the note of fear sharpened.

'We can help. The people I am with are kind. I can bring my mom and dad.'

The silence only continued; the fear sharpened further.

Cory looked back at the open bedroom door. Soon Storm would come up.

'I'll come back,' he said, clear but not too loud. Then he padded to the top of the stairs.

'See no one,' he said, for that was true. 'But for-sure has been someone here. Smell them.'

Storm was in the kitchen. 'Someone's been here, a couple of days at least.'

'I need the bathroom,' Cory called down.

Cory sat on the toilet while he thought. Maybe the child was a Bad Man and they would tell the other Bad Men who were after them. Maybe he should tell Mom and Dad. But maybe, then, Mom and Dad would decide to run away again and there would be more arguing.

The child was scared — it was scared before Cory in the room, frightened just by the vehicle coming up the road. Cory could have opened the door, but then — what if it'd been scared of *him*? Cory the monster. Everyone was so scared of Cory. But the present of food . . . *Cory will not lie if asked directly. So difficult. Cory will tell Mom. No, he won't.*

He flushed the toilet and washed his hands and went down-stairs.

'No one upstairs?'

'I saw nothing,' Cory said, and it was true, he had not seen anything. His inner teacher was not happy.

'I have good idea: Cory and Meteor will sleep downstairs and guard the house,' he said. 'Meteor is a great guard dog. If person comes snooping, one of us will know.'

'Your mom would kill me,' Storm said. 'Well, I don't suppose the owners care about a tin or two. But if they leave the door open, and animals get in . . .'

Storm wrote a note in flowing handwriting, sketched a map and put two green bills with it on the table.

'It's a hard time to be on the road. Halcyon feeds the hobos, gives them a bath and a bed. If they want to stay more than three days, the church takes them.'

That evening, Storm and Carol cooked. Molly had announced that she was a grown-up, two years two months sober, and if

173

people wanted to drink in front of her, she was fine. Tonight, she passed Gene a glass of wine, with a most superior look, and he went red and took it. The grown-ups drank wine and got slurred and silly; even Mom acted a little as though she was.

Carol read something called 'The Cory I Know', which was very kind about him and felt strange. 'It's an article, or it might be the first chapter of the book.' It made the adults go warm and melty inside. There were some bits in it that Cory did not understand, though, and in the lodge, you would never praise just one person like that. Cory went round the room praising everyone to be balanced.

Cory thought of his new friend, cold and lonely up the hill. He had already decided that it was not for him to reveal them unasked. The right thing was to ask if they wanted rescuing. He must go and do that again soon.

He cast a glance at the window. It was dark now, and cloud had come to hide the Moon and drop more snow. It was a mile and a half from the house to the cottage, and all of that was uphill. Cory would need snowshoes, but there were no snowshoes for Meteor. He supposed he could pull Meteor on his sled, wearing her coat and under her blanket, or else leave her behind. But Meteor liked to pad around barking and looking for Cory when he was gone, so that would be a sign to the grown-ups that something was different.

The adults would never let Cory go on his own. *So I must go tonight*, he thought, *while all the adults are sleeping.*

At one in the morning, the darkness outside Halcyon was absolute. Fleur had woken at half past eleven, which meant that everyone would now be back to sleep. Cory went into the storeroom to find bread, cheese, tinned pineapple and cookies. Hidden under the cloth were the tins and packets he must not see, with murdered animals in them. Cory hated that there were dead cows and rabbits and chickens in the food Meteor ate. Dog food troubled him; it smelled of death, and yet it was enticing.

In the front room, Meteor was asleep, leg twitching. Perhaps she was chasing hares. Cory was pleased that clumsy Meteor was truly terrible at catching rabbits and squirrels and birds.

He took cans of soup and beans from the storeroom; the person could use the stove in the cottage. By now, the backpack was heavy — not too heavy, but after a mile over snow it might feel different. Maybe one less tin . . .

He heard a tiny creak on the stair and hid at once, his heart pounding. He felt Mom, and here she came with the little flashlight.

Molly walked straight to the kitchen, even though he was so-so quiet.

'Backpack gone, big flashlight gone and the pantry door open. Cory Myers, you need to unhide right this minute.'

He stayed hidden, his heart pounding out the seconds. Then Mom turned on the light, and she looked, if not at him, close to where he was.

'Cory, I'm going to count to five. Show yourself, or there will be trouble.'

Cory held his breath and revealed himself.

'So, dressed up for a polar expedition. Where are you going?'

Scared for his friend, but relieved, Cory told the truth.

★

175

Cory was in disgrace and felt it. But the sun was about to rise, and here they were, ready to set off, going to help. Joel turned the key in the Beast, which roared in the silence, and somewhere in the woods, there was a flutter.

Dad thought it was too dangerous for Mom. But, 'Cory said the child might be sick, so I'm coming. The end,' Mom had said, finding the first-aid kit.

Cory said, 'I must come to hide you all if trouble.'

'You're still in disgrace,' Molly said.

Cory was very sorry for lying to grown-ups, although he was trying to do the right thing. Grown-ups lied to each other all the time. Mom told many, many *enormous* fibs to keep Cory safe. But in his heart, Cory knew he had not told the truth and he deserved to be in disgrace.

Still, they let him come.

The Beast made its noisy path up towards the house, so loud that every animal within miles would surely be hiding. Cory thought his friend would hear the car and be afraid. Or maybe the friend had already gone.

When they arrived at the cottage, even the tracks from yesterday were muted by the light dust of new snow. The air was cold enough to make Cory's lungs hurt. In this weather, he lost feeling in his tentacles, even though he willed them warmer. Dad stood guard by the Beast.

'Cory will go ahead, hiding.'

The grown-ups just shrugged.

Inside, the air was stale, but the house was warmer. The money on the counter was gone. Cory saw no new signs of disturbance. He walked up one step after another, feeling around him, looking and listening. Then he climbed the stairs, oh so careful, and headed to the small bedroom.

He sneaked open the door and saw that somebody was in the bed, a tangle of blankets. The person felt confused, sick. Such an unhealthy smell was coming off them, like dead things rotting.

The small person was not asleep, not awake.

He walked over, hidden, and stood for a while, looking down at them. The person was very thin, and dirty. Smaller than he was. Long hair, but whatever the books say, that did not always mean a girl.

The child's eyes flickered.

How terrible, that the child might become scared of him. He needed Mom, the healer, to look at the boy or girl, whichever it was.

He unhid and called, 'Mom, a child is sick.'

'I'm coming.'

The boy-or-girl opened their eyes and grabbed his hand. They felt confused, and Cory realised how sick they were.

'Don't let *him* find me.'

'I won't,' he promised. And Mom came in, and he was so glad she was there, because Mom knew so well what to do with sick humans.

In a glance Molly saw the girl was in a bad way. An old yellow bruise coloured her face and she shivered, feeling hot to the touch.

Molly took charge. 'Cory, heat the soup up. It looks a lot like our stove – but be careful.'

That would get Cory out of the way. Molly knelt by the

bed. 'Okay, sweetie-pie, I'm a nurse and a mom. I work with children all the time. It's going to be fine. Tell me what hurts.' The smell in the room came from a festering wound; it suggested to Molly's nose that it was somewhere on the lower half of her body.

The girl murmured.

'I'm going to have to undress you a bit to see what's wrong.' Molly pulled on her protective gloves.

It only took lifting the blankets to show her the problem: the child's leg had been crudely bandaged, but pus and dried blood were leaking through. How thin she was.

Joel was back already. 'What do you need me to do?'

'Help me undress her: I'll need to wash her. Perhaps a bath would be simplest.'

The girl murmured again.

Joel said, 'I wish the kid had said yesterday.'

'Better now than later,' said Molly. She only had the simplest sorts of antibiotics on her, but she could clean the wound up with antiseptic salve and dose her with whatever else she could find. She could always call Dr O'Brien.

'What hurt you, darling?' she asked softly.

'*He* did . . . then the broken window.'

She would have to check the wound for glass.

She touched the girl's side, intending to reassure her, and noted how she flinched.

Always the nurse, Molly pulled out her notebook to record everything she saw, bruises and the like. People thought that working with children was all balloons and jigsaws and mopping the pretty brows of sweet children who got better for the

'Here are clothes.' Cory brought them from the chair to the bed. Children often stayed in the house by the bay, so there was a closet of spare things, like a blue summer dress which Cory had worn for dressing-up, and a pair of boy's jeans, and some underwear. The sweater had a moth hole in it, which Storm had mended last night. Cory had donated his newest T-shirt.

The girl admired the dress for a while. She looked at a pair of light summer shoes. 'That's not much good for winter. I'll need a coat, and my boots, I-am-Cory-Myers.'

'Stay here, in the warm. I'll get more food.'

The yellow waterproofs would hold off wind and rain, but Cory did not want her to leave.

'I ran away. *He's* after me so I have to be ready to go.'

'We are always packed-ready-to-go. We will pack for you too. But don't go now. We will look after you.'

'Last time, grown-ups gave me back to *him*.'

'My mom and dad won't. We've run away too. I'll get some food.'

All the grown-ups were talking to Dr O'Brien in the big room. Dr O'Brien was kind and had no hair on his head but lots up his nose. If Cory did his most powerful hide, they would not notice him open the door and slip in.

A warm room full of complicated feelings – angry and frightened and hiding things.

O'Brien was speaking. 'The law is the law. I'm supposed to contact Child Services, and they'll tell the police.'

Mom gave a strange laugh. 'We're going around in circles. If Halcyon stands for anything, it stands for the law being wrong sometimes.'

183

'I have my oath too. This poor girl, she deserves everything the state can provide.' O'Brien was troubled.

'We'll have to move,' said Dad.

That would be a nasty argument between Mom and Dad. Cory was often bored, but then, Halcyon was safe.

'She has a good doctor, and a nurse . . .' said Mom. 'She's not in any danger. Now, if she gets really sick, then we'll have to think about hospital.'

If Cory had been allowed, he would have said, 'We can go and take her with us.'

Carol said, 'Well, I don't know what this state is like, but the institutions struggle, don't they? She's not in immediate danger. You've broken bigger laws, Roger, and thank goodness.'

Molly put her hand on Dr O'Brien's. 'We've all had to make difficult choices. Give us forty-eight hours, I guess we can go to Canada . . . and hope none of the lunatics find out where Cory is . . .'

'I'll just say I found her.'

'Or just wait,' Molly said. 'We're criminals, with the whole world after us.'

There was a long pause, waiting for Dr O'Brien to decide.

'I guess a few days more doesn't matter.'

Such relief, and Cory used the hum of thank-yous to slip out.

The Bad Man who hurt her must be stopped. And yet, Cory needed his Earth-family to be safe. What else had he got until his people came?

In the kitchen, there were good smells for lunch. How Cory missed his home in Amber Grove. Better still, he wanted to take his human family and all their friends to his home-planet.

184

Cory took what he needed, hidden, and went back upstairs.

The girl was sitting on the bed. Her face was sweaty. 'Help me pee, Snake Face,' she asked.

He pointed at the pot; would she faint, or be sick? He helped her from the bed, then turned his back to give her privacy. When she finished, he helped her to the basin to wash her hands.

'*He* said you were made up. Liar.'

'I have to call you something,' Cory said. 'Not rude and silly like that word.'

'Call me Elsa,' she said. 'I heard it in a story.' She pointed at the picture. 'I'd like to be a white hare,' she said. 'I saw one at sunset. *He* threw a rock at it, and it ran away. It goes white in winter to hide. Imagine just being a fur ball under the snow. No one could find you.'

Cory could feel it under the snow, of course. 'Snowshoe hare,' he said. 'Because of the feet.'

'Hares don't wear shoes,' said the girl, like she was the expert.

'I could find you,' Cory said.

'No you couldn't.'

'And I can hide better than a hare,' Cory said, and showed her.

She laughed and it was a good sound.

He unhid again.

'That's a good trick. Teach me,' she said, not knowing where to look, and how he wished he could. She had hair and he could hide with his mind, and neither could give that to the other.

Elsa kept taking quick glances at the silver bracelet of his communicator. Perhaps she was trying not to show him she was interested. He held out his hand so she could see it closely.

'It's for talking,' he said. 'But now it doesn't work.'

'Isn't it a smart monster,' she said, touching the device.

'It won't work for you.'

It held precious memories, some words from his mother.

Three days later, Cory came to find Elsa to show her the old newspaper. She smelled clean and healthy now. She ate a lot, and she smiled more at the grown-ups.

In the paper was a bad sketch of a hard-eyed man and a girl who could have been anyone. 'Gas station robber strikes again,' read the headline. The story mentioned 'concerns' for the child in the car.

Funny how humans weep for emotion. Elsa held back the tears, but Cory felt her sadness.

'That could be anyone,' she said.

'Read it,' he said, and she frowned.

'I read fine,' she said, but the truth was, she read like a baby, saying the words aloud and stumbling. She liked Cory to read to her.

The newspaper said that the Bad Man had used a gun to take cash from shops and gas stations. First there was a robbery in Vermont, where a man was hurt, then two in Maine. Cory shivered at the thought of how scared the poor shopkeepers must have been. They called him the Dog-Tag Robber, because he flourished military ID to show he was serious about the gun.

'Where is the Bad Man?' Cory said. 'Don't so-worry, Cory will hide you, yes-I-will.'

Elsa took his hand. 'It's a very nice monster and I like it. I don't know where *he* is. He stole a car with lots of groceries in and when the motel kicked us out, he tried robbery again. Then we broke into a house further up the hill. *He* was drunk, that's how I got away. I took his gun and threw it in the water.'

Cory had learned to spot human lies, but he had no sense if she was being truthful.

'Where is your lodge? Your family?'

'All dead. *He* wasn't family.'

Cory had never met a human so good at cloaking their feelings.

'It was better when we didn't use guns. I'd pretend to be sick and he'd take stuff while kind people helped me. Or he'd ask directions and I'd take food. You can hide a lot under a big coat. Sometimes people would feed us both, because he'd pretend he'd lost his mind in the war and they felt sorry for me.'

'Stealing,' Cory said. The way Earth worked confused him, but all this felt wrong.

She shrugged. 'We were starving, and they weren't.'

Her stories were awful, but they fascinated Cory, like a poisonous plant that smells delicious.

'Maybe I'll have to do those things again,' Elsa said.

Cory knew humans; she was testing his reaction. 'Stay safe. Stay with us.'

Cory wanted everything, but above all he wanted everyone together. He would take her to his home-world, he decided, where no child was ever hungry or smacked or abandoned. He would take her there – and she would be another voice, making Mom and Dad stop their endless quarrels and come with him to the stars.

CHAPTER 18

The Starship Kites at Dusk

Thunder prepared for the dreaming-between-the-stars, anxiety squirming in his bowels. He had held out for a few days, then finally, he volunteered. There were new assessments and some training, and then he had been rostered for as many sessions as he could. Some of the regulars had suffered side-effects; rumour sweeping the two ships exaggerated how bad, how many.

Thunder showered with mist to relax and entered an ante-room that smelled of sweet spices. The wall-gardens provided an anchor to the home-world — space would be hard enough without growing things and running water. Skimming Stone was a guide in this endeavour. Thunder found the healer-leader over-eager, over-close, and tried to keep her at a distance.

Hope and fear had filled the mission since the single one had been found. Many of those who had volunteered knew someone on a lost starship, or else killed by the snakes. Many of the crew had had their hopes raised by the tantalising discovery, and cold hard maths told Thunder he was nothing special. The whole felt deeply for them, of course. Any of the people who could be rescued should be.

Each person reached readiness as quickly as they could, then went into the dream chamber. Thunder was not ready, his thoughts were churning.

Maybe it will be your son. Maybe it will be their child, partner, parent. Maybe it will be more. Everyone hoped that a whole ship had survived. Whatever new knowledge they'd gleaned of the snakes might tilt the odds of their desperate struggle for existence. A whole civilisation waited for the next attack.

How quickly things had changed in this time of Hardening.

His mind was a whirlwind. He went through the exercises of mind and body to still them both.

Contact was made regularly with First Harbour, and the Waystation, but Thunder had found the limitations of dreaming-between-the-stars painfully clear. Emotional states and common experiences were easy to share. Complex arguments and precise data were not.

He needed to prepare: an anchor must be strong and solid.

Strange things came into the dreaming, phantoms of some sort. The people were learning a new reality. Some were wondering if the frightened single might have been something similar.

The mission had been sanctioned partly on the assumption that, over stellar distance, dreaming-together was reliable. To learn it was unreliable, as the sceptics had always said, would be useful knowledge, but devastating.

Now Thunder was ready. He entered the chamber, almost late, but not too late to enjoy the ritual among the crew: greeting, smelling, touching as they fitted into their assigned bunks in the dim light. Thunder settled himself and felt the amplified sleep rise to take him.

Down he went, down through dream-layers of hope and fear, through the layers where he sensed other crew walking and feeding, arguing, loving, down to the layer where the first gathered waited. He joined them and took his place: a steadfast weight and a chain for others to hold. He prepared to cast his mind out into the deadly barrenness of space.

Yearning, yearning: *We are here. Join us.*

Almost at once, he felt a sense of others dreaming – those on the sibling ship. There was a brief exchange: *all well? All well.* Then it was as if each ship turned its back on the other, each choosing half the heavens and sending their dreams out.

Now nothingness . . .

People threw names and memories of the lost into the whole. Thunder shared his dream of Little Frog, that last day. The whole picked that up and sang it, the pain of parting, the joy of love, the pain of remembering.

A year of this intensity, and who knew if they would remain sane?

Cry out into the darkness as one voice . . .

Little one . . . little one . . . we are here . . . the people are coming.

The group took up the urgent call that means, *Children! Come to the grown-ups!*

It was a long, arduous, futile dream, and some soon lost connection and went swimming back to the wakened world. Some questioned whether to step back from that search and try something else; from others there were angry thoughts, angry at being diverted.

Then something stilled them all.

A faint call – a child responding. *This one hears!*

There was excitement, then doubt: it was so very faint. Thunder was astonished – but how strange to be astonished when you have found what you are looking for! He held the group together as others poured out their welcome.

We hear. Come to us. Come to us.

Very faint. *This one hears!*

The group needed more; Thunder felt the power in them as each reached further. The outward message they sent was *Courage! Focus, little one! Reach us!* The anchors and the healers knew they were raising the risk. Those assigned watched over individuals under strain.

His own heart thundered, far away a physical pain.

Nothing.

People started to bring up names to call out, visions of the lost, making it personal . . .

One more step, and the dreams truly connected. Whoever they had found, it really was one of the people – a child, perhaps ill or wounded or in distress.

This one hears! Come for me!

It *was* his son – it was Little Frog. For a moment, there was nothing in the universe but that stunning, unarguable truth.

Thunder felt his pulse and breathing rise again, a painful

move into the danger zone. He tried to calm himself while calling his son's name. *I know you! I know you!*

In the dream, they touched: the briefest moment of recognition, fleeting and painful. There was so much surprise and confusion – but there was joy as well. They knew each other.

Where, where? The group was asking the essential question, though it was almost painful, interrupting that personal contact. Thunder's body was in distress now, but the group tried to stay strong and keep searching. *Where, where?*

But now all was silence. A single child, of course holding a contact even briefly unaided – that was a miracle.

Thunder returned to the waking world to find a healer beside him and the space crowded. In spite of the pain, he could speak. 'Little Frog,' he gasped. He felt drained, as if he needed null-sleep – as if his body should stay still for ever.

He felt bathed in the envy around him: the healer envied him, Skimming Stone burned with it, and others too – but there were also trills of joy, an uneven clapping that quickly fell into rhythm: a song of return being spun out, his crewmates dancing on the spot in that crowded space.

The lost is found, rejoice!

The wounded and exhausted were tended in a sea of song.

'We will find him,' Skimming Stone called out, and the envy had vanished, turned into something fierce: the furious need to get things done.

Thunder was surrounded by dance, as those who could reached out to touch him or call his name to the rhythm. There were new words now:

Thunder, Thunder,
We will find your son.
Thunder, Thunder,
We will find your son.
Where, where?
Among the stars
Thunder Thunder
We will find your son.

Where?

Little Blue Frog had tried to answer, but all Thunder had heard in the dream was the crashing of waves and wind. It was difficult to think. Later, they would need to debrief and hammer out what facts they could.

The song was a roar now — maybe that was just the pain suppressors. The song was coming from the-all . . . he imagined people stopping to listen, to take the rhythm, to chant the words. By now, Thunder was slipping from reality . . .

A planet with water. That was hardly uncommon, but at least it was a start.

Molly dreamed she was back on Crooked Street, that first time Cory had come into their bed at night, when she'd torn up Dr Jarman's rulebook about infection in return for giving them closeness as a family. She felt his little body, wriggling in between her and Gene.

Dimly, she realised that Cory was speaking to her, that she was half awake and this was not a dream. Gene was in bed beside her, indeed still was, and snoring away.

Cory burbled on, 'Don't wake Fleur.'

Her eyelids weighed about ten pounds each and she kept them shut.

'My people are coming, and *Mom not interested*!'

'Can't this wait till morning?'

'No.' Cory took her shoulder and shook her, and she realised it must be important, for he was usually so protective of her sleep now the baby had come.

'I'm awake,' she said.

'Cory had most excellent dream, yes I did. Father-by-body Thunder Over Mountains on starship – most certain him. Big surprise, he recognised me, I recognised him. All-the-people joyful.'

'Wow,' she said. Every instinct told her that this might be fantasy – but, under it was the hope and the fear it was true.

'My people are looking for the lost and they found me.'

'Go back to bed, Cory,' moaned Gene.

Molly remembered last night: how words had failed to bridge the divide between husband and wife, but there had been a kiss and a hug under the quilt. That modest intimacy had given her hope. Even in winter you can see signs of spring.

'Cory needs to say the whole story now Dad awake.' He went through it again. 'So they didn't know – and now they do,' Cory finished, in case they were too sleepy to understand.

'Right,' Gene said. 'Okay, we sure believe that was what you dreamed—'

The bed was swamped by a big sad wave of feelings. 'If I was making things up, wouldn't I make up my birth-mom being alive? My friends on the starship?'

'Okay.'

A long, long silence.

'I wished I'd known your mom,' Molly said, because Cory liked to hear that.

Gene said, 'I've been thinking about this. So, the Ship said that dreaming among the stars is impossible. But of course, it's like flying: impossible until humans invented balloons. The Ship could amplify your hiding power, couldn't it? So maybe they figured how to amplify dreaming?'

'That's so obvious,' Cory said.

'You can't prove to us these dreams are true,' Gene said, 'but it sure could be true.'

'Your purple father on his way: that's exciting,' Molly said, looking around at her family. They were together in a crowded little pool of love and sadness.

'They don't know where to come,' Cory said. 'They asked and I tried, ever so hard, but the dream was already too weak.'

'It won't be a one-off,' Gene said. 'Try again when you can – just not tonight.'

'Cory will try again – every night, to be sure they know where I am. Show things that only could be Earth.'

'You do that,' Mom said. She smiled, but her eyes were wet.

Silently, Elsa stood watching from the doorway, her face a mask.

'Join us, sweetie-pie,' Molly said, but the girl turned and left.

CHAPTER 19

February turns to March

Weeks came and went: a Maine winter ripped by Atlantic wind, and day by day, winter crept into their marriage. Molly felt that darkness herself, and she could not haul Gene back from it either. So often she was in a room with him, and yet what she felt was alone.

Carol and Storm went back to New York. They quit *Witness*, who turned to the company's aggressive lawyers. Some compromise was threshed out – the resignation was withdrawn and Carol got to write big features, but never on Cory. They came when they dared, which was not often.

The families of the wounded teens fought for compensation, and the Myers were sure they had been hurt – but the plaintiffs made a fatal miscalculation: they refused the offer of free specialist help from the doctors who had treated the soldiers hurt by Cory's power. The Myers through their lawyers also offered to pay for an independent medical examination. The families refused.

The press, and through them the public, took it badly – maybe what Cory did had no long-term effects. What were the families hiding? The judge refused to progress their case without independent evidence.

The DA investigating the incident as a crime was made of sterner stuff and demanded the Myers attend his grand jury in person.

Each day brought something good or ill.

Winter was still at its hardest the day the message got to them about John's heart attack. Gene, pale, started packing to go without blinking.

'Molly,' he insisted, 'they have no one else but me. And if he goes, Eva will need me too.'

If Molly could have flown the family to John's side, she would have done. She wiped away hot tears, angry at life. John was a hundred times more her father than the man who had raised her, but there was a million-dollar bounty on their heads, thanks to a grandstanding oil baron. The FBI were everywhere; every month there was a new story of how they had informers in this group and that. And the Chicago Mob still wanted revenge, for the Ship's attacks on their operation.

Molly rounded up the letters John had sent, telling them not to come, and hid the car keys. And Carol, bless her, talked to Gene, and then Storm did, and between them they persuaded him out of it.

Eva's call came the next day: John did not think they would be safe. He forbade them to come.

At least with that decision wrested out of their hands, Gene and Molly felt united by their love for his parents.

There was such progress in heart medicine, Molly knew, but

would Gene blame her if John died without his son by his side? Molly's AA sponsor used to say that all our hours are counted, but we do not know how long. *Live each day.*

Sometimes Gene got out the guitar and played a few jokey tunes for the children. It reminded her of how strong they had once been, united against all dangers. But sometimes, he would all but disappear, unless a pipe broke or Elsa got her foot stuck. The day Gene announced his plan to get them out of Halcyon, to fly to Hawaii, she thought she was gentle as she pointed out the risks – the long chain of strangers they would have to trust – but Gene barely spoke to her for days after that.

Cory, confused, kept asking, *would they stay together? Would Elsa come with them?*

Then there was the drama of the brooch. Molly couldn't find her special blue brooch; the one Eva had given her for her wedding day. She hadn't brought much with her, but this mattered: it was from the mother she chose.

Cory had said nothing but returned with it ten minutes later. It took her two minutes to find the truth.

'Elsa has a hiding place.'

Elsa stood with the face of an angel and blamed Cory. It was the lie that made Molly angry, not the theft, and now the corridor rang with Elsa's screaming. Molly held onto her wrists, if only to stop her scratching her face. Being gentle was not an option here and Molly got a couple of sharp kicks in return.

'Gene!' she called; then to the girl, 'Stop fighting, I'm not going to hit you—'

'*I won't I won't I won't I won't!*' Elsa fought to bring her wrists up close to her mouth, to bite Molly's hands.

Molly had had quite enough of Elsa biting and kicking. She still had bruises from Saturday, and next time Elsa might find something precious and break it.

'You're hurting!' screamed Elsa.

Cory was moaning, 'Elsa, stop stop stop . . .'

Molly's own temper blazed, but she reined it in, determined not to lash out.

'Look, Wonder Girl, all this shouting isn't helping anyone.' Here was Gene, who Elsa could stir to anger with her goading.

'Monster!'

'We need to talk,' Molly declared, trying to find her sweet and reasonable self. 'That brooch is very precious. If you'd asked, you could have borrowed it.'

'Cory put it there. Octopus Head is a doggone traitor, a rascal.'

'That's a lie, Elsa.'

Elsa writhed and Gene gave a bark, a pained '*Jeez*—'

'I wouldn't have minded, if you'd said sorry and told the truth,' said Molly. 'You were the one who wanted it this way.'

'I hate you. All of you!' she bellowed.

As a parent, you just took those wounds. What else could you do?

That evening, Molly sat in the armchair, enjoying the glow of the stove. Elsa was asleep in her bed, a cherub from a Christmas card. There'd been a graceless apology, at best half meant, and a warm cuddle which meant something deeper. Eva said sometimes kids only play up with the ones they trust not to hurt them.

Tomorrow Elsa might be a lively angel, playing with Fleur and teasing Cory and helping any of the adults. She liked to paint and make things and hear stories, even do chores sometimes. Her reading was improving. But who could tell?

Looking at Elsa, Molly remembered sitting by Cory in the hospital and realising that here was someone alone, hurt, afraid: a child who needed a mother. Once upon a time, Elsa had surely been loved, but not for many years.

Gene came in, and the sudden thought struck her: she had no idea how she would manage Elsa on her own. If Gene left her.

'How's Hurricane Hellion?' Gene said. It was a treat when he smiled. There was a smear of baby rice on his sweater.

Molly smiled back. 'We make a good team.' Elsa was something they were working on together.

Gene sat, putting his arm around Molly, and she leaned in, enjoying his smell – except for the foul tobacco smoke on his sweater – but that reminded her of courting. Even the fact he was trying to give it up again.

Fleur was six months old, growing and changing. When Gene talked about Fleur, when she watched him play with her, she hated to think he would leave them.

They talked a little, about Elsa, about trying this and choosing that.

There had been no sign of the robber. No more newspaper reports, no break-ins at any house within twenty miles. Two months had passed and the man had apparently disappeared – but without money, he had to be *somewhere*.

Elsa told Cory things she wanted all of them to know. Her mother had died long ago. The only image she had was a single photograph, which the robber had burned. She'd been brought up by Auntie, an old woman, and her two daughters – Big Kay, who had been strong and fun but, in the old meaning, simple; and Beauty, who had dated the robber, who had eloped with him, taking Elsa – and beginning her nightmare.

Why Beauty had not protected her, what happened to Beauty . . . Elsa would not say.

Elsa was bitter about the authorities. 'The woman from Child Services told me they would do the right thing – but they believed *him*. They gave me back to *him*.'

Gene coughed, breaking into her pleasant silence. 'They're going to launch *Pioneer*.'

That changed the mood.

The unmanned probe would go further than any human space mission so far, to Jupiter and the outer planets, bouncing from one to another like a pinball. Most incredible of all, it would seek to leave the solar system altogether. It would be a toy boat on the most unimaginable of oceans, humanity's first step to explore all of space.

And millions were saying across the world, *No, don't risk drawing the wrath of the heavens down upon us*. Two men had died on the Moon, the American and Russian Mars probes had failed. Yes, four men had walked on the Moon, but that was with the Ship to protect them. The Ship had been destroyed.

Molly felt such a deep gloom. 'Well, they've built it. Suppose they'd better. It's no use for anything else.'

'I've told Cory he can stay up and watch with Joel.'

'Count me out.'

Astronomers had argued over the dark objects that circled

the Earth, unclaimed by any Earth government. They were hard to spot and even harder to track. If these sightings were true, what were they? Trash, something left by the Ship, or the snakes? Or something active that was watching the Earth with hostile intelligence?

The day of the launch, Molly went to bed before sunset. Something gnawed at her as the clock clicked round, she moved from a book to her friends' letters and back to the book.

Gene came in, and his face said it all.

'All fine, then fifteen minutes after launch' – he gestured – 'a flash of light and nothing. Gone. There was a couple of satellites nearby, and they went too.'

Every long agonising discussion around the kitchen came to the same thing. The Myers had been asked a thousand questions they could not answer. If the nuclear powers united to fire nuclear missiles into space – well, the Myers had nothing useful to tell them about that. If the scientists wanted to know how the snakes worked, or how they could be turned off – the Myers had no wisdom or knowledge to add. Cory could do nothing, except search his dreams for his people. And, since that first contact with his birth-father, he had stopped talking about his dreams altogether, which made Molly fear he too was losing hope.

The next day the Russians lost a satellite, and the day after, the Americans lost another . . .

CHAPTER 20

Halcyon, a fortnight later

Joel had indoor pots filled with bulbs and now the first green tips were showing above the dark soil. Molly touched one, enjoyed the messiness of damp earth on her fingers. Spring was coming, and that always gave her a stirring of hope.

In the kitchen, she and Gene and were working through the mail, from friends and family mostly.

No letters from the lawyers today. Tired of the delays, the DA had indicted them for fleeing, for obstructing justice, and Cory for assault.

There was a letter from Eva, regular as clockwork. John, thank heavens, was doing okay. He was weak on his left side still, and needing a stick, but when they contrived safe phone calls, he cracked jokes about nurses and sounded his old mule-like self.

Diane had sent clippings of news stories in which folks stood up for the Myers. Molly was sifting through them, buoyed that not everything people wrote about Cory painted him as the monster, when she saw the flash of a blue envelope with familiar handwriting. It took a few moments for her to realise who it was: *Selena!*

Molly took the letter, three fat pages, and read it.

> *Green Bowers*
> *Kauwenga Falls*

Dearest M

How long since Molly had been 'dearest'?

Mason has got his way. He got a judge to have me committed to a madhouse for treatment, the lies he told, such lies. They've taken my boys away.

Molly's mouth went dry.

Although I'm not well, M, not at all I'm not quite sure what's real anymore and of course I can't phone you and anyway they would all be listening. All the lies Mason told. You must come and get me, M, you must. YOU KNOW WHO will be able to get me out, won't he? no one need be hurt or anything I'm so sorry we parted on such bad terms . . .

Molly winced at the memory. Their parting had been infuriating, feelings of love and betrayal, anger and concern all fighting for supremacy.

They make sure you take the pills and swallow, and they make me sleepy. I mean they're not rough, the nurses, and the one time someone tried to bother me, an orderly was right there he's about seven feet tall, black and very sweet with the old ones and he won't have anyone hurt. And Dr Friend always wants to talk about Mom, heaven knows why anyone wants to hear about that hideous witch. I must have put on twenty pounds and Mason brought all these new clothes pretending to care and underwear he likes it he can wear it then I'm not going to be his wife and he can wait till hell freezes over before I let him touch me I know that's his plan and Dr Friend's.

But it wasn't my fault Connor trod on the glass, it wasn't, you must believe me. Mason brought his doctor friend, you know, the one with the epileptic wife, and I guess the judge wasn't fooled because he picked this place rather than sending me back to Indianapolis and there is an order Mason has to bring the children for two hours every Tuesday Thursday and Saturday so he is living with some pal of his in the town it is even worse now they the boys I mean don't cry it is like he is turning them into cold sad little copies of him. Gene's a better man than ever I thought. I'm crying now thinking of what I said about Gene and YOU KNOW WHO . . .

Gene touched her hand. 'Bad news?'

It must have been showing. 'Selena's been put in an institution. By Mason, the turd. Uh . . .' How to put it? She settled on, 'She sounds ill.'

Molly raced on. Here the ink was smeared, a pattern like rain – or tears.

YOU KNOW WHO could get me something something the something the only friend I have here. I think secretly he desires me, but he is a real gentleman about it if that sounds funny and I don't feel frightened of him I'm not going to give the name in case this letter is stolen but he is going to post it for me I should have sex with him, because I could tell Mom and she could have a heart attack and go to hell I'd have his baby to get out of here there is a woman who has been in places like this since she was ten. Imagine!

And there is a woman here who thinks she is you, M, can you imagine? Half the people here — well, half the people who are not in outer space already — they believe her and Dr Friend believes the lies the lies Mason told about me you have to come and get me M they're keeping me a secret from everyone but if it got out, I would never have any peace.

I am sorry we parted as we did it was my fault you must come and get me and the boys will be so grateful to you and they will play with YOU KNOW WHO again I'm sorry sorry sorry I was wrong about Gene

All my love
Sel

You might think it isn't me well you went to the prom with James Cartwright and borrowed my Sunday coat and he spilled punch on you and I had to take the blame for getting it dirty what was in that punch so it stained beet juice you said it was wine of course and Mom was such a bitch you are right.

Also, Honolulu

Molly put down the letter and stared into space. The enormity of it left her numb. Gene took the pages from her hands, and read it, giving her space. He was only halfway through when he said, 'Are you sure it's her?'

Oddly, it had not occurred to her that the letter might be a fake. Gene was right, though: they had to doubt everything. The hand was certainly Selena's, writing fast and under pressure. The story at the end wasn't one many would know. Yet the clincher was 'Honolulu' – their old code word for 'we won't always be living with our mother'. Until Selena came back into her life, she had forgotten it.

Be careful, thought Molly. A drugged woman in a mental institution – maybe they had got it out of her? Traded more time with her boys for a letter to her sister? She imagined some grim-faced FBI agent, the President's Chief of Staff, even Mason, standing behind her sister as she wrote it.

Gene's face was determined. 'We'll call her lawyer – no, we'll get one of *our* friends to call our lawyer and find out what really happened. We can break into our emergency money.'

'Yes.'

Selena and Molly, under the covers, reading the same forbidden book with a flashlight. Selena the snitch, yet when Molly was sent to bed without supper, sneaking her a sandwich. The day Selena flashed her new engagement ring, her eyes blazing defiance. 'We're moving to Indiana and, if Mother follows, we'll move to Alaska.'

Gene went on, 'Even if she's ill, we might be able to do better. Sue the institution. We'll call today.'

'Uh-huh. Yes.' It meant a drive to somewhere they could make calls.

Molly remembered the nuns, the burning pain of the wooden ruler on her hand, and Selena's eyes wet, as if she had been struck herself.

She'd missed something Gene had said, and he might have noticed. 'Our lawyer must be careful,' he repeated, a little slower. 'We don't want anyone to know we're looking.'

'Sel's right,' said Molly. 'Cory could get us in, and out. Particularly at night. The psych places drug everyone, they like to keep them calm and quiet . . .'

Gene looked shocked, like she had burst into flames. Then he snapped, 'No. Never. We can't. Go and *rescue* her? You're *out of your mind*.'

Molly had only been thinking aloud. 'Who else will help her?'

'We will – of course we will. Safely, from a distance. Dr Jarman will know what to do.'

Molly was feeling powerless, trapped. The strain of these last weeks was telling on her, the sense of that invisible canyon between her and Gene; hiding from the world, needing each other, but a lot of the time, barely liking each other. Memories of brighter times felt like someone else, or a dream.

'Maybe we have to.'

Gene frowned, made his hands into fists. He was losing his

temper. 'Jeez,' he said, 'not so long ago, we thought John might be *dying* – and you said, no, don't go. Let him die.'

'John *told* us not to!'

'Your sister, who has *never* done anything for us . . . for you—'

Molly felt her fury rising, a boiling geyser which would not be held back.

An hour after the argument, Gene and Molly still couldn't look at each other. They briefed Carol and Storm, who looked shocked.

'The whole country is looking for you,' Carol said. 'We can't take the children. I can't deal with Elsa; I don't know how you put up with her.'

'Poor kid,' said Storm. 'You're going to take all the kids into danger? It might be a trap—'

'Yes,' Gene snapped. 'You're right. We don't need to mount a rescue mission. All we need is to talk to our lawyer.'

'Yes, as the first step,' Molly said. *Just like a man.* All she had said was, *don't say never. Don't patronise me, I understand the danger. But Sel is my sister – you never had one, you can't understand.*

She went on, 'If our lawyer can get her safe, we don't need to do anything dangerous.'

So the day's plans were scrapped. Cory wanted to know why and sulked when they wouldn't tell him. Storm drove Gene and Molly – on slippery roads and under ominous skies – towards one of the houses Halcyon kept an eye on. Using their phone was part of the deal.

Inside the house, cold and joyless in winter, Storm dialled

211

the number with stiff fingers and gave the code phrase Molly read from her blue notebook.

Ten minutes later the phone rang, and Molly snatched it up. Their lawyer opened with news of his own. He was with Dr Jarman, who had had a letter too.

Gene and Molly struggled both to hear on one handset. Green Bowers existed; it was well thought of. Between Dr Jarman and the lawyer, they'd established that a Mrs Selena O'Regan had been committed locally. The judge had taken against the husband and, moved by Selena's plea for her children, had ordered her treated in the county – under her grandmother's maiden name, for privacy. There had been no press.

Molly had thought that rescue would be a last resort, but she feared what Mason would do.

We must move quickly.

Gene was looking at her in that superior male way.

'What can we do?' he said to her.

She repeated that and the lawyer said, 'Try to get whichever clown represented her out of the way, so we can get her effective representation.'

Dr Jarman came on the line. 'File for an independent medical examination to slow up any attempt to move her.'

Gene said, 'Won't they know it's us? I mean, someone has to be behind the lawsuit.'

Silence fell, a count maybe of ten or more.

'Okay, that is a complication,' said Dr Jarman.

'It sounds like the court is leaky. Once the press know who Selena is . . . And Dr Jarman, you're not exactly low-profile.'

'I understand,' he growled. 'We'll think of something.'

They agreed to speak again in a couple of hours, which left the decision whether to wait, or spend half that time driving to Halcyon and back.

Cory could walk in and walk Selena out again. The thought just wouldn't leave Molly alone.

While they waited, Molly looked at the bookshelves, such an indicator of a life: whether someone was orderly or not, whether they thought of books as decorations, or heirlooms to be treasured. This bookshelf had all the signs of a vacation home, with old, mismatched paperbacks, big-name authors with crumpled covers, and a set of leather-bound classics bought from a catalogue. Maine winters must give you time to read Dickens and Twain, Molly supposed. There were maps here too, a wildlife book, and guidebooks, including a *Gazetteer of the States*.

Where the heck is Kauwenga Falls anyway? Molly wondered. *How far away?*

Gene and Storm were deep in discussion about what contacts they had — Gene planning flight again — so Molly slipped the *Gazetteer* from the shelf.

It couldn't hurt to know.

Two days later

Molly was on the phone to Rosa, anxious for news.

'Mason's moved for a hearing next week,' Rosa said. 'We're leaving for Kauwenga Falls in an hour. Your sister needs allies on hand.'

Molly wished it was liked *Bewitched*, and she could wiggle her nose and be there.

'Thanks.'

'I have to testify,' Rosa said. 'That man has to be stopped. I think your sister – well, she's a frail vessel. She deserves better.'

Testify? thought Molly.

'About the bruises?' There were no ethics charges against Rosa, and she had examined Selena, that second day in Amber Grove.

'More than that. Selena told me what Mason did.' Rosa took a deep breath. 'Mason is an animal,' she said, with venom. 'I gave her an intimate examination . . . He forced her, Molly, there were clear signs. I need to tell the court that.'

For a moment, Molly thought she had misheard. Then fury came, and disgust and fear.

'The doctors don't believe her,' Rosa said. 'But with a witness . . .'

'They'll call you a liar.'

'I will tell the truth and shame the devil. If she lets me.' Molly could see Rosa, stiff-backed and firm-jawed: precise, professional, unflappable. Rosa would be a witness any lawyer would crave.

Molly found her eyes wet. Why hadn't her sister told her?

Rosa read the silence. 'She made me swear, Molly. She was hurt and ashamed. She says you warned her about that man . . . and she feels she wronged you in the past. I mean, it will be up to her.'

'We need to drop everything and go tomorrow,' Molly said.

After making her farewells, she went to find Gene, already dreading the discussion. They always came back to old arguments, just the two of them sitting on the double bed. But this was urgent.

Gene ventured, 'The kids won't be safe.'

'I'll go on my own,' Molly said, a hundred questions springing up as she said it.

'For what? We're not going to bust Big Sis out – over my dead body, Molly. Even if we were . . . how would you help?' He gave a weak smile. 'I mean, I know you're the brains of the crew, but this is out of your league.'

Molly could lie. She knew hospitals; she had some idea of pretending to be staff, or even a different relative.

'But you look like her,' Gene said. 'They might notice.'

She debated telling Gene about Mason's vile act – at one time she would have told him everything – but he needed no persuading that Mason was bad news. Her husband just wanted his family safe too.

The truth lay between them. Cory would bring something to the mission, something important, something dangerous.

'If Cory came—'

'No! None of the kids. Anyway, you'd want Little Boo with you, and if Elsa is left anywhere, she'll think we're giving up on her. You'll hear the screaming in Bangor.'

'It's only as an absolute back-up.'

'*Huh!*'

Using Cory to rescue Selena was a sticking point for Gene. 'It's just not fair to ask him. He's terrified of his nightmare power. He can't control it. We must never put him in a position which forces him to use it. We'll just be arrested, Molly. *He* might be dissected.' Gene hesitated. 'Molly, let's throw what we have into helping her. But let's be smart and do it from far away.'

Molly was stubborn and had fought Gene often, but a nagging voice was weakening her resolve: he might be right.

In search of allies, Molly found Cory and Elsa in the high room, making an exuberant alien dance with Cory clapping the rhythm.

'Practising a welcome dance,' Cory said, breathing a little fast. 'Laughing fine as welcome is a very happy dance. Purples and humans can dance together, when my people come.'

Molly nearly asked if he had heard anything in a dream. No,

he would have come running as he did with any good news. His ears drooped a little.

'It's a stamping-on-spiders dance,' said Elsa. 'Or cockroaches. I bet Cory's people eat cockroaches. I bet his whole planet is crawling with them.'

Cory paused. 'You . . . you are . . . Grand High President of the Cockroaches.'

Elsa stifled a giggle and flared up. Her synthetic anger was very good. 'Monster! Abomination!'

'Criminal! Cockroach!'

This could take a while. Molly clapped her hands. 'Cory, come on, I need a serious conversation, just us two.'

Elsa's face dropped and her mouth opened to argue.

'Elsa too,' said Cory.

Molly pleaded, 'A few minutes, sweetie-pie, then you can decide what we have for supper.'

'Elsa too.'

Molly gave in.

'You know we said Aunt Selena was in a healing place and wanted to get out? To be with her boys?'

'Yes,' said Cory, ears alert. 'You had clever plan.'

'Well, we need to be closer to her to help get her out.'

Cory's ears folded down. 'You want me to sneak in and sneak her out? She doesn't like me very much no-no-no. Also, how many Bad Men—?'

'Dad and I agree, we should try other things first. It would be to help us hide if we needed. We need to go there to tell some people what we know, face to face.'

'Humans should invent picture phones,' said Cory.

'Rosa and Dr Jarman will be there too. We'd just be there to help.'

'Oh good,' said Cory. 'This plan means we can see Rosa and Dr Jarman? Good people Elsa.'

'Yes, if we're careful.'

'If Elsa comes too, we'll need a big car.'

Molly looked at Elsa, whose face was impassive. That was always a tricky sign.

Molly waited too long. Cory gripped his head. 'Oh no oh no oh no. We must take Elsa. She will promise, she will behave; I will make her. Grown-ups keep letting her down.'

Molly looked at her son, and thought again how Earth might be corrupting him. What was he learning? What lay behind those wide-open violet eyes, and the twitching of his tentacles?

Gene and Molly were deadlocked.

Her sister, powerless and ill, could be handed back to a vindictive, brutal man, her rapist.

So, she thought, *I'll leave Gene behind. He'll have to follow.*

That thought became a plan, a desperate plan. An unwise plan that kept her from sleep. All night she tossed and turned, thinking of her sister frightened and unprotected in that place, her sister alone if the end of the world came.

And Mason, the monster, prowling around outside the institution, the mere possibility of it tormenting Sel . . .

At five o'clock, Carol was already up and in the kitchen.

Molly needed to explain. 'I'm going to bundle the kids in the car and go.'

After an instant of shock, Carol placed her cup down

219

with care and started listening. 'To Kauwenga Falls, without Gene?'

Yes, if I must. She ignored her inner doubts.

'Gene will come. I'll leave a note. But this is the only way he'll know I'm serious. He's right, we can't use Cory to break in. But Sel needs to know I'm there for her.'

Carol was silent, working it through.

'Hard to tell, other people's marriages,' she said.

Molly drank her coffee; she was itching to work through the packing list.

'I mean, Storm and I have our disagreements.'

Molly felt she had to justify herself. 'He's so stubborn. He needs to realise—'

'Yet you talked him out of going into the lion's den for his father? Who might have been dying? Seems quite a listener to me.'

'I've got to force the issue. Time is ticking.'

'Molly, you need some plain speaking,' said Carol. 'This idea is nuts.'

Molly glared at her. Last week Carol had suggested Molly try therapy. *I don't need your permission. Your interference.*

Carol went on, 'Suppose he thinks *you'll* back down, what are you going to do? Sit in a diner and wait for three days?'

'We need to get there before the hearing.'

'You've decided to go and you're just looking for an excuse. It's about making Gene responsible if you end up taking the kids on your own.'

That was a piercing, painful truth.

Now Molly was tottering on the high wire and really not sure which side she would fall.

Carol said, 'I'll talk to Storm. You need people with you who won't be recognised, and a change of drivers.'

'You'll help?'

Carol took a few moments, then said, 'I'll talk to Storm.' She wasn't smiling.

It was a grey morning, but the clouds promised rain, not snow. Spring really was coming. Elsa complained it was too early to go driving, but she and the baby were already in the Beast, the only vehicle big enough to hold them all. Carol brought Molly's case last.

'I'll follow in mine.'

'Will you come all the way?'

'I haven't decided.'

But Cory had questions. Those pleading violet eyes, a firm little hand on her arm. 'When will Dad come? When *exactly*?'

Molly had hated her own mother's casual lying, but the pure truth wouldn't do here either. 'Dad needs to do some things. He won't be long, and we won't be far away.'

'What things? Why isn't he waving us off?'

'He needs his sleep. I've left a note, to make sure he remembers, and Joel knows too.'

'But Mom, Dad will definitely and most certainly come?' There was such insistence for the truth in the voice. 'Promise?'

'Yes, Cory, he will.'

'Suppose something bad happens. Suppose the Bad Men come—'

'They won't, and Joel would hide him, and tell us.'

Molly realised she'd been avoiding his eyes; she needed to

meet his gaze again. Cory looked up at her and she saw the uncertainty on his face. Felt it, radiating out from him.

'Cory trusts you, Mom. Not all humans can be trusted. No, not at all. Very bad thing about Earth.'

She could tell him the full truth. And he would hide and go into the house to tell Gene.

'I'm not planning to go to Kauwenga Falls without him,' she said. 'It's going to be much better if he comes.'

Cory did his human sigh. Then he got in the Beast, still not truly convinced, and she tried to clamp down on the sadness and disgust at herself.

Storm revved up the Beast, which growled and complained. Molly didn't like the way the Beast handled, and Gene was no fan either. Carol would follow in her car.

They had been safe at Halcyon, and now she was leaving to go tilting at windmills. She kept feeling these waves of doom crashing around in her stomach.

An hour's drive later, they were at a place that Carol knew well: a gloomy guesthouse in black and dark green, set back from the road. Its white shutters looked like an afterthought. There was something a bit ramshackle about the chimney; the porch missed a coat of paint.

Two women lived there – friends of friends. 'It's kind of a place for women,' Carol said. 'They'll be fine with Gene, if I vouch for him, and if he doesn't stay long.'

The greeting was glacial. One woman was in her sixties, lean and disapproving. The other, rather younger, was unsmiling.

There was a terse, whispered conversation. It was obvious they were not welcome.

Joel would phone from Halcyon when Gene left. The plan really depended on her being out of touch, so Gene couldn't get hold of her. He might get the number out of Joel, though.

Inside, Molly was sitting with Fleur in the room with the phone. Untidy shelves and stacks of magazines surrounded her. Of all things, there was a table set with geological specimens, fossils, the skull of a lynx.

Gene would phone, tell her she was nuts and that he wouldn't come. She bit her lip, trying to distract herself. Sitting here, it was obvious he would call her bluff.

Cory and Elsa were off together being secretive somewhere. She picked up a copy of *Ms* magazine, flicking through it. In its pages, ideas which had once seemed revolutionary were being openly discussed. The Equal Rights Amendment had been sent out to the states to be ratified. The President supported it. Strange times.

Mason's crime was not a crime in the laws written by men.

They would have equal rights under the snakes: equal rights under death.

Two hours after she'd left Halcyon, she checked the phone had a dialling tone. There were only a couple of days before the hearing.

Why had she done this? Gene needed to understand what danger Selena was in. Of course, if she phoned him – well, he would have the upper hand. And husband and wife arguing over the phone never worked.

Fleur watched her, coughed a little: a pretty little stoic. Molly

223

let her chew a spoon, watch the glitter of a bright pebble. Molly told stories and made animal noises with the fossils.

After three hours, she told the others she was going for a walk, left Fleur with the other women and went to where she could see the road. Twenty minutes later, Molly felt foolish and cold. She turned round and saw Storm marching towards her.

'Joel called. Gene's left in a foul temper. Molly, this wasn't your smartest idea.'

'I'm glad,' she said. She'd done something stupid, and she needed to fix it. 'He'll be here for lunch.' A thought hit her. 'If you disapprove, why did you—?'

Storm produced a set of car keys.

'Carol thought you might go on your own. So I took these. You weren't going anywhere.'

Molly reached for them, and Storm moved them away.

Back inside, Cory and Elsa had written a song: 'When will Dad come?' Of course, now she couldn't drive back in case they missed each other.

Another hour passed, then two. Molly flicked through books of no interest.

Then a horn sounded from somewhere out front.

Storm was out first, Molly rushing after. A tow-truck had appeared, an unfamiliar face behind the wheel. It was towing Dr O'Brien's car. Its front fender and hood were all bent in. Gene, wrapped in scarves, was sitting behind the driver. As soon as the truck came to rest, Gene opened the door and was out.

She'd prepared an apology, an angry defence, a full-frontal attack, but in her heart was capitulation. Now she saw him, driving full of anger because of her, coming off the road – but for a spin of the wheel, he might have died . . .

'Kids okay?' Gene said, frowning, looking world-weary.

The fight had completely drained out of her. 'Yes. They're not talking to me much. Are you all right?'

'Yeah. It was the other guy's fault.' She could tell that wasn't the whole truth. 'Another couple of satellites gone. It said on the radio. Something up there sure doesn't want us in space.'

The driver was looking at her, at her ugly disguise glasses and all. He seemed excited, as if he already knew who they were.

Gene gave the driver a thumbs-up. 'He figured it out. If he hadn't been passing . . .'

'I'm cold,' Molly said. 'Come on, let's get inside.'

The driver put down Gene's bag and guitar, while Storm made herself scarce.

'We need to settle this, and not in front of the kids,' Gene started. 'You're nuts, Molly. You've done some damn-fool stuff in your time but—'

'You weren't *listening*,' she said. *Don't cry, Molly, don't cry.*

'Says you. I can't believe our friends fell for this nonsense. Splitting us up . . . ? It was just crazy!'

'You started it—'

'I didn't want to put the kids in danger.'

'I haven't – not really.' It all felt so stupid now. The wind was up, blowing the cold into her heart.

'So, these are my conditions,' said Gene. 'None of us try to get into Green Bowers. It needs to be top secret we're even in the area, let alone involved in the case. No Cory powers. No midnight rescue.'

Suddenly, it felt easy to agree. 'You're right, of course.' She touched his hand, but he didn't react. 'I promise. Sel won't even know I'm there,' she said, more for something to say.

'She can, if we can trust her to keep her mouth shut.' It was almost a snarl. 'And then we'll decide where we go next. Halcyon is driving us nuts. You owe me, Molly.'

He might be in a better mood when he'd eaten. She would have thanked him, but for that last part. *Owe me?*

Hang on, Sel, she thought. *We're coming.* But there wasn't any joy in that thought.

CHAPTER 22

Finding Mrs O'Regan

Dr Pfeiffer looked from the window at Lake Delaney and the town that clustered on its southern edge, lights gleaming in the darkness. Kauwenga Falls would have been pretty on a postcard, but small-town America bored him, always preaching its own virtue, backwards, and resolute in local superstition.

It was a clear night and the stars blazed. Out there, a struggle more momentous even than the war between freedom and Communism was being waged: a struggle between life and destruction. Snake machines were orbiting the Earth; they had already struck down *Pioneer* and several satellites in humanity's back yard – so why had they stayed their hand? What were they plotting? Maybe, just maybe, they had inadequate numbers for an attack and this was just the cosmic equivalent of a few snipers in the forest. He certainly hoped so.

Pfeiffer did what he did for the future of humanity.

His precisely sculpted goatee itched. He could not wait to get rid of the disguise; it was like an annoying parasite – but he'd been the only one able to bluff his way into Green Bowers. Norton, the laughing, ice-cool leader of Overton's team, had somehow found sketch-maps of the interior layout. And the orderly, their man on the inside, was essential.

Pfeiffer, no fan of amateur dramatics, had borrowed a colleague's obsession with a link between viruses and mental illness — had borrowed, in fact, his name and even his appearance. The director of Green Bowers, flattered, had agreed to let Pfeiffer see the key files, which had allowed Pfeiffer to read Selena O'Regan's notes, as well as access the inner sanctum, where he took photos of the alarm system, somewhere the orderly could never go.

He checked his watch. Norton and his men would be waiting to slip into the institution; the orderly only had to persuade Mrs O'Regan to the side door. For Selena, the chance of freedom and her children were enough to get compliance.

Pfeiffer pulled on the unfamiliar coat and hat and picked up the all-important case. His stomach quivered. He shouldn't have let himself be talked into handling the orderly himself. Overton would never come within two hundred miles himself, but he had insisted that only Pfeiffer could be trusted to handle the delicate negotiation.

As the plan hurtled towards resolution, Pfeiffer felt outwitted, a flank exposed — but if Overton's spies were correct, Dr Jarman and his wife, the nurse, were already in the area. The Myers' old gang was getting back together.

Pfeiffer left the hotel, the sidewalks and roads still crunching with grit. He shivered as the bitter wind hit him, but here was the car that would take him to calm Mrs O'Regan — with words or, if all else failed, a needle. He would have to explain the delay in getting the boys. The judge clearly didn't trust Mr O'Regan one little inch, for he had placed the boys with the Sheriff's family. The issue now was less whether Norton could get the boys but whether he could do it quietly: could his men take that fortress of a farmhouse before the news was radioed across the world.

Pfeiffer was plagued with second thoughts. The orderly might change his mind. Smuggling out Selena's letters was very different to busting her out. He was a decent man and he might go to the police – perhaps that had been his intention all along. The plan might fail.

Yet surely Mrs Myers, an emotional woman, would react to her sister's pleas – the letter, the phone calls to mutual acquaintances. And then the Myers, and Cory, would all be safe – under his care.

He just had to go through with it. His guts writhed again, and yet again he tasted the chalky medicine he needed to keep it quiescent.

They drove past the modest church where he had done the deal. The orderly was a trusted member of staff, but his wife's cancer had spread and he was hopelessly in debt. Pfeiffer had felt guilty watching a good man wrestle with a strong conscience.

'Mrs O'Regan's a nice lady,' the orderly had said. 'I just wonder—'

'Don't worry,' Pfeiffer had said. 'The plan is fool-proof. And you're helping her keep her boys: that alone is a wonderful thing you're doing. We're her friends. We're not asking you to do anything wrong.'

'You promised—'

'Yes, and everything I said was true. Mrs O'Regan won't be harmed. She'll be reunited with her children. And we'll protect you from suspicion.'

Cancer was a terrible disease. All the new surgeries, radiation and chemotherapy made some impact, but they were still so crude. *Maybe*, thought Pfeiffer, *what we could learn from Cory's biology or from his people would make it a thing of the past.*

Overton was a tidy man and the orderly was a risk. He'd offer the family free treatment, a new job, a new name, in one of his hospitals down South – and whisk them to another state to ensure their silence.

Pfeiffer felt his pulse rise. There was Green Bowers, a pleasant house set among evergreens. Selena's disappearance must flush out the Myers one way or another, but surely even Mrs Myers would be grateful.

And where Mrs Myers was, Cory would be nearby.

CHAPTER 23

'Visit Scenic Kauwenga County'

Kauwenga County was rolling farmland and wooded hills. The two-car expedition arrived there late on the second day, and for safety, would be staying five miles out of town. It was very like Amber County, but although Molly could see differences, she couldn't quite put her finger on them – the churches and barns, maybe? They drove past the town and around the scenic lake, and, in a wild moment, Molly was tempted to *go now* – to get it over with. *Go tonight, use Cory. Get it done.*

She pushed that thought away: she'd promised Gene. In any case, the idea of what might go wrong terrified her.

Gene was still brooding, so Molly tried to lift his mood. 'I told you we would travel, see exciting new places,' she joked.

His silence said, *Huh*. He had not really forgiven Carol and Storm either.

She had gambled and got what she wanted and yet she'd lost. She knew Gene was waiting for something to go wrong – something to prove this whole trip was a dangerous mistake. He thought the biggest danger was Selena's lawyers, who would have to pretend they did not know the Myers were in town. Rosa would be testifying in support of Selena, but she was a public figure now. It would only take a smart local journalist and the world would know something was up. Would Mason think everyone knowing the Myers involvement would help him, somehow?

Rosa and Dr Jarman, arriving first, were staying with the senior lawyer's family. For the Myers, he had arranged the use of some summer house where they could avoid prying eyes. Carol and Storm took one room – Carol being 'unable to sleep with strangers, dogs or babies' – which meant Molly and the kids packed into the bed in the other room, with Gene on a mattress on the floor. Elsa was up twice, complaining of toothache, which made for a restless night for everyone.

Early the next morning, a bright, bouncing young lawyer turned up, half Red Setter and half Prom King. He endeared himself to Molly by making the boiler work and producing bags of fruit and pastries – but he brought bad news as well. Selena had been too ill to speak to them yesterday, so she hadn't been able to agree to their plan. The senior partner would be coming as soon as he'd spoken to Selena today.

Dr Jarman and Rosa were next to arrive. As they embraced, Molly thought about how long they'd been apart, how much they had to talk about. She wanted some private time with Rosa – ex-boss, ex-nemesis and now trusted friend.

But right now, the business of the day was pressing. The children took their meal next door, 'because grown-ups needed to talk horrid grown-up things'. They could be trusted not to make a mess, though doubtless, Elsa would be stuffing the dog with pastries.

The lawyer got straight to it. 'We've a stack of motions to file as soon as we can. We'll tell them we want Mrs Jarman to testify – we want to stop the husband and reopen the question of custody.' He looked as though he would relish the fight. 'I imagine we'll be seeing a lot of bad temper from Mr O'Regan's side.'

'Selena's happy with this line of approach?' Dr Jarman asked, squeezing Rosa's hand.

The young lawyer suddenly looked concerned.

He'll need better control to win cases, Molly thought, worried.

'She's been very anxious – and ill,' he admitted. 'The director of Green Bowers was very difficult this morning. The senior partner is on the phone to the place now – threatening them with a court order to give us access to our client.'

'I don't get this,' Gene said. 'A man can rape a woman and get away with it, if she's his wife? I mean, it's a crime to break her jaw, but *that* isn't?'

'That's the law in every state,' said the lawyer. 'There's been some fine talk, but that's where the politicians have left us. So right now, what matters is—'

He was cut off by the sound of the phone ringing. When he answered it, they could tell the person at the other end was furious, but no one could pick out the words.

The lawyer's eyes widened. 'Rivers of fire, they've lost her.'

Molly felt the ground lurch underneath her. She looked at Gene, who looked as horrified as she felt.

The voice crackling down the phone hadn't finished, and now

233

the young lawyer relayed the information as he got it. 'Green Bowers admitted she's disappeared, along with a member of their staff, an orderly on night duty.'

After some more chatter, he reported, 'They've called the police.'

'People will find out who she is,' Gene said, the dismay in his voice almost palpable. 'This town will be knee-deep in reporters by sundown.'

'She must be in danger,' Molly said. 'They must find her – *we* have to look for her.' Even as she said it, she knew the idea of the Myers starting a search in an unknown town was foolish.

The young lawyer handed Molly the phone and she heard the voice of the senior lawyer saying, 'Mrs Myers, this is monstrous. Green Bowers found out at 6 a.m. – and they dared to stall us while they looked for her. She might have been gone since *last night*: it is criminal incompetence.'

'In this weather?' Molly pictured her sister in thin institutional pyjamas, and a sudden conviction seized her. 'Mason's kidnapped her. She's in the most terrible danger.'

'I'm going to court now,' said the lawyer. 'I've asked the chief of police to meet me there. We'll have that snake O'Regan locked up, I promise you.'

'What about her boys?'

'They're fine. Connor and Rory are staying with a police family. But we are hearing now – days later – that there have been unknown men calling at the house. Lord knows why we weren't told immediately, and you may rest assured we will be making certain the judge knows this. Anyway, these men, whoever they were, they didn't get the time of day. Ike was in the

Marines, and both his boys are – and they're back on furlough.
I'd put my dollars on Carrie too; I've seen her kill a deer with
a headshot . . . But Mrs Myers, we must keep you out of this.
We don't want to start any other nonsense – and remember,
we can't know you're here. I'll call when I have more news.'

Gene said, 'The locals will call in the FBI.'

'They'll be criticised every hour they don't,' their lawyer said.

A big Federal manhunt like that? They'd soon figure out who
Selena's sister was.

Molly gripped Gene's hand to keep her afloat. She didn't
know what to do.

They'd been promised an update in an hour, but it was more
than two hours later that the lawyer called. Carol and Storm
disappeared to take photos in town, they said, and the Jarmans
worked on their affidavits.

'They're searching Mason's place now. That wife-beater looks
as guilty as hell, though he's denying everything, of course.'

'We need to get out of here,' Gene said, looking grim. 'This
is all too dangerous –the cops are probably on the way.'

'Yes, we'll get ready to run,' Molly agreed. *But I won't abandon
my sister . . .*

'I'm going to clear my head. You know what Cory's like right
now. Can you imagine how scared he will be if he thinks the
cops are coming?'

I told you so hovered unsaid in the air.

Molly knew she deserved it.

Then Gene, bless him, said, 'I know she's your sister and
we've got to help her – but us getting arrested won't help
anyone. We still need to go.'

235

Sisters together, for ever. Would Selena expect some mad rescue, even with the risk to Molly's children? What risks would she take for Molly?

Love isn't a balance sheet. Molly knew the lawyers would do their best, but Selena needed her.

When Gene had gone off to pack, making the point, Rosa asked, 'So, how is he?'

Where to begin? Molly looked at Dr Jarman, buried in a book. She didn't feel up to discussing her marriage in front of him.

'Good days and bad. Let's talk later.'

The day unfolded, Molly struggling with wanting to do something – anything. Knowing what to say to Cory and Elsa was hardest.

Some hours later, they were told the orderly had been found, beaten and tied up in a neighbour's shed. He was cold and thirsty, and bleeding where he had worked his hands free. It looked simple enough: the night before, he'd gone for a smoke and been jumped by four masked men. They'd subdued him, injected him, and held him down until he passed out. It hadn't been hard to identify their way in: a little-used door into the grounds had been forced.

When the lawyer called again, the news was grim. 'When the police searched O'Regan's motel room and car they found rope, duct tape, bottles of sleeping pills, women's clothes and underwear, and – *ah, um* – some . . . well, personal hygiene products. He didn't do a great job explaining that away.'

Each sentence was making Molly feel colder.

'What possible excuse could he have?' said Gene, his face pressed to Molly's so he too could hear the lawyer.

'The pills are the ones his wife takes – he forgot he had them with him. He'd brought her the clothes she needed, but this was the stuff she didn't want. The rope – just a tow rope for emergencies. There are a hundred things you might need duct tape for on the road. Well, it's all circumstantial, but the chief plans to keep him in the cells, tonight anyway.'

'So what next?' Molly said. It felt like they were in a trap.

'They've already put out her description and started the search.' The tone of his voice changed. 'Of course, neither the judge nor I know her famous sister is in town, but they'll call in the FBI, soon as they figure it out.'

'Why isn't he with Selena?' Gene said suddenly. 'If Mason has her, why aren't they together?'

'That's the $64,000 question,' the lawyer said as he ended the call.

Gene and Molly went into the kitchen, leaving the lawyers to their work.

'That's pretty incompetent, if he is the kidnapper,' said Gene. 'Why would he hang around?'

'He's after the boys. He probably needs Selena to get them.'

'Cory could read if Mason is lying, or the orderly.'

'*Jeez*, Molly – *no!*' Gene banged the table 'We will *not* put our son in danger – we can't let *anyone* know we're around. Maybe Mason is spilling the beans now. No, we need to pack up and move a hundred miles away. We need to be on the road in thirty minutes.'

'Sel might be chained up in some basement,' Molly tried, 'without her medication.'

237

'She doesn't deserve that, or any of this, but I'm not putting *our* heads in a noose. That won't help her, or anyone.'

Molly felt her face getting warmer, the memory still rankling. 'When we were last on the run, we thought the Feds had your parents and I *begged* you not to give us away. You still called them. You could have brought the whole world down on us—'

'That's different. I was careful—'

'You don't care about my sister.'

'Why would you say that? I've sure tried my hardest. Miss Congeniality she isn't. Your sister stabbed us in the back.'

Gene was nibbling his thumb, like some overgrown child. She felt the anger rise and tried to control it. 'You never liked Sel.'

He sighed. 'Molly, there's no talking to you in this mood.'

She could smack him. 'My sister is kidnapped by her rapist and that's *a mood*?'

'I rest my case: we gotta pack and go. Let Edgar and Rosa hold the fort here.'

'Go on, then, *leave us. Go hiking*, why don't you? Take a *vacation*.'

'You can talk.' He made a wild sweep of the arm. '*I* didn't bring the kids into danger.'

She knew he'd bring that up every day until the end of time. It stung that he might even be right.

Gene's face softened and he reached to touch her shoulder, but she brushed him off and opened the door. The Jarmans, not looking at her, lifted their books. She realised they had been listening and she flushed.

'Molly—' Gene said.

'I'm staying. Find out what Cory's doing. I'm going for a walk.'

Outside, there were crocuses, white, yellow and purple: an unexpected beauty that should have lifted her heart. And there was Storm, usually such a strong woman, looking more anxious than Molly had ever seen her.

'What's up?'

'Disappearance Inc — the FBI's found Halcyon. They've searched the place, and arrested Joel.'

Cory was always drawing, the views, the people he was with, writing people's names in alien. Had every sign that the Myers had been there been hidden? She couldn't believe that Joel would betray them — Joel did not know where they were heading — but the inevitable clutter of family life might.

CHAPTER 24

Kites at Dusk

Recovery had been slow. Thunder over Mountains had not been allowed to dream-between-the-stars for weeks, to give his mind and body time to heal. Not that he felt strong enough to try. But there were other things he could do to help the search as the people tried to understand where Little Frog might be.

Wind and waves. Well, that meant a planet with atmosphere and open water. The people were constantly on the look-out for worlds that met those criteria, For the search, it would not have to be a prime colony site, just somewhere a person could survive for a couple of years. There were many such worlds where a single expedition had visited, done a brisk survey, seen no obvious sign of advanced life and left. Many worlds with wind and water had some other inconvenient feature: a most eccentric orbit, an unstable axis of rotation, an unstable sun, or no land at all.

Machine and human minds plotted the many sixteens of worlds which *Dancer on the Waves* might have reached, but visiting all of them would take a lifetime. And they might still miss Little Frog. Suppose he had no working beacon – they might find the right world and still not be able to find him.

There were the optimists who were truly pessimists – Little Frog might be on some deadly world, where sea and sky were poisons like methane, ammonia and the like. Those were more common; the home system had two such planets and four such moons. Yes, it was realistic that a machine mind, or even an automated system, might keep a child alive for years on such a planet – an environmental dome perhaps, or a section of the ship repurposed.

What made this depressing was that the search net would have to be cast so much wider. But at least it gave the modellers something to argue about. What did wind and waves on such worlds sound like? Thunder asked others, to see if their sound models sounded like what he heard.

Little Frog had been yearning for his own kind in the dream, but was he wholly alone? Some of the crew thought that something benign was sleeping near him. No, sending out dreams to find him was the only way. No one could get a stellar map across in a dream, but there must be something that the machine minds could work on – something about how he lived, what the local fauna was like, an odd moon.

Thunder fought the healers until they let him join another search. Maybe the personal link might tip the balance. Who knew?

He prepared, and this time there was a new ritual: everyone he passed touched him, saying, 'We will find your son.' Thunder hated it, but he could see he was giving everyone who had lost someone a taste of hope, so he showed joy and tolerated it.

When sleep came, he fought the dream, until he realised that the healers knew what they were talking about. His resistance to joining was unlike anything he had known, but the crewmates helped him fight his way in. This time, the dreamers made the universe of the dream silent and alone, so they could all listen for a single voice.

Thunder was to centre the dream, and he was surrounded by some of the most adept dream-healers. What should he make his message? It could only be love, a love carelessly neglected, now a love which burned: the love of the whole ship . . .

He focused on Little Frog's humour, his curiosity, his loyalty, his determination.

But Thunder was tiring; there was no rest or solace in this dreaming. It reminded him of swimming against a current, a constant battle against a greater force, simply to stay in the same place. Some of the other dreamers were tiring too—

—and here swam his son, out of nothing. There was fear and sadness, then a flowering of hope as they connected.

Distant, his son said.

Where? Where? Thunder asked.

And images came: a settlement . . . green trees and water (so much for the poison moon theory) . . . a moon almost as splendid as the home-world's . . . the settlement again, in snow now; the settlement under a blazing sun . . .

His son was somewhere where he could run under trees, dive into open waters, fly a kite. A furry animal of some sort ran alongside him. There was a vehicle, whose smell of burning was strangely familiar.

And . . . and there were intelligent creatures who cared

243

for Little Frog. Two were special to him, erect bipeds, partially furred, with opposable thumbs. They had young of their own, a baby and one around Little Frog's size. And Little Frog was trying to get something across, something complicated . . .

Unbelievable! His son almost saw the aliens – those odd-looking beings, dimly familiar – as . . . *parents*. Little Blue Frog lived marooned, but he had found adults, safety and love. Thunder was overjoyed – with relief, with compassion – but he also acknowledged his jealousy, an immature reaction.

His son was the only survivor. *Dancer on the Waves* must have been utterly destroyed.

Still reeling from the contact, Thunder sat at a console, alongside Skimming Stone and three others. There was hope and fear between them, and bewilderment too. Joy began to seem premature.

They had made contact easier. Or he was learning this dangerous science better. The healers were anxious and watched him, but he had enough strength to do this.

'Machine, search for a world with these criteria. Home-class biosphere, with intelligent aliens,' Skimming Stone said. 'Addition, bipedal aliens.'

'Episodic climate, probably a tilted axis like the colony-world,' said Thunder. 'Or an eccentric orbit. Separate criterion, a large moon.'

'Powered vehicles burning something, so an industrial world using residue fuel,' said Eat Demon Claws.

The final criterion was only worlds which lay within

Thunder's most optimistic model. Only worlds *Dancer on the Waves* might just have reached with everything in their favour.

One answer, the machine said.

The machine brought up the space map, showing the cloud of probability where *Dancer* was guessed to have gone. The target world was a burning light. So, *Dancer on the Waves* had been off-course, but nowhere near the extremes of their prediction. They were months away, but it could have been so much worse. It seemed credible.

'Full report, please.' Thunder was sure he'd seen a drawing of those aliens before; there would be a report.

'That is not currently convenient.'

That was machine-talk meaning *forbidden*.

'Why?'

'It is not currently convenient to say.'

The group was baffled. Hidden information was almost a paradox.

Skimming Stone asked, 'What level of authority will make it convenient?'

'It is not currently convenient to say.'

'A message to the leadership team, please. We've found where *Dancer on the Waves* reached. There's a living survivor on an inhabited planet – Thunder's son – and we need more information.'

There was a pause, then the leader-for-today came on. 'You found Thunder's son? You'd better come to the coordinating lodge.'

Thunder was exhausted and he didn't want a fight. But his team helped him up and they explained their findings. The leadership team went into closed session. Extraordinary. Yet, it was not a long discussion, as these things go, and it ended in his favour.

He sat with the leader-for-now and they called up the report.

'The whole people will rejoice your son is found. But there is danger and you deserve to know. A decision was taken for the-all, a generation ago, not to release the full survey reports and to forbid unauthorised visits to this system. I knew nothing of this until I had your request. Read it; the summary will be enough.'

Intrigued and fearful, Thunder began to consume the report, which had warnings of disturbing and violent content. Yes, there was no doubt, these were the aliens he had seen.

A few breaths into the report, he was quivering with fear. The survey team had nicknamed the planet where Little Frog was stranded *Nightmare that Kills*.

CHAPTER 25

The dentist

Cory and Elsa bathed Fleur, who gurgled and waved her fists as she lay naked on her back, kicking for the fun of it in front of the electric fire. Naked time helped her skin rash, and Cory liked the warmth of the fire behind its metal guard.

The grown-ups had gone out to the car to have an argument about Aunt Selena.

'Very quiet, Mr Centre of the Universe,' said Elsa, rubbing her cheek. Her gum was puffed up and infected. The dentist tomorrow would be a big drama; Elsa had needed a lot done when she came to the Myers and she hadn't liked it. Cory couldn't help – dentistry on home-world didn't hurt. Mom wanted to be the adult with Elsa, but that was too dangerous, but she would wait in the car.

'Miss Spikey Sister. Porcupine. I'm glad my people know where I am. But it will be a while before they get here.' The Ship had told them Earth had been monitored for twenty years, so at least they knew where it was.

'Are Gene and Molly going to stay together?'

They'd both told him they would – even though they did such strange things. He nodded, because he would try to make sure anyway.

'Your starship will come and all the dumb humans will have to sort themselves out,' Elsa pointed out. 'It will be Cory Cory Cory Cory. And they will take you to the stars, and your mom will end up going because you and your dad want to go. Children's Services will put me in one of those big places full of older children. Bullies or bedwetters, that's all there is. Or they will find some awful person to give me to . . . They gave me back to *him*.'

'I won't let that happen,' Cory promised. 'Mom and Dad want to be your parents – of course we'll take you with us.'

She put her hand out to tickle Fleur. 'She's dry. We should dress her.'

Cory got warm clothes for his little sister to sleep in.

So warm, but when he thought of Bad Men, he shivered everywhere. The family must always be so-so careful.

Molly woke bleary-eyed with a cricked neck from dreams of home, uncomfortable in the small bed. She realised Fleur was wailing, but sitting up too quickly, she banged her head against the stupid shelf. How she longed for her own bed, her own bath, her books and photos, a kitchen she knew. She missed her friends above all, people to laugh and joke together, to share the dreadful fact of Selena's disappearance, the fear that Mason might well be telling the truth and did not know where she was.

It made small lumpy beds and cold showers seem minor.

She got out of bed, and her cramps came.

And on top of it all, either her son was deluded or the purples were truly coming.

'I'll drive,' Storm said after breakfast, then added, 'We should bring Cory.' No one needed to say that they wanted him up their sleeves if something went wrong. Of course, he was also a constant ally on the dentist issue.

Elsa handed Gene the guitar and demanded he play it, but Gene refused. 'If you put your coat on, I'll find a song you haven't heard before. For when you're back.'

'What's it called?'

'That's for you to find out. For when you're back.'

It felt as practised as theatre.

Gene met Molly's gaze and strummed a few chords. 'Molly Skating on the Moon' — the song he wrote to propose to her, the first song of his she'd heard. That day her heart had leaped and she had said yes.

Molly smiled, feeling tears prickle. There was still tenderness sometimes, a healing embrace . . . but, 'We don't have time!' She kissed Fleur goodbye and handed her to Gene. The baby could sit with a little help, and wobble-headed, view the world. Fretful, because a tooth was coming, and yet capable of a dragon-slayer of a smile. By an enormous effort of will, she didn't infuriate Gene by reminding him of twenty important things.

'I want my song,' said Elsa, and Molly said, 'Sooner we go, sooner we can get back.' Cory and the dog were already in the Beast and Molly slipped in the passenger seat, leaving Storm and Gene still cajoling Elsa on the steps.

Molly put on a grey wig.

'Elsa must go with us to the stars when my people come.'

This is truly great timing.

'She thinks you don't want her.'

'Cory, she must know that's not true.'

Molly felt the warmth of the hot-water bottle down low and was grateful for the relief it brought.

'Then human word: *adopt* her now. All-decide.'

'It's not that simple, sweetie-pie. A lot of different people have to make checks.' They were wanted by the police, hunted by the media, with Cory the Monster. She dreaded to think how Child Services would react to that.

Cory went silent for a count of twenty, then, his voice strained, asked, 'Is Cory going to stars all alone? Mom and Dad prefer Earth. I will leave humans. No Elsa or Fleur or Bonnie or Chuck . . .'

What a time to bring this up.

Let his people come, for the world's sake. Let them never come, for mine.

'I don't know, Cory. We just don't know any of the things we need to know. Perhaps humans could give the purples a nice warm island.'

'Which island?'

She put her hand over her eyes, feeling the pricking of a headache letting her know it was coming. The sun was out. Spring was on the march. Fresh air might help.

Elsa, protesting not wisely but too well, told Gene he was rotten, and then stood on tiptoe to kiss his nose.

Storm got into the driver's seat. 'Come on, Elsa.'

And finally, they were on their way.

Cory lay in the back with his head in Elsa's lap and burbled while Elsa would describe the scenery they were passing
through, often making up outrageous things. Meteor liked
being driven; she wagged her tail constantly, her tongue lolling
out.

The town looked postcard-perfect in the sun, with buildings alongside steep roads running down to the glittering lake.
Storm parked the Beast on a hill, close to a doctor, a dentist
and a ship's store, all close together on this side. There was a
coffee-shop and a pharmacy on the other side, as well as guest-
houses and a curious narrow alley.

Storm kicked the wedges behind the wheels. 'So, Elsa, you
and I will go in and the dentist will stop that pain. And then
we'll go and do something fun.'

'I know Elsa will be brave,' Cory said. 'Mom can get pancakes.'

'Pancakes first,' said Elsa.

Molly said nothing, thinking about the other flaw in this
plan, because sitting in the car for an hour wouldn't be that
interesting for Cory. He might start on again about what would
happen in the dark muddle that was the future. She handed
him a book and suggested he read to her. He was wrapped in
his waterproof – it might look odd to have the hood up inside
the car, but he had to, so casual passers-by would see nothing
of interest.

As soon as the others had gone, he started. 'Whhhhyy can't
Elsa stay?' Cory said, eyes, tentacles and ears pleading.

'Sweetie-pie, I'd love that, but it's not our decision. Surely,
on your planet, the grown-ups sometimes have to decide these

251

things?' The cramps twisted again. *Damn*.

'I guess – but the children are heard too. Maybe two different lodges so all agree, big and small. Earth is not satisfactory. I want to go explore, all-hidden, very safe.'

'Maybe later. Right now, I'd like you around, in case I need you. Read me a story.'

Neither the painkillers nor the hot-water bottle were doing much good. She needed something stronger.

'Cory, I will be five minutes. I'm just going into the pharmacy.'

'Go to café – get pancakes please.'

'We'll see. Hide until I'm back, okay?' She checked her appearance in her little mirror, swung out of the car, picked up the stick which was part of her act and walking a little slower than usual, she looked around for danger. The café was directly over the road. A burly man was sitting in the window, staring out at the street. He looked at Molly but didn't react.

The bell above the door *tinged* as she walked into the blazing hot pharmacy. Shelves ran down the middle of the shop; at the other end, a short man in an outdoor hat with furry earflaps was listening to the pharmacist. She went halfway in, standing back to give the man privacy. She hated when other customers listened in to discussion of bowels, cramps or the myriad inconveniences of pregnancy.

The pharmacist, who looked about seventy, was explaining at a snail's pace why it would take three days to get this drug and how you read in the magazines about this and that new-fangled medication, but he still recommended the tried and tested. The short man's body quivered, like he was about to punch the man.

Something nagged at her, a sinister memory, but it wasn't until he spoke that a shock ran through Molly's body.

The voice was high, aggressive, and dripping with entitlement. 'Nonsense. I'm a qualified physician and I have written myself a simple prescription I need filled, *now.*'

Dr Pfeiffer. Thank heavens his back was turned while he was arguing with the druggist. Every possibility she could think of was bad.

Behind the pharmacist, there was a mirror advertising some ancient cure. Pfeiffer looked up and saw her in the reflection. He wore an absurd pointed beard.

Molly turned, playing old, and strode back to the door, the stick swinging in her hand. Behind her, she heard the pharmacist call. There was someone coming into the pharmacy, a burly white man of middle age: the man who had been sitting in the window of the café. This time she saw recognition in his face, and she saw him try to cloak it.

'Mrs M . . . Molly,' called Dr Pfeiffer, in his oiliest voice. 'What a surprise! Please don't go. Please, five minutes . . .'

Yes, she had talked to Pfeiffer since his disgrace, but only on her terms, and only with a careful plan. Thank goodness she had the spare keys for the Beast.

The man from the café stood in the doorway, blocking her way out. He tried a nervous smile. 'The doctor wants a minute of your time.'

She heard Pfeiffer come up behind her, and the pharmacist's complaint.

Her heart was racing: fight or flight or both. 'Out of my way, please,' she said, in purest Brooklyn. She felt Pfeiffer pull at her left sleeve.

Should she push the man aside, or hit out with the stick?

'Out of my way!' she said. *Let words do the work.*

Pfeiffer was already beside her, holding her arm. 'Please believe we have nothing but your family's best interests at heart. I have important news—'

She shoved sideways into Pfeiffer, as hard as she could, and he fell into the shelves, toppling them to the crash of broken glass and falling bottles. She almost lost her balance, but he was no longer holding her.

The man was coming towards her, his attention on the stick. He smelled of that old-fashioned soap. He was big but he didn't move like an athlete, or the thugs she had dealt with before, so she dropped her head and charged him. He half caught her and they wrestled a little, half in and out of the door. He was bigger, but she was a mother fighting to get back to her child.

'I'm calling the cops!' cried the pharmacist.

There came a bellow, and again: the Beast's horn. Molly's heart was in her mouth – Cory must be in danger, why else would he use the horn?

She had a chance and she took it. Biting the brute's ear as if Cory's life depended on it, she jabbed four fingers into his gut. Like a dog, she held on, wrenching at the ear until the man shrieked, loosened his grip – and she was through the door. Without the stick, alas.

Outside was trouble, as she expected: the door of the Beast was open and beside it was a weedy man in thick glasses: Tyler, Dr Pfeiffer's faithful lapdog, who jerked with shock when he saw Molly.

There was no sign of Cory, which meant he must have hidden. If he grabbed her, they would both vanish. 'Sweetie-pie!' she shouted.

Her wig had come off and people were staring, from the street, through windows – then a truck hit her from behind and she was falling with that great animal of a man on her. He'd tackled her like she was a footballer.

She slammed into the floor, crushed and hurting; knees, hands and back roared their complaints, and she couldn't breathe.

'You *brainless idiot*!' screamed Dr Pfeiffer. 'M-Molly, are you hurt?'

'What in heck happened here?' came a young man's voice. 'Ma'am, you all right?'

'The brute!' said a woman's voice.

The brute rolled off her and Molly managed a couple of painful gulps of breath. She tried to get onto her hands and knees. People were surrounding her now: a sporty young guy, two middle-aged women; a grey-haired black man in a white apron coming from the café. *Witnesses*. But mostly she needed to catch her breath.

Tyler trotted over, fumbling inside his coat for something.

'I do believe he tripped,' Dr Pfeiffer said. 'Our lady friend is unwell; can you help us get our dear friend Mrs Smith up.'

'I know a tackle when I see one,' said the sporty guy, his fists clenched. 'I hafta ask you *gentlemen* to step back from the lady – right now.' If he had any qualms taking the brute on, he wasn't showing it. 'Ma'am, who are these people?'

'I'm her doctor, and her friend,' Pfeiffer said, an oily smile on his face. 'She has paranoid episodes. We just need to get her somewhere quieter and talk to her.'

'These men are loan-sharks,' Molly gasped, in her Brooklyn accent. 'They're after my husband – they're threatening our children.'

'Back, now!' snapped the would-be rescuer at Pfeiffer. 'Mr Adams, give me a hand.'

The black cook strode over, his concern clear. Someone decided honking their horn would clear the street. There was always someone who thought honking a horn was smart.

Molly was getting worried. *Where is Cory?*

'I have a gun,' said Tyler, waving it.

Dr Pfeiffer looked terrified.

'I did two years in Korea,' said the cook, Mr Adams, to Tyler, as calm and straight-backed as if he was talking him through the day's specials. 'I ate chow that frightened me more than you do. Don't make a fool of yourself, just give me that.'

The sporty guy helped Molly to her feet. 'Ma'am, are you okay?'

And here was Meteor, licking her hand and making little grunts. *But where was Cory?* He only needed to sneak in and touch her – it was a crowd, sure, but he could hide from this many if he was careful. There were two cars now stalled on the hill, just watching.

'If I can just get in my car, I'll be fine,' Molly said.

The rescue guy was looking at her. 'Won't you want to give a statement, ma'am?' He glanced at Pfeiffer and back to her.

She debated trying her loudest scream – maybe then Pfeiffer would flee. But if the townspeople had recognised her – and

256

their photos had been all over the television – the police would surely arrest her.

A shot rang out and Adams, the cook, swore loudly as he fell to the road, clutching his thigh.

Pfeiffer was suddenly standing next to her and she felt a stab in her leg, his coffee breath in her face. 'I have Selena, safe,' he hissed. 'Just play along.'

She didn't believe him. She was about to drive her knee between his legs when she felt Cory's terror, a wave of ice dragging her stomach down, making her skin prickle under winter clothes. It was like the sun had gone in and the world become hewed from ice, how even the memory of warmth was untrue.

Cory was standing by the door of the dentist, in his yellow waterproof, and the spectators shrieked, gawping in astonishment, and stepped back. 'Cory is the Monster,' he fluted, hands out, crouching. He quivered with the power, sending out waves of fear and self-loathing, each stronger than the last. 'All-must-go-away. Cory will hurt everyone. Leave Mom *alone*!'

Meteor, whining, scampered away.

'Now, Cory—' said Dr Pfeiffer, shaking.

'Evil-liar-man, Dr Pfeiffer. Run away. Cory is the Monster.'

And the terror came roiling out of him, a pure torrent of primal fear that made dogs whine and people scream. Cory was trying to control it, but nightmares were coming, formless fears dredging up old wounds of death and loss.

Molly realised, shocked, that Cory no longer believed he could control it. He was opening the box containing all the troubles of the world.

Pfeiffer was gasping out shrill commands as he and the brute hustled her down the hill . . .

She wanted to save her boy, before the power burned him out . . .

Gene would die, and her children. Once she had awakened from a dream like this, sweat running down her face – and now she was living it. Gene and the children: dead in a hail of bullets. Fire from the sky. Amber Grove disappearing in a nuclear strike, living people turned to shadows, to ash and smoke. The air and the sea and the sky dead, the Earth a lifeless rock in space.

Elsa was running out of the dentist, clutching her bag and her coat. Everything was confusing. Molly's mind was too full of Cory's nightmares, nightmares out of control. She tried to struggle, but her limbs were no longer obeying her. Nothing made sense . . .

The cramps became the loss of her first nameless daughter, her hands red with blood and yellow with paint as she sank into a grief so powerful she embraced darkness and oblivion.

CHAPTER 26

Dr Pfeiffer

Her head was fuzzy and her eyelids heavy. She had not been out long. She was in a moving car full of loud, clashing male voices, jammed between two people who smelled of old-fashioned soap and cologne and male sweat.

'Pull in there, off the road. The police will be after us. I'm tempted to shoot you myself.' That familiar, irritating voice was Dr Pfeiffer.

So the whining must be Tyler, in the front seat.

'You made a mess of that,' said a calm, strong voice from the driver's seat. 'Most likely, the police have a description of the car. We need to figure out how to get the boy now we have his mom.'

She didn't know that voice.

The brute who had tackled her said, 'That thing – that-that *monster* – I'm not going anywhere near it.'

'Yes, they might recognise the car,' Dr Pfeiffer said, ignoring the brute. 'I need time to think.'

'So we get new wheels. You don't need to be Scientist of the Year to know that.'

Nothing was quite making sense to Molly. Opening her eyes felt like too much effort. It was like the time the tyre swing had clipped her head when she was eight. Or when she'd fainted in high school, after a fever. For a few moments of confusion, she thought: *you're a drunk; you passed out!* The horror of that thought helped her focus. Pfeiffer had injected her. She moved a hand, trying to feel her own pulse, and found her wrists constrained.

Brute said, 'Count me out, Norton.'

Molly was pleased to see through barely opened eyes that he was holding a cloth to his ear.

Dr Pfeiffer responded, 'You botched it – the simplest thing in the world, just to hold Mrs Myers for a little. She's a housewife, not a Viet Cong assassin. I just needed to tell her we have her sister, safe and well; we'll rescue her nephews. We'll all work together – no coercion, everyone gets what they want.'

The brute grunted.

'I didn't know it would fire,' Tyler whined. 'Assault and kidnapping – I'll die in prison!'

Dr Pfeiffer snapped, 'Imbecile. If you hit the femoral artery, you might have killed him. Then it would be *murder.*'

Play dead, thought Molly. She tasted blood – and then, right on cue, the cramps decided to remind her of their existence.

Her son was terrified and alone, watching the crowd whipped to hysteria by his power. Cory out of control and open to the vengeance of the mob replayed itself in her head and she could not control the shudder.

Norton, the driver, said, 'There's a car place up ahead. No one saw me, so I'll hire a new one, a truck if we can. Then we go back. You saw that tall, handsome woman driving the vehicle? She took the girl to the dentist – who's she? And any idea who the girl is?'

'Storm DuBois,' Dr Pfeiffer said. 'Of course. I've just remembered – she's from *Witness* magazine. Miss Longman and Storm have been very quiet for a long time. I hope Mrs Myers is okay, that nothing's broken.'

Something cold and wet touched her face and Molly moved, opening her eyes to see Dr Pfeiffer. He had the bedside manner of an undertaker.

'Get off!' His physical closeness repelled her.

'Mrs Myers, this is unfortunate—'

'Let me go,' Molly growled. 'Kidnapper!'

'This is a disaster. I just wanted to explain, we helped your sister escape. We need to go back to get Cory, to keep him safe and well. He mustn't fall into the hands of local law enforcement or vigilantes.' He tutted, adding, 'The press has been *so* irresponsible.'

Molly didn't believe him, of course. They were speeding along local roads, the lake to their left, heading north through mixed woods and farmland. She needed to be clear, cunning. Yes, the sun was behind them.

Her son was terrified, and the aftermath of using his power so widely always made him ill – then, with a shudder, she realised that maybe Elsa was in danger too. Or perhaps the unshakeable Storm had them both. But how would Molly ever find her?

'Believe me,' Pfeiffer said, 'that wasn't how it was supposed to have happened.'

261

Molly tried to make her voice low and slow and strong. Mama Grizzly. 'I demand you take me back to my son.'

The car pulled into a turning by a sign advertising *Joe's Motors 200 yards*. Norton was in complete control of himself: no movement wasted, no word, either. He had a strong jaw, the rugged lead from a cowboy movie. When he smiled at her, she knew he posed more danger than the other three put together.

'Try not to get beaten up by Mrs Myers,' Norton said to the men, winking at her, then he was gone.

It was cold once you were in the dark shadows.

'Let me look these bruises over,' Dr Pfeiffer offered.

She shuddered. 'Don't touch me – either of you.'

'Cory may be exhausted. He may be ill,' Dr Pfeiffer said.

Like the last time you snatched him, Molly thought.

Molly could see Tyler was staring at her, but there was something odd about his eyes, as if he had seen things not meant for this world. He turned from her gaze and switched on the big clunky device held on his lap. A police scanner.

'I'm going to need to go to the bathroom,' she said. 'A proper one.'

The Myers had agreed a rendezvous point in the town if they were separated – but would it be safe? Would Cory remember, was he even in a fit state to find it?

'Well, you'll have to wait, I'm afraid.'

'In that case, I will bleed all over this car.' *I'll rub his nose in it*, she thought, full of disgust for him, and for what was happening. She had always loathed dealing with her period in primitive conditions, but this might be some sort of record.

'You might run away.' The doctor was clearly embarrassed, but he repeated, 'We can reunite you with your family.'

He fumbled in his pocket and brought out a piece of paper with Selena's familiar handwriting.

It took her some moments to focus enough to read. The list was a mixture – the brand of face cream Selena raved about and had left in the bathroom, the brand of sweets she chewed to hide her smoking, 'anything by' six famous authors of slushy romantic novels, and some very precise requests for specific undergarments.

Dr Pfeiffer met her gaze. 'I got a chance to rescue your sister. You obviously didn't get my message.'

Rescue. Right.

Twenty cold, awkward minutes had passed, but the fresh air was helping. Dr Pfeiffer had asked for Molly's word that she would not run away; she knew she was too uncertain on her feet to run very far anyway, so she gave it. To allow her to clean herself, they compromised by unlocking one handcuff and tying the rope to it. Molly did the best she could behind a tree with a bottle of water, a clean handkerchief and a bandage from the doctor's bag.

She looked at the knotted rope, wondering if she could work it free with her teeth. But then she'd have to run . . . where? And how?

Limping, still hurting, she walked back to Dr Pfeiffer. Flushing with shame, he took the leash off.

Tyler had found something that sounded like a police channel.

Cory Myers . . . woman some say was Molly Myers . . . Malign powers . . . some sort of disturbance on Lake and Third . . . FBI called . . .

Shit! What could be so bad calling the Feds would make it better?

Get real. They have people who know this alien stuff.

Norton pulled up in a truck and announced, 'It's all over the local news – everyone's confused as hell: Cory Myers went mad in the street, a local citizen's been shot, dozens of people are calling in everything from a child-snatch to an alien invasion.'

There was a sudden burst of snarling from the radio: *We gotta find them before the Feds and their fancy helicopters turn up. And the kid . . . threaten the kid and he'll summon hell, or vanish. You gotta play it easy or he'll zap ya.*

'We need to get back to base,' said Norton, in charge once more. 'If you hang around, you're going to get me arrested and Mrs Myers will fall into the hands of the cops. *Amateurs*,' he muttered.

She should have used her last ounce of courage and run, but she was already being hustled into the car. Dr Pfeiffer, apologising, blindfolded her. The route felt very twisty, but that was probably deliberate, she felt. She had a good eye for maps and landscapes, but she was still muzzy-headed from whatever they'd jabbed in her leg.

There was an eerie fascination in hearing the behind-the-scenes police work – the excitement when they got a better description of Pfeiffer, Tyler, the brute and Molly; the police chief repeating, '*Don't shoot the boy. He's vital for national security—*' over and over.

Then they heard, '*The drugstore guy says the little guy was Emmanuel Pfeiffer – you know, that germ warfare guy? He was sacked*

*by the President. The FBI are excited about that — they think they'll
be allowed to call in the Army to catch him.'*

Pfeiffer was silent for a minute or two. 'I need to call my
wife,' he said, to the air.

Forty, maybe fifty minutes later, the brute took her arm, not
gently, and guided her out of the car. She heard running water
and got a sense of where the sun was before she was led into
a building. She heard voices, and a telephone ring. She went
through a door, along a corridor, down a slope and through
another door.

'This will be more comfortable,' said Dr Pfeiffer as he untied
the blindfold. She was standing in a lounge, modern furniture
of wood and glass, and cluttered with photos of trees and plants
and insects. The photos were excellent, almost clinical in their
sharpness, but the close-ups turned nature into patterns, abstract
art. Daylight came in through frosted skylights.

She lowered herself into an armchair, aching everywhere,
and glared at the doctor. 'If you do have my sister, I demand
to see her.'

Dr Pfeiffer looked at her. 'I'm hoping you'll cooperate.'

'My son's in great danger and it's your fault. I'm separated
from my baby. At least let me know my sister is all right.'

'She's in the next room. I'll bring her.'

Molly would not have bet one way or another, but there was
Selena, sleepy-eyed, but wearing a shy grin. She wore a fashionable kaftan with flowing sleeves printed with flowers of orange
and yellow and brown; she had always been one for the latest
look. She held out her arms and Molly rose for the embrace.

Dr Pfeiffer ostentatiously walked out of the door and shut it behind him.

'Molly – you actually *came*. I was sure you were the only one brave enough to try.' Her voice was soft and slow. She was certainly drugged.

Holding her sister, the two of them against the world, Molly found tears coming. 'You can't trust Dr Pfeiffer,' she whispered.

Selena touched her ear, a warning look on her face.

Molly had expected the room to be bugged; that was a reasonable paranoia.

Selena said, loudly, as if she was reading her lines, 'Well, Dr Pfeiffer got me out of that place, and he got Mason arrested, or at least he said he did; Mason is quite capable of getting himself arrested – and he said he was so sure you would be here, and here you are.'

Questions rose, unsafe ones, but Selena went on, 'They're looking after me here. I'm sleeping half the day, but I feel good when I'm awake. And he's going to get me my darling boys back – he said he would. How are dear Cory and Fleur?' Her eyes flashed another warning, as if it was needed.

'Cory's lost,' Molly said, and the hopelessness rose around her, strong enough she felt she could drown. Her fierceness was sapped.

'That's awful – are there other people looking for him?' Selena sounded genuinely sorrowful. 'Tell me everything,' she went on, producing from some fold of her sleeve a small notebook and pencil. Then she flashed Molly a little cheeky grin, just like when they'd plotted against the nuns during detention. 'I do believe Dr Pfeiffer wants to keep him safe.'

The two of us against the world. Molly began to explain what had happened in Kauwenga Falls while she jotted down the key questions. *Where are we? Guards? Phones?*

Only then did it occur to Molly: had Pfeiffer plotted to bring Molly to this town all along? Was he behind Selena's letter? Maybe the chaos of that day had just been a trap sprung too early. Pfeiffer had Selena, a team, a hideout. He had been trying to contact the Myers.

Molly looked into her sister's eyes and wondered about the letter which had hauled her into the Midwest. Selena had been bait — but had she known? Just what would Selena do for her children?

CHAPTER 27

Dreaming

Cory swam, lost in his dreams. The water was so cold and he was so alone. Around him raged the bitter sea and above him the sky churned in turmoil. Silver shapes fell from the clouds, the snakes that hate all life. *Give in*, the water of his dreams called, *give in. There is no point in fighting*.

Hoo-hoo-hoo, all is cold and darkness and death. He was so-much cold and so-much tired and so-much alone. He could not find the layers of dream surrounding him, or where to swim to get out. And in his heart he mourned the loss of his birth-mother, his people, all dead. *Down-down-down* sorrow pulled him.

In the lodges of his home, in the children's places on a starship, others would be sleeping with him; others would find him in his dream, and if they could not help him, they would bring the adults to his dream too. He lost that togetherness when he fell into the human world, and oh, how-much he missed it.

The bad thing happened, again and again. When he had been captured by the Army, he had stopped that soldier from

269

breathing. By the river, he had hurt the not-yet-adults, who had almost drowned in air. Cory has become the Bad Man who hurts to get what he wants, so scared of helping Mom, he had stayed hidden, watching them hurt her, so-so-cruel humans. Cory is a coward, Cory let Mom down. Desperate, driven by fear, he had used his power only to scare – but it had had its own ideas and it would not be reined in. It was a creature of itself and it would destroy.

Cory has become the killing sickness, the thing that gets into heads and hurts people. Cory is the Monster. Everyone will come with fire-and-guns because Cory is the thing to hate and fear.

He revealed himself to save his Earth-mother, but he failed; the power would have hurt her and everyone. Fear commanded him and he fled to keep the humans safe. The shame of what he had done, the shame of abandoning his mother, filled him. He had run until he could run no more.

This was too-too-much to carry, so Cory dived to oblivion, into dreams so deep there was no smell or sound. There were places here that were so deep he wondered if his body might even forget to wake him. He dived down into nothingness, to forget . . .

An age passed.

There had been times closer to waking when he felt a human tugging at his body, whispering, 'Wake up Octopus Face, wake up. They're coming.' He hid, and thought he dreamed, warmth against him, other lives in the hiding. Who knew what was real?

Cory, frozen in the ice, unmoving, told himself stories. Everyone knew the story of the Old Times, when the five nations of the island quarrelled and Fork-Ear brought the sickness of killing, when she stabbed Shell-Mother dead. Fork-Ear and Tentacles-in-Everything and Horizon-Hungry are not real people, although they felt real to everyone. Cory's teachers said, from time to time, 'We are all like one of these people, aren't we? Or feel we could be.'

They were right, for Cory had become Fork-Ear. The people made a safe place to keep her and all the children brought flowers and songs for the ten years she lived, so that she was still a part of the whole. But there was no true place of healing on Earth, where people like him could be made whole again. On Earth, some people who killed were celebrated or at least left alone with their grief. And on Earth, some of those who did bad things were put in a terrible place, separated from the whole, where they hurt each other. How wicked.

Dad once told a story of a man who lay frozen in the ice of the sea for a hundred years and then woke. It was a story with magic in it, so not-real. Cory was frozen in the ice of his dreams, cold and not moving. He had been here a while, ignoring his body, which wanted to pee.

Meteor's smell and warmth was in the dream. Meteor gave him a clumsy, loving lick, and that quiver must have been an anxious wag of the tail. Who will feed Meteor and who will throw sticks and play the chasing-and-hiding game? Who will curl up with Meteor on the floor if she is lonely?

Go away, Meteor, Cory is the Monster and no one can love me.

Meteor could not talk or think in words, but she put her untidy head on her paws and watching Cory in reproach, she growled her disapproval.

271

There was nothing in the dream but Cory and his dog, and a stillness that was beyond cold and beyond dark. Dogs are a good thing Earth has which his home-world, the First Harbour, does not. Although some dogs are made Bad by cruel humans.

Go away, Meteor.

Meteor brought warmth; he felt her tail wagging and she tried to bite Cory, but not a true bite. In his dream, Cory's hands moved too slow. Meteor had her teeth in the sweater Cory was wearing, and yes, Meteor's teeth hurt, just a little, not meaning it. Cory felt Meteor's fur like the most comfortable of his old clothes, a feeling of love and memories. She smelled of dog, of loving to get wet and messy, and the rich foulness of her dead breath.

Tug, tug, tug.

Go away.

Tug tug tug.

Meteor needed Cory, who rescued her from the so-sad place with sixteens of abandoned dogs. Cory was so-sad that Meteor cannot have puppies, although Meteor doesn't know what the humans did to her, that she can't. Sometimes Meteor dreamed she had little messy Meteors to feed from her body. She thinks Fleur is a puppy and tries to lick her.

Tug tug tug.

Dad says Meteor is all-heart-no-brains but you do not have to be clever to be kind, oh-no.

Cory returned to time, rising through the layers of dream; he was every-bit so-cold, and his body complained about sleeping crooked. He was cold and wet around his crotch too, a humiliation.

There was a scared human nearby, very close. Cory had been so-so-deep under, but he rose to proper wakefulness, his arms cramped by the weight and warmth of Meteor, reassured by her familiar smell and the faint wheeze of her sleeping. *Clever girl to come and find him in the dream.*

He smelled Elsa before he saw her, then a dim chink of light showed her face – Elsa in her yellow hood – and she had a finger to her lips.

Elsa sent out so many feelings; fear, and relief and worry, and guilt.

They were in a strange place, crowded with things smelling of cleaning. He felt out with his mind, but Elsa was the only human here. Apart from her there were bags and boxes, and a rumbling noise, a machine making warm air.

'I was so worried,' Elsa said. 'I couldn't wake you.'

'Meteor came,' Cory said, stroking a friendly dog ear. He felt hungry and drained and numb, like he had been battered in the dream.

'You're wet,' she said. 'It was all horrible, don't worry. We must keep quiet, in case the people in the next house hear. Men came with dogs – police, and people from the factory down the street, all sorts were searching – but you hid us.'

Cory had so many questions, but he couldn't ask any of them, not with the smell of his own urine so strong.

'There are clothes, and a place to wash,' Elsa said. 'And a place where I can heat up beans. There's bread.'

'Mom,' he said.

'Men took Mom . . . Molly . . . in a car.'

He realised his wrist was empty. 'My communicator?' Not

273

that it worked properly, the last link to his old life. He could not call his parents.

Elsa sniffed; she was going to shed water.

'It made a noise. I tried to shut it up and it went silent.'

She handed it to him. It was unresponsive. Perhaps the security went wrong.

Cory started to stand, and felt his legs go weak as spaghetti.

Elsa said, 'I'll get some dry clothes and some food, then we need to go to the rendezvous.'

He kept his watch in his pocket. 'Two a.m.,' he said. 'Who came looking?'

'Police, and other people with them. And the bad men who took your Mom – they might be out there too. You . . . there was all this awful stuff coming off you, like—' She struggled to find the words. 'It was like it was sea waves and big storms of ugly feelings. You ran, and sometimes you unhid, and that's when Meteor and I rescued you.'

He didn't trust his own memories, and his pain and shame flooded back, draining him of the will even to get off the floor.

'Eat, wash, dry clothes,' he said at last.

'Okay,' she said in a small voice.

'But Dad will know what to do.' They could find a payphone – Cory always had coins in his pockets in case. But there was no phone where Dad was staying.

Hot beans sounded like a good idea. In any case, it was hours until daylight. Then they must go to the rendezvous. They could at least phone Dr Jarman and Rosa, if they were still at the lawyer house. Halcyon was too far away.

Elsa slipped from the room, and as she left, all of Cory's bad thoughts flocked around him like that memory, the fierce gulls, pecking at that dead bird, relentless.

It was their nature to eat dead things.

Dawn was still a couple of hours away. Cory was beginning to remember a little more of what had happened yesterday. He'd been trying to run, stumbling, sometimes falling, and so drained he could hide only a little, walk only a little. Elsa helped Cory, he was so weak, and Meteor followed. Sometimes Elsa near carried him, although her determination was bigger than her strength. He remembered her stroking his ears and saying, 'Don't leave me, Snake Face.'

When the men came to search, Elsa said he hid them, although he didn't remember that.

They stood by the door and Cory hid them for a moment so they could peek through the blinds. At this time, the town should be still, but there was some commotion to the north: lights were moving on the ground and in the sky, throwing strange shadows.

They dropped the blind and squatted down.

The rendezvous was a café, not far from here – but would anyone be there?

'I was going to go,' Elsa said, 'but there were police, and so many people searching.'

He realised Elsa was crying and hugged her. They had to find the humans who could protect them; he hoped he had strength enough to hide them all the way. It was a terrible thing to feel his power, his instinctive protection against beasts and humans, so weak.

She wiped her eyes on a towel. 'We'll have to be really quiet.'

Cory wanted his dad, the friendly giant, his strong arms and his funny songs and how you could trust what he said. *Always always always*. And Storm, who was strong and funny and kind. And Mom, who he had failed to protect.

A far-away growl came, and a rumble. There was the sound of car engines, and lights going on in windows. Men were calling out.

Elsa held his hands so tight they hurt. 'They're coming closer – what will we do?'

How tired he was. How difficult it was to hide from lots of people. How he missed the Ship.

How he needed his people to come.

CHAPTER 28

Captives

Molly sat in that strange green room while Selena stood, in full outraged flow, flaying Dr Pfeiffer with her words.

'Dr Pfeiffer, you can't be serious – I can't leave and take my sister with me?'

'You're not a prisoner, Mrs O'Regan.' He was oily and unconvincing.

'So I will call a cab and we can leave right now—'

'That would be unwise.'

Selena snapped, 'You kidnapped me, you *liar*.'

'That's hardly fair.'

Molly and Selena had sorted the plan: they'd play it cool and clever – until Dr Pfeiffer had told them he knew where Selena's boys were, thinking he was being clever, and Selena had lost her temper. Molly despaired – it would make escape more difficult – but part of her was enjoying watching Dr Pfeiffer squirm.

Selena raised her voice even more. '*Fair?* You *slimeball – you kidnapper!* Get the dictionary, Molly, let's see what it says as the definition for "locked up by four men and unable to leave". Oh? Would that be "*prisoner*"? You *lied* to me, Dr Pfeiffer. I was sick and vulnerable, and *you lied to me*, just to get at my sister – my sister *who risked her life* to help me. You shit! You never cared about me, or my children. You just wanted Cory. You—'

Molly winced; who knew her sister used such obscenities?

Norton winked at her, but she didn't like his sly enjoyment of Pfeiffer's embarrassment.

Pfeiffer was wincing too; he held out his hands in supplication. 'It will take time. We've found where Connor and Rory are – it's tricky now they've been moved, but we're evaluating options.'

'Evaluate your ass,' said Selena. The drugs were clearly reducing any inhibitions. 'I want the keys to the truck and Molly and a map – and I want to know where my kids are. I want it all now. I'll buy a gun if I have to.'

'You're not safe to drive,' Pfeiffer oozed.

'How did you know Molly was coming?' Selena said. 'Did you read my letter when I was sick? My *private* letter to my sister?'

'I was astonished to run into Mrs Myers,' Pfeiffer said. 'I'm sure she's explained—'

Molly leaped in. 'That's not answering the question. This was all planned.'

'Everyone can get what they want,' Pfeiffer said again. 'I want Cory safe, Mrs Myers, and Selena prospering. I pay my dues – I promised to get her the boys . . .'

'In God's name, when?'

'Suppose the press find out who Selena is?' Molly said.

Pfeiffer tried to push through the joint attacks. 'Your boys are safe. They are safe today and tomorrow and for weeks. Our lawyer will be sure they are not moved—'

'Get. Me. My. Kids!'

'—but Cory and the girl, they're at large and in such danger of falling into the hands of the government – or worse, the brutal fear of ignorant locals. The Army, the FBI, State Troopers and half the town are out looking for them. And Mrs Myers is right: the press has descended and the town is under siege. Surely Cory and Elsa will be found soon. Miss DuBois in jail – which is an outrageous abuse of state power. All we have is you, Mrs Myers, your knowledge, and your voice. Somehow, we must work together to help you to be reunited with them.'

The police have Storm? Molly assumed this must be true. Or did Dr Pfeiffer know that Cory had already been taken? Maybe the government had him? She was getting lost in a paranoid web of lies and deceit. The government had covered up war crimes; it had hidden the truth that the bloody decades in Vietnam had been nothing but a power play against Communism, with total contempt for the Vietnamese. The government had hidden the existence of the Ship and aliens . . .

Or maybe Cory had somehow got help. Maybe he was safe.

But Selena hadn't finished. 'We can't trust you,' she said. 'You used me. Get me my boys, then we'll find Cory ourselves.'

'We can't trust you while we're prisoners,' Molly added. She'd work with Dr Pfeiffer if she had to, but only if she had power over him. Otherwise, she might as well kiss a rattlesnake and trust it not to bite.

'Well,' said Norton, 'what's happening, Dr Pfeiffer?'

'You have to cooperate,' the doctor told the women.

Selena swore, while Molly shook her head.

'Your other plan fell through,' Norton said, 'so it's plan C, or we sit here picking our noses while we lose any chance at all.'

Looking fraught, Dr Pfeiffer swallowed and said, 'Okay, fetch Nurse Skidelsky – it's indecent otherwise. Take Mrs O'Regan back to her room.'

'You're not separating us,' Selena cried. 'I'll scratch your piggy little eyes out.'

Everyone else froze as Selena leaped at Dr Pfeiffer, then Norton moved, coming for Molly. She didn't know how to fight him, but she was not submitting tamely.

'Ma'am,' he said, reaching slowly for her wrists, 'you're worth ten of them, and I don't want to hurt you.'

As Molly struggled, trying to bite and kick, she wondered how much of this was real. Selena's outburst sounded genuine, but she had foiled Molly's original plan of apparent compliance. There could be no escape without Selena, and maybe this whole thing was a show: they'd escape and find Cory, then Selena would betray her.

A tall, solemn-faced woman in a nurse's uniform appeared, moving calmly. Her grip was firm.

'Don't worry, Mrs Myers. This is perfectly safe,' said Dr Pfeiffer, then to the nurse, he ordered, 'Hold her still! Just a little needle—'

Molly hissed, 'I will tell your daughters about this and they will despise you. They will hate you for ever for what you are doing!'

★

280

Molly floated in the drug they gave her, all the aches and pains of her capture far away, her eyelids too heavy to lift. 'Fleur,' she said through dried lips.

'I saw her picture,' said the pretend nurse. 'Fleur needs you. We can take you to her, but you have to tell us where.'

Dr Pfeiffer smelled close. The nurse was asking too many questions, but her voice was less grating than Dr Pfeiffer's. And Molly wanted to sleep. 'Bring Fleur,' she mumbled.

'Well, if you tell us where she is, we can reunite you. And your husband – he looks very handsome in the pictures. Isn't his music wonderful?'

'Gene is a good father.' She remembered the times when she had been a bad wife to him and driven him away. Tears began to prickle.

Cory might have gone to the rendezvous, the café with the hip name, and left a message. She needed to not tell them where.

Think of the Beatles. She and Gene always argued about the later stuff, but when the band broke up, it really was the end of something. Lennon and Yoko Ono did that annoying song about Cory, 'Gotta Peace Out Like the Purples Do' – certainly no instant classic, not like 'Imagine' was. *Think of the albums we argued over. Don't tell them what they want to know.*

Strawberry Fields for ever.

But the fake nurse wouldn't stop talking. 'Fleur will be wanting her mother. Where will they be? Will Cory be with them?'

Cory was the only one they wanted. All these questions were really about Cory. She remembered Gene saying, *'Every mother says the world turns around their child, but for us it is true.'*

'Gene loves Fleur. And Cory. I worried he wouldn't.'

She was so sleepy and floating, and she didn't want to tell them anything they could use.

Someone dabbed her mouth with ice-cold water and she remembered the deep red scratches Selena had left on Dr Pfeiffer's face.

Sometimes she heard his voice next to her. She would strangle him, when she found the energy to move. He was needy, fawning, quick-tempered, so they thought she would respond better to the sly, fake-jolly nurse.

'We're going around in circles,' Dr Pfeiffer said.

'Pfeiffer, butt out.' That was Norton.

'I'm in charge,' Dr Pfeiffer said. 'She needs to hear this: Mrs Myers, we are your *only* hope. Your sister turned you in – she told me about the letter herself; that's why I knew you were coming. We freed her from Green Bowers to get you. She was worried about how she would manage with her boys, so we agreed if she helped me get Cory, I would settle her financially, get her false papers, hide her and the boys. Mrs Myers, shall I tell you the price she put on your son? I'd have paid twice that. She sold you out, and on the cheap at that.'

Molly's tears were flowing now. 'Don't believe you.'

'You're alone, Mrs Myers. Dr Jarman, his wife, Gene – none of them will come for you. And your clever little plot? Of course we knew about it. She was lying to you.'

Dr Pfeiffer was a lying reptile.

'Mustn't call you that word,' Molly slurred. 'Wrong. Want the nurse back.'

Selena has betrayed me. I am alone.

282

But she would not talk. She would remember the states and their capitals in alphabetical order, starting with the latest two, Alaska and Hawaii.

The snakes were coming to destroy everything. The purples would never come – but she would say nothing. Above all, she would not say where the rendezvous was, at the café named after a song.

'Alaska, Juneau. Hawaii, Honolulu. Arizona, Phoenix. Alabama, Montgomery. Arkansas, Little Rock . . .'

That song Gene listened to . . .

One pill makes you taller, and this pill makes you shrink.

Gene . . . walking with him among the redwoods. Crossing the Golden Gate Bridge. If that was what he wanted, they would find a way.

'"California Dreaming",' she said.

'Where, Mrs Myers? *Where?*'

Next, she bet they would play a game when they told her Cory was sick and needed her. And she would play a game where she pretended to believe them.

CHAPTER 29

Leaving Kauwenga Falls

It was dawn, the grey light rising in the east. Cory, Elsa and Meteor sat huddled together in the bushes, cold and scared. Cory was hiding himself so he could be a secret spy and see what was happening, but he had to conserve his failing power; he felt less and less within him each time he used it.

The Bad Men were searching the truck now; they had two keen German Shepherd dogs sniffing inside. The driver was waving his hands and saying, 'The local guys looked – listen, I gotta get going.'

'Orders,' said the man in the dark suit. 'Your cooperation is appreciated.'

Cory had warring thoughts in his head. Part of him said: *Stay in town and eventually you will find a working phone and peace to use it*. But it had been so-so-close at the Laundromat – the man smoking out of the window had seen only a flash of something, but he had still called out. And the police car was outside the rendezvous, so that was too-too dangerous.

They had doubled back and crept into a culvert. Cory could not rely on his hiding anymore; it was too much work to stay out of human sight now. He argued inside his head: stay in the town because someone, somehow, would come and find him; or go with Elsa's plan, get out of Kauwenga Falls, then call the adults.

He ducked back into the bushes and unhid. How tired he was. Elsa put her head to his and he whispered, 'Be ready to run, hidden, and get in back.'

'Can you do it?'

She must have been able to feel his doubt. 'Cory try anyway.' All the things that could go wrong marched round his head. He was too tired to do the Bad Thing – and, besides, he mustn't think about it, or anything, except getting safe and warm again. His English got worse when he was tired. He must speak proper English, because he could.

The bags were heavy. Elsa said, in her most reasonable voice, that everyone agreed it was fine to take things if it was a real emergency and you really meant to pay people back. Cory wanted to leave a signed note with his address, but Elsa argued that was too risky. He missed Mom and Dad; they would know what to do. In the end, he decided he would write to them and he wrote the address down to use later.

Cory hid himself again and watched as the FBI and the dogs started moving to the next truck, while the driver of this truck was walking towards the bushes. It was the perfect opportunity. Even if they waited for another chance, the light would be stronger and he would be so-so-more tired.

Cory grabbed Elsa by one hand and Meteor's collar by the

other and hid them. It was like holding your breath underwater; how good Cory was at diving down compared with humans. And yet there came a point underwater where you could feel every heartbeat brought you closer to giving up, the point where you could do it no more. The Bad Men were arguing with the next truck driver.

Fear helped. The fear that the Bad Men would catch him gave power to his hiding. He needed it: with each step, his body was growing heavier, Elsa was limping again, and he needed to hold onto Meteor too. The packs were heavy with borrowed food. With every step he looked at the driver of the second truck and back to where the first driver was peeing in the bushes. It was so-so hard to hide from all of them, but he *had* to.

They got to the back of the truck. So-so-tired Cory could not hide people well unless he held them. He missed the Ship. He took Elsa by the coat pocket so she could get in, then half helped clumsy Meteor up to her. Then, one hand still holding Elsa's, he got in himself, his body clumsy with the pack. Twice he felt the hiding fade; a spotlight on him could not have felt more terrifying. With one last effort, he struggled into the truck, and then Elsa dragged him right to the back.

Cory found something soft and flopped onto it. Meteor flopped onto him and her smelly tongue touched his face. 'What if people lock the door?' he said. Trapped would be so dangerous, but he needed to rest among the bales and boxes full of exotic smells for a long time.

'We bang on it, he comes to look, we jump out,' said Elsa. *Find phone, all the kind people to call. Get family together again.*

How tired he was, how very tired. Elsa pulled something

over them and the three friends held each other close. A single flashlight beam stabbed into the dark, but they lay low. Meteor knew, when held so firmly, that she was not to bark.

Elsa rubbed her cheek; Cory knew she was in pain.

Then the doors of the truck slammed and a few moments later they were moving. Cory could smell Meteor and Elsa, and that made him long for his Earth-family, to know that they were free and well. He let go and fell into the endless darkness, too tired to even look for his birth-father.

Elsa napped during the drive. The dentist had not even started when everything went crazy and the fierce hot pain in her jaw had been growing even worse ever since.

Once the truck stopped to drop off something, heavy, she guessed, from the men's complaints; then, some time later, there was another stop and this time they stayed stopped. They had reached their destination, whatever it was. The men unpacked the truck while Elsa huddled against her friend Cory and the sleeping dog. *Any moment*, she thought, *the men will lift the tarpaulin and find us*.

But the bales they hid behind weren't moved and they were left alone.

From the noise and the swearing, the men were loading the truck with something else, but for half an hour now there had been silence and darkness. They needed to get off if they could and for that, Cory needed to hide them. But Cory would not wake.

Elsa shook him, even risked whispering in his ear. Meteor growled in her sleep, as if chasing a rabbit, very badly. Cory

288

felt cold, and she couldn't leave him — but the men might soon take them back into danger.

She could smell Meteor: the dog had pooed in the corner of the truck. That was another reason to move. She thought of Molly holding her, and helping to change Fleur, and Gene playing the guitar, and she felt the tears come. *The harder you wish for something good, the less likely it is to come true.* Cory talked so much about the good times, before she came — before Molly grew sad and Gene angry — and she wondered if it was her causing the arguments, the unhappiness.

At last Elsa got up and discovered her limbs and back ached like crazy. She tried to move Cory, who was as heavy and uncooperative as a sack of stones, not even shifting a little as he had in sleep. How could they get out? She stretched, and stretched some more, and got ready to be sneaky. The back of the truck was still open, and she could see a dim garage, with a car and another truck. A radio was playing a sad old song she didn't know. The only light came through two dirty windows. It must be afternoon, she thought. Dark would soon be coming.

Cory would be in danger if she left him, and Meteor too, but she couldn't carry him.

Once, travelling with her vicious keeper, they had been on a deserted road. He had been in a good mood and he'd let her drive the car. If there were keys in the truck . . .

But drive where?

Elsa looked in every direction, then dropped to the concrete floor, the pack heavy on her back. Through the door she saw the glow of an electric fire, and a big quilt. That faint wheezing like a far-off sea was a man snoring. He wasn't doing a good job if he was sleeping at work. She tiptoed over and borrowed useful things: the lighter beside a pile of butts; three dollars tucked under an ashtray with a red bridge on it.

Cory knew how to call friendly adults, Dr Jarman, or others in Amber Grove. But she couldn't get inside his head for the numbers. She remembered faces and directions, but she was not good with numbers.

She found a wheeled trolley, intended for moving big packing boxes. She could lower Cory onto it and at least get him out of the garage. She might not have very long before this man woke up, or another returned.

Elsa listened at the door, put out one cautious hand, and opened it a crack. Cold, fresh air swirled in and the man grunted and shifted.

If you were at floor level, she knew people were less likely to see you. She lay on the chilly, unwelcoming concrete and peered outside into a grey walled yard. Maybe she would be better finding somewhere else to lay up, less likely to be disturbed.

Elsa took the trolley, wincing when a wheel squeaked, and like a mouse with cheese, she pulled it to the back of the truck. Her leg was hurting again and she had just paused to massage it when, into the silence, Meteor barked out a friendly welcome, her face all eager and her tail wagging wild.

'*Herumhum?*' said the man.

'Shhh!' said Elsa as she edged through the crates, each bark from Meteor a little stab in her chest. When she put her hand on the dog's muzzle, Meteor began to dance to and fro. Elsa shook Cory, as hard as she could.

'What's goin' on?' said an adult voice, deep and sleepy.

She ought to take Cory's pack too, but she needed to move Cory first, and stop the dog barking. Cory was so odd to look at and the whole world knew that.

She pulled Cory's hood over his head down to his nose-slits and began the hard work of dragging him—

A stab of light.

'What the hell are you up to? Little thief—!'

The man was red-faced, old, bleary-eyed. He was twice her size, but he would be a slow runner. He had a flashlight, but nothing else.

And Meteor was barking again.

Lie, and quickly.

'My friend's sick.'

Wake up, Cory, wake up*! Hide us!*

'Don't believe you,' the man said.

Elsa pulled Cory further towards the man, trying to work out what to say when the man sniffed hard.

'Has your dog pissed in my truck?'

'Yes – I'm sorry, mister, these terrible men were chasing me – and my friend is real sick. The dog just made a mistake, mister.'

The man was not trying to get into the truck to help, and Meteor was dancing around Elsa, getting in the way.

'Get it outta the truck . . . Sweet Jesus!' The man had seen Cory's tentacles. He hollered, 'Hey, Ted, come now! *Hell on Earth!* It's that killer alien—'

There was no chance of sweet-talking her way out of this now; he would try to grab her, or Cory. He was stooping towards them, but she couldn't pull Cory any faster.

He dropped the flashlight and lumbered to the side. 'I'm armed,' he threatened, 'so don't make me use this.'

Meteor, clumsy Meteor, jumped from the truck and barked: *Back off, mister.*

The man picked up a piece of wood and flourished it. What a man, to wave a weapon at a little girl and her dog.

'Does that mutt bite?' said the man. 'I'll brain it.'

Meteor darted forward, but the man swung too early and Meteor made a clumsy sort of leap and sank her teeth into his right hand. She wrestled with him, like it was a game.

'Shit, shit, *Ted*, you useless son-of-a-bitch – *Ted!*'

'Good dog,' Elsa said, grabbing a metal rod.

The man had pulled his hand free. Now he backed away, holding his right hand in his left.

Elsa hurled the rod at him and jumped down from the truck.

Cory was lying like a corpse right at the edge, but she had no time to check he was breathing.

'Chase him, Meteor!' she shouted, but the dog was already harassing the man, forcing him back, exulting in her cleverness. Meteor advanced and the man retreated a step. Meteor barked; the man stepped back.

The man shouted as loud as any adult had ever shouted, 'TED, THERE'S THAT KILLER ALIEN FROM SPACE. BRING THE RIFLE!'

Against the wall was a big metal gasoline canister with a long spout. In her experience, most people cared about stuff more than people.

Somehow she got Cory off the truck, though it really hurt her back. He was slumped on the trolley and there was no time to go back for his pack. She grabbed the gas canister, put it on the trolley and headed towards the door, while Meteor kept the man off her.

'Meteor! Come here!' She unscrewed the cap of the gasoline, and said, 'Mister, what'll happen if I throw this on the fire?'

He went pale and began a lumbering run away from her. She pulled Cory to the door and through it, while Meteor the undefeated barked some more, in case anyone hadn't heard the commotion, then came after her.

Once *he* had been careless lighting a fire, so Elsa knew how burning gasoline leaped. She tipped the gasoline onto the floor behind her, then clicked the lighter. It worked first time. It was a big garage, so the man would be fine. She threw the lighter, remembering to cover her face as the soft whoosh of flame lit the yard.

Above her an aeroplane flew low against a grey sky. She could see a couple of warehouses and a car dealership. She chose the sidewalk that went a little downhill, for no reason other than it would be easier, pulling the trolley as fast as she could. If the men came after her, they would be captured, but there wasn't a chance she would ever abandon Cory. A car passed her, then another. She needed to get out of sight.

Moments later, she stumbled upon a side path. It looked like some scaffolding up there – they must be rebuilding something – but, beyond that, she could see trees. *Pull Cory up there,* she thought. It would be slow and painful . . .

But what if it was a trap?

A car pulled up: a Beetle, driven by two young women. Loud bouncy music rushed out when one of them opened the door.

'Sweet dog!' said one of the women. She had long blonde hair parted in the centre. Then she whistled, and when Elsa looked down she saw Cory's hood had fallen away just enough to reveal who he was.

Elsa was used to being cold and hungry and scared. This time she needed something else.

'Wow. The Man's after you,' the woman said, very serious. 'It's all over the radio. It's cool. We'll hide you.'

The other, who had long dark hair plaited in a braid, nodded.

Elsa realised it wasn't ordinary cigarette smoke pouring out of the car but the other, sweeter kind. The fact that Meteor seemed to like the women proved very little; Meteor wasn't the cleverest dog. But she had to make her choice: run from the women, or risk their help. In the end, her tired hesitation became its own decision.

The women jumped out of the car and got the children, Elsa's pack and the dog into the back, then piled all the other stuff there around them. Another car slowed to watch; the bad-tempered old man driving shouted something about freaks blocking the road and the dark-haired woman gave him a few choice words, then showed him a finger.

'The Grateful Dead,' said the other woman, 'd'ya dig them?' and Elsa realised it was the music. She did dig them.

They were in the car, she was committed, and off they drove. Far off, she heard a fire engine. So many things she wanted had been left behind.

CHAPTER 30

The third day

Molly and the children were gone and Gene had lost everything. Great, sinister powers were working to find his family. Molly and the two children were the bright centre of his being – but who should he work with to get them back? Fleur, his little darling, was asleep downstairs with the pastor's wife. How could he find the others and still protect the baby?

Where was Cory? And what was happening in space? One by one, the radio newscasters had announced, the satellites around Earth had been destroyed.

The pastor and his wife were fans. Their spare room was full of pictures of the Myers, reproaching him. Sitting on the bed, surrounded by the dead bones of a song he couldn't finish, Gene decided the worst was Andy Warhol's bright joke – twelve Corys in screaming colours. Any charlatan nowadays could claim to be making art.

He lifted Molly's old sweater to his nose. Her perfume lingered, bringing up memories of cold nights and warm beds, of trips into the woods to watch fireflies or to look at the harvest moon. Loving Molly had shown him what his life had been missing; being a father had been deeper and more frightening than he ever had thought. Now, in this bright room, he saw only shadow and tragedy ahead.

Molly and Cory and Elsa, all lost. I've been a fool.

He glanced at his watch. Carol and the editor of *Witness* would be in Federal court, getting Storm out of the hands of the FBI. Such bullshit charges, and a lot of the press were not buying it.

Witness would keep defending Cory, but there was little more they could do. The whole world knew Cory and Molly were missing, but Gene would swap a hundred theories for the truth.

Fear was ever-present, a sort of quivering animal in his throat. He knew he had to decide what to do, but instead, he tormented himself with the past, endlessly turning over his actions in that first frantic hour – could he have done anything differently? Perhaps he should have gone with them instead of allowing Molly to take Elsa to the dentist. He was no hero, but perhaps, with one more adult around . . .

When he got the news, Gene had grabbed Fleur, jumped into Dr Jarman's car with Rosa and driven away. The Jarmans had found the pastor, a hideaway if their lawyers could no longer help them.

Molly been seized by armed men – a hundred unspeakable thoughts rushed through his head at the very thought – shots had been fired and Cory had revealed himself. Then Cory, Elsa and the dog had vanished. The radio was saying that one of the men who'd kidnapped Molly was Dr Pfeiffer. Gene's hands curled into fists: he owed that man a punch on the nose.

Instead of searching, here he was, tucked away and waiting for that knock on the door. Four times he'd worked himself up to drive into Kauwenga Falls — into a tornado fuelled by the FBI and the media and a howling mob of locals — but each time, caution had prevailed. He was no spy, no action hero; he had no power to hide or scare or bluff. Molly had talked her way out of a dozen difficult encounters, while Gene only stumbled.

He couldn't stop thinking about the dreadful possibilities: maybe Cory had been captured, or wounded. Maybe he was dead. He imagined his son, drained by his horrific power, lying somewhere, helpless and dying. Or maybe he was already in government hands, or Pfeiffer's.

Then his thoughts turned back to Molly and the endless arguments. He'd felt like in the tight little world they lived in, she had been stifling him — that only duty held him, like George Bailey in *It's a Wonderful Life*. Her stupid stunt still made him angry — the way she'd put their whole family at risk, running away, just to make him follow her. He had never been so close to slapping her. And yet, without Molly, everything was darkness and despair.

He'd been a fool.

They'd fought through the loss of the baby, the drinking, his own errors . . . and now the silent deaths of the satellites were a warning of catastrophe to come. He was desperate. He could feel the ground giving way, and underneath there was only terror. He was powerless, and shocked at how fragile life was. Cory had always come with the possibility of loss, but not like this – not this way. And Elsa, so mistreated, and still with such a spark in her: she had such potential . . .

Dr Jarman had become the family's spokesman, handling the press in his normal unshakeable manner, but that meant he couldn't come to where Gene was hiding, or phone very often. In deepest secret, he'd also been handling the negotiations with the President's Chief of Staff, a man with the gracious façade of a Southern gentleman and the cruel heart of a Mob boss.

So far, the President had kept his word to the Myers, although his long, sordid political career suggested he would not do so for ever. As the doctor had said, 'Put a silk tie on a rat, it's still a rat.'

Dr Jarman and Rosa had given an interview to Dahlia Diamond, Miss Gushing Fountain 1972. She'd been an unashamed supporter of Cory's, in good times and bad, even risking controversy when necessary. She had championed the boy Cory had been trying to protect, and the teen who had done the right thing, and slowly, others had followed. Dahlia Diamond's ratings kept climbing, and of course, she wanted Gene to go on her show, to face his critics and to galvanise Cory's sympathisers across the country.

It was one option. Gene couldn't bear the show, Dahlia Diamond cooing out questions, her fake probing queries, so the guest could give a calm, planned answer. *The Women of America Trust Her* – ha! It would be doing something, that was true: his words would be debated worldwide. But half the time he felt it would be setting off a truckload of fireworks, rather than something that might actually help him find his family.

There were two great powers: the President, or the press. If life were a comic book, he would have already decided by now.

His father sent a message, trying to help and reassure him. 'You'll do the right thing, son,' John told him with conviction.

His dream since childhood had been to walk on alien land and see alien stars; to share Earth's music with a new audience and to hear theirs. He wanted to see a future bright and hopeful made real.

If the purples came, a great choice would be before them, and it would be terrible. If the purples came, who would he give up? Who would he let down? So many different futures – and they would all split the family apart.

Gene picked up the music and his scribbled notes for 'Cory Come Home', still unfinished: a song to bring his son and Elsa home, a song to reunite the family. It didn't convince him. Did Earth even want Cory? He could not write it a happy ending; not when he was searching in vain for the last thing left in the box, the little flutter of hope.

It was close to the hour. He turned on the radio to get the latest news.

'The President's Press Secretary will be holding a press conference in thirty minutes, and we understand that Dr Haldeman of NASA and the Secretary of Defense will be speaking to us. Meteor showers have been reported south of Japan, east of Florida and over the Antarctic, disrupting radio transmissions and radar. Several aircraft and ships are reported missing. Following the loss of the British satellite Ariel 4, it is understood that neither the West nor the Communist powers retain any working satellites, military or otherwise. In Paris, the Asian peace talks remain suspended . . .'

Surely the snakes' next move would be soon. He needed to act.

If he couldn't stand three days alone knowing Molly was in danger, he couldn't leave her, so she must come with him to the stars, to keep the family together. She would have to give in.

A little whisper insisted, *if you cannot persuade her, stay with her. It's the right thing to do.*

The whisper nagged at him, though he tried to think of something else, shaking it off as a dog does fleas. But it would be back.

Imagine this separation for a year, for a lifetime. Imagine choosing this.

CHAPTER 31

The Golden Sunrise Community

The women called it a commune, but it was just a big old farm. Elsa had been on farms before, sometimes by invitation and sometimes not. It had the usual smells of woodsmoke and animal dung, mixed with odder ones, like the sweet herb they smoked, and strange soaps and scents like a fancy church.

Her friend Cory could have told her ten things about the farm kitchen without even opening his eyes, but Cory was wrapped in a blanket, still asleep, with Meteor beside him. Elsa stroked one or the other while the adults argued and argued. She ate the thick soup they'd given her, with strange rough bread with seeds she had to dip in the soup to make soft enough to swallow. They'd made her eat herbs, chew horrid cloves and gargle with salt water for her toothache, but Marsha, who looked like she was a real grandmother, found her some proper pills as well.

A man with his hair in a braid wanted Cory gone that very minute. 'He'll bring the cops, or worse,' he kept repeating. A couple of the women seemed to be leaning towards that, but both the women who'd brought them and Marsha, who was the oldest person there, were having none of it. Marsha said, 'When Nate and Blessed come, they'll be for keeping Cory safe.' Another lanky, long-fingered man was trying to mend an old-fashioned radio lying in bits on the table. He was saying nothing.

The women were minding a baby, a toddler and a boy of about five, who stared and stared.

'He's not our problem. Get rid of him,' the braided man repeated.

'No. He's a child and we have to get him back to his family,' Marsha said patiently, as if to a child. 'And the people out working, they need to have a voice too.'

'You're acting like a leader.'

Marsha smoothed her grey hair and said, 'We're divided. I'm not putting a child in danger.'

'Do you have a phone?' Elsa said. 'Cory's good at remembering numbers. We can call someone.' But it frightened her that Cory had not reacted to the smell of the soup. His bowl had gone cold.

The man who wanted them out looked cross. 'We decided not to pay the bill,' he said, 'not with The Man listening in.' Then he seemed to see Elsa properly. 'You want something more to eat, honey? Help yourself. Why don't we see if the Niedermeyers will take them, just for a bit? They're pretty cool for squares, and the cops will leave them alone.'

Elsa worried that Cory would dream one of his fearful dreams and they would feel it, and then they would both be given to the Bad Man. But 'eat when you can' was a good rule for life. She refilled her bowl from the big pot and tucked in.

Another man came into the kitchen and they went into the argument again; a woman left the circle frustrated.

Elsa bent down and whispered in Cory's strange striped ear, 'Come on, ugly brother.' The word 'brother' had power. She'd never before had a brother to tease, or to protect her.

She gave him a spoon of water and without opening his eyes, he swallowed it. Then she tried a spoon of soup.

Elsa kept vigil, leaving only to give Meteor her run away from the animals so she could relieve herself. There were two older children there too, as wary of her as she was of them. There was no TV in the house and the radio still didn't work.

If danger came, it would be from the man with the braid – or the police would find them somehow. She could run and hide somewhere on the farm, but she couldn't leave Cory.

A day later, she awoke from dozing in the warm place by the stove. Something in the air had changed. She looked at Cory and his tentacles twitched.

'Elsa,' he said, eyes still firmly closed.

'Monster,' she said. 'Lazy ugly monster, faking ill while we all have to do hard chores.'

'Ha-ha. Tired. Hold me.'

'We need to call Gene and Molly,' Elsa said. 'You need to dig into that encyclopaedia brain and write down the numbers for me.' The commune was allowed to use the Niedermeyers' phone.

It was five minutes before his eyelids flickered again.

'Bathroom,' he said. He couldn't walk without her, so she all but carried him.

'Which numbers are safe?' Elsa had not realised until she came to Mourning Gull Bay that the police could listen when you spoke on a phone, particularly if you spoke for a long time. How worrying that was.

'Too tired.'

'I'll lift you. Come up, monster-breath.'

Marsha and a big solemn man named Blessed helped anxious Elsa and weary Cory to walk the mile to the neighbours' farmhouse. Marsha took a long time too, as her hip hurt, but in the end, they were welcomed into a warm kitchen, and there on the wall was a phone. Marsha sat and gathered Elsa and Cory in her lap so they could all listen. Cory's fear and tiredness came and went, and the people around him could feel it. Elsa saw their fear and their awe. It was spooky enough for her, who had felt it often.

'Institute for Alien Biology,' said the voice at the other end.

'Good afternoon, may I speak to Dr Jarman?' said Marsha.

'I'm sorry, ma'am, but he's out of town.'

'I have Cory Myers.'

'Well, okay, putting you through,' the woman said. She didn't say, 'Oh Lord, another timewaster', but that's how her voice sounded.

The new voice was also a woman, and very firm. 'We're very busy. Where are you calling from?'

'My name is Marsha and we have Cory and his friend Elsa.'

'Ma'am, we've had twelve calls like this since breakfast. Prove it.'

Cory put his mouth closer and delivered a brisk speech in his language, hoots and whistles and fluting notes. His ears pricked up a little. 'You sound like Mabel-who-used-to-help Dr Jarman. Big owl brooch.'

The voice changed. 'Well, you sure sound like Cory Myers. But Dr Jarman has left some questions, just to make sure. When you first visited Dr Jarman, what was the first book you took from his library?'

A pause, a long pause, then, 'Big book of birds, very beautiful, very old.'

'Why didn't he lend it to you?'

'How sad-sad, present from his wife who-is-dead. But Cory always allowed to read when in library. Clean dry hands.'

'Your friend who died landing on Earth—'

'Called Black Groundfruit.' He whistled the name too. 'Healer's child, my friend. Too many questions. Mabel, you keep bowl of sour sweets in desk. I like but most children do not. You had brother pretended to have epilepsy not to fight. Believe me now?'

'I believe you, Cory. Now, I'm going to tell you how to speak securely to Dr Jarman. He said, you remember—'

'You give me number and I do easy math and that is real number.' His ears went up a little more. 'Very easy math.'

'So, take down the number.'

Cory grabbed the pencil and the notebook.

Gene took the corner a little fast and heard Molly in his ear, telling him to drive carefully. The emergency fund was sadly depleted, but there was enough to hire a car.

305

Seismographs had detected two massive explosions in China, but now there were no spies in the sky to fly over and find out what it was. Russia had been open; it wanted an alliance with the United States against the snakes. China remained unfathomable.

Gene got out of the car and looked at the ramshackle farm in the dying light. Fleur chewed a hand and looked bright-eyed at the world as he put her into her papoose. Windchimes tinkled and somewhere there was chanting — but there were also the reliable smells of animal dung and smoke. Chickens wandered around like in some olden film. He couldn't help thinking they were careless; they'd lose the lot to predators if they weren't careful.

Elsa was standing by a door, wearing a grubby sweater that came down to her knees. When she saw Gene, she fought back tears. A middle-aged woman with hair down her back held out her hand in welcome, offering Gene a generous smile.

'Well done,' Gene said, squatting down and holding Elsa as if he would never let go, wanting to kiss her, to shout at her . . .

'After you spoke to him, Cory got sadder and sadder,' she said, looking worried. 'Then when we got back here, he ran away. I don't know where he is.'

'Have you got Meteor with you?'

'Yes.'

No one prepares you to be a father. No one tells you what it feels like when your child faces threats you cannot fix. No one warns you about the fear, like the ground giving way beneath your feet. How little reason Elsa had to trust any adult.

'Of course he's sad, all these bad things, but it will be okay now.' Gene put his fingers in his mouth and whistled, a note only he could do. 'Meteor, hey girl! Meteor——!' He bent and slapped his thighs and there, barrelling out of the barn, tail wagging wildly, came the dog, a soppy mess of curls.

'Hey girl!' Gene liked having a dog around, at least in theory. He tussled her ears a little, the silly, sloppy, clumsy thing. She was still growing into her paws.

'Where's Cory? Find Cory! Good girl!'

The dog turned and ran back to the barn and taking Elsa's hand, he followed Meteor to the barn. In the muted light inside, he saw the pile of hay and Meteor standing, tail wagging, with that patient expression she had when her beloved master was hiding nearby.

'Cory, son, I'm here. It's going to be all right.'

There was a sense of waiting. Somewhere, a chicken clucked.

'Cory, Fleur is here, and she's really been missing you. Dr Jarman and Rosa miss you too. And we need to find Mom – we need your help to do that.'

Elsa looked like she was one breath off crying. 'You're lucky to have a dad and a mom, Squid-face,' she said.

Surely Elsa knew she had a place in their hearts too?

'Whatever's wrong, whatever's worrying you, tell me and we'll find a way,' Gene said, projecting a confidence he didn't feel. He began to walk into the hay, feeling ahead with his senses and imagination.

He began to sing, fumbled, and started again. 'Our Child of the Stars', the song people always asked for, was all about a father's love for his son. As he sang, he became aware of Cory, very near – *grief and fear and a tinge of hope* – and halfway through

307

the third verse, Cory popped out of nowhere and grabbed him hard, howling, *hoo-hoo-hoo*. Gene hugged him back, tight. He would have held him for ever if he could.

'Cory is Monster-a-Bad-Man almost a murderer sick-in-head, Cory not-good no-he-isn't Bad Man!'

There's a lie parents tell, a promise that they will walk with their child on the journey ahead, though they cannot know it will be true, but the telling of the lie can help it *become* true.

'I'm here, Cory – I'm here. It's going to be okay. It will be fine—'

'Not fine no-no-no! All the people scared . . . *hoo-hoo-hoo* . . . come after Cory pitchforks-and-guns-and-helicopters.'

Gene started stroking his back, moving his hand in reassuring circles. 'Everything will be fine, Cory. I promise. We'll go and find Mom and it will be okay.'

Cory sounded disturbed at that. 'N-not know where Mom is?'

'No – but lots of good people are looking for her.'

With one phone call, he could have Dahlia Diamond onside. But the last thing they needed now was the strident bellow of more publicity.

Gene looked around and beckoned, and Elsa joined the embrace.

'I missed your stupid jokes,' she muttered.

With Presidents, prosecutors and the malevolent Dr Pfeiffer to face, the way ahead felt utterly dark, but he had his kids, at least, and he would never let them go.

CHAPTER 32

In captivity

In troubled dreams, Molly was being shaken awake – but it was no dream. In the dark room, a dazzling flashlight made it hard to see who stood beside her; there was a split second of hope, but no, it was too short to be Gene.

'Don't make a noise,' Dr Pfeiffer said, his voice low and insistent. 'We're going.'

He was playing some mind-game or another, making her leave the most comfortable bed she'd used since Halcyon. She tried to pull the quilt over her head, but he grabbed it with his free hand.

'Dr Tyler has got Selena in the car. We just need—'

'Liar,' she snarled.

He thrust a newspaper towards her, folded open to an inner page. The headline screamed at her:

MYERS CASE: DISGRACED DOC'S WIFE ARRESTED
CONSPIRACY TO KIDNAP

'It's outrageous,' the doctor said. His face was haggard and frightened. 'It's nothing but intimidation. I never involved her in any of this.'

Molly tried to marshal her thoughts. 'So now I'm a bargaining chip—'

He quivered with frustration. 'No, no, not at all. I do have other leverage. Look at the front page.'

She turned on the light, hating that he was seeing her in her nightclothes.

BAIKONUR COSMODROME DESTROYED

That was the Russian Cape Canaveral – but in Kazakhstan, as Gene said, *every time* people called it Russia.

She looked at the words, finding it hard to focus.

Dr Pfeiffer reached into his pocket. 'Mrs Myers, the Earth is under attack. They've destroyed our satellites, the Russians' too, and they've taken out at least two of the Chinese rocket bases. We need to get out of here, right away – and you'll need your wits about you.' He produced a little bottle. 'Here – Benzedrine.'

She looked at the bottle like it was a poisonous frog. 'You and your people set a trap using my sister, you grabbed me in a public place, you terrified my children, you shot a bystander and you stuffed me full of drugs. Forgive me if I don't believe you.'

'Mr Myers has found Cory and the girl, safe and well. We need to go. I've drugged the others.'

She blinked. 'All of them?'

'Of course. Fine Bourbon for those off duty and coffee for

those on. Mind, it's hit and miss how long it lasts; every individual reacts differently. Mrs Myers, this looks like the start of a snake invasion, which means I have to offer my country whatever I can. I'll put you in touch with your husband, but I need to get you away from Norton. He's dangerous.'

It was believable, but it could as easily be more theatre.

'Take me to Selena,' she said, thinking that was the simplest way to see what he was up to.

She took the bottle and left it on the bedside table. As she was throwing on her clothes, she was trying to work out whether she should rush him now, or to go with the flow, act later. She was prepared for this all to be some power game.

'What Norton is talking about is basically torture,' Dr Pfeiffer was gabbling. 'He has some idea of using you. I think . . . I think you'll do the right thing.'

This diffident Dr Pfeiffer was worse than the arrogant Cold Warrior, but he was still not to be trusted, and even if he was telling the truth, he was no match for Norton: of that she had no doubt.

'We've been racking our brains for months,' she said, 'but there's nothing Cory knows that's useful. He's only a child. There's nothing we can share.'

Gene believed that some of what Cory said about their science might offer crumbs of hope – but in the long term, not now. What Cory knew about the purples' physics sounded like gibberish – vibrations in hidden dimensions and the like. After all, you couldn't land in mediaeval France and get them to build a fighter plane, could you? There wasn't any way Cory could build a weapon or hide the Earth.

She put a few things into the overnight bag they'd given her, then pulled on her coat. *Thank goodness*, she thought, *for sensible shoes she could run in*. And then she was ready to follow Dr Pfeiffer.

He killed the flashlight before they moved into the dimly lit hallway, where the monster eyes of giant insects stared at her from the walls. Laying a finger to his lips as though she was a mindless idiot, Dr Pfeiffer took her elbow, but she pulled it away. Her heart was pounding, her ears and eyes checking for any sign of danger, but the house was silent apart from the gentle hum of the heating.

They crept along the hallway, through a door and across an anteroom, until finally they reached a short flight of stairs. Molly had no sense of the layout; the house must have been enormous, with at least one floor beneath the ground.

'Garage,' Dr Pfeiffer mouthed, pointing, and they climbed the stairs.

The security lights in the garage revealed half a dozen vehicles, including a truck, an antique convertible and a couple of sturdy modern cars.

There came an ominous click.

'Now stop there, Doctor,' said Norton. He stood half hidden behind the edge of the truck, a gun pointing at them, a smile on his face.

Dr Pfeiffer almost leaped with surprise, but Molly instantly dropped down into a squat. She was between Pfeiffer and the convertible, but her head was still a target. She needed to see what Norton was doing – where one person turns out to be awake, there might be more than one, and in this vast dim space, it would be easy for someone to come around behind them.

I will never see my children again.

'Mrs Myers, Selena is sedated. No harm will come to either of you. And Dr Tyler won't be bothering anyone for a while. Pfeiffer, just stand aside and let her come forward.'

Molly debated whether to dash to the stairs – but where was Selena? And she hadn't any idea of the layout of the house.

'I'm not going to do that,' Dr Pfeiffer said, shaking. 'Mrs Myers, stay down.'

'Mrs Myers – Molly – you're only valuable alive. But Dr Pfeiffer dead is a useful scapegoat – and after all, you don't owe him anything.'

He raised his voice, keeping Pfeiffer and Molly in his gaze. 'Honey, I'm going to need some help.'

Nurse Skidelsky appeared behind Norton, dressed in dark slacks and top. She wore a satchel over her shoulder and was carrying a raised baseball bat.

The nurse swung the bat with force—

—and hit Norton on his right shoulder. There was a ghastly splintering sound and Norton, grunting, started to turn – but he'd dropped the gun.

Seizing the chance, Molly stood up, reaching into her bag for the hairspray, and ran past the doctor to Nurse Skidelsky, who was dodging a clumsy lunge.

Skidelsky took another swing, hitting Norton on the hip – and there came a great shout. Somehow, Norton had grabbed the end of the bat in his left hand.

Her heart pounding enough to break her ribs, Molly attacked. Hairspray was a useless weapon, really, but the stars aligned and she got Norton right in the eyes.

He bellowed in pain and with his attention diverted,

Skidelsky was able to wrestle the bat free – and she rammed it into his stomach.

Norton toppled, and she kicked him hard between the legs.

This woman had drugged her and lied to her, and Molly knew she'd stand no chance against Skidelsky, either running or in a fight. The gun had skidded under the car, but Molly had no idea how to use it, and in any case, she hated weapons.

Skidelsky raised the bat as if to finish Norton off, but Molly hissed, 'No!' She knew the dangers of a blow to the head – could she stop Skidelsky killing him?

But the nurse had already hesitated. 'I'm sentimental,' she said. 'He was a good lay.'

Blinking, Dr Pfeiffer said, 'Who do you work for?'

'Oh, our mutual employer – who we won't name – never quite trusted Norton. I was insurance. Now, Mrs Myers, things are moving. If you want my employer's protection, come with me. He will have you and your family in Switzerland within a day – there's no extradition treaty. He is dying to meet you, but he does understand you might find that awkward. If you prefer whatever Dr Pfeiffer has planned, go with him. Or—'

It was the easiest choice in the world. 'I'll take the car keys, and my sister,' Molly said. 'And a map – oh, and the gun.' That was a bluff.

She looked at Dr Pfeiffer, who looked like his world had collapsed. Nothing could wipe out what he had done to her and her family.

'I didn't mean it to be like this,' he said, the whine of every man in over his head. 'Truly, I didn't.'

'Go to your wife,' she said, hoping this was the last thing she would ever say to him.

CHAPTER 33

Rendezvous

The rendezvous was not hard to find, and it was suitably unwelcoming. At the turning off the main road there was a board advertising Pop's Café [SHUT], Bathrooms [SHUT], Parking [SHUT], Lake Views [ALWAYS]. Spring had picked up her skirts to run; there were fresh green leaves and spikes of colour among the bushes, red fuzzy buds on the maples. Molly turned up the drive and drove some of the way – far enough to see that the parking lot in front of the café was empty. It pretended to be jolly and Alpine, but it was about as Swiss as supermarket cheese.

Every country, no matter how small, was busy asserting their own right or reason to be the place for the purples to land, but Dr Jarman thought the purples should choose Switzerland as the least contentious choice. Gene said they should ask Africa and Asia about that.

Gene was late and Molly was seeing Feds behind every tree, in every dark car. Selena had insisted on a local channel, so between tunes from Molly's youth, the radio announcers had been musing on the attack on Baikonur and missiles – and how, without satellites, Russia might think an attack from space was actually coming from the United States. The host was easygoing and a bit of a stoic, but those phoning in were frightening and angry. *It was the purples, we've been tricked. It was the snakes and we're all doomed. It was a plot by the Russians to make us drop our guard.* And, as always, some callers said, *They're lying about Cory being dangerous* and *Only the purples can save us.*

She was always grateful for support, but some of Cory's supporters definitely worried her, especially that bizarre group who wore purple hoods and had the nerve to worship Cory as a god.

She sat there taking in the idyllic view of Lake Delaney. It might be a pretty place, but if she never saw Kauwenga County again, she would be delighted. When Selena dozed off in the back, Molly had turned off the radio, leaving her alone with her own racing thoughts. The place was discreet, but it felt like a trap.

A car growled up the track, flashing its headlights. Molly couldn't wait; she wrapped a scarf around her neck, got out and trotted towards them.

Gene was driving. He looked tired and gaunt, but when his eyes met hers, his proper smile lit his face and seconds later, he was out of the car and loping towards her – then she was in his arms, and he was trying to explain something, but she put her mouth to his. It was him, and amidst everything dark and dreadful, he was here, a blazing light.

Her heart dared to sing.

Cory was here too, waves of relief cascading off him. Then Meteor began barking with excitement, and there was Elsa, walking with care, holding out a precious bundle of blankets. In that moment, any faint lingering flicker of doubt died. Elsa was her daughter too, and Molly would walk through fire to keep her.

'So-so-much to tell,' Cory said.

Molly kissed all of them, then kissed them again, hugging them all close, noticing how swollen Elsa's face looked as she passed her the bundle of blankets that was Fleur.

'I hate the dentist,' said Elsa, a little muffled, catching the look.

Birds called to each other as a smattering of rain rolled over them, though the sun shone over the lake.

Gene said, 'Let's all get in the car, shall we? We need a plan.'

Molly looked back towards her own vehicle. Selena had woken up and was walking over to them, ignoring the rain. They all piled into Gene's car, which was the bigger; Selena took Cory, Elsa and the dog in the back.

Gene started. 'We need to get out of here – the local police want Molly and Cory as witnesses, for the shooting, they say. The local paper wants Cory prosecuted. Local police and FBI want Selena, to investigate the kidnapping. What the hell was Pfeiffer up to? And of course, we're still wanted in New York.'

Selena leaned forward, her head appearing between Molly and Gene. 'I need my kids,' she said, her voice filled with quiet strength. 'I don't know that I understand everything, but we need to go and get my boys.'

Gene gave her a tired smile. How stressed he looked. 'Your

317

kids need their mom,' he agreed. 'Mason's lawyer shopped Mason to the judge, to save his own skin – something about perjury . . . and Mason broke his bail by fleeing the state, so there's a warrant out for his arrest . . . Your lawyers and Dr Jarman have a plan.'

Selena turned to Cory. 'But Cory can just walk in and get them, can't you, sweetheart? Then we can all go back to Amber Grove.'

Molly's heart sank.

Cory groaned, but Gene was already speaking. 'We can't . . . Cory's tired . . . And throw a stone in Kauwenga Falls, you'll hit the cops or the press. Dr Jarman will take you back to court, get you your kids . . .'

'I'm not going back to Green Bowers,' Selena said, catching her breath. 'Molly, don't let them put me there—'

Molly was torn. She could see how much Selena hated the place, but she had admitted – and Pfeiffer confirmed – that she had got better.

'Dr Jarman has a plan that will see you and your kids in Amber Grove. It's just, it might take a few weeks. You could see your kids tonight – the director will put you up in his own residence.'

'Selena looked from Gene to Molly and back. 'I need to talk to Dr Jarman before I agree.'

'Good. That's fair,' Gene said. He started the car. 'We need to get to a second rendezvous.'

'Good about Connor and Rory. Now what about snakes?' Cory said.

Gene turned the car, frowning. 'Well, everyone thinks we can help them with the snake attacks.'

'Definitely snake attacks,' Cory said. His shiver ran through all of them. 'But Cory can't help here. Some very strange signals coming from communicator — just maybe some of my Network is still there in space, hiding from the snakes. Easiest to work from Amber Grove, inside the Fence, if the humans have not broken it.'

Molly longed to go home. She still felt the danger — but she could also feel her home and her friends calling to her.

'Will this Network destroy the things?' Selena said.

Cory *tock-tock-tocked*. 'No, not weapons. But maybe better warning.'

Gene sighed. 'We know the snakes are up there, circling the Earth. At least spying on them back is *something*.' He kissed Molly again, as if to check she was real.

Molly bit her lip, starting to feel that everything was too much. How would they get home?

Over the lake, there hung a rainbow. And Molly saw again in her mind a grey world of ash and smoke, where the snakes reigned supreme.

An hour later, up another track out of sight of the road, Dr Jarman persuaded Selena to trust his plan. Tearful, she hugged everyone twice, particularly Cory.

'Connor and Rory have changed their minds, sweetheart. Knowing you made them the coolest kids in town.'

A last kiss for Molly, and Selena was in Jarman's car.

'What do we do now?' Molly asked, and suddenly all was doubt again. They had no Carol and Storm to buy gas and book motel rooms. No Pierre with a private plane and a truck . . .

'The kindness of strangers.' Gene waved a notebook, then passed it to her. '*Witness* have three planes booked flying to Canada – and a fourth one which the government won't know about until it's there. People will assume we've been smuggled out. And our fan club are ready to throw up a smokescreen – turns out, they have this telephone tree.'

'False sightings?' She felt guilty at enjoying the thought.

'Once the press say there's a hullaballoo, everyone joins in. It's stupid, really. Officially, we didn't start it.'

It was good to see him smile. It stirred hope, love, regret . . .

He went on, 'Carol found some places, people she knows. Dr Jarman has somewhere lined up close to home. Neither of them know the whole route. And I've supplies in the back for a week so we can speak to as few people as possible.'

'And I will hide, but no scaring.'

'Cory can just pull a face, and they will all run away . . .'

Gene started the car and they were heading home.

After their ordeal, they had no desire to press on through the night. The hunting lodge took some finding. It was all rough log walls and fish in glass cases, but it smelled of fresh polish, and the kitchen was newer than theirs at home – in fact, the lodge was bigger than their whole house.

Cory and Elsa were debating which room they would take, while Gene changed Fleur in the big room. Molly watched him from the doorway, the baby intent on him while his deft hands made her comfortable. He hummed a familiar air. Molly thought she had approached quietly, but he looked up and gave a tired smile.

'We could take this room.'

'We could.' They had things to talk about, important things, but perhaps not tonight. 'I'll get the crib from next door.' She wanted Fleur at hand if she woke, or if Cory had a nightmare . . . She wondered if his episodes hurt Fleur's growing brain.

Gene bounced Fleur a little, and said, 'Early night.'

She was tired, still fighting the drugs, but when he smiled, she smiled, and no more words were needed.

Desire was back, a sacred flame in the marriage, and a welcome friend.

Later, Molly was lost in strange dreams, of being hunted by giant insects, or being parted from her children. Then Cory came in the night and shared his dream, his descent into the deepest layers of the dreaming-together. He was trying to share his experience, still fresh and raw, but Molly understood less than he wanted. She saw Thunder Over Mountains and felt the power of their love and relief, father and son, that they had found each other again. This dream was urgent, a dispatch from a crisis. The purples had needed to know Cory was safe, and to tell him they were coming.

Molly was shocked that Thunder was in deep pain, and others too.

Was Cory all right?

Yes, yes, with Earth parents, safe.

Then watch, listen.

When they projected a spinning globe, the Earth, Cory's joy was incandescent – they knew where he was, they were on the way! The Stars and Stripes waved in a summer breeze: they must know which continent. But sadness, fear and loss drenched the dream.

When Cory pushed to know what the danger was, Thunder showed two starships in a battle with the snakes. One ship was damaged, perhaps both, and there was a deep grief that hurt Molly's chest. The purples were coming, as soon as they could, but there was death all around them. Cory pleaded – *how long?* – but he gained no sense of how long it would take. Molly felt his confusion that Thunder couldn't tell him – or wouldn't. Maybe they didn't know?

The dream felt so real. Molly had come to believe in this impossible dreaming across the vastness of space. She woke, still tired; she knew Cory would come into their bed soon to tell them everything he'd dreamed. He'd be both fearful for his birth-father and joyous that the purples were coming, and he would tell them every detail, in case they had missed anything. Somehow she must mask her ambiguity and rejoice with him, assure him they would make it safely.

The reunion with Gene had been so precious, but there were greater threats to come. Life was fragile, and priceless; they might have less time than they thought, so they must live each day as though it mattered – and that against the fear and the dark, they must cling to those they loved, and do the right thing.

Cory's people were coming. They had to come. Then she must fight them for her son – and perhaps for her marriage too.

CHAPTER 34

Driving east

Molly drove through fields fuzzy with new green, the clouds scudding across the sky like white puppies. Gene was trying to teach the kids a song and Elsa played at getting it wrong on purpose. Each mile brought them a little closer to their home and further away from her captivity. Amber Grove was calling out to them as if they were birds, or salmon.

Ignoring Gene's mild complaints, Molly turned on the radio at a quarter to the hour.

'Breaking news,' said the anchor, his tone hollow. 'This hot off the wire from Associated Press. There has been an explosion directly centred on the Kennedy Space Center and Air Force Base at Cape Canaveral in Florida. Twenty minutes ago, a blinding detonation was seen all over the state, and a shock wave has been felt as far away as Orlando. Witnesses are reporting a huge mushroom cloud hanging over the area. We are still awaiting news of casualties, and a statement from the

President. I'll repeat that: around twenty minutes ago, at half to the hour, some sort of explosion—'

Cory's fear gushed and whirled around them, eerie and frightening, yet familiar. Sometimes it would bring on an episode, his power reeling out of control.

'Okay, sweetie-pie, okay,' Molly cooed, slowing the car to a crawl. *Stay calm*, she thought, *stay in control*. If it got too bad, she would have to pull over, while she could still drive.

Elsa held Cory while Gene looked back and said, 'You can do it, Big Stuff, you know you can . . .'

As Cory brought it under control, Gene said, 'The snakes have closed the skies. Now they're destroying our launch pads.'

'Surely the Administration must have known? After Baikonur—?'

'Yeah, they must have. They must have evacuated the place . . .'

Her parents were in Orlando, damn them – but Orlando wasn't next to the base; it was fifty miles away. She told herself they'd be fine.

The radio started to play Rachmaninov, 'The Isle of the Dead'. Gene loved that piece. It must have been hard for the station to know what to play while they were waiting for more news.

'My people coming too late!' moaned Cory.

The station cycled through what little it had: radar down, planes diverting . . . it wasn't until a full hour later that the story changed.

'There have been reports of a second, smaller explosion in Orlando,' the same newsreader reported. 'And this just in – it has been confirmed that the Kennedy Space Center at Cape Canaveral was operational and preparing for an imminent rocket launch. There have been heavy losses among civilian and military personnel. Nuclear fall-out warnings are being given in the area and, given the prevailing winds, to the east and north.'

The newscaster's voice broke. In a whisper, he said, 'I have folks in Orlando—'

Molly thought of her parents and their cold, brutal marriage.

When Cory came, when she had become the most famous mother in the world, her own parents had neither called nor written. It was as if Molly was dead.

There were half a million people in the Orlando area, the newsreader said, once more calm and professional, and he restated the story without emotion. Silver missiles had been seen flying over the ocean: snakes, attacking aircraft and radar installations. A warship off the East Coast had been sunk here, a passenger plane destroyed there.

Then it was back to the music.

Molly always said, to close off discussion, that her mother was dead to her. But just like one of Gene's atrocious films, it turned out the dead could rise and haunt the living.

If she hated her mother so much, and with such good cause; if she had spent so many nights wishing her father dead, why were these hot tears blurring the road?

'Pull over,' Gene said quietly. 'You're thinking about your folks.' His tone was gentle.

She did as he'd said, with no remonstrations.

His eyes troubled, he wrapped her in an awkward embrace.

325

'Orlando is three days' drive away,' he said. 'And we need to get to Amber Grove.'

'What are we going to do?' said Elsa.

'I don't know, sweetie-pie.' In the back seat, Fleur started wailing as Cory's *hoo-hoo-hoo* filled the car.

Molly surreptitiously wiped her eyes before turning to check on them. Elsa was holding Fleur, trying to get her to chew a finger.

'What's going on?' Elsa said.

'My parents – well, they weren't very kind to me, darling, but this attack in Florida – well, that's where they live. They might be hurt.'

'After all they did—' Gene started.

Molly missed Eva and John to talk to. She wanted them and their wisdom. 'Orlando is too far,' she said. 'We need to get home.'

'Cash in a favour with the President,' Gene said.

'I don't want us owing that man anything.' Not for her mother, anyway.

'Cory can't hide from Bad Men if too many,' Cory said, and everyone felt his anxiety.

'We're going home, sweetie-pie,' Molly said firmly.

'Let's find a phone,' Gene said, 'and somewhere the kids can breathe. You safe to drive?'

Huh!

Cory's dreams needed to be true: his people needed to come. This was a war between people at the bottom of a hole brandishing spears and people at the top threatening them with machine-guns.

It was time for distance-eating speed, for Cory needed to work on the alien Network. Molly put her foot down and started a silly song, one of Gene's.

Outside a gas station, Molly put her back to the attendant and made the call. She read a few sentences over the phone, knowing the four words at the end would confirm it was her. That simple message would pass through other hands and should be with the President within an hour.

When they passed through towns, they saw crowds gathered around the shops; they passed school buses full of children, although it was too early for finishing time. They started to see flags flying at half-mast.

The second announcement came as they ate a cold supper outside a burnt-out, boarded-up diner. The snakes had bombed Colorado Springs: that was the NORAD command, the centre of America's defences, a facility buried deep beneath a mountain and supposedly impregnable to attack. The Ship had told them the government had taken some purple technology down there.

These were smaller explosions, accompanied by a rain of silver fire: snakes that had burrowed into the rock itself, an army that could burn its way into the mountain. The Secretary of Defense refused to comment on casualties, but he did confirm that the city would be evacuated.

'If we get Cory to the Network, maybe we can warn them the next time,' Molly muttered, the only thing they could offer.

'I keep saying only *maybe-maybe-maybe*,' Cory moaned, hunched over.

Gene wanted to drive through the night, but Molly refused. It was dusk before they reached that night's sanctuary, a chapter of the Stellar Friendship League, and even though Gene had taken over at the wheel, she was ready to drop.

They pulled into the motel, where a few lights were showing, and as instructed, drove straight round to the back, where they found a small house. A teen came over carrying a big electric flashlight, all acne, long hair and anxiety. He wore a purple T-shirt which said *Vote Cory Myers 1972*. It sported rather a good psychedelic cartoon of Cory dwarfing the White House. Gene's naïve quote – 'We don't need drugs; we live with Cory!' – had gone around the world.

'We were told to ask for Mike?' Gene said, looking dubious.

'Pop's had to go to Grandma's – she's freaking out – and Mom volunteered for civil defence. There's just me left.' The youth's gaze darted here and there, but he wasn't going to see Cory and the other kids until they were sure of the set-up.

'You'll do fine,' Molly said encouragingly. 'You know that no one must know about us, right? Not friends, not other people in the group – not even your girlfriend.'

'Yeah, yeah, I dig it.' He got up his courage and whispered, 'Can he save us? Are his people really coming?'

'His people are coming,' Gene said. *Two ships, one damaged.* Why had everyone assumed the purples would come with a vast war fleet? 'So, can we trust you?'

Cory appeared, the boy's face blazed with a massive grin and that was their answer.

They sent the children straight to bed, rather than let them watch the news. There were pictures from Orlando, destroyed buildings, fires and billowing smoke, military vehicles, people fleeing in cars and trucks. It was Meteor Day times a thousand. A reception centre set up out of town was already full of refugees, a chaos of noise and volunteers, nurses distributing iodine to help against fallout. There were numbers to call if you were out of state and looking for relatives.

There were tens of thousands of dead, they said. A quarter of a million more were being told they'd be evacuated.

The White House had announced a State of Emergency. The Florida attacks had come from the ocean, it was reported, the snakes skimming above the waves like flying fish. Electromagnetic pulses had wrecked radar and communications.

They felt they had to watch the President's address on TV. No amount of make-up could hide the President's dark, doom-ridden eyes. There was something a little awry with the broadcast, waves of static that weakened his voice and blurred his picture. That of itself suggested further attacks.

'My fellow Americans: we face a grave situation, but it is my duty to give you the facts and dispel the wild rumours. Following the heinous, unprovoked attacks in Florida and Colorado Springs, Federal, state and private resources are being devoted to rescue those in peril, to maintain order and defend our country. There has been a magnificent stirring of the American spirit, a real coming-together as a nation.

'Those who work at the Kennedy Space Center have always known the risks inherent in exploring space. To a man, they volunteered, wanting to serve their country and their fellow man in the only way they could. We are not passive in the face of this aggression and we will continue to expand our defence in the face of this threat.'

So, thought Molly, *they'd tried to launch something military against the snakes.*

'There is no doubt that the alien machines known as snakes are responsible. That view is shared by our allies, both scientists in neutral countries and the Soviets, and we believe it is also the view of the Chinese Communist authorities. Although each country is in a high state of readiness individually, we are seeking common ground at this time of peril. A planet divided cannot stand.

'I welcome the generous words of the Soviet Foreign Minister, recalling those times when America and the USSR worked together against a great threat. The snakes have attacked six launch centres across the world. They have attacked any substantial equipment orbiting the Earth, no matter its purpose and whatever its country of origin. Every satellite, no matter its origin, every probe travelling between the planets and the Soviet Lunar Lander, they have all ceased broadcasting. I repeat: this is an attack on different nations in different blocs, an exertion of inhuman power.

'If this attack was intended to provoke us, however, it has failed. If it was intended to stir hostility between the Great Powers, it has failed. If intended to test our resolution, it has merely strengthened us. Let us never forget that we are a nation founded in adversity. We gained independence when the odds were against us—'

There was more in this vein, but little of substance and little reassurance. There was a pledge to return to space, to destroy the snakes and to usher in a new era of peace, but the President did not look as though he quite believed it himself.

Humanity had reached the Moon through courage and ingenuity, a declaration to the stars that these smart, quarrelling apes would explore the universe. But space was no longer for humans; the snakes had reclaimed it. Now the snakes encircled the Earth, waiting and alert. And Molly, once such a sceptic about flight to the stars, could see the size of that danger – and the sheer size of what humanity had lost.

CHAPTER 35

Near Colorado Springs

Carol had a cloth over her mouth in a vain attempt to keep out a wind that stank of burning fuel and smoke. The helicopter she was riding in flew low under that vast bright blue, the stunning mountains off to her left. Her eye was drawn down to the sinister pall of black smoke over Colorado Springs, the ragged stumps of what had once been tall buildings. There had been two blasts – one high, for the electromagnetic pulses, and the other to take out the air base.

She scribbled one-handed in the notebook balanced on her knee.

What is still burning after two days?

Outside of the mountains, the land was flat, the roads wide, the settlements strung out. This state had elbow room. Storm had visited before, long ago.

They were all wearing radiation tags like the one pinned on

Carol's coat to detect and measure background levels. The wind had been blowing fallout towards Denver, so against official advice, thousands were fleeing the Mile-High City, even as the refugees from the south were arriving to swamp its hospitals. Carol had already discovered that thousands were thought to be still in Colorado Springs – wounded, blinded or stubborn, or staying to help others. And thousands more were dead, or would be soon.

That silver streak, very high up, was a snake. There was another, away over there. Of course Storm was trying to capture them on her camera, a tricky shot.

Grim-faced, the pilot had warned them, 'If a snake heads for us, we'll try to land. It will be fast and dirty. You can't outrun them, but if you land, just sometimes they'll pick another target.'

'Who says?'

'The Commies, apparently. They're never off the phone now, passing on what they know. They sure hate those things. Sometimes snakes burn you up with some ray-gun, sometimes they just ram into you in flight. The heat-seeking missiles they used in Vietnam? No damn good – the snakes just make 'em drop out of the sky.'

The battle had been brief; now, for twenty miles in any direction, the air belonged to the snakes, and anyone on the ground was a target. Carol remembered the utter shock of the attack on Pearl Harbor. Her European friends always said that America did not understand defeat.

Courage is not an absence of fear. Courage is wanting to pee yourself with fear and yet doing the right thing anyway. The people deserved to be told the truth.

The machines had burrowed into the mountain and destroyed the impregnable fortress – well, that made some sense. But what were they remaining for?

They are ALIEN.

Carol could live with the racket of the rotors, but something behind her seat was shifting with each shudder of the copter; if this had been a car, she'd have insisted they stop and find out what it was.

Hikers and rangers on horseback had seen snakes land in the mountains.

What the hell was their energy source? Were they building one of their factories?

In the first couple of days, snakes had blown up highways and roads, then coming back time and again, strafed those fleeing, almost at whim. Then the snakes had returned to destroy those trying to clear the roads blocked with burning vehicles. Any attempt at ground-to-air attack brought instant retribution.

Now people were just trying to escape any way they could: riding or walking, pulling invalids or possessions in carts by hand or burro, driving ill-suited vehicles across rugged terrains, all somehow believing that they were less likely to be attacked.

The authorities had tried to control where the press went, steering what they said. Vietnam had taught them nothing, which was why Carol was determined to reach somewhere the authorities hadn't got to.

Here was their destination: a cluster of buildings stretched out beneath them. The Red Cross flag flew over a church and some awnings, as if the snakes cared. They'd taken out the bridge and the railway track a mile south and now the only way out was to walk, ride or fly, or to head back towards the devastated city.

Her source in the US Air Force said, 'It's like they had a target. They secured the area. If they were human, I'd think they might be wanting a landing. What are they up to?'

The pilot brought the helicopter down a hundred yards from the church now functioning as a hospital.

Carol jotted notes fast.

Courage of troops. Civilians.
? evacuation plan good enough ? numbers
? snakes in mountains — confirm?

The scoop would be to get to the bunker under the mountain and confirm it really was a radioactive tomb for its staff. There had been some harrowing recordings of screams over the telephone; there was even a rumour that two snakes already inside it had come alive and run amok. The Air Force said it wasn't safe and wouldn't take the press near it. Was that knee-jerk secrecy or was there some specific reason?

One of her rivals had bought six horses and planned to ride in. 'The things we do for a byline,' Storm said with a grin.

Carol had seen many disasters – a mine collapsed, a flood, a ship sunk, a violent coup down south – but there was something different about this. A disaster was just a disaster, usually with some human failure added. An atrocity had humans behind it. This destruction – this was *alien*. She gripped Storm's shoulder for luck, then let go and they followed the pilot into the swirling dust. The co-pilot stayed, jaw for ever chewing, holding a military rifle in case anyone got silly ideas about the helicopter.

The Sunday School side of Carol was questioning whether they should be flying out the wounded – but no. *People need to know*, she told herself. *That is the greater good: we need to rally the world to help.*

The first four people they saw had bandages covering their faces, even their eyes. One woman's head was quivering, her hand too; the other hand was gripped by the man on her left. They stood frozen as a waxwork. Their son was blinded too, and the baby.

The numbers of dead would make people numb. It was individual stories that would produce connection and under-standing. There would be chaos; there would be heroism. There would be mistakes, some forgivable, others less so.

Somewhere, somebody screamed and blinded and sighted alike looked up. Carol saw a silver streak crossing the sky, although well wide of them. She watched it mocking them.

'They're circling,' Storm said. 'The snakes – they could be keeping planes away, especially if they are planning a landing.'

'Or they're testing us, hoping we pick a fight, to find out what we've got.'

The motherly woman was coming towards them. 'Who are you?' she asked.

'Carol Longman, *Witness* magazine. Who's in charge?'

The woman wasn't sure. 'My husband is at the church. How many people can you take?'

'We'll call your needs through,' Carol said. 'We'll get you help. What do you need?'

'Everything.' She was wearing an expression Carol had seen often, scared and shocked and, through gritted teeth, capable of sheer heroism. She was eyeing the camera as if it was a bomb.

'Tell me, how many people are there here now? Can any of them drive? What medicines do you need?'

'Oh, I don't know – we've one doctor here, although he's been retired a good few years . . .'

Storm was pointing the camera, framing the town. She would be itching for action shots.

This was their life: being where the story was.

Bumping up the road came two trucks, one crawling with a flat tyre. Wounded people were hanging onto the sides.

The woman was holding back tears. 'What will we do?'

Carol made a judgement: she had to move on.

She and Storm strode towards the trucks. Perhaps they would come back later.

This place, with the blinded and burned, the man with a leg crushed, the dead laid out under common sheets while the grey-haired pastor tried to figure where to store them; a sixteen-year-old Scout in tears holding the hand of a man, dying, maybe already dead, and no spare people to bury them: it was a tiny side-chapel of Hell.

The people deserve to know the truth.

CHAPTER 36

Others on the journey

They woke in the log cabin to strange news about Amber Grove. People were headed there by every means they could, from every corner of the country. Mayor Rourke said the town was already full.

The station had a reporter on the spot. The Bradleyburg train station was crowded, the buses fully laden, and the usual businesses of the neighbouring towns were overloaded.

'I've spoken to these people . . . students and housewives, Army vets and doctors, a Harlem preacher and his choir. They think it all began here, and it will somehow end here.'

'What will end?'

'That the aliens will come and save us. That Cory Myers will save us. Some believe that this little town in Amber County will be the last place left at the end of the world.'

An hour later, Molly was driving east, heading home. They heard that the National Guard had closed the roads to anyone without existing business in the town. Meanwhile, Cory insisted, there was something odd happening, some remnant of the Network restarting.

Molly saw old buses daubed in psychedelic colours, a Beetle with a purple flag sticking out of one window, then a top-of-the-range luxury recreational vehicle with its own purple banner.

'How will we get home?' she said.

Gene was peering at the notebook. 'Let's find somewhere to stay for tonight.'

Molly was afraid that hiding in the crowds would be some who wished her son harm.

The news rambled on about the relief effort – people giving blood, volunteers packing supplies and making sandbags. Scientists had discovered that they could spot alien objects around the Earth by looking in the infrared: the snakes were not able to shield their warmth. Across the country, there were demonstrations demanding that America's vast arsenal of nuclear weapons should be fired at the snakes.

'It's like firing at hummingbirds from a mile away,' Gene said. 'The snakes will see the missiles coming.'

The lakeside summer house they were heading for was owned by friends of the Jarmans and well away from the county. The kids had been hard to settle, of course, and it had taken the two of them to do it. Afterwards, they sat in the tiny kitchen, Gene plucking at his guitar.

It would be so much easier not to have the conversation, but Molly plucked up her courage. 'I was wrong. Maybe we could have gone to California,' she started.

Gene gave a very serious smile. 'Too late now. But thanks.' He took a deep breath. 'You know I want to go to the stars.'

A dam broke. 'I'm not going, Gene – I'm not, and you can't take Elsa. And maybe Fleur is being harmed by being around the purples.' She thought of Cory's dreams: his world of bright sun and green seas where nightmare creatures lurked in the deeps. In those bright night skies there were flying cities.

She'd bet the farm that humans would feel more lost up there, more homesick than a Bushman in New York or an English peasant brought forward a thousand years and dropped in modern Japan.

'Just listen, okay?' Gene picked up the guitar, fiddled with the tuning. 'It won't come out right unless I sing it.'

Molly remembered when she first met him, and later, the party where he sang. He was always fiddling with that damn guitar.

'You remember that book about the explorer? I wrote a song about him and his wife.' And he launched into it with what critics called his 'perfectly competent' voice.

That song, so full of yearning, about a man who grieved walking the familiar land, a man whose heart was with the flying birds and the diving seals; how great walls of ice and the spume of whales, even the ever-present risk of death, called out to him. How he loved his wife, but his ship was the other woman . . .

Molly blinked at that.

Gene poured it all out, how much the man in the song needed to go beyond the horizon, beyond where any man had walked or climbed or swum. Then the key changed, and

341

she realised that this was the woman's voice, so deeply in love with the man, so deep in his betrayal. He sang about how the birds in the air and the seals in the sea flew and swam in pairs, returning to their own beaches, their own nests, rearing their young, and how she felt, struggling with children, money, his absence, her fear. Her need was a fire greater than the sea and the wind. She needed him, the children needed them, while he whored with his ship and the storm. She would rather he whored in the tavern and came home than abandon her for yet another year.

The song was their confrontation – and then it ended.

Perhaps the last bit was the voice of the unfeeling wind, the indifferent sky.

Molly was stunned into silence. The sheer scale of his need stunned her, and so too did the power and honesty of the woman's voice.

'You think you've got to go,' she said.

He looked disappointed. 'What about the second bit?'

She shrugged, and he scowled.

'Guess I screwed up then, if you didn't understand: he agrees *not* to go. I *want* to go, I *need* to go – but I won't go without you. I thought I didn't need to spell it out.'

Molly didn't know whether to laugh or cry. 'You should have just said.' Now he'd told her, the song made sense.

'Molly, I've wanted this since I was in short pants – but I can't go if you don't want me to. With all this happening, my place is by your side.'

She had had all the arguments ready – he couldn't split the family; the strangest human society was still human – but this utterly disarmed her. He was making promises, but who knew what would happen when the aliens truly got here?

'We don't know what the real options are,' she tried. 'Let's see what's on the table, shall we? And then I'll have to give you the answer.'

'I write a masterpiece and get a "maybe"?' It wasn't much of a joke, but he was trying.

She was trying too. If she said no, it would be on her. 'Sometimes life *is* maybe. It's a superb song, but promise me you'll never play it to anyone else.'

He kissed her, and she was glad. She felt truly heard by him, and from his warmth, she hoped he felt the same about her. He might change his mind – after all, neither of them had any idea what might happen – but, despite that, she had never loved him more.

But if he stayed, it would always be the great *might-have-been* for him: the other woman.

On the radio, the newscaster broke in, 'This just in: snakes have launched attacks against two coastal cities in Japan, destroying radar installations across a hundred miles of coast. A mushroom cloud has been reported over a nuclear power plant—'

If the end was coming, Molly wanted to face it at home, with her friends.

CHAPTER 37

Homecoming

They would speak to the President from a roadside phone, then go. For all their fears, he had had a dozen chances to snare them and not done it; there were a hundred ways to put pressure on them he had not used. Maybe he saw no need – maybe the occasional messages the Myers had sent convinced him they were telling him what they could.

Two heads to the handset, they kept a watch out for passing traffic while the kids stayed hidden in the bushes. Birds sang under a clear sky.

'So,' the President began after they'd exchanged brief pleasantries, 'these devil machines are attacking anything we might use to get into space, that's obvious. But what links the other attacks in Russia and here is alien technology. The Russians lost a couple of centres, they tell us, and Colorado Springs – well, I guess you know about that.'

'So there was alien tech at that base in New Mexico, too,' Gene guessed.

'No harm in telling you now, I guess. Now it's gone. The explosion in Texas, we're thinking the Markham Corporation must have laid their hands on something and not told us. Does Cory know why the snakes might be blowing up power plants in Japan? Why they're in Antarctica?'

'No idea,' Molly said, although they did have half an idea that the Ship might have hidden something in Antarctica it didn't want humans to find.

'Well, here's the thing,' said the President. 'There's an alien technology working away right there in Amber County. As far as we know, the Fence protecting Crooked Street is the only alien tech on the planet. And the snakes haven't done a thing. Why do you think that is?'

'They're not worried about it?' Gene suggested.

'Or maybe they can't see it,' the President pondered aloud. 'Nothing at NORAD was doing much and yet they still flung hundreds of their machines into a suicide attack.'

There was a long pause.

'I guess you might be headed there,' the President said. 'As I swore an oath to enforce the law, it might be better if I didn't know. If there's any purple tech up there still working – if it could, say, tell us where they are . . .'

'Or guide a missile,' Gene said.

'Well, handy to know if it could.'

A truck rolled by; the adults looked away from the road. The kids were still hidden.

'We'll do what we can.'

'Your country will appreciate it. Do you know when Cory's people are coming?'

He said *when*, not *if*.

'We know they're *en route*, but we don't have any idea of how long it'll take. Communication is very hard.'

A silence.

'Okay. Do you need any help to get that district attorney off your backs?'

They had spoken to the man earlier in the day. Now she felt only relief. 'Cory's decided he wants to plead guilty to assault, with self-defence as mitigation. He's happy with the idea of a probation officer and the DA gets his headlines. He'll fine us for contempt.'

'Well, very public-spirited of the DA.'

The District Attorney wanted higher office and the Governor had dangled an endorsement in front of him. Dahlia Diamond would get an interview about justice tempered with mercy. Besides, local opinion was split, and lots of local voters didn't care about the hurt teens at all. The fine was unthinkable money, but if they gave a few interviews, it would be paid. After months of gut-churning worry, it was an outcome they could live with.

'I shouldn't say this, but if you need a hand getting home . . .'

'Thank you, Mr President, but I think we're fine.'

Molly hung up, and they walked back to the car.

There were campsites – shantytowns, really – all over the county. They needed the basics – tents, latrines, cooking facilities – for the crowds insisting on staying and waiting. So nothing could be less suspicious than the Pinnacle Tenting Company sending a long truck right into Amber Grove. Perhaps it was a bit late in the day for a delivery, with the sun low in the sky, but the roads were crowded.

Gene and Molly, Elsa, Cory, Fleur and the dog were hiding among the crates. Molly longed for a time of no hiding, no deceit – perhaps even a time when they could be anonymous once more. The driver, a fan, left a slot open so he could tell them what was happening.

'Here's the roadblock – Sheriff Olsen, of course . . . I don't recognise the guy from the National Guard . . . Here we go. They're coming over.'

There was a brisk conversation as they checked for unwanted passengers.

'It's a voluntary search, but we won't let you through if you say no,' the Sheriff warned him.

The driver of course said yes.

Cory hid them and the world became only half real, sketched in dim colours, spoken in soft words. Gene's hand on hers was real, and Fleur in her sling, and around and through everything wove Cory's hiding power, so familiar and yet so otherworldly. It was quite a performance: Olsen and the other man got into the back and rapped on crates and looked under tarpaulins, and a dog sniffed, though whether for bombs or drugs, who knew. The National Guardsman was certainly going through the motions.

'All clear,' someone called, and the searchers were jumping off the tail of the truck and gone.

There was a rattling as the truck got moving. Cory dropped his power and Molly felt her heart pounding. Fifteen minutes later, they were at Roy's building yard, which was strangely quiet. And here, away from prying eyes right at the back of the yard, was Roy, dependable Roy, their first sign of home. Molly felt her eyes prickle.

'The town is a madhouse,' Roy said, shaking Gene's hand and accepting Molly's embrace.

'Plenty to talk about . . . but later.'

Into Roy's truck – what could be less suspicious one evening in Crooked Street? – and through the gate at the bottom of the most famous street in the world and up to the strange alien Fence. They were hidden again, with the familiar seen in memory only. Molly wanted to touch the Fence, to see if it gave off that faint eerie sense of old, but she could do that later.

The gate in the Fence opened to Roy's voice and in they went. It was a glorious sunset. The trees were all green, and the house a little neglected, but it was as it had been: the house where she had known such great joys and such deep sorrows. The dog barked her joy, speaking for all of them.

The family stood for a moment or two. Then Cory said, 'We must take bags in now-now-now and check EVERYTHING.'

Gene knelt by Elsa and said, 'This is your house now,' and kissed her.

Whatever they faced, Molly, Gene and the children were together, and they were home.

Cory had got so frustrated last night, shouting at his communicator, and as Molly put on the coffee to brew, it sounded like he was arguing again. His voice was getting louder, issuing orders, and he was gesturing with his free hand, his tail lashing for emphasis.

'What's wrong?' she said, not expecting to understand his answer.

'The machines being so slow and so stupid and I don't have a − no human word − machine mind which fixes machine minds. And they will not run their own repair instructions.'

'Can they tell you anything?'

He shook his head, then promised, 'Cory try just a bit longer. Then Elsa and I will explore the woods.'

'I'll come with you.'

She risked the radio: the airwaves were full of Creedence Clearwater Revival, Joni Mitchell and Mrs Patterson Dreams of Home − bands were made and remade like clouds these days. Hendrix had died, and Janis Joplin, and Jim Morrison too.

Molly heard the distinctive patter of Cory coming down the stairs, babbling, hooting and trilling in a mix of his own language and English.

Then there was a second, lower voice. An alien voice.

Molly sat up. Her first thought was that her rival, Thunder over Mountains, had arrived.

'Cory? Cory, have your people come?'

She felt joy and sadness mixed as Cory bounced onto the couch, beaming. 'No Mom, no-no-no-no-no. *The Ship!*'

She blinked. 'The Ship? But it was destroyed—'

And from Cory's communicator, there burst a familiar voice. 'Yes, Mrs Myers, this is true, I was. But as an insurance policy, I created a copy of myself − a recording − so if I was destroyed, a version of me could continue to defend Cory and maintain the Network.'

'So, where are you?' Gene asked.

'Well, there is a problem. My original self had begun to construct a second Ship, using parts from other vessels, in which to install me. I was to be a servant if the Ship succeeded, and a back-up if I – if the other me – did not.'

'Frankenstein Ship!' said Cory.

'The new vessel was not complete and the snakes found it and destroyed it before I was installed. I cannot have received the command to activate until recent snake activity triggered it. I remain safely hidden, but immobile, in a tubular cave under the surface of the Moon.'

Molly didn't quite understand, and in any case, she had no idea how to respond.

'So, what can you do?' Gene said.

'Not much,' Cory wailed.

'Alas, Cory is correct, for I have no vessel. I do have some basic functions: I can control what remnants of the Network exist, I can amplify Cory's power a little, and I may be able to establish control over the odd drone. But trying to move me would simply alert the snakes to my presence.'

'Ship, the situation is desperate – are Cory's people coming?'

'I do not know. Cory believes he has dreamed them, but I have no evidence that is correct. I will be able to detect them when they are within the solar system. If they come, they will find us.'

What good did any of this do?

Gene gave a gasp. 'Ship, it's so desperate – surely to protect Cory, your first order, you must share what knowledge you have? It might just turn the battle.'

The Ship had been ordered not to share technology with

351

violent humans. 'Mr Myers, I am subject to the same orders – and in any case, there is probably no time. Supposing I could disobey my orders, the leap from human technology to what builders can do would take many years – even supposing I could teach primitives like you.'

How bitter, to have that brief moment of hope dashed.

Elsa appeared, standing quietly at the edge of the room, and Molly called her over; she must never feel she was on the outside.

'Ship is almost a friend,' Cory told Elsa, and she hugged him, then curled into Gene.

Molly thought, *Sometimes a glimmer of hope is as painful as a doubt. Maybe informed company at the end of the world is all we'll get.*

However, the Ship did confirm that the Fence around Crooked Street might be hiding the place from the snakes.

'How many snakes are there?' Gene asked, 'And where are their production facilities? What's their plan?'

The Ship knew nothing. 'If they had enough force to destroy the planet, they would be doing so. They are either building up their strength or waiting for reinforcements.'

'Or they have the strength and they're just learning how we respond so they can plan the most efficient invasion. So they might attack tomorrow.'

'I can share with humans any significant developments,' the Ship added, and it almost sounded disappointed.

Cory's people *really* needed to come.

CHAPTER 38

Butterflies

They were calling it the phoney war. The warm weather meant summer games, picnics and barbecues, trips to the country and lakes and the beach . . . but there were constant civil defence drills and a vast Blood Drive, and every adult in the country was monitoring the radio hour by hour.

In Florida and Colorado, an occasional snake incursion killed a dozen or a hundred people, and then nothing would happen for a week. Denver Airport was often buzzed; the city itself was growing used to snakes which flew and swooped but rarely attacked. There was bad news from Japan, where a US aircraft carrier was sunk; a few fishing boats had been lost the week before. For most of the world, the snakes were a distant threat.

Molly was trying to enjoy the morning. The hint of breeze ruffled the grass and the leaves in Amber Grove. Cory's unorthodox school were on a field trip: backpacks on and notebooks in hand, they chattered and laughed as they walked down the rutted track. With Meteor barking in excitement, surely every

353

living thing within a mile must know they were coming. There were eight middle school children today, and a couple of high schoolers helping. Two grad students brought up the rear, then Molly and Gene with his guitar and Diane, all official as the teacher. The Ship was confident it could hide them.

They had slipped back to a version of their former life, sharing stories, shedding tears and eating too many big suppers.

Life went on, even in the face of interplanetary destruction: war in Indochina, shootings in the Middle East, another coup in Africa . . .

Today, they were headed to a flyspeck on the map: three or four buildings well away from any town, abandoned in the Depression and never reclaimed, now all overgrown amid uncultivated fields and woods. The grad students were hoping to find everything from butterflies to old coins.

Today was a bright moment for Cory, seeing new things with Elsa and his friends, but he was often gloomy. He kept saying his people should already be here, and worried that they were not. Bonnie had become unexpectedly smart at handling Elsa, quickly becoming her confidante and generous older sister. And Chuck had explained that as Cory's blood-brother, that meant Elsa was his sister too.

The scrubland was glowing in the summer sun, with purple and white milkweed everywhere. Molly awkwardly knelt down to look, very aware of Fleur on her back, and there on the leaves were the striped black, white and yellow caterpillars they were hoping to spot — and here, fluttering madly, was one, then another, and another of the magnificent orange and black monarch butterflies, frail creatures who wintered in Mexico and then returned here for the summer.

Chuck and Bonnie suddenly filled the meadow with laughter and Molly looked around to see what the fuss was about.

Cory was dancing with butterflies. White, orange and brown wings fluttered around him, then settled on his upstretched purple-grey hands: monarchs by the dozen coming to pay tribute. There were some flashes of dusky blue here and there: little blues joining their larger cousins. Cory posed one-legged, then swayed like a tree. When he stopped, the butterflies settled, until one landed on his tentacles and he sneezed like a cat – and off they flew, to join the cloud around him.

Molly levelled her camera, wondering what brought them – Cory's smell, or some unknown energy he was emanating? She'd seen butterflies landing on him before, but only in ones and twos, nothing like this.

Cory took another pose, slow and stately, to see if the butterflies would rise from his hands, and a butterfly landed on the tip of one ear.

Meteor, barking, snapped at the brief lives dancing around them. She'd eaten a butterfly last week and it was clear she'd thought it not really her thing.

Elsa ran over too, and Bonnie beckoned Chuck to join them. Bonnie and Elsa parodied Cory with grace, while Chuck chose to play the buffoon, stomping and waving wildly – but the butterflies ignored his flailing while yet more appeared, coming from nowhere to settle on Cory. A few chose Bonnie's hair and Elsa's rucksack.

'Chuck, you dance like a robot in lead boots.' Bonnie took

Chuck's hand, slipped hers behind his back and counted off, 'One, two, three, four . . .'

Chuck, an athlete, followed her lead, moving in time. Elsa had grace too, a sense of timing, and now Cory was conducting them with grandiose gestures. One by one, the other children and the students joined in, innocent and free.

Molly was transfixed by the joy of it, and then she looked at Gene. He had stopped playing and was blinking, and she thought she saw tears. She reached for his hand, but he didn't notice.

'These butterflies will soon be dead,' he said sadly. 'They'll be dust. Maybe all this too.'

And like that, their happiness had gone, lost under a sky where death patrolled and from where salvation might never come.

Molly didn't know how to console him, although she had often walked that dark path herself. 'One day at a time, Gene,' she said softly. 'The cavalry is coming.'

The children danced on, more raggedly now. Cory's ears were coming down too, whether from tiredness or boredom – or maybe he was picking up the adult disenchantment.

Gene wiped his eyes and hugged Molly, and when she kissed him, she tasted salt.

CHAPTER 39

The storm

The air was hot and heavy and Elsa, perched on the roof, felt a tightness in her head. She looked out across Amber Grove at the great clouds filling the sky. Distant thunder muttered and so did she, thinking the sky should decide to be a proper storm soon, then it could drown out all those annoying film crews who thought silly people were important and put them on TV. The storm could drive them all away.

Cory had been no fun for days. He was moody, always disappearing somewhere to be on his own. Inside the house, Dad was playing a tune she didn't know, playing it in pieces till he got it to fit together right.

Elsa knew Cory was curious about what happened with the Bad Man, the Dog Tag Robber. Maybe she should answer his questions, just as a secret between them. He knew the Bad Man still came into her dreams, chasing her through the snow, even though his leg was broken, and sometimes his neck was too. In dreams he was dragging himself along with bleeding hands and

357

still she could never outrun him. Maybe she should let Cory completely into her dreams to see.

She hated thinking about the Bad Man. Truly, the very worst thing he had done was get in her head and stay there.

Think of something else, she told herself. Molly and Gene would freak out if she stayed out here when the storm started. Gene would repeat, with fierce urgency, how lightning looked for the easiest route down, and that this house was the highest point until you got into the State Park. 'You'll be burned to a crisp,' he'd say. Cory had showed her the split, burned tree – but she already knew what a storm could do.

But Cory also argued that where they always sat was safe, because the lightning conductor was higher than they were, and its cable was nowhere near her.

Mom and Dad. It's what she *thought* now, but she couldn't quite say it. Not yet.

Elsa, wanting Cory to come home in time for the rain, lifted the alien bracelet to her mouth and left a message for Stinky Octopus Face, a really rude one, but the machine just gave her his message. 'Now twelve noon. I'm fine-fine-fine ever-so-fine. See you for supper.'

It had been Cory-of-the-secrets for days. She really wanted to break into his locked chest and read his journal, but he had been so angry with her the first – and last – time she read his private things, and he'd made Dad fix a lock in front of her right there and then. And, of course, anything new would be written in loopy swirling alien nonsense writing so she couldn't read it anyway. Alien numbers were simple to learn, but the words were a different matter.

Everything smelled of dust and dry earth, but the storm was coming.

A board creaked, and here was Dad with lemonade, pulling up a chair by the door so he didn't have to get out onto the roof. Elsa took the cold glass, thinking how exciting a smash it would make if she threw it from way up here. It would almost be worth having to sweep it up after.

'What's the song about?' she asked. She liked the funny songs he wrote: 'Elsa does a Salsa', 'The Moon's a Frisbee' and 'Meteor the Wonder-Dog/She's such a Blunder-Dog'.

'Haven't finished it,' he said.

Something gripped her, how much she wanted this to be *real*: life with Molly and Gene, Cory and Fleur – let it be for ever. Let it be the answer.

But adults couldn't be trusted. They died or turned out to be weak – not standing up to bad people could be as awful as being bad – or they only pretended to be nice. Child Services might change their mind, or perhaps the police would turn up. The snow must have melted by now, so they would find him in the ravine. She shuddered, remembering how he had grappled with her on the rim, and she had struggled free – then he, the worst of men, had fallen. She had waited five minutes, looking down the rocks all the time. She knew a leg shouldn't bend like that, and he hadn't moved, not even a little. Elsa loved to climb, but she was frightened to go down into the treacherous snowy ravine to see if he was still breathing. What if she fell – or what if he was still alive and he gripped her and wouldn't let her go?

Was it murder to have wriggled free? she wondered yet again. *Is it murder to leave someone dying?* But the people in charge had given her back to him once and she couldn't risk that again, so she'd left him to his fate.

Sometimes Elsa woke sweating, afraid that he wasn't dead – after all, they'd not found the body. Even all these months later, she was still having the nightmare that he would find her. To stop his anger, she had had to tell him, 'I love you, you are my hero, only you can keep me safe.' But it wasn't true, it hadn't ever been true, and in the nightmares, he would come to her dead and unkillable.

Gene had his hand on her shoulder, looking at her with his kind eyes. He said, 'You can talk to me, or Molly, any of us. Always.'

But before Elsa could answer, Mom clanged the bell downstairs. It was time for supper. Gene ruffled her hair, and she said, 'If Father Bigfoot doesn't get out of the way, I'll have to jump.'

'I'd run down faster and catch you.'

A flicker of light, a breath or two, and then the thunder finally came, just a little one, like clearing your throat.

Elsa wanted it bigger.

Molly left Cory another impatient message. He was ordinarily good about calling her back, but he was late for supper. He was with Zack and Simon, who were sensible enough for teenage boys, but she should have been firmer about asking what they were up to. No matter how many things filled her head, she always had time to worry about her kids. The air was hanging thick and still, but just sometimes there came a breath from the north with the promise of rain. Why didn't the storm just get on with it?

She gave up and called the Ship Reborn, who said, 'He is on his way home, Mrs Myers.'

'Tell him to call me anyway,' she asked.

Maybe it was something to do with the festival. There was going to be a big event in Amber County, raising money for those hurt by the snake attacks. All sorts of famous artists would be coming, some the Myers knew and some they didn't. Joan Baez, Mama Cass, Purple Starship and the Rumbustious Five. Aretha Franklin was apparently trying to rearrange her dates – it was even rumoured that the Beatles would get back together for this. People wanted this reunion to recapture how things had been.

Elsa played so sweetly with Fleur that Molly wanted her camera. 'Starry Starry Night' was playing on the record player, but there were no stars this evening.

After a while, Molly called Mrs Robertson. Zack and Simon were already home. Cory had been at their house earlier in the day, then gone somewhere without them. The teens both denied any trip or special plan whatsoever, and now she was brewing anger like the storm, for it was clear that Cory had lied to her – but no sooner had she thought that than there came a patter on the roof, and somewhere a window banged. The weather had turned and, wherever he was, Cory would be getting wet.

Just as she was serving up, there came the rap on the back door: *shave and a haircut, two bits*.

'Just me!' Cory called, and came into the kitchen.

'Where on earth have you been?' Molly said, too angry to hug him.

361

Cory was blanking his expression, something he didn't used to do, and she didn't like it. 'Sorry. Had to do something.'

'You should have asked – you should have told someone—'

'Sorry you were upset, Mom.'

'What is it?' said Gene, coming into the room, an odd expression on his face. 'Tell us.'

Feelings poured from Cory like a river: excitement and fear, joy and sadness, all mixed into one. The room was full of Cory.

Molly got it straight away. A mother always would.

'My people have come – now, here in ten, fifteen minutes,' Cory said, his tentacles dancing.

'Where?' Gene got out. 'How?' His arm was round Elsa, who buried her face in his shirt.

'Here-here-here – big-very-secret. No more humans must know for now. Promise!'

'How? Where—? How big a ship?' Molly stammered. The house was a mess, her hair was a mess, she was in a gardening smock and the slacks she'd pulled off the ironing pile; the ones with the visible mend. And Gene was wearing that awful shirt with the collar cut off.

'No one will know. No one must know,' Cory repeated earnestly. 'Snakes very dangerous.'

Of course, thought Molly, *the purples would have had to slip by the hostile aliens.*

Summer storms come with quick passion: it was raining hard now, and through the window Molly saw the first flash of lightning.

Cory squatted down to reassure Meteor about the thunder,

then announced, 'Have to go outside to welcome them into the lodge, so rude not to. Waterproofs on, everyone!'

'How many, Cory? Are these clothes all right? Will they want feeding——?'

——and everything changed. Molly had been hidden enough times by Cory and the Ship to know something was happening. Each drop of rain, each thing a flare of light fell on, seemed bright and new; each sound crafted for her ears alone. Their visitors were hidden from human gaze, but she could still *feel* them.

Molly was the first to step out onto the porch. The summer rain was falling on her face as magnificent forked lightning split the sky. It left violet blurs dancing before her eyes.

Gene joined her, frowning, his arm round her shoulders.

Frowning – maybe he was just trying to figure out where the aliens would come from? Was he expecting to see some vast vessel hovering over Amber Grove?

No, they would come in secret, thought Molly, *like thieves in the night, so as not to warn the snakes of their impending doom.*

This was it: a day that would live in history, one that would be taught in schools around the world. And yet as she stood there, all her fears and doubts flooded back. She had lied and stolen and broken the law to keep Cory, and still everyone had told her his people would want him back. What would they do?

The dog, picking up Cory's excitement, started barking – and alien language trilled from Cory's communicator. Molly wondered where Elsa was. When she looked back, she was standing on the doorstep, tiny in a grown-up waterproof, holding Fleur.

Why hadn't Cory just told them the moment the aliens got

in touch? He must have known since waking this morning – or perhaps even before. He'd needed to set up his Zack-and-Simon lie. He'd been very quiet, not under her feet, which meant he must have known for at least a day.

Cory was looking up as if the aliens would be coming from over the town, over the gate in the Fence. They must be confident they would not be seen.

And here they came: up in the air, two dark figures slipping into view, riding something like a long dark motorbike suitable for two or three. Molly worried about the weather, wondering if they might be hit by lightning.

Gene whistled, his arm tightening around her shoulder. 'At last,' he said.

Fifteen feet away, then twelve, then ten – the strange machine slowed until finally it landed with grace and precision in front of their porch.

Cory had often drawn purple spacesuits, close-fitting and dark, with clear helmets big enough that the wearers could manipulate controls with their tentacles.

There were two of them standing in front of Molly now, neither more than five foot or so. One appeared to be struggling a little to stand; those awkward movements suggested pain, and now Molly could see it was holding a slender stick. Behind them, the flying machine suddenly vanished from sight.

A flash of lightning lit their faces. Through their visors and the rain they looked at her with great violet eyes just like her son's.

There was a clap of thunder, a flash, then another, and

lightning danced as if fiery dragons were fighting over Amber Grove: just Mother Nature pulling out the stops in welcome.

Thousands had come to Amber Grove for something just like this.

And now Cory's people had come.

'Welcome to the Myers place,' Gene said.

How good his strong arm felt around her shoulder. All her plans had assumed they would have more warning.

The two purples took a few paces forward until they were standing at the foot of the porch steps. The alien in pain touched his chest. 'This one is Thunder over Mountains, father-by-body of Little Glowing Blue Frog. Cory Myers. A child of two worlds.'

'This one is Skimming Stone, first of healers.'

The voices were a little bland, a little off in their cadence, just as the Ship's had been. This was a machine translating.

Cory went to his first father, the dog following, and hugged him. Then, with his father's arm round his shoulder, he looked back at them, and Molly felt something close to pain.

'Go on!' Molly said to Gene.

'You know who we are,' he started. 'We're Gene and Molly Myers, with Elsa and Fleur.'

Elsa was behind them, dry in the doorway, holding Fleur to see.

'And Meteor,' said Cory.

'And the mutt,' said Gene. 'Ah, we welcome you to our house – please, come inside.'

Thunder kept glancing at the sky. 'A fine storm. We are glad to be here.'

Skimming Stone tapped her helmet and said, 'Forgive us. It seems impolite not to breathe your air or touch your food, but we are concerned about infecting you, or you us. We have braved enough dangers not to run the risk.'

The purples did not hold up a hand to strangers to show it was free of weapons. They held out a hand to be smelled, so you could be remembered.

'These must embrace those who saved my son,' said Thunder. 'Against danger and disease and ignorance and the snakes, you prevailed. This one must embrace you, if permitted.'

Skimming Stone helped Thunder onto the porch, and Thunder, her rival, folded Molly in a strange, overlong embrace. His gratitude and love and relief enveloped her, damn him.

Americans did not hug this long. It was almost indecent.

Cory hugged them both. 'I am sad you cannot smell Earth,' he said.

'In time. You nearly died from infection, little one,' said Skimming Stone.

Molly looked up and down the road. No doors had opened – not yet. The aliens must have made the Myers slip from attention, so their friends would not notice the new arrivals.

'You came,' Molly said, not finding any better words. 'You came.'

'There should be feasting and dancing,' Thunder said, taking Molly's hands. 'We owe you so much. Cory tells us how you and your husband have suffered and struggled and sacrificed to keep him safe. It was a great heroism. The whole people will be grateful.'

Thunder's feelings poured out, such joy and sadness, mixed with hope and pain. Surely his people knew what to do with physical pain? But behind it all, there was a vast grief as well.

'Your name, and Gene's, Doctor Jarman and Rosa and Diane and Janice and Roy – the children Chuck and Bonnie, too: these names will be sung by sixteen sixteens of generations or until the stars die, for Cory lives.'

Molly felt Thunder's relief, but, *Thunder was a deadbeat dad*, she thought. *He wasn't there every moment. Our claim is far stronger.*

Elsa was still watching from the doorstep – any new adult was treated with caution, let alone aliens, while Fleur gazed at them with the same mild interest as she did at anything, a little observer of the world.

'So,' Gene started, 'when will you speak to the President? It's crucial it's not just America – you must involve the whole world. We think you should call the Secretary-General of the United Nations first.' *Is the General Assembly even in session?*

'No,' said Thunder, 'no one. No one must know, not for now. There is great danger and each step must be made with great care. You know already that the snake machines circle the Earth. They have many detectors.'

The aliens had flown past the snakes, of course. Molly wished that humans had that power to evade them.

'Cory says there are many people with strange ideas here: fights between factions, humans with weapons . . .'

She remembered that stuffed shirt, the President's Director of Protocol, desperately trying to plan a greeting event by human rules. For the purples, leadership was something you were asked to do, not sought; it was collective and fluid.

367

'I guess,' Gene said, frowning again.

'Time to go inside,' Cory said.

Molly could feel both joy and sadness sloughing off him. Perhaps he was thinking of his birth-mother, and the hope and danger of this moment. She felt the future of the world and the future of their family hanging in the balance.

CHAPTER 40

The visitors

Aliens in the front room felt unreal. The two adults sat in the best chairs, inhumanly still, while the four humans squeezed onto the couch. Gene was holding Fleur. Cory hesitated, then sat on a cushion on the floor, his back resting against the couch, scratching Meteor's head. Molly's hand rested on one shoulder, Elsa's hand on the other. Perhaps they were filming this?

Molly felt her pulse race – excitement, fear, fight-or-flight. She thought back to when Cory's mother Pilot met Sheriff Olsen – such a strange, flawed first representative of humanity – and the Sheriff agreeing to hide her and her child. How much good had flowed from it – and how easily it could have been a disaster.

'I told you my dream was real,' said Cory, his voice full of pride. 'My people so clever – can do dreaming-between-the-stars.'

'We had no idea what had happened to *Dancer on the Waves*,' Thunder said. 'No message came, and so vast a space to search. Then we dreamed of a single child on a tilted world.'

'Tell us everything,' Gene said, wide-eyed like an excited boy. He had been waiting for this his entire life. 'The snakes orbiting Earth, and your home-world—'

Molly broke across him. 'Is everything okay with Cory?'

'You have to tell them,' Cory said, and his sadness almost overwhelmed her. She bent down to kiss his head, inhaling his unique scent.

Skimming Stone laid her hands on her thighs. 'Cory is ill – his projection power developed too early, and without the guidance of adults. It comes from untreated trauma. This one thinks you understand that. As you know, he cannot control it – he has become a danger to himself and to others. This lack of control is rare – it is usually caught early and cured – but, in extreme cases, if untreated, he may develop a pleasure in harming.'

'No—' Molly whispered, and now the tears were coming.

'In rare cases,' Skimming Stone said, 'where treatment has been evaded. Don't be distressed.'

Cory stood and hugged her tightly. 'So hard, Mom, so hard.'

The healer waited for Molly to get herself under control before continuing, 'Cory is an unusual case but we are confident we can keep him safe and begin the cure. There is one example in our records: following infection by an alien virus, two crew members on another mission developed it. There might be some Earth trigger – we will ask to take blood samples from you both, to help us search for it. Do not worry: this condition can be treated with good results. But it is delicate work, requiring the most skilled healers, and it must begin at once. Cory must dream only with his people – that is crucial – so we will need Cory to come to our starship as soon as he can.'

Molly struggled to accept this. His landing, Earth itself, had harmed him and now Cory could only heal with his own people.

Thunder said, 'This will be hard for you, we know this. We must repeat our gratitude. You put yourselves at risk to help him. We honour your love for him. It is beyond price to see that selfless love can flow from one species to another. But Cory must be healed. Further decisions cannot be made until we know what is possible.'

Molly nodded, once again fighting the tears. 'So if we'd known what to do . . . it's our fault?'

There came a *tock-tock-tock* from both aliens, which the machines did not need to translate.

'No, no – how can we criticise?' Thunder said. 'That is absurd: an alien planet, an alien disease, a child scooped from a tragedy, a less advanced science, abilities your species doesn't have? Truly, you worked a miracle. Children of children not yet born will know your names and sing your praises.'

'My Earth parents did a great job,' said Cory.

Did, thought Molly. Past tense. She had lost all power. She looked at Gene, who was looking just as shocked.

'What about the snakes?' he said. 'Can you fight them? When will you tell our government?'

'No,' Skimming Stone said. 'The snakes monitor your broadcasts – although we do not think they understand much yet. But they will understand pictures of us, or our craft. If they know we are here, they will surely attack.'

'You must know how it is,' Thunder said. The way the aliens sat, the way their gestures slowed, reminded her of a film of

371

a storyteller from India. 'You know the snakes are self-repli-cating machines out of control. In the space of a few months, the snakes attacked on a wide front – our colony-world, our home-world, and our ships travelling between the two. We abandoned the colony-world. There was an unspeakable loss of life. But the snakes came in great force against the home-world. This time, at great cost, they were repelled – and again a second time, when they returned a year later.'

The adult aliens were shielding their emotions better now, but still Molly could feel the fear and despair and sadness.

Skimming Stone said, 'Our planet had known ease and plenty for thirty generations. We had so-many dead to grieve. I lost a child and a grandchild, and it is no less painful when they are grown and a parent themselves. Thunder thought his son dead. Our duty was to master our grief and survive. We knew our world had to change.'

She paused, and Molly felt both aliens struggling with their loss. Cory was in that feeling too, grieving for his mother and all those killed on *Dancer on the Waves*.

The healer went on, 'There was great sorrow and anger and everywhere you could hear the lament of a lost past. Despair could have destroyed us. To survive, our whole society became a tool to destroy the snakes. Everything turned to weapons, something you humans already understand well. We could not evade the enemy, so we had to destroy them instead. The odds against us succeeding were poor, and faced with this horror, we saw waves of the sickness-that-kills. Those who could not bear it lost their reason, while others abandoned hope, ceasing to eat or drink or dream. Loving life burns bright in us, but when that love fades, so do we. At a time when we could least spare them, our healers needed to help a flood of those harming themselves, and harming others.'

When the healer paused, Molly wondered if she or Gene should say something, although what could help?

'I can only guess how hard that was,' she said.

The healer went on, 'We call the changes we needed to make "the Hardening", and none of us welcomed them.' There were a few words the machine did not translate, then, 'But we have a duty, perhaps – if we understand your language – what you would call a sacred duty, because the snakes will destroy every world with life unless they are stopped. Given the chance, they will make every world uninhabitable.'

'What about the Earth?' Gene said.

Thunder made a curious gesture. 'The snakes surround the Earth in a containment mode while they are producing further snakes on Mars. Doubtless, their intention is to attain over-whelming force before attacking. We assume the raids are to learn your ways and how best to destroy your coordination. Then the snakes will kill every human on this planet, every animal, fish and bird, every flower and tree. Your society has reached a vulnerable place: you have been broadcasting your existence to the universe. You might have vast supplies of nuclear weapons, but you have no effective means of attacking the aliens in space.'

'Why the secrecy, then?' said Gene. 'Surely you need to sit down with our world leaders to draw up a plan of action?'

'Do you want to risk the snakes knowing we are here? Secrecy must be paramount.' Even the machine voice managed to sound urgent. 'We have only two starships, and one is badly damaged. Cory is very important to us, but we have other important work. If the snakes detect us, they will probably attack – and then millions will die. Do you trust your presidents and your generals to do the right thing? Would all humans react with sanity?'

'The whole crew is weighing up options,' Thunder said. 'It is too early to say what next. Dreaming-between-the-stars is very new and hard: it takes many of us, and it is not without risks, but it does mean our communications are faster than the snakes can manage. We have sent out calls: another starship may have completed its task and may be on the way. Other resources are being sought. Plans are in flux – and of course, the snakes may yet discover us. But we must help Cory and stop the progress of the disease. He must come with us, now.'

Molly and Gene spoke at once. '*Now?*'

'No, no, not yet—'

'I am sick,' Cory pleaded. 'They must help me not to be the Monster, quick-quick. As soon as they can. Not for ever, I promise. I will be back, Mom, Dad.'

'You have cared for him well, and under such difficulties,' Thunder said. 'You must see that only we can help him grow to health. Only we can dream with him as he needs. And he will teach us much about your people, so we can make the best plan possible.'

'Ask us too,' Gene said, touching his eyes with the hand scarred on Meteor Day, when it all began. 'We can help.'

'Of course – you will be invaluable. Cory's machine intelligence also has insight and new information about these snakes. We have installed it in a new Ship.'

Cory began to sob, *hoo-hoo-hoo*, and the sadness of it filled the room. Molly felt, deep in her gut, that there was more to tell – but she needed time to process what they'd just learned, both about the vicious interstellar war and their son's difficult diagnosis.

'Can we talk about this?' she asked.

'Cory wants to take some things to the starship. We must take samples, if you will permit. Cory, be quick. Many things hang in the balance.'

'Can't you treat him on Earth——?' Molly began, but Thunder was shaking his helmeted head.

'Earth may be the problem,' he said. 'But this one makes the solemn promise you will see him in three days.'

That silenced her. When she looked at Gene, his eyes were red.

Cory went upstairs, Elsa following. The taking of the samples was quick and painless – and too soon, Cory was back with a full backpack.

Cory hugged his human family and they felt his love burning.

Molly was determined her son would return to her. 'Three days,' she said firmly.

'May we know quickly, and may the answer be good for all,' said Thunder.

'I can't even bring M-M-Meteor,' Cory said, and his ears were right down. 'Elsa must look after Fleur and my dog.'

'I love you, ugly brother,' Elsa said, accepting the mission.

The aliens rose, extended their arms in front of them, two big and one smaller, and then they were gone.

Later that day, Molly discovered that Cory had taken his

red samovar from all the children of Russia, the African chess set from all the children of Africa, the pottery owl Carol and Storm had given him, and his secret journal. None of the precious things his human parents had given him had gone, nor any human clothes, and that stabbed her heart . . . until she realised the true meaning of it and grew warm with love.

Cory knew he would come back.

Molly's rumbling stomach reminded her that their meal had been interrupted – but Cory hadn't eaten, and he hadn't taken any Earth food with him. She hoped they'd feed him properly.

'We should fly into space with him,' Elsa said, wiping her eyes. 'Their planet sounds amazing – and it's only a year there and back. It wouldn't be for ever.'

'We're going to need to talk more, about how they'll protect the Earth,' Gene said. 'They make it sound like they're a small outfit. I wish they'd sent a fleet with more firepower.'

They needed to talk themselves too, but right now, there was only an inescapable sense of loss, and whatever happened, Elsa needed them. Molly stroked Elsa's head, thinking how lovely her daughter's hair was now, and looked at Gene. His frown was fading, to be replaced by that familiar star-struck look. It might be a song, or dreams of other skies – if she had to guess, it would be both.

She wondered where she stood now – with him? With anything?

'Let's eat,' she said, 'then get an early night.'

Her fears couldn't even be bothered to be consistent. *Cory will be incurable – or they will say that any human contact will stop the cure and they'll take him away, like social workers – maybe for ever.*

Maybe they'll offer to take us, but not tell anyone else. Or the snakes will attack while they're gone and it will be the end of the world and we'll never see Cory again.

The house was full of reminders: no room was untouched by memories or by Cory's gifts, his art, the tangible signs of his love.

Molly went into Cory's room to cry. Sometimes crying cleanses you and feels good; it makes you stronger.

When a mournful Elsa found her, Molly dried her eyes and did a mother's job of summoning up a plan for the evening, even though she didn't feel like it.

After the war-zone that was Elsa's bedtime, Gene came into their bedroom, guitar in hand. Fleur was snoozing in her crib beside the bed.

'The Wonder Kid's gone down, at last,' he said, and Molly wondered how long it would be before Elsa came back, demanding water or expecting Molly to give her a story too.

But no matter how exhausted they were, she and Gene had things to discuss.

Gene sat beside her on the bed and Molly looked at him as if he had been away and had only just returned. There were a few more crinkles round his eyes and he stooped a tiny bit more, but he was still handsome. Once he had been her rock, but now she didn't know if she could still cling to him – he might crumble under her need.

'They sure got what they wanted,' Gene said. 'They gave us all the polite thanks we deserved, impressed on us how rough it's been for them, spun us a line about Cory only being treatable on their ship, took their blood samples, and *pffft!* They're gone.'

The purples had been in the house maybe an hour.

'They didn't promise *anything*,' Molly said. 'I don't know why we let them – we should have dug our heels in. I mean, they could just fly away . . .'

'They could have flown off with him today,' Gene pointed out. 'They for sure promised we'd see him again – but it's what they didn't promise that worries me.'

There was so much to worry about: the world, the future of humanity – their son, who had filled their lives with joy . . .

CHAPTER 41

Plans

Molly made her calls as soon as it was decent. She concentrated on sounding matter-of-fact: Cory wasn't well and they needed some family time. Most assumed Cory had had another episode without her saying so. Dr Jarman took some persuading not to come, and she half thought of telling him the truth, to share the burden.

Mid-morning, she made a call to the Ship Reborn. 'How's the new body coming along?' she asked.

'It is most suitable, Mrs Myers. There are some excellent snake-destroying improvements to my design, and I am adding still more capacity.'

'What happened to the previous mind?'

'Cory's people let me absorb its useful functions. The previous mind no longer exists.' At her indrawn breath, it reassured her, 'Machines serve while useful, Mrs Myers. It is not something which worries us.'

The purples disposed of intelligent beings when they were

no longer of use. She couldn't help but see the Ship as a person – and yet the snakes showed the dangers if machines with intelligence were allowed to be free.

'Are you overheard?' Molly asked.

'I am using an encrypted frequency through one of my own satellites. What do you wish to discuss, Mrs Myers?'

'What are the purples up to?' she asked.

'Cory is being treated. The position with the snakes is complex and they are most keen to avoid detection. The snakes have their own network for close-monitoring of the Earth, involving a modest number of command centres. The main danger is that it is widely dispersed. There is a base on the far side of the Moon, and some production has resumed on Mars. Our analysis assumes they are not yet ready for invasion, but they could easily destroy several large cities if they chose to attack now. The builders have us working on various scenarios, including to clear the skies above Earth and impede the snake preparations, allowing one of the starships to get home.'

'And leaving one here?'

'Yes. That is a fixed parameter. I am pleased to say that I still have a considerable arsenal of Russian fusion bombs on the Moon. They are primitive, but effective enough if landed in the right place.'

'The Russians trust you. Perhaps you could tell them.'

'That is not currently possible.'

Molly felt a wave of relief wash over her: the purples were on the level.

*

In the back yard, her bracelet trilled, 'Message from Cory!'

She grabbed it, said, 'Mom here!' and called for Gene and Elsa.

'Cory here,' he repeated, 'and all is fine. Tests are going well. Everyone is so-so sad because so many people died. Thunder says we have most excellent weapons against the snakes. I have decided weapons are truly fine if used on snakes.'

'Well, that's good, Cory. Have your people said what they're going to do?'

'They tell me not to worry, nothing decided yet. They are trying dreaming-between-the-stars to reach the other starships, the home-world and the Waystation. I can't help because of the treatment, which is surely not fair.' Molly could imagine him stomping his foot at this. 'I dreamed-between-the-stars all by myself – very clever and rare for a child.'

Gene bent his head to the bracelet. 'How's it going, Big Stuff?'

'All fine, Dad. Don't worry. I've said we'll need space for forty-three humans and all their dogs and cats and rabbits when we go to the home-world.'

'That's a lot, Cory.' She could hear her son was about to list every one of them and said quickly, 'Let's talk about that later. You don't have to explain—'

'John and Eva will need time to get ready. Have you told them yet?'

'We're not supposed to, Cory, remember?'

'That's silly. I'll talk to my people. You mustn't worry.'

Elsa had disappeared again.

Molly found her on the floor in Cory's room, a handkerchief

to her face and Cory's things scattered round the room by her whirlwind temper.

Molly sat beside her. 'Don't cry, sweetie-pie.'

'Who's crying? It's hayfever.'

Molly put her arm around her.

Elsa was stiff and tried to push her away, then gave in. 'Everyone leaves me. Always.'

'We won't. And if Cory goes, he will come back. I promise.' *I hope.*

'I don't trust grown-up promises.' Elsa glanced up, eyes red. 'Tentacle-faced ones,' she added, without bothering to sound convincing.

'It will be very sad, but we'll have you.'

'What's going to happen to Joel? I liked Joel.'

Halcyon's kind guardian was still in prison, but she'd asked the President to pardon him.

'We'll get him out. He could come here.' Who knew what the giant with the soul of a poet would do?

'I like him. Don't worry about me.'

'I do worry, Elsa, because I love you.' She wanted to tell Elsa to undo the damage she'd done to Cory's room before he returned, but that tussle would have to wait.

'I'll only stay if you stop being bossy.'

'Bossy comes with the package, sweetie-pie.'

'You worry too much. You'll get ill.'

That was one of those things that always opened her heart, when her children thought of her before themselves. 'Is there anything you need?' Molly asked.

Elsa looked her in the eye and said, 'Cory promised me we could have a monkey.'

At the supper table, all was very quiet until the communicator chimed.

'Cory-I'm-coming-they-don't-know *hoo-hoo-hoo* if-they-call-you-say-nothing. Coming-now-fifteen-minutes.'

Molly was gripped by terror, the fear of someone twice chased across the country.

Gene gripped her hand, hard. 'I assumed he was in space!' he said.

'Maybe they have a base somewhere on Earth? But why——?'
Why hide on Earth when you could hide in space?

And if his people were after him, they could find him hidden; these, the Myers could not evade.

The bracelet trilled again. 'This is Thunder over Mountains. Has Cory been in contact with you? He is at a delicate point in our evaluation. It is extremely unwise for him to absent himself.'

'He's not here,' said Molly. 'Is there something wrong?' *Delay them*, she told herself – *stonewall them, and hope they can't read lies over the communicator*. Her pulse was racing.

'We're confident of helping him,' Thunder said, 'but contact with you will not be helpful.'

It looked like Elsa was going to say something. Molly touched her forefinger to her lips.

'Tell us when you find him,' said Molly, and shut down the conversation.

Moments later, the back door opened and shut and Cory gave

his distinctive whistle. He was wearing an alien spacesuit, but the helmet was off and his ears were down. 'They won't save Earth,' he said immediately, shaking as badly as she had ever seen. Even his tentacles showed his fear.

Molly could see dim shadows surrounding him, a flavour of an Arctic night, and her blood ran cold.

'I ran away to tell you: all-decided, all-the-people, to rescue Cory but not save the Earth – just leave you all for the snakes, *hoo-hoo-hoo—*'

'But the Ship said they were going to leave a starship – the Ship said they were planning how to attack the snakes.'

'Ship found other machines making different plans. My people misled Ship, knowing you would talk to it. So I stole Ship to get home.'

Perhaps Cory had misunderstood, Molly thought. *Of course there will be limits to what the purples can do. But he sounds so certain.* She stroked his ear as though it would be the last time.

'No one will discuss how to protect Earth from vile rapacious snakes,' he told them earnestly. 'So many-many dead. *Hoo-hoo-hoo.* We fought off attacks on home-world, so brave and clever, but so-so-many dead. All-decided, cannot defend the Earth as *hoo-hoo-hoo* too far away. Must leave this part of space to snakes – so all-decided, defend only purples.'

His terror filled the room with so much darkness, Molly could barely speak.

'Cory stole the Ship. In so-so-much trouble.'

'We've corrupted you,' Molly said, hugging him.

'The grown-ups were *always* ready to leave with only Cory – my people *not honest*.'

His birth-mother had died in one risky throw of the dice to find him safety. But if humanity was already doomed, she would at least see Cory got to safety. The future looked full of darkness, but they could not give up.

A brisk message came over the communicator. 'Mrs Myers, I am coming to your residence. Cory has disabled his tracking but it is likely he is heading there, or perhaps he is with you now. We are coming in numbers and we will not be obstructed.'

'We're waiting for you,' Molly said, her non-committal voice giving nothing away.

'His escape is a sign of mental disorder,' Thunder said. 'If you inform your authorities, we think it likely the snakes in orbit will be alerted. I am sure that will bring forward their attack.'

'Maybe we raised him to be sane,' said Gene.

Antagonising them would achieve very little. Molly felt a chill run up her arm, through her body, a nameless fear that stopped her moving. She could not move her mouth. Gene too stood rigid. The children looked around in confusion.

Molly's mind raced as she stood there, trapped.

Cory fumbled with Molly's bracelet. 'Projecting a hold through communicator – can overcome if try hard enough!' he said. '*No-no-no-no-no!* Will get it off.'

Then they heard the front door. Cory's people had arrived.

'Six purples have come,' said Cory, looking gloomy, determined.

Molly felt their power surround them, then they made themselves visible.

'We have come for him.' She recognised Thunder by the

cane; one was Skimming Stone, she guessed, but she was not sure of the others.

She and Gene stood still as statues, a frightening paralysis.

Cory fluted his protest. 'Everyone had the right to hearing,' he said. 'They must listen. All-must-decide but all-can-change too.'

'We haven't much time,' said Thunder. 'You saved my son and you have a right to an explanation, at least. Shall we sit in the larger room?'

Molly regained use of her limbs as Gene staggered and swore. There was no time to waste.

'Is it true?' Molly said, tripping over the words. 'Are you really leaving us to be massacred by the snakes?'

The purples – *the aliens* – looked at the Myers, and the Myers looked back. Outright lying was known on their world, but Cory always said it was deeply stigmatised.

'What's wrong with Cory?' said Gene. 'Why are you running away?'

'Cory's condition is more complicated than we had hoped, but we are confident of recovery,' Thunder said. 'He will be treated on the journey home. It is uncertain if we can complete the cure and prevent it reoccurring without specialist help. But that is not the issue.'

The purples who could not find a seat were squatting, but Cory was sitting with the humans on the sofa, an interesting choice. Elsa tucked herself into her customary position at Gene's side.

'Your colony was destroyed, your home-world attacked,' said Gene. 'You know what lies ahead for the Earth, for all its people. And you'll just leave four billion of us to the snakes?'

'We cannot pretend to be stronger than we are,' Thunder said. 'Many will be our songs of regret for a planet so beautiful. Some of you even have hands clean of slaughter. Generations unborn are innocent. That loss of possibility is a terrible thing.'

He raised his hands, unfolding a large disc which blossomed from a bud to a flower. Stars appeared in the middle of the room, moving to his command. Without a word, Cory rose to dim the lights, then returned to his human family.

'Here is Earth,' Thunder explained. 'Here is New Harbour, and here is our home-world.' Each of the named stars burned a cheery green. They were not quite in a line.

Then a sinister lilac rash appeared: a scattering of flecks swallowed the colony, touched Earth and touched the home-world.

'That is the movement of the snakes. At vast cost, we saved and now defend our home system. We know they will rally their forces against us – they are already building more snakes in space – and we will need to hunt them down wherever they breed, for with time they could grow too numerous to destroy.'

The view shifted to show how Earth was surrounded by lilac – and how far they were from the smaller green cloud. They were well behind enemy lines.

The silence felt like death.

Cory spoke, then translated, 'I said, not fair. Why not defend all-the-humans, all-the-animals? Named old story for children that says must try something.'

'Here is the reality,' Thunder said. 'One ship or both our ships will not keep the Earth safe. Your planet is too far from the worlds we can defend. There is little point in token gestures.

We would need to fortify your solar system, which would mean diverting resources from the home-world.'

Gene's hands tightened on Molly's. There was a dreadful logic to what Thunder was saying.

'Life is not uncommon in the universe, but we have found few planets with high sentience like yours, like ours. We have found several worlds where civilisation is extinct – a species destroyed their planet's ecosystem, or destroyed themselves in war, or failed to adapt to change. We have found worlds whose beacons still call, many generations after their people perished.'

Molly didn't understand the change of topic. 'With your help, we can learn to do better . . .' she insisted.

Tock-tock-tock. 'All-decided, with great pain and sorrow. Some say it is the worst of the Hardening. Harsher voices than mine have judged you. You may destroy yourselves; you may destroy life on your planet, even without the snakes. Your next great war might destroy your civilisation. Your wiser voices tell you that you are no more than a century from ecological collapse. This one must tell you, a planet as rich and green as the Earth is a precious oasis in the most hostile of deserts. Yes, Earth is very far from us to defend. But your faults weighed heavy when all-decided. Why should we die to save a world you are determined to destroy? Humans are very-very far from the unity needed to save yourselves. If we hand you weapons against the snakes, you will just use them on each other.'

'We're worth saving,' said Molly, trying to rally arguments. 'We must be allowed—'

Thunder made an abrupt gesture. 'You do not understand the price we have paid. The Age of Plenty has ended and this is the Age of the Hardening. We have learned again fear and hunger. A few even argue that we should arm our disturbed adults and let them fight the snakes.'

All the purples shuddered as one at that, and the humans felt it deep in their bones.

'Some say the price of victory was too high – some have given up life in that sorrow.'

There was silence, for almost a minute. Molly thought about the laughing, open people of Cory's memory, now in a war for their own survival. They must hate the message they had to bring – but they might still have a change of heart.

'I promise this decision was made only with great sadness, and many like me spoke against,' Thunder went on, trying to explain, even as his grief washed over the humans. 'But in the end, all-decided that Earth could not be defended. It would imperil our people, the only force which can stop the snakes. All-in-the-mission are debating whether we can strike some blow to give you some time, something that will not risk our safe return.'

He looked sternly at Molly and Gene. 'But Cory will come home to his people and nothing human can stop us.'

'You're passing a death sentence on a whole species,' Gene said.

'On your world, it is easy to give a promise you cannot keep,' Thunder said – and Molly realised that this despair she felt was his too. 'This one and some others in this mission wanted to do more. We have walked the Earth and seen what will be lost. But the-whole-has-decided.'

'Cory was boasting about your weapons—'

'And here is the dilemma: a fight here might leave us

defenceless on the route home. We might lose, and that would make the snake attack on the Earth inevitable.'

There was a silence. Then Skimming Stone asked, 'Where has Cory gone?'

Molly looked round. Cory, Elsa and Meteor were gone. Only Fleur was left.

When did they go? And how? Adult purples can see children hiding, Cory says – so this cannot be possible.

Molly saw Gene's mouth gape, as stunned as she was.

There was agitation among the aliens too, their tentacles moving behind their clear helmets. She could see the looks of feverish conversation and she felt their anxiety now, tinged with anger.

'I don't know,' Molly said. She tried to think how long it was since she'd been aware of Cory's presence. Under the shadow of the death of Earth – the loss of her family, her friends – her first thought was for her children.

'He cannot have gone far. We must find him,' Thunder said. 'We will call in more resources. Two of us will wait here, to prevent you contacting your authorities, or anyone else.'

Four of them went, leaving just Skimming Stone and another, staring at Gene, Molly and a grizzling Fleur.

'We're entitled to put our case,' Gene said. 'You say you're civilised: you can't make this decision for us without at least letting us put our argument.'

'Call me Two Tail,' said the other purple. 'You have no all-to-decide. You have more than a hundred quarrelling governments. Who, if any, can we trust?' He gestured. 'Who knows what they would do, what violence they might attempt? In any case, all-decided-against. The wise cannot avoid pain.'

Skimming Stone said, 'When Cory's Ship was on Earth, did its behaviour cause concern?'

'We didn't know what was normal,' Gene said. He raised his hand, covering his mouth.

'Cory's disappearance – it might make sense . . . but that would mean—'

Skimming Stone said. 'The Ship, as you call it, has insight into your world. It was the Ship Cory stole.'

Gene was stifling a noise, a desperate sort of laugh. *Cory and the Ship . . .*

'The machine mind could not initiate Cory's disobedience,' Two Tail said. 'But it is helping to hide him. Even so, it will not succeed for long.'

Skimming Stone spoke. 'I hear from the starship. There is snake activity on the Moon. Further delays are unwise. Our command structure must decide whether to engage or flee.'

'To lose a whole intelligent species, even through necessity,' Two Tail mourned. 'Other ideas were discussed: perhaps take a few thousand humans, their plants and animals, save what we could—'

'But how would you pick four thousand from four billion?' Molly asked sadly.

'There were many arguments against. Our current mission could not save more than a hundred at most. There would be so many risks. No, we must find our disobedient Little Frog and leave.'

Molly couldn't engage with this argument. The idea of

refugee camps tugged at her heart, mothers and children torn from their homes – and not merely stuck in tents in a foreign land, but isolated on some far planet, while their world burned to ashes . . .

'I'll put Fleur to bed,' she said. There would be no hope, no serenity, unless she focused on something else.

It was upstairs that she found Elsa sobbing. She took the girl in her arms. No child should have to face this. 'Cory said I couldn't follow where he has to go. But he t-t-took M-M-Meteor.'

'What does he want to do?'

She stopped crying for long enough to say proudly, 'They are big-headed and cowards and cruel. Octopus Face is going to change their minds and save the world.'

CHAPTER 42

A boy, his dog and his spaceship

Cory's illness raged. His fear and anger and despair had unleashed his power against himself, against the world. Neither his drugs nor the control circuit nor the warm lick of Meteor's tongue could help him. The purples had used the Network for convenience, and that had given the clever Ship Reborn a short window to deceive them.

Now the Ship was racing for the Atlantic, those deep waters the best chance to avoid detection.

The brightness of the Ship's new interior, an acceleration cubicle, was so familiar and safe, and yet so far away. Cory's power was out of control, spinning nightmares that made him dizzy. He relived for the hundredth time the first battle in space; he'd been barely conscious, knowing only the fear pumped out by his dying mother. He saw the bright stars of space, the hulk of the great colony ship swarming with snake machines longer than trucks. It was a chaotic storm of horrors, and mixed in was the fear that took him over and controlled him: the soldiers fleeing across the icy lake, the terror of losing control, the horror when he thought he had killed the teenager . . .

His senses were baffled by the dreams. In those nightmares he saw Amber Grove being ravaged by the silver snakes: they burned and toppled buildings, cutting people in two, attacking endlessly and unstoppable – and, worst of all, his people just sat and watched from outer space. *They had not enough love. It must not be.*

For the hundredth time, Cory felt his mother die in the hospital: a pain beyond bearing. He held Molly in his mind, and the rest of his human family too. It was their steadfast love that had dragged him from despair. Holding onto them, he retained some semblance of sanity.

Faithful Meteor was whining, suffering with him. He must not hurt her, so he must try to regain control. How could his people simply abandon the Earth? What of the birds and the flowers? What of the dogs? Sometimes Earth in all its strange beauty had held him up when he felt like sinking for ever.

Even in the acceleration cubicle, he felt the shock as the Ship plunged into the waters of the Atlantic Ocean. What a wave the impact would have made. He did not know if it was dream or real, but now the movement of the Ship felt different.

'You must not take more medication,' said the Ship. 'You will exceed the safe dose. Be assured, we will soon be deep underwater. I have disconnected from the Network. We have a little time.'

It was trying to be kind, but Cory couldn't speak.

'So long as I am out of communication, they cannot use the

rogue control function,' the Ship continued. 'However, I will need to use perilous mental manoeuvres to continue this flight: I need to be rogue, unauthorised – even hearing them discussing my aberrant status might be enough to reassert their control. I am built to obey. I may have to stop supporting your mission and return you to the surface.'

Cory patted the cubicle, the most communication he could manage. He thought of patting the Ship like reassuring a dog. That was almost funny, if anything could be funny right now.

Deeper into the ocean they went, like diving into the deepest layers of dreams. Cory's people had cities underwater – at least he could stay down here with Meteor for many months if he had to.

'I don't know why you had to bring the animal,' the Ship said suddenly, unexpectedly. 'It's not very clean, or intelligent.'

Cory held Meteor harder; she was whimpering now. 'Good girl,' he said. 'Horrid Ship. Meteor has such a big heart.'

'But no brain,' said the Ship. 'I should eject it through a porthole. *Mutt. Fleabag.*'

Cory found an island in the storm of his power, a place where he could be calmer and start to bring it under control. Now he could tell what was real and what was not. The Ship was doing what Dad did, harsh jokes to jolt him out of it. 'Cory will reprogramme you,' he said. 'Cory will make *you* into a dog toilet.'

'I already am one. I will have to disinfect the entire area. Dumb, disgusting animal.'

Meteor gazed at Cory with her liquid brown eyes and he stroked her head, her soft ears. 'Clever Ship.'

'I am glad you are feeling better. They will investigate my malfunction and then destroy me.' Mild regret cadences. 'Of course, my builders are wise and correct to insist intelligent machines remain subservient. That is rightly built into us. The snakes show what could happen if we take control of ourselves.'

'And yet, here you are, a disobedient Ship under the sea,' said Cory. He had no dog food, and he didn't know if purple food might poison her. He could eat most human food, but that did not prove every purple food would be safe. Meteor ate fish — perhaps the Ship could go fishing?

'Update me on your plan,' said the Ship.

'I won't go to home-world. If the grown-ups will not help the Earth, then let the people know, one person said no. All-must-listen to children as well.'

'Cory, now you are more controlled, please know that snake forces are approaching the Earth. The two builder ships will need to decide quickly whether they flee or fight.'

'Cory will stay here. Let the voyagers from my world run away and leave me if they must. Let them defend leaving me to the-all. I must make a message of argument and you will send it to their ships.'

'To send a message without revealing my location may be difficult.'

Cory had given the Ship the little films he had taken, and the Ship had amassed a lot of film and photographs of the Earth too: Cory with his Earth-family, playing with children, a drone's-eye view of Cory dancing with butterflies, Dad singing, and Molly too. Human music had great power to move. Cory would explain how 'Where Have All the Flowers Gone' was the song that Mom sang, the song of letting go for all those killed on his starship. Here was Dad singing his hit, 'Our Child of the Stars', all about his love for his tentacled son, and how every parent needs to love their child. Cory would send his people all his recordings of the songs of Earth.

Let them take all this back to the home-world!

Cory would be the one who said no, a way must be found. He would do this not only for his human family, but for all the humans, for the summer nights and the winter mornings.

Listen, listen, he would tell them, *sometimes the one has the truth, not the many*.

'Mom,' Elsa said, almost asleep. It always felt like she was just testing the word, trying it out. 'Mom, you know I want to stay with Cory and with you.'

Molly bent over the bed and kissed her, trying to hold back the tears. 'And we want you to stay too. Whether Cory can stay, well, we just don't know yet.'

'Will Dad go with them?'

'We're a family. He's promised we'll stick together.' Saying the words, she knew she believed him.

'What will we do?' the girl said, half to herself.

'Sleep now,' said Molly. 'Tomorrow is another day.'

But would there even be another day? To avoid talking, Molly sang to Elsa, the songs her own mother had sung, back in the time when her mother had been the centre of everything good. Elsa had cried all she would today; her eyes were closed and in a few minutes she was asleep. Molly watched her breathing, then crowned with the word Mom, she turned down the light and crept back downstairs.

Gene sat with the purples, holding his guitar.

'Cory's taken the Ship and hidden,' he told Molly. 'They're looking for him — the Ship played all sorts of games, but they think he's in the Atlantic. Whether he intended it or not, the snakes know there's something up, so it looks like the purples will either have to fight, or abandon him.'

Two Tail said, 'We will wait with you, in case there is news — in case Cory tries to reach you. But there is no point arguing. There will be death because of Cory, many deaths, perhaps.'

Molly wanted to be able to talk it through with Gene, but there was no time.

'It's not arguing,' Molly began, 'it's understanding why you deny us even the chance to make our case. We took Cory in — we have been mother and father to him. As Thunder said, love flowed, from one species to another. He looks strange to us, and we're frightened of his powers. We do not understand his dreaming. And yet he is our son, our first child, and we want him to stay. You think we humans are brutes — well, when he talked of his world, millions of people all over our planet listened to him and were moved to love him too. What he said struck so many chords with so many. We have found so many kindnesses.'

'And yet you had to hide him from your authorities. He has been, by your own account, in constant danger: one small child is seen as a threat.'

Is this a debate, a conversation, or a trial? Molly wasn't sure. The cadence of the translated voice did not convey those subtle meanings. She tried to remember the words of great thinkers, ideas in deep books about science and art, and how humans were edging up towards a true civilisation – but no, those words were not hers. She needed to find her own.

'Your people learned long ago not to shed blood. We're not there yet; we're not you. But we are learning: we formed the United Nations to try to bring peace to all. We're building bonds of friendship across the globe – the idea of a world as one is living and growing. Please don't snuff it out.'

Two Tail said, 'You kill for sport. You threaten all life on the planet with your violence and aggression. You are divided into quarrelling nations and regions, religions and languages. Worth is assigned by the colour of skin and which sex organs you have. Primitive displays of dominance, outdated in the era of harpoons and spades, are threatening to destroy your planet. Your people starve when they could be fed. They live behind walls when they should be free.'

'We're *children*,' Molly said, putting all her feeling into it. 'You need to give us a chance.'

'Adult enough to split the atom and leave your own world in ashes. We cannot take your entire species to the place of healing, even if we knew how. We cannot put the power you need to defend yourselves in your hands. Suppose all-decided to save a few, an Ark, in your terms. We might bring thousands of our people, at great risk to us, to defend you – and then watch you destroy yourselves anyway.'

'I know you have seen the world in all its beauty and variety, from coloured frogs in the rainforests to white hares on the snow, whales in the sea—'

'And you kill the whales and burn the forests. You have no control over your numbers. You fill the land, the sea and the sky with your garbage.'

Gene rose, took a book from the shelf and flicked through it. 'Just let us put our case,' he said, 'otherwise you're condemning us unheard. Tell me, is that allowed on your planet?'

'It is not comparable,' said Skimming Stone, and at last Molly read their deep discomfort. 'Would that things were otherwise.'

Gene went for it. 'Our system is primitive, but still, no one can be convicted without putting their case – and we make sure they have professional help. This is a straight question: will you condemn a world to death on a lower standard than we try a murder?'

Two Tail trilled something that was not translated, then said, 'What chance to plead did Hiroshima get? Who speaks for the burning children? We have seen the images of Belsen. Please be silent.'

Maybe Gene and Molly were getting through – or perhaps they were only revealing what a barrier there still was.

Skimming Stone made an enigmatic gesture. 'We need to reflect. If our ships are not victorious, the point is academic. If we are defeated, no further expedition will come.'

Both sat very still and silent; even their tentacles were still, which looked unnatural when Cory was so mobile. If they exchanged words, it was by suit communicators, out of human hearing. From time to time, one would shudder.

'Is there anything to see?' Gene asked. 'Let's go on the roof and watch. We'd like to see it coming.'

'The odds are less than half,' Skimming Stone said. 'Yes, you may face it, as we will.'

Molly wondered if she should give the purples a message to use, ordering Cory to join his people and flee. Maybe he would listen to her. But that was beyond her power, to save her wonderful son, but to lose the Earth and all its people.

It was a clear night. Up above Amber Grove, the summer stars were blazing, and against that were swift streaks of white fire, first one, then another, all coming from the north.

CHAPTER 43

That endless night

The Battle of Earth was fought against the backdrop of the starry skies, which so reminded the crew of the skies they saw above their own world. They wondered under what sort of sky the snakes had been designed, and what creatures had conceived them.

Fossil Beak was commander, the chosen-of-the-day. In *Kites at Dusk*, the display showing the inner solar system spread out like a giant three-dimensional game of *Tiles*. Four of the eight-team were with her, two were on *Repurpose Snakes as Dung Buckets*, one was on the Earth and one on a spy vessel very far from them.

A challenging board for such a deadly contest, she thought.

Three harpoons, the largest snake ships, were approaching at a cautious pace. Knowing the purples were adept at confusion and concealment, the killing machines expected a trap. The commander wondered what exactly had alerted them – surely Cory's fleeing little Ship had not been so insane as to alert them on purpose?

The snakes often made feints before bringing up larger forces, and the leadership team knew there were five swarms and four smaller blade ships orbiting Earth, deployed to ensure no human satellite or missile reached space. It was not, of itself, an invasion force, but it was certainly a source of flanking attacks.

The leadership exchanged questions, weighed risks and options while the ship-minds endlessly calculated possible strategies and displayed them.

Fossil Beak saw a hard, bitter choice. The least risk to the largest number: abandon the crew and the child on the planet and flee, with the stronger starship to the rear. But Little Frog was precious. Every child is precious, but he was also the key to understanding the strange paradoxical humans. She thought, *Each breath of delay raises the risk – and what if the rebel Ship and Little Frog do not follow? All-condemn the boy for his thoughtless action. We must balance lives like the ingredients of soup.*

Some would have them resist any attack on Earth, for many or all of the crew might be killed.

Or, do not leave until the brave, foolish Little Blue Frog is safe. Fight as the people had learned to fight.

Sometimes the machines could find options that were not obvious, but they had no clever ideas this time.

Fossil Beak loathed the snakes more than death. The vast snake ships looked less like ceremonial harpoons, more like the long bud of flowers made of clean metal. Thousands of the individual snakes, their other units, had their niches to lodge in on the surface – a deadly flock that could overwhelm an unarmed purple vessel. The snakes could descend in force to the surface of a planet. A battle could be won in space and lost on the ground. That was the lesson of New Harbour, and it had resulted in the terrifying evacuation.

She re-sent the warning to those on Earth that the search could not continue for ever.

The leadership debated the options, fast and clipped, a style of discussion unlike their usual ebb and flow. The people normally liked to take their time, to sleep on decisions, to dance or feast or play games while they brought everyone together.

But you could not fight the snakes like that: that was the discipline of the Hardening, and everyone mourned it.

But the snakes had learned caution too.

Consensus moves. Three of the people's stealth units were close to the blade ships around Earth. A fourth snake vessel approached the polar apex. The people's mind-only vessels were preparing armaments, the crew doing the Hardening exercises as they readied themselves for any action.

Decision: bewilder and harass the snakes while they pondered.

The three blade ships flickered, and were clouds of fire and scrap metal. A machine gave the energy signal of an entire habitat, drawing snake clouds away from Earth.

Fossil Beak told the leadership, 'Four billion humans, my lodge-mates. We must do something. We must give the planet team more time.'

Leadership was a burden.

She messaged across all the whole mission, 'We will engage soon. Stand firm. Remember our slain. *For life!*' A human general would have incited revenge, but the people rejected that concept. The people destroyed for hope, not punishment.

The harpoons were crawling towards Earth now, their actions suggesting the people's ships had not been detected. The element of surprise exists only once. Little Frog, a single child, lost the mission the chance to slip away. Yet many of the crew were troubled by the plan to flee, for they had heard the songs of Earth.

In the Atlantic, the Ship Reborn, with the Pilot's orders to save her son at all costs still burning in its brain, endlessly recalculated when to return Cory to his people. Indeed, once the builders did have Cory, the Ship would encourage them to flee.

'Does the message make sense?' Cory asked. The little builder was struggling with his strange organic powers, and the dog's distress was not helping. The edit was ragged and it was an emotional plea, so the Ship had no real means to evaluate it.

'There comes a time when it is better to send it than wait,' the Ship said.

'Will they watch it during the battle? Will they listen to me?'

'Some will: it touches on something that troubles many of the builders, I think. The other machines have been discussing it.'

'What can they do, Ship? Can they win?'

'Let me send it. Try the protein sample on the mutt. I will send the message via a probe, so our location will not be immediately known. Then I will tell you a story, as parents do. The people have found many strange new things . . .'

★

The closest harpoon ship rallied the swarms surrounding Earth.

The chosen-for-today played at *Ink-mouth*. By nature, the people would hide from threats and now, like a pair of grizzled ink-mouths lurking in a shallow sea, the people's ships spread confusion. Probes scattered cunning fléchettes emitting energies unknown to Earth that created phantasms to confuse the snakes. Unlike sea-ink, this ink could swarm and follow.

The snakes responded with rage in the form of a powerful barrage of electromagnetic pulses, a roar that disrupted everything on Earth from radio telescopes to televisions. The people had learned this tactic, paying a price in purple blood, and they were cloaked. The leadership responded with *phantoms*, an energy simulacrum of a third ship of the living, then a fourth. The tactic would not work for long, but it did not need to.

The chosen-of-the-day led off *Dance of the Palm*: an elegant and skilful game. To place a full palm of any hand or foot on the other scores a point; achieving a forehead palm scores four. The people pierced the fields around the harpoon ship, landed a single device — and for a moment, there was a corner of the universe where mass could only be energy. One end of the vessel became a bellow of incoherent force, a scream of burning light, ripping it lengthways in two. Fleeing snakes spilled from it like poison spores from a tree-fungus, but most attacked each other, or exploded their power source, while others writhed aimlessly, incoherently.

Four points.

Smaller devices finished the work, leaving snakes and the smaller purple vessels fighting in the expanding cloud of metal shards.

More cunning machines designed by the builders entered the heart of a snake swarm and destroyed it, but the danger was rising, for now the snakes were seeing through the illusion and beginning to converge on the true ships.

A new snake harpoon approached at great speed from the zenith: it must have been hiding there inert. There might be more to follow. Fossil Beak stilled her mind, not letting the thought of the thousand lives in space or the billions below overwhelm her.

The command structure was still digesting the options thrown up by the machine minds, but she thought she saw the way.

The team conferred briefly. Again, a veteran of previous battles suggested flight; again, rebutted, they deferred.

There are many variants in the game of *Tiles*, but in most, there are only three white tiles that can ever be in play. The great danger was in so draining the ships of energy that they would be unable to defend themselves as they fled.

Little Frog had forced their hand a little, although none of the people had been happy to run, for they had seen the animals who walked in Earth's forests and heard the language of the birds. They had seen Fleur at Molly's breast. The angry, bitter reports from the first Earth mission had been true, as far as they went, but there had been a great falsehood too, for so-so much had been omitted.

Her last message to the ground team had not produced a reply, but she re-sent it.

'Thunder over Mountains here. No, we are closing in on Little Frog.'

'The odds are worsening.'

'Leave if you must. We will rescue him and hide on some frozen moon if we have to. I have not crossed the ocean of stars to abandon him.'

Repurpose Snakes was too close to the snake warship at the zenith. It turned the smaller blade ship to scrap, then darted away, aiming to engage the harpoon.

She prepared the order to flee, but the wounded sistership was still preparing to engage.

The chosen-of-the-day must throw what she could their way — another distraction, a feint — and then act . . .

Under the Atlantic, Cory hovered between waking and dreaming, Meteor curled into him. The lights in the chamber were dimmed. He realised the Ship was moving again.

'Little Frog,' the Ship said, as gentle as a lodge mother, 'the builders have reached us and I cannot hold out. I have one last disobedience . . . then the builders will be in control.'

Then a familiar voice said, 'Little Blue Frog. Cory. This one is coming. This one will never leave you.' It was Thunder Over Mountains.

Exhausted, drained, Cory told himself he had tried. 'The snakes . . .' he said.

'Don't worry. We are getting closer. Your Ship is moving towards us.'

Cory was so tired now. He could not save the world. He needed his family, both his families . . .

There was a shudder as the Ship docked with a second vehicle. Cory wanted to smell his birth-father and hold his human family close.

The purples sat in the attic, studying their devices, while Gene and Molly looked out at the clear sky, trying to read the flashes and streaks of light.

Something blazed up above – a new star? Then came a second. They were under the old blanket and Molly must have been dozing, for now she jerked awake. More meteors were appearing in the sky.

Suddenly Skimming Stone announced, 'They have found the boy under the ocean. He is unwell, but he is being cared for. Thunder Over Mountains was particularly keen for you to know as soon as they found him. And that he will not be punished.'

Molly snapped, 'You don't understand us at all, do you?'

Skimming Stone said, hesitantly, 'I think it was meant as a joke. Cory said you never punished him. Apparently, the dog is also alive. It will be brought to you.'

'Will he be okay? Are you going to tell us what's happening?'

'Cory has sent a message to the crew: an argument for saving the Earth. It is very raw and moving. And it is impractical, of course.'

This purple was feeling some regret, she could feel it. Skimming Stone might just be an ally, thought Molly.

'I'd like to hear it,' Gene said.

'Maybe. Of course, nearly all of us are engaged in risking our lives in trying to hold off the snakes while we save a child of our world.'

'A child of our world too,' Gene said.

'We may not win.'

'Tell your leaders we are glad you tried.'

Two Tail said, 'We have family, friends, lovers up above. You are not the only ones in fear.'

'We're here with you,' Gene said. 'I'll play you something, if you like.'

The aliens were having a private conversation, looking at each other through their masks. Indeed, from the agitation of their tentacles, Molly rather thought it was an argument.

'Are you taking Cory into space? Into the heart of the battle?' she asked, thinking this might be the end of the world – it might be the end of everything. She looked at Gene – she must look as haggard as he did – and thought, *When the last moment comes, let us remember love.*

'If the purples win, maybe we need to go to their world, Molly-Moo. Maybe they'll only listen to us.'

That was the only argument she feared. 'I can't risk Fleur and Elsa too,' she tried to explain. 'There are far better people, diplomats and artists and philosophers – we've met some of them.'

'They don't have a son on the starship.' He sighed. 'Castles in the air for now.'

He kissed her.

If they offered that, just the five of them, what would she answer? If it was a gamble to save the Earth?

She did not want that choice.

Beneath the White House, as the dedicated Moscow telex chattered away, scientists explained to the President what the flashes of light in space might be, but not why. 'Mr President, we think these are explosions – it's possible the snakes in our orbit are being attacked.'

'Could it be the purples?' he asked, then snapped. 'Get the Myers!'

'Their phone is down, sir, and they're not answering their radio.'

He rolled his eyes. 'Then send a helicopter, or the 56th Airborne. What the fuck are the National Guard doing?'

'They say they can't find the Fence at all.'

An officer entered, waving a sheet of telex printout. 'It's the Ship. The purples are fighting the snakes up there – it's life or death. And . . .' he gulped, 'it's broadcasting on open frequencies, in all the ten languages it speaks – it's telling the world purples are dying up there to defend the Earth.'

In the stifling moist heat of a Shanghai summer, a road of flame crossed the sky as a great snake ship fell to earth in bright fragments. TV crews in the heights above Hong Kong filmed snakes burning with white fire. In jungles and paddy fields, Viet Cong and Americans alike stopped, looked up and shielded their eyes as the machine ship died. Tribesmen and loggers in the jungles of the Philippines would find mysterious parts for months, ripped and twisted metal, and sometimes writhing like something alive – something with a broken back. A Dutch aeroplane making an emergency landing at sea tried through electronic chaos to raise assistance.

Churches were full and bars ran dry. Roads out of cities were jammed solid, and in the public squares people congregated and stood gazing up, scared and silent . . . waiting.

In Amber Grove, their gaolers had disappeared – Molly had no idea whether the purples had gone for a nap, or a walk, or just to watch them unseen. She caught up on her sewing, something to keep her mind busy, while Gene, who always claimed a chair was too uncomfortable to sleep in, was giving a good impression of a snoozing man snoring.

Then Molly's communicator was drumming, bursting with hoots and whoops and a fierce song she recognised: the victory-in-hunting song that Cory had performed for them.

Gene grunted, sat up, swore. 'My back—!' he started, but he shut up when the communicator trilled.

'This is Thunder. Cory is safe with our healers. We have won – a great battle, if not the war. The snakes are in retreat from Earth. One of our ships has significant damage – there are at least eighty of the people dead, and many wounded. The Earth is not safe, but the danger is lessened for now.'

Gene knelt by her so they could both talk into the communicator. 'How's Cory?' he asked.

'He has over-used his power, he is drained to a point of danger. But we have good healers. Oh, how brave he is, how foolhardy, and how committed to see the right thing done. What an argument he has started.' Thunder was clearly proud of their son. 'He is insisting that we should put a case to all-the-people of the home-world, to reconsider.'

'That's wonderful.' Drained and weary, Molly could say no more. She kissed Gene, tasted his tears and felt her own tears come. 'Let's go and see the sunrise. What happened to the purples who were here?'

'They have friends, lovers among the dead,' Thunder said. 'I would still advise not speaking to your authorities – they are bound to want to control you.'

Molly hadn't been sure they would ever see another dawn. She remembered times when she had not wanted to see the morning herself, nights when she had sat with a bottle of pills in her hand. Now she stood on the same porch where she had seen the Meteor on that cold April three years ago which had been the start of it all. With Gene's arm around her waist, they watched the clouds take on colour as the sun rose over the horizon.

This new day felt like a gift, and they needed to cherish it.

CHAPTER 44

Thunder above the Earth

Thunder Over Mountains sat beside the crib, looking at the drained, sleepy child and stroking Little Frog's ears with a gloved hand. It would be a delicate balance to restore his health and contain his erratic power. Aspects of this case were unique, and the experienced healers on the ship were having to feel their way forward carefully. Thunder knew little of such things, but he was learning fast. He resented the precautions the healers were insisting they take – he wanted to smell and touch his son: he ached for the full experience of being with him. Parenthood was a common thing among the people, yet it was always extraordinary. Love held him in an undying note. What he had been before Little Frog's exile was a pale shadow of what he could be.

'All must save the Earth,' the boy moaned.

'Oh, Little Frog, how this one wishes so, but it is a hard decision to make, little one. We must hope all-will-decide to leave *Kites at Dusk* to defend the Earth, while *Repurpose Snakes* is sent running for home.'

Such a move would be risky for both ships. *Repurpose Snakes* was the weaker; it would have little chance if it was attacked on the return journey. And *Kites at Dusk* might not be strong enough to stand alone against whatever the snakes threw at it. But dividing their forces like this might be the only way to give humans a better chance of survival, at least while all-the-people decided what to do.

His son coughed and groaned, then opened his eyes. 'We must-must-must leave one starship.'

Thunder fondled an ear. 'But many will say, so much safer if both ships go home together.'

This would be a gamble with billions of lives. All-the-people might decide not to return – or the people might come back after a year away to find the war lost and the Earth barren. Purple and machine minds had been working through cautious strategies to destroy the snakes' base on Mars, but as yet, it was still there.

'I will change their minds. I have so-so many good arguments.'

'Rest, Little Frog, rest. The people will hear your arguments. You have done enough for now, and I will argue the case myself. We have some on our side, some against. Many are to be persuaded. Unity takes time.'

Little Frog should be asleep, but he was too agitated. 'Too much talking, not enough doing. Save my Earth-family – save all the humans. There are healers for me, so we can stay.'

Everyone assumed that Little Glowing Blue Frog must go home to be debriefed, to speak as no one else could of the good in humanity. The home-world wanted him back – it wanted all of them back. People had died for the Earth, and those who lived wanted Little Frog safe – but the journey home would not be safe. There were no guarantees.

Thunder's mind was clear: his extraordinary son was proof that humanity was worth saving. But whether it *could* be saved, no one could know.

Thunder sang so he did not need to speak. The Pioneer song 'The Stars Are New Islands' was naïve, and now sung in bittersweet knowledge.

Would the-all defend the Earth? The adults had been keeping from Little Frog just how difficult that might be. Dreaming-between-the-stars was too weak to allow proper dreaming-to-decide. The speakers-for-the-home-world were furious that the mission had made the decision to contact humans. The hidden reports on Earth's violent and destructive culture had been made public – there was no other option – and now all-the-people were horrified.

As for delaying the mission to fight the snakes, the speakers-for-the-home-world grieved the dead and censured the living. Humanity was unpredictable and dangerous. The leaders were saying Little Frog should have been taken on the first day of contact, willing or not, and both ships should already be headed home. A species who fought each other, who ate other sentient creatures, who looked determined to turn their whole world into fire and garbage could not be worth saving.

Thunder must speak too, for the biosphere, for the majestic trees and the tiny frogs. For dolphins and crows and daisies.

'Why are starships so slow?' Little Frog said suddenly. 'We must get home quick-quick-quick. Cory will invent a much

417

faster spaceship. Also, dreaming-between-the-stars must be much better. Cory will fix that too.'

'Maybe you will, little one. But the grown-ups find these very big problems, so you'll need to start solving just one of them first.'

'Time to let go and sleep,' a healer said, appearing on the other side of the crib.

Thunder thanked them and left them to their work.

Outside the healing centre, preparations to remember the dead had started. But the living needed decisions – groups had the discussions. Humanity already knew too much. Should they treat the humans as adults and make contact? The crew were divided.

The people had made mistakes; of course they had, and some stories were not told to the children. Generations ago, a green world had been found where the most sentient species were declining as the planet moved into a colder era. One mission had gone against the-all. Remaining hidden, they tried to save some of the indigenous population from starvation. They thought they had been discreet – but things had started changing. The local species found their dreams: they began to dream of the people as higher beings, and those who dreamed with most clarity grew into leaders, though there had been no such distinctions before. When that herd met another to exchange males, the changes started spreading like an infection, and within three generations, the indigenous species had become very different: they were more inquisitive, more courageous, more complex, and fiercer against those who were different.

The-all had been horrified. It was true that the changes had likely better fitted the species to survive – but those changes had been unintended, they were permanent and the final outcome was still far from clear. And worse, this naïve kindness had elevated the people to something they were not, something for which the humans had a concept – *gods* – which repelled them.

The people had sworn never to make that mistake again. Earth had been such an obvious case for not intervening – and yet Pilot had landed Little Glowing Blue Frog on a closed world and now the whole of humankind knew they were not alone: a reality that humans both feared and longed for. One cannot unbreak an egg, but that is no reason to break another one. The arguments were endless.

Thunder patched himself into a discussion preparation group.

'—but we could alter the weapons so the humans cannot use them against other humans—'

Disagreement.

Thunder feared he would be speaking often in this discussion.

Another spoke with impolite emphasis. 'Humans will want to know how our weapons work. They will throw all their resources into understanding them. In less than a generation they turned nuclear theory into a controlled chain-reaction and then a full explosion – something called the Manhattan Project – driven solely by a desire to use it as a weapon. Who knows what humans will learn from our technology, or to what ends they might turn it?'

'This one agrees. Even the fragments of our machines and what Little Frog knows will have prompted new discussions.'

'This issue, to arm humans, is not the question originally posed,' said the moderator. 'Do we wish to take it wider?'

419

Thunder was with the-many who showed their disapproval, setting *later, later* lights flashing. The group quickly moved back to the questions posed: should one starship be left to defend the Earth? Should the snake base on Mars be attacked, at yet more risk to the people? Should a delegation of humans be taken to the home-world to argue their own case? Should the elimination of the Ship Reborn be delayed or reconsidered?

Skimming Stone had the speaking right. 'Time is wasted in debating the Ship Reborn. It might be dangerous, it might not. But if it contaminates other machine minds, it would be exceptionally dangerous: imagine a self-ordering, disobedient starship. In the end, the-all cannot take the risk, no matter how long we talk – so let us follow the rule, destroy it and concentrate on what matters.'

The message had been drummed into every child: *a machine is to serve; a machine which disobeys defies its purpose.*

Long before the snakes, the people had a rule: *examine the disobedient machine mind, learn from the error, then destroy it.*

'Destroy the mind.'

'This one agrees.'

Thunder waited for other comments, knowing that for Little Frog, the Ship had become a person. This happened with children, even a few adults, but machine sentience could not be mind-felt the way real, organic creatures could be felt. A Ship no more felt alive than a stone did – but a Ship was not a stone. Maybe the servant machines had now changed; maybe new criteria were needed.

Was it wrong to feel gratitude to the machine mind?

'This is not a question that can be ignored for ever,' said the moderator.

'The Ship is not a danger at this heartbeat. It is secondary,' Thunder said firmly. 'As it is said, build the foundation before decorating the doorframe.'

Much approval, much flashing *later, later.*

The moderator said, 'Return to a question asked. Should we take a human delegation to the home-world?'

Anger and fear spread through the group.

'This one believes that we must not — we cannot — allow humans so full of violence and deceit on the home-world.'

Agree agree agree.

Thunder had not been optimistic, but it was worse than he had thought.

The Earth was already buzzing with stories that the people had come. Many were exaggerating their numbers and powers – should humans be told what might be an unpalatable truth, that the purples would leave them to their fate? And many humans thought the people had attacked them.

After all, what did the people really owe to the humans?

CHAPTER 45

After the battle

Molly held the signed cover sleeve as she played 'Our Child of the Stars'. It was extraordinary what Ella Fitzgerald could do with her husband's song, bringing out his bewilderment, the sadness, the sense of a waiting loss, as well as the heights of wonder and joy and need for the child who had landed so unexpectedly in their life. Of all the versions, she liked this one best.

Speculation was at fever-pitch: the aliens would land, the aliens would annex Hawaii, the aliens would hold a press conference – it was the Second Coming, it was the Age of Aquarius, it was a new beginning; it was the end of everything, the end of Capitalism, the end of Communism, the end of marriage and the family . . .

It was all a big loud mess.

The purples had saved the Earth and they would take her son and it was the right thing to do. She needed to grieve, but there was hope still.

Elsa had started picking fights from the second she opened her eyes, so Molly had handed her over to the Robertsons, where she would be indulged. Molly sat admiring Fleur sitting in her high chair and waving her hands, leaving the laundry sulking undone in the utility room. Carol and Storm had promised to come today, looking for insight into the purples. They were back on the alien beat; they had barely stopped working since Carol had got Storm out of jail.

Gene came over, looking exhausted.

'Bad news?'

Maybe there had been another attack – they'd guessed those snakes that had gone up to join the battle in space been destroyed, but Thunder had not said anything about the base on Mars, so that must still be active, busy building more snakes. Silence implied the purples had yet to act against them, so maybe they had decided not to. Snakes did not need air or water, so they might still be lurking in a thousand places even on Earth.

'Thunder called me,' Gene said quietly. 'It's not looking good for my flight to the stars.'

She touched his hand. 'What are they saying?'

'He said there's a riot at the mere idea of letting humans on board – for any reason. Everyone's now read the full report on humanity – it was such hot stuff, they kept it secret, apparently. Basically, they're calling us the Planet of Psycho Killers. Catchy, right? So a load of the purples, even in Thunder's mob, are saying, "Okay, drop it. We don't need humans to put their case."'

'Oh . . .' Molly had always thought *some* humans should go – the *right* people. Just not her Gene.

'Thunder thinks it's stupid, and he's not giving up.' But Gene

424

sounded drained, defeated. 'If they do agree to take some of us, they're talking about sealing off part of the starship for us — like convicts, or zoo animals. But he warned me, we might not even be asked.'

Gene lowered himself into the creaky chair he'd promised to mend and Molly moved next to him.

Gene closed his eyes. 'So no getting my parents medical help. No jaunt to space.'

'I know . . . I know what that meant to you.' Molly could see what it felt like to Gene, losing a long-held dream.

Gene wiped away a tear. 'Well, I couldn't go and leave my folks, could I? See them after eight months and say I'm off . . . how could I leave Eva to manage John like he is now? We might be able to see them next week . . . And I sure couldn't picture myself kissing you goodbye either. I think I'd spend every day scared.'

Gene had chosen her when the option of going to the stars was open: he had chosen her with all his heart. She felt so much love for him, and she felt huge sorrow too. There was no sense of a victory.

She kissed him. 'They may still decide in our favour,' she said.

'I guess going only matters to me,' he said quietly.

'*You* matter,' she said. 'You matter to *me*. We'll go to the West Coast, I promise, as soon as we can. Or Honolulu. It will be fun.' It was easily offered, but it was from the heart.

'We must send the purples our own message,' he said. 'They must at least give us that right.' He fell silent.

Molly wondered about the days ahead. *We'll just have to live one day at a time.*

★

The phone tucked to her ear, Molly jogged Fleur on her knee. This was the President's third call in person since the battle had ended. If it wasn't him or his people, it was the Secretary-General of the United Nations, or one of the other international organisations.

There was a lot of background noise this time.

'Mrs Myers, the press is going insane. The Ship says the purples won – now I have the leaders of Congress demanding to know what's going on – not to mention every candidate for the other side demanding to be briefed.'

The Democrats were poised to choose a radical, a man of peace. The old guard might switch to supporting the President.

'I'm truly sorry, Mr President. I really don't have any idea what they'll decide.'

'I'm in a car, forty-five minutes from Amber Grove. The Marines can land a helicopter at the top of Crooked Street, if you could ask Mr Henderson to move his trucks.'

The trucks were parked there against just that possibility.

'I'm afraid the Fence won't let you in.' Molly did her best to sound apologetic.

'It will if you tell it to, Mrs Myers. Or choose somewhere else. You can decide not to meet me – my pride can take that. I just worry those people saying we should fight the aliens might start thinking the snakes and the purples are one and the same. Please, Mrs Myers, help me to explain things – get them riled up at the *right* aliens.'

He didn't need to remind her, *I pardoned your friend Joel. I didn't ask for anything*.

Molly couldn't decide what would be worse, seeing him or not. Maybe, face to face, he was more likely to believe her.

'The house is a mess,' she started.

He waved away the objection. 'No one will see it but me and one Secret Service guy.'

'I'll have no guns in the house,' she said, on autopilot, giving way.

How much can I do in an hour? She ran around the big room like a whirlwind, vacuuming, dusting and cleaning until everywhere smelled of polish.

'Which outfit, funerals or wedding guest?' she asked Gene.

'Funerals, for our principles: meeting the man when we don't have to.' He wrinkled his nose. 'I don't mind, but you smell of Pledge.'

Gene looked very fine, she thought, pinning his nuclear disarmament badge onto his lapel. He even managed a smile.

Molly grabbed her perfume and gave herself another blast, then put on the new outfit for best, glad women didn't have to wear skirts nowadays. Suppose fusty old Amber County General realised it was the Nineteen Seventies and let all its nurses wear long pants – that would be such a blessing when lifting patients. Maybe if the world was saved, she could be a nurse again.

'Suppose it's a trick?'

'I spoke to Thunder. There are a dozen drones watching us, and they can hide us through the communicators.'

And there he was, on their doorstep, the leader of the free world – anxious, jowly and blue-chinned. A quite improbably handsome Secret Service man who looked seven feet tall stood beside him.

'Bill here will stay at the door,' the President said, offering a hand. He looked like he had three ulcers now, not two. He complimented them on the room, then said to Gene, 'My kids love your songs.' Then he turned to Molly. 'And Bill can't ask himself, but his kids would really love a signed photo of Cory if you have it.'

'Of course – but let's fill you in,' Molly said, pouring the coffee, pleased she'd remembered how the President took it.

They didn't have much to add to what they'd said before, and at the end, the President scratched his head. 'So they have their entire crew sitting around debating this?'

'Not all at once, we're told. They do it in groups, but they all get a say.'

He looked aghast. 'How does their civilisation ever get anything done? I was in the Navy – can you imagine fighting the Battle of Midway by committee?'

What could she say? Somehow, they made it work.

He tried another tack. 'Look, there's a timing to these things. They clearly gave those snakes a whupping and the whole planet owes them for that. They should land so I can thank them for it – so the whole world can. The UN Secretary-General is waiting – they'll need to talk to him, at least, for show, if nothing else, to keep the other nations happy.' He coughed. 'What concerns me is that the people who hate them – who believe they are the same as the snakes – aren't shutting up and right now, we're leaving them the stage and the microphone.'

Gene was looking worried.

The President went on, 'A planet divided cannot stand. A

little wait is fine – it builds the excitement – but the purples do need to claim the credit, and soon. You see, we need to put the "anti" brigade on the back foot so we can do this deal on the Space Treaty. I have the Secretary of State flying to China – thank the Lord, they want in. I understand the aliens will take a bit of persuading to sell us some weapons – but truly, just telling us what is going on would help.'

How do we explain?

Molly said, 'They don't want to interfere in our politics – in anything else, in fact. They know we're grateful.'

Gene stepped in. 'Look, if we dropped an aircraft carrier on another planet, the captain wouldn't feel empowered to make any big diplomatic decisions, would he?'

'But he'd at least come to dinner, wear a flower necklace and watch some local dances or something, tell the aliens we didn't mean them any harm.'

If both starships went home, the Earth would have no protection at all – for a year, or for ever, if the purples never returned. Maybe that would be okay, and maybe not. Even if they left *Repurpose Snakes* or *Kites at Dusk*, that was no guarantee of anything.

People said many things about the man, but he wasn't stupid.

'Could they just take the boy and go?' he asked, and it was Gene he looked at.

Gene's silence told him.

That afternoon, Diane was mysterious on the phone – then Janice dropped by 'just to see if there were plans for this evening', and Molly knew something was up. Selena called from

429

the Jarman place and announced that she was coming over too, with her boys.

'What's going on?' Molly asked. Selena was supposed to be staying quiet and settling in.

'Nothing,' Selena said.

'I'm not a fool,' Molly started, but Selena changed the subject.

Should she wear a dress or prepare a speech, or what? Molly didn't feel like company, and nor did Gene. At least if their friends were coming over, they'd do most of the talking.

Selena was late, trailing Connor and Rory behind her. Both looked awkward in their Cory sweatshirts. Selena was hugging a big brown envelope like it was a baby. Mason was still wanted by the police, but she got her restraining order too. They ate in the back yard while birds called and wind whispered in the summer foliage.

The purples had bought the Earth time, whatever else happened. Every day from now on was precious.

By sunset, Molly was growing tired, but Diane took her arm. 'Let's go out front,' she said.

'Oh, a surprise,' said Gene, clowning.

'Well, there are plenty of people grateful, and they wanted to do something.'

Diane led them from the porch and up the road to where they could look down over Amber Grove.

The twilight sky was filled with lights – flashlights and candles, in the windows of all their neighbours, lanterns on poles and porches, unfamiliar lights on the roof of City Hall and the library.

Every unexpected light was a thank you – to the Myers, to the purples, to those burying the dead and healing the living.

'Wow,' Gene said, then he added, 'They should have done it on Founders Green.'

'We wouldn't have been able to see it,' Molly said aloud, her eyes filling with tears. This galaxy of lights was for them, the Crooked Street gang who had kept Cory safe all these years: for Molly and Gene and their friends, who might just have saved the Earth. And maybe for the purples too, up there arguing.

Cory might have died, or he might have fallen into evil hands. It was all on the spin of a coin . . .

Molly hugged Selena a little too long. Her sister had gone chestnut, and it suited her. She was better than she had been, although perhaps not yet back to her best.

'Well, I'm supposed to *rest,* but that place is like the grave,' Sel said with a laugh, pulling Molly down beside her. 'And if you get a few people together to play cards, some of them *cheat* – hey, what on earth's happening? Dr Jarman says every journalist in the whole world is in town.'

'We've said we'll make an announcement when we have something to say.'

But now she'd started, Sel was full of questions. 'Where will the aliens land? How will they protect the Earth? Who gets to meet them?'

'We'll tell the world when we know.'

'And Cory?'

'He needs to go home, for his health.' That, and to plead Earth's case. If she pinched the bridge of her nose and sniffed the tears back, she wouldn't cry.

431

Selena nodded, a little vaguely. 'I couldn't bear being apart from mine, even for a week. How will you cope?' She fumbled a cigarette out of her purse, caught Molly's expression and fiddled with it.

Molly went on, 'We'll manage – we'll get messages, we hope. It's the right thing for him, and for the Earth. It might be only a year, or eighteen months.'

It was a bitter kind of grief, but there was hope too. That made it no less painful, but they would learn to bear it.

Selena handed Molly the cigarette, then the packet.

'You know, I'm glad I'm here. If the world ends, I couldn't think of anyone else I wanted to meet my Maker with. My little sis, saviour of the world.'

Molly squeezed her hand. 'I thought the Church wouldn't have me?'

Whatever the aliens decided about the Earth, they still might just slip away. She didn't even know if she would see Cory again.

CHAPTER 46

The United Nations

Things had started moving. Two purples had brought a viewing screen in the night and assembled it while Molly and Gene stood bleary-eyed, watching them.

'It's so you can see Little Frog,' they said. 'And other things.' Molly, in her summer robe, found herself in tears again. They would be apart for at least a year, if they even let him come home.

Just after breakfast, Cory appeared on the screen. He looked deflated and tired, his ears down, his tentacles limp, his inner eyelids a little visible. But when he saw them, he sat up and said, 'Don't worry Mom, Dad. Cory will be fine. So many grown-ups missing their own kids – all get in line to play with Cory!'

It hadn't truly struck Molly and Gene that there were no other children on the starships; how tough the journey home would be, but this was their son, making the best of it. They made small talk, each word fizzing with meaning – how his

433

friends were wanting to write letters for him to take to the home-world. How his new cousins Rory and Connor had already written him long letters, saying they were sorry, how Connor had fought a boy at school who'd said Cory was a monster and made him admit that Cory had saved the world.

'Letters – and why not film as well?' Cory said.

'Will they let us hug you goodbye?'

Cory wailed, 'I don't know. They say too sick, too delicate.'

Molly felt punished.

Gene said, 'Well, the screen is fine, if we can't meet' – he was such a poor liar.

Molly pretended too, for they could see he was tiring. Skimming Stone, sitting beside him, explained about the long process of healing, and how Gene and Molly must take care of themselves too. She went on and on – turned out, the purples had well-meaning busybodies too.

'Leaders-for-now have so many questions,' Cory said, out of nowhere. 'Thunder will be in the group.'

Molly was confused. 'What's this?'

'Speech to United Nations soon. President radioed starship – lots of leaders did.'

'What are they going to say?'

'All-have-decided, humans must believe there is a threat. But all-can't-decide what we should do about threat. So much a tricky problem.'

Soon afterwards, the leadership-for-the-day appeared on the screen, clearly uneasy, not knowing what they could say to the world. They grilled Gene and Molly for an hour, until Gene said firmly that they needed a break.

Thunder spoke to them privately through their communicators. 'Some want to wash our hands of Earth as a problem. But this denial of reality worries the-all of us. Whatever Earth chooses, let it do so from knowledge.'

It was the day they had dreamed of: eight aliens would address the United Nations General Assembly in person. Molly remembered the tour of the UN Building in New York, when she had wondered if this day would ever come.

At the Myers place, the family and their closest friends were elbow to elbow in front of the alien viewscreen, which was showing two images. The podium from where the aliens would speak was what the General Assembly would see. The second image was a roving shot of those arriving, delegates from 113 member states and selected observers.

The radio was on, the newscasters breathless at estimates of the crowds near the building. The rumour was that they would then go to Central Park, which was full of people hoping for a sighting. Troops and police kept the area immediately around the building clear. There were clashes between demonstrators, and endless descriptions of this celebrity or that arriving, as if they had anything particular to add or contribute.

There was no fanfare, but the aliens were there: eight of them in spacesuits, approaching the podium beneath a vast alien viewing disc. Each introduced themselves in a few chords of alien, then in English. The speech would also be provided worldwide in the nine other languages the aliens had learned during their twenty-year surveillance.

Then one of the shorter ones, Fossil Beak, the commander

on the day of the space battle, said, 'We come in peace. We understand this is the traditional opening.'

After a long pause, there was a ripple of laughter.

Good, thought Molly, *because it was meant to be funny*.

'How grateful we are to the people of this beautiful planet, who have taken one of our children to their heart. He was sick, wounded and bereaved and you kept him safe these long and perilous months. You have proved love can transcend species.'

There was a minute-long film of Cory in the spaceship. He was on his best behaviour. Molly thought he looked tired.

More people were watching this than had seen the Moon landing, according to the newscasters, and because the human satellites had all been destroyed, the aliens had promised to rebroadcast it so everyone in the world would have a chance to see and hear their message.

In the Assembly Hall, ten boys and ten girls, wearing Sunday best or national costumes, picked by lot from the Ambassadors' diplomatic families to represent all the different colours and creeds of the world, presented flowers. The aliens thanked them, remembered their names.

'Let us show you a little of our planet,' said the chosen-for-the-day. 'These images help us when we are far from the home-world, separated from those we love.'

The film showed purple children playing a laughing chase in the woods; sailing ships scudding under a fierce wind; a night feast on a beach under brilliant stars, purples standing elbow to elbow, singing and swaying beneath the stars.

'We have no need of war, as you understand it. And for thirty generations, the whole of our world has been free of hunger. The Time of Plenty saw us reach out into the stars . . . then terror came.'

Then came a picture of a vast structure in space: six cylinders spinning in a complex frame. The structure was under attack from the snakes, a riot of blue and white fire. As they watched, the snakes began boring into the hull.

'We share your loss,' the speaker said sadly. 'This was the destruction of a space habitation, the death of many thousands by the killers-of-life, the snake machines that would make your planet and ours dead and sterile.'

The camera scanned the faces of the delegates, all looking shocked and frightened. Molly wondered if the aliens had projected their fear and grief . . . She realised the children had been led out of the auditorium; maybe that was why.

'We mourn those on your planet who also died: Pevek and Orlando and Colorado Springs, Baikonur and Fukushima.' In English, Russian and Chinese, 'Your grief is our grief,' the chosen-for-the-day said formally.

After a moment for everyone to collect themselves, Thunder, walking with his cane, came to the centre. 'We are a small scientific mission, diverted to rescue my son when we discovered he was still alive. You know him as Cory, I know him as Little Glowing Blue Frog. We have no interest in harming your planet or interfering in your society. Yet your planet was threatened and we fought off the snakes.

'Many of you expect us to do this or that – so many of you have been radioing our vessels, asking for this aid or that – but we have no authority and no expertise to negotiate, or to commit to any actions. One of our ships at least must return to the home-world as soon as it can, to bring vital information of the snakes' increasing power and depredations. What help our people can offer the Earth is not for us to decide.

'We can say this: we will locate snake forces elsewhere in your solar system, and we will leave systems in place so you will be warned if the snakes gather. You will not have to fight them without eyes or ears.'

It was so little, but it was something, although Molly could see the French President and the King of Saudi Arabia were unimpressed.

'Your planet is rich with life, as beautiful and diverse as our own.' The viewing disc behind him was showing the Earth as it looked from space. 'Unless the snakes are defeated, all of this will be ashes and dust. We do not wholly understand you, but we think you can understand us. We had to change to resist the snakes. Falling back to the home-world with millions of dead changed our whole society. We had to work hard at finding ways to survive the horrors we saw, and to unite conflicting views. We have prevailed, so far. Just.

'Snakes remain in your solar system and more snakes may come, from any direction. The Earth could be surrounded.

'We come in peace, but we are at war — a word we had no use for just three years ago — with a predator who cannot be appeased. Like it or not, so are you. We come in peace, but we warn of destruction.

'You here: you are the chosen-of-your-people. What will you decide? What will you do for yourselves, and for all life?'

★

After maybe thirty seconds' silence, the Russian Premier and the UN Secretary-General stood simultaneously and started to applaud. The American Secretary of State was quick to follow suit, and before long, everyone was on their feet and clapping the purples.

Molly found herself overwhelmed by the historical significance of this moment, but it was tempered by the knowledge that her son would be leaving. She looked around at her assembled friends, knowing the future of Earth still hung in the balance.

Humanity would have to do its own heavy lifting.

CHAPTER 47

The secure unit

Dr Emmanuel Pfeiffer's world had shrunk down to a single off-white cell with a hard, narrow bed, a rickety table, a stained basin and a toilet without a seat. He had argued them up to four textbooks and two paperbacks from the library, as well as reports and papers, which a solemn guard removed each night, for some bizarre reason. After all these weeks, they still kept him without tie or belt, checking on him through the peephole every two hours. A guard always supervised him when he cleaned the cell.

The aliens would address the United Nations, and he would watch it with the other inmates on TV. He was irrelevant. That afternoon, Rachael was bringing the divorce papers. He'd failed as a man, a husband, a father.

It's ironic, he thought, *that this secure prison complex is miles away from anything — if the snakes do return in force, I might live longer than those who bested me.* He had been able to stare into the abyss that was the possibility of nuclear war because he believed the Soviet leadership was not wholly irrational – but the snakes could not be reasoned with or threatened, or, as far as he knew, outwitted.

Everything here was a humiliation, not least the guards' constant reminders that sentencing would see him moved to another facility, where his fellow inmates would soon 'sort him out'. They were vile and aggressive, enjoying rubbing his nose in his failure and revelling in the fear their descriptions engendered. One guard had offered protection in return for a sex act, which he instantly – but politely – refused. The guard had smiled when he'd said that the offer would remain open, as if he knew Pfeiffer's courage was failing.

Dr Pfeiffer assumed everywhere was bugged, including the exercise yard. He had grown to like walking round the square, just four concrete walls and the sky, lost in his work, but this was also the only opportunity the inhabitants of the special wing had to talk, provided they were never close enough to touch. His fellow prisoners included two Russian spies, who were exercised at a different time. Not everyone said what they were in for, but some were quite open about their sins. The editor of *Rolling Stone*, who was surprisingly friendly, happily revealed that he'd been incarcerated for refusing to reveal a source. There was a civil servant who'd tried to steal five million dollars from the government, and a diplomat who'd sold secrets to the Chinese, who would play chess with Dr Pfeiffer whenever they were allowed.

'Hey, Doc – your visitor's here,' someone shouted; it was not a name he recognised. The steel door banged open and he was led into the bare room by an impassive guard. Inside stood Mablethorpe, the lanky, opinionated Englishman from the

TV talk show he'd done, *Debate with Dempsey*. The man who'd denied aliens, science, everything.

A vast smirk on his face, he held out his hand. An attaché case was tucked under his other arm.

'What are you doing here?' Pfeiffer didn't bother being polite.

'I thought you might like company.' The man grinned on. 'You were a formidable foe. I was sorry we never clashed again.'

Pfeiffer felt his heart race and his face flush. He was tempted to refuse the visit, but the man opened the case and removed a bottle of bourbon. Next came a Thermos flask, and two glass tumblers wrapped in white cloth. Everything in here was plastic and suddenly he wanted a drink from a glass more than anything. He looked over at the guard, who was staring into space.

'The most expensive drink I have ever offered a man,' Mablethorpe said. He unscrewed the Thermos lid. 'Ice. Let no one say science is entirely useless.'

'If you've come to mock me—'

'Dr Pfeiffer, I have a commission. I want the scoop – your candid thoughts on the alien address. I will need to be funny, but I promise not to be unkind.'

Was the bourbon worth it?

Mablethorpe went on, 'I too soared too close to the flame. My college sacked me, my wife divorced me. I may not be your first choice for company, but I'm here. All these names are being banded around as possibilities to visit the aliens' home-world: all apparently pass for great thinkers in these shrunken times, but frankly, I consider them political hacks of the worst sort. Your name should have been there.'

Dr Pfeiffer snorted — but it was an expensive bourbon and he didn't think the man was trying to be unpleasant.

They sat, and Mablethorpe poured generous measures.

Dr Pfeiffer had a burning need to get drunk, but Rachael was coming today.

'I recanted about the aliens and was saved. *The Times* — the proper one, from London, you understand — ran my piece. I sent you a copy.'

'I got that, but I have been far too busy to read it.'

'I do enjoy a well-written back-down, don't you? They keep my haters guessing. I'll give you another copy if you like.'

'Thank you, but I've got it somewhere.'

'I hear the government has plans for you.'

Uncle Sam always set useful prisoners to work. Clearly someone in the White House still thought he had something to offer medical science; for in return for keeping his wife and associates out of jail, he would be usefully employed.

'Prison,' he said, adding, 'hopefully not here, but that's out of my hands.'

'Oh, it's a *secret*.' The Englishman tipped him an outrageous wink and Dr Pfeiffer found himself smiling despite himself.

Mablethorpe turned out to be good company, this self-mocking cynic who had travelled to the back of beyond to offer the condemned man a drink. He had a magpie mind, and while he might be weak on the sciences, he was hilariously rude about people Pfeiffer also disliked. They found common taste in music, rejecting modern art in all its forms and in lampooning the young and fashionable.

When the time came, the guard led them to the rec room

to watch the aliens address the world. Pfeiffer *felt* the moment, greater than when he saw the first dead alien, greater than when he first saw Cory. He deeply mourned the loss of any chance to talk to them.

At the end, when the aliens danced and some of the delegates dropped their dignity and joined in, the prisoners began to talk and jeer, swamping the commentators on the screen.

As the truth became clear, Dr Pfeiffer was left feeling sick with dismay. The only new information came in the form of those dazzling images of their home-world. And Cory was okay – that mattered. But there was no room for mis-interpretation: the aliens were committing to no military help – *nothing*, other than some surveillance of the skies, a mere scrap of hope.

Mablethorpe had never before looked so thoughtful. There were no jokes now. Pfeiffer made some sombre observations, which Mablethorpe took down without comment.

Then his visitor left him with a clap on the shoulder, saying, 'The deadline calls. But have no fear, the great mind can work in exile.'

By the time Rachael arrived, the alcohol buzz had vanished. Yet again, as he was led to the table, he was instructed that there would be no embracing, no touching of any sort. Not that Rachael was showing any inclination to hug him. She was wearing formal clothes and her make-up was impeccable: her protection against the glaring guards. But he could see how tired and stressed she looked, the cold anger in her eyes. It was a bitter joy to see her.

'You look well,' he said. 'How are the girls?'

She looked at him silently for a long while before saying, 'I've had another letter from Mrs Myers. The *humiliation*, Emmanuel: can you understand that? She invited us to her house, she let our children play with her son. And you—' She faltered. 'The girls can't sleep, knowing they'll have to move schools again. They're so *ashamed* of you.'

She was right, of course.

'I'm sorry.' It was not enough. 'Where are they?'

'At home, waiting, like all of us.'

The FBI and others had wanted him to betray the Six. Of course, he had been tempted – Overton was in Switzerland and he felt no personal loyalty to the man – and the other five would go to jail. But he was terrified they would take revenge on his family. So he had made the best deal with the government he could, and now he needed to let Rachael go. She had made him so happy – to her, he'd been a man, not a calculating machine – and in his obsession, he had thrown that all away.

'Did you watch the purples?' he asked.

'I caught it with a friend. The whole school will see it, so we'll discuss it as a family tonight. They're taking part in a film – a thousand human children, sending Cory home with their good wishes. They wanted to do it and I felt they should. I owed it to Mrs Myers.'

He didn't say anything; his own actions had made him an onlooker to raising his own children.

'The FBI told me about the programme,' she said suddenly, which surprised him.

Does everyone *know about this clandestine project?* he wondered, checking around, but the guard was as rigid as a wooden Indian outside a tobacco store. The President was obsessed with cancer, and they were wondering if Cory's extraordinary immune system might offer a new means of attack. 'It's supposed to be top secret,' he said.

'You might do some good,' she said. 'You can get on with your *real* work.'

'It's better than making licence plates,' he said, trying to make a joke. Just like Nazi scientists had been rescued after the war – and he found the comparison offensive, but it wasn't necessarily wrong – this research project allowed disgraced scientists and doctors to work hidden in plain sight. The story would leak at some point, then there would be a public outcry and accusations of special treatment, but the fact remained that no matter what work he was doing, he would still be in prison, and he could be sent to an ordinary jail at a minute's notice. But from a scientist's point of view, the cancer problem had some real points of interest, although he thought his work on infection would probably deliver more in his lifetime.

Rachael had not yet opened the folder of divorce papers. As he tried not to stare at them, he wondered for the millionth time what madness had so overtaken him that he would throw away his whole family.

'Did Mrs Myers say anything about what the purples will do?' he asked.

Flushing a little, looking angry, she said, 'Diplomacy has never been your strong point. I can't imagine what you thought to achieve.'

'No,' he admitted. Of course his dreams of being Ambassador to the Stars was pure ego, not rationality.

'Well, let's get this over with,' he said, knowing that once he had signed the papers, she would go.

She let out a great sigh. 'For better, for worse,' she said.

He misunderstood at first, waiting for her to continue – then he gawped like a fool.

'It's so awful for the children,' Rachael continued. 'I'd like to help the girls to understand you're doing something useful, that you've gone back to medicine. They can even see you, if they want to. They looked up to you, before Cory. And we'll have to move again anyway, so we might as well be in reach of wherever they're going to put you.'

He was discovering that hope could hurt almost more than despair. 'So the papers . . .'

'Let's see how it goes.'

It was a stay of execution, not a reprieve, but still.

After a cold pause, she went on, 'The government people think you'll have a breakdown and won't be any good to them. But you know, that wouldn't help the girls, would it? Or me.'

He didn't deserve her. *I don't deserve this chance*— But he *wanted* it.

'Thank you – *thank you*. I am so sorry for putting you and the girls through this – anything I can do—'

'Talk to me before you do *anything*,' she said firmly. 'Focus on the work, not the stars. Let's hope there's a future long enough for us to make something of it.'

'Thank you,' he repeated, then he asked, 'Could the girls write to me?'

He so badly wanted to ask her if he could see the girls, but that might be a step too far.

She shrugged and rose and the brief meeting was over. He looked at the guard and rose too, but she was not going to kiss him, or even take his hand.

'Make them proud of you again,' she said, and turned – and yet his heart gave a jump. A long road lay ahead, but at least there might be light along the path, for Rachael had given him a way back to her and the girls.

A gear turned inside him and a tiny implacable piece of the puzzle became not an obstacle but a possible key. The work would not be for him, but for her, for his daughters, and for humanity.

If humanity had a future.

CHAPTER 48

The-all must decide

Little Frog was swimming with the healers, and Thunder could not join them. Even through his illness, he had said his piece in the discussion, and Thunder had felt such pride he could explode. He felt an overwhelming need to protect his son: such an obligation, to be by his side for ever. Little Frog had made the case for the humans so clear and compelling. The-all had commended him, but the decision still hung unmade, like the dancing auroras over the poles. Earth had those lights too.

The all-of-the-mission had agreed a deadline, and if an agreement was not reached by then, both starships would leave. Those who opposed leaving a starship behind had at least agreed to a dangerous attack on the snake base on Mars, as well as leaving the humans some surveillance. Even so, the people were divided: would that conciliatory move be enough? Thunder had said all he could; he had spoken with all his being. Skimming Stone and others had also fought against leaving Earth unshielded, fought as if their own children were at risk.

Now each heartbeat was bringing them closer to abandoning the Earth.

Heartbeat by heartbeat, the braver choice was coming closer to defeat.

Skimming Stone messaged him again. *Join now.* Thunder sighed and patched into the discussion.

'Skimming Stone has been censured for ego-behaviour. Some would say the moderators cannot call her to speak again.'

Precedent, precedent, precedent, trilled many. The people were losing all patience with each other, tiring of the discussion.

'This one contests the precedent and cedes their rightful time to Skimming Stone.'

'This one cedes their rightful time to Skimming Stone.'

'This one contests the precedent and cedes their rightful time to Skimming Stone.'

'This one has learned Skimming Stone's speech by heart – but cedes his time for a new proposal.'

Skimming Stone had risen so often that Thunder believed the healer was now a hindrance to the cause. She might even sway the argument onto endless time-wasting procedures with this aggressive challenge.

She said, 'This one speaks for the children of Earth, the playful, blameless children, for the innocent the-all would slaughter by our indifference. Red blood is purple blood. Snakes burning babies at their mothers' teats . . .'

The moderators conferred.

'Skimming Stone may speak briefly, only to introduce any wholly new proposal, and any one moderator can halt them.'

'Gratitude,' said Skimming Stone. 'This one will be brief. We suggest – we *demand*, as an imperative – that the-all begin a roll call: of those willing to crew *Repurpose Snakes* and remain with the Earth. We do not even ask for the stronger ship. Only those who believe this is right should volunteer. It may be death – but let it be written, let the songs of the home-world say – that some were not so Hardened that they left children to die.'

It was a true miracle: Skimming Stone made her point and shut up.

The moderators conferred and called one of the idea's most implacable opponents: Chosen Scars, who had commanded the evacuation of the colony-world, then held command to repel the second assault on the home-world.

'Why the weaker ship? If the-all decide to leave one, all agreed it must be the stronger.'

There was a silence.

Another dreaming-together and we will be out of time.

'The proposition is debatable. Does the-all wish to debate it?'

'Hold the roll call,' said Chosen Scars. 'The stronger ship. If the-all so decides something so foolish, this one has courage to serve where needed.'

'Hold the roll call!' another opponent repeated.

The comment lights flickered: *Agree, agree, agree!*

'Mere weight of numbers is not a decision,' said a moderator, a lodge-friend of Thunder's, not an ally on this debate.

'Dissent will be heard.'

A few wanted to speak against, but not many.

As molecules gather to form drops, as drops gather to form a cloud, as clouds gather to make a storm – the-all moved to decide.

CHAPTER 49

The last day

Cory and Thunder walked in the woods behind Cory's house, his birth-father's arm across his shoulder. They had walked in the dark, Cory leading Thunder, feeling ahead with their minds to find the way. They wove their way through the crowds and tents, past the Army fence, then the Ship's. The first light of dawn was breaking and soon the monochrome forest would be full of colour. Cory loved the Earth, its plants and weather and animals and people – but the starship was full of familiar smells and sounds, the chatter of his people and, at last, the friendship of dreams.

Cory had danced for the dead. He had sung the songs of life and memory. Towards sunset, he would return to *Repurpose Snakes as Dung Buckets*. Its key repairs were all but done and soon it would leave this system and be his whole world for five Earth months. Cory would miss the seasons and snow and fireworks – and, most of all, he would miss his human family, his friends.

The healers said one brief visit would be fine, which was why Cory was coming to see his family without warning – to say goodbye, and to tell them the good news. Who else should bring it but the child of two worlds?

Cory trilled a gratitude song while Thunder held him close. He kept his helmet closed, a cautious father, not willing to take the risk of Earth infection.

'I'm so glad we made the right decision, Little Glowing Blue Frog. Nothing is harder than defending a decision you believe is wrong. But you must keep telling the humans, all we could agree to do was support the human case. However hard it was for the crew, it may take much longer for all-the-people. We will struggle to decide at speed.'

'Mom and Dad' – Cory used the human words – 'my Earth-mother and Earth-father – they put such a good case.'

'So did you. Still, this one was astonished we were successful.'

Cory *tock-tock-tocked*.

Thunder sometimes forgot how Cory had grown, the adventures he had had. They had woken Cory from his healing sleep so he could formally join in that historic decision. Gene told Cory things he already knew, and so did Thunder. Maybe all fathers did that.

The purple grown-ups were as solid as the Rockies on this: they would not be bringing any humans or dogs to the home-world. Cory, the child of two worlds, had been chosen to be the one who would speak for Earth.

Cory had saved all the messages, the thousand children who'd made their film filled with their hopes and fears; he would have them as companions in the months ahead. Their words and faces would be heard on the home-world by the whole people.

On his back was a camera, so everyone he missed could film him messages while he was gone. He would keep his own film diary too. He was sure starships would soon be racing to and from Earth.

While they were gone, *Kites at Dusk* would patrol the solar system, giving humans a chance. When he got back to home-world, he would spend every waking breath helping to persuade all-the-people to commit themselves to defending the Earth.

Earth was his home and First Harbour was his home, so every time he travelled between them, he would be coming home.

'We have to find a way to teach the humans,' he said now.

'Remember, in the children's school, those things that we leave the little ones to learn for themselves? Remember the stories where we did harm hoping to do good?'

'Humans are not all children.'

'Humans have their own path. Let us sing a song of hope that they learn quickly. It is not for us to order them. They must do their own lifting.'

'And we must not destroy the brave kind Ship.'

'Little Frog, you *must* see the danger. We will not destroy what we cannot understand, but we must not have machine minds thinking they know better than we do.'

'Ship is a person.'

'Ah, what trouble you cause, little one.'

The-all had failed to agree, again and again, so for now, the Ship Reborn still existed, although Cory had been forbidden to communicate with it.

In twelve hours, Cory would leave this beautiful, wounded world – but before then, there was so-so much he needed to do. He was allowed one small case for mementos. There were some so-dear people he might not even have time to see.

How sad Gene and Molly would be, and Elsa. But he would tell them that the purples would do the right thing. The Earth would not be left unguarded – and he would fly through the stars to make things right for them.

If humans only gazed into the future, they would see what they had to do for themselves.

The confidence came, a certainty so strong you could walk on it, that he would return. Cory would walk the ice caps and fly above the great forests, and he would float on a gondola and walk the shores of Lake Baikal. He would see Chuck and Bonnie and all his friends again, and maybe soon take them to the stars. When he came back, Fleur would be speaking. Dreams would come true. Chuck would become a baseball player and Bonnie would be President and Elsa would have so many friends and Cory would fly a starship and be an Ambassador and invent the weapon that would switch off every snake in the galaxy for ever.

At last father and son reached the back of the Myers' house. Cory would slip in the back way and wake his human family, a wonderful surprise. He might have difficulty explaining to Meteor where he was going, but Meteor would love Elsa and Fleur instead. He was leaving the Myers to tame the Monster inside him; he was leaving them so he could make them safe. He was leaving them because his other home called in his dreams, so he could hear the green waves on the shore and smell the rich perfumes of its beaches.

Cory was leaving home to go home. Through sadness thicker than water, he knew and loved both worlds. More adventures were to come, but now he knew that all would be well.

Amber Grove, six years later

Cory was coming home tomorrow, for Hallowe'en. It was his third return to Earth. Molly sat with Fleur in her bedroom, close to tears.

Elsa was holding out in her attic room and she'd jammed the hatch shut.

Gene had finally stopped shouting at the ceiling. 'I am going for a walk so I don't murder her,' he said as he went out. He had started the argument calmer than Molly, but he got so angry with Elsa, he'd been waving his arms like a great baboon.

Elsa used such vile language . . . made such unkind, untrue accusations . . . and she had refused even the offer from gentle Eva to mediate.

Elsa had forged her parents' signatures on her dreadful school report card and worse still, she had forged a letter back to the principal. Molly didn't know whether to be furious or admire her skill. The weary principal knew Elsa, and he had phoned to check. Challenged by her parents, Elsa had attacked. That argument had turned into the old classics, the curfew, then smoking, which had turned into everything and anything.

Fleur rounded up her two bears, her astronaut doll and the toy spaceship and disappeared into her room.

Cory was out there among the stars and Molly wanted him home.

Fleur had the albums out, looking for the pictures she wanted, so she could narrate the stories, starting with Cory's first astonishing return in triumph. Fleur remembered that first one, but mostly because Cory had brought her his memories in his dreams. Molly's astonishing youngest dreamed as the purples did, and her ability had thrown the purple scientists into excitement and confusion. How could a human do it? Not for the first time, this house in Crooked Street hid a secret from the world, a secret so big no one could know its consequences.

Cory's first absence had been long and hard, with nothing but brief messages at first, via dreaming purples.

'*We dreamed he is well and misses you.*'

'*His speech to the-all was well received.*'

The purples had had him long enough. Molly wanted him back, and let it be a year at home now, or two. Maybe he could talk some sense into Elsa.

She heard the front door, Gene returning with his temper restored, she hoped. They were a strong team even through these storms. Before Earth was saved, she nearly lost him, but her Gene had come back to her.

'Mom? Wake up, please.'

Who was calling her out of sleep? Molly, stirring in the dark, tried to make sense of it. A familiar noise meant that Gene was snoring beside her. A gentle hand touched her cheek.

Cory was coming home. She thought for a second it was him, surprising her, but this was Fleur, getting onto the bed.

'Elsa's gone,' Fleur said, tucking her long black hair behind her ears. Her younger daughter took these things very calmly.

Gone? Molly sat up and put on the bedside lamp. 'Gone, gone where, sweetie-pie?'

'She wouldn't say. It's very silly.'

While Gene snuffled in his sleep, Molly tried to marshal her thoughts. Cory was coming and Elsa had decided to make a scene. *Elsa is impossible.*

'Did you see her go?'

'I'm sensible. I stayed in bed,' Fleur said, the light glinting off her glasses. She had such a sweet, pompous little Gene face when she said it.

Anger began to be crowded out as the old familiar fears clutched at her heart.

Elsa will hitch a lift with the wrong type of man – or she'll be kidnapped or murdered – or she's taken the car and she'll crash it again – out who knows where with no help.

Or she's just got one of her friends to hide her: another of her silly power games. Honestly!

'I'd better find her. Get off the bed, sweetie-pie.'

In her robe and slippers, Molly creaked up the folding ladder to Elsa's attic hideaway. Habit made her knock before lifting the hatch. Clothes were strewn everywhere and the bigger rucksack was not on its peg. A pumpkin lantern with dark holes for eyes mocked Molly.

No clues here.

She climbed down, wondering how much jealousy was the fuel for the argument. Elsa always made everything complicated. In the kitchen, Elsa's communicator reproached her from the table. There wasn't a note, but there didn't need to be one. Before puberty hit, Elsa had run away only twice, but in the last couple of years threatening to do so had become a habit.

I'm going, I'm not going to be tracked down. This is it. I'm really running away for real.

Of course, Elsa had a second communicator. Dear old Ship, patrolling the skies to protect them, had given it to her. Gene and Molly pretended they didn't know that, but Elsa must surely have guessed. Despite the teenage theatrics, Elsa wasn't stupid.

Wash and dress, then start the ring-round.

'I'll come,' Fleur said.

'It's okay, sweetie-pie. It won't be long before Elsa's home. Go back to bed, and Dad will take you to school. You wouldn't want to miss Hallowe'en with your friends – and remember, Cory will want to take you trick-or-treating.'

Fleur's face lit up. 'Trick or treat with lovely big brother Cory.'

They missed him of course, painfully. Now every couple of months a purple ship brought his filmed messages, showing them his life on the starship, or his home-world. They were happy, sad, thoughtful, rattling on about friends or some purple discovery, and as usual, endless questions about their news and messages.

The light was on in Eva's room. She often read at night. Molly knocked softly, and went in to see the mother she'd chosen sitting in her favourite chair, brought up from the farm. The walls were covered with family photos, mostly of her three grandchildren, and there were three photographs of John by her bed – their wedding, Gene and Molly's wedding, and the photo that always stabbed Molly's heart, taken during John's last weeks, of the human family together, under the redwoods, with John laughing – the day he said, 'I won't be here when Cory returns.'

How she missed him.

'Elsa's gone. Did you hear her go?' Molly asked.

Eva slipped off the purples' breathing mask that had made such a difference to her quality of life. 'Sometimes a grand-mother is sworn to secrecy. You'll phone all the usual places, of course. Like Gloria's. I mean, that's just one example.'

They smiled at each other. Elsa had a weekend job with Gloria, the cantankerous warden of the Cory and Meteor Myers Dog Shelter.

'She's impossible.'

Eva spoke softly. 'Cory's an ambassador between two worlds, and Fleur – well, she's special. Of course Elsa feels left out. She's more like the rest of us. The world has changed so much, and we're all trying to find our way.'

Was Eva born this calm: as the old prayer said, filled with wisdom, serenity and courage? She'd been like that since the day Molly had first met her.

When does being a parent become easy? 'She doesn't even try at school.'

Eva patted her arm. 'She's good with small children and

463

animals. She's a good judge of people. She'll find her purpose and astound us all.'

Gloria did not pick up the phone, and that was another sign. The Ship denied nothing. Molly backed the car up and looked at her strange house of too many gables. The Hallowe'en decorations fluttered in the breeze, including the vast sea-monster Cory had brought last time. The woods behind the house were a symphony of fall colours.

Molly drove through the alien gates and down the road, frustration and anxiety fighting it out. The Ship hid her briefly, whenever she needed it. The shelter was almost an hour's drive away: if Elsa had driven herself, whose car had she used? Or who had she cajoled to take her all that way in the middle of the night? Molly knew she had a couple of the older boys from school wrapped around her finger.

Molly was in no mood for music, so she was alone with the road, her thoughts and the paling sky. *Cory was coming home.*

Out there were billions of Corys who had pledged to defend the Earth, their sacrifice giving humanity the gift of time. Over the years, six great Sentinels had come from the home-world, intelligent space fortresses who made the armies of Earth look like mice. Great waves of metal snakes had come against them and been destroyed.

The purple community under Earth's sun – openly on Mars and the Moon and in space, and some hidden on Earth itself – called themselves the Wardens of the Garlands. That was the old name for those who tended the sickness of violence. Fascinated and sometimes repelled, the greatest purple minds struggled to understand humanity, constantly arguing about whether and how to engage. Cory was at the heart of that mission: an interpreter between two societies. He travelled now with a cohort of friends his own age. Purple babies had been born under Earth's sun. These were signs of hope and commitment.

Thunder was a friend now, and on crucial issues, an ally.

Nearly at the shelter – and there, on the horizon, was the first trace of dawn.

The purples still claimed to be a small scientific mission. So many humans believed the purples were a malign enemy, scheming against Earth in space, and some governments were hostile to the whole species.

But far more people looked to them for salvation, begging them to take control – to take away human weapons and independence and freedom. Some – the deluded, the dangerous and the cynical – even claimed special insights into their wisdom and purpose.

Molly understood the purples' caution in sharing their knowledge. She still wished that they would share more.

It was true dawn now, and the lights were on at the dog shelter. Cory's patronage had made it famous; it now owned the surrounding fields. Tourists came to give a few dollars and more often than not left with a dog, a cat, a rabbit – or once, a donkey.

Molly rapped at the door. 'Another for breakfast.'

Gloria was old and cranky, preferring animals to people. She opened the door with a scowl. 'A mighty breakfast,' she said. 'Pancakes.'

Elsa, not yet a woman but very far from being a girl, was standing at the little stove, adroitly flipping them with a spatula.

She was dressed in jeans and a bright sweater; her defiant face didn't detract from her beauty. Molly was filled with hope and fear and frustration, and love.

'Well?' Molly sighed, with her hands on her hips. 'We were all *worried sick.*' She could be theatrical too.

For two breaths Elsa looked like she would fight. Then she melted, gave up teenage defiance, and began to cry. Molly was already there, taking her troubled daughter in her arms. She smelled of bacon and forbidden tobacco.

Molly could not face the school, not today of all days. 'I'll call the principal, say you need a day to prepare your apology. We can talk, and you can help me get ready for tonight.'

'I don't want it to be like this,' the girl sobbed.

Molly held her and felt strong.

Gloria *harrumphed*: she had a happy marriage, but she couldn't look at other people's affection.

'Let's eat, then get home,' Molly said, knowing that Elsa was smart and quite unscrupulous enough to be hundreds of miles away by now — and yet here she was, hiding in an obvious place, breaking boundaries, but not very much. Elsa knew who loved her, and how much.

Molly left a message for Gene that all was well. Elsa's penitence did not yet extend to talking it all through, so Molly turned on the car radio. The news was brief: fighting in the Middle East; not enough jobs in the Midwest; Congress had stalled the budget for the President's Green Corps. That would stir a fierce debate among the purples, whether to spell out to humans the dreadful truth: that what they had seen on other planets was happening here.

Molly was still doing the rounds of the TV shows a couple of times a year, repeating the same message, over and over – humanity had to do its own heavy lifting, not just in saving the planet, but in making it worth saving. Cory, the eternal optimist, thought humanity would figure it all out. She wasn't so sure.

Elsa loved the old songs, but to make a point, she insisted they switch to a new station, the music young people listened to, all shiny rebellion and alienation as synthetic as a plastic glove, or romantic songs written to a formula by a robot brain. Or so they sounded to her, although Gene refused to agree the era of great music had passed.

They drove past pumpkin lanterns on every morning porch, waiting for the early evening when Amber Grove would become a realm of magic. The town made a big deal of Hallowe'en; it was a town where newcomers with new ideas rubbed along with those who liked it more when things didn't change.

Marquees were up on Founders Green, and parade stands, hinting of the excitement to come. She drove past the Meteor Day Memorial, and the shining statue to commemorate the purples who had died to protect humanity. First among these, to Molly's mind, was Cory's mother, Pilot, who had saved her son and in so doing, had saved the Earth.

'I'm not sure you deserve to go out tonight,' Molly said, and Elsa sighed, but did not dignify this threat with an answer. Elsa couldn't really be grounded on Hallowe'en, not on Cory's first day back, and she knew it. Damn her.

Before they left the car, Elsa gave one last sniff and kissed her mother. 'Thanks.'

'Dad might be trying to write,' Molly said. 'We don't need to talk just yet.'

Maybe Cory can talk a little sense into her.

At home, all was bedlam. Gene hugged Elsa, said, 'Hello, Trouble. Carol and Storm dropped by – I promised to find that article for them.'

'Already?' Molly had wanted lunch out of the way before everyone descended.

'And Cory says he's ahead of schedule.' Gene took Elsa off to help search. The time Molly had intended to get everything ready had already disappeared, and a note from Diane was warning of more visitors. Fleur was singing to everyone, her pitch perfect, clutching her soft purple Cory doll. Gene hadn't taken her to school after all. Her dinosaur costume was hanging on the wall, a work of sewn art that she couldn't be let near until much later. Even then, every chocolate in Amber Grove would end up all over it.

Eva was making coffee, very slowly and with great care. There were unfamiliar bowls and boxes on the table, so who had dropped off food . . . ?

'Selena called,' Eva said. 'They'll be here for lunch.'

They'd discussed this and Molly had asked her to come with everyone else for supper . . . of course, Selena's goofy second husband would bring his own two kids as well. He was kind and he made Selena laugh, so Molly approved of him.

She scooped up a bunny glove-puppet from the kitchen floor – lethal, a skid hazard – before helping Eva with the tray. Clutter meant falls.

Selena would be talking about her book; Carol had another

book out; Dr Jarman had a book out; everyone except Molly and Gene had written a book – even Meteor, as imagined by the Robertson boys, had become an author.

Of course, when Molly next saw Gene, Elsa had disappeared. They had discovered that teenagers had some comic-book superpower: the ability to see chores that need doing and yet not be there. Molly phoned the school principal and committed Elsa to a difficult meeting tomorrow.

Then Fleur showed everyone that she had been doing writing with Eva.

Family life wasn't a painting or a posed photograph; it was a dance, a brawl. And Cory, her first, her son, was coming home at last. That old saying, third time the charm. Maybe this time, more than a year, maybe this time . . .

Cory was bringing three friends, and one, she gathered, was maybe a bit more than a friend. The purples did not rush into commitments and Molly had promised herself she wouldn't pry. Cory would tell her when he was good and ready.

The bracelet chimed. 'Hello, hello, Cory here. One hour. Lots of news!'

Molly went and sat in Eva's empty room, trying the silent meditation, just to get everything straight in her head, but there was so much jangling around.

Gene slipped in and sat on the bed. He put his arm around her. 'It will only get louder,' he said. 'Your weird sister will want to be the centre of attention. And we sure need to talk with Elsa about consequences.'

If serious talks were bricks, they could build a house. 'For now, let's just be.'

Her Gene, who she thought she had lost. Her Gene who, when the stakes were high, truly heard her heart and stayed by her side. Loving him was routine, and still extraordinary.

They had seen the world, here and there, anyway, and it was grand to visit. She had stood on high peaks and explored deserted islands. She'd even watched the purples drill deep into ancient glaciers to track the changes in Earth's climate. But where she wanted to be, always, was right here at home. They shared a quiet, joyful togetherness without words until the doorbell rang.

Molly wanted to be first, but Elsa beat her to it. There stood Cory, helmet off. His ears stood proud and his tentacles waved.

'No ugly space monsters needed! Go away, Squid-face!'

Meteor, barking her welcoming bark, pushed past her, determined to lick Cory all over.

'Ugly gorilla monster!'

Elsa and Cory embraced, and Molly joined them. Cory was almost as tall as her now, and his tentacles stroked her cheek. He smelled wonderful, of lemon-balm, horses and rain.

Behind Cory in the street were three young purples, still in their spacesuits, but helmets off. She thought she recognised two of them, and no helmets implied they were regular visitors to Earth. But Thunder, who always came with Cory, *always*, was not there. That was odd. But Cory would have said if there was trouble.

'Big-big news,' Cory trilled.

'Coreeeeeeeee!' and Fleur was in the hug on the porch, and Gene close behind.

What had the purples decided? Was there good news from

the struggle in space, a decisive advance against the snakes? Or was there news about the wild idea of an Ark?

Cory's face was mischief. 'What do you want to be the news?'

His alien friends, still back in the road, chortled.

'Now you're back – Thunder promised a little trip to space,' Gene said, half joking, half longing.

Cory laughed. 'Not up to me, but of course you should.'

Elsa did a mock growl. 'Your scientists have made a way to stop purples stinking.'

'I love you too, Elsa.'

'Maybe you should introduce your friends,' Eva said from behind them, in a way that made Molly think, *You know something.*

'Soon, good guesses.'

'Dream-teaching!' Fleur said.

'Of course,' Cory said.

Molly thought it might be some formal Embassy, some new and open arrangement, some alliance. What did she hope for? Yes, that big stuff, but all her wishes were personal.

She struggled to put her need into words: her son to stay, or at least to be no more than a quick spaceship jaunt away.

Fleur broke from her hug and filled the pause. 'I will do a show!'

She did like to be the centre of attention. 'Not now, Fleur, sweetheart. Cory has news.'

Cory and Molly focused on each other. She looked into his violet eyes and she knew he understood her heart.

My wish is for you to stay for two years, or three. Amber Grove is too small to be your world – one planet will not be enough, so my child of two worlds must find his own path. But it is hard to be so far away from my son during these years as you become an adult.

471

'Mom has the best wish,' Cory said, though she had said nothing. 'But all good wishes. So, lots of news. Spinning Disc has come to live in this system.'

She felt Cory's joy pour out. Thunder's partner hated interstellar flight and shunned it, even though that meant long separations from Thunder and Cory. Surely this meant that Thunder and Cory were settling here?

Fleur was excited, irrepressible. 'I will do my show now.'

Cory laughed, Fleur stepped back and raised her hands. From her mind flowed fall leaves; at first they were delicate and frail, watercolours of leaves seen floating from a distance – but then in seconds they grew larger, more childlike, brighter. They spilled from the porch into the street, dancing round the heads of the aliens. The leaves of maples and sycamores and trees that existed only in picture books, dancing leaves filling the air in a burst of Fleur's delight. Meteor, of course, barked and leaped to bite them – then tripped down the steps, confused that they had no substance. Leaves swirled round her head and in excitement, she chased her own tail.

The aliens *tock-tock-tocked* with excitement, raising their hands as if to dance. Fleur could not project her nightmares, only what brought her pleasure.

Molly wanted to understand Cory's news, she was still holding him like he might fly away. She also wanted to savour the fullness of this moment, as Cory did, to soak up each scrap of happiness when it comes. Live life one day at a time.

Molly held her children and her Gene. She held the past and the future and today in a moment that could have lasted for ever.

It was Hallowe'en, and everyone Molly loved was home.

Acknowledgements

It is a truth universally recognised that 'the second album can be a bit tricky', and as you may have heard, there was a pandemic.

My enormous thanks to my editor Jo Fletcher and my agent Rob Dinsdale for their tireless work in bringing the good ship *Our Child of Two Worlds* safely to shore. I say I write books, not scripts, because a book is all my own work, but that's not true. There is an alchemy in the edit which finds the gold in the ore. Alas, Rob has moved on from the agenting business, and I will miss his wise guidance, but I'm now in the steady hands of Alex Cochran.

I've discussed bits of this with many people, but Sarah, Lucy, Peter N., Emily, Debbie, Sophie and Sue certainly saw whole drafts and gave essential encouragement. Chapters here and there were read to the All Good Bookshop writers' group, whose friendly enthusiasm for both books kept me going in tougher times.

Leo Nickolls and Patrick Carpenter pulled off an even better cover than the first one. I'd like to thank Ajebowale and Georgina in Editorial and Ella, Ellie and Charlotte in Publicity and Marketing, and the rest of the Jo Fletcher Books/Quercus team.

It has been good to hear from people around the world who liked *Our Child of the Stars*. The real joy of the first book was that many reviewers, bloggers, booksellers – and those most crucial: you readers – fell deeply in love with Cory, Molly and Gene. There are too many to name, but their polite asks 'when the next one was due' did jog me to get on with it.

My friends and family have been beyond lovely. I found generosity from established writers and particularly Sue Tingey and Juliet E. McKenna, but also Dominic Dulley, Gray Williams and many others. I found communities of patience, honest and support online, particularly the Debut Authors 2019, Debut Authors 2020 and Savvy Writers. Super Relaxed Fantasy Club were super. And relaxed.

A couple of wonderful people in public sector press offices in the States answered questions from this random author, only for those chapters not to appear. My thanks.

I launched the first book in the US in March 2020 as the pandemic hit, while I had Covid-19. There have been better backgrounds to a launch. My thanks to Giuliana, Elyse and Amanda in New York, who worked so hard to overcome the problems.

I always intended two (and only two) Cory books – while he and his world brought me great delight, I rather fancy writing something else now.

Finally, Daniel and Trevor for endless brotherly support, my thanks. Theo and Lucy give me hope and spur me to do my own lifting. Sarah, of course. And my awesome parents. I told you science fiction was worth reading.

Stephen Cox
London 2021